KNOW YOUR RIGHTS

READER'S DIGEST

KNOW YOUR RIGHTS

And How to Make Them Work for You

 The Reader's Digest Association (Canada) Ltd.
Montreal

Editor
ALICE PHILOMENA RUTHERFORD

Associate Editor
ANITA WINTERBERG

Designer
ANDRÉE PAYETTE

Art Director
JOHN McGUFFIE

Copy Editor
GILLES HUMBERT

Research
ENZA MICHELETTI
WADAD BASHOUR

Editorial Assistant
ELIZABETH EASTMAN

Production Coordinator
SUSAN WONG

Production Manager
HOLGER LORENZEN

CONSULTANTS AND
CONTRIBUTORS

Chief Legal Consultants
NELSON BROTT, BA, BCL
(McGILL UNIVERSITY)
OF BORENSTEIN, DUQUETTE,
BROTT & SHEA

&

ROSS ROBINS, BA, LLB,
BARRISTER AND SOLICITOR
OF BERGMAN, ASPLER &
ASSOCIATES

Copy Editing
JOSEPH MARCHETTI

Resources and Index
ROBERT RONALD

Canadian Cataloguing in Publication Data

Main entry under title:
    Know your rights, and how to make them work for you

Includes index.
    ISBN 0-88850-558-2

        1. Law—Canada—Popular works.   I. Title: Know your rights.

    KE447.K59   1997   349.71   C96-901025-7

For information on other Reader's Digest products or to request a catalogue,
please call our 24-hour toll-free Customer Service hotline at 1-800-465-0780.
You can also visit us on the World Wide Web at http://www.readersdigest.ca

Printed in Canada

97 98 99 / 3 2 1

CONTENTS

YOUR MONEY

269

YOUR CAR

349

YOUR CONSUMER RIGHTS

377

YOUR RIGHTS IN ACTION

439

ABOUT THIS BOOK

"I know my rights!"

You've heard these words time and time again. In moments of frustration, fear, or anger, you may well have uttered them yourself. But do you *really* know your rights? And even if you do understand the legalities, do you have the knowledge to use that information to get what you rightfully deserve?

Very likely you have had the experience of believing that you were entitled to something—a refund for a faulty product, a service from a real estate agent or a physician, a response from one of your children's teachers—only to discover that either you were not legally within your rights, or if you were, that you had no idea how to take effective action.

KNOW YOUR RIGHTS was conceived to solve this kind of dilemma. An action-oriented guide, it explains what you need to know about that awesome entity, Canadian law, and then it shows you how to use that legal knowledge to get the best results. Covering hundreds of situations that ordinary Canadians encounter every day—from the negligent dry cleaner to the unfair boss to the belligerent policeman—KNOW YOUR RIGHTS tells you how to avoid hassles, negotiate disputes, solve problems, and get a fair shake—all with maximum speed, efficiency, and economy.

Furthermore, this problem-solving book will prevent that numb sensation of helplessness and hopelessness that can strike when you must deal with life's problems, whether it's a question of getting your neighbor's pesky puppy to stop barking or making sure the Government of Canada, or your provincial government, pays your rightful benefits. In other words, it gives you confidence and power.

KNOW YOUR RIGHTS is organized by topics in seven major areas: your home and community, your marriage and family, health care, job, money, car, and consumer rights. The last chapter, "Your Rights in Action," tells you how to assert yourself and take the decisive steps necessary to ensure corrective action whenever your rights are infringed.

The information is readily accessible: *Easy-to-read boxes* appear on practically every page, giving you handy checklists of facts you need and steps to take in order to secure your rights. *Detailed charts* help you compare and contrast important options. *Sample letters and forms* show you what to say and how to say it, whether you are complaining to a manufacturer, hiring a nanny, or resigning from a job. *True-to-life scenarios* give you insights into the way real people cope with real problems. At the back of the book, a *directory of resources* lists scores of organizations that offer further information and help.

Although no single book can cover every facet of the law, KNOW YOUR RIGHTS does tell you what your rights are and how to take action to secure them. Because, at times, you may nevertheless need the services of a lawyer, this book also advises you when professional help is necessary and how to work effectively with a lawyer to save both money and time.

"You can't fight city hall!"

This is another expression that you, no doubt, have heard a thousand times. But don't you believe it. The fact is, you *can* fight city hall, and this book gives you the know-how to do just that—and to win.

YOUR HOME AND COMMUNITY

*Owning a house or apartment may be the biggest
financial responsibility you will ever assume,
so secure your home by understanding your rights.*

HUNTING FOR YOUR HOME ■ NEGOTIATING
AND SETTLING ■ PAYING FOR YOUR HOME
■ MANAGING YOUR HOME ■ REPAIRS AND
IMPROVEMENTS ■ NEIGHBOR PROBLEMS
■ ENVIRONMENTAL CONCERNS ■ CONDOS,
CO-OPS AND PLANNED COMMUNITIES ■ RENTING
■ OWNING A SECOND HOME ■ HOME OPTIONS
FOR SENIORS ■ MOBILE HOMES
■ SELLING YOUR HOME ■ MOVING

HUNTING FOR YOUR HOME

Knowing your rights and responsibilities while house hunting could protect you from costly mistakes now and in the future.

KEEPING AN EYE ON THE BROKER

Real estate agents or brokers occasionally resort to shady tactics in their eagerness to make a deal for a seller. As a buyer working with a traditional seller's broker, you should be wary of:

1. A broker who asks you the top price you are willing to pay for a house. It is unethical, and can lead to abuse, especially if the seller is willing to sell for less than your top price.

2. A broker who creates a sense of urgency or false intimacy by revealing personal information about the seller, such as a pending divorce or financial woes. These claims may be pressure tactics meant to hurry your decision to buy.

3. A broker who tries to exhaust or confuse you. This is done by showing unsuitable properties and saving the best—and highest priced—choice until last.

4. A broker who keeps showing you homes you cannot afford. If you learn from neighbors that houses in the area are available within your price range, question the broker.

5. A broker who insists that your offer is too low. The broker should give you advice, and has a right to disagree about a price, but is legally bound to present your offer to the seller.

Working With Real Estate Brokers

Whether you are a first-time home buyer or back in the housing market after many years, you will need to find out what houses are available in the location you want, at a price you can afford, with the features you desire. While some buyers find suitable properties through word of mouth, classified ads, or "For Sale" signs, most enlist the services of one of three types of real estate professionals: real estate brokers, Realtors, or real estate agents.

Real estate brokers are licensed by the province to negotiate real estate transactions between a buyer and seller for a fee; Realtors are brokers who belong to the Canadian Real Estate Association; real estate agents, who also must be licensed, sell property on behalf of a broker or Realtor and share the fees with his employer, unless of course he is an independent agent who works for himself. Traditionally, someone wanting to sell a house hires a broker or agent to advertise the property and find a buyer willing to pay the asking price. For these services the broker receives a commission from the seller—usually 5 to 6 percent of the sale price.

Because brokers generally advertise properties in a computer listing that other brokers can access, the broker who lists the house may not be the one who brings in the buyer. When this happens, the broker who brings in the buyer takes half the commission from the broker who listed the property. If you are a buyer, note that a broker showing you a house may not necessarily be representing your interests but simply trying to get a commission. Note, too, that you are not legally obligated to a broker just because he spends a lot of time with you: in fact, you are free to change brokers or use several simultaneously. Once you decide to make an offer on a specific house, though, you are obligated to deal through the broker who first showed you the house.

FINDING A BROKER

To protect home buyers from the false impression that a broker is working in their interest, most provinces have laws requiring brokers to tell buyers whom they represent. However, the majority of provinces do not require this disclosure

until after the first round of house hunting. If you are looking for a house, take the time to search for a reputable broker through friends, associates, a mortgage lender, lawyer, or the local board of the Canadian Real Estate Association.

While some house hunters may only feel comfortable working with a traditional real estate broker, others may find advantages in using an alternative broker, such as a discount broker or a buyer's broker. These alternatives can provide knowledgeable buyers with savings in money or time—or both.

ALTERNATIVE BROKERS

Discount brokers or consultants, like traditional brokers, are hired by the seller, but at a lower commission (three or four percent of the selling price rather than the standard five to six percent). Because the broker takes a reduced commission, the seller can lower the asking price on the house and thus create savings for the buyer. Discount brokers cost less because they do not show buyers properties or negotiate the final deal. In fact, they do little more than give the buyer a seller's name, address, and telephone number. While you may not mind looking at houses on your own, understand that the discount brokers will not provide the services traditional brokers offer, such as helping to get past an impasse in a sale price.

Buyer's brokers are gaining great popularity nationwide. Working as independents or as employees of a traditional real estate company, they differ from traditional brokers and discount brokers in that they are paid by the buyer. For a fee, they try to find exactly what the buyer is looking for and negotiate a favorable purchase price.

Like any other broker who brings a buyer to a seller's broker, a buyer's broker may divide the commission with the seller's broker. This 2.5 to 3 percent payoff usually serves as the basic fee for a buyer's broker. But a buyer's broker may also charge a retainer fee or want the commission based on an hourly rate or a flat fee. In the end, you could pay hundreds of dollars more to a buyer's broker than you would to a regular (or seller's) broker. On the positive side, buyer's brokers claim to save as much as 20 percent average on selling prices by negotiating hard on a client's behalf and working to get discounts from sellers for such things as defects or potential repairs. Buyer's brokers also save busy clients time by weeding out inappropriate properties.

YOUR RIGHT TO FAIR HOUSING

In any house-hunting situation, you are protected by your provincial human rights charter or code, which prohibits discrimination based on race, national origin, religion, or gender. Under these laws, it is illegal for a broker to discriminate by

---

What to Expect of a Buyer's Broker

Buyer's brokers are expected to provide clients with specific services and guarantees:

✔ **Exclusivity.** A buyer's broker should work solely for the buyer and should not represent the seller in any way. Some brokers try to do this in order to collect both the listing broker's fee and the buyer's broker fee on the sale of a house. Called fee splitting, this is illegal in some provinces and is unethical everywhere.

✔ **Contract.** A buyer's broker should provide you with a contract explaining services, fee structure, any bonus provisions, and the time frame of the agreement. Be sure you understand all its elements.

✔ **Basic fee.** A buyer's broker's basic fee may be expressed in terms of a flat fee, an hourly rate, a percentage of the home's list price, or a percentage of the purchase price.

✔ **Retainer fee.** Besides the basic fee, a buyer's broker's contract usually calls for a retainer fee, covering a period varying from 30 days to six months. If the broker fails to find the buyer a suitable home within the time period, the client has the right to an immediate refund of the retainer fee.

YOUR RIGHTS TO INFORMATION FROM A SELLER

As a prospective buyer, you have the right to certain key information from the seller. Some Realtors will not show a property without a detailed written disclosure form from the seller. Still, most Realtors and most provinces require only verbal disclosure by the seller—and only if he is asked. Be sure to ask questions and get full answers before agreeing to a contract. Some key information to dig out:

1. Does the house have any structural or property defects not obvious to the naked eye?

2. Which appliances and fixtures are included in the sale price? Add these items to your purchase agreement.

3. Does the house or property have easements (allowance of property use by others), zoning violations or restrictions, or building-code violations against it? Are there any construction liens registered against the property?

4. Are there any environmental hazards that may affect the quality of the house or environs? Since a seller may be unaware that the home harbors hazards such as asbestos, radon, or urea-formaldehyde foam insulation, take full advantage of your right to a home inspection.

5. What is the full amount of property taxes and other assessments on the home? Are all tax payments up to date?

refusing to negotiate or to falsely deny that there are suitable homes available for sale or inspection. It is also illegal for the seller of a house to discriminate by refusing to negotiate the sale of a house that is on the market, setting different terms or conditions of sale for different people, or falsely denying availability. If you feel you have been discriminated against, contact your local provincial Human Rights Commission.

If You Find the "Perfect" House

After many days of house hunting, you finally find the house you want to buy. In your enthusiasm, you might eagerly instruct your real estate broker or lawyer to start drawing up the purchase agreement. But before making any commitments, you need to get prepurchase information about defects in and around your future home. You can then incorporate this information into the negotiating process or, at worst, cancel the sale.

Although a house may look fine to you, it takes a professional home inspector to make sure that the basic structure is in good shape and that the heating, plumbing, and electrical systems are sound. Many mortgage lenders require a prepurchase home inspection, and the lending institution may insist on an inspector of its choice. Usually, however, the buyer hires the inspector and pays for the service.

In most cases, home inspectors do not have to be licensed engineers or architects; so before you hire an inspector, ask about his professional affiliation. Expect to pay $100 to $300, depending on where you live and the condition of the home. Older houses generally cost more to inspect because they are assumed to have more problems. An inspector should set the fee in advance and provide a written report upon completion.

Most homeowner associations can recommend an inspector to members, and the Yellow Pages usually have listings of private consulting and inspection firms.

ADVANTAGES OF A HOME INSPECTION

If you worry about getting your money's worth, ask the inspector if you can join him on his rounds. Most inspectors, as a matter of professional courtesy, encourage buyers to do so. The two- or three-hour examination will probably be well worth your time and money. It will give you a quick education about the way the house is put together overall, and introduce you to its structural peculiarities and unique features. Your guided tour will alert you to major problems, which can be used as leverage in your purchase negotiations or could even make you decide to back out. You will also discover if there are minor defects or conditions—a water heater too small to supply your two teenagers, for example—that could affect you immediately upon moving in. Knowing about these problems can bolster your position at the bargaining table, and help you anticipate the nature and extent of repairs and maintenance in the months to come.

Your home inspection may also reveal problems that should be examined more carefully by a specialist. For example, a general inspection may reveal termites, which are often found in older homes in British Columbia and southern Ontario. In that case, you should hire a certified pest control inspector to estimate the cost of repairing the damage and eradicating the infestation. Similarly, tests for carpenter ants, asbestos, radon, urea-formaldehyde foam insulation, lead in drinking water, and other environmental hazards should be conducted by specialists whom your home inspector can recommend. Keep in mind, however, that you can make your inspections only with the cooperation of the occupant.

Only after these inspections should you make your deal with the seller. If you have already started negotiating, be sure any purchase agreement is conditional on the house passing a building inspection. Then, if major structural problems are discovered—if the foundation of the house sits on sand and is clearly unstable, for example—you can break the purchase contract without penalty.

An expert is someone who knows some of the worst mistakes that can be made in his subject and how to avoid them.

WERNER HEISENBERG
Physics and Beyond

Make Sure Your Home Inspector Does His Job

A professional home inspection is the best way to uncover any flaws in the structure or systems of a house you plan to buy. The following checklist highlights the areas a good inspector must evaluate in his written report to you:

• **Foundation, basement:** Structural stability; moisture, cracks; infestation by termites and other insects; accessibility of crawl spaces, musty smells.

• **Attic:** Accessibility to attic and crawl spaces; insulation, ventilation; condition of chimney; infestation by squirrels.

• **Exterior walls, roof, and gutters:** Basic construction. Condition of siding materials, trim. Fans, vents. Roof leaks, condition of shingles, sun damage, sags, skylights. Leaks in gutters, drains.

• **Windows and doors:** Condition of glass, screens, storm windows; caulking, weather stripping; sashes, frames, hardware shutters, insects.

• **Interior:** Condition of walls, floors, stairways, ceilings, insulation. Presence of leaks, cracks, moisture, squeaks, sagging, insects. Closet space.

• **Electric, plumbing, heating systems:** Capacity and condition of grounding; fuses; circuit breakers; outlets. Capacity and distribution of heating and cooling systems throughout the house; effectiveness of thermostats. (Buyer would do well to ask for prior heating bills.) State of septic system, pipes, faucets, water heater, kitchen, laundry room; water pressure.

• **Outdoor structures, grounds:** Condition of garage, barn, and other structures; pool, pool surround; fences, walls; drainage, septic-tank location, troublesome trees.

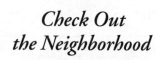

Check Out the Neighborhood

Your own investigation of the area around your potential new home is as important as an inspection of the house itself. Before buying check:

✔ *The neighborhood.* Consider the quality of the house- and lawn-care of homes on your street, space between lots, street lighting, traffic.

✔ *The overall community.* To determine the quality of a community, get information from the chamber of commerce, real estate brokers, and local residents. Find out who your neighbors will be and what they think about crime, police, and fire protection and the quality of hospitals and schools in the area.

✔ *Development plans.* Ask the seller and other local people about any upcoming development plans for the community. An unsightly fast-food restaurant or shopping mall could affect the enjoyment or value of your property.

✔ *Zoning laws.* Do restrictions prohibit building a deck or other sorts of remodeling? Are noisy businesses allowed next door? Can you have a home office on the property? If your home is in a planned community, is it subject to zoning restrictions on pets or parking, for example?

✔ *Environmental factors.* Do power plants, garbage incinerators, or airborne pesticides from farmland affect the area?

Once you have found the "right house" and had it inspected, have the property surveyed by a provincially certified surveyor. The survey will set out the actual location and boundaries of the property, and describe any easements (servitudes, in Quebec), such as a right of way. Often the seller does not know the exact boundaries of his property, and an existing fence may not mark the actual dividing line between lots. The survey will clarify this, and show if a fence, driveway, garage or garden shed is encroaching from a neighboring property.

Even if there is an old survey available, you would be wise to have it updated. This way, decks, garages, or other extensions or additions to the property will be clearly shown.

WHAT THE SELLER MUST TELL YOU

Although a prepurchase inspection can uncover essential information about a future home, no one knows the quirks and tics of a house better than the people who have been living in it. Until recently, the premise of *caveat emptor* (let the buyer beware) generally applied, and buyers almost always had to pay for major property defects discovered after purchase. Today's buyers benefit from legal trends that make house sellers responsible for disclosing problems before a sale. Therefore, would-be buyers should inquire about a house's defects. The seller might be asked to complete a written disclosure form, or merely to answer honestly any questions from the would-be buyer. A buyer may be able to cancel a sale or sue for repair costs if a seller knowingly conceals defects or purposely misrepresents the condition of a house. (See "Managing Your Home," page 30.)

Avoiding New-House Woes

Just because a home is new does not mean it is perfect, as is evident from the high volume of litigation involving owners of newly built homes. Some provinces have enacted laws to protect new home buyers. For example, all new home builders in Ontario must be registered with that province's New Home Warranty Program. British Columbia offers a similar program, but builder membership is voluntary. Other provinces have what is called implied warranties of habitability and fitness that guarantee the house will perform as expected.

The majority of complaints about new homes cite the use of inferior materials, low-quality construction, or a combination of the two. The high cost of raw materials and the pressures of competition may tempt some builders to substitute cheaper products than the contract specified—to use particleboard instead of plywood, for example. Pressure to finish the home on deadline or on budget may result in low-quality construction work. But whatever the cause, shoddy workmanship can result in all sorts of ills, from malfunctioning electrical, plumbing, and heating systems to misaligned doors and windows, and from poorly ventilated bathrooms, kitchens, and laundry rooms to dirt trapped under a polyurethane floor finish.

Because of these potential lapses, it is wise for anyone buying a new home to have it examined by a reputable home inspector and, if necessary, a structural engineer. If these professional prepurchase examinations reveal problems, insist on having them fixed immediately. If necessary, you may have to renegotiate the terms or timing of the sale or even cancel it.

Concerns With Older Homes

Older homes may well offer charm lacking in newly built houses. What's more, the fact that a house is older does not necessarily mean that it is not in good physical condition. The soundness of a building depends on its original quality and how well it has been maintained. A 20-year-old house may be in better condition than a 10-year-old structure.

Nevertheless, an older house may host a roster of problems that could translate into major repair bills for a new owner. Whether a building is 20 or 200 years old, a buyer should learn as much as possible about its structural soundness through prepurchase inspections and information from the seller.

Be particularly aware of evidence of termites or wood rot, inadequate or antiquated electrical wiring, plumbing weakness because of old pipes and rusty fixtures, leaky roofs and useless gutters, and wet basements. While these problems usually can be identified in prepurchase inspections, the extent of the problems may not be clear until you take possession of the house. Wood rot, for example, may have been concealed with a couple of coats of paint; or an electrical system that adequately serviced the house's existing equipment may not be able to cope with the high-voltage demands of your appliances. Depending on the situation, you may get some redress through the courts, since most provinces have laws requiring disclosure of defects.

However, anyone buying an older house, especially one more than 30 years old, should expect to make some repairs. Major problems found before purchase often can be negotiated into the sale price. But buyers who agree to take a house "as is" must accept responsibility for all repairs and maintenance, unless the seller made false misrepresentations about the state of the property.

Warranties: Legal Protection for Newly Built Homes

A variety of warranties are included with the purchase of a newly built home.

✔ *Express warranties.* These first-year guarantees of good workmanship from some builders or developers come free with new homes and are spelled out in the sales contract.

✔ *Implied warranties.* Almost every province guarantees implied warranties of habitability and workmanship, which legitimize the reasonable expectations of homeowners that a new home is safe, sound, and well constructed. For example, a sinking patio might breach the implied warranty of workmanship.

✔ *Extended warranties.* An extended warranty covers a home against major design and structural defects for five years. It may come free with a house when its builder belongs to a warranty plan such as the Ontario and British Columbia New Home Warranty programs.

✔ *Product warranties.* Products in a new home under written warranty from their makers are included in the first-year warranty of a builder or are covered by the implied warranties from the builder.

Do You Really Want to Build?

❖ 1 2 3 ❖

HOW TO CHOOSE AN ARCHITECT

These criteria can help you choose an architect to design a custom-built home:

1. Word of mouth. If a friend has a house you admire, find out who designed it. Ask your provincial Association of Architects about architects in your area.

2. Interview and compare. Meet with at least three architects to discuss your plans. (Ask first if they will charge for consulting time.)

3. Find out about fees. Some architects charge fixed fees plus expenses; others get a percentage of the cost of the house. Pin it down before going any further.

4. Explain your own ideas. Go to the interview with your own concept and priorities, including size and style of the house, budget, and special needs. Make sure the architect responds to your vision.

5. Ask how she works. What is her specialty? Would she execute the design of your project, or use assistants? What priority would your project take in her schedule?

6. Consider personality. You will be working with an architect for a long time. Is her company congenial?

7. Discuss the contract. Be clear about your payment terms and the architect's responsibilities. You might get a lawyer to look over the contract.

A custom-built home may be the answer to your dreams or it may be a financial and emotional debacle. Taking certain precautions can help protect you from disasters and arm you with legal recourse for worst-case scenarios. Before engaging designers and builders for your custom home, take time to plan. Decide what kind of house you want, how big it should be, and how much you can spend on it. If your design requirements are unique and your budget is ample, you may want to hire an architect. Interview several before choosing one, and consider their reputations and finished projects before making a decision.

Many custom-home builders can provide both design and construction services. Some builders keep files of house plans they have designed, but with the builder's permission and payment of a small fee, you can use them for your own home, modified to your needs. Full-service builders will not only design and construct the house but can advise you on interior design as well.

If you use builders to design your house, make sure the contract spells out who owns the design plans if you use another builder; the cost breakdown of design and building; what kind of changes can be made once construction begins, and at what cost. You might save money by buying one of thousands of house plans available in home and trade magazines. This can be cheaper than hiring a builder/designer or architect, but the plan may also need tailoring (if your land is sloping rather than level, for example). Make sure all specifications, including electrical and plumbing, are included, and that they meet provincial and local standards. Otherwise, you will end up paying to have the plan redesigned for you.

YOU'RE THE BOSS

No matter whom you hire to design and build your home, you are at the helm of this mammoth undertaking. Before you begin, determine—and contractually specify—the chain of command. Does the builder defer to the architect? Who hires—and is liable for—subcontractors? A builder must follow not only your design plan but also the National Building Code, and building codes set by your city and province. These codes vary from one jurisdiction to another. Some forbid functional fireplaces in new homes, others prohibit the use of wood as a structural or siding material, and some insist on copper piping for plumbing. Since you are ultimately responsible for any building-code violations, review the requirements of these codes with your builder before construction begins.

Other Ways to Own a Home

Though the classic image of "home" may be a single-family residence on a private patch of land, there are other options available to potential homeowners. These include buying homes in a planned residential development, condominiums, cooperative housing units, co-owned properties, and rental properties that include an option to buy. Planned community developments, once the venue of retirees, are popular with those who want to eliminate some of the burdens and responsibilities of ownership.

PLANNED COMMUNITIES

A planned community of single-family residences often offers conveniences such as complete lawn service in summer and snow shoveling in winter; amenities such as common swimming pools and other recreational facilities; limited maintenance and repair service for the home; and on-site conveniences such as grocery stores or banks.

If you are considering buying a home in a planned but not yet completed development complex, investigate the reputation of the developers, the past projects they have completed, and their financial backers. Also, if you have seen only a model home, find out which features and fixtures will actually be included in your house. Ask specifically about such things as the dishwasher, carpeting, and lighting and bathroom fixtures. Take into account whether they are part of the overall price or whether you must pay extra for the ones you particularly want.

Be aware that rooms in the model home are often larger than those in the homes yet to be built. Similarly with the materials used: they, too, may be of better quality in the model home.

CONDOS AND CO-OPS

Condominiums and cooperative apartments are also gaining popularity. A condominium is a type of ownership, not a type of property. Whether a condo is an apartment or town house, you own the dwelling plus an interest in the common property. You contribute toward, and are jointly responsible for, building maintenance, lawn care, and shared amenities. A cooperative apartment, alternatively, is not owned individually: A person buys shares in a corporation that owns the real estate, and holds a long-term lease on a particular unit.

Residents in planned subdivisions are automatically part of the homeowners associations that govern their common properties. These associations are legally entitled to enforce rules and regulations on residents. Since these rules may both benefit and constrain members, consider them carefully before

Keeping It Cool With Co-owners

The details of co-ownership of property vary in complexity with the parties' relationships and their province's laws. For unmarried co-owners a good way to avoid ambiguities and squabbles in the future is to sign a written agreement, separate from the deed or other ownership documents. Here are some points of potential trouble that it might nail down:

✔ *Mortgage.* How much of the monthly payments will each owner pay, and who will deal with the lender in business relating to the mortgage loan?

✔ *Maintenance.* Will the costs of keeping up the property be spread among the owners as they occur, or is there a joint repair and maintenance account? How will each owner's nonfinancial maintenance contributions be compensated?

✔ *Disputes.* How will arguments over dealing with the property be resolved? Mediation? Arbitration?

✔ *Incompatibility.* Who gets to stay in the house if two partners find they can no longer get along? How will that decision be made? And if one partner does leave, will the other have first option to buy his or her share?

✔ *Survivors.* What happens to the property if a co-owner dies? Will it pass to the other co-owner, or must it be transferred through a will?

making a commitment to buy. You should also get a copy of the condominium association's deed, bylaws and covenants, the engineer's report and management agreement, and, in the case of new condos, the condominium developer's prospectus, and read them carefully before signing any legal documents.

Another option for prospective home buyers is to share a property: parent and child, two sisters, an unmarried couple, or several friends might pool resources for a joint property. Specify in advance how ownership will be divided—who pays what proportion of which expenses, who will act as managing partner, and how the co-ownership arrangement can be dissolved. Sharing a property is always risky since there is a good chance that the direction of some partners' lives will change. What if one partner decides to marry or move? What if she loses her job and is unable to keep up with the payments?

With the high cost of real estate, some sort of joint ownership may be the only way new home buyers can hope to finance a home. It can be a legally intricate business, however, so hire a real estate lawyer to advise you.

Buying a Foreclosure? Beware!

Some home buyers look for value in properties whose mortgages have been foreclosed by lenders because of the owners' financial distress. You should know that houses in foreclosure may not be the bargains they seem. Watch out for these common difficulties:

• **You might not see what you get.** When homes fall into foreclosure because of unpaid taxes, they are boarded up and advertised for sale in local newspapers. The winning bidder may buy the house sight unseen—and then may find it a shambles, thanks to former owners who have taken everything they could, including the kitchen sink. If the foreclosed property is offered by a private lender in public auction, however, you usually will be permitted to tour the property before bidding at auction—obviously a safer alternative.

• **Former owners may buy back the property.** Homeowners are sometimes able to buy back their homes even after a foreclosure sale, depending on provincial foreclosure laws. Most provinces permit homeowners to regain possession of their homes within periods ranging from 60 days in Ontario to one year in Quebec after foreclosure for unpaid taxes. If you are the new owner of a home purchased under these circumstances, you may not be able to take final possession of the home until this period expires. Even if you are allowed to occupy the home in this period, you may be required to vacate once the taxes are paid by the original owner.

• **The paperwork is highly complex.** Buying a house in foreclosure is a complicated legal procedure with rules that vary from province to province. Wherever you live, you must have a real estate lawyer help you navigate through the muddle.

• **A home may be riddled with financial woes.** Many foreclosures come with outstanding debt attached to the property. Mechanics' liens—claims against the home by unpaid former workers—can put in question the title of a home itself, not the credit of the previous owners. Keep in mind that mechanics' liens and any unpaid property taxes must be paid off before title to the house can be transferred. Both of these sorts of debts can be tracked down before purchase by a real estate lawyer.

• **You may need cash on hand.** In some foreclosure sales, the full payment is required immediately, within a week or 10 days of sale. Most mortgage lenders will not finance foreclosure purchases. Therefore, you will need to make sure you have cash on hand when you are lining up the purchase of a foreclosure.

NEGOTIATING AND SETTLING

You finally found the right house, and now you have to come to terms with the seller. Know what your rights as a buyer are—and sharpen your bargaining skills.

Key Concerns in Negotiation

When your house hunting leads you to a home you want to buy, you can start negotiating the sale with the seller. This process typically entails three stages: the bids, the counterbids, and the agreed-upon price. The buyer then presents a final purchase offer accompanied by a deposit, called "earnest money." When this is accepted by the seller, it effectively becomes what is known as the binder, or deposit receipt. Often the binder becomes the purchase contract. If changes are needed, the buyer and the seller set a date to create the final sales contract.

To prepare yourself for the negotiating process, you must define your priorities. First, know the top price you can afford to pay and the top price you will pay for the house under consideration. Second, determine which aspects of the house would be negotiable: perhaps the seller could be persuaded to include the kitchen appliances in view of the fact the house needs new carpeting. Finally, consider your requirements for particular features of the deal, such as a certain moving day.

HOW TO CALCULATE AN OFFERING PRICE

In order to calculate your initial bid, you must assess the fairness of a seller's asking price. You may well have looked at other properties in the area and thereby have firsthand knowledge of the asking prices for comparable homes. In addition, the real estate broker who showed you the house can prepare a list of homes similar in age, condition, size, and property called a "comparative mortgage analysis." The list should compare only similar homes in the same neighborhood sold within the last six months. (If you are not using a broker, you can look at deeds at the municipal clerk's office stating location and sale price of homes, then scout the area to find those of comparable size.) Be sure to factor in any value differences, such as the added worth of newly renovated bathrooms.

At this point you may have sufficient knowledge of comparable homes to make an appropriate offer. But if you are not confident of your own analysis, you may want to arrange for a professional appraisal. A provincially licensed home appraiser assesses the current market value of your home. An appraisal

Do You Need a Lawyer?

When it comes time to close on a house, many home buyers turn to a family lawyer to handle essential documents. Other buyers feel they can manage by themselves, since it is not mandatory to have a lawyer represent you when buying a home. In Quebec, however, a notary must draw up the deed of sale.

But to ensure that your interests are promoted and legally protected, from purchase offer to title transfer, your best bet is to hire a real estate lawyer.

Your lawyer can help draft a purchase offer that protects you with contingency clauses, unlike a standard purchase offer or one drawn up by the seller's broker or lawyer.

A real estate lawyer can also conduct a title search on your prospective house; arrange an appraisal of the house; and review your mortgage lender's agreement. When you get to the final sales contract, the lawyer can add items that protect you, brief you on the complex procedure of closing on the home, and finally represent you at the closing itself.

Some real estate lawyers advertise a low flat rate for closing on a house but do not offer services over the course of the home-buying venture. Other lawyers charge an hourly rate, a flat fee, or a percentage based on the purchase price of a home.

service can cost several hundred dollars but may save you thousands if it identifies an inflated asking price. Note, however, that mortgage lenders require home appraisals by appraisers of their choice, paid by the buyer, so you may prefer to wait until you apply for a loan to have an appraisal; otherwise, if your appraiser is not one of those normally used by the lender, you may pay twice for the service.

MAKING A PURCHASE OFFER

If you have been dealing with traditional real estate brokers, you are likely to be given their agency's standard purchase-offer form when you find a suitable house. While provincial laws mandate some provisions for the final purchase agreement that will be part of these standard forms, these provisions may not protect you enough. A buyer's best protection is to hire a real estate lawyer to write the contract. You can ask friends or the local bar association to recommend one. (See also "Do You Need a Lawyer?" page 19.)

Some basic points to include in a purchase offer, besides names, addresses, description of the property, and the offering price, are any other financial details, such as the amount of earnest money deposit and the down payment requested, and amount of mortgage loan to be sought. The offer should also describe any conditions, or contingencies, upon which the final sales agreement depends, such as home inspection, seller disclosure, loan approval, and so on.

THE IMPORTANCE OF EARNEST MONEY

The most effective purchase offers are accompanied by earnest money. You are not required by law to make a deposit, but sellers tend to judge the sincerity of buyers by the size of their deposits. In one way, less is best since you may lose your money if the deal falls through (this may depend on a contingency clause in your purchase offer about breaking the deal at the last minute.) Alternately, a big earnest money deposit might encourage the seller to agree to a lower purchase price.

Most real estate brokers expect to have a deposit cheque in hand when presenting your offer to the seller. The cheque should never be made out directly to the seller, however, but to the real estate brokerage as trustee or fiduciary agent—one of those terms should be part of the payee's name on the cheque—or to an escrow service that holds your money in trust. Decide with your broker or lawyer where your earnest money will go until the purchase is final. If it is a big deposit, your purchase offer should stipulate that it be held in an interest-bearing account with interest credited to you. The offer should also set a date for refunding the money if the seller does not accept your offer or if you withdraw it before he accepts.

MAXIMIZING YOUR POWER TO NEGOTIATE

To clinch the best deal, you should arm yourself with firm facts about the local real estate market. You also must be careful not to reveal any clues that might give the seller leverage.

1. Before making an offer on a home, have a real estate broker (your buyer's broker or the listing agent) prepare a comparative market analysis. This will show you recent sales prices of similar homes in the area. When you then consider both the added features and notable problems of the house you are looking at, you can determine whether the asking price is fair.

2. Avoid talking to the seller about why you are buying a house. If a seller knows that you must buy quickly because you are relocating for a new job, he can use your urgency to his advantage.

3. Be sure the seller knows that you are considering other houses, even if his is the one you want most. The threat of competition for your interest will encourage him to keep his price and conditions within fair market value.

4. If you are home shopping with your spouse or a friend, save any show of enthusiasm for a particular house until you are in private. If the seller knows you really like the house, he will have an edge over you during negotiations.

Dealing With Final Details

After you complete your purchase agreement and before the closing, or settlement date, you need to make sure that the seller is the true owner of the home, that no claims exist against the property, and that the seller has the right to sell the property. If problems do arise, you might be able to renegotiate the terms or timing of your final contract and still complete the sale.

When someone owns real estate, he is said to hold "title" to the property. Bad or defective title to a property occurs for a variety of reasons: liens (financial claims) against the property; an unpaid second mortgage; an heir of the previous owner suddenly appearing to claim ownership; or a violation of community association standards.

To ensure that a house does not have a defective title, you need a "title search." This can be conducted by a title insurance company or a lawyer. The search traces the history of the

Put Legal Protections in Your Purchase Offer

Contingencies in your formal purchase offer are particular conditions that allow you to break or to renegotiate the purchase contract if certain aspects of the deal are not met to your satisfaction. Remember, the purchase contract—or binder—can become the final contract. So negotiate the following issues before you sign your purchase offer:

• Set a limit on the seller's response time to your offer. By giving him 48 hours, for example, you keep the seller from waiting for better bids from other buyers while keeping you in limbo.

• Make your purchase offer contingent on the results of a professional home inspection by an inspector of your choice. This may include a termite and environmental inspection.

• Insist that the seller provide you with a written disclosure of defects in the property before you agree on a final price.

• If you are applying for a mortgage, include an escape clause that lets you pull out of the deal if your loan is not approved within a designated time.

• If the purchase of your new home depends on selling your current residence, try to add a clause that frees you from the purchase contract if you cannot sell your home within a designated time.

• Establish the dates for settlement (closing) and for taking possession of the house.

• Enumerate exactly which features and fixtures of the home will be included in the purchase, such as kitchen appliances, lighting fixtures, carpeting, bookcases, or a backyard swing set.

• Include a description of the condition you expect the house to be in at settlement time. Ideally, the house should be "broom clean," or swept of debris, and completely intact.

• Agree in advance to a specific amount of penalty if you need to back out of the deal or if you learn something about the property (other than a defect in the house, for instance) that makes the deal untenable for you. Known as a "liquidated damages clause," it is part of most purchase offers. Try to limit liquidated damages to the earnest money deposit; do not agree to a clause requiring more money.

• Watch out for arbitration clauses in purchase offers prepared by brokers. These clauses oblige the broker, buyer, and seller to arbitrate any dispute. If you agree to this and the offer becomes binding, you forfeit your legal right to sue.

property, determines whether there are any current claims or encumbrances against the property, and tells you what problems must be cleared up before you can have "clear title" to the property. You can then decide whether you want the seller to fix the problems (such as paying the property taxes due), or whether you should cancel the sale. Some title defects are simply due to recording errors (such as failure to show a paid-up second mortgage) and are easily fixed.

Even with a title search, most buyers opt for the protection of title insurance. There are two types: lender's and owner's. Lender's title insurance—required by lenders, paid by buyers—protects lenders from faulty title. Owner's title insurance protects the buyer from claims against the property that predate the buyer's ownership. Both policies carry a one-time fee, usually half a percentage point of the purchase price. The buyer might pay for both or negotiate to split costs with the seller.

GET THE VITAL DEED

Besides clear title to a home, a buyer needs a valid "deed." A deed is a written document signed by the seller that describes the property and confirms title or ownership. Deeds are held at the county recorder's office. If the signature on a deed has been forged or falsified, it could invalidate your right to ownership—even if you have already bought the home.

To protect against bad deeds, buyers usually require a general warranty deed (also called "full covenant and warranty"), in which the seller ensures legal soundness of the title of the home. While general warranty deeds allow the buyer to sue the seller if claims against the home are discovered, suing is a minor consolation to losing a home.

Other types of deeds offer less protection for the buyer. A "quitclaim deed," for example, merely transfers the seller's ownership to the buyer and does not guarantee clear title. A "grant deed" is more definitive, but does not include a promise by the seller to defend the buyer against future third-party claims. Be sure to clarify the type of deed you will receive from the seller before closing the purchase.

Strategies for Closing Day

When the purchase offer evolves into a final sales contract, the buyer gives the seller a down payment. Then the buyer works to secure a mortgage (see "Paying for Your Home," page 25), and the "closing," or settlement, date is set. This is also the time for a buyer to ensure the best deal possible with certain last-minute efforts. These include a final walk-through of the home, whether owner-occupied or newly built, which should occur a day or two before closing. You should look for glaring new problems (a floor badly damaged by the seller's moving service) or discrepancies with your purchase agreement (the seller removed a lighting fixture that was part of the contract). Insist that problems be remedied, or prepare to negotiate a repair or replacement fee with the seller at closing.

A Bad Time to Change Plans

PROBLEM
Doug and Mary made a purchase offer on a newly built custom home, put down an earnest money deposit, and agreed to a final sale price with the builder. A week later, because of changes in their anticipated job transfers, they decided not to buy the house. Are they entitled to a refund of their earnest money?

ACTION
Because the builder was unusually generous, Doug and Mary got back their deposit though they could have ended up in court. While contingencies in purchase offers normally protect buyers from penalty if their mortgage falls through or other conditions aren't met, buyers who change their minds have to forfeit their earnest money deposit. If they hadn't been so lucky, Doug and Mary's builder could have sued them for damages arising from their breaking the contract. If he had, they could have tried to settle out of court by agreeing to pay the costs of the building plans and site work.

Before closing date, the buyer needs to buy a home insurance policy to protect the new investment in the event of damage or destruction. This insurance also protects the mortgage lender's investment, and at closing the buyer must provide proof of purchase of the policy to the lender. (See also "Managing Your Home," page 30.)

On closing day, the least anxious buyers are those who are well prepared. They have attended to all the prepurchase concerns discussed on the preceding pages and are fully informed about what will happen during the closing. In some provinces, a mortgage lender must provide the buyer with an itemized estimate of settlement costs and a detailed account of closing procedures and terminology. Brokers can also convey or supplement this information, but a buyer should rely primarily on the advice of a lawyer, or a notary in Quebec.

The home buyer's closing costs typically include:

- Balance of the purchase price not covered in the deposit and in the mortgage amount being borrowed.
- Items payable in connection with the mortgage, which might include the lender's home appraisal fees and prepayment of insurance and property taxes for the year.

TEN CONTRACT ESSENTIALS

Be sure a contract includes:

1. A formal description of the property and its boundaries, including the physical terrain and the boundary markers, preferably done by a licensed surveyor.

2. Identification of features and fixtures that the seller is obliged to transfer to you as part of the property sale.

3. Total purchase price, including the amount of earnest money deposit, down payment, and the balance due in your mortgage loan.

4. The identity of the escrow agent who holds the earnest money deposit.

5. Agreement between you and the seller on who pays what costs, through what date, for municipal assessments such as property taxes.

6. For the purchase of newly built homes, the builder's guarantee of habitability and good workmanship.

7. Assurance of clear title to the home, unencumbered by claims against the property.

8. Promise of a valid deed that entitles the present owner to sell the home to you.

9. Firm date of occupancy. Without this you may have to leave your old home before the seller has left your new one.

10. A detailed written description of the house and contents upon occupancy.

- Title charges, for title search, and both owner's and lender's title insurance.
- Government recording and transfer fees, for recording property documents at the county courthouse.
- Property and pest inspections (both buyer's and lender's).
- Buyer's broker commission, if applicable, and lawyer's fee.

Along with vigorous cheque writing to cover these costs, you also engage in final rites with the seller. These include: coordinating the payment of utilities; calculating property tax payments so that you pick up the tab where the seller leaves off; making adjustments for any missing fixtures. You should also be able to produce proof of property and fire insurance (for the benefit of the mortgage holder who may be the seller). Once the closing is completed, advise the municipality that all tax bills should henceforth be sent to you. Also make new contracts with hydro and heating supply companies, and advise credit card issuers and Revenue Canada of your new address. Last but not least, remember to get the keys!

Closing Costs You Can Negotiate

Closing ceremonies of a home sale consist mostly of the buyer writing cashier's cheques to various parties. While local custom often dictates whether the seller or buyer pays certain one-time fees at closing, buyers should know that most of the following costs are negotiable:

• **Mortgage loan fee.** You can suggest that the seller pay your lender's fee for issuing a loan (usually about one or two percent of the total loan). After all, the seller gains if your loan is expedited. If you are buying a new house, try to get the builder to pay this fee to free your cash for the down payment.

• **Title insurance.** Lender's and owner's title insurance can both be paid by the buyer, or in some cases, they can be shared by the buyer and seller. Your final contract should clarify who pays which costs.

• **Credit report.** Lenders charge a nominal fee to explore your credit history. You can try to add this fee to other expenses charged by the lending institution and propose that the seller pay all or part of the costs.

• **Transfer fees.** If you are buying a home from a current occupant, the local municipality charges small fees to record the transfer of ownership into public records. Either buyer or seller can pay, so you could ask the buyer to accept responsibility for this cost too.

• **Escrow fees.** When you make an earnest money deposit, you normally leave it in the hands of a neutral third party, such as an escrow agent. This third party charges you for the safekeeping of your money. Since this money eventually goes to the seller as part of the sale price, you might want to ask the seller to pay for all or part of the escrow service.

• **Statement of adjustments.** If the closing date falls between billing cycles of property taxes and basic maintenance bills such as oil and hydro, you and the seller must negotiate the fair division of these costs. If you are signing toward the end of the month, you might ask the seller to pay the month's property tax, for example.

• **Property survey.** If you had a qualified surveyor survey the property before purchase, you could ask that your part of the survey costs be shared with the seller.

• **Lawyer/notary fees.** Your mortgage lender runs up legal expenses in closing your loan. Although the buyer would normally pay this cost, there is no harm in asking the seller to split it with you.

PAYING FOR YOUR HOME

Most home buyers cannot afford to put down the total price of a house. Mortgage loans are the answer, but finding the best loan is no easy chore.

Prequalifying for a Mortgage

Most home buyers make a deposit on the home they want to buy and then apply for a mortgage loan to help finance the deal. If the buyer has trouble settling the loan, the closing date for the purchase may be postponed or the sale canceled. To avoid these problems, it is smart to "prequalify" before applying for a loan.

Prequalifying for a mortgage loan means finding out how much money a lender is likely to loan you, based on an analysis of your monthly income and outstanding debt. Lenders use two traditional ratios: they compare the anticipated monthly housing expense—mortgage payment plus property taxes and home insurance premiums—with the borrower's gross monthly income; and they compare the borrower's overall monthly debt (mortgage loan payments, credit card debt, car payments, and so on) with gross monthly income. Generally, lenders want monthly house payments to stay below 28 percent of gross monthly income and total monthly debt to stay below 36 percent of gross monthly income.

You can ask a mortgage lender to prequalify you at no cost. The lender states the amount it would be willing to put up, and you can search for a purchase that falls within the correct range. Prequalifying for a mortgage is not a promise that a loan will be made, but it does get the attention of real estate brokers, who can be more confident that a client is good for the money, and it also lures sellers, who want to deal with buyers financially qualified to purchase their homes.

Making the Most of a Mortgage

A mortgage is a legal agreement with a lender whereby you give a promissory note and receive a loan to buy a house, and the lender gets the right to own the house if you do not repay the loan as agreed. This arrangement between lender and homeowner is commonly referred to as a mortgage.

In a traditional 20-year mortgage, you pay fixed, monthly payments that in early years return mainly interest profits to

The Mortgage Prepayment Option

What if you have a sudden increase in cash flow and want to pay off your entire mortgage loan before it is due? Although you might think lenders would be glad to get their money back as soon as possible, mortgage prepayment actually deprives them of profit from the interest you would otherwise pay.

In many cases it is wise to prepay your mortgage, especially if interest rates have dropped below the rate you are now paying. But unless you have a clause allowing for prepayment, the lender may charge you a three- to six-month penalty, plus expenses. In Alberta, British Columbia, and Ontario, a lender need not accept prepayment, unless you have negotiated this "privilege" before signing the mortgage deed.

So it is important to inquire about prepayment provisions, including partial prepayments at specific intervals, when applying for a loan. The flexibility of being able to pay off the loan sooner than later can save you thousands of dollars in interest payments.

The prepayment option also becomes crucial when a homeowner wants to refinance the mortgage. A harsh prepayment penalty in the original loan could offset the significant benefits of refinancing in a period of low interest rates.

TYPES OF MORTGAGES/PROS & CONS

When you are considering the manner in which you are going to pay for your home, the primary financial concern is the type of mortgage loan you should assume. Mortgages come in myriad forms: fixed and variable, 5-year to 20-year, government-guaranteed or privately funded, all with varying interest rates,

Type	Definition
Fixed-Rate Mortgage (FRM)	Fixed-rate mortgages are available for anywhere from 5 to 20 years to maturity. The borrower makes a fixed monthly payment for the life of the loan, paying a much higher proportion of interest to principal in the early years.
Variable-Rate Mortgage (VRM)	Interest rates on VRMs are based on a financial index such as the prime rate set by the Bank of Canada. Because these rates fluctuate over the life of the mortgage loan, a borrower's monthly mortgage payments may change frequently. Most lenders impose caps (limits) on these changes.
Wraparound Mortgage	This mortgage covers an existing mortgage and the balance to be paid. If a property priced at $150,000 has an outstanding $60,000 mortgage, a purchaser with a $20,000 downpayment would probably fare better taking out a $130,000 wraparound mortgage than taking out a second mortgage for $70,000.
Balloon Mortgage	Balloon mortgages offer equal monthly payments based on a fixed interest rate, with one large final payment at the end of a relatively short term, usually 5 or 10 years. Monthly payments typically cover interest, while the last payment repays all the principal.
Government Loans	Canada Mortgage and Housing Corporation (CMHC) administers National Housing Act loans and grants and insures mortgages from private lenders. Provincial programs, such as Ontario's Home Ownership Saving Plan (OHOSP) and British Columbia's Home Purchase Assistance Act (HPAA), also apply in some areas.
RRSP Mortgage	First-time home buyers may borrow from a self-directed Registered Retirement Saving Plan (RRSP) without penalty provided the loan is paid back in 15 years. Each spouse may withdraw up to $20,000.
Shared-Equity Mortgage	Friends, relatives, or business partners buy property together and share down payments and/or monthly mortgage payments, but only one partner occupies the residence. Partners either share profits from the sale of the house, or one buys the other's share. This mortgage also known as a mortgage on undivided interests of property is most common in commercial property investments.
Assumable Mortgage	An assumable mortgage is passed on to the new homeowner at the former owner's interest rate. Generally, VRMs mortgage loans are assumable, while fixed-rate loans are not.
Graduated-Payment Mortgage (GPM)	This type of fixed-rate loan is a crescendo of monthly payments that start small and rise steadily, until leveling off for the duration of the loan. Designed for younger home buyers with growing earning power who will not be able to afford higher payments for 5 to 10 years.
Vendor Take-Back	In times of high interest rates, the current owner may offer to finance the new owner's purchase, using the home as collateral. In effect, the seller takes a first or second mortgage on the property while transferring ownership to the buyer.

repayment requirements, and monetary boundaries. In addition, each one has advantages and disadvantages for you depending upon your financial situation, age, desires, and needs. If you are among the many borrowers who have trouble understanding their mortgage options, let alone figuring out which is best for them, this chart is designed to help. It describes the 10 most common types of mortgage loans and briefly discusses the most relevant pros and cons for each type of loan.

Pros	*Cons*
The borrower has the security of predictable monthly mortgage expenses.	Lenders often charge a higher interest rate on FRMs than other types of mortgage loans to protect their interest income in periods of higher interest rates.
Initial interest rates of VRMs are two or three percent lower than fixed rate mortgages, and borrowers have lower monthly mortgage payments when interest rates go down.	When interest rates go up, so do mortgage payments. Even with caps on monthly increases, a steep rise in rates could cause mortgage payments to soar beyond what you can afford.
The buyer's borrowing costs for a $130,000 first mortgage are probably less than if he assumed a $60,000 first mortgage and a $70,000 second mortgage. And if interest on the $130,000 exceeds interest on the original $60,000, the lender also benefits.	In the case of a wraparound mortgage, you may be prohibited from prepaying the loan.
Starting costs and monthly payments are low, making this option especially attractive for first-time home buyers who have no profit from selling a former residence.	Monthly payments are mostly interest, so the borrower gets no equity in the home until the loan is paid. The final payment may be so big that it requires refinancing. A dangerous option.
Lower interest rates, easier qualifying requirements, and lower down-payment requirements make government loans attractive to many qualified borrowers.	Loan amounts average less than non-government (conventional) loans. Homes eligible for CMHC loans may not cost more than $250,000 in Ontario and British Columbia, $175,000 in major centers, and $125,000 in other areas.
Interest and tax savings are substantial. You save the interest you would ordinarily pay to a lending institution, and all your repayments to the plan are not taxable until you cash in your RRSP.	In the short term your RRSP plan is greatly reduced. Also the loan must be guaranteed by the CMHC or the Mortgage Insurance Company of Canada.
One partner helps make the purchase possible and gets tax advantages and, hopefully, profit, while the other partner gets to live in the home and gets help with mortgage payments.	Resident partners give up equity in the property, while investor partners may lose anticipated profit if homes or other real estate do not gain value. For both parties, equity sharing entails complex legal and tax issues.
In a period of high interest rates, a buyer who can assume the seller's lower-rate loan pays less total interest and smaller monthly payments. The seller enhances the value of her home.	Lenders may charge a fee for assuming a mortgage. Depending on the outstanding balance and the interest rate of the old loan, assuming the seller's loan can cost more than a new loan.
In the early years of the loan, when new homeowners can least afford monthly mortgage payments, rates are lower than average fixed-rate loans. Later, when you can better afford it, rates are higher.	If your income does not rise as anticipated by you and your lender, or you unexpectedly get laid off, you may have trouble keeping up with the escalating monthly payments.
For the buyer, the interest rate of a take-back is usually lower than market rate, making this loan a no-lose prospect. Sellers can sell homes more quickly and still obtain their equity.	Take-backs usually require a final balloon payment, which the buyer may have to refinance. Sellers who do not arrange take-backs through traditional lenders assume financial risk.

What Makes Lenders Wary?

When you apply for a mortgage loan, the lender checks your financial history, and will note unfavorably any unusual cash flow within the previous six months. Lenders are looking for a steady income, not fluctuating highs and lows. As a result, home buyers who accept financial help from relatives or friends to make a down payment might be dismayed to find that gifts can hinder their eligibility for a mortgage loan.

If you get financial help from someone, ask her to write a "gift letter" to your lender confirming that the money is a gift and not a loan. This assures the lender that you are not going further into debt and jeopardizing your ability to repay the lender's loan.

Prospective borrowers who sell pricey personal assets, such as a boat or car, to fund the down payment may also be viewed unfavorably by lenders. Plan to sell personal assets more than six months before applying for the loan.

Lenders are also reluctant to lend money to people already in debt, so you should use any available cash to pay off your credit-card debt before applying for the loan.

If you are strapped for cash, consider trying to get a mortgage from Canada Mortgage and Housing Corporation or your provincial mortgage and housing authority if your province has one. They offer lower interest rates, and their mortgages are generally easier to qualify for than conventional mortgages.

the lender for your use of its money and in later years repay primarily the principal—the amount of money you actually borrowed. Through the process of "amortization," or paying off your debt, you increasingly gain equity (ownership) in the property. Variable or adjustable-rate mortgage loans offer different payment schedules and more flexible interest rates.

Mortgage loans are offered by a number of sources: (1) commercial banks; (2) mortgage bankers specializing in mortgage loans; (3) the government-run Canada Mortgage and Housing Corporation (CMHC); (4) credit unions; and (5) private individuals, often the seller of the property. Once you have decided which lender offers the best mortgage options and made your application, the lender will find out if your income is sufficient to cover monthly mortgage payments and other debts, determine if you have enough assets to close the loan, investigate your credit history, and appraise the property value of your prospective home.

Meanwhile, you should try to get a loan commitment letter from your lender with a "lock-in agreement" stipulating the exact interest rate of the loan. This agreement protects you from rising interest rates during the application process. You may be charged a fee by your lender to lock in an interest rate.

GETTING INFORMATION FROM A LENDER

The Bank Act and most provincial consumer laws require the lender to itemize all loan costs and provide you with a statement clearly showing the amount of capital borrowed and all costs associated with this, including interest. You can expect this information shortly after you receive a commitment letter from the lender—formal receipt that your mortgage loan application is being processed.

Loan costs include points (a one-time fee of several percentage points of the total loan); a loan application fee; credit check fees; home appraisal, home inspection, and escrow fees; mortgage insurance; lender's title insurance; and title search fees. The lender must also tell you the finance charge (interest) on the loan and the annual percentage rate (APR) for the loan. Because lenders charge different points and interest rates, the APR is the closest thing consumers have to a standard measure of comparison (see also YOUR MONEY, page 278).

Many mortgage lenders sell mortgages to private investors, mutual fund, or private firms. By selling the loans, lenders get cash back to reinvest, while those who buy the loans, referred to as the "secondary market," get the right to receive the principal and interest paid by borrowers. When you apply for a loan, lenders should tell you whether they intend to sell your mortgage. If so, be sure to ask what effect, if any, that would have on you.

WHAT IF YOUR BANK SAYS "NO"?

If you are rejected for a traditional mortgage, it may be that the size or steadiness of your income is insufficient, your overall debt is too high, or the cost of the home is more than the lender thinks you can afford. Or you may be the victim of discrimination. The Bank Act and some provincial housing laws dictate that if a lender rejects your loan application, he must tell you why. The lender also must give you a copy of the credit-bureau report that was used to gauge your qualifications. The credit report includes your history of on-time payments, the amount of credit available to you, and other pertinent information. Since credit bureaus make mistakes, borrowers should not hesitate to question their accuracy. (See also YOUR MONEY, page 295.)

If you cannot get anywhere with traditional mortgage lenders, you might consider government-sponsored or other lending sources. But be careful. Generally, the less proof of credit verification a lender requires, the higher the cost of the loan to the borrower—higher interest, extra fees, or larger down payments.

If you were a victim of discrimination by a federally chartered financial institution, complain to the Federal Human Rights Commission. If the lender is not federally chartered, consult your provincial human rights board.

Who Needs Mortgage Insurance?

When you are accepted for a loan, you may be required to pay for mortgage default insurance. (This is different from "mortgage life insurance," an optional policy that pays off your debt if you die before the mortgage is paid off.) Mortgage default insurance protects the lender from borrowers who default on their loans by covering the lender's losses. The entire first-year premium on the insurance is often paid for by the buyer at settlement, with subsequent premium payments paid from the escrow account your lender sets up to cover this and other periodic costs.

Lenders normally require that mortgage default insurance on loans cover 80 percent or more of the cost of the property. In other words, the down payment is less than 20 percent of the appraised value of the house.

Although the purpose of this insurance is to protect the lender, it can also help borrowers buy a home with less money down. Once you have acquired 50 percent equity in the home, your lender should no longer require you to maintain the default insurance.

Foreclosure: A Frightening Concept

A specter that haunts many homeowners with mortgage loans is the fear of default and foreclosure. The laws and rules governing procedures are dauntingly complex, but some salient features of the process are:

✔ *Default.* An owner can default on a mortgage loan by missing a payment or simply being late with one. Lenders generally overlook one or two late or missed payments, but do not have to.

✔ *Acceleration.* Once an owner is in default, the lender has the right to demand the entire amount of the loan at once.

✔ *Workout.* The owner should contact the lender immediately to try to work out a solution; such as a new loan schedule. The lender, anxious to avoid the laborious foreclosure process, may be willing to negotiate.

✔ *Foreclosure.* If the owner cannot pay the debt or work out a solution, the lender usually must go to court to get a foreclosure judgment against the owner. The owner may be able to defend against it, but will need a lawyer to do so.

✔ *Last resort.* Before the actual foreclosure sale, an owner usually has the right to get the home back by paying the mortgage debt and costs. One way of doing this might be to refinance the mortgage with another lender.

MANAGING YOUR HOME

Insurance, taxes, building flaws, mortgage lenders, utilities, and greedy governments may all have to be dealt with as you settle into your new house.

1₂3...

FILING A PROPER CASUALTY CLAIM

In the wake of burglary, fire, or any other disaster, you can take these steps to file a complete casualty insurance claim:

1. Call your insurance agent or company immediately to report loss or damage. They will send you a claim form and arrange for an insurance adjuster to inspect the damage.

2. Insurance companies will ask you to supply reports of loss or damage as soon as possible. Be as accurate as you can—and if you later discover something additional that was stolen, amend your list of losses.

3. Don't have permanent repairs made until the insurance claims adjuster has seen the damage. If you must have immediate work done, such as new locks or windows, keep receipts and take pictures of the damage.

4. Your claim form will ask you to itemize damaged or stolen possessions, including the original purchase price (or appraised value of an antique or high-value gift) and current replacement cost. Document your information with receipts, canceled cheques, appraisals, pictures, and videotapes that identify the damaged or stolen belongings.

How Much Home Insurance?

As long as you owe money on a mortgage loan, your lender will require that you maintain a homeowners insurance policy. This insurance does more than just protect a lender's investment—your home—if it is damaged or destroyed. A homeowners policy also protects your stake in the property and your finances in case you are sued for accidents that occur on your premises.

A homeowners insurance policy should include two types of coverage: "casualty protection," which covers you in case of loss or damage to your home or personal property; and "liability protection," which guards you against lawsuits for injuries that occur to others on your property. You can buy one or several standard policies and supplement them with additional coverage, if needed. For homeowners insurance to be effective and worth the price you pay for it, you need to start with an appropriate amount of coverage and keep increasing it as your property increases in value.

CASUALTY INSURANCE

Three standard home casualty insurance policies, HO-1 (HO stands for homeowners), HO-2, and HO-3, protect you against a variety of perils that might damage your home and personal property. The HO-1 policy affords the barest protection of your property and possessions from 11 common perils including fire, windstorms, and theft. The more popular HO-2 offers protection from 18 perils, while the most common policy, HO-3, protects the dwelling but not its contents from all other perils except certain standard exclusions. For an extra charge you can always add a clause (endorsement) which would cover your personal property up to 10 percent of the value of the insurance on your home. Earthquake or flood damage, for example, is covered only by separate, more costly policies. HO-4 covers renters, while HO-5, like HO-3, protects a dwelling and also covers its contents.

Homeowners must guard against being over-insured—paying for excessive coverage—as well as underinsured—risking inadequate coverage during crisis situations. You can determine the right amount of casualty insurance you need by assessing how much it would cost to rebuild your house if it were completely destroyed. This "replacement cost" is different from the market value (likely sale price) of a home, because market value includes the value of the land and its location within the community. If your ocean-view home that could sell for $300,000 is destroyed by fire, you may have to spend $180,000 to rebuild it. Because the fire has not diminished the value of your ocean-view lot, your casualty insurance need only cover the replacement value of the house and belongings. (It can also work the other way: An old house might well cost much more to replace than it could fetch on the current market.)

You need an appraiser to assess the value of your house, but you can calculate the value of your personal belongings by making a complete inventory of items, from furniture to clothing, including purchase date and price. Since standard policies limit reimbursement for damaged or destroyed personal property, you may need extra insurance, or "floaters," for valuable assets such as jewelry, art, or furs. A floater is either a separate policy (for an art collection, for instance) or an extension of a stan-

Preventing Accidents on Your Property

According to personal injury law, you can be held responsible if someone is injured on your property. The degree of your fault depends on how serious the injury, how dangerous the conditions that caused it, and what you did to correct those conditions.

• Occupier's liability law requires homeowners and renters to take reasonable care to prevent injuries to third parties on the property. Reasonable care, though not precisely defined by law, means using common sense to foresee and prevent problems, such as warning visitors about a temporarily exposed wire or a pet that may turn violent.

• Generally the duty of care is higher for an invited guest or certain type of worker, a meter reader for example, than for an uninvited salesperson, but the distinction between invitees, business persons, and innocent trespassers is gradually disappearing in Canadian law. Ontario, for example, has passed the Occupiers Liability Act and the Trespass to Property Act to supplant the common law by statute, so that a duty to care applies to all visitors unless the occupier of the property has restricted or modified his duty, or the visitor has assumed the risk of entering the property.

• A homeowner can be held responsible for intentionally causing harm to anyone entering the property, including trespassers. If a passerby is injured by touching an electrified fence that had no warnings, you may have to pay her damages.

• The courts are tougher on homeowners when children are injured, since children lack the judgment of adults and are therefore more vulnerable. You may be responsible if a child enters your property without permission—perhaps sneaking into your backyard, diving in the shallow end of the swimming pool, and cutting his head.

• You are personally responsible for on-the-job injuries of household employees, defined as anyone you pay to do part- or full-time work where you provide materials. A babysitter or secretary for a home business, for example, is a household employee. You should consider carrying workers' compensation insurance for these workers to protect yourself from lawsuits. The coverage is mandatory if the person works for you on a regular basis. You may also need separate insurance for the home business.

• If you are sued for an accident and injury that occurred on your property, consult your lawyer and your insurance company immediately. Smaller insurance claims are routinely settled outside of court, even if the homeowner concerned is not legally at fault.

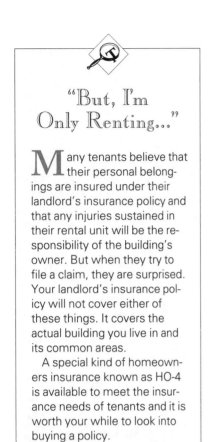

"But, I'm Only Renting..."

Many tenants believe that their personal belongings are insured under their landlord's insurance policy and that any injuries sustained in their rental unit will be the responsibility of the building's owner. But when they try to file a claim, they are surprised. Your landlord's insurance policy will not cover either of these things. It covers the actual building you live in and its common areas.

A special kind of homeowners insurance known as HO-4 is available to meet the insurance needs of tenants and it is worth your while to look into buying a policy.

A tenants policy will insure your belongings against the same perils regular homeowner's insurance covers, including: fire; riot; vandalism; theft; weight of ice, snow, and sleet; freezing of plumbing systems; certain leakage; and damage to some heating systems. This coverage also pays for living expenses you incur as a result of these perils. If your home is damaged by fire, for example, you may be covered for the cost of accommodation and living expenses while repairs are being made.

HO-4 liability coverage applies to injuries or damages caused by you, a family member, or even a pet in your home. For example, if a guest slips and falls in your home, your insurance will cover any expenses she incurs and your legal costs if you are sued.

dard policy and may cost from several cents to several dollars per $100 of coverage.

Along with floaters, many standard policies offer complementary coverage for certain perils, including floods, earthquakes, hurricanes, and riots. Insurers impose higher premiums and deductibles on these high-risk policies, and sometimes even refuse insurance. If you feel you have been unfairly denied coverage, contact your provincial superintendent of insurance. This office regulates the prices companies charge, the policies they offer, and whom they can refuse.

LIABILITY INSURANCE

As a homeowner, one of the risks you assume is that someone might be injured on your property and hold you financially responsible for damages. Liability insurance protects you from this risk. It pays the legal costs and actual damages of a claim against you (and your family) for bodily injury or property damage that you, or your pets, may cause to others on your property. Unlike casualty insurance, a liability policy does not require you to pay a deductible amount before the insurer covers your losses. However, your liability coverage may be limited, typically to $200,000.

Occupier's liability law, as defined in nearly every province, requires homeowners to exercise reasonable care to prevent injuries to third parties on their property. If you are sued, and your liability insurer agrees that you have acted reasonably to prevent injury to others, your legal expenses and any damages should be covered by your insurer to the limits of your policy, after which you are responsible for costs incurred.

If you have a net worth greater than the limit of your liability insurance, you should consider extra, or "umbrella," coverage. This comes separately and pays for losses beyond the limits of a standard policy. You are covered, for instance, if a delivery person slips on your front steps, breaks an arm, and sues you for an exorbitant amount because he thinks you are wealthy. Umbrella coverage also protects against suits for libel, slander, or invasion of privacy.

VARIATIONS ON STANDARD POLICIES

Variations on standard liability and casualty insurance are also available for owners of condominiums, cooperatives, older homes, and vacation homes. As with traditional single-family dwellings, it is important for owners of other types of homes to buy the appropriate homeowners insurance policy in order to avoid being overcharged on premiums and underinsured in the event of damage or disaster. Homeowners 6 (HO-6) is the standard casualty policy for condo and co-op owners. It protects the personal possessions and interior space of the owner.

It does not provide insurance coverage for the structure itself. That is usually covered by the condominium or co-op association. (See also "Condos, Co-ops, and Planned Communities," page 66.)

Property insurance companies offer different casualty policies for older homes, defined differently by each company, but usually 25 years and older. Because older homes are more likely to have outdated wiring or other systems and may not be modernized to meet new building codes, insurance companies often charge more for these policies. The standard older home casualty policy, HO-8, covers the basic perils of the HO-1 policy, such as fire and theft.

HO-8 does *not* cover a multitude of perils that are covered in newer homes: freezing or bursting pipes, electrical damages, collapse from weight of snow, and others. Historic homes—50 to 100 years and older—are the most difficult to insure, since architectural details may be irreplaceable or prohibitively expensive to replace. For insurers that specialize in historic homes, contact your local Heritage Foundation.

Owners of vacation homes and second residences need to purchase liability and casualty coverage separate from their primary residence policies. Although casualty coverage generally protects your property against burglary and theft, for example, policy restrictions often apply to homes that are not occupied for 30 days or longer. (When you leave even your primary residence unoccupied for a month or two, your policy may require you to notify your insurance agency.) As with any type of coverage, you need to decide, with the help of an insurance agent or broker, which policy is most appropriate for you.

When to Challenge Property Taxes

Home ownership generally includes the obligation to pay property taxes. Collected by local governments (cities, towns, villages, counties), these taxes pay for such public services as sanitation, fire and police departments, streetlights, sidewalks, schools, parks, hospitals, and more. Property owners pay according to the value of their property, as determined by government assessment.

The assessed value of a citizen's property is multiplied by a tax rate usually set by the local government. This determines each property owner's tax burden. While provincial budgets set a limit on taxation, local governments can adjust the tax rate periodically to fit their budgetary needs. They can also charge special assessments to fund one-time expenses, such as a new public library. Your local board of property tax assessors must notify you about the status of your property taxes

Refuting an Unfair Insurance Settlement

If you feel your insurance company shortchanged you in settlement of a claim, here are measures to take:

✔ *Reread your policy.* First you must know what situations your policy covers, as well as its financial limits. Only then can you decide if you are getting a proper response from the insurer. Does your policy have a large deductible? Check if you are insured for replacement value or depreciated cost of the lost or destroyed object.

✔ *Compare your estimate.* Add up your inventory of damages and losses and their approximate replacement value; compare your figures with the insurance adjuster's estimate. Then discuss the discrepancies with the adjuster.

✔ *Gather and offer evidence.* Before contesting your insurer's settlement, you must harness all evidence supporting your case. This includes written and pictorial evidence, such as the receipt for a stolen ring or a picture of an antique you inherited.

✔ *Talk to the boss.* If talking to the adjuster does not solve the problem, ask to speak with the claims department manager. Most companies will pay for an independent appraiser or arbitrator to help settle the disagreement.

✔ *Get government help.* If you are still dissatisfied, contact your provincial superintendent of insurance, who regulates the industry and often provides free mediation services.

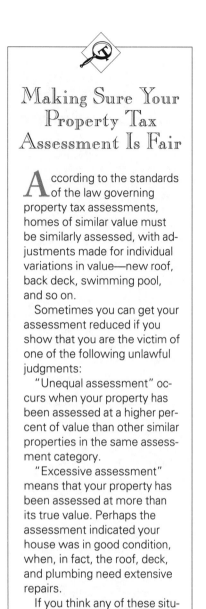

Making Sure Your Property Tax Assessment Is Fair

According to the standards of the law governing property tax assessments, homes of similar value must be similarly assessed, with adjustments made for individual variations in value—new roof, back deck, swimming pool, and so on.

Sometimes you can get your assessment reduced if you show that you are the victim of one of the following unlawful judgments:

"Unequal assessment" occurs when your property has been assessed at a higher percent of value than other similar properties in the same assessment category.

"Excessive assessment" means that your property has been assessed at more than its true value. Perhaps the assessment indicated your house was in good condition, when, in fact, the roof, deck, and plumbing need extensive repairs.

If you think any of these situations apply to you, call your local tax assessment board or contact a real estate lawyer.

and assessments for the upcoming fiscal year. (For fiscal years starting in July, tax-assessment notices are sent between November and January.) You have very little time—sometimes only 10 days—in which to challenge an unfair assessment.

According to legal standards, property tax assessments should be fair and just for all citizens, but the evaluations are often politically charged and economically complex. For example, a town losing money in commercial property taxes proposes major hikes in residential taxes.

MAKING SURE AN ASSESSMENT IS FAIR

Along with political and economic factors, it is common for assessors to make mistakes in calculating the value of your property. An assessor might inaccurately record the square footage of your home; mistake the size of your lot; see value-enhancing improvements where you made necessary repairs.

If you believe your property tax assessment is inaccurate or unfair, there are a number of steps you can take:

- Gather evidence to verify that your taxes are unfair. If the assessor's report incorrectly states that you have a two-car garage, take a picture of your garage to prove otherwise.
- Examine public records at the local assessor's office listing property values and taxes you and your neighbors pay.
- Join an organized community protest against tax increases or attend the next town meeting on rate hikes.
- File an appeal with your municipality, in writing, stating why the assessment is in error and include evidence; or meet with the local tax board and make an appeal.
- If necessary, appeal the decision of the tax board in court. A lawyer may take the case on contingency, collecting a fee only if you win.
- Hire an independent property-tax consultant (ask your accountant for a recommendation) instead of a lawyer to contest your assessment with the local tax board or in small claims tax court.

Your Escrow Money

A portion of a homeowner's monthly mortgage payment goes into a reserve fund, or escrow account, that holds sufficient sums to pay upcoming property taxes and homeowners insurance premiums. Your mortgage lender, who manages your escrow account, calculates your contribution based on anticipated yearly tax and insurance costs. The yearly cost is distributed evenly among your monthly mortgage loan payments.

Lenders generally review escrow accounts once a year to determine whether monthly payments need to be adjusted and then send you an annual notice. If you do not normally receive this notice from your lender, you can request one.

Homeowners should guard against two common problems with escrow accounts: inflated monthly payments and misappropriated interest earnings. Attorneys general in some provinces have successfully filed suit on behalf of homeowners against lenders guilty of cushioning escrow accounts. Some mortgage agreements allow for a one-month cushion or none at all. Thus if a homeowner's yearly tax and insurance costs are $1,200, monthly escrow charges should be $100 plus the stipulated one-month cushion. If the mortgagee is actually paying $250 a month for escrow, the lender is overcharging.

Mortgage lenders have also been found guilty of withholding interest profits from homeowners. Some mortgage deals, however, do not require lenders to pay property owners the interest from their escrow accounts. In other words, lenders benefit from the extra cash pool of escrow accounts and also make a profit from the interest generated from them.

Undercharging on escrow accounts also can be a problem. A lender may collect too little every month, then hit the homeowner for a large lump sum when taxes or insurance premiums are due. Or, if property taxes rise suddenly, lenders can impose an increase in escrow fees and require immediate cash payments. Homeowners unable to provide the lump sums in such situations risk defaulting on their mortgages.

Where large sums of money are concerned, it is advisable to trust nobody.

AGATHA CHRISTIE
Endless Night

Resolving Disputes With House Builders

If you discover structural problems in a house that is less than 10 years old, try to resolve the problems with the builder or developer. Even if you are not the first owner, you may still have recourse under provincial laws. Here are some steps to take:

• Review your homeowner's warranties to determine whether your complaints are covered. Then talk to the builder and try to compromise on a fair solution for repair or replacement.

• If your builder is unresponsive, find out from your municipal planner's office whether it has a statement of intent and agreement from your builder. This statement cites the builder's responsibility for property repairs and improvements.

• Contact your local Better Business Bureau (BBB) for information on the builder's company and any complaints filed against it. The BBB in many areas offers mediation services that are free to homeowners. After a homeowner files a complaint, the bureau asks the builder for a written statement, and tries to work out an agreement between the parties. It may take a month to reach a settlement. Sometimes no agreement is found, but it is worth trying. The local homeowners association may also be able to mediate a complaint.

• If mediation fails, the BBB or homeowners association may also offer binding arbitration that is enforceable by the courts. This process may last a couple of months. If settlement seems unlikely, see a lawyer about suing the builder or developer.

• New Home Warranty programs in several provinces will compensate owners of defective new homes.

MORTGAGE REPAYMENTS

Even a difference of one percentage point in mortgage rates can add up to thousands of dollars over the life of a mortgage. Here is some information to help keep the balance in your favor.

1. Ask your lender for a computerized repayment schedule. This way you see exactly where you stand in regard to your repayment.

2. You will pay down the mortgage faster, and at considerable savings, if you repay it in weekly or biweekly installments, rather than monthly.

3. Take advantage of any prepayments permitted by your mortgage agreement. Making 13 payments a year instead of 12, or paying off an extra 10 percent of the balance each year will shorten the term of your mortgage and save thousands in interest payments.

4. Try to have the interest part of your payment compounded monthly rather than semiannually. But in any case make sure that it is compounded. The compounded interest will save you thousands of dollars over the life of your mortgage.

You can analyze your own escrow account at any time by reviewing your original loan contract and then comparing it with the lender's annual statement of your escrow account. Also check your mortgage contract to determine whether it specifies a maximum amount of money the lender may maintain in your account. Or you can hire a private mortgage monitor who will analyze your escrow account and flag any irregularities.

Structural and Property Defects

When you buy a home, the law acknowledges your right to assume it will be decently constructed and safe to inhabit. As with any product you buy, your home should be free from major problems, defects, and dangers. Almost every province guarantees so-called implied warranties of habitability and workmanship with the purchase of a new home, and thousands of homeowners every year invoke legal protections in their claims against manufacturers, builders, and others responsible for a panoply of problems.

Owners of newly built homes have the most recourse under the law for complaints of major structural problems and property defects. But even if you bought a previously occupied, or older, home, you have a variety of options for recourse. Recourse can be based on two types of flaws: "material defect," which is a major physical problem that might prevent someone from buying the property or that significantly diminishes its value, such as seasonal flooding; or "product defect," such as a broken stove or bad house paint.

Seeking redress will be easier if you take measures immediately upon discovering a defect in the house or property. Contract laws in some provinces may allow you to sue for up to six years after contract agreement, but claims may need to be brought within one year of discovery. You may have a claim even 10 years after purchase if the problem is a "latent defect," a problem you could not have known about until it became obvious at a later date—such as discovering that the house was built on land that had been used as a toxic waste dump.

LEGAL PROTECTIONS

Depending on the age of your house, major structural problems may be repaired or replaced free of charge under the terms of a written home warranty you received at settlement. If your home is newly built, you probably have a first-year warranty from the builder or developer that guarantees good workmanship. An older house that is less than 10 years old may still be covered by builder's or seller's warranties.

You may also have bought an extended-term version of this warranty (typically 10 years, renewable annually) that continues to cover some major design and structural defects, but to a lesser extent than in the first year. After the first year, for example, your warranty may not cover all repair service calls. You may be responsible.

So, for a plumbing problem too minor to be covered by your home warranty, but which still requires a plumber, you will have to pay for the service call on top of the cost of the warranty. But if your furnace breaks down and requires an expensive replacement part, that major expense would most likely be covered by the home warranty.

Dream House Turned Nightmare

PROBLEM

Nine months ago, Sara and Barry bought a one-family home on a new development site that was part of a larger planned community. At that time, other homes in the development were in various stages of completion. Except for Sara and Barry's landscaped yard and one other lot, the grounds throughout the site were still unsodded, without trees or vegetation. Heavy rains caused major drainage problems, ruining Sara and Barry's new sod and causing water damage in their basement. When they bought the home, the developer and real estate broker had assured them the site would be finished within three months of the settlement date. What recourse did they have?

ACTION

Early residents of unfinished developments with barren lots must often wait for completed landscaping until the developer sells or completes more homes. But Sara and Barry's problem was a property defect, and because they were the first owners of a newly built home, they had a good case for legal recourse. Upon the advice of a lawyer, they wrote a letter to the developer explaining the situation and requesting reimbursement for the damage. If the developer had not cleaned up the damage or made financial reparations, Sara and Barry could have sued him successfully.

Even if you do not discover a problem until several years after your purchase, you may have a valid legal claim if you act immediately. (The time period in which a lawsuit must be initiated varies from province to province.) First gather whatever pertinent evidence you have, such as home and product warranties, purchase contracts, correspondence with the seller or builder, photos or videos that document physical damage, and records of any mediation efforts between you and the party you consider financially responsible.

You might also keep notes on conversations you have with neighbors with similar problems and whose houses were built by the same contractor. These records will give your lawyer a more viable case.

What to Do About Defective Products

Every home is built and equipped with hundreds of manufactured products—doorknobs, dishwashers, ceiling fans, air ducts, plywood, plumbing, wiring, and so on.

If one of these products fails to function as it should, a homeowner may be legally protected by one of three warranties: (1) a written warranty from the manufacturer; (2) a homeowners warranty from the builder of the house, called an express warranty, which protects the first owner and sometimes subsequent owners of a newly built home; (3) an implied or express warranty from the builder or seller of the home. (See also :"Warranties: Legal Protections for Newly Built Homes," page 15.)

Product failure might be a breach of one of these warranties. If a problem occurs, contact the manufacturer to see if its warranty still applies.

If the company refuses to repair or replace an item, try the contractor, who may be even harder to pin down than the manufacturer. Next ask your provincial consumer affairs office about any implied warranties that might apply to your case. Finally, consult a lawyer, who will consider your case under both federal and provincial commercial product warranty laws.

If a home product causes injury or illness to someone, the manufacturer could be responsible under a personal injury liability law. If such an injury occurs in your home, contact a lawyer immediately.

Your Right to Challenge Utilities

123...

TAKING ON YOUR UTILITY

If you think your utility bills are inordinately high or suspect that you are being charged for someone else's service, here is what you can do about it:

1. Before contacting anyone, make sure you have a viable complaint. If it is the electric bill that worries you, turn off all lights and electrical appliances (don't forget the furnace and the refrigerator), take a flashlight, and look at the electric meter. If it is still running, you have fodder for a case that you are being wrongly charged.

2. Contact your utility company, explain your situation, and ask for a meter inspection. This is a more thorough examination than a meter reading. Industry Canada will verify your electric and gas meters at no cost. The telephone number is in the Blue Pages of your telephone directory.

3. If you plan to withhold payment of your bill while the utility responds to your complaint, put the complaint in writing and make sure that service will be continued in the interim.

4. If the utility company ignores your complaint, contact your province's public service commission, which regulates utility companies and investigates billing disputes. You can demand a formal hearing on your claim.

5. You can sue a utility company if the firm has denied you a fair hearing for your complaint. A letter from your lawyer may be enough to get the attention of the boss so that you won't have to sue.

Every homeowner relies on utility companies to provide basic services, including gas, electricity, oil, water, and local telephone service. Utility providers, whether Crown corporations or private companies, often hold local monopolies or near monopolies on these essential services. This means you can neither choose utility service providers from a competitive pool nor contest their rates.

Apart from telephone rates, which are governed by the federal Canadian Radio and Telecommunications Commission, the provinces regulate most utility companies. Despite this watchdog surveillance, homeowners are still subject to a host of errors and unfair practices.

Problems may arise because of technical or computer errors, inefficient or unethical business practices, lax laws, or environmental factors. Inaccurate billing is more readily detected in provinces that require utility companies to provide detailed bills. But wherever you live, it is worth scrutinizing your bill periodically for irregularities.

If you do question your bill and get into a dispute with a local utility, the utility company does not have the right to terminate your service without a fair hearing. Although unscrupulous utility companies have gone so far as to illegally enter residences to turn off service, a utility is supposed to use due process, and should terminate your service only after it has investigated your reason for not paying.

Most provinces require a detailed investigation of your complaint before service can be terminated. Should this happen, contact your province's utility regulator. Your service must be reinstated immediately, and remain "on" while the dispute is being investigated. If you experience problems, you may want to consult a lawyer about taking legal action. Bear in mind that you are not entitled to reinstatement of services pending an investigation if you failed to pay your utility bill. This, of course, would be a breach of contract on your part.

Battling Expropriation

Federal, provincial, and local governments, and some utility companies have the right to take your property for public use as long as they give you fair compensation. This governmental right to claim private property to serve the public good is called "eminent domain." This right is severely restricted by law and often hotly contested in practice. The Federal Expropriation Act, as well as similar provincial laws, protects private property from being taken "for public use without just compensation."

Private property can be taken for such "public use" projects as the construction of railways, highways, schools, hospitals, sewage systems, parks, airports, urban renewal housing, pylons for an electrical system, and pipelines.

Homeowners, neighborhood associations, and environmentalists have increasingly challenged government development plans on the grounds that a project is taking more property than necessary, that the plans are not well enough formed to warrant condemnation, or that condemnation does not serve a legitimate public purpose. So far, however, the government has nearly always managed to persuade the courts that it is justified in taking private property for public use.

ON THE LOSING END

If the government decides to take your property, it will make an offer of compensation based on its appraisal of your property. Compensation will be based on the current fair market value, not the replacement value of a home. You may be compensated for the cost of moving, of financing a new mortgage on another home, or for the devaluation of the rest of your property because of the government's new utilities.

You can contest the government's compensation offer in an expropriation hearing. Because expropriation proceedings vary by province and can be complex, consult a lawyer who specializes in this field.

I believe that every right implies a responsibility; every opportunity, an obligation; every possession, a duty.

JOHN D. ROCKEFELLER
American oil magnate
and philanthropist
1839–1937

Your Right to Contest Expropriation

Before the government or a public utility can legally take your property for public purposes, it must negotiate with you a fair price of compensation. If you do not agree on a price, these are steps you can take to reach more acceptable terms:

• Arrange your own professional appraisal to determine the current fair market value of your property. The best approach is to measure your property against comparable homes in the neighborhood. If your appraiser's figure is higher than the government's, you can present this evidence in condemnation proceedings.

• Enlist your neighbors' support. If their properties are also targets of condemnation you believe is unjust, you might consider joining forces for a class action suit against the government.

• If only some of your property is to be taken, you are entitled to request severance damages in addition to compensation for property taken. This may take the form of monetary compensation or alternative benefits that you can suggest, such as new grass and hedges for the border of your property next to which a school will be built.

• If you are dissatisfied with the decision of the expropriation board, you can appeal the case. Some expropriation cases have been fought all the way to the Supreme Court of Canada.

• If you feel the compensation offered is inadequate, contact a lawyer who specializes in condemnation proceedings. You may not have to pay the lawyer unless you win your case. These specialists sometimes work on a contingency basis: they take a percentage of the compensation fee.

Repairs and Improvements

Whether you are fixing up your home or just coping with wear and tear, you need to know how to finance the work, get someone to do it, and stay within the rules.

Home Equity Loans: Your Best Bet for Improvements?

When you renovate your home, make essential repairs, or do some home maintenance, you have the option of financing these projects with several kinds of bank loans that use your house as collateral: a second mortgage, or home equity loan; a home equity line of credit; or a reverse mortgage. The amount of the loan is based on your "equity," or degree of ownership, in the home. Before you do any renovations you should always request permission in writing from the mortgage lender. Most mortgage deeds prohibit any alteration to the building while the mortgage remains unpaid. A renovation could be considered a default under the loan agreement, just as would be the case if you dropped the insurance or missed a payment.

To determine how much you can borrow, lenders generally calculate your equity as the appraised market value of your home minus the amount you still owe on your mortgage loan. Therefore, the more you have paid off on your first mortgage loan, the more money you can access. Lenders usually offer loans for nearly the full amount of your equity (75 or 80 percent). You can also qualify for these loans, of course, if you have no mortgage.

Many municipalities and provinces provide incentive programs for major renovations or improvements. Check out the subsidies available by calling your provincial housing ministry or provincial association of building contractors. Subsidies may also be available from the federal government.

BORROWING FOR A NEW KITCHEN

A traditional second mortgage loan is a fixed-rate loan of a limited amount of money, repaid on a schedule of equal monthly payments for the life of the loan. Fixed-rate second mortgage loans often suit homeowners who need a lump sum for a set purpose, such as remodeling the kitchen for $10,000.

Although second mortgages are often referred to as home equity loans, home equity loans may be based on an adjustable interest rate rather than a fixed rate. This can give borrowers the advantage of lower interest rates in a favorable economic climate, but it leaves them vulnerable to unpredictable fluctuations and unfavorable rates.

Unlike a second mortgage or home equity loan, a home equity line of credit allows you to use the collateral of your home as a new source of cash up to the limit of your credit line. As with credit cards, you can borrow from and repay your credit line as often as you like. Typically, the lender gives you a chequebook, and you are free to write cheques against your account (the loan) and make deposits (loan payments) to the account at any time.

Reverse mortgages are usually available to homeowners age 60. In a reverse mortgage, your home is collateral for a loan that the lender advances to you in regular monthly installments—like your first mortgage loan in reverse. The debt is paid back when you sell your home, or, in the event of your death, is settled by your heirs. Reverse mortgages are more commonly used for supplementing pension income or Old Age Security benefits, but may also be used to increase cash flow for home improvements and other expenses.

Whatever kind of home equity loan you choose, remember that your home is on the line. If you are careless about spending and repaying the loan, the convenience of a home equity loan can become squandered equity and, at worst, foreclosure. Borrow cautiously and compare lenders' terms as carefully as you did for your first mortgage loan.

Complying With Building Codes

When you reconstruct or add on to your property, whether building a shed or converting an attic into a home office, you have a legal obligation to comply with local codes. National, provincial, and municipal building codes set standards for construction materials, and electrical, plumbing, and other home systems in order to protect the welfare and safety of residents. If your renovation or remodeling is going to alter the structure of your home or even change the use of a room, you will be expected to comply with building codes.

Building permits are the government's way of making you comply with building codes. You probably would need a building permit or other type of professional permit for projects ranging from converting a porch into a bedroom to installing a new dishwasher or building a tool shed. To get the permit, you will have to agree to abide by electrical, plumbing, and fire-safety codes, as well as rules governing height, distance from property lines, and location of any structures you build.

How to Get a Building Permit

Before you start a major construction or renovation project, you will need a building permit from your municipality's buildings department. Permits are the way local governments enforce compliance with health and safety codes. Localities issue permits when they are assured that the construction will be done according to local standards.

To obtain a building permit, you must submit an application that describes the planned project along with a nominal fee. For some projects, you may have to submit architect's or builder's plans with detailed specifications. In some areas, obtaining a building permit is so complicated that architects, engineers, or contractors include it as part of their service—perhaps at a price.

Once you have the permit, you may need to arrange with the municipality for on-site garbage receptacles or another method of disposing of construction materials. When construction is under way, you may receive visits from your local building inspector, who ensures the project is in compliance.

If you proceed without a permit, the municipality can halt construction or fine you or both. If you finish the project without a permit, you may be denied an updated certificate of occupancy, a vital document certifying the house meets local health and safety codes. This could be considered a latent defect, a major problem should you want to sell the house.

THE DANGERS OF CHEATING

Homeowners sometimes ignore building codes under the false assumption that a little change in their own house is nobody else's business. If your house bristles with scaffolding, though, or is trafficked by contractors, an official may notice the activity and take steps to penalize you for noncompliance.

INVESTIGATE ZONING CODES

Zoning codes divide municipalities into districts for specified use: commercial, industrial, residential, rural, and others. Zoning decisions are made locally by zoning boards composed of professional city planners and local citizens. When you are planning a renovation or addition, you will have to observe zoning laws as well as building codes.

For the most part, zoning codes are local and specific, and they change with time. So whether you live in a new neighborhood or inhabit a three-generation homestead, you should explore zoning codes before altering your home or how you use it. Your city or town hall houses the official zoning maps and regulations, which are available for public reading. The

Renovation Considerations

In recent years, rather than buying another house, more and more property owners have opted for renovating their present homes, or adding new additions. Here are some things to check out before you begin the job.

• Notify your mortgage lender of the work you have in mind. Usually the mortgage deed prohibits any alteration to the structure, so any unauthorized addition or renovation may constitute a default: the lender could then demand immediate full payment of the loan. You may think that your plans will increase the property value, but this may not be the case. A built-in swimming pool, for example—an improvement in your mind—may actually lower the value by reducing the lawn.

• Will the renovation contravene any zoning bylaws? You may have a problem, for example, if your municipality does not allow commercial activity in your neighborhood or on your street, and you want to build an additional room for use as a dentist's office or hairdressing salon.

• Zoning bylaws usually have "set back" restrictions, which set out minimum distances required between any kind of construction, and between any construction and various lot lines. Will your new room, terrace, or other planned extension be closer to your neighbor's home or to the city sidewalk than the minimum "set back"?

• If your renovation infringes on a zoning bylaw, you could ask your municipal zoning authority for a variance that would legalize your project. If refused, you have a right to appeal, and for this, you should consult a real estate lawyer.

• Remember that new construction could give rise to construction liens on your property. If your contractor did not fully pay the subcontractors and other workers, a lien could be placed on your property, sometimes without your knowledge. In most provinces construction lien acts require the owner to withhold about 15 percent of the contract until the subcontractors and other workers are paid.

• Generally the Goods and Services Tax (GST) does not apply to the purchase of older homes. However, it does apply to the purchase of a "substantially renovated" older home. If you are making major renovations to your property, an eventual buyer may be obliged to pay at present an extra 7 percent GST which will make your home less attractive. If you do not charge this 7 percent, you will be required to pay it yourself. Consult a lawyer to see if you can avoid this tax altogether.

maps will indicate how zones are divided and subdivided. Residential zones may distinguish among single-family home districts, condominium and apartment districts, historical home districts, and so on.

Zoning codes commonly regulate what you may build on your property, where you may build it, and how you may use a new or altered structure on your property. Planned communities, condominiums, and cooperatives usually add other rules (see also "Condos, Co-ops, and Planned Communities," page 66). If you ignore zoning regulations, you could be fined or, in a flagrant case, be forced to demolish offending structures. At the least you will have difficulty selling the property.

SETTING UP A HOME BUSINESS

Whatever kind of business you plan to set up in your home—day care, word processing, tax preparation, massage therapy, hair care—you should first investigate local zoning laws. Most problems occur when a home business attracts too many visitors, makes the neighborhood noisier than before, increases commercial traffic to the area, or uses advertising on the property. As the number of Canadians working from home increases, community regulations on home businesses are being reevaluated. You can help shape your local zoning rules by attending community and city council meetings on the subject.

The Value of Keeping Records

Whenever you make a change to your house or property, you should always keep accurate records of your expenses, using two categories: repairs (necessary maintenance) and improvements. The distinction matters most in taxes: local property-tax appraisals and federal income-tax calculations after a sale of property take into account expenditures on repairs and improvements. Although there is no capital gains taxes to pay on the sale of single family residences, this tax does apply to the sale of duplexes and apartment buildings. Home repairs also increase your property value and therefore increase your property taxes.

By property tax standards, a home improvement is work done to a home that fulfills at least one of three goals: (1) It increases the home's value (you convert a closet into a bathroom); (2) It extends its life (you modernize the entire electrical system of an older house); and (3) It changes and enhances the use of the property (you convert a garage into a rental apartment).

Important Records to Keep on File

Protect yourself against construction problems, tax challenges, and lawsuits. Keep records of home-construction projects until several years after selling your home.

✔ *Construction and design contracts.* Contracts with architects and contractors should indicate work and payment schedules and who takes responsibility for what.

✔ *Before-and-after photographs.* Pictures of the construction area can solve later problems with a contractor.

✔ *Names of suppliers, subcontractors, trade inspectors.* You should know who installed and inspected your electrical, plumbing, and heating systems.

✔ *Name of on-site city building inspector.* If you are found to have violated a building code, the city official who signed off on the project may be partially responsible.

✔ *Personal journal.* Keep records of conversations you have with contractors as evidence of oral agreements.

✔ *New product information.* From new wiring to new walls, make sure you keep all warranties and receipts.

✔ *Receipts of payments.* Keep canceled cheques of payments to contractors. If you pay cash, keep a written receipt signed by both of you.

CHOOSING A CONTRACTOR

Many people think that the most important decision you will make when building or re-modeling your home is picking the right contractor. Here are some suggestions as to how to go about it:

1. Check with local building agencies. Many cities offer a builders' exchange that matches licensed, reputable builders with clients.

2. Comparison shop. Let each prospective contractor know that you are obtaining several bids on your project.

3. Talk to former clients. Reputable contractors should willingly give the names of at least a dozen satisfied customers.

4. Make sure a contractor is licensed, bonded, and carries both workers' compensation and liability insurance.

5. Ask for a bank reference to verify that the contractor is solvent and responsible.

6. You may want to choose a contractor who is a member of your provincial contractors' association. Those bodies regulate the industry somewhat.

7. Find out how many projects the contractor is currently handling, and whether he can keep to your schedule.

8. Ask how extra costs or charges for special services are calculated. A contractor may bid low for part of a job (plastering a wall), then offer to finish the job (painting it) and overcharge you badly.

In contrast, home repairs are changes that merely maintain the house's normal condition. Repairs include fixing a leaky faucet, patching a hole in the roof (but replacing the roof is an improvement), or repainting the chipped exterior of the home.

Homeowners and Revenue Canada or local property-tax assessors sometimes disagree on what constitutes an improvement or a repair—hence the importance of keeping accurate records of any construction or alterations. For example, the local property-tax assessor sees that you put new windows on one side of the house—a value-added improvement that raises your tax basis. You might argue and present evidence to the local tax board to prove that the windows were damaged during a recent storm and had to be replaced. Thus qualified as repairs, they should not result in higher property taxes.

Some home improvements qualify for special tax breaks, such as property-tax credits for improvements on older and historical homes. Or, if you add a work space to your house, you may qualify for federal tax deductions for home offices. A tax accountant can best advise you on these complicated matters—and he will want complete records of the project.

Hiring a Contractor

To take care of major home repairs and improvements, most homeowners hire building contractors. In such circumstances, keep the following standards in mind: (1) The contractor should complete work according to the terms of your contract, and the quality of materials specified. (2) He should be careful not to damage your property or cause personal injury. (3) His costs should be fair. (4) He should not be negligent or engage in unethical behavior.

Unfortunately, these standards are not always met. While licensed contractors are generally honest and capable, consumer-protection agencies can cite a huge number of homeowners' complaints against unscrupulous and unqualified contractors. This is true partly because some provinces require no more than a registration fee for a contractor's license. The home builder is more protected in those provinces that have strict performance standards for contractors. Even better are the provinces and local municipalities that require contractors to be licensed, bonded and carry liability and workers' compensation insurance. A bond is a sum held by a third party (usually a bonding company) as a guarantee of good workmanship. These are among the most common types of bond:

■ **Contractor's license bond.** Required by most provincial construction boards as a qualification for licensing, these bonds

can range from $2,000 to $20,000, depending on the type of contractor and the volume of work performed.

- **Performance bond.** This option guarantees that funds will be available if your contractor does not complete the job stipulated in your contract. The fee that a contractor must pay for this bond is normally passed on to the homeowner.
- **Payment bond.** These bonds assure subcontractors that they will be paid by the general, or head, contractor. Payment bonds mean that no financial claims, or "liens," for labor or materials will be filed against your property. However, they are costly and often duplicate other protections.

Your contractor should also carry two types of insurance: liability and workers' compensation. The first will protect you if the contractor damages your property or causes injury to someone on your premises. Workers' compensation, required in all provinces for the contractor's employees, covers the treatment of injuries incurred on the job.

WHAT TYPE OF CONTRACTOR DO YOU NEED?

If you are planning a big repair or improvement project, you probably should consider hiring a "general contractor," the generic term for the person who maintains overall control of and responsibility for a project. The duties of a general contractor include meeting with you to discuss the plans and specifications for the project; preparing a bid, or estimate, for the project; and acting as liaison between you and an architect, interior designer, or subcontractors on the job.

A specialty or subcontractor works in one trade—as a carpenter, roofer, locksmith, or plumber. General contractors often have a roster of reliable subcontractors with whom they work. But when you take on small projects, such as replacing a heating system, you will probably hire the specialist directly. Meet the person, conduct a background check, and solicit bids just as you would when hiring a general contractor. When hiring any contractor, remember that the better you define your expectations, the more successful the project will be.

Dealing with Contractors

Just as knowing what you want in a project helps determine whom you hire for the job, knowing how much money you expect to spend protects you from committing to a financially draining affair. You can negotiate the costs and specifications of a project, such as the quality of materials to be used, when a contractor submits his bid to you for the job. Then compare that bid with those you get from

The Protection of Cooling-Off Laws

Provincial consumer protection laws provide for cooling-off periods to guard consumers from the pressures of aggressive sales techniques. These laws state that you have the right to change your mind about certain purchases of goods over $25 within 3 to 10 business days if the contract was signed in your home.

The protection applies only to goods, not to services (except in certain cases to dance studios, fitness clubs, and some educational services), and the laws are aimed primarily at importunate door-to-door salespeople. But they also apply to someone already working for you. Suppose that while a contractor is painting your living room, he suggests you install new molding. You like the idea and place the order. But if you change your mind, you may cancel the order within the "cooling-off period," without penalty, because you made the purchase away from the seller's place of business.

You must notify the contractor in writing: send the notice to an address that the contractor must provide and use certified mail with return receipt requested. The contractor must respond to your letter within 10 days of its receipt.

The cooling-off laws do not apply if you made a purchase or ordered a service over the telephone, by mail, or in the contractor's place of business; nor do they apply to contracts for emergency home repairs.

WORK ORDER

HOMEOWNER

Name _____

Street _____

City/Province/Postal Code _____

CONTRACTOR

Name _____

Street _____

City/Province/Postal Code _____

DESCRIPTION OF JOB (2)

_____
_____
_____
_____

MATERIALS REQUIRED AND SUPPLIERS (3)

_____
_____
_____

Total _____

COSTS

$ _____
$ _____
$ _____
$ _____

LABOR REQUIRED AND HOURS (4)

_____
_____

Total _____

$ _____
$ _____
$ _____
$ _____

TOTAL COST OF JOB (5) $ _____

WORK /PAYMENT SCHEDULE (6)

Progress payments will be made in the following amount on the following schedule:

Work Stage and Date Completed:

1._____
2._____
3._____

Amount to Be Paid:

$ _____
$ _____
$ _____

(7) The homeowner hereby authorizes the contractor to furnish all materials and labor required to complete the job. (8) Any alteration or deviation from the above specifications involving extra cost of materials or labor will be executed only upon written orders for same, and will become an extra charge over the sum mentioned in this contract. (9) All work will be completed in a workmanlike manner according to standard practices, within the time period specified. A penalty of $XX will be charged for not respecting the completion date. (10) The home-owner agrees to pay the amount mentioned according to the payment schedule above. (11) All disputes will be settled by arbitration by a lawyer. (12) The contractor shall carry proper fire and liability insurance.

(13)

Agreed: Homeowner _____
Date

Agreed: Contractor _____
Date

A Sample Work Order for a Small Project

This simple work order could be used for any straightforward project. It includes: 1. Names and addresses of homeowner and contractor; 2. A detailed description of the job; 3. A list of materials, suppliers, and costs; 4. The type of labor, hours required, and cost; 5. The total cost; 6. The payment schedule. Clauses also specify: 7. That the contractor has authority to hire workers and buy supplies; 8. That any changes be in writing; 9. That the work meet standards of quality and time and what penalty applies if schedules are not met; 10. That the homeowner will pay when work is completed satisfactorily; and 13. Signatures proving that both parties agree. If you are planning extensive construction, your contract should also include: 11. A provision regarding arbitration; and 12. A provision regarding fire and liability insurance.

other contractors. (If you plan to compare several contractors' bids, supply the same information to each.) You can compare their tenders against the following criteria:

- **Presentation.** Is the contractor's estimate scribbled on a piece of paper or neatly typed on letterhead? Is it supplemented by brochures or other materials pertinent to your job? A contractor who presents a well-organized presentation probably has a higher standard of professionalism on the job than someone who looks at your kitchen for five minutes and announces that the remodeling will cost $30,000.
- **Price estimates.** Bids will vary among different contractors, but should fall within about a 10 percent range of one another. If they deviate more than that, and you provided comparable information to each, it is possible that the low bidder forgot to include a certain element or is underhandedly trying to lure business with a low bid that will later rise.
- **Detailed measurements and materials.** Contractor bids should spell out the specific sizes of rooms, windows, doors, and the like, as well as the quantity and quality of the various materials that will be needed. If you specified a certain product brand, model, or quality level, make sure an inferior material has not been substituted to lower the bid price.
- **Installation.** If your bid includes the price of new carpeting, does that price include the usual fee to install it? Specify the same for dishwashers, cabinets, windows, and so on.
- **Payment structure.** To ensure your job is completed on time and within the budget, structure your payments to tie completion of a specific task with periodic payments. You will have to pay a certain amount of money before the job begins and then make specified payments at specified times, as the work progresses. Be sure to withhold a percentage (usually 15 percent) until the job is completed to your satisfaction.

Since this information will appear in your final contract, clarify as many details as possible in preliminary bid negotiations with prospective contractors. Otherwise you leave yourself vulnerable to bids that can be interpreted in the contractor's favor. Along with details on materials and costs, a homeowner should base the choice of contractors on personal appeal and responsiveness to your preliminary concerns. All else being equal, you want the contractor with whom you communicate best and whom you trust the most to work in your interest.

SIGNING THE CONTRACT

Once you have weeded out the competing bids for your job and checked licensing and references, you can select a contractor and sign a contract. Although it is always in a con-

---

HOW TO DEAL WITH POOR WORKMANSHIP

What if your contractor turns out shoddy work or fails to finish the job? Here are some ways to deal with him:

1. Talk to the contractor about the problems, then put your complaints in writing. You will soon discover whether or not he can rectify the problems.

2. Gather proof that the contractor did not live up to the terms of your contract. Include records of all written and verbal agreements and correspondence, and photographs of damage or poorly done work.

3. File complaints with your local homeowners' association and Better Business Bureau. They can provide information on any other claims against the contractor.

4. Call your provincial contractor's license board to see if it provides any compensation to homeowners whose licensed contractor has not performed as promised or has defaulted on the contract.

5. Sue the contractor in small claims court. The court cannot make the contractor redo or finish the job properly but, if you win, it can order him to pay you damages.

6. If the damages you claim are more than is allowed in small claims court, hire a lawyer to sue the contractor in a higher court.

sumer's interest to have a lawyer review a written contract, you also can manage the agreement yourself, especially on smaller jobs. Be sure to spell out in the contract all basic information about the job, including timing; price; materials; responsibilities for insurance, permits, and cleanup; and a schedule for making payments.

Because few construction projects progress precisely as planned, your contract should stipulate how changes will be mutually agreed upon by you and the contractor. Changes from the original contract agreement should always be confirmed in writing so that you are protected in potential disputes. Most contractors use a "change order form" that refers to a specific alteration of an item listed in the contract—for example, "Substitute oak doors for pine doors in closets. Additional charge for materials, $600."

Homeowners should also include a contract clause on work stoppage. It ensures that if your contractor simply fails to show up for the job and stops answering your telephone calls for a certain period of time, you can send written notice that you consider his actions a work stoppage and that you are implementing the part of the clause that permits you to hire another contractor and/or take legal action.

WHERE DOES YOUR MONEY GO?

Your new home improvement project begins, and after your second or third payment all you see is a pile of rubble and a gaggle of subcontractors yanking wires and pulling up floor-

Where we cannot invent, we may at least improve.

CHARLES CALEB COLTON

English clergyman
and writer
1780–1832

Reducing the Risk of Construction Liens

A contractor, subcontractor, worker, or supplier has the right to put a lien, or claim, against a homeowner's property for unpaid bills. Even if you have paid the contractor in full, you are vulnerable to liens if he has not paid subcontractors. Protect yourself with these measures:

• In most provinces, the right of a contractor to issue a lien can be waived upon request by the homeowner if the contractor agrees. Ask the contractor for a lien waiver or release before work begins. The waiver should state that the contractor forfeits any rights to file a claim under construction lien laws.

• The contractor's lien waiver pertains only to his own work and not to that of subcontractors and suppliers. So you should insist that your contractor provide you with lien waivers from all such persons involved in the job. Withhold payments at each stage of the project until you have received notarized lien waivers from the subcontractors and suppliers involved in that stage attesting that they

have been paid in full and agreeing to release you from any obligations under provincial lien laws.

• Rather than make the contractor responsible for obtaining lien waivers from subcontractors and suppliers, you can arrange to pay these parties directly. This way there is no risk of the contractor using the suppliers' money for other purposes.

• If the contractor is handling payments, talk to subcontractors and suppliers regularly to make sure they are getting paid according to the terms of their agreement. Most provinces require that the owner keep a "hold back" of about 15 percent in a trust account to pay for unpaid suppliers, subcontractors, and workers.

boards. What exactly is happening, and where are your payments going?

The money you give contractors is funneled into four major categories: contractor's labor, cost of materials, cost of subcontractors, and profit percentage. Most contractors, when estimating the cost of a job, total the costs of material and labor, then add a percentage to cover their overhead costs (licensing, building permits, paperwork, taxes, and so on) and profit. The percent of profit contractors charge is typically around 10 percent, but may vary from 5 percent to 25 percent depending on the local marketplace, the contractor's popularity or specialty, and the region of the country.

CONSTRUCTION OR BUILDER'S LIENS

Construction (formerly mechanic's) lien laws are designed to protect workers and suppliers from contractors and homeowners who fail to pay for work done or supplies received. The laws put ultimate responsibility for these payments on the homeowner—even if he has already paid the contractor for work done by a subcontractor or for supplies delivered.

Warding Off a Lien

PROBLEM
Julian hired a contractor to put a new roof on his house and build a small deck. After the job was done, and Julian had paid the contractor in full, he decided to ask the bank for a home equity loan to build a swimming pool. But before he could do so, Julian received notice that a claim for $2,000 was being filed against his property by the carpenter who had built the deck as a subcontractor. The carpenter said he had not been paid and was basing his claim on the construction lien law, which puts responsibility for paying the debt on the property owner. Julian, aware that if the lien was applied to the property he would have trouble getting a loan, had to make sure the lien was not approved.

ACTION
Julian went to the contractor, who admitted he had spent Julian's money to pay off debts and had nothing left to pay the carpenter. Acting on his lawyer's advice, Julian offered to settle with the carpenter for $1,500. Realizing it was probably the best he could do, the carpenter accepted the offer and signed a release of his mechanic's lien. Then Julian filed a suit in small claims court against the contractor for $1,500. Persuaded by Julian's proof that he had paid the contractor and the carpenter's testimony that he had done the work but secured no money from the contractor, the judge ordered the contractor to pay Julian.

Lien laws exist in all provinces, although they vary widely in terms of the procedure a subcontractor or supplier must follow and in the degree of protection given to homeowners. Subcontractors generally have a certain amount of time after not

Beware of Improvement Rip-offs

Provincial consumer affairs departments are inundated with homeowners' stories, especially from senior citizens, of unscrupulous contractors.

Common tales of woe include gaping holes in walls, unfinished roof and siding work, disconnected gas lines, driveways blacktopped with oily gunk that washes away with the next rain.

Even more painful is the contractor who spends two months building an addition to your home, cashing your payment cheques along the way, then skips town, and leaves you with an unfinished room.

Other typical scams involve your property's landscaping. A self-proclaimed contractor, seeing that your lawn is bare, claims he has topsoil left over from a previous job that he will offer you at a cut rate. What he really has is low-quality soil at an inflated price. Or you may encounter a tree "expert" who offers to trim your trees, then hacks away at your favorite maple before absconding with your deposit.

After a natural disaster, homeowners are particularly vulnerable to on-the-spot improvement offers. No matter how badly you want a job done, do your homework first: check references, licensing, and the Better Business Bureau for a record of complaints. Never pay cash in advance. Your home and finances are at stake.

being paid (one to three months) within which to file a lien claim. Although it seems unfair, a homeowner may well end up paying the subcontractor even if he has already paid the contractor for the work done. If a lien claim is found to be valid in court, the lien can become an encumbrance on the property, making it very hard to sell or borrow against.

being paid (one to three months) within which to file a lien claim. Although it seems unfair, a homeowner may well end up paying the subcontractor even if he has already paid the contractor for the work done. If a lien claim is found to be valid in court, the lien can become an encumbrance on the property, making it very hard to sell or borrow against.

To protect yourself from construction liens, you may be able to have contractors and subcontractors sign a waiver of lien right (see "Reducing the Risk of Construction Liens," page 48). If a construction lien does get filed against your house, it will be recorded with the county clerk. When the claim has been settled, it is very important—and entirely up to you—to get the lien taken off the record.

Can You Do It Yourself?

The popularity of do-it-yourself home improvement manuals and television programs indicates the enthusiasm homeowners have for making their own repairs and renovations. For major construction projects, you can act as your own general contractor by registering for an owner/builder exemption at your building permit office. The exemption endorses your legal right to act as a contractor when building or improving structures on your own property for your own (and your family's) use. Without this permit, city officials could request that you cease construction or be fined.

Be realistic about the work you can, or should, handle. Before you try rewiring the electrical system in your attic, for example, call your local construction or buildings department for information on city codes. Systems that are subject to municipal health and safety standards generally require the work of qualified trade specialists.

PICK YOUR HELPERS CAREFULLY

If, as owner/builder, you hire subcontractors to help you, you must still comply with provincial labor and other laws. You will have to meet all provincial requirements on workers' compensation insurance, liability insurance, and unemployment insurance payments. You might also have to contend with legal minimum wage and overtime rates.

Avoid hiring unlicensed subcontractors, even if they seem competent and offer you a low rate. If anything goes wrong— if they damage your property or cause negligent injury—you have little legal recourse, since these workers probably do not have enough assets to make a suit worthwhile. Bear in mind, too, that most provinces require all construction workers to be licensed by the construction industry commission.

BUILDING IT YOURSELF

Homeowners acting as their own contractors for home improvement jobs should understand these key issues before committing to a project:

1. Being your own general contractor makes you responsible for hiring subcontractors, such as electricians and plumbers. For each, you need to solicit bids, check credentials, draw up written contracts, confirm insurance coverage, and monitor work.

2. Construction jobs are extremely time-consuming. You may find yourself constantly juggling schedules, buying materials, conferring with workers to solve unexpected problems, and more.

3. When you are the boss, you assume all responsibility for unforeseen problems. If you order the wrong materials and thereby delay a subcontractor who charges you a penalty for wasting his time, you have no legal recourse.

4. If you apply for a loan to finance your home improvement project, you may find that lenders are reluctant to risk an unprofessional remodeling project that could actually lower the value of the home.

5. You must arrange for building and zoning permits and all other details, such as garbage disposal, that a contractor would normally organize. Be aware that owner-contractors are often more carefully scrutinized by city building officials.

Neighbor Problems

Uncertain boundaries, delinquent dogs, late-night noises, trees, and trespassers all cause unneighborly friction. The law deals with most of these vexations.

Getting Your Boundaries Straight

Most homeowners have a basic idea of their property's limits, or boundary lines, and they generally respect their neighbors' boundaries. But the precise limits or boundary lines are often unclear and can become a source of conflict when someone believes his neighbor has transgressed his property line.

Property boundaries are detailed in the deed to your home, which you received at the time of your purchase. (Deeds are also available for review at the county recorder's office.) It is not uncommon for boundaries to be imprecisely recorded, since most boundaries are not simple, straight lines but irregular or undulating. Even boundaries marked by more permanent features, such as a stream or large rock, can change through time—as when a stream changes course or a rock is removed for construction.

Ownership boundaries apply also to the space above and below ground, with limits set by provincial and local laws. (Air rights, for example, vary by hundreds of feet in different areas.)

When boundaries are unclear or erroneously recorded in public records, homeowners have several options for clarifying their property lines without involving neighbors. These are:

- **Title insurance.** The title search conducted when you bought your home describes the boundaries of the property and is backed by the title insurance you bought. Title insurance guarantees that the purchaser has legitimate ownership of the property described in the deed. If this turns out not to be true, you can make a legal claim against the insurance company.
- **General warranty deed.** If you have this type of deed, the previous owner has assured you that the property description is true and accurate. If you discover that the property boundaries were misrepresented, you may be able to take legal action against the seller.
- **Quiet title.** If you discover an error in the recording of the boundaries of your property, you can take action to correct, or quiet, the title. The action to quiet title must be presented to a judge and is best managed by a lawyer.

---

1 2 3

IF NEIGHBORS BLOCK A VIEW

If your neighbor builds or plants something in the middle of your favorite vista, consider these points before taking action:

1. The law allows your neighbor to block your view as long as the blocking item is useful to the property owner and not built specifically to annoy you. You have a valid case if you can prove malicious intent, as in the case of a so-called spite fence—an unnecessarily tall fence erected to irritate you.

2. City ordinances occasionally protect the view you had when you bought the property. You must have proof, such as photographs, that your original view has been blocked.

3. Municipal zoning laws usually include setbacks (distance between structures and property lines) and height restrictions—typically four feet for a front-yard fence, for instance, and six feet in back. See if the neighbor's addition that blocks your view is in violation.

4. An "easement" ("servitude" in Quebec) formally establishes a specific right-of-way between your and your neighbor's land. If you arrange a solar access easement, for example, your neighbor agrees not to block your sunlight.

If your neighbor builds or maintains a fence that is unsightly or excessively large, you can take these measures to rectify the situation:

1. Before complaining to local officials, go to the county records office, a county law library, or the public library and read local fence ordinances to see if your neighbor is really breaking the law.

2. If a neighbor's fence does not comply with local rules, approach him in a friendly manner. He may not realize he is breaking the fence law.

3. If the neighbor tells you to mind your own business, you can complain to the city planning or zoning office. Officials will look into the matter, and if they agree that the neighbor has violated an ordinance, they will send written notice of that fact and request compliance.

4. If the town planning office decides you are irked by a minor violation and refuses to help you, you can sue the neighbor in civil court to have the fence removed. Be sure to consult a lawyer, however, before plunging into legal action, because you may not have a case. Courts look for substantial noncompliance with local fence ordinances and do not usually order a fence removed for a minor violation, such as being a few inches too high.

- **Homeowners association.** Properties in planned developments and subdivisions are usually well defined, but if you find an error, contact the developer or association board.
- **Ordinances on water boundaries.** Property lines defined by streams, lakes, or oceans may change as the water's edge moves. Normally, a homeowner owns the land up to the water's edge, and in some cases to the center of a lake or stream. The federal or, in some cases, provincial government owns navigable waters, and it and local governments may not let you build a dock or overhanging deck on the water.

BOUNDARIES MARKED BY FENCES

Whether white-picket or hand-hewn stone, fences are a clear way to mark territory. Because fences are at times the source of boundary conflicts between adjoining property owners, most provinces have fence statutes. These apply to all types of boundary fences. In rural areas, fence statutes usually impose either an open range or closed range policy. In open range areas, cattle, sheep, and other livestock wander freely, and neighbors may erect fences to protect their properties; in closed range areas, the livestock owner must fence in the herd.

Urban and suburban fence statutes usually regulate fence appearance, height, and location within the property. Planned communities often impose additional restrictions. In practice, few cities waste time enforcing fence violations. As long as no one complains, nonconforming fences may stay put for generations. In general, with the exception of subdivision rules, local laws allow you to determine how your fence looks, and as long as the materials used are not hazardous to passersby, a fence can be made of whatever material you choose.

SHARING THE FENCE EXPENSE

When a boundary fence is shared by you and your neighbor, it is subject to both provincial and local laws. Most provinces have statutes recognizing that a preexisting fence used by both of you belongs to both of you equally. You must share the cost of maintenance or replacement, and neither of you may remove it without the other's permission. If your neighbor refuses to contribute to necessary repairs after your verbal and written requests that he do so, you can sue him for half the costs in small claims court.

A more amicable solution if your neighbor does not want equal responsibility for maintaining the fence—perhaps because it is not visible from his house, but is quite close to yours—is to agree in writing that you will take primary or even full responsibility for it. If one neighbor moves out and a new homeowner moves in, however, the situation regarding the boundary fence reverts to local laws on mutual ownership.

If your neighbor erects a fence on his property, but at the edge of the boundary between your properties, that fence remains his property. But if you then use the fence to enclose your property on one or more sides, many provincial laws provide that you pay your neighbor a portion of the fence's value.

Occasionally, a homeowner will build a fence intended to put neighbors out of sight and mind—and out of sorts. A "spite fence" is likely to be a high, unsightly barrier constructed at the property edge, and under certain circumstances, it may be against the law. Several provinces give a neighbor the right to sue the owner of such a fence on the grounds that it is a nuisance with no reasonable use to the owner.

To avoid disputes with neighbors, build the entire fence on your property as close to the boundary line as possible.

*Good fences
make good neighbors.*

ROBERT FROST
Mending Wall

Troubles With Trees

When trees grow on or near property boundaries, issues of who owns or cares for the trees often arise. Provincial laws on boundary, or "line" trees, are based on the premise that the trunk determines ownership. If the trunk is on your side of the property line, even if roots or branches extend into your neighbor's yard, the tree is yours. If the trunk straddles the boundary, in most provinces you and your neighbor are legal co-owners and should negotiate equal shares of maintenance and care.

Settling Boundary Disputes

If any boundary question arises with your neighbor that cannot be clarified in your property deed, take corrective action right away. Legally, anyone encroaching on your property without your objection has the right to continue such use after a certain number of years.

• **Make an agreement.** If you and your neighbor do not know your exact boundaries, and one of you wants to build on land that is in question, you can agree, in writing, to a new boundary.

• **Sign a quitclaim deed.** A more formal agreement is a quitclaim deed: Each neighbor waives any right to the disputed property on the other side of the boundary. (If it is recorded in public land records, the agreement is binding even on future owners.) Be aware, though, that some lenders demand full payment of a mortgage loan if the borrower transfers any interest in the property.

• **Hire a surveyor.** A licensed surveyor will determine the exact dimensions and location of your property boundaries. If the survey conflicts with earlier surveys and one neighbor is found to be on the other's property, consult a lawyer.

• **Try mediation.** Local government building departments or other municipal agencies may offer mediation for disputes between neighbors. Planned communities also may provide mediation services.

• **File a lawsuit.** To correct a disputed boundary line, you may have to file suit in court. If your neighbor is building on ground that a recent survey shows is yours, and the neighbor does not respect the new boundary description, you may need to file a civil lawsuit.

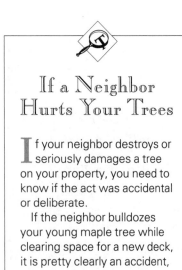

If a Neighbor Hurts Your Trees

I f your neighbor destroys or seriously damages a tree on your property, you need to know if the act was accidental or deliberate.

If the neighbor bulldozes your young maple tree while clearing space for a new deck, it is pretty clearly an accident, and he will likely offer to pay for damages. But if he refuses to take responsibility, contact your homeowners insurance company. Many policies cover trees damaged unintentionally by others. Your neighbor's insurance may also cover the problem.

If insurance will not cover damages and your efforts to receive compensation from your neighbor fail, you can sue for the amount of actual replacement value. Some courts additionally compensate tree owners for aesthetic loss and diminished property value.

If your neighbor deliberately injures or destroys your tree, civil penalties in some provinces provide punishment. In other cases, criminal penalties apply to the act of intentionally harming someone's trees, shrubs, or saplings.

Thus a spiteful neighbor, irritated by the blossoms falling in his yard, could be charged with a criminal violation for chopping down your cherry tree. To file a complaint, you might need a witness to the desecration or some other evidence.

When you and your neighbor co-own a tree, each of you has the right to cut limbs over his own property as long as no harm is done to the tree or the other person's property. At best, neighbors can agree that one person will arrange for the tree to be trimmed and bill the other for his share. But sometimes problems arise—for example, if you believe a costly procedure is necessary and your neighbor disagrees or refuses to share the expense. As long as it has been established that the tree is a boundary tree, you can take action if the problem falls into one of these categories: legal necessity (conforming with a height ordinance), essential maintenance (protection against disease), or safety (attending to potentially hazardous falling branches).

Explain to your neighbor why the work should be done, if necessary with an expert opinion, such as from a tree service, to back you up. If he still refuses to share costs, make at least two written attempts to secure his cooperation. In your letter, refer to your prior requests for his cooperation, provide an estimate of the work needed, state your intention to have the work done, and bill him for half the amount. If your neighbor still won't cooperate, you might suggest mediation or file suit in small claims court to recover your expenses.

OVERHANGING BRANCHES

You may have the right to trim branches of your neighbor's trees that overhang your property. If your neighbor's trees interfere with your ability to use your property fully (if a newly planted tree throws deep shade on the garden from which you sell cut flowers, for example), some provinces recognize that you have a legal claim. Other provinces recognize a legal claim only when the trees cause serious harm to your property, as when their roots cause your driveway to crack.

In many provinces, you have the right to cut the roots of your neighbor's tree if it encroaches on your property, especially if there is any risk that it will damage your underground drain pipe. Sometimes such problems arise from city trees growing on city-owned land adjoining your property. If such trees cause you damage, you may sue the city.

If a neighbor's tree is diseased or hazardous, you should alert the tree's owner and can trim branches within your property boundary if the owner does not. Generally, however, you may not enter your neighbor's property to trim or destroy the tree except in an emergency situation (such as a violent storm or fire when a branch poses an immediate threat of danger). But courts increasingly are holding owners liable for damage caused by trees they know to be unsound or dangerous.

Therefore, if an obviously rotten limb of your neighbor's tree falls on your garage, you can sue for damages if you can prove the owner knew, or should have known, that the tree's condition made it hazardous. As in all relations with your neighbors, however, first try direct communication and then mediation before going to court.

Problems With Trespassing

A trespasser is anyone who intrudes physically onto your property without permission or privilege, and you have the right to fend trespassers off the premises by putting up a sign or a fence or by telling them to leave. An unwanted door-to-door salesman who keeps ringing your bell is invading your property without permission. And if you find an unfamiliar neighbor lounging at your swimming pool, he too is invading your property without permission. But all social guests and household workers come onto your property by "permission," and firefighters have "privilege" to enter your property without permission to save your burning house.

But what if the trespasser is your pleasant neighbor Betsy who has extended her garden a few feet onto your property, or who regularly takes a shortcut to and from work through your yard? These are incidents of repeated trespass, or "encroachment," to which you should respond, even if the encroachment does not bother you. Why? Because in almost every province, a trespasser can legally acquire ownership of your land by occupying it if you do not object.

By the laws of England, every invasion of private property, be it ever so minute, is a trespass. No man can set foot upon my ground without my licence, but he is liable to an action though the damage be nothing.

CHARLES PRATT
English jurist

Keeping Your Neighbors' Pets Out of Your Yard

What can you do if your neighbor's prized poodle has a penchant for eating your petunias? Pet owners are responsible for the behavior of their trespassing pets and in general must adhere to local ordinances. If you have a persistent problem, here is what to do about it:

• Dog and cat owners are not normally held responsible for their pets' occasional trespassing into your yard. But if a pet causes significant damage to your property—such as digging up new, expensive sod—you may be able to seek monetary compensation in small claims court under nuisance laws.

• Most towns have leash laws, or running-at-large laws, that require dogs to be restrained when they are not on their owners' property. If the owner of a dog that ranges around your neighborhood does not respond to your request to abide by leash laws, you have the right to report the dog to the police or dogcatcher, and the city might impound the pet.

• So-called pooper-scooper laws require pet owners to clean up immediately after an animal defecates on another person's property or on the street. If your town has no such ordinance, and if your neighbor's Great Dane seems to hang out in your rose garden, and if your neighbor is unresponsive to your pleas to keep his dog on his own property, your only recourse may be to sue him for nuisance or property damage.

• Local ordinances often restrict the number of animals allowed per household and usually restrict certain species as well, such as ducks, goats, reptiles, and other animals that might wander onto a neighbor's property. Check the laws in your locality, and don't hesitate to assert your rights.

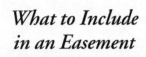

What to Include in an Easement

If you decide to grant an easement, or legal right-of-way, on part of your property, you or your lawyer need to prepare a written document that includes the following:

✔ *Names of both parties.* Identify yourself and the person to whom you are granting the easement, and make sure both of you sign the document.

✔ *Purpose.* You should describe the exact nature of the easement and the reason for it, such as providing a shortcut to the beach or using land for building a storage shed.

✔ *Property description.* Include the precise location of the area within your property affected by the easement and its exact dimensions.

✔ *Special use, duties, or conditions.* Clarify, for example, that the builder of the storage shed agrees to maintain the trees surrounding the shed as part of the easement agreement, or that your neighbor must pick up after her horse as a condition for granting an easement for a riding path.

✔ *The price paid to you.* The exchange of money legitimizes the easement as a legal contract. You and the easement holder can negotiate the amount.

✔ *Duration.* You can stipulate that the easement is effective from the date of signing until five, 15, or 25 years later.

Under this legal doctrine, called "adverse possession" or "prescription," the homeowner who allows someone to trespass for years (in some provinces, 10, in others 20) without giving permission, complaining, or taking legal action loses rights to the land. In 15 years Betsy may actually own the strip of land on the edge of your property where she planted that garden, simply because you never said anything.

AVERTING ADVERSE POSSESSION

As a homeowner, you have several options for preventing unwanted visitors, including neighbors, from gaining a legal claim to ownership of any part of your property. Fences, gates, and "No Trespassing" signs are basic measures. You may also need to "clarify," or claim, your property boundaries for the trespasser. For example, if your new neighbor, unsure of the boundary, innocently installs a swing set for his children in part of your backyard, you should quickly set him straight. You may let him leave the swing set, but you should ask him to sign an agreement that grants him and his family permission to use your property. The agreement should describe in detail the portion of land involved and state clearly that you have the right to revoke your offer at any time. If the bit of land in question is sizable—say he builds a playhouse next to the swing set and you have noticed that the kids are playing baseball every day in the area—you could suggest that he pay rent for it as well as signing the agreement.

EASEMENTS

Homeowners commonly grant, or sell, the right to use part of their land for a specified purpose, called an "easement" ("servitude" in Quebec). Unlike the agreement temporarily granting your neighbor permission to use a strip of your land for his child's swing set, an easement becomes part of the property and applies to the property no matter who owns it.

Easements are recorded in the title or deed to your property and are filed in the county records office. Cities and utility companies commonly hold easements allowing them to haul garbage, install telephone poles, build sewer systems, and so on without constantly asking property owners for permission.

Homeowners can issue private easements to their neighbors, but problems often arise when a new owner is subject to an unexpired easement granted by a previous owner. (Easements can, but do not always, have a start and end date.) Thirty years ago the owner may have issued an easement for his neighbor to run a water pipe under part of his property. Now you own the home, and you start to build a driveway and run into the pipe. You must, by law, respect the right-of-way of the easement and work around the pipe. To eliminate the easement, you can seek a written release from the easement holder. You should first consult a real estate lawyer for advice.

A lawyer can also help you grant an easement. (To be effective, the grant must be in writing.) You have the right to sell a right-of-way or other use of your property. The amount may be a token to legitimize the easement, or it may be a significant sum if the easement diminishes your property's value.

Noisy Neighbors

In addition to trespassing, homeowners sometimes experience noise, odors, and other intrusions that are defined as "nuisances" under the law. Playing music loudly in your home at midnight, letting your dog howl at the moon, and revving up your lawn mower early on weekend mornings may appear to be privileges of ownership, but when your neighbor is trying to sleep, he may consider them nuisances.

Two types of nuisances are recognized by the law. A public nuisance is an offense against a whole neighborhood or community—such as excessive noise from a nearby airport—and legal action to correct it is usually taken by a public entity, such as the city or county government, against the offender. Private nuisances usually involve homeowners complaining about their neighbors, such as a barking dog or loud music, and complaints are filed by individuals in civil court.

Generally, a homeowner must show that the neighbor is responsible for an activity that interferes with the enjoyment or use of the homeowner's property, and that the annoyance has caused harm, such as property damage, physical injury, or mental anguish. If his evidence is sound, the homeowner can seek redress for injuries inflicted by the neighbor's annoying activity and seek a court order to have it stopped.

FAMILIAR NUISANCES

Many of the annoyances that cause conflict among neighbors are common enough that laws are usually in place to forestall lawsuits. Almost every local community has ordinances prohibiting excessive, unnecessary, and unreasonable noise. (Homeowners associations may have noise prohibitions even stricter than municipal rules.)

Basically, the annoyance must be substantial enough and of a sufficient duration that any reasonable person would have the same angry response that you do. You would not have a valid complaint because you are unusually sensitive to loud noise, or because you cannot abide hard rock. Noise ordinances are enforced by the police, and occasionally by special environmental noise-abatement organizations.

123...
KEEPING THE NOISE DOWN

If your neighbor's noisiness interferes with your domestic peace, there are steps you can take before taking legal action:

1. Approach your neighbor amicably and discuss the problem. She may be unaware that her TV set, turned up so she can hear it over the vacuum cleaner, blasts directly into your office.

2. Visit city hall or the public library for a copy of the local noise ordinance. Then write a letter to your neighbor, citing the ordinance, pointing out that her noise violates it. Keep a copy of the letter.

3. Check with other neighbors to see if anyone else is having trouble. You may want to join efforts.

4. Try mediation. Dispute-resolution services are free in many localities, especially in urban centers and in planned community associations.

5. If your neighbor still continues to agitate you, call the police or the department of environmental protection while the noisy activity is occurring.

6. Consider filing a nuisance claim in small claims court for monetary damages or in civil court if you have suffered major injury, such as loss of business. First, however, have your lawyer write a letter threatening legal action which may stop the noise before you have to go to court.

BLIGHTED PROPERTY

Among the list of woes that one neighbor can wreak upon another is poorly maintained, unsightly property. Most local ordinances regulate the appearance of property to some degree by prohibiting "blighted property," or property that has fallen into a state of disrepair. Ordinances typically forbid a homeowner from maintaining a property that creates a danger to others or is such an eyesore that it diminishes the value of neighboring homes. If your neighbors paint their house bright blue with yellow shutters, you may shudder at the sight but have no legal recourse unless you can prove that their color scheme actually reduces your property value, or unless neighborhood zoning laws prohibit the colors.

Quieting the Neighbors

PROBLEM

Jim and Linda had just retired and moved to a small house in a new neighborhood. They introduced themselves to their next-door neighbors, Bob and Katie, personable young newlyweds. Unfortunately, the newlyweds were also fans of popular music and played their high-tech CD system loud and long into the night. Jim and Linda liked to go to bed about eleven, but found that many nights they were kept awake by the music until two or three in the morning. Jim and Linda complained gently to Katie and Bob, and the music stopped for a few weeks. But when it started again, Jim and Linda found the situation untenable.

ACTION

First, Jim and Linda researched their local noise ordinance at the local library and the county clerk's office and decided the late-night noise was a violation of local law. They also kept careful notes on the times they were kept awake by the loud music and the ways in which they tried, vainly, to get Katie and Bob to do something about the problem. Then they took their problem to the local community dispute-resolution board, which formally mediates such cases. The board persuaded Bob and Katie to turn the music down six nights a week, and Jim and Linda agreed to put up with it until 1 a.m. on Saturday nights. Had no mediation group existed in their community, Jim and Linda could have reported the problem to a local government office or the police. As a last resort, they could have taken Bob and Katie to court.

Blighted property ordinances may also require that driveways and sidewalks be clear of debris and in good condition and not cracked, or that sidewalks and fences be free of graffiti—or even an innocuous hopscotch board. Communities usually regulate weeds and rubbish separately as health and safety hazards, although the trimming of high, unsightly weeds may be included in a blighted property ordinance. Planned communities often impose additional aesthetic restrictions on yard and home appearance and maintenance. (See also "Condos, Co-ops, and Planned Communities," page 66.)

Before You File a Nuisance Claim

Can you prove that your neighbor has caused substantial interference with your use and enjoyment of your property? Have all your efforts to correct the matter failed?

If you answer "yes," then you may choose to file a nuisance claim. However, be prepared to face the common (and effective) defenses that (1) you must have known about the nuisance when you moved into the neighborhood (the "We were here first" logic), or (2) that the neighborhood has tolerated the nuisance for so long that it has, by inaction, endorsed it.

The party you accuse may say she is not responsible, or is only partially responsible, for the offense. For example, if her dog's howling occurs only when two certain neighborhood dogs get together, not when her dog is alone.

When you file a nuisance claim you must not only be prepared for effective defenses, but you must produce sufficient evidence that a nuisance definitely exists. Proof may take the form of testimony by neighborhood witnesses, expert or specialist witnesses, photographs, videotapes, or other factual evidence.

ENVIRONMENTAL CONCERNS

As the hazardous side effects of modern technology grow more serious, homeowners have gained certain rights—but have just as many responsibilities.

Fighting Pollution on the Outside

Along with a house and the lot on which it stands, homeowners gain incidental rights to the use and enjoyment of the airspace above, the earth below, and the water that flows on or under their property. To protect these rights, the federal government and all the provinces have introduced strict laws in recent years.

Federal laws such as the Environmental Protection Act, the Arctic Waters Pollution Prevention Act, and the Fisheries Act attempt to limit air, water, ground, and noise pollution. Typical of provincial efforts at environmental protection are Ontario's Water Resources Act and Environmental Bill of Rights, and British Columbia's environmental protection law, Bill 26. Regulations that give substance and procedure to Bill 26 are contained in a book the size of a city phone book.

In Canada, environmental law is one of the fastest growing fields of law for lawyers. Still, homeowners who want to sue for pollution damages face a daunting legal battle. Often you may be better off joining local citizens' action groups to press for change or, if you live in Ontario or Quebec where class actions are permitted, file a class lawsuit.

NOISY NOISE AND DIRTY AIR

While homeowners own the airspace above their home, upper airspace is controlled and regulated by the federal government to facilitate airplane traffic. When residents live near local airports, the noise generated by airplane traffic may be aggravating enough to justify a claim against the government for the taking of property (see "Managing Your Home," page 30), or against a privately owned airport for nuisance. If you feel that airport noise is impinging on your right to use and enjoy your property, talk to your neighbors about a joint action, or contact a lawyer.

Another common intrusion into homeowners' airspace is harmful or noxious emissions from local industrial plants. Despite protection of the Canadian Environmental Protection Act and similar laws, enforcing the legislation is often difficult and unsuccessful. The rules require precise and detailed proof that the accused company is emitting harmful substances that

Are Electric Power Lines Dangerous?

In this electronic age, the health risks of electromagnetic fields produced by everything from toaster ovens to high-voltage power lines have become a subject of major controversy.

Several independent scientific studies have linked physical proximity to high-voltage power lines with unusually high rates of cancer in adults and children, including childhood leukemia. Other scientific opinions, however, say the evidence is inconclusive.

Because research is incomplete, the federal government is unable to define for homeowners what level of exposure may be dangerous. (Some utilities give homeowners meters to measure the electric fields around their houses, but the readings do not mean much without a definition of safe exposure levels.)

Meanwhile, parent and community groups have pushed local governments and utility companies to reduce the possible dangers of electric fields by keeping high-voltage power lines away from schools and densely populated areas.

are causing, or will surely cause, damage to local residents or devaluation of their properties.

One recourse is to bring a private nuisance lawsuit against the offender. For example, you could sue a nearby meat-packing plant creating noxious odors or a textile mill expelling excessive levels of dust. Other common pollutants that provoke complaints are pesticides sprayed by crop-dusting planes, fumes and ash from garbage incinerators, and offensive smells from municipal landfills or composting facilities. A homeowner, living near a contaminated lot of land whose air is fouled by industrial pollution, can suffer a major depreciation in the value of his property, and might even be unable to sell his home.

In fighting polluters, the help of private environmental consulting firms can be very useful. These companies can assess air quality, contaminated site remediation, and make environmental impact assessments. Armed with detailed scientific reports, anyone may present a case to their provincial ministry of environment and energy (the name may vary from province to province), which will investigate the alleged polluter. With the proper evidence, the province should be able to enforce antipollution laws and regulations quickly and successfully.

Ontario's Gasoline Handling Code, which covers problems related to underground fuel tanks, is a model for ensuring success. Administered by the Ministry of Environment and Energy, the code requires that a professional engineer certify that the cleanup meets all applicable laws, regulations, and guidelines.

The nation that destroys its soil destroys itself.

FRANKLIN DELANO ROOSEVELT
President
of the United States
1932–1945

How to Fight for a Healthy Home Environment

From individual lawsuits to government intervention, there are numerous methods of recourse for homeowners who suffer personal or property damage as a result of pollution, both inside and outside the home:

• Local environmental and citizens' action groups can provide valuable information and assistance on local polluting culprits and pending cases. They can help connect you with others suffering similar damage from polluters.

• If you know and can prove who the polluter is in a local situation, you can file an individual lawsuit claim on grounds of trespass or nuisance. You need to show that you or your property has suffered actual harm or damage.

• The provincial minister of the environment will represent citizens in severe pollution cases, as when homeowners must leave their properties because of hazardous waste leakage.

• Under the access to information acts, homeowners can obtain information on government-monitored pollution. If you suspect a local plant is dumping hazardous waste that is contaminating your well water, you can file a request for documents of government agencies that regulate the company, and these may confirm your suspicions.

• The Canada Environmental Protection Act and other federal laws allow individual homeowners to sue a polluting company for compensation for damages and decreased property value. But because these lawsuits are very complicated, they are prohibitively costly for most homeowners who are better served by first addressing these complaints to their environment ministry.

DANGEROUS WATER

Your incidental rights as a homeowner extend to the water below your property, and being sure that water is clean is a critical matter if you pump your own drinking water. That vital source can become polluted by underground chemical and fuel storage tanks and by farm pesticides. Environment Canada found in the early 1990s that up to 20,000 underground tanks, about 10 percent of all such containers, were leaking. Provincial legislation has since begun to address the issue of underground tank disposal and placement. Provisions in fire prevention acts and fire code regulations recently enacted in provinces such as Ontario, Quebec, and Saskatchewan are designed to prevent problems from occurring, and to contain those that do arise.

Contaminants in the Home

Environmental problems just as likely lurk inside your walls as outside your home. The myriad products that go into the construction of a home are regulated to some degree by federal, provincial, and local laws that require testing and elimination or removal of dangerous products. Still, materials in your home may threaten your and your family's health and safety. The most common home contaminants are asbestos, formaldehyde, lead paint, and radon.

- **Asbestos.** A mineral fiber found in rock, asbestos was used in a variety of household and building materials—from appliances to floor tiles—to strengthen the product and provide insulation and fire protection. Asbestos can cause lung and stomach cancer if inhaled repeatedly over time. Banned in new products, asbestos is common in older homes. A homeowner can contact her local health department for advice or she can hire a qualified asbestos abatement contractor to survey her home and determine whether there are asbestos-containing materials that should be removed.
- **Formaldehyde.** This chemical is widely used in building materials and household products such as pressed wood and carpeting. (Canada banned urea formaldehyde foam insulation several years ago.) Formaldehyde can cause burning sensations in the eyes and throat, breathing difficulties, headaches, depression, or exhaustion. Emissions are highest when products are new and when temperature or humidity in the home is high. Mobile homes tend to have higher-than-average, and often excessive, levels of the chemical. You can test for formaldehyde with a dosimeter avail-

Watch Out for Radon Scams

By no means are all firms that test for and deal with radon contamination unscrupulous. But some are, and they take advantage of homeowners' concerns about the dangers of radon. Here are things to watch out for:

✔ *False fears.* Some dual-service companies, which offer radon testing and radon reduction services, have been known to exaggerate radon levels, then convince panicky homeowners to pay for costly radon reduction services.

✔ *Immediate cure.* Because radon levels fluctuate daily and seasonally, and in different areas within the home, even the quickest tests should take at least 48 hours. Long-term tests that provide the most accurate average radon levels take several months.

✔ *Scare tactics.* Beware the radon reduction contractor who insinuates that other homes in your neighborhood have tested high in radon. Certain communities do have higher-than-average radon levels, but neighboring homes often have greatly varying levels. Arrange an impartial professional radon test from a private pollution consulting firm, or call your provincial health or environmental ministry for advice on detecting and removing radon.

✔ *Do-it-yourself kits.* These are easy to use, but may be misleading. Ask your provincial health or environmental protection agency what models it recommends.

able from health and safety industrial suppliers, or through city or provincial health agencies. Excessive levels of the chemical can be controlled by removing the offending product and increasing ventilation.

- **Lead paint.** Most homes built before the mid-1970s were coated with lead-based paint. If sweet-tasting lead paint chips are ingested by children, or dust from the paint is inhaled, lead paint can cause brain damage. Victims of lead paint exposure can sue the paint manufacturers, but must determine which lead-paint company is responsible. While total removal of lead paint from a home is costly, special sealants may reduce the hazard. Renovations that require disturbing the paint should be done by a specialist. Call your provincial health department for information.

- **Radon.** A colorless, odorless radioactive gas that can cause lung cancer, radon occurs naturally. It is released from the breakdown of uranium in the soil and rock on which many homes are built and enters the home through cracks in floors and walls, openings around sumps (basement drains), and through water wells. Call your provincial health department for information on radon detection kits and how to remove radon from your home. You can also hire a certified radon tester.

For more information about household hazards, contact Health Canada's Environmental Health Directorate, your provincial environmental ministry, and local environmental groups.

Is Your Drinking Water Pure?

Most bacteria and parasites once present in drinking water have been eliminated through 20th-century technology. Nevertheless, North American homeowners are still vulnerable to the contamination of their lakes, rivers, groundwater, and other essential water sources.

Modern-day toxic chemicals, from industrial, agricultural, and municipal sources, can pollute water, causing cancer and other serious health problems. In the 1970s, environmentalists forced governments to recognize the links between toxic substances in drinking water and elevated cancer risks. As a result, environment ministries were established, every province passed clean water laws, and the federal government enacted various pieces of protective legislation, most recently the Environmental Assessment Act, regulating pesticides and restricting the amounts and kinds of waste that industry could release.

Your Right to Information About Your Water Supply

Under federal and provincial access to information acts, and other laws such as Ontario's Environmental Bill of Rights, you can find a lot of information about your drinking water. Water quality is also constantly checked by municipal inspectors. Here are some facts you should know.

✔ *The source.* Most public drinking water systems are regulated by the provinces, using guidelines established jointly by federal and provincial governments. You have a right to be told where the water comes from and how it is purified.

✔ *Contaminants.* You are entitled to know the precise contaminants for which your water has been tested.

✔ *Violation notices.* If contamination occurs, the municipality must give the public an explanation of the violation.

✔ *Potential health risks.* The notification of water contamination should include a clear description of the potential adverse health effects.

✔ *Corrective measures.* Your municipality must spell out what steps it is taking to correct a contamination problem. It should also indicate whether alternative water sources, such as bottled water, are necessary, and if so, for how long.

TRYING TO GET IT CLEAN

The standard purification method used in Canada's water treatment systems involves sand filtering the water and disinfecting it with chlorine. Yet this rigorous process is not foolproof, and the water that gets to your tap may not be as safe as you think. Some chemical by-products of chlorination have the potential to cause cancer. However, contaminant limits have been adopted jointly by federal and provincial governments and suppliers of drinking water must make periodic tests to ensure these guidelines are kept.

Lead leaching into water from lead pipes and lead solderings in older buildings can also contaminate water after it is treated. (Lead pipes and solder were banned in new construction in the late 1980s.) Most provinces now require that large-scale water systems add lime or other chemicals to the water to minimize the amount of lead, but homeowners with older houses should test their own plumbing systems for lead content in the water.

TESTING THE WATERS

Even when public drinking water meets national and provincial standards, it may still contain pollutants that you cannot see or taste, such as pesticides or herbicides, industrial solvents, disease-causing bacteria, parasites, or radon that leaks into wells. If you have a private well, you are responsible for the quality of its water. Your local health department may provide free testing of your tap water, especially if you have specific cause for concern. Or you can pay a provincially certified water testing lab for a thorough private test.

If you find that your water needs to be filtered or treated, there is a wide range of water treatment systems available. Be careful, however, not to buy the wrong product or become prey to deceptive sales practices by unscrupulous water treatment companies. Before investing in a water treatment system, you should consult a qualified water-quality contractor or plumbing inspector on the most appropriate treatment for your specific water problems.

The Hidden Dangers of Lawn Care

Pesticides, herbicides, and insecticides can help eliminate unwanted rodents, weeds, and bugs from agricultural crops and suburban lawns, and can greatly increase the productivity of farms and the beauty of private and public landscapes. But they can also damage human immune and nerve systems and cause cancer. Although some pesticide toxins have been banned by Agriculture Canada,

---

Pesticide Warnings

Landscaping companies that take care of people's lawns and gardens typically spray mixes of pesticide and fertilizer. When many lawns in a neighborhood are treated this way, the toxic chemical sprays remain, drifting about the neighborhood and permeating the air you and your family breathe.

In response to pressure from concerned citizens' groups, many communities now require lawn care companies to give local residents warning prior to, or while, pesticides are being sprayed. This right to fair warning about spraying allows residents—especially those with children, who are hypersensitive to pesticides—to vacate the area or stay indoors during spraying.

If you hire a lawn service, you have the legal right to know what your alternatives are when choosing a termiticide, pesticide, or herbicide, including nonchemical treatments. Insist on a thorough explanation of the health implications for the suggested chemical treatment.

You can check with your local environmental protection agency or an environmental group. Then refuse to have any chemical you consider hazardous used in and around your home.

Homeowners can maintain a healthy lawn without pesticides by using a number of nonpolluting methods, such as fertilizing with organic products. You can also check with your local environmental group for information on low-maintenance varieties of grass that grow in your climate.

others are still legal and are commonly used in lawn pesticides at legally allowable levels. Toxins are present in some pesticides prepared for use by home gardeners and, more potently, in sprays used by lawn care and landscaping companies.

The cumulative effect of chemical lawn and farm sprays contributes to air pollution, and water runoff from treated lawns and fields is suspected of contributing heavily to the pollution of enclosed bodies of water. Because the toxic chemicals in pesticides are colorless and odorless, many people suffering symptoms of pesticide exposure may misinterpret the cause. Some learning disabilities and certain forms of depression, for example, have been linked to pesticide "poisoning." Clinical ecologists can often diagnose pesticide illnesses, and poison control specialists may be able to link physical symptoms to specific pesticide ingredients. Federal and provincial environmental departments, Health Canada, and Agriculture Canada are working together to reduce the use of harmful pesticides.

Too Much Garbage

Canadian homeowners produce millions of tons of garbage every year—garbage containing organic waste, plastics, paper, glass, metal, and all manner of toxic materials. Local sanitation departments and private haulers truck this garbage away, and for many homeowners that is the end of it.

Yet garbage continues to affect citizens as it is processed into the local environment and ecosystem. More than two-thirds of our garbage goes into landfills, whose effluents pollute local soil and trickle down into the groundwater supply. Some garbage is burned, polluting the air with toxic emissions and creating potentially toxic ash residue. Sometimes garbage is illegally dumped into local waters.

DEALING WITH TOXIC WASTE

Besides the environmental impact of the sheer tonnage of garbage produced by Canadians, there is also the problem of dealing with everyday products that are in themselves toxic. The federal Hazardous Materials Act sets safety standards for household products, and local pollution laws often require that certain hazardous fluids, such as oil and automotive antifreeze, be treated separately from other garbage.

Several municipalities have instituted hazardous waste collection programs for things such as treated wood, lead waste, and unused paint, and recycling programs for papers, metals, and plastics. But even where there are programs for disposing of hazardous wastes, many homeowners still pollute public

---

Taking Action Against Polluters

If a neighbor or local business is polluting your area, it may be up to you to take action. Every situation is different, and the law is complicated in this area, but here are some things you can do:

✔ *Try negotiating.* If your neighbor is dumping motor oil into the gutter, for instance, you may be able to deal with him directly. He may not realize that he is breaking the law.

✔ *Check local ordinances.* If your neighbor's yard is strewn with rubbish, or his front lawn is piled with leaves and trash, he may be violating local laws. Go to the library or check with a city hall clerk to find the appropriate agency to contact.

✔ *Report polluters.* Some areas have complaint lines that you can call and report activities such as illegal dumping. Check the Blue Pages in your telephone book or call the department of sanitation or your provincial ministry of the environment.

✔ *Class action.* If you live in Ontario or Quebec, you can file a class action suit. In 1990, the Quebec Court of Appeal awarded $21 million to 24,000 members of a class action who had successfully sued an aluminum company for polluting the air with bauxite.

✔ *Ask for help.* If your problem is important, but you don't know where to turn, contact local or national environmental groups or your provincial ministry of the environment.

waters and city dumps by casually dumping excess paint strippers, pesticides, and other dangerous products down drains and into garbage cans. These homeowners, along with irresponsible industries, effectively pollute their own, and their neighbors', home environment—water, air, and earth.

TAKING ACTION AGAINST HAZARDOUS WASTE

Private citizens who want to reduce toxic waste in the local environment can reduce the amount of hazardous products they purchase. They can also work to stem the tide of hazardous industrial waste by joining local governments, business leaders, and citizen groups in searching for community solutions to waste management. You could address such issues as:

- Setting up community programs for recycling, composting, and collecting hazardous household waste.
- Community importation of garbage from other communities. Usually this is a revenue-raising program by the local government.
- Ensuring that landfills are lined to prevent leakage into surrounding soil and are monitored for leaking toxins.
- Initiating or supporting plans for source-separated waste facilities, such as separate programs for yard waste, food waste, and other materials that can be composted.
- Setting up a forum on solid-waste management that creates a dialogue between business and industry, government, environmentalists, and other concerned citizens.

Nobody can be in good health if he does not have, all the time, fresh air, sunshine, and good water.

FLYING HAWK
Oglala Sioux chief

Homeowners' Pollution Primer

The crazy quilt of local rules governing waste disposal in Canada defies generalization. Homeowners can do their bit, nevertheless, not only by observing their local rules but by reducing their use of toxic materials. For the sake of your home and community, you can:

• **Recycle.** Some communities have passed laws requiring citizens to separate and recycle materials such as corrugated cardboard, colored paper, cans, glass bottles, plastics, and newspapers. Fines levied against violators can be high. To find out about recycling programs in your area, contact your municipality.

• **Limit your use of hazardous materials.** Some drain cleaners, air fresheners, rug and upholstery cleaners, pesticides, and even certain laundry detergents contain chemicals that can cause ills ranging from dizziness or nausea to cancer. Local environmental groups, provincial environment ministries, or Health Canada can provide information on which products are unsafe and suggest alternatives.

• **Dispose of garbage properly.** Abandoning materials such as mattresses or appliances not only pollutes the environment, but may be illegal in your area. Many communities make periodic pickups of items too large to place for regular garbage pickup. Contact your municipality or look in your local Yellow Pages under "Garbage Collection" or "Rubbish" to find out about such services.

• **Dispose of hazardous substances properly.** In most communities it is illegal to dump motor oil, certain paints, petroleum, and pesticides into the public sewer system via your drain, street gutters, or a local waterway. Call your municipality or health ministry to find out about proper disposal of hazardous waste in your area.

CONDOS, CO-OPS, AND PLANNED COMMUNITIES

These innovations in home owning offer many benefits—and a few pitfalls.

Key Concerns When Buying In

Condominiums, planned developments, and cooperative housing organizations are shared-interest communities that have gained great popularity among homeowners in the past 30 years. There are thousands of such communities in Canada today, and by the year 2000 as many as one quarter of all homeowners may live in shared-interest communities instead of individual, independent homes.

Planned housing developments and condominiums are the most popular and widespread type of shared-interest community, while cooperatives are less common. The rules of ownership vary: Buy a condominium and you own a unit in a building or complex (of apartments or townhouses, for example), with full ownership of your unit. Buy a single-family home in a planned development and you get rights of ownership to your house and property. Buy a cooperative apartment and you own shares in a corporation that owns the property and you get a proprietary lease for your unit.

All three types of shared-interest communities are governed by homeowners associations consisting of members of the community, but usually run by an elected board of directors or board of managers. When you buy property in a shared-interest community, you are legally agreeing to abide by the governing rules and regulations set by the managing board. It is vital, therefore, that you understand the legal ramifications of those regulations—and the possible limitations of your rights—before you finally buy a house or an apartment in a shared-interest community.

WHAT HOMEOWNERS ASSOCIATIONS DO

The homeowners association of a planned community is like a government. It imposes regulations on members, and offers protections and advantages to you, your family, and your property that you would not otherwise have. Courts of law accept the independent power of a homeowners association to rule its own territory, within the limits of certain federal and provincial laws. Most provinces have laws that specifically govern condominium and cooperative operations and management.

Since a homeowners association is self-ruled, it is able to impose a wide degree of control over the daily lives of community members. It can place restrictions on what your house looks like; whether you may have pets; the hours during which you can perform noisy home repair work or play loud music, and so on. These rules are described in the declaration, the by-laws and the rules and regulations which must be made available to members and prospective members of condominiums, according to the various provincial condominium acts.

While the rules and regulations of homeowners associations constrain residents to some degree, owning a home in a planned, controlled environment offers a number of advantages over independent home owning. These benefits may include special facilities and services such as on-site security, swimming pools, playgrounds, parks, party rooms, social events, health care, tennis courts, golf courses, parking facilities, exercise rooms, and more.

WITH SO MANY OWNERS, WHO PAYS FOR WHAT?

To pay for the myriad services and facilities, homeowners associations charge each unit owner a monthly maintenance fee. In condominium developments, each unit—everything within and including the four walls, floor, and ceiling—is owned individually, while common areas and services are owned and paid for jointly by all unit owners. Many condo declarations limit the owner's boundaries of exclusive ownership to the space within the walls: technically, you cannot paint or place a picture on the walls. In most declarations, however, the condo owner owns up to the midpoint of the walls and so can do most things to the interior walls, and the condo corporation has the right to maintain the exterior walls according as it wishes.

Condominium owners pay a monthly fee based on the size and value of their individual units in relation to the whole development. Part of the payment is applied toward the building's mortgage and property tax costs. For cooperative property owners, who do not own individual units but own a share in the property-holding cooperative, the co-op board pays all the building's mortgage, taxes, insurance, and maintenance and repair expenses. The co-op owner's monthly maintenance fee, proportional to shares of ownership, goes toward these expenses. One major difference between condos and co-ops is that if the condo owner defaults on the condo fees or other expenses, a lien can be placed on his property, which can be sold to recover these costs. If a co-op member fails to meet payments, then the other members must make up the shortfall.

Property owners in planned developments pay their own taxes and other expenses, and they also pay monthly maintenance fees for common buildings and common grounds.

123...

WHAT TO DO BEFORE BUYING

Looking at a home in a condominium, a cooperative, or a planned community? Take these steps before buying:

1. Get copies of the binding agreements, bylaws, rules, and conditions to which you would be subject if you bought into the community. Make sure the unit boundaries include at least one-half the thickness of the walls.

2. Check the most recent financial statement from the homeowners association, or condo/co-op board. Look for unpaid assessments from shareholders who defaulted on common cost payments. If the homeowners association is cash poor, it may offer you a lower initial maintenance fee, then raise it steadily after you move in.

3. How big is the operating budget for routine maintenance and repair, and how big is the reserve fund for unanticipated expenses? Find out the general pattern of maintenance fee increases.

4. How many units have already been sold? How many are occupied by renters? (Renters do not have the same stake in the association.)

5. Find out if there are any liens or pending lawsuits against the condo, co-op, or housing association corporation.

6. Find out about selling restrictions. Will you have the right to sell the unit back to the corporation from whom you originally bought?

Part of the monthly maintenance fees for all three types of common-interest ownership is kept in a reserve fund, or account, to cover emergencies such as a main water pipe rupture or broken elevator. Unit owners may be asked to pay occasional special assessments for unforeseen or new circumstances, such as lobby renovation or enhanced landscaping. These extra costs, and the necessity for incurring them, are often the source of conflict between individual unit owners and the homeowners association or condo or co-op boards.

Constraints of Community Rules

Homeowners association rules can affect many aspects of daily life. The color you paint your house, the trees you plant, the mailbox you put up, the lettering style of your house number, your kitchen remodeling, where your cat plays outdoors, which relatives can visit for extended stays, how loud you play

The Duties of Association Directors

Like any corporation's board of directors, the managing board of any homeowners association (which includes condo and co-op boards) has legal obligations to the shareholders of the corporation. Most provinces have specific statutes governing these associations, and some apply regular corporate laws, but all agree that an association board has several basic obligations:

• **Duty to adhere to the governing documents of the association.** These documents, including the declaration of incorporation and its bylaws, define the relationship between the unit owners and the association. A board may take action only within the authority allowed by these documents. If your condominium bylaws call for a two-thirds majority vote of shareholders to change or add a rule, the board may not make a rule in any other manner.

• **Duty to conduct activities responsibly.** The homeowners association must perform the activities it is chartered to do with diligence and due care. Without specifying what duties are owed, courts generally describe a duty to act responsibly as an obligation to act prudently and avoid negligence in management activities. An association board would be exercising due diligence by keeping the reserve fund sufficiently financed to cover emergency and ongoing costs.

• **Duty to act in good faith.** The board is acting on behalf of the corporation and its shareholders. Management decisions must be made in the best interest of all unit owners and not based on personal gain or self-interest. Board members must be legally disinterested in the board's action, and there should be no self-dealing. Some condo laws, such as Ontario's Condominium Act, allow unit owners to cancel management agreements between the co-op corporation and the project developer (who usually also supplies the manager) upon giving a 60-day notice and obtaining a 51 percent vote.

• **Shareholders assume the same responsibilities.** Owners who are not on the board but who make occasional management decisions are subject to the same rules. In condominium and cooperative associations especially, unit owners and shareholders are often given the power to approve actions that, in a typical business corporation, would be approved solely by the board. For example, owners may be asked to approve increased maintenance charges or to change the rules on swimming pool use. In condos, voting rights are given equally to each unit regardless of size and price; in co-ops, voting rights may be pro rata to the monthly charge each member pays.

music, the time of day you do home renovations, and whether or not you can hang signs—all are examples of the kinds of free choices you might have to forfeit when you become a member of a shared-interest property.

Community association rules, restrictions, and conditions are generally concerned with these basic issues: who occupies and uses your home, how you use it, how you alter its appearance, to whom you rent and sell it. Here are some specific areas in which an association's rules and restrictions might apply:

- **Members of the home.** Although most provincial human rights charters and codes prohibit discrimination in the sale of housing, homeowners associations have been permitted to prohibit roommates or unrelated adults to live in the same unit, limit the number of household members in a unit, and, in some cases, exclude children. For example, a condominium community might require that residents be at least 55 years old, and limit visitation by children under the age of 16 to no more than 60 days per calendar year. This type of restriction may often be successfully contested since discrimination because of age is prohibited in most provincial human rights legislation.
- **Pets.** Pets may not be welcome in many planned communities. Associations may impose an outright ban on pets or limit the number and kind of pets. They also may prohibit certain breeds of dogs, such as pit bulls, and nontraditional pets, such as geese and snakes. Associations that allow pets usually enforce restrictions such as leash laws, even for cats, and cleanup rules. Conflict may occur when pet rules change, as when a "No Pets" ruling is added to the association's declaration and bylaws after a resident has moved in. In this case, residents are usually allowed to keep their current pets but may not replace them when the pet dies.
- **Use of the home.** Associations often regulate zoning issues, such as whether home businesses are allowed. If your work is invisible to the community—you are a writer, for example—you will probably have no problem, but if your business requires visitors to and from your residence or bothers other shareholders in any other way, the association can require that you cease your home-based business.
- **Roommates.** Unit owners sometimes clash with their associations over roommates and unmarried partners. Generally, unrelated adults may stay for an unlimited period of time unless the bylaws of the association deem otherwise. However, the shareholder-tenant in a co-op usually must use the apartment or house as a primary residence and in most cases cannot turn it into a commercial enterprise by inviting consecutive roommates to pay rent.

Your Rights When Rules Change

Condo, co-op, and subdivision unit owners have argued in lawsuits that it is unfair for a homeowners association to change rules governing individual units if the rules adversely affect the unit owners. Some disaffected owners have claimed that other shareholders should not be able to deprive them of rights that existed at the time of purchase—by suddenly prohibiting dogs, for example.

But courts have rejected that argument if the amendments were adopted by the board of directors following approval by a majority of members voting in accordance with the bylaws. The courts have pointed out that provision for amendments was set out in the corporation's original declaration and bylaws. The unit owner should have read these carefully before buying the unit. (Voting rights may also be exercised by the mortgagee or lender, especially in matters affecting the security of the mortgage, such as insurance, maintenance, and finance.)

Alberta is among provinces that require unanimous consent for certain changes affecting the number of units, unit boundaries, common areas, and the voting power of each unit. Other provinces have different limits: the requirement in British Columbia, for example, is 66.66 percent; in Ontario, it is 51 percent. But if the board has acted legally and fairly, and the vote meets the provincial requirement, a unit owner will probably have to succumb to the majority or propose a viable alternative.

HOT SPOTS OF CONFLICT

Cooperative associations enforce and amend rules that sometimes conflict with the needs and desires of shareholders. Watch out for these common points of conflict:

1. Pets. Association rules on pets are usually more stringent than local municipal laws. Some associations restrict pets altogether; others tolerate only certain kinds of pets.

2. Architecture. Most associations have a committee that enforces the architectural restrictions of properties. You may not be able to add a porch to your subdivision home or plant a certain type of tree.

3. Parking. Associations often limit the number of parking places allotted each shareholder and may further regulate the type and weight of vehicle permitted.

4. Access to amenities. The use of common facilities is regulated by homeowners associations. In an attempt to limit its insurance liability, for example, a board may impose strict rules on the use of a common swimming pool.

5. Age. Condominium and subdivision associations sometimes have rules that restrict the age of residents to serve the needs of a certain age group, such as 55 and older. Generally, there must be a legitimate reason for the age restriction—a no-children rule preserves the peaceful environment of a retiree community, for example. However, this type of restriction may be challenged before provincial human rights tribunals.

- **Home appearance and alterations.** Architectural restrictions may not let you maintain your condo or co-op house and yard as you wish. A shingled roof may be mandatory and certain colors may be forbidden; other rules may specify the height and style of a fence, whether you can have a television satellite dish, or whether you may build a shed. All structural changes, even something like adding a skylight, usually require association approval.
- **Renting.** Condominium and cooperative developments often restrict unit owners from renting or leasing their residences to a third party. Those that do typically set parameters, such as a rental period not less than six months (to minimize traffic), only two rentals per year, no pets, board approval for the tenant, and so on. In addition, unit owners must sometimes pay a fee to the association for the right to sublet. Since these restrictions are spelled out in the association bylaws to which an owner has agreed, courts generally uphold them.
- **Resale.** Homeowners associations usually extend considerable control when a shareholder decides to sell a unit. They often have the first option to buy a unit (the "right to first offer") before it goes on the public market. They can charge a so-called flip tax, a one-time fee (often substantial) paid to the association when a shared-interest unit is sold. Provincial statutes generally impose no restrictions on these practices and no limit on the amount of fee charged, as long as these rules are explicit in the bylaws and do not conflict with other laws (on discrimination, for example).

When shareholders have challenged resale or other restrictions, courts have usually held that property owners of shared-interest communities have reasonable grounds for wanting some control over who lives in their building or complex. As long as an association has acted reasonably and in good faith, homeowners have little or no recourse. The courts acknowledge that community members are financially interdependent, and must share facilities, and preserve a certain desired character of community. Above all, the courts recognize that homeowners consent to these rules when they buy the property.

Handling Internal Conflict

While homeowners associations are granted much legal leeway in imposing and enforcing their governing rules and restrictions, sometimes they overstep their authority. Property owners may have valid legal cases against their association, not just differences of opinion.

In some cases, you may be able to negotiate exemptions from a rule or find creative ways to work around it. If advertising is prohibited, you may find a central but discreet place where all residents can post signs. One ingenious resident of a planned community that did not allow advertising to be posted in front yards put a sign in his car window saying, "For Sale, $120,000: House Included."

Organizing your neighbors can be an extremely effective way to influence the association. As fellow shareholders, they may share your grievance and be eager and happy to help. Once you have joined forces, you can approach the board as a unified lobbying force against a new or unpopular ruling. (For more information about joint action, see YOUR RIGHTS IN ACTION, page 464.)

Instigating Change

PROBLEM
Ida and Moe had been living in their condominium for three years and had adhered to all homeowner association rules. As a gift, Moe received a basketball hoop and net and decided he wanted to hang it from the wall over his garage door. Ida pointed out that installing recreation equipment outside their unit was against the association rules.

ACTION
Moe and Ida talked to a few of their neighbors and found that not only would they not mind a basketball hoop, they would welcome one. Moe and a group of residents drafted a proposal to put before the association board. They asked that the rule regarding hanging equipment outside each unit be repealed. After negotiating with the board, Moe and his group compromised, and part of the often-unused guest parking lot was converted into a basketball area for the use of all residents.

WHO IS LIABLE FOR INJURIES?

Courts have recognized homeowners associations as distinct legal entities with responsibilities to both unit owners and to outsiders. For example, if you are seriously injured on the common-interest property of your planned community, you may be able to take legal action against the association. A number of provincial laws assert that a unit owner may sue an association for any act of negligence on the part of the association for injuries suffered in a common area.

Complications may arise if a third party, such as a visiting friend, is injured on common-interest property. Courts have ruled that individual unit owners do not have control over the maintenance and management of common areas and are thus not considered liable when a third party is injured in a common area. The association, however, can be found liable

Making Changes From Within

A handful of municipalities now require condo and co-op homeowner associations to set up in-house mediation services. These services give disputing parties the chance to resolve differences outside of courtrooms. Where they exist, in-house mediation and arbitration services have significantly reduced the number of shared-interest property owners filing lawsuits.

If you have a conflict, find out if there is a mediation or arbitration clause in your association's rules. Settling your dispute may be much easier than you thought.

Before any mediation or arbitration hearing, assemble whatever documents you need to present your case. Although the proceeding may be less formal than a court hearing, you still should have proof to back up your claims, including copies of contracts, agreements, photographs, and statements from witnesses. (See also YOUR RIGHTS IN ACTION, page 465.)

Keep in mind that another way for a shareholder to influence board decisions is to join the board.

because, to the extent that it controls common areas, it acts like the owner of those areas. Even if the co-op, condo association or homeowners association carries its own liability insurance, you should also be insured for accidents to third parties. You should also have proper fire insurance to cover your unit and its contents. It often happens that in the event of an accident both you and the association will be sued.

WHO PAYS FOR REPAIRS?

The lines of responsibility for repairs in condominium and cooperative units are often blurred. Although condo and co-op associations are responsible for problems in the major structural systems of the complex, including main water pipes and electrical wiring, the unit owners must pay for problems inside the four walls of their units. Suppose your bathroom ceiling suddenly cracks open because of water damage. If the main water pipes are faulty, the association is responsible for repairs. But if your upstairs neighbor let his bathtub overflow, then he may well be responsible.

To determine the source of a repair problem, hire a qualified contractor or other home professional, such as a plumber or electrician, and get a detailed written report. Damages caused by other unit owners may be covered by their homeowners insurance or yours. If the association is at fault, it should foot the bill. If either the association or another unit owner refuses to pay for damages you believe are his responsibility, see a lawyer specializing in shared-interest properties.

If a rule is reasonable the association can adopt it; if not, it cannot.

ONE JUDGE'S RULING

Do You Have a Case Against Your Association?

If negotiation and arbitration with your home association have failed, and if the board's actions have violated one of the following conditions in your case, you have a chance to succeed in challenging the association. Talk to a lawyer who specializes in community association law.

• **Unauthorized rule making.** If the board does not have authority either under provincial laws, such as a condominium act, or under the governing documents of the association, the rule you dispute may have been made by the board without authority.

• **Arbitrary and capricious rule making.** If the board makes a rule that is not related to the health, happiness, or enjoyment of property of unit owners, courts may consider the rule invalid. For example, if for no apparent reason a board imposes a new rule that limits the size and weight of vehicles residents may keep in a spacious parking area, a unit owner who uses a minibus for business might have a legal case.

• **Discriminatory effect of rule making.** Boards may not make rules that isolate, discriminate against, or are unfair to the minority shareholders. A condominium board may not impose higher maintenance fees on the minority of condo owners who do not live in their units year-round unless it is specifically granted that power in its bylaws.

• **Unfair lien.** What if your association board fails to pay a landscaper who did major yard work, and he files a mechanic's lien or financial claim against the entire shared property? You may have a case against the board if you can prove it did not act in good faith—if, for instance, it had money in reserve that it used instead to refurbish a rooftop patio used mainly by several board members.

RENTING

Because the landlord-tenant relationship is often contentious, many laws and regulations exist to protect the rights of both sides.

Your Rights As a Tenant

If you rent rather than own a home, you are protected by provincial and local laws that govern landlord-tenant relations. Although these laws vary considerably depending on where you live, there are certain basic concepts with which you should be familiar in order to know when your rights are not being recognized.

First you want to formalize a rental agreement with the landlord. Your tenancy and many of its conditions can be established by either an oral agreement or a written lease. A verbal agreement is usually sufficient for short-term stays, such as week-to-week or month-to-month tenancy. In an oral understanding, the landlord agrees to rent the unit for a fixed term at a fixed price, and you agree to pay the rent. The agreement remains valid for as long as you keep paying rent.

Some provinces require landlords to give written notice of termination of such an agreement, while others allow for reasonable verbal notice of termination, such as one rental period.

LEASES LONG AND SHORT

Written lease agreements may bind you and a property owner for any length of time, from a month or less to one year or more. Because a written lease is always enforceable in a court of law, it is to your advantage to sign one in case your landlord transgresses your rights or reneges on his obligations. The landlord may not include in the lease any provisions that negate your rights granted by federal, provincial, or local law.

For example, a landlord might be permitted to limit the number of people living in your apartment. He cannot, however, add a clause to the lease to the effect that your rental agreement will be terminated if you, as a guardian or parent, have children under the age of 14 living in your apartment. Such a restriction contradicts your right to fair housing under provincial human rights legislation.

Landlords do have the right to impose certain other restrictions on the use of their rental properties. A landlord can prohibit you from using a water bed, ban pets, forbid cooking with a barbecue, and prevent you from using part of your rented house or apartment for a small business. If challenged, how-

1 2 3...

WHAT SHOULD BE IN A LEASE

A lease should be written in such a way that it avoids misunderstandings and can provide proof before a tribunal. It should include:

1. The owner's name, or his agent's, his address, and his telephone number. You will need this information in an emergency, or to file a complaint.

2. The date you take possession and the date you start paying rent. If your landlord enticed you with a free month's rent, make sure these two different dates are acknowledged in the lease.

3. Terms for refund of security deposit and interest generated from the deposit. Some provinces require landlords to pay tenants the interest from their security deposit accounts once or twice a year.

4. Permission to sublet. If the landlord allows subletting, you will have to agree to be responsible for the rent and that the sublessee will abide by the lease provisions.

5. Condition of the premises. If repairs are needed, include in a rider the landlord's duty to complete the work by an agreed date.

6. Pet rider. Some landlords dictate conditions of pet ownership. Make sure you agree to the terms before signing.

ever, such rules and regulations usually are measured by these criteria:

- The regulations promote the convenience, safety, or welfare of all residents;
- The rules are reasonable in relation to their purpose;
- The rules apply equally to all residents;
- The regulations are clear and unambiguous;
- The rules have not been designed to evade the obligations of ownership.

You have the right to be notified of any regulations that will apply to you as tenant at the time you sign your rental agreement. If your landlord subsequently changes a rule or regulation, you should be given reasonable notice of the change. Normally no charge can be made to your lease while it is in effect.

Standard rental leases often include "riders," or additional provisions. If the rental property offers a parking space you want to use, a garage and vehicle rider to the lease will clarify the terms and conditions under which you rent the space; the additional rental amount, if any; whether you must pay a deposit; and allowable vehicle size.

You, as tenant, can propose adding a rider or extra clause to the lease. For example, if you prefer your own stove to the one in the rental unit, you can ask the landlord to add a clause stating that you will use your own stove and be responsible for moving and maintaining it. Otherwise, the landlord could later claim that it is part of the rental property, and you would have to leave it behind when you move.

WHAT TO EXPECT AFTER YOU MOVE IN

Once you move into your rental property, both you and the landlord must comply with local building and housing laws on health and safety. You cannot clutter common hallways with your bicycle and other personal objects, nor can your landlord allow garbage to pile up in the building lobby. If you believe your landlord is violating health or safety laws, complain to the local department of health or other government agency.

Although various provinces set different standards of the conditions a tenant may expect from a landlord, usually the landlord must:

- Have the unit ready for the tenant to move into at the time and in the condition agreed upon;
- Provide safe, healthy premises;
- Make necessary repairs to keep the premises in a livable condition;

What About Making Repairs?

Your lease agreement, provincial statutes, and local health codes determine how landlords must handle repairs. The general guidelines are:

✔ **Emergency repairs.** If repairs are needed to correct a critical problem, such as a leaky pipe, the landlord may enter the unit immediately. (This is one reason a tenant may not change the locks of a unit without giving a key to the landlord or his agent.)

✔ **Repairs related to health and safety.** If the problem is not an emergency, the landlord must start repairs within a certain number of days, set by municipal officials, after your notice. In some locales, you may be able to have the repairs done and deduct the cost from the next month's rent.

✔ **Miscellaneous repairs.** Landlords are bound by a good faith obligation to effect nonemergency repairs as soon as possible. Some provinces set a time limit during which a landlord must begin repairs after a tenant's notification.

✔ **General maintenance.** If the owner neglects standard maintenance chores, such as collecting garbage, you can report him to your local health or housing department.

✔ **Damages caused by tenant.** If you cause damage in your rental unit, you are responsible for arranging for the repair and paying the cost.

- Maintain all electrical, plumbing, and other facilities in good working condition;
- Provide receptacles and arrange for frequent removal of garbage (single-family residence renters usually must provide their own garbage containers) and be responsible for rodent and cockroach elimination;
- Provide hot and cold running water;
- Provide weatherproofing, such as unbroken windows.

If you are injured on the common property of the rental building or complex because the property has not been well maintained—say you trip on a loose stair and break your ankle—you may have a liability case against your landlord. In all provinces except Alberta (where rented premises must comply with the province's Public Health Act), landlord tenant laws require rented premises to be in a "state of good repair."

YOUR RIGHTS WHEN YOU MOVE OUT

You are obliged to leave the apartment in the same condition as you found it, except for ordinary wear and tear. If you have adhered to your legal obligations as a good tenant, you then have the right to reclaim your security deposit. However, the landlord has the right to apply part or all of your deposit to costs incurred for damages beyond ordinary wear and tear.

For example, if you soiled the carpeting to the degree that it has to be replaced, your landlord can deduct the replacement cost from the security deposit. Any repair costs must be

For a man's house is his castle...

SIR EDWARD COKE
English jurist
1552–1634

Renters' Basic Legal Rights

Generally, the law dictates that your rental property should be safe, healthy, and livable, in compliance with local health, housing, fire, and safety codes. In addition, renters are entitled to certain specific conditions guaranteed by local legislation on tenants' rights:

• Like a homeowner, you have the right of quiet enjoyment of your rental property. That means you should be able to live in your dwelling without unreasonable interference by your landlord.

• Your landlord must respect your right of privacy. If he needs to enter your apartment for non-emergency repairs or maintenance, he must give reasonable notice—at least 24 hours—and may do so only during normal business hours.

• You have the right to complain to your landlord if he neglects his legal duties, such as keeping common areas of the building safe and sanitary. The landlord may not retaliate against you for complaining by raising your rent or decreasing services.

• You have the right to join with other tenants to bargain the terms of the rental agreement. If your landlord imposes an unreasonably stiff penalty for late rent payments, you can appeal to your provincial residential tenancy board or rent control board for cancellation or reduction of the penalty.

• Your landlord may not take your personal possessions for the purpose of recovering overdue rent. In some cases he may, however, withhold part of your security deposit when you leave.

• As long as you do what the rental agreement and the law require of you, you have the right of exclusive possession of the property until the lease expires.

THE DUTIES OF TENANTS

Besides paying the rent on time and meeting other specific conditions of the lease, tenants owe a landlord these considerations:

1. Tenants may not disturb other tenants with excessive noise or disturbances, such as nightly trumpet practice.

2. Tenants may not run a high-traffic business from the apartment when they have signed a residential lease.

3. Tenants may not house relatives or friends in numbers that would violate local health standards. If a tenant says he will be living with his son, he cannot also put up the son's girlfriend and two children without written approval.

4. A tenant who damages the refrigerator, windows, carpet, or other items of the landlord's property in the apartment must repair or replace them.

5. A tenant cannot conduct illegal activities, such as drug dealing, on the premises. If a landlord is aware that illegal activity is going on in the rented premises, he or she risks having the property seized or boarded up.

6. When a tenant moves out, the property should be in the same condition as when he took possession except for ordinary wear and tear.

7. Tenants who plan to leave at the end of the lease must give prior notice in writing (from one to three months). Otherwise, the lease is automatically renewed.

itemized for you, with copies of receipts included. After your lease expires, the landlord must give you notice of any repair costs within a period (about 14 days) specified by provincial law. If you do not get timely notice, you have the right to reclaim your entire security deposit, regardless of damages—but you must take action within one year of the end of your lease.

The Snoopy Landlord

PROBLEM
A few weeks after Betty moved to a new apartment, she realized that the landlord had come into her apartment when she was out during the day. One of her locks was left undone, and only the landlord had extra keys. When she confronted him, he said he was showing the place to a contractor making bids on renovating the building. Betty was furious, and when it happened again, she threatened to take action against the landlord.

ACTION
First, Betty called her local residential tenancies board to complain about the landlord's behavior, and was told that a landlord must respect a tenant's right to privacy. In an emergency, or when the health and safety of residents are at stake, most rental laws tend to allow a landlord to enter a rental unit irrespective of the wishes of the occupants. But in nonemergency situations, a landlord must give a tenant reasonable notice—usually 24 hours —for limited purposes: to inspect the premises, make repairs, or show the unit to prospective tenants. (Written notice is required in Alberta, British Columbia, Ontario, Prince Edward Island, and the Northwest Territories.) Even then, a landlord is restricted to entering during reasonable hours. Armed with the board's recommendation, Betty confronted her landlord again and warned him that if he continued to invade her privacy, she would seek a court injunction against him on the basis of unreasonable entry. This convinced the landlord to stay out of her apartment.

Security deposits, which are prohibited in Quebec, can range from half a month's rent (in British Columbia, Manitoba, Nova Scotia, Newfoundland) to a month's rent (in Alberta, Ontario, New Brunswick, Prince Edward Island, Yukon, and the Northwest Territories). In weekly rentals, one week rental is usually the maximum security deposit allowed. The tenant can also claim interest ranging from 1.5 to 10 percent.

Your Rights As a Landlord

Whether you lease a portion of your home, rent out your vacation property, or lease multiple-unit investment properties in exchange for money, you take on the legal obligations of a landlord. Local municipalities regulate the actions of anyone who rents out property. In many cities, certain legal exemptions are made for owner-occupied rental properties and other properties containing only two, three, or four units.

As a landlord, you are also entitled to certain rights. These rights begin when you first select tenants to occupy your premises. Although you must adhere to federal and provincial laws banning discrimination based on race, religion, age, gender, sexual orientation (in some provinces), social class, or nationality, you can otherwise refuse rental to anyone you do not want as a tenant.

Unless your city has rent control laws, you have the right to set any rent you choose. Additional charges, such as for parking, should be included in special clauses, or riders. You also have the right (but not the obligation) to charge a security deposit to cover potential losses, such as damage, failure to return keys, or a breach of the lease agreement. Depending on your provincial laws, a security deposit is usually less than or equal to one month's rent. If, at the end of a tenant's lease, you have lawful grounds to retain all or any of the security deposit, you must give the tenant written notice of the reasons for retention, with all costs itemized.

WHEN THE TENANT MOVES IN

Before a new tenant moves in, the property should be put in good condition—a broken air conditioner replaced, a fresh coat of paint applied, and so on. After you sign the lease and before the tenant moves in, you should inspect the rental property together, noting slight damage, such as a dent in a wall, that does not warrant repair. Record these facts on an inspection form, and co-sign it with the tenant; this document protects you both if you later argue over property damage.

Your tenant is legally obliged to maintain the premises in reasonable upkeep, which means operating electrical and plumbing fixtures properly and maintaining appliances in good working condition. The tenant may use or alter the space only within the limits and regulations set in your lease agreement, and must notify you promptly of problems with the property or its major systems, including electric, gas, water, or sewage.

Should your tenant notify you of broken or damaged items that need to be fixed, you must give reasonable notice that you, or a professional service such as an electrician, will enter the apartment at a certain time to remedy the problem. After fair notice, you can enter the dwelling to inspect, repair, make improvements, or supply necessary services.

DEALING WITH NON-PAYERS

Your rental agreement probably states what day of the month rent is due and sets out a grace period for payment, if any. If rent is late, send tenants a reminder letter. If your lease allows

Renting Out Your Home

If you are moving to a new home but having trouble selling your old one, or if you own a second home that you rarely use, you may want to convert your home into a rental property. Along with the financial benefits of rental income, you gain certain tax advantages, such as writing off all the business costs of renting the property.

Finding a good tenant is key to ensuring that you get a steady rental income and that your home is not damaged. You can advertise in your local paper or list your rental with a real estate agent. Ask applicants to fill out a form with their employment, credit, and rental histories. Tenant screening services are available through the Yellow Pages of your telephone book. Follow up by checking the tenant references thoroughly.

Once you have found a tenant you want, your obligations as landlord will include general repairs of the property, lawn upkeep, and responsibility during "emergencies," such as flooding. You may want to hire someone to handle these chores. You should also consult a lawyer and insurance agent about liability protection, and an accountant about how your rental income will affect your taxes.

If renting out your home, be careful not to lose the status of "principal residence" or you may be subject to capital gains tax when you sell. If you rent out your second home, the interest on its mortgage loan is tax deductible.

you to charge a late fee (usually a week or 10 days after rent is due), send a late-charge notice on the day the charge is effective. Eviction is your next recourse. Most provinces require a formal notice requesting rent due as the first step in an eviction procedure. If the tenant does not pay, you can sue to evict.

You must first notify the tenant in writing (notice period varies from one day in New Brunswick to 20 days in Ontario), by certified letter in some provinces. If the tenant still does not pay the rent due, you will have to make a court appearance. In most provinces a landlord does not need a lawyer for eviction proceedings, although you may want to hire one to improve your chances—especially since the burden of proving that the tenant should be evicted rests with the landlord, and the law generally protects a tenant's right of occupancy.

If the court determines the tenant should be evicted, she must leave voluntarily or be physically removed by local officials. But this does not guarantee you will receive your money, even if payment was ordered by the court, so consider hiring a collection agency to track down the delinquent tenant.

How to Handle a Dispute With Your Tenant

Although local and provincial landlord-tenant laws and ordinances clarify most of the obligations of both parties, you and your tenant may disagree on issues that are not clearly defined. In many provinces the procedures for negotiating disagreements with tenants are clearly spelled out. You should consult a lawyer before taking any legal action.

• **Legal notice.** If your tenant is not complying with a provision of the lease or is the source of complaints by neighbors, ask your lawyer to draft a letter to the tenant. The letter should clarify the lease clause that you feel the tenant is violating and request a stop to the offending activity within a certain time.

• **Arbitration.** If you are in dispute over a matter concerning the physical condition of the property, you and your tenant can agree to have a neutral third party inspect the property to determine whether or not you are conforming to your obligations. You can agree that the findings of the arbitrator will be binding. Your local rental authority may be able to suggest arbitrators.

• **Termination of lease.** You can usually cancel your tenant's lease by giving notice of cancellation within 30 days to three months (depending on your province) prior to the end of the lease agreement. You can also cancel according to some other provision of the lease. Or your tenant might voluntarily offer to terminate the lease before the end of the rental period, in which case you can

simply accept the termination. (In some provinces, under certain circumstances, you cannot terminate a lease even at its end without legal cause.)

• **Termination notice.** If your tenant continues to violate your lease agreement for any reason other than nonpayment of rent, and you have carefully notified the tenant of the violation, you can issue a notice of termination of the lease. The notice must reiterate the reason for the termination, which must be based on substantial breach of the lease and not be simply a ruse to take back the premises. The termination notice document must also set a time frame for the tenant to quit the residence. A lawyer can advise you on your provincial procedures for delivering a termination notice.

• **Eviction.** If your tenant disregards your legal notices, you may have to sue to evict. Eviction involves a court proceeding in which a judge determines whether the tenant has truly violated the lease and deserves eviction. You may never physically evict the tenant yourself—that is done, if necessary, by a sheriff, or bailiff, under orders of the court.

OWNING A SECOND HOME

Whether your second home is for pleasure, business, or both, you should be aware of different options for dealing with renters, property managers, and Revenue Canada.

Defining How You Use a Second Home

Homeowners buy a second residence for a variety of reasons. Urban dwellers may own a home in the country and a condo in the city. A young couple might buy a houseboat on the bay and use it as a vacation hideaway. Older homeowners may buy a home that will serve as their retirement retreat in a few years. And a few lucky people have the financial means to afford two or three residences in favorite areas of the country or the world.

Buying a second home is much like buying your primary residence. However, a unique set of concerns arises in terms of maintenance of the home and tax implications.

If your home away from home qualifies as a second residence that you rent out when it is unoccupied, you can deduct the mortgage loan interest for the period that this house is rented. However, if you do not rent out your second home, be sure your first home does not lose its status as your "principal residence." Of course it is up to you to decide which home should be so regarded. You might be wise to give the designation to your second home if it worth more than the first. (See "Renting Out Your Home," page 77.)

IS IT FOR WORK OR PLAY?

In addition to scrutinizing mortgage loan interest deductions, Revenue Canada is interested in whether you use your second home as a personal residence or a business property. The distinction is this: If you rent your home, you become a landlord and must report rental income. That in itself does not make the home a rental property provided you can prove that you also use the place for your own enjoyment.

If you have designated your second home as your principal residence, and it loses this status, the property would be liable for capital gains tax. You would also lose the capital cost allowance (up to 5 percent of the property value you may claim as an annual expense) used to offset rental income.

Of course you must include rental income when you file your tax return, but you may claim deductions for such things as

What Kind of Vacation Home

A vacation home can serve several purposes. There are various ownership options:

✔ *Personal use.* If you can afford it, a second home offers a cherished weekend or vacation getaway from the workaday life.

✔ *Investment.* Buyers often choose resort area condos and town houses for a mix of business entertaining, personal use, and selective rental periods. At best, the property earns money, is enjoyed, and is a tax shelter.

✔ *Fractional ownership.* This option allows the advantages of a vacation getaway without the full costs or responsibilities. A quarter share usually means you get the property every fourth week.

✔ *Time-shares.* Ownership in a time-share is usually divided in 52 parts. If you buy three parts, you get three weeks in the unit per year. Or the property developer remains the owner, and you buy a limited lease. Time-shares may be fun, but generally are not good financial investments.

What You Should Know About Time-Shares

Visitors often fall in love with a particular vacation spot and then are seduced by the notion of a "time-share" in a condominium, chalet, or beach cottage. A time-share is a fractional piece of ownership in a particular property.

You pay not only the purchase price of your share but also a proportional share of maintenance costs for the unit and its grounds. These fees are set by the developer of the time-share property, and he can raise them whenever and as much as he wants. He can even change the basic terms of your agreement.

Some time-shares entitle you to a prescheduled time slot each year in a specific place and may include a deed to that fraction of property that you own. Other arrangements offer a floating time slot or an alternative choice of units in which you can stay.

Some time-shares are part of a vacation club, where you buy access to different destination choices. Your choice may be reduced, however, by a developer who rents out time-share units to non-time-share owners in the most popular seasons.

If you try to sell your share of the unit, you probably will not succeed. You will be competing with the developer, who is probably using the same lures that brought you into the time-share. Most time-share owners who try to sell cannot find a buyer and take a loss on their investment.

mortgage interest, insurance, property tax, and heating for the period when your home was rented. If you have divided your house into two or more dwellings, or made other major structural changes to make it into a rental property, it may lose its status as a principal or personal residence, be deemed a commercial property, and be subject to capital gains tax upon disposal. If part of your home was so altered, that part of your home will no longer be considered the principal residence or personal property.

In some cases, where you have been obliged to move to another town in search of employment or because of a job transfer, you may be able to rent your principal residence for up to four years without losing its "principle residence" status. You can even get an extension beyond four years in certain circumstances. If you rent out the home long enough to qualify it as a business property, you can often claim a significant tax loss on the property. But because these tax issues are especially complex and subject to change, you should consult your tax accountant or adviser before deciding to look to a second home as a tax shelter.

MAINTENANCE ON A SECOND HOME

If your home is for personal use only, very little maintenance may be required—locking up the home, turning off the water and draining pipes for winter, and other seasonal or occasional concerns may be the extent of your efforts. But if you rent or loan the home to others and constantly keep it in use, you are more likely to have additional maintenance and repair concerns, as well as landlord obligations.

You should clarify in a written agreement with a renter what her responsibilities are, such as calling the local plumber if a toilet clogs or a pipe bursts. If the situation is more complex or costly—if the plumber decides you need a whole new plumbing system, or a ceiling needs replastering—the renter should be obliged to contact you.

Because of the difficulty of managing a property far from home, many owners of second residences—particularly those that they rent to others—hire a local property manager. If your residence is part of a resort area, it should be easy to find a professional on-site property manager. If your home is tucked far away in the woods, you may need to find a trusted local person through the recommendation of neighbors or the real estate office through which you found your property.

You can make a contractual arrangement with the property manager to check on your house regularly when you are away, to be on call in the case of emergency, and to personally handle or hire workers for routine maintenance chores such as lawn mowing.

To protect yourself from injuries to others on your property, you will need to carry homeowners insurance, just as you do on your primary residence. The same principles of liability apply to your second residence as to your first. That is, you are responsible for maintaining the property in a safe and habitable condition and for correcting any potentially hazardous situations that may arise.

Resort Vacation Options

When you buy a vacation home in a resort area, the value of your property is dependent on the viability of the resort. So before buying a ski chalet or a condominium on a golf course, you should determine the quality of the resort. If it is a publicly held development, you can ask for copies of quarterly statements and annual reports. These will give you some indication of how financially sound the resort is.

If it is a private development, you can ask the opinions of local realtors, current residents, and employees of the resort. If the employees tell you they have not received paycheques in a month and management is in turmoil, the long-term outlook is not promising and you may want to reconsider investing there. Ask your banker or lawyer to research the financial stability of the resort and its owners.

If your vacation house is affiliated with a resort, you should also know exactly what rights of access you will have to the resort facilities. Do you have unlimited access to ski slopes, or do you have to pay extra usage fees? Are your privileges limited if you are not a year-round resident or if you do not use the property for a specified number of days each year? Put your agreements in writing.

A MOVABLE TREAT

Greater concerns arise when your vacation property is not a fixed location but is part of a time-share arrangement that offers a choice of locations. These vacation clubs are a popular choice for people who want to enjoy different properties and locations in different seasons.

As a member of an international time-share network, you can trade your ownership interest with another time-share owner—your week in the tropics for a week in the Alps. Be sure to clarify your privileges and access to amenities. The last thing you want to hear upon arriving at an expensive beach resort is that you have to use the public beach a mile down the road because the time-share owner you traded with used up this year's private beach passes.

123..

SHARING A SECOND HOME

If you decide to share the expense of a second home with a friend or relative, watch out for these potentially contentious issues:

1. How will ownership be divided? This should be specified on the deed. You will also have to calculate each partner's proportion of the down payment, monthly mortgage loan payments, maintenance, property taxes, and other operating expenses.

2. Who gets to use the property when? Rather than find yourselves arguing over desirable holiday time slots, arrange your schedules in advance.

3. How is voting power distributed? If it is not distributed equally among the partners, be very clear about which partners' opinions count the most.

4. Who will manage the property? Management includes not only physical upkeep but also the necessary bookkeeping. If you decide to hire a property manager, you must make it clear which owner the manager will report to.

5. What if one partner wants to sell her share? Decide ahead of time how much advance notice you must give each other and how you will determine the buy-out price.

HOME OPTIONS FOR SENIORS

More and more elderly Canadians are taking advantage of imaginative housing schemes that pool their resources and help ward off the loneliness of old age.

A New Beginning

For many Canadians, a 65th birthday begins a period of major adjustments. The work that occupied their days for much of the previous four decades is no longer there, and neither is the income that employment netted. Since many people can now look forward to living well into their eighties or nineties, today's retirees have to think hard about the kind of life they want to lead for the next 15 or more years and see how their aspirations stack up against their retirement income.

With a positive frame of mind, retirement can be that inestimable blessing—a chance for a new beginning. This can be the opportunity you've dreamed of for filling your days with new enriching activities—travel, a study program, a second career, a new business, a part-time job in a special-interest field, volunteer work. At age 65 you may find you are entitled to many special deals and discounts on public transportation, movie and theater admissions, plane and train fares, and bank services, and so on. Some local governments also provide free lawn care and snow clearing services to seniors, as well as reductions in their property taxes.

Of course the retirement goals you set will have a major bearing on whether you stay put in your existing home or seek other living arrangements. It may also be that the location of your home is far away from stores, hospitals, and parks and you would like to live in an area where these services are more accessible. Other considerations of course are how well your house and neighborhood will meet your needs as you age. Are you near family, friends, and your place of worship? Have you easy access to public transportation, and community and health care services? Do you feel secure in your home and walking in the neighborhood? Does the house seem too big and empty now that your children have grown up and moved out?

Your financial situation will be one of the weightiest factors in deciding about retirement housing. Many older people feel they would be better off selling their homes and investing the proceeds in something that would increase their own monthly incomes. But moving out of the home you have lived in for many years, a home that was the scene of much joy and filled with memories, is naturally a very big decision filled with stress and anxiety. You need to consider all the alternatives. Where will you find the most suitable alternative accommodation? When is the best time for you to move? And what are your options if you decide to remain in your home?

Consult your children, your friends, and a trusted doctor, lawyer or bank manager before making your final decision. Enroll in one of the counseling programs sponsored by the Canadian Association of Retired Persons, or one of the workshops given by community colleges, public libraries, senior centers, and community Ys. You will discover that you have a wide range of options to choose from.

House sharing, for example, can be an economic and social blessing for seniors who find the family home too big, too lonely, and too expensive to maintain on their own. The housemate could be a friend who not only shares expenses, but meals and leisure too. It could also be a student who shares household chores in exchange for low rent. A self-contained apartment within the home for a friend or relative, perhaps one's adult children, could be the answer for those reluctant to share their living quarters, who like to have company nearby.

Other retirees may be only too willing to abandon the responsibilities and expenses surrounding the upkeep of the family home and eager to move from the city to a smaller town or resort community. Even if you have a particular place in mind, it would be unwise to finalize your plans right away. If you have always dreamed of retiring to Vancouver Island, rent

I heard my father say that he never knew a piece of land to run away or break.

JOHN ADAMS
Autobiography

Sale and Leaseback

North America's senior citizens own as much as $2 trillion in home equity, but many remain cash poor. If you are a home-owning parent, you might consider this popular strategy for staying in your home while cashing in on your equity:

• **The strategy.** Sale and leaseback is a method whereby owners over age 55 sell their home to their children, who in turn lease it back to the parents for life. The deal is often seller-financed, meaning parents receive a down payment and monthly mortgage payments from their children, then return some of it in rent payments.

• **Advantage for you as seller.** You stay in your own home, free of ownership responsibilities, with a steady income. The profit from selling your home is tax-free since there is no capital gains tax on the sale of your principal residence.

• **Advantage for your children.** They keep the family home in their possession. They also earn rental income, against which they can deduct, for tax purposes, the expenses of being a landlord.

• **Alternative solution.** In some cases, older people find it advantageous to apply to a bank or other financial institution for a reverse mortgage. In this type of mortgage a bank may lend you a certain amount of money, say $50,000, for example, paid to you at a monthly rate over 20 years or so. Your fully paid up home is their security, which they can realize when you decide to sell, or on your death.

• **For more information.** Consult your accountant and lawyer. The Canadian Association of Retired Persons also provides information on this and other home equity conversion options.

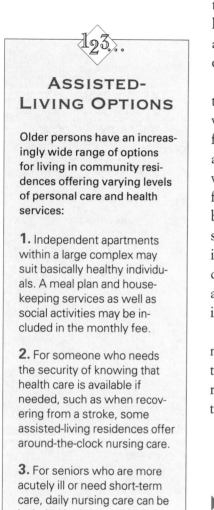

123..

ASSISTED-LIVING OPTIONS

Older persons have an increasingly wide range of options for living in community residences offering varying levels of personal care and health services:

1. Independent apartments within a large complex may suit basically healthy individuals. A meal plan and housekeeping services as well as social activities may be included in the monthly fee.

2. For someone who needs the security of knowing that health care is available if needed, such as when recovering from a stroke, some assisted-living residences offer around-the-clock nursing care.

3. For seniors who are more acutely ill or need short-term care, daily nursing care can be included in the monthly rent at an assisted-living residence, along with the meal plan and other services.

4. Long-term health-care services in residential complexes can combine the level of care found in nursing homes with the continued comfort of private living quarters.

5. In facilities with several tiers of service, a person who needs full-time nursing care after a hospital visit and then becomes more self-sufficient can stay in the same apartment. Only the monthly fee changes. Seniors who need and can afford the extra health care often prefer this more congenial community atmosphere to traditional nursing homes.

there for a year to make sure that is where you really want to live. Gather information about creative housing alternatives and places where retirement prospects are good. Talk to real estate agents about this, at home and when you travel.

For some older people with infirmities moving into a continuing-care or supportive home with many services is an ideal way of alleviating loneliness and stress. While everyone hopes for good health in retirement, it is wise to explore living arrangements that provide housekeeping and health-care services help if needed. This type of accommodation is often found in life-care communities, a name given to apartment buildings and other housing complexes, which encourage seniors to be independent, while guaranteeing them increasing levels of supportive and medical care as their health declines. Services in such communities range from educational and recreational activities and shared meals in communal dining rooms to 24-hour nursing care.

Although there are many housing developments and apartment buildings catering exclusively to older people, their status is uncertain: under federal law and most provincial human rights legislation, it is illegal to discriminate against prospective owners or renters because of age.

Shared Housing

The steady increase in the number of Canadians over age 65 has generated many new housing options that offer alternatives to the often sad choice of living alone or, when necessary, in a nursing home. Federal, provincial, and local government agencies, health policy experts, families, and senior citizens are seeking and supporting housing innovations that are affordable, safe, and comfortable. Three increasingly popular options are group-shared housing, matchup services, and adult foster care. (For more about these services, see YOUR MARRIAGE AND FAMILY, page 151.)

Group-shared housing consists of apartments, condominiums, or houses in which several unrelated adults, including healthy, independent older people, live together and share expenses. Most shared-housing complexes are funded primarily by the residents' rent payments and private donors, but some are government funded, some are run by private nonprofit organizations, and others are profit-making ventures.

VARIED ASPECTS OF SHARING

Shared-housing developments take different forms. They can be clusters of duplexes of two apartments each, for example, with each four-bedroom, two-bath apartment occupied by four residents. Or a large Victorian house, with separate, private rooms and common living areas, may serve as a group home. Residents pay rents, called "sharing fees," which may be quite low in homes where members make their own meals and are otherwise independent. In homes offering meal preparation, laundry service, or housecleaning, fees are much higher.

Like the homes they occupy, members of group-shared housing are a diverse lot. Some still work full- or part-time outside the home. Some are fully retired and living off their retirement income. Still others may need the help of a part-time nurse. All share common facilities and spaces such as backyards and dining rooms. The agency with which they are affiliated may offer no social services except an occasional visit from the residence supervisor. For groups whose health or disability requires more help but not full-time care, a house manager can help shop, cook, and clean.

Group-shared housing for the aging occasionally conflicts with zoning regulations and raises objections from local communities. Some zoning boards object to shared housing between unrelated adults on the grounds that group homes increase traffic flow.

MATCHUP SERVICES

Matchup programs bring together individuals in need of housing with homeowners seeking someone to share their home and rent (or mortgage payments). The matchups are usually between an older and younger single person. Most often the homeowner is an elderly person who wants added income, security, and companionship. The younger adult is often enticed by rent that is lower than market rate. Some renters perform light household chores in exchange for free rent.

ADULT FOSTER CARE

Foster families are paid by the province to care for semi-independent older adults, providing them with the amenities of home living and limited personal care. Provincial laws vary, but foster families are usually allowed to care for up to three or more adults aged 65 or older.

The cost of adult foster care is about a third that of nursing-home expenses. Government or nonprofit agencies match families with foster adults and pay for care costs. In some programs, elderly people pay from their Old Age Security benefits or pensions. Provinces are sometimes allowed by the federal Medicare program to apply nursing-home funds to adult foster care. Foster families are screened by participating social service programs. Elderly participants can relocate if their match does not suit them. For more information, contact your local social services department.

The Benefits of Home-Care Social Services

Full-time private home care is of course the ideal way to look after the frail or elderly—but it is also extremely expensive. For those who cannot afford private care, health-care maintenance programs may be the best alternative.

These innovative programs merge medical care, home care, and social services into a comprehensive package for seniors who live at home but are not fully self-sufficient. Privately run, publicly funded, and affiliated with local hospitals, they require elderly participants to sign over their Old Age Security benefits in exchange for unlimited access to health-care professionals.

Comprehensive care services help relocate seniors to new apartments that are wheelchair accessible. The service is responsible for sending an aide twice a week to clean the apartment, help bathe the resident, and pick up groceries. The service sends doctors on house calls; and transports participants to a day center twice a week, where they join others in social activities.

Participants are guaranteed free health care for life, including hospital and nursing care. And because their health is so closely monitored, participants are hospitalized only about half as frequently as other adults over 65 years of age. For more information, contact Health Canada or your provincial social service department.

MOBILE HOMES

Not-so-mobile "manufactured housing" is an inexpensive alternative to more conventional housing—but owners' rights are not well protected.

What to Look for in a Lease

If you rent a plot in a mobile-home park, try to get a long-term lease for a year or more. The lease should clarify the following:

✔ *Security deposit.* How big a deposit is charged, and under what conditions will it be returned to you?

✔ *Extra fees.* Are you charged an entrance fee when you move in? An exit fee on leaving? What if you sublet or resell your mobile home?

✔ *Utilities.* Are your expenses comparable with residential rates in the area? How does the park operator calculate each resident's share?

✔ *Basic services.* Are yard maintenance, septic systems, garbage collection, and other services included in your rent?

✔ *Extra amenities.* Does your rent include access to on-site swimming pools, tennis courts, clubhouse, and other facilities?

✔ *Children.* Are there any regulations on age or the number of children allowed?

✔ *Pets.* Are pets allowed, and if so, what kind and how many per homeowner?

Affordable but Vulnerable

Mobile homes, also known as manufactured housing, are factory-built residences made for year-round living. Unlike recreational vehicles or travel trailers that are towed along the highways, mobile homes travel only from factories to retailers to home sites chosen by consumers. Most of them never move again.

Because they are so much more affordable than conventional housing, mobile homes are an option that many people choose. Yet because they make up such a small part of the housing industry, and perhaps, because those living in mobile homes often have little economic clout, mobile-home owners in general have fewer rights than conventional homeowners.

A scarcity of provincial laws and local regulations leaves mobile homeowners vulnerable to shoddy workmanship and unscrupulous salespeople and site operators. Manufacturers of course must meet minimum federal standards for such things as electrical, heating, plumbing, and other elements that could affect health or safety. These, and appliances such as stoves, heaters, and refrigerators must conform to Canadian Standards Association (CSA) standards. Meantime, industry activists are working with the federal government to improve regulation standards and establish fair practice rules. Nevertheless, mobile-home owners and renters must be on guard to avoid being exploited.

FINDING A PLACE TO SETTLE DOWN

Before you buy a mobile home, you need to find somewhere to put it. If you want to buy a plot of land in a residential area, check local zoning laws. Some municipalities have passed laws preventing zoning discrimination against mobile homes, yet some regions still do so on the basis that they do not conform to local architectural standards and overburden municipal services such as garbage collection and water supply.

Most mobile-home owners settle down in mobile-home parks. There are hundreds of these communities in Canada, some owned by mobile-home retailers or manufacturers and others independently operated. Even so, there is still a shortage of mobile-home sites, which gives park operators an advantage over their prospective tenants. So watch out for unscrupulous park operators who require that you buy a mobile home from them as a condition of renting a site on their property, or who charge more rent if you do not buy from them.

Negotiating a lease may also be a prickly matter. Some mobile-home parks offer tenants leases of at least one year. In others, tenants have to negotiate their leases month to month. This leaves them exposed to frequent rent increases without legal recourse.

If you are lucky, you will find a well-established, cooperative park community where residents, not a developer, are the rule-making owners.

GETTING THERE

Once you are ready to move your mobile home to the park site, your main concern is the safe transportation and installation of your home. To date, neither manufacturers nor dealers are fully responsible for damages to the mobile home incurred during transportation. For the mobile-home owner whose home arrives on-site damaged, the result may be additional expenses for repairs or a legal battle.

When it comes to installing your home on site, use only professional, fully trained installers. Many structural problems have been traced to improper installation, and most provinces and municipalities have set installation standards. Lobby groups are working with government agencies seeking new legislation that would mandate a five-year warranty on installation.

A house is a machine for living in.

LE CORBUSIER
Vers une Architecture

Things to Know About Mobile Homes

A single mobile-home unit is usually 14 feet wide, may be anywhere from 32 to 80 feet long, and comes complete with carpeting, draperies, and appliances. Attractive as they may be, by the nature of their construction, mobile homes are not as safe as conventionally built homes.

• New mobile homes typically cost between $30,000 and $50,000. Anchors, awnings, base slabs, jacks, patios, stairs, and transportation to the site may add another 15 percent or more to the purchase price. Mobile-home owners also must pay for the cost of renting or buying a site for the home and associated maintenance fees. Even so, mobile homes cost so much less than conventional homes that they are especially popular among young couples, retired persons, and other low- or moderate-income families and individuals.

• Manufactured homes that have been built in the last 20 years must conform to the National Building Code. In most provinces, the buyer of a mobile home is protected by the Sale of Goods Act and often by provincial consumer protection legislation. Common problems in manufactured homes include weak caulking, disintegrating siding, improperly installed windows, inferior or nonexistent insulation, inadequate electrical systems, leaking roofs (especially in multisectional units), and improperly connected heating ducts.

• Most mobile homes are financed with personal loans, although you may be able to qualify for a traditional mortgage if you undertake to purchase the mobile-home site as well. Canada Mortgage and Housing Corporation will not give direct loans for mobile homes but it will sometimes insure such mortgages.

SELLING YOUR HOME

Putting the house you live in on the market is a challenge, both financially and emotionally, and is best tackled with professional help.

⟨1⟩⟨2⟩⟨3⟩...

YOUR CONTRACT WITH A BROKER

An employment contract with the real estate broker you hire to sell your home, called a "listing contract," should clarify these points:

1. Exclusivity arrangement. With an "exclusive right-to-sell" contract, you pay the broker's commission even if you find a buyer on your own. With an "exclusive agency" arrangement, you list your property with one broker but pay no commission if you find the buyer.

2. Length of contract. A relatively short listing period of 30 to 90 days is common, although it may take six months or longer for some homes to sell. Elect a shorter commitment with optional renewal.

3. Cancellation agreement. What if your broker does not perform a satisfactory job? Avoid contracts with penalty fees for sellers who cancel.

4. Commission agreement. Broker commissions are negotiable. You may be able to bargain below the typical 6 percent commission.

5. Showing the house. Will your broker bring interested buyers to your home individually? Do you need to be there? Will there be an open house?

Sell It Yourself or Get Help?

When it comes time to sell their homes, most homeowners choose to hire real estate brokers to handle the many details involved in taking a house sale to its closing rather than spend the time and effort themselves. Sellers find many advantages in using an experienced broker, who can:

- Advertise your home on the Realtors' computerized network—called the multiple listing service, or MLS—expanding sales potential to real estate offices nationwide;
- Offer advice on preparing your home for sale (from repainting and recaulking to repairing broken electrical switches and cleaning gutters);
- Write effective advertisements to sell the home, using tricks of the trade that maximize your home's fine points and mask deficiencies (by emphasizing, for instance, the historic authenticity of a house with small rooms and low ceilings);
- Use her experience, including knowledge of the neighborhood and local marketplace, to help you set the appropriate asking price;
- Screen buyers, weed out browsers who are not ready to buy, and assess their financial ability to make the purchase;
- Advise you on offering incentives in a slow economic market, such as paying for extra home improvements;
- Help review the buyer's offer and negotiate the best deal.

These pluses alone usually make a broker worth the typical commission of 6 percent of the final sale price of the home. If you are in a seller's market where there are more buyers than sellers, the broker may be able to sell your home for at least 6 percent more than the original sale price, meaning that you essentially receive her services for free. (See also "Hunting for Your Home," page 10.)

If you have spoken to several brokers and found one you like, you should sign a contract that clarifies both your rights and obligations. You can choose from a variety of arrangements. An open listing agreement guarantees the broker a commission during the contractual time frame—even if you or someone else brings in the buyer—in exchange for the broker's dedicated effort to sell the home. This option is preferred by sellers who want the broker to do all the work involved in selling a home.

In contrast, an exclusive agency agreement exempts you from paying the commission if the broker does not find the buyer. This is often the best arrangement when the seller has a likely buyer or is willing to make the effort of finding a buyer by handling queries about the property and showing the home.

If you sell the property later, but to a person who was introduced to you by your agent, you will, in most cases, be obliged to pay the agent's commission.

Whatever your arrangement, a hardworking broker should stay in frequent contact with you. At all times, a broker hired by you has a duty to protect and promote your interests.

BROKER ALTERNATIVES

Discount real estate brokerages offer services midway between full-service, full-price brokers and selling a home by yourself. Discount services charge either a set fee or a reduced commission of 2 or 3 percent to list your home in the local marketplace and provide skeletal services. Discount brokers require you to do most of the marketing and all showings of your home. For an extra fee, sellers can also have their homes listed in the MLS electronic marketplace.

Another way of selling a home is to contact a local realtor and arrange an "open agency agreement." This is a nonbinding invitation for the broker to sell your home without listing it on the MLS and without performing even the minor services of a discount broker.

In an open agency arrangement, you do all the sale-end advertising and showing yourself, but agree to pay 3 percent of the sale price to any broker who brings in the buyer (that is, half the usual 6 percent a broker would receive for advertising the home and bringing in the buyer). This increases the flow of potential buyers to a seller's home. Sellers who choose this arrangement should advertise their homes as "for sale by owner with brokers welcome at 3 percent."

SELLING YOUR OWN HOME

Sellers sometimes choose to save the cost of a broker's commission by orchestrating the sale of their own homes with the aid of a few key professionals. If you are considering selling your home yourself, be prepared for a time-consuming task that will require much effort, patience, and flexibility. You will need to assess and set a fair sale price and calculate the value and condition of your home's main systems (electrical, plumbing, and so on), appliances, and other features. Then you will

Tips for Selling Solo

In any economic climate, but particularly when sellers are competing for scarce buyers, homeowners who sell their own homes should keep these points in mind:

✔ *Set priorities.* Do you want a quick and easy sale at the risk of a lower price, or will you hold out for top price even if it means your house stays on the market longer?

✔ *Advertise wisely.* To create an effective newspaper ad, include a full description of the house that emphasizes its best features. Include the price, with your address (if you are having an open house) or telephone number. Put an eye-catching sign in your yard for passersby.

✔ *Remember fair housing.* Federal and provincial laws prohibit discriminating against potential buyers on the basis of race, gender, religion, and other criteria. Avoid judgmental statements that might be construed as discouraging buyers.

✔ *Get a home inspection.* Find out about problems that buyers might notice, before or after the sale, and either have them fixed or reconfigure your asking price.

✔ *Offer incentives.* Any inducement that adds value to a buyer's purchase works in your favor, from offering a home warranty to lending part of the down payment. Do not, however, represent the value of the house or the neighborhood falsely.

If Your Buyer Does Not Get the Loan

When you sign a purchase agreement, or binder, with a buyer, the final sale may be contingent upon certain conditions that must be met by a specified deadline. One of the most common contingencies involves the buyer's securing a mortgage loan. If your buyer has not done so by the deadline, you have several courses of action.

The option most preferred by buyers is to renegotiate a deadline for financing. Sellers should keep in mind that for buyers to secure a mortgage, they must not only be approved for the loan but also accept its terms, such as added points or fees. As the seller, you should know what constitutes an acceptable loan for the buyer. The terms should be spelled out in your purchase agreement.

If the market is slow for sellers, you will probably be anxious; so if your buyer has not secured a loan by the deadline, you might consider altering your arrangement. You could offer to pay for one of the loan points or other up-front fees, such as title insurance. This will make it easier and more appealing for a buyer to secure a satisfactory loan.

Finally, if you are wary of your buyer's sincerity or ability to secure a loan and one of the contingencies of your agreement has not been met, you have the right to terminate the purchase agreement and look for another buyer.

have to advertise and market the home, respond to inquiries, screen potential buyers, and make appointments to show the home. Finally, you will negotiate financial agreements with the buyer and arrange for a sales contract.

To determine a reasonable sale price for your home, you will need to assess the current state of the housing market in your area. You should also be aware that while home improvements such as a new water heater or insulation add value to the sale price, home decorating, such as the new wallpaper in the master bedroom, does not. In the long run your best bet probably is to hire a professional home appraiser. For a few hundred dollars, using both objective calculations and personal opinion based on experience and familiarity with the area, he can assess the value of your home within a specific price range.

The Buyer and You

Before you open your home to prospective buyers, walk through each room with pen in hand and make a list of necessary improvements and minor repairs. Since you cannot anticipate the details buyers will notice—they may ignore the bathroom tiles you painstakingly regrouted while they peer at a tiny chip in the tub—focus on sharpening the overall condition and appearance of your home. Repainting, removing clutter from rooms, waxing floors, repairing dripping faucets, mowing the lawn, and other basic chores will make your home sale-ready.

Sellers should greet interested buyers with a fact sheet about the house. Include the dimensions of each room and the property; the average monthly costs of fuel, water and electricity; property taxes; and a brief history of recent value-enhancing repairs and improvements. Also have on hand all the relevant papers for appliances and other products, such as a water-sprinkling system that might still be under warranty.

SELLER TELLS ALL

Not only is it good business to be candid about the condition of your home; in many provinces, it is the law. Disclosure forms and disclaimers about the condition of the seller's home are becoming a requirement in many provinces. You must tell the buyer the truth about all the physical defects of the house. Most provinces also require sellers to tell buyers about lead-based paint in and around the property, as well as the presence of radon and asbestos (see also "Environmental Concerns," page 59). Since more and more buyers are suing sellers for problems not disclosed before the sale (and since more courts are favoring these buyers), you should protect yourself with a disclosure statement, even if it is not yet the law in your province. Many agents will not show a home without a disclosure form, as they, too, are being increasingly sued along with sellers.

One strategy is to hire professional home inspectors. You can attend to any problems they find in the structure or systems of your home, reduce the sale price, or make another financial deal, such as a buy down, to offset the probable cost to a buyer of repairing the defects.

By disclosing the problems, you lessen the chance of being sued for concealing a defect—potentially a much greater drain on your finances than a few repair jobs. To protect yourself against any inaccuracies in your disclosure form, you can get errors and omissions (E & O) insurance for sellers.

NEGOTIATING THE VARIABLES

Eager buyers will make bids to buy your home in response to both your asking price and their assessment of what your house is worth. While your asking price should be reasonable for the market, you can set it 2 or 3 percent above the current market value in order to leave room for bargaining. If you know that other sellers in your area with comparable homes are getting many offers, you might set your price at 5 or 6 percent over market range. In this way you can give in a little more on the price to make buyers think they are getting a deal, and still sell your home more quickly for an acceptable price.

While in the "offer" stage, you can accept offers from more

No man acquires property without a little arithmetic also.

RALPH WALDO EMERSON
American author
1803–1886

Offering a Better Deal With a Buy Down

One incentive that can be offered by a seller who is having trouble finding a buyer is a buy down. In this arrangement, the seller agrees to reduce, or buy down, the interest rate on the buyer's mortgage loan for the full term of the mortgage. Here is how it works:

• A buy down is an extra incentive provided by the seller whereby he pays for, or buys, an agreed-upon percentage of the buyer's mortgage loan. For example, for a one percent buy down, you would pay the equivalent value of one percent of the interest on the mortgage, based on current interest rates. Thus if current interest rate on mortgage loans is 7.5 percent, your one percent buy down on a $100,000 house would be $7,500.

• At the closing of the sale, the seller writes a cheque for the buy-down payment to the buyer's mortgage lender. The lender puts the money in an escrow account and applies it evenly to the buyer's monthly mortgage interest payments over the period of the loan,

• A buy-down offer reduces the buyer's cost in buying the home. Rather than paying the buyer a one-time fee, however, the seller's buy-down money is distributed over time into the buyer's mortgage payments, thereby lessening the buyer's monthly mortgage loan expense.

• The buy down also benefits the seller obliquely by making the property more attractive to a buyer who might otherwise not have taken it. A buy down is actually a reduction in the sale price.

• You can also offer to be mortgagee (lender) to the buyer by having a balance of sale, say 20 percent, which the buyer pays to you on a monthly basis at an interest rate set by you and the buyer.

Watching Improvements Pay Off

If you have kept careful records of improvements to your home over the years, you will reap rewards when you sell it. Remodeling projects add value that translates into quicker sales, greater leverage for pricing, and tax reductions. Remodeled kitchens, for example, typically return as much as 94 percent of their cost if the house is sold within a year of the job.

A major kitchen renovation might include new cabinets, flooring, laminate countertops, energy-efficient oven, ventilation system, custom lighting, and a central island of counter space. A minor kitchen job might entail refinished instead of new cabinets.

Along with updated kitchens, the highest-value remodeling projects are sun-space additions, which open up the house visually and can double as an office or family room; family-room renovations such as adding glass doors, a fireplace, or more floor space; and bathroom remodeling that might mean a new bathtub, a vanity counter with molded sinks, and new flooring.

Homeowners spend billions of dollars a year on home repairs and improvements. To the extent you can afford them, you can enjoy these improvements and add value that pays off at sale time.

than one buyer at a time and make multiple counteroffers. You are free to take the best deal. All offers and counteroffers, whether negotiated through a real estate broker or directly between you and a prospective buyer, should be in writing.

Saved by an Escrow Account

PROBLEM

Rose, widowed for five years, decided to sell the old house she and her husband had lived in for many years, and move to an apartment she could afford. Through a broker she put the house on the market, and when a couple showed serious interest, she began negotiating for her new place. Then a house inspection commissioned by the buyers revealed that her home's electrical system might not be able to cope with their modern demands. Rose was devastated when they threatened to withdraw because of the potential expense the problem might lead to.

ACTION

On the advice of her broker, Rose got an estimate of the cost of replacing the electrical system and immediately offered to put that much, and a little more, into an escrow account out of which the buyers could draw to refurbish the electrical system should the old one fail within the first year of their ownership. Reassured, the buyers accepted her deal. Rose got less money than she had hoped for (since some of the sale money went back into the escrow account), but she still had enough to relocate and had rid herself of a property that could have turned into a serious financial burden.

When evaluating a purchase offer, be aware that the sale price alone does not convey the full value of an offer. For example, if a buyer offers less than your asking price but is willing to make a high down payment, or to accept the house without certain necessary repairs, it may be a worthwhile offer. Pay special attention to time limits. If an offer specifies that the seller has two weeks to respond, and you sign, you cannot then accept other offers or sell the property to another buyer for two weeks.

GETTING CLOSE TO MAKING A DEAL

If you have a buyer who is really interested, you should be amenable to allowing a home inspector of his choice examine your home. The report of a professional home inspector can actually help shift some liability for future problems from you to the professional. Show the buyer your disclosure statements. Make no guarantees—you can say the roof is five years old and under warranty, but do not promise it will not leak.

Negotiate a deadline, such as a day or two, by which you agree to make a counteroffer. You could use the time to weigh multiple offers, if you have them, and drive up the final sale price. Do not keep interested buyers waiting too long, or they may withdraw their offers. Also, buyers can take back any earnest money deposited in an escrow account if you do not make a counteroffer or accept their offer by the deadline. When you do accept a buyer's purchase offer, or the buyer accepts your counteroffer, you enter into a purchase, or binder, agreement, and you must stop accepting other offers.

Final Concerns of Selling

The purchase agreement is a legally binding contract that will become a sales contract (or the basis of a sales contract) when the conditions, or contingencies, of the agreement are met. Since it is a legally binding contract, you should have a lawyer review the agreement and include certain legal protections.

If you and the buyer agreed that a certain known defect— say, loose floorboards in a bedroom—will remain unrepaired, you should state this specifically in the contract so the buyer cannot later blame you for concealing or neglecting the problem. Your purchase agreement should also clarify your agreement with the buyer as to which fixtures come with the home, such as laundry machine, dishwasher, and ceiling lights.

SMALL COSTS, BIG PROTECTION

There are a number of up-front costs to a home purchase that a buyer may have negotiated for you to pay, including title insurance and home warranties. You might offer to pay the title insurance costs not only as a sales incentive and goodwill gesture but because it protects you from being sued by the buyer in case of an error in the boundary records.

Similarly, home warranties protect the seller from unanticipated problems. Warranties guarantee the basically sound condition of a home's major systems, from heating to plumbing, for a limited number of years after the sale. Home warranties do not cover structural elements, such as the foundation, and are harder to obtain and less comprehensive for older homes.

Still, for a relatively low, one-time premium fee, home warranties can protect the seller from responsibility for undiscovered defects that might later prompt a buyer to file a lawsuit.

CLOSING IN ON THE CLOSING

Once a purchase agreement has been signed and a date of closing set—usually a month or two away to give the buyer time to secure a mortgage—there is not much left for you to do besides pack your belongings and make whatever repairs you have agreed to. You have the responsibility of leaving the house in a clean, habitable condition.

The Facts About Sellers' Tax Breaks

When you profit from the sale of a home other than a single family unit, a duplex for example, you owe Revenue Canada a capital gains tax. There are several ways of easing, delaying, or even avoiding, the payment:

✔ *Calculate adjusted basis.* You do not simply pay taxes on the sale price of your home. You pay taxes on the difference between the price you paid for it and the price you sell it for, plus the value of home improvements, minus losses from fire or other damage. This is called the "adjusted basis" of the home.

✔ *Deducting sales costs.* Sellers can deduct many expenses incurred in preparing a home for sale, including repair costs to the part of the house that was not occupied by you, say the upper part of your duplex, real estate broker's commissions, advertising, and legal fees.

✔ *The GST* Be aware that if your property has been substantially renovated—for example if the floors and windows were changed, a room or new kitchen added—your home may be subject to the federal GST. Ask your tax lawyer or accountant what you can do to reduce or avoid this tax.

Closing, or settlement, day should bring few surprises to home sellers. To ensure this, have your lawyer check with the settlement agent (usually chosen by the buyer) a day or two before settlement to make sure all the proper elements are in place, including the buyer's mortgage loan. If you hold joint title to your home, remember that your co-owner needs to have signed the deed to the property before settlement day.

Gather the items you will need at settlement, including:

- Documentation that any contingencies you were responsible for have been fulfilled, such as repairs completed;
- Your homeowners insurance policy, if the buyer is taking over your policy for the home;
- The deed to the property to transfer the title from you to the buyer;
- Prorated expenses, such as property taxes and gas, water, or electric utility bills, with a copy of receipts indicating your most recent payments.

Do not expect to walk away from the settlement with a lot of cash or even freshly written cheques. Settlement lawyers often hold on to buyers' cheques until the necessary legal documents have been recorded, such as the deed in the county records office. Make sure your lawyer has discussed with the settlement lawyer or agent exactly when you will receive your cheques. You can write these dates into the sales contract.

A friendship founded on business is better than a business founded on friendship.

JOHN D. ROCKEFELLER
American oil magnate
and philanthropist
1839–1937

Selling a Property You Co-Own

Co-owners are two or more people who purchase and inhabit property together; they may be married with joint property, owners in a tenancy-in-common arrangement, or joint unmarried owners. When they sell the property, special concerns for each form of ownership must be addressed:

• Married couples usually own property in joint tenancy, each having an equal undivided interest. If they sell the property, any profits are shared equally. If married co-owners are divorcing, the sale of the house is part of the bigger issue of property acquired during marriage. Provincial laws vary widely on community property and equitable distribution. Your divorce lawyer can advise you.

• If you own property with someone not related to you by marriage as "tenants-in-common," and if your co-owner wants to sell the property, you could be forced to sell against your wishes. A co-owner may sell his individual interest in the property, and in some instances, through a "partition lawsuit," force a sale of the property.

• Property law has not addressed many contemporary issues of joint ownership by unmarried persons. Such co-owners themselves need to address certain legal issues in a contract they write at the time of purchase. The contract between unmarried co-owners should clarify, for example, whether a joint owner has a first option to purchase the share of an owner who wants to sell. Another contractual consideration should be who will retain rights to live on the property if the joint owners can no longer live together.

• Any contract between tenants-in-common or joint unmarried owners should also specify how the fixtures, furnishings, and appliances in the house are to be distributed if the property is sold.

MOVING

A final step in the long process of finding a new home is getting your possessions from one house to another. Learn what you can do to minimize the cost and anxiety.

Avoiding Problems in the Move

About six to eight weeks before you want to move out of your home, you should start planning the move. You will want to compare the services of several moving companies. Check the movers' qualifications with your consumer protection agency, or your local Better Business Bureau if the move is local. Ask for the mover's motor carrier license—without one, the mover is not authorized to carry goods. For moves to another province, the mover should be licensed by Transport Canada.

To compare movers, ask for an estimate, either nonbinding or binding. A nonbinding estimate is the probable cost of your move, based on an on-site evaluation of what you are moving, and how far. The actual cost may differ, based on the total weight (or sometimes volume) of your goods. A binding estimate is a guaranteed final cost based on the company's inventory of your possessions. There may be an extra charge for this guarantee. Binding estimates tend to be the best deal for consumers because they allow fewer variables in pricing.

MAKING A COMPLETE INVENTORY

Moving companies comply with a standard set of rate charges, based on weight of goods and distance transported. There are also set charges for packing, unpacking, and other services— all of which should be explicit in your job estimate. Walk through your house with the movers as they inventory your belongings to ensure an accurate assessment. Note any damaged items and insist on a statement in the estimate declaring that all other items are in good condition.

Be thorough, for belongings the mover did not see, such as boxes in the attic or bicycles in the basement, will cost extra.

On moving day you will receive the actual contract for the job, called the "bill of lading." Read it carefully for any deviations from the estimate agreement. If the cost of your move is based on weight of goods, you have the right to watch the movers weigh the goods. Unscrupulous movers have been known to overload the scales.

Unless you have paid for private delivery, your belongings will probably be moved with other families' goods. In this case,

WHAT MOVERS CHARGE

1. Line-haul charge. This is the basic charge for a move, based on weight of goods and distance traveled.

2. Packing charge. Boxes, bubble wrap, packing tape, and the labor of packing and unpacking boxes are all extras.

3. Distance fees. If the movers must carry your goods more than 75 feet from truck to building, you may pay more.

4. Waiting time charges. If you are not ready when the movers come, you may be charged for delaying them.

5. Stair carry. You may not be charged for one flight of stairs, but any steps above the first flight usually carry a charge.

6. Charge per mover. Companies usually charge an hourly rate for each mover.

7. Additional charges for heavy furniture or appliances. Pianos, whirlpools, refrigerators, and other difficult or heavy items generally cost more. Get a price breakdown.

8. Special services. If you want your goods delivered quickly, you may decide to pay for exclusive use of a vehicle rather than wait for other customers' goods to be loaded with yours.

Regulating the Movers

Moving companies are licensed by their provincial transport ministry. Those who do business interprovincially must also be licensed by Transport Canada and are often registered with transport ministries in all provinces where they do business. Those who do business in the United States and overseas are also registered with the Interstate Commerce Commission, a U.S. federal agency, and the Federation of International Movers, and other moving industry boards and associations.

These industry federations set standards for packing and shipping and may provide arbitration committees that help resolve problems between disgruntled customers and the moving company. In some provinces, the provincial consumer protection act may regulate such matters as estimates.

If you are not dealing with one of the larger well-established moving companies, make sure your mover is licensed, can offer insurance by a private insurance company and has a good record for reliability. Check with your Better Business Bureau or local consumer affairs office for previous complaints.

delivery is made within a specified range of days. The mover must notify you of any delay. When the movers arrive at your new home, be there. Open any crushed boxes and make notes on the inventory forms about any damaged items inside.

MOVER'S LIABILITY

Your own homeowners insurance may be sufficient protection for your possessions, so check with your insurance agent before signing a contract with a mover. Be aware, however, that unless you take out special moving insurance, under Transport Canada rules, the mover is liable for only 60 cents per pound per article. Under such circumstances, if your $5,000 fifty-pound stereo system is damaged, the mover need only pay you $30.

Movers offer valuation insurance, which is different from full insurance, in that you have to prove liability before the mover will pay. Valuation is the amount of value you place on your shipment; if something is damaged or lost, you can get reimbursement or replacement only if you can prove that the mover is at fault.

For items of extraordinary value, get a separate written appraisal. Movers offer different rates and deductibles for items of extra value. Your best bet is to move precious items yourself or hire a specialized service, such as art movers.

FILING DAMAGE AND LOSS CLAIMS

Because you have to prove the movers caused the damage to your belongings, your inventory list is the first piece of evidence you need. It cites the undamaged condition of goods before the move. You also need your notes from the delivery day, specifying any damages you and the mover noticed on-site. To prepare your claim, make sure you have your bill of lading (contract) number, a written assertion that the mover is responsible for damage incurred, and a dollar amount of replacement or repair value for items in question. File your claim as quickly as possible for best results.

The mover must, by law, acknowledge receipt of your claim within 30 days and either deny or make an offer to settle within 90 days. If the company fails to respond in time or you are unable to resolve the claim with it, consider arbitration.

TAX BREAKS FOR MOVING

Moving may not be quite so expensive as you think. If your move is for employment reasons and is at least 40 kilometres closer to your new place of business, some of your expenses, such as the cost of trips to the new area, may be tax deductible. However, these regulations change from time to time, so check with your accountant, or ask Revenue Canada for tax form TI-M, which set out the current criteria.

YOUR MARRIAGE AND FAMILY

Nothing is more personal than your marriage, your children, and your family. But knotty legal questions can intrude on even the most private situations. Knowing your rights can help you find the best answers.

MARRIAGE ■ FAMILY PLANNING ■ ADOPTION ■ PARENTING ■ CHILD CARE ■ EDUCATION ■ DOMESTIC PARTNERSHIPS ■ DIVORCE ■ REMARRIAGE ■ ELDERCARE ■ FAMILY PETS ■ DEATH IN THE FAMILY ■ PROTECTING YOUR FAMILY

MARRIAGE

As well as being a sacred institution, marriage is also an important legal relationship. It brings great benefits and entails even greater responsibilities.

Can You Marry?

Marriage has been expected to last a lifetime. Yet the law requires very little from you or your prospective spouse before you enter into this civil contract. Perhaps the most basic requirement is age. Age regulations were originally based on the belief that marriage candidates should have reached puberty: the bride was required to be at least 12, the bridegroom 14. Today most provinces require a couple to have attained the age of majority, so that marriage marks the union of socially and physically mature people capable of supporting themselves.

Most provinces, however, permit minors to marry if their parents consent. Since marriage is considered good for society, often the consent of one parent is sufficient and will override the objection of the other parent.

THOU SHALT NOT

Even if you are old enough to marry, you cannot necessarily marry anyone you want. Marriage between members of the same sex is not legally valid in any province (see "Domestic Partnerships," page 131), and you cannot marry someone who is already married. Nor can you marry certain close relatives. While marriage between first cousins is permitted in some provinces, every province bans marriages between a parent and child, brother and sister, grandparent and grandchild, great-grandparent and great-grandchild, uncle and niece, and aunt and nephew. Marriage between a stepbrother and stepsister is also prohibed as are marriages between stepparents and their stepchildren. In fact these types of marriages are considered to be incestuous and punishable by law. The federal Marriage (Prohibited Degrees) Act, passed in 1990, augments restrictions in the various provincial statutes, and also prohibits marriage between adoptees and their adoptive parents and siblings.

Provincial laws also restrict marriages when one or both parties lack mental competence, generally defined as the ability to understand one's legal responsibility and, therefore, to give consent. These laws are intended to protect the incompetent person, but they are sometimes an area of dispute because incompetence is not always clear-cut or easy to define.

Marriages can be voided or annulled for incompetence or failure to meet age requirements. Marriages can be voided because one or both parties withheld pertinent information—such as being underage, the woman's pregnancy by another man, physical incapacity, impotence resulting from disease, malformation, or a defect that precludes the husband from consummating the relationship. Marriage can also be annulled for error as to the person—if a man holds out that he is a successful businessman when he is actually a professional criminal. It would not be grounds for annulment, however, if one party pretended to be rich but was only of meager means.

Forms and Formalities

You have never been more ready for marriage. You have applied to the county clerk's office or marriage license bureau for a license, and paid the fee. (Marriage licenses are not required in Quebec.) Yet,

---

Sharing Your Life, Financially

Making the right financial decisions with your mate is important to your partnership's success. In money matters, it is never too soon to begin. The following tips will get you started financially and legally:

• **Joint bank account.** Once married, many couples decide to open a joint bank account, with shared responsibility for its activity. Each spouse can make deposits and write cheques. You and your spouse may also maintain separate bank accounts. Many couples, particularly those with two incomes, choose this option to clarify where the money is coming from and where it is going.

• **Credit cards.** If you already have your own credit cards, you are not required to make them joint if you marry. When a husband and wife do open a joint credit card account, they both become responsible for it, no matter who actually incurs the charges. More and more, married couples consider it prudent to maintain at least one account in the name of just one of them to establish a separate credit identity and history.

• **Life insurance.** If you do not already have life insurance, marriage may provide the impetus to get it. If you are young, healthy, and have no children or large debts, you may not feel you need insurance just yet. But you should definitely start considering it. Many couples take out two policies, one for the wife, naming her husband as beneficiary, the other for the husband, naming the wife as beneficiary. If you already have insurance, you should probably reconsider the amount of coverage you need and whom to name as the beneficiary. (See also Your Money, page 304.)

• **Health insurance.** Most company and private health insurance plans make provisions for family members. If you both already have coverage, you may want to maintain separate coverage, or it may be more cost-effective to switch to joint coverage under one policy. Check with your employer, and carefully read the provisions of your policies.

• **Income tax.** Joint income tax returns are not permited. However, if one spouse is unemployed, or has a low income, the employed spouse would be entitled to a deduction for caring for his or her partner.

• **Joint decisions.** You may want to share all financial responsibilities, or you may decide that one of you can handle them better. But it is important to make this decision and stick to it. Whatever you arrange, you should both know where all your legal and financial documents are located.

depending on your province's "cooling-off" period, you will have to cool your heels for one day or maybe an entire week.

Suppose you and your beloved decide to marry in a foreign country. Will your marriage be valid in your home province? Yes: provided it was conducted with a license from and according to the laws in that locality. If, however, in order to evade your own province's restrictions, you go to another province or to the United States to marry your first cousin, your marriage could be deemed invalid when you return.

MAKE IT OFFICIAL

You can marry practically anywhere—in a church, in a court office, on the beach; some couples have even tied the knot while skydiving. But wherever you choose to hold your wedding, you must find a person authorized by law to officiate at it, and by law the ceremony must be completed in the presence of one or two adult witnesses in addition to the presiding official. The license must be signed by you, your spouse, the witnesses, and the official, and finally recorded with the appropriate county office. Not every legal union requires such a civil contract, however. In provinces that recognize common-law marriage, couples do not need a license for a marriage to be legal, although other requirements pertain.

In recent years, before entering a marriage, some couples have written a premarital (or prenuptial) agreement, setting forth certain agreed-upon conditions concerning property, support, children, or other important areas of their life together. While some premarital agreements may not be enforced by the courts, these agreements have become more common among couples marrying later in life and those who remarry with significant assets. (See also "Remarriage," page 146.)

Rights and Obligations

Historically, under common law, a wife was considered to be literally the property of her husband, totally dependent on him and subject to his will. Today's laws, increasingly gender-neutral, grant both spouses full civil rights to own property, get credit, negotiate and sign contracts, engage in business, and keep wages.

Moreover, while the law recognizes the right of a wife to be financially dependent on her husband, it also allows a husband to be the dependent spouse and rely on his wife's earnings. Both partners are legally responsible for supporting each other, the basic legal obligation of each partner being to provide necessities: food, clothing, and shelter. This assumes, of course, that he or she has the means to do so.

WHO OWNS WHAT

In all provinces, you can keep individual control over any property you take into a marriage. However, many provinces are now "equitable distribution" jurisdictions, which means that most property accumulated during a marriage is subject to division upon divorce, regardless of how it is titled, particularly if it has become commingled over the duration of the marriage. In some provinces literally all property (except that acquired by gift or inheritance) is shared, including a legal, dental, or other professional office, or a share in a partnership.

In provinces that maintain the community of property concept, property acquired by the labor or skill of either spouse during the marriage is owned jointly and equally. Each spouse owns one-half of the property and if one spouse dies, the property does not pass onto the other automatically. It is distributed to heirs named in a will or according to intestate laws.

Issues relating to these laws usually do not come up unless the partners divorce and must divide their assets. Even so, when you and your spouse want to own property jointly—a house or stocks, perhaps—you may have to choose what kind of "tenancy" will be involved. ("Tenancy" here is used in a legal sense and does not refer to renting.) Married couples usually own property through "joint ownership," either through "joint tenancy with the right of survivorship," which guarantees a survivor the deceased partner's share, or "tenancy by the entirety," which forbids one spouse from selling the property unless the other gives permission.

In both of these cases, if one spouse dies, the other becomes the sole owner of the property. Joint owners cannot sell without permission from the other, although they each own equal, individual shares in the property. Some couples may be "tenants in common," each owning separate legal title to an undivided interest in a property. A tenant in common can sell off her part of the property. After death, it passes by will or intestate succession laws to the next of kin. "Sole tenancy," or titling the property in one person's name, may also be an option. In some provinces, however, real estate purchased by one spouse will be considered to be owned by both spouses, even if there is only one name on the title. This is especially true of in the case of the matrimonial home.

THE SPECIAL NATURE OF MARRIAGE

Married couples are granted certain rights indicating the law's recognition of the "special nature" of the marital relationship. They are entitled to the right of privileged communication: a spouse generally cannot be required to testify in court about confidential information exchanged with a partner, although a spouse who wants to testify against the other may do so.

Changing Your Name

Many people still assume that a married woman automatically takes her husband's name. That notion is derived from the long-past days when a married woman had no legal existence apart from her husband. In fact, it is only when the wife uses her husband's name that it legally becomes hers.

If that is your preference, you may want to change the name on your driver's license, credit cards, and other identification. Some women opt for using their spouse's family name in social situations, and their maiden names professionally and on official documents such as passports, or when involved in civil litigation. The courts usually insist on birth name on court documents.

Husbands sometimes want to take their wives' names or both husband and wife may decide to use both surnames hyphenated. Or a couple may decide to take an entirely new name together. In most provinces you do not need the approval of the court to take a new name; just begin to use it.

To avoid any confusion, however, or problems with government or other agencies that may insist that you use your "real" name, you may want to formalize the change. Every province has legal procedures for changing your name. In a divorce, women can minimize potential problems by including their name-change intentions in their final decree.

FAMILY PLANNING

Having a baby can be one of life's most satisfying experiences. But when to have a child is a matter to be thought about carefully. It carries legal consequences.

Birth Control by Sterilization

Sterilization is North America's second most common form of contraception after birth control pills. To date, hundreds of thousands of Canadians have chosen tubal ligations or, in the case of men, vasectomies. Candidates for the surgery are required to give written, informed consent. Depending on provincial laws, anyone under 18 or 19 years of age or mentally incompetent may not give such consent.

If a woman becomes pregnant because the sterilization procedure failed, she may file a wrongful pregnancy suit, charging medical malpractice. Such cases are difficult to win, however, since the birth of a child is rarely seen as a harmful act. Besides, no surgical intervention or device to stop pregnancy can be considered 100 percent effective all the time. No Canadian has yet been awarded money for the care and upkeep of a child born after sterilization was performed.

For many women and many men, sterilization procedures cannot be reversed. Before consenting to sterilization, make sure you have thought the decision through carefully and have discussed the procedure extensively with your doctor. There is no law that requires a doctor to inform the other spouse that one spouse has been sterilized by means of tubal ligation or vasectomy.

Deciding About Pregnancy

Birth control drugs and devices are now readily available across Canada, and the majority of women between the ages of 15 and 44 use some form of contraception. Health Canada is responsible for certifying the safety and effectiveness of birth control devices and drugs before they go on the market. However, every form of contraception involves a combination of benefits, risks, and side effects that should be weighed with the help of your doctor.

If you are seriously injured by using a contraceptive, you may in some circumstances have a claim against the manufacturer. In the case of an intrauterine device (IUD) known as the Dalkon Shield, hundreds of injured women successfully sued the A.H. Robins Company when it was determined the company knew about, but did not communicate, the potentially harmful effects of its IUD.

ABORTION

In the landmark *Morgentaler* case of 1988, the Supreme Court of Canada struck down the section of the Criminal Code that prohibited abortion. The court held that by making it illegal to have an abortion, the law conflicted with the federal Charter of Rights and Freedoms, which gave women the "right to life, liberty and security of the person." In a futher decision of 1991 the court also concluded that only a child that was born, that is, delivered from his/her mother's womb, was a "person" who could have rights.

Certain provinces then tried to impose restrictions, saying that abortions may only be conducted in hospitals and not in clinics. Dr. Morgentaler, however, opened clinics in those provinces and was successful in having the courts rule that abortions may also be performed in clinics, providing the operation was done by a competent licensed medical professional.

Some provinces have reacted by proposing that abortion be excluded from procedures covered by Medicare or that Medicare pay only the doctor's fee but not the clinics' "facility fees," nor the cost of equipment, towels, bandages, medication, etc., that may be necessary in an abortion operation.

Meantime, the larger issue of whether or not abortion should be allowed at all continues to be a touchy matter that arouses strong feelings in people on both sides of the issue. The question is very far from being resolved in the public mind, and the federal government appears reluctant to stir up even more trouble by enacting new and clear legislation in this matter.

NOTIFICATION AND CONSENT

The issue of notification and consent is one of the biggest areas of controversy regarding the state's right to place restrictions on abortion. Notification is not an issue among adults, since a doctor is not required to inform a woman's husband or companion about an abortion. In the case of minors, it is another matter. For the most part, the law is still a gray area. For example, a minor's right to medical treatment, her right to give an informed consent, and her right to confidentiality regarding her medical file, are often diametrically opposed to the doctor's duty to inform her parents prior to making any medical intervention.

Although one becomes an adult in most provinces at age 18 (19 is the age of majority in British Columbia and Nova Scotia), the problem of notification is most prevalent in the case of 16- and 17-year-olds. Doctors confronted with such underage patients seeking abortions must use their own judgment. Many consult their ethics committee.

If the girl is under age 16, her parents are usually notified. With 16- and 17-year-olds, the doctor must assess the maturity of the child, the danger the abortion may pose to her health, and other factors that may affect her health. The definition of health most often used is that of the World Health Organization, which declares health is a state of complete physical, mental, emotional, and social well-being, not merely the absence of disease and physical well-being.

Dealing With Infertility

Advances in reproductive technologies have changed the odds for couples who want children but have had trouble conceiving. In 1978, Louise Brown made international news as the world's first test-tube baby, conceived outside a woman's body. Today, a number of clinics offer in vitro fertilization, a process by which a woman's eggs are fertilized with a man's sperm in a glass dish and then transferred to a woman's uterus.

Medicare does not cover the costs of in vitro fertilization, which has only a moderate success rate. Large amounts of money are required for the procedure since often several

Rights for a Pregnant Teenager

What should you expect if your teenage daughter becomes pregnant and considers an abortion?

✔ *Must a parent be told?* In some provinces, minors can obtain abortions without the consent of their parents. However, in the case of younger children, say 14- to 16-year-olds, doctors are hesitant to perform abortions unless they have parental consent.

✔ *Giving your permission.* If you agree that your child should have an abortion, you should contact the doctor and sign a consent form. If you do not agree, then you should state this clearly (preferably in writing) and inform the doctor of your opposition. But if your child insists, the abortion may nonetheless take place, especially if the hospital ethics committee feels an abortion is in her best interest.

✔ *A judge's decision.* If time permits, a minor can seek approval for an abortion in a court hearing rather than from her parents. Judges are asked to assess her maturity and ability to understand her decision. Most cases dealing with teenage abortions are held in camera, that is in private.

attempts must be made to achieve fertilization, and success can never be guaranteed.

ARTIFICIAL INSEMINATION

Each year thousands of women whose partner's sperm is not viable are artificially inseminated. In most cases, the couple relies on the sperm of an anonymous donor, but if they are married, the law presumes that the husband is the legal father of a child born during the marriage. Several provinces have legislation that prohibits the male spouse from denying that the child so conceived is his. The father has all the rights and obligations toward this child as if the youngster were born into the marriage in a natural way. The donor has no rights and no responsibility to the child unless he is known to the mother and acts as the father. Records related to anonymous donations are considered confidential.

The risk of contracting disease through donated sperm is an increasing concern. Sperm banks usually screen donors for such diseases as HIV, gonorrhea, syphilis, herpes, and hepatitis B. To further decrease the chance of infection, the sperm is typically frozen for a period of time. Anyone dealing with a sperm bank should insist on these precautions. The sperm bank should also perform a complete chromosomal analysis before accepting a donor. If the recipient gives birth to a child with a screenable genetic deformity, such as Tay-Sachs, she may have a legal claim for damages against the sperm bank. The bank may also be liable if she is inseminated with the wrong sperm.

🐚

The history of man
for the nine months preceding
his birth would, probably,
be far more interesting
and contain events of greater
moment than all the three-score
and ten years that follow it.

SAMUEL TAYLOR
COLERIDGE

Miscellanies, Aesthetic and Literary

🐚

Fertility/Infertility: A Glossary of Terms

As more couples wait longer to have babies, infertility has become a growing problem. New technology has made childbearing possible when it had not been before, but the advances involved have caused a growing public debate on legal, medical, and ethical issues.

• **Artificial insemination.** Semen is deposited in the vagina by artificial means rather than intercourse. It is typically used in cases of infertility and for single mothers.

• **Sperm bank.** This is the depository that maintains sperm given by donors, who are usually paid a fee and promised confidentiality.

• **Frozen embryos.** These are fertilized ova, or eggs, that have been removed from a woman's ovary, fertilized with a man's sperm outside the human body, and then frozen, to be implanted later in the woman's uterus. If all the embryos are not used, the remaining ones may be the source of custody disputes.

• **In vitro fertilization.** Also called IVF, this phrase literally means "in-glass fertilization." The woman's mature egg is removed from the uterus with a thin needle, fertilized with the man's sperm in a petri (glass) dish, and then reinserted into a woman's uterus.

• **GIFT.** A variation on in vitro fertilization, GIFT, or *gamete intra-fallopian transfer*, involves combining the egg and sperm and immediately inserting them in the fallopian tubes (not the uterus) for natural fertilization rather than fertilizing them in a petri dish. ZIFT, or *zygote intra-fallopian transfer*, is a newer procedure in which the egg is first fertilized in a petri dish before being placed in the fallopian tubes.

Recommendations for regulating and licensing these new techniques are set out in a report by the Royal Commission on New Reproductive Technologies. Another good source of information on this subject is the Ottawa-based Infertility Awareness Association of Canada.

SURROGATE MOTHERS AND THE LAW

Surrogate motherhood, infrequently chosen yet widely reported on, remains an area of great dispute. A few provinces have laws regarding the contractual arrangements between parents wanting a baby and a woman who agrees, either to be artificially inseminated with the husband's sperm or to have an embryo implanted and carry the baby. Even though contracts where the object is a human being would be illegal in ordinary contract law (because human life can never be the object of a contract), formal and informal arrangements are often made about surrogate motherhood. A sister, say, may undertake to bear a child for her brother-in-law and infertile sister. Money paid for this "service" is illegal, although money may be exchanged to cover the expenses and inconvenience of pregnancy. Should the surrogate mother refuse to relinquish the child at birth, it is hard to imagine how such a contract could be enforced.

Whose Rights Come First?

As pregnancy progresses, questions of rights under the law can become distressingly complex. Physicians are required, for example, to get the informed consent of patients before performing surgery or other medical interventions. But it is also a woman's right to refuse medical treatment, such as having a cesarean section, even if her refusal could jeopardize her fetus. Since the Supreme Court's 1991 decision that a fetus is not a "person" and, so, has no rights, the mother's rights are the only ones that can be considered. Even so, in the later stages of pregnancy, a doctor could refuse to carry out an abortion since the life of the mother could be placed in great danger.

IS IT CONFIDENTIAL OR NOT?

The same ambivalence applies to a patient's right to confidential medical records, promised by laws in all provinces. Yet if traces of an illegal drug are found in the bloodstream of a pregnant woman or a newborn baby, health-care workers in some provinces are mandated to report it on the grounds that the child has been abused. As a result, the provincial Children's Aid Society might decide to move the child to a safer environment, where illegal drugs are not used.

Cesarean Sections

Some 18 percent of all childbirths in Canada are by cesarean, or C-section, a surgical procedure for delivering a baby through the abdomen rather than vaginally. The rate has just about tripled in the last 25 years, and there is widespread disagreement regarding the reasons for this upward trend. Some believe that a physician's concern about a malpractice suit if a birth becomes unexpectedly complicated may be one factor driving this increase. Others blame it on the policy of performing repeat cesareans for all women who have once experienced a surgical birth (although this practice is diminishing).

Prior to labor, if your doctor advises a "C-section," you are entitled to seek a second opinion. Another doctor and another hospital may be less inclined to perform it. You can also ask your doctor early on when and why she performs cesareans. You may or may not agree with her reasons.

While most women prefer not to have a C-section, in rare cases, a woman may request one. She may fear the pain or stress of labor or may have had complications in an earlier delivery. A doctor generally will not perform a C-section for other than medical reasons, but if you have concerns, you should discuss them with your doctor. Severe stress or fear may indeed be a medical reason to perform one.

ADOPTION

Adoption has long been a means of creating or augmenting a family. But adoptive parents are required to prove their special fitness for parenting.

Entering the Adoption Maze

Perhaps you want to have your own child, but your partner is infertile. Perhaps you have two boys, feel too old physically to try again, but always dreamed of having a girl. Perhaps you are single, doubt that you will ever marry, but really want to be a parent. Adoption represents a viable way to form or extend a family and to provide a family for children whose relationship with their biological parents has been terminated.

Yet many legal, financial, and emotional hurdles stand between you and a successful adoption, and they dictate that you carefully research your province's adoption laws, whether you are working through an agency or on your own. And every adoption agency—public or private, for profit or nonprofit, religious or nondenominational, local or foreign—has its own requirements. Each of these agencies has developed criteria it hopes will ensure that adopting parents possess the personal qualities and financial resources to best serve the child's welfare. While natural parents can raise their children with the expectation of only minimal government intervention, adoptive parents are required to give clear evidence of their parenting potential.

AGENCIES, PUBLIC AND PRIVATE

To begin the process, you will want to find out what agencies are available in your area and what services they offer. The Adoption Council of Canada in Ottawa can supply you with answers to your questions (for address and telephone number, see RESOURCES, page 469). Every province has agencies funded and run by the province. Private agencies may either be for profit or nonprofit. At a public agency, you can expect to encounter extensive waiting periods and sometimes strict eligibility requirements. If you are seeking a healthy newborn, you may discover that there is a multiyear waiting list or even that no applications are being accepted at the present time.

Most public agencies almost exclusively place children who have already been given up for adoption and need parents. If you are prepared to adopt an older child or particularly a child with "special needs" (one with physical or mental disabilities, or possibly from an economically deprived or minority background), you can expect greater opportunities to adopt more quickly and with less stringent applicant requirements through a private agency especially in the case of international adoptions.

Private agencies associated with a specific religious group may or may not consider applicants who fall outside that faith. They may, however, be more open than other private agencies to couples with limited incomes and may offer their services for a lower fee. In both cases, that of public or private adoption agencies, the provincial child welfare department will investigate the living condition and other factors when an adoption takes place.

It is easier for a father to have children than for children to have a father.

POPE JOHN XXIII

Independent Placement

More than half of the infant adoptions today come about through placement outside of the private and public agency systems. Most provinces permit prospective adoptive parents to connect directly with a birth mother or her intermediary. Subject to court approval, you can expect to pay "reasonable fees" for adoption services and legal expenses. In some provinces, you may pay for pregnancy-related expenses, such as transportation, housing, maternity clothing, and counseling. If, however, you meet someone who offers to "find you a baby" or "place your child" for a fee, you have probably found a criminal.

Bringing a Foreign Baby Home

Thousands of Canadians decide to look overseas to find a child to adopt. The process is not quick—it can take 18 to 36 months in all—and it may cost $10,000 or more. Each agency and country will add a layer of procedures, but here are the basic steps and documents involved:

• **Legal documents.** To obtain a foreign adoption, you or your lawyer will need proof of the child's identity through a birth certificate, evidence that the birth parents have relinquished their parental rights, and receipt of an adoption decree.

• **Passports.** You may have to go to the foreign country for court proceedings or to pick up the adopted child, although perhaps an intermediary can act on your behalf. Have passports for the child as well as for yourselves.

• **Foreign adoptions.** Each country prefers that the adoption be made according to its own laws although some permit the adoption to be completed in Canada.

• **Adoption petition.** You will have to go through adoption proceedings in a provincial court even if you have completed the adoption in the child's birth country. You will need the child's personal documents, proof of Canadian citizenship or legal permanent residence of at least one adoptive parent, evidence that the child was less than 18 when adopted, and an adoption petition.

• **Naturalization.** The adopted child must have a visa to enter Canada. To qualify, the child must pass certain medical tests and the prospective adoptive parents must supply the Canadian Immigration Office in charge of that foreign country with proof of their financial ability to support the child.

Some provinces restrict independent adoptions to relatives and stepparents of the biological parents. But, as with any adoption, the adoptive parents must be approved by the provincial child welfare agency and they must obtain an adoption judgment from the courts. There are no set fees for the adoption process but costs for adoptions in the province (as opposed to foreign adoption) can easily pass the $5,000 mark.

With stepchildren, or a relative who has been living with you for a number of years, the adoption process may be simplified. In these cases, adoption is not necessarily the best option. For most purposes, obtaining guardianship or custody from the courts is a viable alternative that does not require consent from the biological parents and avoids other emotional and familial conflicts.

If planning a private adoption, you should consult an experienced social worker or lawyer to help you get background and health checks of the birth parent, to provide counseling and doctor referrals, to assess any potential legal difficulties, to assist the social worker who processes the case, and to prepare legal documents and appear in court when necessary.

Seeking a Special Child

Some adoptive parents wait years for a healthy infant. Meanwhile, tens of thousands of children are waiting for adoptive parents to choose them. Not everyone can or should adopt a "special needs" child, but you will want to consider whether you have the tolerance and the capacity to care for such a child.

No exact list of conditions defines special-needs children. They may have physical, mental, or emotional disabilities. They may have suffered physical or sexual abuse in their birth families. Children who test positive for the HIV antibody, who were born to HIV-infected mothers or possessed traces of cocaine at birth, may all come into the category and so might those who are part of a sibling group that needs to be placed together.

Older children are another special group, because every province has laws requiring that older children consent in writing to the adoption, although in special cases the court can dispense with the consent. This "age of consent" varies from 10 to 12 years old. Often these children are living within the provincial foster-care system, which provides a temporary home either in a government-run institution or with private, subsidized foster parents. Foster care is not intended to be a permanent parenting arrangement, but it sometimes becomes an intermediate step to adoption. (See also "Parenting," page 112.)

BE PREPARED FOR THE HOME STUDY

Anyone who adopts must go through a home study. This is a series of detailed interviews conducted by a social worker to evaluate your "appropriateness" for adopting. Here is what to expect:

1. You may have to write an autobiographical statement and answer detailed questions about your life: education, family, work, religion, friends, and child-rearing ideas.

2. You will be asked for a report of a physical exam, including a tuberculosis test.

3. To make sure you have no child abuse or criminal record, a form with basic personal data will be sent to your provincial child welfare department and police agencies.

4. To verify your income and financial status, you will need copies of your tax returns and other financial records.

5. You will be asked to identify three or four people who know you well and who can provide references as to your suitability as an adoptive parent.

6. Be prepared during the home visit for the interviewer to inspect the child's bedroom and make sure there are safety features such as smoke detectors and a plan for exiting in case of an emergency.

A NATIONAL NETWORK

Finding a special-needs child can be as simple as contacting a local adoption agency, either public or private. These agencies are usually linked to exchanges—provincial, regional, and national—that match families and special-needs children. Many of these exchanges provide photos, biographies, and other relevant information.

You may be eligible for a financial subsidy if you adopt a special-needs child. This subsidy is available when reasonable efforts to place the child have been unsuccessful, the child cannot be returned to his parents, and a subsidy may make the placement attractive or will help pay for the child's particular special needs.

The Rights of Birth Parents

First and foremost, the birth parents have the right to give or withhold consent for a child to be adopted. This is the linchpin without which no adoption can be completed. A birth mother may decide before giving birth to have her baby adopted, but most provinces, recognizing the inherent emotional complexity of this decision, have laws that prohibit her from giving official consent until after the baby is born.

Many provinces also insist on a waiting period after the birth, that varies from province to province. (See "When a Birth Mother Can Change Her Mind," page 110.) In most provinces, a licensed social worker may witness the written consent; others request only that a notary public witness the consent. Some province laws are more stringent, requiring that the birth mother appear before a court.

THE BIRTH FATHER'S RIGHTS

Most problems in adoption proceedings involve the question of consent. Although the birth mother's consent is primary, the position of the birth father must also be considered. If he is married to the birth mother who wants to give up her baby for adoption—a rare situation—his consent is also required.

In the majority of cases, however, the father is not married to the birth mother. Legally described as the "putative" or "alleged" father, he too must consent to the adoption of his child. Should he refuse, his consent may be overridden by the courts, especially if he has abandoned the birth mother and the child, or if the court finds that his refusal to give consent is not in the "best interests" of the child.

Notice of the adoption must be given to the father, through a newspaper if his whereabouts are unknown. If the father does

---

Being There at the Beginning

If you have arranged an open, private adoption, you may be able to be present at the baby's birth if you want to be. Some adopting parents are reluctant to observe the delivery because the birth mother has not yet signed her consent. Otherwise, the decision rests entirely with the birth mother. Here are her rights:

✔ *Access.* Although she needs to get doctor and hospital approval, the birth mother may invite anyone she likes into the delivery room.

✔ *Consent.* It is the birth mother's baby until the consent form is signed, and it is up to her whether or not she decides to see the baby before giving consent.

✔ *Counseling.* A hospital social worker will check on the birth mother. The mother does not have to talk to her, but the worker will ask whether she has received or at least been offered adoption counseling.

✔ *Naming.* The birth mother is entitled to name her baby and receive a copy of the birth certificate. Later, when the adoption is complete, the certificate will be amended to show the child's adopted name and to identify the adoptive parents as the parents.

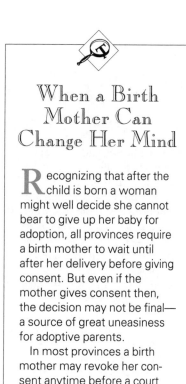

When a Birth Mother Can Change Her Mind

Recognizing that after the child is born a woman might well decide she cannot bear to give up her baby for adoption, all provinces require a birth mother to wait until after her delivery before giving consent. But even if the mother gives consent then, the decision may not be final—a source of great uneasiness for adoptive parents.

In most provinces a birth mother may revoke her consent anytime before a court grants a final judgment in adoption. This means a waiting period of at least six months, the specified minimum time that must pass between the court's first judgment, which is interlocutory or temporary, and the final judgment.

In some cases even a final judgment could be set aside and the child ordered returned to his/her biological mother. This could arise if the mother was underage when she gave consent or if consent was not "free and voluntary." This might be the case, for example, if the young mother was promised large sums of money to give up her child, or if her consent was given under pressure, from her parents "forcing" her to give up her child. Delay for the adoptive parents can be prolonged further, if the birth mother appeals to a higher court to set aside the lower court's judgment.

For the adoptive parents, getting through this final waiting period often takes tremendous patience and nerves of steel. But, for most of them, this is a small price to pay for the joy of finally having a child.

not file an objection within a certain period of the adoption notice being mailed or published, most provinces permit the father's rights to be terminated.

As well as vetoing an adoption, unwed fathers can seek full rights to custody. Usually fathers who seek this from the courts will have tried to establish their parental rights prior to the adoption petition. To ensure such rights, a man must prove he is the biological father; sign the birth certificate; support, communicate with, and try to act like a father to the child; and obtain a court order establishing his paternity.

Completing the Adoption

To complete the adoption process, you must prepare and file a petition. This document is usually filed with the provincial or family court where the adoptive parents reside. Its exact contents vary from province to province, but generally the petition includes:

- The date and place of the child's birth;
- The date you placed the child with the adoptive parents and the adoptive parents' names;
- The new adopted name of the child;
- The name, age, length of residence in the province, and marital status of the adopting parents;
- A statement attesting to the adopting parents' desire and ability to care for the child and accept the rights and responsibilities of parenting;
- The name of anyone whose consent is required but has not yet been received.

If you adopted through an agency, the home study conducted by the agency when you applied for adoption may be a sufficient report. (See "Be Prepared for the Home Study," page 108.) In some instances, however, if you have made an independent adoption, you may have to let a social worker inspect and report on your home environment after the child's arrival.

At the court hearing that follows the petition, the judge usually grants an interlocutory decree, which is a document giving you temporary legal custody. After a certain waiting period, typically six months, the judge will grant a final decree. Finally, the adoption is complete: the child's name is changed, and a new birth certificate is completed giving his new family name, the date and place of his birth, and the occupations of his adopting parents. The old birth certificate is sealed and filed away with other confidential adoption records, which usually can be opened only by court order.

A Child's Right to Know

Courts have increasingly recognized the desire of adopted children to know more about their biological parents and of biological parents to learn about their natural children. Most provinces now permit adoptive parents and adult adoptees to receive such information (not including names and exact locations) as medical and genetic histories of the biological parents, and the general circumstances of the adoption. Most provinces require that adoptees seeking access to confidential records provide sufficient reason for their release. Various volunteer organizations, most established by adoptees, will help adopted persons find out about their biological parents. Some organizations will arrange meetings between the estranged parents and the child.

A DELICATE BALANCE

Some provinces have "search and consent" guidelines for an agency or other intermediary trying to find the birth mother in order to obtain consent to a reunion with the child. If the mother refuses, the adoptee may still be able to have the adoption records opened by petitioning the court.

Most provinces now have mutual-consent registries, where adult adoptees and biological parents can voluntarily list their names. If one party requests release of records, the registry will show if consent has been granted by the other.

At every step the child should be allowed to meet the real experiences of life; the thorns should never be plucked from his roses.

ELLEN KEY
The Century of the Child

Tracking Down a Parent

Eventually, your adopted child will have questions about her roots. The knowledge may be important to psychological well-being, or she may need to know her medical or genetic history for health reasons. The following steps will help her track down her biological parents.

• The very best approach is to plan ahead. If you know from the beginning that you are going to want your child to meet her biological parents, you can probably make arrangements at the time of adoption for future information or contact.

• If you have to start from scratch later on, ask the agency or intermediary that handled the adoption to try to get in touch with the birth parent. If the province has "search and consent" rules, the agency may be able to contact the birth parents and get permission to reveal their identity.

• Write to your province's department of vital statistics, which can sometimes provide additional birth data, including the name of the birth parent.

• Register with your province's mutual-consent adoption registry if one exists in your province, or with a national registry service; the birth parents may have registered, too.

• Supply the Department of Social Affairs with a name and any other identifying data. If you have sufficient cause, they may be able to provide you with the address of one parent's last known place of employment.

• Besides "search and consent" guidelines and mutual-consent registries, some provinces keep identifying information about siblings of deceased adult adoptees or deceased biological parents who consented to a release of records.

PARENTING

The law recognizes the special, private nature of the parent-child relationship. But it will step in when parents fail to provide basic care.

When Discipline Becomes Abuse

Child abuse is never tolerated by the law and any form of corporal punishment of a child (even an occasional spanking) is now controversial. The law considers excessive or "unreasonable" force abuse—and if parents are found guilty of it, their children can be taken from them. Although no two provinces have identical child welfare legislation, most laws dealing with child abuse have common elements and generally include:

✔ *Serious injury.* If a child suffers serious physical injury at the hands of a parent, especially if hospitalization or medical care is needed, nearly every child welfare agency considers it abuse. Sexual molestation and intercourse are also abuse.

✔ *Potential threat.* Besides statutes against bodily harm itself, some provinces have laws that prohibit placing a child in a situation where he will be at risk of serious injury or psychological abuse.

✔ *Injury is injury.* Laws in some provinces consider any physical injury—not just "serious" injury—to be grounds for suspecting abuse.

Taking Care of Your Child

In the belief that it is not the state's business to interfere in the private sphere of the family, the law's role in how you raise your children remains relatively slight. Legislation seeks only to ensure that every child's basic needs are met. Food, clothing, shelter, and usually medical care and education are the minimum necessities parents must provide under provincial laws. Child welfare agencies will only step in if—through neglect or abuse—these basic parenting duties are not being met.

Child abuse and neglect is also prohibited by the federal Criminal Code. Failure to provide the "necessaries of life" to one's children is a crime. Although the code permits "reasonable force" in disciplining a child, this often conflicts with provincial child welfare laws that prohibit force at all times. Furthermore, "reasonable force" may mean different things to different judges. Fear of an assault charge is enough to keep many parents from hitting their children for disciplinary purposes. In one widely publicized case, an American father visiting Canada was charged with assault (but later acquitted) for spanking his young daughter after she shut the car door on her younger brother's hand.

SUPPORT UNTIL EMANCIPATION

Both parents are responsible for support. Should one parent lose a job or leave town, for example, the other parent must see to the child's support and care, thus minimizing the risk of the child becoming a public charge. This dual responsibility persists at least until the child has reached the age of majority or has been "emancipated," that is, gets married, joins the military, or is otherwise living independently.

Technically the Criminal Code requires parents to support their children up to age 16. Most provincial laws set no age limit to obligations to support one's dependents, and they apply even if the parents are not married or are minors themselves.

The laws that govern the tricky matter of determining whether parents have neglected to care properly for their children are narrowly defined. The court still has great discretion to evaluate each case individually. But child neglect—which, along with abuse, can lead to the termination of a parent's rights—is generally recognized to mean that a child's safety or health is put at risk. Child neglect includes leaving a child without proper supervision, letting a child's wound or illness go medically unattended, allowing a child to suffer malnutrition, and parental drug and alcohol abuse that jeopardizes a child's emotional or physical safety. Some provinces consider a parent's failure to send a child to school to be neglect.

It is not only the parents' actions that dictate the appropriate care for the child. Parents may themselves request foster care because they cannot handle a child's difficult behavior, such as frequent acts of truancy or juvenile delinquency. But the court will not take action to begin outside supervision until a petition is filed and a court hearing has been held. The petition can be filed by a parent or a guardian, a police officer, a social worker, or even a citizen with a complaint.

Going Solo

The rise in the number of single parents in recent years has led to greater social acceptance of and respect for this often difficult and demanding parenting role. Whether they are alone because of divorce, death, or because they never married, single parents have the same responsibilities to provide basic care and support for their children as two-parent families, although they usually have to do it with more limited resources.

Second Thoughts About Single Parenting

PROBLEM
Before the birth of her son, Margo told his father, Rick, that he did not have to worry about taking care of the child. With or without Rick, she decided, she wanted to have the baby. But in the first months after the arrival of her son, Margo began to have second thoughts. Only then did she realize the full burden of single parenting and of the unfairness to her child—emotionally, financially, and in terms of time. She tried to talk to Rick about it, but he refused even to take her phone calls.

ACTION
Since Rick was the father, Margo had the right to make him provide support, whether he wanted to or not—but first Margo had to prove his paternity. She went to family court, and the court requested Rick to take a blood test which he consented to undergo. On the basis of the tests, circumstances, and Margo's testimony, the court decided that Rick was indeed the child's father and ordered him to accept his legal obligation of child support and related parental responsibilities. (If Rick fails to pay, Margo has the right to ask the court to garnishee Rick's wages.)

123...

TIPS ON PARENTAL LEAVE

When your baby is born or when you adopt a child, you, as father or mother, may be entitled to 12 to 34 weeks of unpaid leave from your job.

1. Since the leave is unpaid, you might not be able to afford the time off.

2. You must give your employer prior notice of leave, such notice varying from two weeks in Alberta to four weeks in most other provinces.

3. In most provinces, the statutory amount of parental leave may be further extended by periods ranging from two weeks in Alberta to six months in British Columbia, Ontario, and Saskatchewan.

4. The various provincial laws governing parental leave require employers to guarantee their workers the same or an equivalent job when they return. But you may find that you are unhappy with the "equivalent" position you get upon resuming work.

5. In most provinces, you are entitled to all benefits but in several provinces your employer does not have to pay pension contributions during your leave.

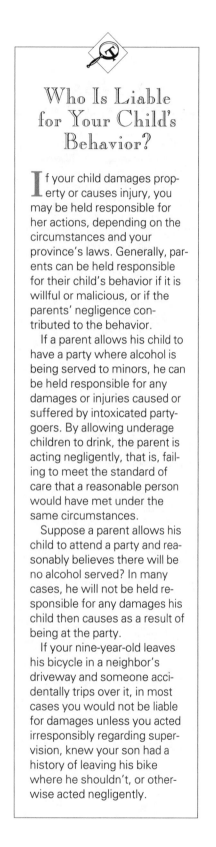

Who Is Liable for Your Child's Behavior?

If your child damages property or causes injury, you may be held responsible for her actions, depending on the circumstances and your province's laws. Generally, parents can be held responsible for their child's behavior if it is willful or malicious, or if the parents' negligence contributed to the behavior.

If a parent allows his child to have a party where alcohol is being served to minors, he can be held responsible for any damages or injuries caused or suffered by intoxicated party-goers. By allowing underage children to drink, the parent is acting negligently, that is, failing to meet the standard of care that a reasonable person would have met under the same circumstances.

Suppose a parent allows his child to attend a party and reasonably believes there will be no alcohol served? In many cases, he will not be held responsible for any damages his child then causes as a result of being at the party.

If your nine-year-old leaves his bicycle in a neighbor's driveway and someone accidentally trips over it, in most cases you would not be liable for damages unless you acted irresponsibly regarding supervision, knew your son had a history of leaving his bike where he shouldn't, or otherwise acted negligently.

Following a divorce, the noncustodial parent will probably be entitled to visitation rights. This is not only the parent's right, but also the child's. Visits can be frustrating and may cause confusion, but they should not undermine the primary parent's role. The custodial parent generally maintains major responsibility for deciding on education, religion, medical care, place of residence, and other such basic parenting matters unless the courts have deemed otherwise. Nevertheless, one parent's primacy in decision-making does not absolve the noncustodial parent from financial obligations to provide child support. (See also "Divorce," page 135.)

If a single parent is a mother who gave birth out of wedlock, she can take steps to obtain the support of the natural father, whether he wants to acknowledge his paternity or not. Furthermore, if a single parent dies, the surviving parent automatically becomes responsible for a minor child's continuing care and support.

Your Children's Rights

Like all Canadians, children have certain rights which cannot be interfered with. For example, they cannot be subjected to illegal search and seizure. If brought before the courts, they have the right to a lawyer and to be informed of their rights. Society, however, also recognizes that children lack a certain maturity, so most minors charged with a crime are tried under the federal Young Offenders Act. Sentences under this act are somewhat more lenient than in regular criminal courts. Minors charged with breaking a provincial law, such as the Highway Traffic Act or Liquor Control Act, will usually be charged with an offense of the provincial equivalent to the federal Young Offenders Act.

For the most part a young person's rights and obligations toward society are the same as an adult's, once the young person has reached the age of 12.

EMANCIPATION

The laws that establish the age of majority and the right to emancipation are the clearest indications of when children can assume most adult rights and responsibilities. At emancipation, a young person is no longer legally restricted by parental control or limited by the province in terms of age. Under most circumstances, he is also no longer legally entitled to support from his parents.

A child can be emancipated without a court decree by reaching the age of 18, getting married (with parental consent if necessary), or entering the military, all of which confer automatic

A Child's Life, Legally Speaking

Children reach adulthood, with most of its inherent rights and responsibilities, at the age of majority, which in most provinces is 18. Before that, unless children have been emancipated or have established independence from their parents, their rights are mostly contingent on their age. Here is how that affects them in various circumstances as they grow up:

• **Contraception.** Anyone of any age can purchase over-the-counter contraceptives. Some provinces require parental consent for prescription birth control devices if the buyer is not of age or emancipated. Provinces also vary on consent for abortion, tubal ligation, or any surgery.

• **Criminal courts.** Persons under 18 who commit a criminal offense are usually charged under the Young Offenders Act and tried in youth court. For serious crimes, such as murder or rape, a young offender may be treated as an adult.

• **Curfews.** Local laws may restrict access to streets and public places after a certain time at night by people under a certain age. Although curfew laws vary widely, they usually allow young people to be out after hours in the company of an adult or to go to work. Some permit them to be out with a parent's permission. Many curfew laws are facing legal challenges in court.

• **Drinking.** Every province prohibits persons under age 18 from buying alcoholic beverages by making either the sale or the purchase of alcohol illegal, sometimes both. In some provinces it is illegal for a minor to drink or possess alcohol outside the home or in a public place.

• **Driving.** Most provinces set 16 as the minimum age to get a driver's license. In Ontario and Quebec, minors get restricted permits which only allow them to drive if accompanied by an adult with a license, and only between certain hours.

• **Gambling.** In most provinces, a person must be at least 18 to gamble in a casino and at least 18 to bet in a lottery or at the racetrack.

• **Guns.** Federal laws prohibit the sale of handguns to minors and allow minors to use handguns only for hunting or target shooting. Selling or giving a handgun to a minor is punishable by prison.

• **Marriage.** In most provinces, marriage is legal without parental consent at 18 and with parental consent at 16. Some provinces have even lower age limits. A marriage that has taken place before the required age may not be valid. In most provinces it becomes valid if it remains unchallenged until the required age has been reached.

• **Medical treatment.** Most provinces require that a patient be 18 years old or the age of majority to give consent for medical treatment. Some provinces set the age at 16. Parental consent is not required for emancipated children and in cases of emergency.

• **Pornography.** It is illegal for dealers to sell or distribute to minors any materials deemed obscene, indecent, or pornographic, including books, films, and magazines.

• **Schooling.** All provinces have laws regarding compulsory attendance of school-age children in either public, private, or home schools. All provinces allow children to be educated at home as long as certain provisions (which vary by province) are met.

• **Sex.** The Criminal Code establishes the age at which a person may legally consent to sex. As a general rule, the age of consent is 18 years, but there are many exceptions. Sex with a person under 12 years old is always prohibited and it is no defense to say one believed that the other party was older. Having sex with a 12- to 14-year-old is not a crime, provided the other partner was less than two years older than his/her partner. It is also illegal for someone in a position of trust, a teacher, guardian or clergyman, for example, to have sex with a person under 18. It is also illegal to buy sex from a minor.

• **Smoking.** In Canada, it is legal for 16- to 18-year-olds to possess and smoke cigarettes or other tobacco products. But it is illegal accross Canada to sell or give them such products.

• **Voting.** In federal elections all citizens (even prisoners) may vote at age 18. In provincial elections however the voting age is 18 or 19 depending on the age of majority in your particular province.

• **Working.** Federal and provincial laws mandate work restrictions concerning age, type of work, and hours of employment. Minimum-age exceptions include such jobs as baby-sitting, yard work, farm work, golf caddying, and delivering newspapers. (For more information about child labor laws, see Your Job, page 246.)

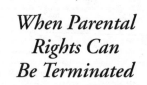

When Parental Rights Can Be Terminated

The law has great regard for the parent-child relationship. Courts are reluctant to intervene and terminate a parent's rights. Yet they will do so. When is such a move deemed necessary? The state needs solid evidence that the parent is not acting in the best interests of the child and is therefore unfit. Following are examples of parents whose parental rights could be terminated by the courts:

✔ *The abusive parent.* A parent who inflicts physical injury or commits a sex offense against a child will be deemed unfit, as will a parent who allows physical injury to be inflicted on a child or allows a sex offense to be committed.

✔ *The neglectful parent.* A parent who fails to provide a minimum level of care—proper food, shelter, clothing, and medical attention—is considered guilty of neglect and therefore unfit. So are parents who are incarcerated, and parents who use drugs or excessive amounts of alcohol.

✔ *The absent parent.* Typically, a parent who is away from the home or otherwise fails to provide normal supervision may be considered neglectful and deemed to have abandoned his or her child.

emancipation in most provinces. If the parents and their child agree, emancipation can also be established if the child creates an independent household or otherwise establishes self-supporting independence.

Minors can also petition the court to be emancipated. But the law requires that the child, if living apart, be 16 or older, derive his income from legal pursuits, and have his parents' permission to live separately. Furthermore, the court must be convinced that granting emancipation will be in the minor's best interests. If emancipation is granted, he is free to establish residency, apply for a work permit, enroll in college, buy or sell real property, consent to medical care, enter into binding contracts, and sue or be sued in his own name.

Taking Over Custody

When parents cannot care for their children, the provincial ministry responsible for child welfare will take over that obligation. If it appears that the child must be placed in foster care for more than a couple of days, that placement must be approved by a family court judge. Courts transfer this responsibility reluctantly and only under compelling circumstances. Such judgments are applied only when there is strong evidence of neglect, abuse, unfitness, or abandonment.

Except in a life-threatening emergency, no child can be removed from her home without a court order. The parental role can usually be terminated only after the child has been removed from the parents' custody and the parents have not tried to maintain contact, or in other ways have failed to serve the best interests of their child.

The criteria governing this legal action vary from province to province, but in every case, clear and convincing evidence that a parent is unfit must be demonstrated before a court will order final termination of parental rights.

GIVING PARENTS A CHANCE

In some provinces, the child must be removed from the parents' custody and under government supervision for three to six months before termination proceedings begin. Many provinces will not approve termination until a situation remains unimproved for a certain period of time. The courts will also consider whether or not the parents have tried to maintain contact with their child or have attempted to rehabilitate the relationship.

In most provinces, no warning or waiting period is required if conditions in the home are particularly grave—when, for example, a parent habitually abuses drugs or alcohol, or has a severe physical or mental disability that undermines fitness.

FOSTER CARE

If a child needs a custodian because injury, death, neglect, abuse, or another situation has rendered the child's parents unable to provide care, the child can be placed temporarily with another adult—a relative, a friend, or a stranger appointed by the court.

If the court decides to place the child with a stranger, the child will be placed either in an emergency home where he will stay for a few days while awaiting a court hearing or in a group home (with two to eight children) run by a public or private agency where he will live for a longer period.

Foster care is viewed as a temporary solution even if the child's stay in a foster home lasts for several years. A child may be placed in foster care with the consent of the natural parent. But in cases where abuse or neglect of a child is either suspected or proven, foster care is more likely to be involuntary and ordered by a court.

Typically, a local social services agency is legally charged with placing the child in foster care and is presumed to be acting in the child's best interests.

FOSTER PARENTS

Unlike adoptive parents, foster parents do not have legal custody of the children in their home. Some foster parents do begin proceedings to adopt their foster children, but the arrangement presumes that the natural parents will eventually obtain custody of their children, or that the foster children will be transferred elsewhere within the foster-care system, or that they will be adopted.

The children remain in the custody of the state, and the foster parents usually have no special advantage over others if they want to adopt them. Some children remain in foster care for a number of years or until they reach emancipation.

Foster parents and foster homes must be licensed according to the standards of their province. This usually involves training the prospective foster parents to meet the special demands of foster children and a careful examination of the parents' physical health and personal characteristics, as well as checks that would reveal any criminal background.

The licensing procedure also includes an inspection of the health and safety standards of the home itself.

AFTER TERMINATION

When a parent's rights have been terminated—whether they are curtailed voluntarily by the parent or involuntarily by pub-

---

1·2·3

YOUR DUTY TO PROVIDE LIFE'S "NECESSARIES"

Your duty to protect and provide for your children and other dependents is set out in sections 214, 215 and 218 of the federal Criminal Code. The following are excerpts:

1. You may be found guilty of abandonment or exposing a child to harm if you are legally bound to take charge of a child and willfully fail to do so, or you deal with a child in a manner likely to leave the child exposed to risk without protection.

2. Whether you are a parent, foster parent, guardian, or head of a family, you have a legal duty to provide necessaries of life for a child under the age of 16 years.

3. Everyone who has a legal duty to another commits an offence if he fails in his duty when the other person is in destitute or necessitous circumstances, or if his failure endangers the life of the person to whom the duty is owed, or causes the health of that person to be endangered permanently.

4. Anyone who illegally abandons or exposes to harm a child under the age of 10 is liable to a prison sentence of up to two years.

lic authority—a legal relationship no longer exists between the parent and child. The parent is not required to provide child support, cannot gain custody or visitation rights, and has a limited right to participate in the child's adoption. The state as guardian has full power to approve the child's placement. The state also becomes fully responsible for the child's support, and may declare the child eligible for adoption.

WHO INHERITS WHAT?

A child who is given up for adoption cannot automatically inherit from the biological parent if there is no will. Provincial laws vary on an adoptee's rights to inherit from biological grandparents who died intestate after the parental rights of her natural parents were terminated. Some provinces disallow any inheritance from anyone in the natural family after termination, but the right to inherit may still be available in other provinces. An adopted child is entitled to inheritance without a will from his adoptive parents and grandparents. (For more information about inheritance, see YOUR MONEY, page 342.)

What Are the Rights of Parents?

Along with the duties of parenthood—to provide food, clothing, shelter, and medical care for their children—parents also have a basic right to their children's custody and many other rights as well, starting with the right to name them. Here are some of the other rights:

• **Consent.** Before medical treatment can be administered to a minor, the parents' consent is required. This is true for most types of medical care, with some exceptions, such as abortion and birth control. Parental consent is usually required in various other areas of a minor's life, such as marrying.

• **Religion.** It is left to the discretion of the parents to choose the religious training their children will get. If your child refuses to go to church, however, you have no legal means to make him do so. The state will step in if a parent's religious beliefs physically harm the child. If a parent refuses to consent to a medically necessary procedure on religious grounds, a court may determine that the parent is neglecting his child and intervene. This may be done when a judge believes that the parents' action (or lack of action) will be harmful to the child's health or welfare.

• **Education.** Parents are responsible for making every reasonable effort to see that their child attends school regularly, whether it be a public or private school. Parents have the option of educating their children at home if certain conditions

are met. (See also "Educating Your Child at Home," page 126.)

• **Place of residence.** Parents can choose the place where they and their children will live, up to the age of the child's majority or emancipation. (Under a divorce order, however, a custodial parent may be prohibited from moving more than a certain distance away. At the time of writing Parliament is preparing to amend the Divorce Act to deal with "mobility rights" in divorce.)

• **Life-style.** Parents can decide the standard of living of their children, assuming that basic needs are met. Should a marriage end, the courts will assess child support and will take a hard look at the financial capability of both parents to decide on an appropriate living standard and life-style.

• **Guardian choice.** If one parent dies, all rights of decision and control fall to the surviving parent. The surviving parent should name another guardian immediately. This choice is subject to the court's confirmation in the event of the surviving parent's death. In some cases, the preference of the child will be considered.

CHILD CARE

All parents worry about getting the best possible care for their children. Provinces may set standards, but they cannot replace a parent's personal evaluation.

Choosing Home Day Care

Parents entrust their children to private-home day-care services more than any other kind of child care. Parents typically choose home day care over a day-care center because it offers flexible hours, a home setting, and relatively small numbers of children. And it usually costs less than having a baby-sitter come to their own home.

Nearly every province has established regulations for those providing care in their homes. While the regulations vary widely from province to province, they establish basic safety and health standards, such as the number of children a provider can care for at one time, what kind of home inspections are necessary, what health and safety standards must be met, and what training or other qualifications are required. These regulations do not guarantee your child quality care, but they do provide some direction. Examples of such legislation follow:

- Most provinces set the maximum group size for day care in a home at no more than eight children including the provider's own children;
- Nearly all provinces require children in home day care to be vaccinated against illnesses such as polio, diphtheria, measles, and mumps;
- Most provinces require smoke detectors or fire drills or both in the home, and some also ban smoking;
- Day care providers may not discriminate against children because of race, religion, creed, or social class, when deciding who they will admit;
- Some provinces require that the staff be trained in CPR or first aid or both;
- Some provinces require that providers have special training or professional experience in child care before they set themselves up as a day-care business;
- Some provinces require that a certain amount of space be available for facilities or recreational equipment.

At the very least, government standards offer parents the choice of providers who are licensed, certified, or registered. While no exact statistics exist, the majority of private-home

---

Checking for Safety

Although a day-care home may be regulated, that does not ensure its strict adherence to safety guidelines or cover all your concerns. It is important that you personally check the building where you will leave your child. Here are some things to look for:

✔ *In case of fire.* Are there fire extinguishers, smoke detectors, multiple exits, an emergency plan?

✔ *Risk of exposure.* Are radiators and electrical sockets covered? Are there exposed electrical appliances or sharp kitchen utensils? Are medicines kept locked up?

✔ *Home improvements.* Does the home need repairs? Is it well ventilated and well lit? Have window safety guards been installed on second and higher stories to prevent a child from falling out?

✔ *Domestic animals.* If the provider has pets, are they healthy and friendly?

✔ *Cleanliness.* Are the bathroom, the changing room, and the sleeping area clean? Does the provider wash her hands after diapering? Is there any evidence of infestation by mice or insects?

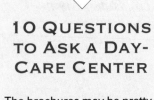

10 QUESTIONS TO ASK A DAY-CARE CENTER

The brochures may be pretty, and your friends may give you strong referrals, but nothing replaces a visit of your own and a meeting with the day-care center's director. Some questions you should ask:

1. How long has the center been in operation, and what do the neighbors say about it?

2. How is the building cleaned and maintained? Are radiators and electrical outlets covered? Can all closets, refrigerators and cupboards be opened from both inside and outside?

3. How long have the teachers been on staff?

4. What are the training and experience requirements for the staff?

5. What is the maximum group size and the teacher-child ratio?

6. What are the policies concerning discipline?

7. Does the staff have first aid and CPR training?

8. What is the policy about taking sick children? When are they not allowed to come to the center?

9. When are the fees due, and is payment required even when your child is absent because of vacation or illness?

10. Are parents free to visit at any time and join in a child's activities?

day-care providers still operate outside the regulated system. When providers are regulated, the government may require the provider to make an application and pass an on-site safety inspection before obtaining a license.

For example, an inspector may go to the provider's home to check for fire extinguishers and smoke detectors. But some provinces permit providers to register by providing their own reports and conducting their own inspections. No regulations can determine whether the provider possesses the character or other personal qualities you want for your child.

Whether or not your day-care provider is licensed, get receipts for the fees you pay. When filing your income tax returns, you can claim up to about $4,000 per year for day-care expenses. Also be sure to inquire about late charges, in the event you are unable to pick up your child on time.

DAY-CARE CENTERS

Each province licenses day-care centers and sets minimum standards. These centers, nonprofit or for-profit, may be connected to a church or synagogue, a school, or a corporation, or they may operate as independent commercial enterprises. As with family day care, government regulation is intended to guarantee parents a certain minimum level of care, but the standards vary widely from province to province. A crucial issue for parents to evaluate is the staff-to-child ratio, which affects the amount of attention you can expect your children to receive.

Every province sets guidelines that vary according to the age of the children. In some provinces, day-care centers must provide at least 2.3 square metres (25 square feet) of play space for each child. There must also be an adequate number of toilets and sinks (generally one toilet for 14 children) and these must be appropriate in size and height for the children's ages.

A WELL-TRAINED STAFF

Nearly every province requires staff members to practice good hygiene and refrain from smoking, and most insist that staff members be trained in CPR and first aid. Most provinces also require personnel to complete some training in child care or possess professional experience before being employed and to continue training thereafter. Nearly every day-care center undergoes government inspections at least once a year.

Still, no regulations can substitute for a parent's own judgment about the quality of a center. Do the caregivers personally greet each child in the morning? How do they discipline bad behavior? Is staff turnover heavy? What protection and cautions are there in case your child has allergies? (Allergies to peanuts, peanut products, and some seafoods can cause great harm and even death in a surprising number of children.)

Chicken Little Day-Care Center
1001 Oxbow Lane, Burnaby, B.C. V3X 1O9
Wendy C. Peters, Caregiver • (555)-111-2222

AGREEMENT FOR DAY-CARE SERVICES

Child **①**

Name of child

Birth date

Child's allergies, medications, special conditions

Parents **②**

Home address

City/Province/Telephone

Father (daytime telephone):

Mother (daytime telephone):

DAY-CARE SERVICES **③**

Days of care

Hours of care

Vacations/Holidays

Materials/Services provided:

FEES **④**

Payment dates

Hours of care

Overtime charge

If child is absent

EMERGENCY INFORMATION **⑤**

Name of close friend or relative: (Include address and phone number.) **⑥**

Name of pediatrician: (Include address and phone number.)

I grant consent for emergency medical treatment. (Parent's signature and date) **⑦**

Signature of caregiver

Date of agreement

Signature of parent

Date of agreement

Agreement for Day Care

To make sure that your child gets the best care, pin down the details of your arrangements with the center by executing a document like this one. The document can originate with the center or with you, but should include: **1.** Your child's vital statistics, including food or medicinal allergies; **2.** Phone numbers where both parents can be reached during the day; **3.** A detailed yearly schedule, including holidays. (Check for holidays that do not mesh with your work holidays, and make appropriate arrangements); **4.** A clear statement of fees, including charges if your child stays late or is absent; **5.** The telephone number of a friend who can be called if there is an emergency; **6.** Your pediatrician's name and phone number and written permission for emergency medical care; **7.** Signatures that indicate both parties understand and agree to the services provided.

121

Answers to these questions will indicate the level of care. For example, low staff turnover indicates good management and the likelihood of strong bonding with the children. One guideline, however, is always valid: never put your child anywhere you cannot drop in and visit any time you want.

Some centers (particularly if they are nonprofit) offer rates based on what parents can afford. Day-care center fees generally range from about $50 to $400 a week, with infants on average costing about $150 and fees for older children running to about $100 a week. Often, the better the facility is, the higher the fee. Of course, high cost does not guarantee quality care.

Hiring a Baby-sitter or Nanny

In-home help offers parents the most control over their children's care. It is usually the most expensive, averaging $200 to $400 a week in major cities. The in-home child-care provider could be anyone from a professionally trained nanny to a recent high-school graduate with limited experience. She may live in your home full-time or work a regular daytime shift. As the employer, you will have to determine what qualifications you need, what kind of care you can afford, and what your responsibilities are.

Finding the right person is not easy. You can try to do it on your own, by advertising or networking with your friends or business associates. Or you may use an employment or "nanny" agency that charges a fee to find and screen candidates, typically conducting a background check for any criminal or abuse-related record and to weed out aliens ineligible for the work.

THE "AU PAIR" SOLUTION
Some agencies specialize in placing so-called au pairs. Typically Western Europeans, these young women may be permitted work visas and receive about $150 for a 45-hour week. The agencies get a fee that includes the expense of transportation, health insurance, continuing support, and administration. Consider these issues when hiring a baby-sitter or nanny:

- What are your obligations regarding deductions and an appropriate salary? Check with your province's department of labor or employment standards commission.
- If you expect the worker to drive, make sure her license is valid, particularly if she is not a citizen or permanent resident. Find out if she is covered by your insurance policy.
- Clarify all employment terms: salary, overtime, raises, and benefits such as vacation, paid holidays, and sick days. You may also have other expenses, such as disability insurance.

An Employer's Responsibilities

Once you start paying someone to take care of your child in your home, you have legal responsibilities as an employer. These include:

✔ *Taxing matters.* You are required to withhold income tax from your employee's paycheque. If you don't, you can be held liable for all sums due to the government.

✔ *More taxing matters.* You must also deduct from your employee's paycheque an amount for the Canada (Quebec) Pension Plan, Employment Insurance, provincial health insurance and, in most provinces, Workers Compensation. You also must pay an employer's contribution for these deductions, a sum roughly equal to the amount paid by the employee.

✔ *Legal evidence.* Your employee must provide you with her Social Insurance Number (SIN), so that you can properly file the necessary taxes and deductions. Her SIN also assures you that she is a permanent resident or citizen of Canada, or has a work permit. Knowingly hiring an illegal resident and not paying the proper taxes can lead to a lot of trouble and expense.

EDUCATION

The right to free education is a cornerstone of Canadian society, but it is often hard to sort out the duties and responsibilities that come with that right.

Who Gets a Free Education?

Every child living in Canada has the right to a free education. This historically has been true whether or not the child is a legal resident. This right continues through high school and until the student reaches the age of 16 or 18, depending on the province.

Although education is a provincial jurisdiction, the right to an education is also guaranteed in section 23 of the federal Charter of Rights and Freedoms. This section of the charter also states that citizens of Canada, whose first language was English or French, or who received their primary education in one of these two languages, have the right to have their children educated in that language. However, this guarantee is conditional on whether there are sufficient numbers to warrant the opening of a new school in the minority language. (In Quebec, children of new immigrants must attend school in French.)

All parents are responsible for ensuring that their children attend school, be it public or private, religious or nonsectarian. Parents may educate their children at home, provided they meet certain, sometimes stringent, requirements. (See also "Educating Your Child at Home," page 126.) Parents who refuse to enroll their children in school or who do not ensure in some other way that their children are educated act in violation of provincial law and, in extreme cases, may face criminal prosecution.

ATTENDANCE

Although your child has a right to attend school, schools are not forced to accept students who have not been vaccinated against such illnesses as smallpox and diphtheria. Parents who refuse to have their children vaccinated are unlikely to find recourse through the courts, since public health policies in most provinces support compulsory vaccination laws.

Eligibility for attendance typically requires that the child and her parents or legal guardian reside within a given district, which may be defined by the town, the neighborhood, or the community. Moreover, school officials are permitted to decide which schools local children will attend, based on such factors as school size and student population; the choice may not be the school closest to the child's home. Parents may make a

Giving Your Child a Day Off

With the stroke of a pen, parents can excuse their children from school. Maybe Alice has a head cold and really should stay at home. Then again, maybe you decided to take her to your family reunion—and write a note saying she had a cold. A day's absence rarely leads to disputes with school authorities.

It grows more complicated, however, if you want to take your children on a two-week trip to Europe in the middle of the school year. Provincial policies may set the ground rules for whether you can get approval for such an absence.

If during informal discussions with teachers or administrators, you can plan how the missed classwork or related exams can be made up, the school will often excuse the absence.

Should the school refuse your request and you take your children away anyway, they may face lowered grades or loss of course credits. Schools may turn to provincial laws or local school regulations to justify their action. (School attendance until age 16 is compulsory in almost all provinces and frequent absences from school could cause the child welfare agencies to intervene.)

request to transfer a child to another school within the local district, but school officials can reject it. Parents may also try to enroll their child in a school situated outside their community, but local officials can require the family to pay tuition if space is made available.

Absences from school are recognized as a reality of life. Children get sick, families sometimes get called away, and other special conditions occur whereby the parent and teacher must agree on the acceptability of the child's absence.

Students with unexcused absences, however, are considered truant. In such cases, particularly when unreasonable absences become habitual, child welfare authorities may require parents to explain the absences in court and even place them under bond to help ensure proper attendance. In extreme cases, habitual truants can be placed in group homes or other government supervised institutions.

Rights at School: A Primer

It is the right and often the duty of provincial legislatures and school boards, as well as teachers, to establish general guidelines and regulations that govern the activities and comportment of students. Of course, the right of schools to regulate the appearance and behavior of their students often results in conflict between a student's right to freedom of expression and school rules.

Usually, such behavioral matters as truancy, tardiness, hairstyles, type of dress, use of vulgar language, abuse of alcohol and drugs, and possession of weapons are dealt with under school regulations. Such rules may also extend to off-campus events such as field trips.

Administrators in private schools have greater freedom than public school staff and boards in making regulations affecting student behaviors. Private schools may also find it easier to expel a student for not respecting the regulations.

The Ontario Court of Appeal ruled in the late eighties that Scripture readings, obligatory prayer, and other "suitable" religious ceremonies, formerly prescribed by that province's Education Act, were contrary to the Charter of Rights and Freedoms. Even though the act allowed students to refrain from participating in religious exercises, the appeal court ruled that classroom peer pressure rendered this right ineffective.

Since then courts in many other provinces have also declared that mandatory religious instruction or prayer was no longer to be used in public school classrooms. As a result, schools that insist on beginning the day with prayer have come under "attack."

SHORT HAIR AND UNIFORMS

Although hair and dress styles can be considered a form of expression, the courts have been split over the rights of students in public schools to dress as they please. Some school boards prohibit any regulation concerning hairstyles unless the school can demonstrate the rule's legitimate educational purpose or the hairstyle results in a substantial disruption of the school's activities. In such instances, the school may contend that a hairstyle can distract other students or cause discipline problems. Other school boards allow regulations based only on health and safety concerns.

Some school boards require that students follow a certain dress code but this rule can sometimes conflict with a student's religious observance. In one case, a 15-year-old student at a private girls' school in Montreal was asked to remove her chador, an Islamic *hijab* or headscarf, and complained to the provincial Human Rights Commission. The commission has not yet ruled on her charge of religious discrimination.

When Your Child Is Disciplined

The federal Charter of Rights and Freedoms, as well as provincial human rights legislation, has asserted students' right of due process—in layman's terms, the right to be treated fairly by government agencies—before any serious punishment can be carried out in a school. Schools must follow "minimum procedures" before negative action can be taken against a student.

No national, uniform procedures exist with regard to discipline, but for the suspension or expulsion of a student, most schools provide oral or written notice of the charges to students or their parents, stating the evidence of the misdeed and noting the family's permission to respond to it. Some provinces have more extensive formal procedures, particularly for expulsions and suspensions of more than 10 days.

Under Ontario's Statutory Powers Procedure Act, a student subject to discipline is entitled to legal representation. Even if the hearing appears to be flexible and is held by school board members in an informal manner, a certain level of procedural fairness must be observed. Where a principal's decision, especially one concerning expulsion, is to be reviewed by a school board with authority to confirm or overturn the principal's decree, the student must have a fair opportunity to provide and to set out his full and entire defense.

The procedure of appeal from school board hearings varies from province to province. In Ontario and Manitoba, for example, the decision of the school board is final, but Alberta and

Injuries at School

Teachers and other school workers must act with reasonable care to protect students from injury. But injuries happen anyway, and some of them make schools, and perhaps their employees, liable for damages. Here are some legal issues that apply:

✔ *Reasonable care.* A teacher of a woodworking class using power tools can reasonably be expected to take extra precautions. Should he fail to give clear instructions and warnings and provide close supervision, he can be found negligent. If the school knew the teacher was unqualified to teach, it could be held liable as well.

✔ *Foreseeable danger.* Teachers are not presumed to be able to foresee extraordinary accidents. A math teacher in whose class a desk suddenly breaks and fractures a student's wrist is not likely to be held liable for injuries.

✔ *Student's contribution.* Even if a teacher or coach is found to be negligent, the school may argue that the student's deliberate and possibly careless action contributed to the injury—if the student, for example, was injured because he knowingly disobeyed a safety rule in shop.

✔ *Court awards.* If you prove negligence, a school or teacher may have to pay damages equal to the amount of loss the injury caused and additional money if malice, fraud, or reckless disregard for a student's safety is proved.

New Brunswick permit a further appeal to the Minister of Education. Most other provinces allow school board decisions to be appealed to the courts. In fact, students in any province can appeal to the courts if there is evidence of procedural unfairness in handling their case.

Authorities may take various measures to enforce school rules. Expulsion is typically considered a last resort. Schools are generally required not to expel a student unless they have failed to modify the inappropriate behavior through counseling or alternative disciplinary measures. Expulsion is the principal's prerogative in most public school systems, but his decision is subject to review by the local school board or district superintendent of schools. Some provinces prohibit schools from expelling students on the grounds that barring them from school denies them the right to an education.

IS CORPORAL PUNISHMENT ALLOWED?

Almost all provinces bar corporal punishment in schools, but some allow it in their schools as an instrument of control, training, or education. In those provinces, the schools may be required to notify the parents, include an adult witness, or rely on the principal to carry out the punishment.

Should the corporal punishment seem excessive or unreasonable, however, criminal charges can be brought against the teacher or educator who used it. The court would then evaluate the various factors concerning the student and the offense to determine whether the punishment was reasonable.

Educating Your Child at Home

Every province and territory has compulsory education laws to encourage able and productive citizens. All allow you to educate your children at home if certain conditions are met. If you want to pursue the idea of home schooling, here are some of the problems you may encounter:

• School officials may evaluate the teacher, the teaching methods, the curriculum, and the materials used in your home teaching program. This evaluation is designed to confirm that the home instruction is comparable, or substantially equivalent, to public schooling. It does not, however, have to be identical.

• School officials are permitted to assess the amount of time devoted to the home schooling and the tests and teaching materials used. The officials have an obligation to ensure that compulsory attendance laws are being fulfilled.

• School officials may request an occasional home visit to evaluate the "school setting." These visits, whose purpose must be to evaluate the nature and quality of home education, should be infrequent and unobtrusive.

• Some school boards require children schooled at home to take standardized tests or may insist that a school inspector review the students' work. Other boards require that students be tested by an independent evaluator.

• Provincial laws may require the parents or teacher to have a certain level of training or hold a certified teaching certificate. Some exceptions can be made if circumstances so require, as may be the case where there is a shortage of teachers or where the student's home is in a remote area.

When a Student Has Special Needs

Since education is compulsory, school boards are required to provide free and appropriate education for all children with a wide range of disabilities. These include hearing, speech, visual, and physical impairments, mental retardation, learning disabilities, emotional disturbances, and a number of other chronic or long-term health problems.

Getting Your Child in the Right Place

PROBLEM
Barbara thought that the best thing for her deaf son, Russ, was to attend regular public school. Aided by a sign-language interpreter, Russ could take any class, join clubs, and develop the skills he would need in a world that relies on speech and sound. But after a few months Barbara saw that Russ was having difficulty reading lips, did not speak clearly, and found the other children impatient with him. His self-esteem was low. Now Barbara wanted to switch him to a school for the hearing impaired, convinced that Russ needed a few years in classes with teachers and peers who consistently supported him. But because Barbara had consented to Russ's inclusion in a regular school and agreed to the school district's individualized educational plan for him, school officials resisted her desire for change.

ACTION
First, school officials asked Barbara to consider letting Russ finish the school year where he was, at which time they would review his individualized education plan. But Barbara believed that was too long to wait and asked for a review right away. Again, the officials demurred, so Barbara exercised her right to demand an impartial hearing by the department of education. The official who presided at the hearing decided the boy's plight was serious enough to require quick action and ordered the school officials to transfer Russ immediately.

Besides education, some provinces require that related services be made available. Speech therapy or physical therapy, medical diagnosis, vocational training, transportation, and parent counseling are among those services.

In the case of disabled students, their parents should receive written notice of the school's intentions and must give consent before the school can conduct any evaluation of the child's abilities or needs. In some cases, parents may also be able to have their child tested independently at the school's expense. Schools then must let the parents participate in the design of an individualized education plan and, again, get their consent before placing the child in a special program.

The practice of placing seriously impaired children into a class where the other students do not have physical or psy-

---

School Plan for Special-Needs Students

The individualized education plan developed by your special-needs child's school will set the course for his education for the entire school year. Before signing off on a program, make sure to check the following:

✔ *The classroom.* Visit the classroom where your child will spend his days. Talk to teachers and other staff members about how the plan is to be implemented.

✔ *Goals.* The plan should include clearly stated, measurable goals. For example, a goal could be for your child to learn her times tables by the end of the term.

✔ *Services.* Your child will receive only the services mentioned in the formal plan. Make sure it is specific, including, for example, speech therapy twice a week and daily bus transportation to and from school.

✔ *Equipment.* Make sure the plan includes any equipment your child needs, such as Braille textbooks for a blind student.

✔ *Your acceptance.* If you disagree with anything in the plan, ask the school to change it. If the school will not cooperate, you can ask for a hearing before an impartial administrator or committee, and if that does not help, you can file a complaint with your province's department of education.

chological problems is often called "mainstreaming," and can lead to controversy if a mainstreamed child is disruptive in the classroom to the point that other students have trouble concentrating on their studies.

When it comes to higher education, universities and colleges are required, under various provincial laws protecting the rights of disabled persons, to take all reasonable measures to enable such a student to complete his education. This might mean that the school allow extra time for these students to write exams, provide equipment such as computers and books in Braille to enable blind people to work effectively, or it might be a matter of altering the institution's structure in order to make it wheelchair accessible.

Special programs exist for gifted children as well as for those with handicaps. IQ and achievement tests are used to identify students for these programs.

Parental Action

If your child is suspended and you feel the punishment is unwarranted, you can appeal the school's action. If your child is a slow learner and the school wants to place him in a special education class, you can reject its decision. In other matters, too, parents have recourse when they disagree with a school's action. But the law gives school officials substantial decision-making power, and a parent's ability to effect change is limited. It helps to know your legal rights.

On an individual level, you are entitled to examine your child's school records, something you may want to do at least once a year to determine whether the contents are fair and accurate. You also can take advantage of parent-teacher conferences to discuss your child's needs or your complaints. If dissatisfied with the teacher's response, you are entitled to take it up with the school's principal and, if the problem is serious enough, all the way up to the superintendent.

STRENGTH IN NUMBERS

On a broader level, you can join forces with other parents or groups like the Parent Teacher Association to pursue change affecting school policy. School board meetings must be open to the public, and parents have the right to be notified about them. At meetings, school boards can be petitioned, and question-and-answer sessions can provide a forum to raise issues.

Although parents have the right to take their grievances to court, the courts may be reluctant to circumvent a school district's authority over daily operations such as absenteeism, gross misconduct, or violation of laws or regulations. According to

---

123

EXPECTING QUALITY FROM TEACHERS

If you believe that your child has an incompetent teacher, you have the right to express yourself. Where do you start?

1. Meet with the teacher. Try to work out your grievance between yourselves. It will help if you have a specific complaint to discuss rather than general discontent.

2. Take it higher up. If you are dissatisfied with the teacher's response, ask to meet the principal or another school administrator. You can contact the school's superintendent or even the school board if you think the situation is serious. But school officials are unlikely to override the principal's judgment.

3. Try for a reprimand. If you are convinced that the teacher is seriously negligent, you can attempt to have him reprimanded or even removed. But in almost all cases, such decisions reside with the school's administration, and the process could take years. Your child may end up suffering as a result.

4. Consider alternatives. If you do not get satisfaction from the school, consider other possibilities. For example, could you have your child reassigned to another school?

provincial education laws, education officials and local school boards are responsible for choosing curriculum and texts, opening or closing schools, defining district boundaries, hiring and firing teachers and administrators, deciding on disciplinary codes, and settling disputes between parents and teachers.

Private Schools

Unlike public schools, private schools have the right to set standards specific to the kind of education and students they want. Unrestricted by the demands of public funding, they may, by and large, admit only females, males, or Roman Catholics (although these limitations may be overruled in court on grounds of discrimination), or they may require their students to wear uniforms and keep their hair short. They can set severe penalties for bad behavior and require high intellectual aptitude for admission. They can charge huge fees.

You may not want to send your child to private school. But if you are thinking of it, consider your objectives and requirements. How intellectually demanding should the curriculum be? How open or traditional should the teaching methods be? Do you prefer a racially, economically, and ethnically diverse student body? Is the school you have in mind certified by the education ministry? Certification requires at least equivalent standards to those set by provincial regulations.

Once you have found the right school, you will have to figure out whether you can afford it. While financial aid is widely available for colleges and universities, aid for private secondary education is more limited. Every school offers some scholarships, usually based on need and sometimes on merit. Most private schools do offer some financial aid, but you may have to calculate if you can afford one of the extended tuition-payment plans. Offered by the schools themselves or by banks or other lending institutions, these allow you to pay the tuition in monthly installments.

Paying for Higher Education

With annual bills that can run into thousands of dollars, it is no wonder that many parents doubt they can afford to send their children to university. Higher education has never cost more—current annual fees range from $8,000 to $11,000—but financial aid is available from the university itself, and from the Canada Students Loan Plan, a federal program established in

---

Finding the Right Student Loan

Student loans are available not only to those who want to go to college or university but are also available to students who want to attend private institutions where they can take computer courses or learn a trade. If you are applying for a loan, these are some things to consider:

✔ *Apply early.* Complete and submit your loan application early, in May, say, if you wish to study in September. Late applications may mean that you will not be able to get your loan in time to pay tuition.

✔ *If you have already graduated.* If the interest on the student loan you obtained some years ago is higher than today's interest rates, try to obtain a new consumer loan to repay the outstanding debt. If you can put up collateral for the loan, the amount you will eventually repay will be considerably less than that of the original loan.

✔ *Student line of credit.* If you have this arrangement with your bank, you will pay only the interest on your loan while studying. Unless you possess substantial assets and are otherwise "creditworthy," you will probably require a guarantor to sign the loan application for a student line of credit or other student loan plan from a bank.

1964 and administered by the provinces and territories. Quebec, which opted out of the federal plan, operates its own system of student loans and bursaries.

There are certain eligibility requirements that must be met in order to qualify for a student loan. Usually the financial situation of the student's parents is taken into account. If the applicant's parents are well off financially, a government loan is often refused. There are many exceptions, however. Special consideration will be given to a student who has not resided with his/her parents for a number of years and who is considered totally independent, and to situations where the student has no reasonable expectation of parental aid.

If a student loan is granted, the government will pay the interest to the lender (usually a bank) during the period of study and for about a year after. Under recently revised federal legislation, the nine banks that grant student loans, rather than the government, will become responsible for collecting outstanding loans. The new measures may be bad news for graduates who have been tardy with repayments: banks are generally more zealous than governments in collecting loans and renegotiating repayment schedules. Student loans typically require total repayment within 10 years after graduation.

Some banks offer a "student line of credit," an arrangement, in which you pay only the interest on your loan while studying. Such arrangements are almost always more expensive than government backed loans, but they are an option if you do not qualify for government assistance.

If you think education is expensive, try ignorance.

DEREK BOK
Former president
of Harvard University

Is This School on the Up-and-Up?

It could happen: You sign up for a course in a trade school and pay the fee, then discover that the school is not legitimate and cannot deliver what it promised; or, worse, that it has closed its doors altogether. Ask the right questions before you hand over your money:

• **Is the school certified?** This is good to know but be aware that while certification means the school has obtained a provincial license, that may mean only that administrators filled out a few forms, paid a small fee, and, perhaps, bought a fire extinguisher and a smoke detector.

• **Is the school accredited?** Accreditation is the result of a more elaborate evaluation conducted by independent and respected educators who are trained to judge the educational quality of the school. Accreditation represents a meaningful stamp of approval.

• **What kind of background do the teachers have?** The school's instructors may have college degrees, but no practical experience in the trade you are studying. If so, you probably will not get the concrete, technical training you are looking for.

• **How long has the school been in business?** A school without a track record is a risk. You want to be sure that the school can deliver what it says it can, and you can determine that only if it has been operating for a number of years.

• **How have previous students fared in the job market?** If few of the school's students have actually found employment in their chosen field, that is a red flag. If the school is reluctant to give you such information or to put you in touch with previous students, think twice about attending.

DOMESTIC PARTNERSHIPS

Couples living together outside marriage have gained greater legal protection, but they still are denied the full benefits extended to married couples.

Domestic Partnerships

U nmarried couples were once stigmatized by society as well as the courts. But in the last two decades, attitudes have changed as more and more people opted for nontraditional arrangements. There are many reasons why some 10 percent of today's couples are living together without marriage. In some cases, one of the parties is still married and does not want to risk losing certain benefits by getting a divorce, or may have religious reasons for avoiding divorce. For some "common law" couples, marriage is a nondemocratic, paternalistic institution.

Although all provinces and territories have laws that deal with property distribution in case of marriage breakdown, there are no laws that so protect people in a common law marriage. In such situations, the courts have used the judicial doctrine of "unjust enrichment" to assure some sharing of property when an unmarried couple breakup. For compensation under this doctrine, there must be proof that one party benefited or was enriched, that the other party underwent a corresponding deprivation (through not being able to pay into the Canada/Quebec Pension Plan because he/she was not gainfully employed, for example) and, finally, that there was no legal justification for the enrichment by one party at the expense of the other. In the case of an unmarried couple who, before the breakup, operated a farm or small business, such as a convenience store, the doctrine of unjust enrichment would allow the courts to order a more or less equal sharing of property acquired during the relationship.

Anyone in an unmarried relationship would be wise to enter into a cohabitation agreement, spelling out obligations to one another during the relationship, and specifying what financial support and property each one receives in the event of a breakup. The matter of support is especially important if you have children.

Laws in British Columbia, Manitoba, Quebec, Ontario, New Brunswick, Prince Edward Island, Newfoundland, and Yukon specifically allow these agreements. Although cohabitation agreements are not specifically mentioned in Alberta legislation, courts in that province give great weight to the terms of

Some Benefits of Tying the Knot

Unmarried couples have become more widely accepted, but the law still provides advantageous status, including the following, to those who have made vows:

✔ *Property benefits.* Both parties are entitled to share in the assets of the other, particularly in the matrimonial home.

✔ *The Divorce Act benefits.* In the event of divorce, either party to a marriage may be ordered to pay the other a support payment, a lump sum payment, or both, according to the particular circumstances of the case.

✔ *Succession Law Benefits.* A spouse is able to inherit from the other even in the absence of a will. This is not the case with an unmarried couple.

✔ *Company and fringe benefits.* Private health insurance, air miles and company pension plans usually automatically include coverage for legally married spouses.

✔ *Health benefits.* A legally married spouse may give consent to treatment for her/his incapable spouse, and may also have more liberal hospital visiting rights and consultation with the other's doctor.

COHABITATION OR COMMON-LAW MARRIAGE?

Many people assume that couples who live together for a long time inevitably become common-law husband and wife. But not all couples who live together and who engage in sexual relations will be automatically considered to be in a "common-law marriage." While laws vary by province, to establish a common-law marriage, generally the following criteria must be met:

1. Both partners must meet the same basic legal requirements as for marriage: they must be single, mentally competent, and old enough to marry.

2. The couple must specifically present themselves in public as husband and wife by introducing each other as "my wife" and "my husband," for example, or by using the identifiers Mr. and Mrs., with the expressed intent to create a marriage.

3. The couple must live together for a specific period of time—from one year to five years, depending on the province.

4. The relationship must be shown to be stable and include some type of commitment between the parties. Simply living together to reduce living expenses, even if this arrangement includes sexual relations, lacks the commitment needed to qualify as a common-law marriage.

such agreements. Some provinces require these contracts to be made only during cohabitation, not before, and not all provinces recognize clauses dealing with child custody and visiting rights. The courts have the power to override any cohabitation agreement that is unconscionable or grossly unfair, or where a signature was extorted or otherwise not freely given.

SAME-SEX COUPLES

Same sex marriages are not recognized under Canadian law, which defines marriage as a union for life of people of the opposite sex. Traditionally, one's sex is considered to be determined at birth. Such a determination might well prove a hindrance to marriage plans by someone who has undergone sex-change surgery.

Ruling in the *Egan* case in 1995, the Supreme Court of Canada found that homosexual couples are not entitled to spousal benefits under the Old Age Security Act. In rendering his decision, the Hon. Mr. Justice John Sopinka said that although he found discrimination justified in the *Egan* case, according to the Charter of Rights and Freedoms, the definition of "spouse" was discriminatory.

In 1996, Parliament approved amendments to the Human Rights Act, prohibiting discrimination based on sexual orientation. Many see this as a first step in same-sex couples' rights to spousal benefits.

The Risks of Joint Assets

Many couples who live together outside of marriage may not adequately consider the financial ramifications of their arrangement. Perhaps they start out intending to keep their financial lives separate or think that having a small joint fund for household expenses will be enough to keep things running smoothly. But gradually they discover that living together can easily create more interdependence than they thought. Questions arise. Should we open a joint bank account? Co-sign a rental lease or a bank loan? Purchase an automobile?

While the law confers special rights and benefits concerning property and finances on married couples—particularly when a spouse dies or becomes incapacitated, or the marriage ends—unmarried partners lack the same protections. For example, if your partner's name is the only one on the title to your condo, even if you can prove that you contributed to the maintenance and mortgage costs for years, you might not be able to claim any ownership. Or if your partner suddenly dies without a will, his or her property will be distributed accord-

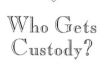

ing to the laws of intestate succession. These generally specify that property is distributed to such blood or legal relations as spouses, children, parents, brothers, and sisters.

It is therefore important for unmarried couples to keep written records of all financial agreements. Without such written evidence of ownership or interest, it would be difficult for an unmarried partner to assert her individual rights in court. If you open a joint bank account, for example, avoid disputes by keeping records of what each of you puts into the account and how the money is spent. Be aware that one partner could empty the joint account at any time, and the other would have little or no recourse. A cohabitation agreement can help document who owns what and how assets are to be divided in the event that you break up. (See also "Put It in Writing," page 134.)

KEEP THINGS SEPARATE

Unmarried partners should also be aware of their liability for each other in joint agreements. Any jointly owned property, any jointly shared credit accounts, any co-signed lease makes both partners liable for payments. Let's say you both signed a lease or mortgage, pay 50-50 shares on it, and then your partner loses his job. You would become liable for the full amount of the money owed.

Unmarried partners should take special precautions when making purchases together. If you are buying a car, for example, will it be jointly titled? If so, both partners will be responsible for payments. If it is not jointly titled, an unmarried partner who owns the title could sell or take the car without the other partner's knowledge or agreement. Making a formal agreement from the outset can help avoid later problems.

If You Have a Child

Children born outside of marriage can be legally recognized as the offspring of both parents if the father asserts in writing that he is the father, the parents marry each other, the father openly acknowledges the child as his own and accepts him into his home, or the father is so-designated in a paternity action.

Once, children born out of wedlock were severely stigmatized and were cut off from benefits given children born during a marriage. They were limited in seeking financial support from their biological father, for example, or in sharing in his estate when he died. Today such a child is generally entitled to those rights as long as paternity can be proved. Most provinces and the territories have enacted legislation doing away with the distinction of children as legitimate or illegitimate. In Alberta,

Who Gets Custody?

Unmarried parents who break up have an equal right to custody of their child if paternity has been acknowledged. The father does not have that right, however, unless he acknowledged paternity in writing or legitimized the child in some other way, such as by having his name included as father on the child's birth certificate.

Unmarried parents can decide between themselves who gets custody of the child. Usually the courts will not question that decision unless the child's welfare is in doubt.

When parents cannot agree on custody, courts recognize the "primary parent" concept, which weighs in favor of the parent who has had primary responsibility for meeting the child's basic needs (food, clothing, hygiene, nursing, and so on).

These duties are still primarily assumed by mothers. Thus in the majority of cases, the mother becomes the custodial parent. But the final decision belongs to the judge who is responsible for determining the "best interests of the child."

which retains the distinction, children are automatically legitimized if their parents marry.

A father acknowledges paternity when he declares in writing, on private or public documents, that he is the father of the child in question. This may be accomplished by signing the child's birth certificate, declaring the child a dependent on his income tax return, or acknowledging paternity in communications with hospital or school authorities.

If the father denies his paternity, the matter can be resolved by the court which would recognize that he is the father by the results of blood tests, DNA tests, or by a careful examination of the circumstances surrounding the birth of the child. If the man was cohabiting with the mother for about 10 months before the birth, continued to live with her during the pregnancy, visited the hospital and brought gifts to his partner at the time of birth, and continued to live with the mother and child after the birth, the court would most likely find he was the child's father. Each case, however, is judged according to its own particular circumstances.

WHEN THE PARTNERSHIP FALTERS

When unmarried partners separate and cannot agree on child support, custody, and visitation rights, the courts will have to decide for them. One parent, or a public agency such as the welfare department, can sue the other parent for child support. A noncomplying parent can be held in contempt of court and face stringent collection procedures.

> *Love is the wisdom of the fool and the folly of the wise.*
>
> **SAMUEL JOHNSON**
> *Johnsonian Miscellanies*

Put It in Writing

Unmarried partners who live together without any written agreements risk getting saddled with debts and losing property. Since oral agreements are hard to prove in court, it is best to clarify the terms of the relationship in writing. Consider drafting the following types of agreements:

• **Written agreements.** An informal agreement can lay out the basic details of your arrangement, from who bought the stereo to who pays the rent. This document can clarify expectations and, if clearly drawn up, is enforceable by the courts. Written records of joint property, household finances, and debt become critical if you split up. Your agreement can pin down who pays the mortgage and taxes, and it can define how property will be handled if the relationship ends. Consult a lawyer for advice.

• **Parenting agreement.** Not necessarily enforceable in court, a parenting agreement can detail support obligations and responsibilities for decision-making regarding the care of a child.

• **Medical proxy.** A medical proxy enables unmarried partners to take responsibility for medical decisions, consult with doctors, and visit in the hospital should the other partner become sick or injured.

• **Durable power of attorney.** This type of agreement allows a partner to take over financial decision-making should the other become mentally or physically incapable.

• **Will.** A will helps ensure that your partner receives your property when you die. Without a will, the courts automatically make your next of kin the recipient of your assets. Even if you have a will, it may be contested, so make sure the will is carefully written and properly executed.

DIVORCE

Even though no-fault divorce has helped reduce abusive, name-calling battles, divorce is almost always an emotionally trying experience.

Ending Your Marriage

The statistics speak for themselves: one out of every two marriages will end in divorce. To be sure, divorces are now easier to get, and the process poses far fewer legal hurdles, but rarely, if ever, is a divorce painless. By clearly understanding your options and obligations, you can reduce the difficulties of ending your marriage.

ANNULMENT

Not all failed marriages are dissolved by divorce. Annulment is a way of legally invalidating a marriage as if it had never existed. In most provinces the courts will grant an annulment if you can prove that one of the following conditions existed at the time of the wedding: one partner was underage, incurably impotent, legally insane, or married to someone else; or one partner forced the other into the marriage under duress or misled the other by fraud. Duress may involve the use of violence, blackmail, or intimidation. Fraud means that one partner concealed relevant information, such as drug addiction, criminal convictions, venereal disease, or homosexuality.

To get an annulment, you should seek the help of a lawyer. Each province sets time requirements for filing an annulment, ranging from 90 days to four years, depending on the grounds. Usually only the parties to the marriage can file for annulment, but in some instances parents or guardians can do so.

SEPARATION

Some couples separate to test whether they really want to divorce. Some separate legally and never live together again, but for religious or economic reasons never divorce. Other couples—with children or debt or serious financial issues—use a separation to quickly and formally settle their affairs in writing, and so prevent the divorce becoming a long and costly court battle. Whatever the reason, once you have completed a voluntary separation agreement, the divorce process is significantly simplified. For your document to be binding, you must file a petition with the court, and a judge must sign the court order. You may file for divorce without having legally separated if, for economic reasons, you live under the same roof, but live "par-

---

123

THE SEPARATION AGREEMENT

A separation agreement is the blueprint for a divorce. It resolves in writing your legal concerns, sets out a legal plan for living apart, and can be a framework for your divorce decree. You and your spouse can write a first draft, but you should also get a lawyer's help. Here are the general areas your agreement should address:

1. Distribution of assets. This aspect of the agreement concerns the way assets will be distributed. This may include furniture, photographs or wedding presents, as well as cars, money, investments, and real estate.

2. Children. This involves not only the question of custody, but also child support, visitation rights, medical costs, housing, and education plans.

3. Spousal support. The intimidating list of financial matters your agreement should deal with runs from insurance to income tax—and who pays for what. If alimony is to be paid, the terms should be decided. The agreement requires analysis and disclosure of both spouses' assets, including pension funds and financial investments, and should also spell out details concerning inheritance rights.

Some Common Divorce Issues

Divorce has become much more straightforward since the law was revised in 1986. Even so, there are some aspects of the legislation that may surprise you. For example:

✔ *Prior behavior.* In granting spousal support, the court will not consider the behavior of the parties during the marriage. If one partner was abusive or even physically violent toward the other, this will not increase or decrease the amount of the support the court will grant.

✔ *Prior agreements.* The court is not bound by a prior separation agreement, nor by an agreement made up especially for the divorce settling property and custody matters. The judge will give close consideration to such agreements, but has total discretion as to whether he will be bound by them, especially in matters concerning children.

✔ *Bars to a divorce.* Condoning a straying spouse can cost you a divorce. If you have previously forgiven your spouse for adultery, you cannot use this as a later ground for divorce.

✔ *Period of separation.* If you have begun divorce proceedings but, in an attempt at reconciliation, you have lived together for several periods totaling less than 90 days, your divorce action is still valid. However, if the period or periods together exceed 90 days, your divorce application will be dismissed and you will have to start new proceedings.

allel lives." Usually this means you do not engage in sexual relations, do not go out together, do not socialize or have most meals together—in other words, you do not live as husband and wife. But before getting a divorce, you will probably be required to live physically apart for one year.

GROUNDS FOR DIVORCE

As the Divorce Act (1985) is a federal statute, the rules and conditions for divorce are the same across Canada. Before the present act went into effect, divorce was granted only if one partner proved the other had committed a "fault," or if the couple had lived separate and apart for three years (if the petitioner was the abandoned spouse) or five years (in the case of the spouse who left the common domicile). Grounds for divorce under the former act were adultery, mental or physical cruelty, and separation for the required period.

Under the present act, breakdown of the marriage is the only ground for divorce, which can be granted even if one partner objects. Consent of the other partner is not required if the applicant proves the marriage has broken down. This can be proven if there is adultery, if there is mental or physical cruelty, or if the couple lived separate and apart for at least one year. However, you do not have to live separate and apart for a year before beginning divorce proceedings. In fact, you can file for divorce the day after your marriage and be granted a divorce one year later provided you lived separate and apart in the interim. You can only file for divorce in a province where one of the spouses has been domiciled for at least one year.

The vast majority of divorces are now granted on the ground of marital breakdown by virtue of one-year separation. This avoids the financial and emotional stress of proving adultery or airing your dirty laundry before the court by submitting medical records or witnesses. In some provinces, you can obtain a divorce by filing proper affidavits and thus never appearing before a judge, if you have already settled the matters of custody, visiting rights, spousal and child support and the division of property. For your protection, such an agreement should be drawn up by a lawyer familiar with divorce.

CAN YOU DO IT YOURSELVES?

Some couples seek to simplify their divorce—and minimize the cost—by doing it themselves. Using a do-it-yourself kit, although certainly cheaper than hiring a lawyer, should be considered only by spouses who both consent to the divorce, have been married a short time, have little property to divide, are both working and in good health, and have no children. In those cases, the process is relatively simple. One spouse initiates the divorce and sends a notice to the other through the court. Depending upon how he received the notice, the receiving spouse has 20 to 40 days to respond. Then the spouse who initiated the divorce will appear in court, state the circumstances of the case, petition dissolution of the marriage and, if there is property, file a property settlement, which both spouses must sign before the court grants a decree of dissolution. The judgment becomes final 30 days later. During this period you can file for appeal or ask that the judgment be set aside.

One Lawyer or Two?

PROBLEM
Max and Dana Diamond, though divorcing, thought they could avoid conflict and settle their differences themselves. Yet after they began making outlines concerning their property, debts, spousal support, and visitation plans for their baby girl, Lillie, Max realized how complicated it all was and hired a lawyer. At first, Dana agreed to this, but she gradually began to feel that Max was trying to take advantage of her, and decided she should hire her own lawyer. But she had already verbally accepted, although reluctantly, most of the terms suggested by Max and his lawyer. She also knew how angry Max would be when she announced her intention. What should she do?

ACTION
Even non-adversarial couples frequently hire two lawyers to be sure that each understands his or her rights and that someone is advocating their individual interests. The moment Dana felt uncertain about whether her interests were being protected, she should have hired her own lawyer. Even if she had signed an agreement with Max, she could withdraw her consent and renegotiate, but, as it was, she had signed nothing. Braving Max's displeasure, she hired a lawyer, and they began their negotiations all over again. In the end, the basic points of their settlement did not change much, but Dana went through the divorce proceeding confident that she was getting a fair agreement.

When looking for a lawyer, choose someone experienced in matrimonial law. You are entitled to a written statement concerning fees, and you can also ask for a periodic expense reports. Especially complicated and protracted divorces can generate huge legal fees. What will happen if you run out of money? (See also YOUR RIGHTS IN ACTION, page 455.)

Settling Finances and Property

Every province has its own guidelines to determine how a divorcing couple should equitably divide their property. These establish broad parameters, and judges will use them if you, your spouse, and lawyers cannot reach agreement outside of court. For couples without children, the hardest task will involve assessing their

---

1 2 3

ORDERS THAT RESTRAIN AND PROTECT

Sometimes in the upheaval of divorce, assets disappear and tempers flare. You can seek a temporary restraining order to protect your assets until final division or an order of protection to safeguard yourself and your children.

1. If you suspect that your spouse might try to remove joint assets—money in a joint account or a safe-deposit box, for example—you can get a restraining order or seizure before judgment to prohibit the removal, sale, or transfer of that property.

2. If your spouse asks other parties—such as a financial manager, a broker, a banker, or anyone who has access to your assets—to help gain control of your assets, the restraining order or seizure can be served on them too.

3. If your relationship has been violent, or you feel you or your children might be threatened with physical harm during the period of divorce or separation, you should seek an order of protection. In most provinces, victims-advocacy groups or court personnel can help you file the papers to get protection. Your spouse can be restrained from coming near you, your house, place of work, school, or other defined location. You might also be awarded temporary exclusive occupancy of your shared home. If the order is violated, your spouse can be arrested and jailed.

joint and separate holdings and deciding who gets what. All provinces and territories, through their various matrimonial property acts, or married women's property acts, regulate what interests each party may have in the property of the other, or in common property.

These laws were passed to remedy the situation where, upon divorce, a spouse (in nearly all cases the wife) was almost left destitute, since in most traditional marriages the wife worked at home and did not earn money to buy anything. Under these matrimonial property acts, the judge deciding the case has a discretion to order an unequal division of property where the circumstances justify it.

Definition of property to be shared equally varies. In some provinces, common property includes a spouse's private pension plan, a business or professional practice, investments, and almost always the matrimonial home. Usually property that was inherited or acquired by gift by one spouse remains that spouse's property, although interest or the increased value of such property from the time of acquisition is usually shared.

Can Mediation Settle Your Differences?

Mediation can offer divorcing couples a less harrowing way of settling their differences than fighting it out in court. Mediation uses a neutral third party trained in conflict resolution to facilitate communication and to resolve disputes over property, custody, and other areas of disagreement. It is not the answer for everyone, however. Can mediation work for you?

• **An amicable parting.** Maybe you have already worked out child custody, most of the property issues, even who gets the beloved pet. But, because you are living 200 kilometres apart, you cannot agree on a visitation plan. Or, with little shared property, you have agreed on a basic separation arrangement but need help fine-tuning the details. The mediator can help clarify your options.

• **No substitute for lawyers.** Perhaps you want to keep down your costs, and see mediation as an alternative to a lawyer. But mediation is not a substitute for legal advice, even though with the court's final approval, it can become legally binding. The mediator will not represent your interests in particular (her job is to remain neutral), nor is she necessarily a legal expert. In divorce cases, lawyers are bound to inform their clients about mediation services. In some provinces, such services are attached to the court and often the service is free.

• **Future benefits.** Couples who use mediation are generally more satisfied than those who do not, and there are fewer post-decree problems

with mediation settlements. In mediation, the parties "own" the agreement and have tailored it to fit their situation.

• **Not for the abused.** If you are a victim of domestic violence, mediation as the means to work out a divorce is not always the best choice. Because it depends on conversation and negotiation, mediation can be a mistake if you are in a particularly aggressive or coercive relationship.

• **Not a substitute for therapy.** You should not look on the process of mediation as an opportunity to air grievances, to deal with lingering anger or bitterness against your soon-to-be ex-spouse. Mediation is no place for this kind of behavior, and the process will probably break down if you or your spouse enters into it in this spirit.

• **May be a money saver.** If a court has a mediation service, the service may be free or nominal in cost. Even if there is a charge for the service, you may spend fewer hours with your lawyers—and incur smaller bills—if you try mediation before going to court.

The judge will usually consider certain factors:

- The length of the marriage;
- The age, health, and future earning potential of each spouse;
- Contributions by each spouse toward acquired property. Domestic duties and the raising of children are considered as substantial contributions;
- What property each brought into the marriage;
- The needs of the parent who has custody of the children.

With the help of a lawyer, you can assess your holdings and appraise their value. But you may want to complete much of this work before you spend long, billable hours with a lawyer. You will need to gather together financial records, including bank statements, tax returns, insurance policies, and deeds, plus pension, retirement, and profit-sharing plans. You should also make an inventory of physical property, such as television sets and stereo systems, furniture and jewelry, kitchen appliances, cars, and, of course, your home itself.

KEEPING A HOUSE A HOME

The sticky issue of who gets the house gets more complicated when young children are involved. If one parent receives custody of them, the courts, to minimize disruption in their lives, may grant that parent possession of the house and mandate that it not be sold until the children reach a certain age.

A divorcing couple without children or with older children might agree to hold on to their house until the real estate market improves. No matter who lives in the house, your court order or separation agreement should detail who is responsible for the monthly mortgage, maintenance costs, taxes and deductions, and repairs. And, even though you might expect a 50-50 split when the house is sold, a judge may decide in this case that "equitable" does not mean equal shares.

Your lawyer can help clarify the tax consequences of your divorce on homes and other property matters. While you may or may not benefit from such changes, they should be incorporated into the final terms of your settlement.

Spousal Support

Into the 1970's, the awarding of alimony was a natural extension of the traditional marriage arrangement. The husband was the breadwinner and provider; the wife was the homemaker and caretaker of the children. If the marriage ended, any alimony awarded went to the wife—usually for as long as she or her former husband lived (or until she

---

Joint Credit Card Debt: Who Pays?

Like many couples, you and your spouse may have tangled over the credit card bills every month. Now that you have decided to call it quits, be sure you do not simply put that memory out of your mind. Old debts, like new ones, can be a continuing financial burden.

If you are worried that your spouse may run up new bills with unused credit, contact the credit card company immediately and ask it to close the account. Generally the creditor will demand that you pay off the balance first, but you can ask that the card be made inactive in the meantime.

Credit card debt, like other joint marital property, is a shared responsibility. So you and your spouse must work out how it will be paid. You can sell off joint property and apply the proceeds, or one of you can pay the debt in exchange for a greater share of the property. You may decide to split it all down the middle, but be aware that if your partner declares bankruptcy later, you will be left holding the bill.

Furthermore, a divorce decree will not protect you from debt collection if credit was granted to you jointly, even if the court has assigned your spouse sole responsibility for a particular debt; the creditor can still collect from either one of you. If you end up paying a bill assigned to your ex-spouse, you may have to go back to court to force your ex-spouse to reimburse you.

remarried). Today, the law aims to be gender-neutral, allowing either spouse to claim alimony, and taking into account who has the greater income or wage-earning capacity. Statistics demonstrate clearly that the living standard of the spouse with custody of the children will drop precipitously.

Alimony, or "spousal support," is rarely awarded for a lifetime anymore, except where there has been a marriage in excess of 20 years in which one partner was the wage earner and the other a homemaker. Since each spouse is required to become as financially self-sufficient as possible, support payments may be limited to a specific period of time or until a certain event occurs—the completion of studies plus six months, say. By and large, the support period does not exceed the length of the marriage. Judicial decisions generally reflect the belief that a spouse needs support only for as long as it takes to get back on his or her feet. The courts generally consider the following:

- The length of the marriage;
- The earning capacity of both spouses and their ability to pay;
- The age and health of each spouse;
- The work experience, skills, and education of each;
- The couple's standard of living during the marriage.

If you are awarded spousal support, you may be offered a choice between one lump-sum payment or periodic payments. Each option has its risks. Should you find at a later time that the lump sum is inadequate to cover your needs, the courts are highly unlikely to add to the earlier agreement. Spouses paid periodically, on the other hand, often receive late cheques or no cheques at all. If you are the one making payments, you might try tying the amount of the payments to your own fluctuating financial status or that of your spouse. The payments would rise when you earn significantly more, for example, or go down should you lose your job.

There may be a late-payment penalty built into your support agreement, but you still might have a tough time collecting your payments. This is a common problem, along with unpaid child-support payments. Some spouses incorporate clauses to help secure payment.

Each province has its own method of enforcing payments. These range from loss of driver's license to garnishment of salary, and ordering payments be made directly to the court officer whose sole function is to see that court-ordered support is paid. Each province respects the support judgment rendered by another province. As well, most provinces have treaties with many governments in the United States and in other countries, whereby these foreign jurisdictions will enforce support orders rendered in Canada.

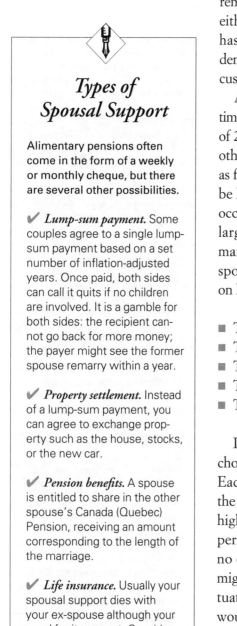

Types of Spousal Support

Alimentary pensions often come in the form of a weekly or monthly cheque, but there are several other possibilities.

✔ *Lump-sum payment.* Some couples agree to a single lump-sum payment based on a set number of inflation-adjusted years. Once paid, both sides can call it quits if no children are involved. It is a gamble for both sides: the recipient cannot go back for more money; the payer might see the former spouse remarry within a year.

✔ *Property settlement.* Instead of a lump-sum payment, you can agree to exchange property such as the house, stocks, or the new car.

✔ *Pension benefits.* A spouse is entitled to share in the other spouse's Canada (Quebec) Pension, receiving an amount corresponding to the length of the marriage.

✔ *Life insurance.* Usually your spousal support dies with your ex-spouse although your need for it may not. Consider negotiating for an insurance policy on your ex-spouse's life. In most provinces, the deceased spouse's estate can be ordered to pay support for a certain period.

Child Support

Parents are responsible for supporting their minor children, and divorce does not end that responsibility—although, unfortunately, the noncustodial parent, usually the father, frequently acts as though it does. Unpaid child support represents billions of dollars annually, a fact that has enormous social consequences.

Federal and provincial laws are focusing more and more on increasing compliance with child-support orders, and punishments for nonsupport will likely continue to get stiffer. Enforcement provisions are the same as for spousal support— loss of driver's license, automatic garnishment of salary upon first failure to pay, and direct payments to a court officer. All provinces respect support judgments rendered by another, and most provinces have agreements with many American states and other countries so that support orders rendered in Canada will be enforced abroad.

If the noncustodial parent of a child is in arrears, the custodial parent is entitled to request back payments or ask for the seizure of assets to pay off the support owed. If the delinquent parent cannot be located or has no income or assets, there is not much to be done about getting back payments.

If the delinquent parent has a steady income or sufficient funds, however, the court can issue an order to his employer to withhold money from his wages, or a judge may attach funds the delinquent parent may have in savings accounts, stocks, or other assets. A delinquent parent whose reasons for nonpayment are not valid can be held in contempt of court and even be jailed in very aggravated cases until payment is made.

MODIFYING THE SUPPORT ORDER

A judge may alter a child-support order if there is a significant change of circumstances in the status of either parent. Such changes might include a major increase or decrease in one parent's income; increased expenses, such as for a new child in the household; a change in the child's needs; or the loss of a job. To have the original order modified, the reasons for change and supporting evidence must be presented at a court hearing.

As of May 1, 1997, new legislation will require judges to award child support according to a defined schedule that takes account of the payer's income and the number of children. For example, an Alberta parent earning $40,000 a year will pay $363 a month for one child or $783 for three children. In Nova Scotia, corresponding amounts will be $348 and $759 respectively. For complete charts and explanations of the law, write to Finance Canada for "The New Child Support Package."

Finding a Deadbeat Parent

Canada is a big country, and finding a father who has skipped out without making his child-support payments can be a daunting task. Still, there are ways to track him down. (More and more women now pay child support, but the vast majority of delinquent parents are fathers.)

Armed with the name, social insurance number, and an existing support order, your provincial child-support-enforcement agency can contact Revenue Canada: any tax rebates or other money that would otherwise be sent to the delinquent parent could be sent to that agency for payment to the parent with the support order.

Locally, your provincial child-support-enforcement department can search records of motor vehicle registration, employment insurance, income tax, and correctional facilities for information.

You can also hire an investigator—but it's best to do so only after other options are exhausted. Try to arrange to pay the investigator on a contingency basis to provide incentive and to protect yourself from paying more than you collect.

If you find the deadbeat, consult a lawyer or your local welfare or child-support-enforcement unit. They may be able to help you get a court order to force the delinquent parent to pay what he owes or have his wages garnisheed.

Alicia Munnie
1 Park Avenue
Toronto, Ont. K1O 3Z5

June 29, 1995

Mr. Harry Munnie
1214 Brewery Boulevard
Moncton, N.B. A4N 101

Dear Harry:

This letter is a reminder that you are behind in your support payments for our child.

As stipulated in our divorce decree dated April 10, 1994, ① you are required to pay $350 by the 7th day of each month. ② As of today, you are 22 days late. ③ You also know that the decree stipulates a late penalty of $50 for each month you are behind. ④ In total, then, you are now $400 in arrears.

According to the terms of the court's child-support order, your wages may be withheld if payments fall 30 days into arrears. ⑤ I want to avoid involving the court again to resolve this. But you know that I very much need this money to provide the proper care for Molly. Please take care of this as soon as possible before the problem becomes larger and other enforcement efforts become necessary.

Sincerely,

Alicia

Putting Pressure on Your Ex

If your ex-spouse has gotten behind in his child-support payments, act swiftly to avoid bigger problems later on. Start with a letter like this one. Specifically: **1.** Make note of the date of the final divorce decree, which is useful information should this letter be handed over to a judge as evidence later on; **2.** Include details of the decree to preclude any misunderstanding with your ex-spouse (and to jog the judge); **3.** State the exact amount your ex-spouse is behind, including any penalty; **4.** Carefully calculate the total; **5.** Make it clear that you are acting in good faith, that you prefer to handle the problem amicably. You do not want to turn a temporary situation into a permanent problem. You might give your ex-spouse a chance to explain why he is behind, but don't let him forget that he has an enforceable commitment to you and his child.

Child Custody and Visitation

The courts are charged with the responsibility for establishing child custody according to the "best interests of the child." But too often custody disputes between acrimonious parents become emotionally exhausting tugs-of-war. In the best circumstances, divorcing parents decide between themselves on a reasonable plan for custody and visitation. This agreement is then put in writing—with schedules, financial obligations, and so forth—for the court's approval. Couples may want to try mediation, arbitration, or other resources to help resolve impasses before the plan is presented to a judge for final approval.

When the court is called upon to weigh the best interests of the child, sole custody is most likely to be awarded to one parent. Some judges rely heavily on information about which parent has been the day-to-day "primary caregiver." In today's society, this most often has been the mother. Judges sometimes request that a social worker provide the court with a report on the family. Some judges may require parents to meet with a court-monitored counselor, who then prepares a custody evaluation to aid the judge in making a decision.

Although there is conflicting evidence concerning what custody arrangement is really best for the development of the child, several judges now affirmatively support joint custody. Courts distinguish joint legal custody from joint physical custody. In joint legal arrangements, both parents must jointly make major decisions about the child's health, education, and religion. Where parents share joint physical custody, the child may spend significant time living in each parent's home or, in rare cases, the parents will take turns living in the home where the child resides permanently.

A BALANCING ACT

Most judges require parents to spell out exactly how they will implement such a joint arrangement. Other judges will not finalize the joint custody until the parents have shown it can work. In a growing number of cases, a court order may prohibit a custodial spouse from moving more than 150 kilometres away from the noncustodial parent unless she has a compelling reason to do so. The Supreme Court of Canada ruled in May 1996 that when the noncustodial parent has established a good relationship with the child, the other parent cannot destroy this relationship, even if there is such a compelling reason for the move as the remarriage of the custodial parent.

If one parent has been granted custody, it is a criminal offense for the other parent to remove the child. The charge

---

ASSESSING THE CHILD'S BEST INTERESTS

If parents cannot decide on child custody and visitation arrangements, the courts must determine the "best interests of the child." It is a difficult job with wide room for interpretation. Here are six factors judges may consider:

1. Who is providing primary care? The courts will consider which parent can best provide day-to-day care.

2. What does the child really need? Maybe the child is emotionally troubled and needs a lot of attention. Dad often travels for work. Mom freelances at home—and gets custody because of that.

3. Are Mom and Dad healthy? The courts are unlikely to grant custody to a parent who is physically ill or mentally unstable.

4. What about siblings? Judges resist splitting up brothers and sisters, especially when they are close.

5. Should the child leave home? Divorce is hard enough on children, and the courts hesitate to make them adjust to a new home, school, and neighborhood as well. If Mom plans to move away, a court might decide that Dad can offer more stability.

6. What does the child say? A child under 10 is unlikely to be asked his or her preference. But in many cases a teenager's opinion (given privately) may be considered.

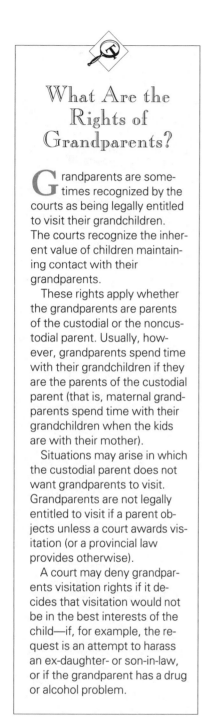

What Are the Rights of Grandparents?

Grandparents are sometimes recognized by the courts as being legally entitled to visit their grandchildren. The courts recognize the inherent value of children maintaining contact with their grandparents.

These rights apply whether the grandparents are parents of the custodial or the noncustodial parent. Usually, however, grandparents spend time with their grandchildren if they are the parents of the custodial parent (that is, maternal grandparents spend time with their grandchildren when the kids are with their mother).

Situations may arise in which the custodial parent does not want grandparents to visit. Grandparents are not legally entitled to visit if a parent objects unless a court awards visitation (or a provincial law provides otherwise).

A court may deny grandparents visitation rights if it decides that visitation would not be in the best interests of the child—if, for example, the request is an attempt to harass an ex-daughter- or son-in-law, or if the grandparent has a drug or alcohol problem.

would be kidnapping and the penalty could be 10 years imprisonment. Even in the absence of a court order it is illegal for one parent to arbitrarily abduct a child who is residing with the other parent.

A parent dissatisfied with a judgment concerning custody may ask the court to change the order if he can show that the custodial parent is not fulfilling her parental duties properly, or that changing the order would be in the best interests of the child.

VISITATION

In the best circumstances, divorcing parents include their agreed-upon plan for visitation in the divorce settlement or decree. They can detail the length and the frequency of visits—for instance, every other weekend plus certain holidays. Such an agreement is preferable to leaving the decision up to a judge.

When the parents cannot agree, the courts will decide visitation rights for the noncustodial parent and include the plan in a visitation order. The court may be asked to intervene, particularly after a bitter divorce or custody battle, if the custodial parent continues to refuse to abide by the order. If visitation becomes a problem, these are things you can do:

- Document refused or missed visits and their circumstances;
- Write a letter to the custodial parent, stating your concerns;
- Contact a mediator, social service worker, or lawyer to act as an intermediary;
- Make sure you continue support payments, even if visitation is denied;
- Request that a counselor talk to your child if she refuses to see you;
- Ask the court to reconsider the custody and visitation arrangement if the refusal continues;
- Obtain a court order enforcing your visitation rights, but only as a last resort.

If you are the custodial parent and your ex-spouse is abusive or there is another good reason to refuse visitation, you can ask the court to terminate visitation rights or to supervise visits. If your former spouse refuses to visit, the courts cannot force the issue. You might, however, get the court to increase your child-support payments to offset the loss of the noncustodial parent's caretaking services during regular visitations.

REPORTING CHILD ABUSE

If you suspect physical or sexual abuse of your child by her parent, you can deny visitation while you talk to a lawyer, minister, or mental health professional. Most provinces have mandatory reporting laws that require certain professionals (such as police officers, mental health professionals, and teachers) to report suspected abuse.

A report of child abuse can lead to criminal charges being filed and even imprisonment. Reporting mere suspicions of abuse is a dramatic measure, however, and you may want to have a confidential conversation with your lawyer. (Lawyers are not legally obliged to contact investigating authorities.)

Happiness in marriage is entirely a matter of chance.

JANE AUSTEN
Pride and Prejudice

After the Divorce Is Final

In most cases, unless fraud was involved, there is no right to modify your property-settlement agreement, although if your ex-spouse agrees in writing to changes, the court will in most cases approve them. A judge might consider extending spousal support beyond the agreed-upon termination date, but judges generally are unwilling to grant spousal support if you did not originally ask for it.

Child-support and custody and visitation issues are modifiable under certain circumstances until your child reaches the age of majority. Both a custodial parent seeking an increase in support payments and a noncustodial parent unable to pay can file a petition for a hearing to show why a change is needed. Changing a custody ruling is much harder. You must show a significant change of circumstances and rebut a presumption that favors the custodial parent's retention of custody.

Starting Over: Changing Your Personal Records

With a certified copy of your divorce decree in hand, you are ready to begin a new life. And since you are in effect establishing a new identity as well, you want to be sure to make the necessary changes on various personal and legal documents to avoid any troubles later.

• **Property records.** Record documents for transfer of ownership or interest in real property with the county recorder's office. This may include the deed to your home if it was jointly owned during your marriage. You may also have to change the title to your car with the provincial department of motor vehicles.

• **Name change.** If you decide to take back your maiden name or otherwise change your name, notify all the institutions and firms that have your old name on file, such as Medicare; the Canada (Quebec) Pension Plan; the Department of Motor Vehicles if you hold a driver's license; all banks where you have accounts; credit card companies; and stores whose charge cards you hold.

• **Joint bank accounts.** Close and divide joint bank and investment accounts as agreed in your property settlement.

• **Creditors.** Inform your creditors—banks, credit card companies, and so on—as to who is responsible for any debts that are outstanding from your married days. If you are not responsible for the debts, ask the creditors to remove your name from the account.

• **Beneficiaries.** Check the beneficiaries of pension plans and insurance policies and make necessary changes. If you want to alter the way your estate is to be settled, don't forget to have a new will drawn up and executed.

REMARRIAGE

The second time around you know more. But to make it work, additional obligations demand that you understand your options and responsibilities.

Should You Combine Assets?

Being careful about finances is important in every marriage, but particularly in a remarriage when your former spouse and children from a previous marriage require continuing support. One important decision will be whether to combine all resources with your new partner. Consider the following:

✔ **Spousal support.** Your former spouse is entitled to sue for increased spousal support. Your and your new spouse's combined incomes and expenses will be evaluated.

✔ **Child support.** A stepparent's income or savings are rarely considered in resetting child support.

✔ **Debts.** Money you put into a joint account could be at risk if your new spouse has lingering debts.

✔ **Inheritance.** Your new spouse is entitled to a share of your combined assets, as are dependent children from this and any previous marriages. To maintain control over how your estate is to be divided, you need to rewrite your will or make a marriage or prenuptial contract excluding your new spouse from any right to your property.

How Remarrying Can Affect Your Finances

Many marriages today are remarriages, an encouraging statistic for many who are divorced and widowed. But it is a sobering reality that remarriages, often weighed down by complicated responsibilities to both a new family and a previous one, are even more likely to end in divorce than first marriages. Even if you are entering into a second marriage without children or financial obligations to your previous spouse, you will be faced with the challenge of coordinating complex new domestic arrangements.

If you currently depend on spousal support, be prepared to forgo that support if you have not negotiated an exclusion in your original divorce decree. Typically, such payments cease when you remarry. If you currently pay spousal support, it is highly unlikely that it will be reduced, even if you can provide evidence that your new marriage cuts into your ability to pay. Also, the courts will consider your new spouse's income in assessing your responsibility.

INSURING BOTH BROODS

With the additional responsibilities of a new family, you will need to reevaluate your life insurance coverage. Perhaps you can be carried on your new spouse's health insurance plan—or vice versa. You can change the primary beneficiary of a life insurance policy to your new spouse, but a stepparent is not always under a legal obligation to provide for your children in the event of your death or otherwise, unless he or she has acted like a parent to them over a certain period of time.

To ensure that both your new spouse and your children from a previous marriage will be provided for, you may have to take out a second policy—one that will benefit your new family—and keep the existing policy that protects your children from a previous marriage and perhaps your obligations to your former spouse according to your divorce settlement. Also, with two families depending on you, you may need to increase your disability insurance.

Older people are especially sensitive about losing assets that they—and perhaps a deceased spouse—spent years accumulating. Or, their children may resent a new spouse's arrival. Legally, they have a reason to be concerned: if there is no premarital agreement, a spouse cannot be disinherited and can make a claim of one-third to one-half of an estate.

Can You Protect Your Inheritance?

PROBLEM
Irene Oliver, a widow, named her only daughter, Jackie, as the sole heir in her will. But after she decided to accept Joe Anders' proposal and marry again, she worried that once she was married to Joe, Jackie's inheritance might be jeopardized.

ACTION
Although she trusted Joe completely, Irene asked a lawyer how she could make sure Jackie was her sole heir. The solution was a contract or premarital agreement between Irene and Joe in which he waived his statutory inheritance rights as a widower to Irene's assets if she died before he did. Joe also consulted his own lawyer. Irene had to list her assets, giving a full and fair accounting of her financial condition. She and Joe signed the contract drafted and reviewed by their lawyers before they married. Irene also made a new will which clarified her intentions to leave her estate to Jackie—referring to the premarital agreement and her intention not to leave her assets to Joe.

One way to balance the rights of your new spouse and the expectations of your children is to write a premarital contract (with the help of a lawyer), spelling out the disposition of the assets you take into the marriage. Another is to leave property in a will by "life estate." This arrangement enables you to leave the long-held family home to your children but ensures that your spouse can go on living there after your death. The children cannot force a sale and claim their share before your surviving spouse dies.

If you and your new spouse buy property together, you may want to establish the title as tenants in common. This allows you to leave your share of the property to anyone you want.

What About the Children?

As a reflection of the nationwide scale of divorce and remarriage, thousands of Canadians are stepparents. Yet despite these numbers, stepparents do not have the same legal rights and responsibilities as biological parents. Even if the stepparent chooses to provide financial support or education, the courts generally consider the position of the natural parent to be primary.

HOW REMARRIAGE AFFECTS CPP AND OTHER BENEFITS

Any Social Security benefits you earn in your own right are yours whatever your marital status. But what happens to your spousal or survivor's benefits if you remarry?

1. Certain restrictions apply when you claim benefits from the Canada (Quebec) Pension Plan after your second spouse dies. One is the length of time you were married to your second spouse. A person cannot collect full survivorship benefits from two or more deceased spouses.

2. If you remarry, you must inform the Canada (Quebec) Pension Plan what name (your maiden name, or one of your married names) you want used for pension plan purposes. This is to ensure that payments as well as possible future benefits are registered correctly. It is not uncommon for people to lose a large part of their pension benefits because they were not correctly registered with the Pension Plan Office.

3. The Guaranteed Income Supplement and widowed spouse's allowance, payable under the Old Age Pension Security Act, may also be affected by remarriage. Contact your local old age pension security office (you will find the number in the Blue Pages of your telephone directory) for more information.

STEPPARENTS, STEPCHILDREN, AND THE LAW

The legal relationship between stepparent and stepchild is a tricky one. Legislation varies widely from province to province, but the law's basic position is that a child's biological parent takes precedence in legal matters over a stepparent, even if the latter is closer and more important to the child. Here are some examples of how the law can further muddy the complexities of stepparenting:

1. A stepparent cannot authorize basic medical treatment for a stepchild unless a biological parent gives specific permission. Experts recommend having on hand a notarized document in which the biological parent authorizes the stepparent to order medical treatment of the stepchild.

2. Generally, the law does not recognize a stepparent's right to visitation with a stepchild if the remarriage ends in divorce. Some judges, however, now recognize that a relationship may be close, and grant visitation rights to a stepparent if it is in the best interests of the child.

3. As a rule, stepchildren cannot inherit from a stepparent who dies without a will. If you want a stepchild to have some of your estate, it is vital that you make a will specifying that wish.

4. If you have company or private insurance, check out whether or not stepchildren are included as "family" when your coverage includes family coverage.

If you pay child support, your payments continue until your children reach the age of majority, unaffected by remarriage of either parent. You can seek a modification of the court order if a change of circumstance affects your ability to pay. But most courts will not allow a modification just because a noncustodial parent remarries. If you stop the child support without permission from the court, collection efforts can be taken against you. (See also "Divorce," page 135.)

STEPPARENTS AS CARETAKERS

Under most circumstances, a stepparent is not financially responsible for supporting stepchildren—the biological parents are. But the courts may require a new spouse to provide support under certain conditions: if the biological noncustodial parent refuses or is unable to pay, or if the child is at risk of becoming a public charge, for example. However, the courts are holding an increasing number of stepparents responsible for financial support of stepchildren in cases where the stepparent acted *in loco parentis,* this is, acted like a parent toward the child.

Child support may be your main concern if you want to begin a new family. But there are other matters you should consider. If you have minor children, you may want to rewrite your will after remarrying. If you were to die, it is unlikely that the courts would give a stepparent custody of your children. The biological parent is entitled to custody unless he is deemed unfit. If you designate your new spouse to have custody in your will, your preference is not controlling, but it could be taken into account if custody must be determined by a court. You can also name a stepparent as guardian of your child's financial affairs if you wish.

ADOPTING STEPCHILDREN

To strengthen the family bond and provide continuity should your spouse die, you might consider adopting your stepchildren if their other biological parent is no longer living. Adoption overcomes the legally weak position of stepparents: even if they choose to give financial support or in other ways participate in the raising of stepchildren, stepparents legally remain unable to assume a full parental role. Adoption gives the stepparent the same legal rights and financial responsibilities as a natural parent, whether or not the marriage lasts.

Because the courts are very reluctant to deprive a natural parent of his legal parenting rights, stepparent adoption is generally possible only if the noncustodial parent has died or has given written consent. However, if you decide to undertake the often difficult process of separating a child legally from his biological parent, you should by all means speak to a lawyer. Then

you can begin the process by serving the parent with a formal adoption request.

If the natural parent refuses to consent to the request, you then must be able to give reasons why his parental rights should be terminated, such as that he abandoned the child or is otherwise unfit. (See also "Parenting," page 112.) If you succeed in adopting a stepchild, you may suggest that the child maintain his birth-family name as a middle name, to minimize the inevitable feelings of divided loyalty.

If your marriage breaks up, you are highly unlikely to obtain custody of your stepchild unless you can give evidence that both natural parents are unfit. While visitation rights may be granted in a some cases, they are generally not given to stepparents. (See also "Stepparents, Stepchildren, and the Law," page 148.)

Premarital Agreements

No one enjoys preparing a premarital agreement. But it can be an important way to clarify ownership and define financial expectations for the future, especially for remarriages, when both partners are more likely to enter the union with assets and children. Nearly every province now enforces premarital or prenuptial agreements under certain conditions.

This increased enforcement of premarital agreements reflects the growing belief that couples who think about financial matters early on can minimize or avoid courtroom property disputes later. You may be among the many couples who reject the expense or the pragmatism of a written agreement that addresses the prospect of divorce. Yet a frank discussion about your finances can help build the foundation of a healthy relationship. It can also be important and useful if one partner should die unexpectedly.

MAKING IT STICK

If you do want such an agreement and want it enforceable, the key requirement is full disclosure of financial information by both partners. What property, stocks, cash, or other assets do you own? What debts do you have from credit cards or other loan accounts, child support, or alimony? How much is your income? By listing all assets and liabilities, you can clarify what ownership and interest existed before the marriage took place and avoid any suggestion that the agreement is based on false or misleading information.

You also should be aware of other reasons an agreement may be questioned. If, for example, the court determines that you

---

What About Marriage Contracts

Although all provinces and territories now have married women's property acts, or similar legislation, a marriage contract enacted during the marriage (or a prenuptial agreement entered into before the marriage) often ensures greater control over certain property rights should the marriage end through divorce or death of one of the spouses.

Not all provinces expressly recognize these domestic contracts. Even in British Columbia, Saskatchewan, Ontario, Quebec, the Maritime provinces and Yukon, which do, the legislation is not uniform. But courts in every province will usually respect such contracts unless some clauses are unfair or unconscionable, are not in the best interest of the children, put one party at risk of becoming a public charge, or a spouse's signature was obtained by fraud or duress.

In some provinces, marriage and prenuptial contracts must be registered with the courts to be effective. These contracts are particularly useful when one of the spouses is a partner in a business or professional practice. (See also "What Goes Into a Prenuptial Agreement," page 150.)

gave up your right to alimony in the agreement without understanding the law, the agreement can be deemed invalid. Some provinces may reject outright any agreement that waives all rights to alimony; such action is considered against public policy because it risks making the spouse a public charge.

The premarital agreement also can be denied if you agreed to receive one-tenth of your partner's property after his death without knowing that provincial inheritance laws generally provide a surviving spouse with one-third or one-half.

BUT IS IT FAIR?

Lastly, courts may evaluate the agreement on the grounds of fairness and reasonableness. Both parties need to have legal representation. Was the agreement entered into voluntarily and with full disclosure? Does it undermine the living standard of either party at the time of the marriage? Does the agreement create an incentive for divorce or separation? Does it strongly favor the spouse who has the most assets? Answers to such questions will weigh heavily in the court's evaluation.

What Goes Into a Prenuptial Agreement?

Some prenuptial agreements simply list the assets that each partner owns and will keep if the marriage ends and state that everything acquired during the marriage is shared equally. If your holdings and responsibilities are complex, you may need a more complicated agreement. Here are some questions you should be prepared to ask, or answer, when you meet with your lawyers:

• **Premarital assets.** What assets does each partner own before the wedding? What property do you want to maintain separately? What do you want to include as shared family assets?

• **House and car.** If you live as a couple in the house you now live in alone, will it become jointly owned? How about the car you now drive? How will you distribute any increased value of property you owned separately before your marriage? Will you split that 50-50 or keep it separate?

• **Life insurance and pension.** Who are the beneficiaries of your life insurance, pension, or other retirement benefits? Will they change, or do the current arrangements meet the terms of a settlement from a previous marriage that requires certain insurance be maintained for an ex-spouse or children? Should you consider buying another life insurance policy?

• **Joint accounts.** Will you have joint chequing and savings accounts? Do you want to have joint credit card accounts? Who will ultimately be responsible for the bills?

• **Debt.** Are you coming into the new marriage with old debt or other liabilities? Will your spouse be compensated if joint marital assets are used to pay off your preexisting debts?

• **Children.** Do you and your new spouse plan to have children? If so—and even if you do not plan it—how will that affect the terms of this agreement? Will you participate in the support of your new spouse's children from a previous marriage?

• **Divorce.** How will you divide jointly owned property or property acquired during the marriage if there is a divorce? If there is a divorce, will one partner pay spousal support to the other?

• **Death.** What percentage of your premarital assets will your spouse be entitled to if you die first? Will the percentage change with the length of the marriage? (For example, the percentage might rise with each additional year of the marriage, up to a certain ceiling.) How do you plan to change your will to reflect the changes your new marriage may bring to existing family relationships, particularly children?

ELDERCARE

Whether or not you are the primary caregiver of your aging parents or relatives, you need to know your rights and their rights—to ensure protection.

Planning for Eldercare

Illness, physical disability, and the other inevitable changes brought on by aging can make life for the elderly—and their adult children—both difficult and confusing. While your aging parents may be perfectly capable of taking care of themselves and making decisions at the moment, you as their child can raise issues and express concerns in order to help them make their later years more comfortable.

Begin by asking your parents if they have begun to make plans in case of incapacity or death. Find out the names of their lawyer, insurance agent, and banker and the location of any important documents such as title deeds, stock certificates, insurance policies, their chequebook, and other financial information. Encourage them to make a list or write a letter detailing all of their assets and monthly income. Ask if they have a will, where it is kept, and the executor's name, and find out if they have already made arrangements regarding funerals. Although you may be reluctant to bring up such issues, remember that having this information will only make things easier for both you and your parents.

Protecting Assets

Whether your parents are rich or poor, you should encourage them to make a properly executed will. If they die without a will, their assets will be distributed according to the laws of the province they live in. These decisions may or may not be consistent with their wishes.

If their estate is relatively small, they may be able to write a will on their own, using a do-it-yourself kit available at many book and stationary stores. Make sure all laws for your province are followed. If you are unsure of anything, or if large sums of money and property are involved, contact a lawyer. If the will is being made with a do-it-yourself form, neither of the two witnesses required may benefit from the will, nor may they be married to a beneficiary. Thus as a son, neither you, your spouse nor your adult children should sign as witnesses.

Easing Stress With a Letter of Instruction

If a parent dies or gets seriously ill, loose ends may have to be taken care of quickly. A letter of instruction from the parent will make those chores easier. Here is what such a letter might include:

✔ *People.* A list of the names, addresses, and telephone numbers of doctors, family members, neighbors, lawyers, financial advisers, insurance agents, stockbrokers, and bankers.

✔ *Documents.* The location of birth, marriage, and divorce certificates; a will; powers of attorney; military discharge papers; a deceased spouse's death certificate—and, if there is one, the safe-deposit box.

✔ *Financial data.* Records of stocks, bonds, funds, and chequing, savings, and other bank accounts.

✔ *Health information.* The location of insurance policies.

✔ *Household documents.* Mortgage information, the title deed, and the homeowners insurance policy. The location of car registration and insurance information, as well as the keys to the car.

123

THREE TYPES OF POWER OF ATTORNEY

If you are going to need to handle real estate, banking, insurance, health care, or transactions on behalf of your parent, you need a power of attorney. Consider these three types, but keep in mind that none of these is a substitute for a properly drawn up will.

1. Power of attorney. With this document, one person (the principal) gives another (the attorney-in-fact) authority to act on his behalf. An attorney-in-fact can make almost any type of decision and can sign legal documents for the principal. This power of attorney can be canceled anytime by the principal, and is valid only so long as the principal is alive.

2. Durable power of attorney. Generally, a power of attorney expires automatically if the principal becomes mentally or otherwise incompetent. A durable power of attorney remains in effect if the principal becomes incapacitated. It ends only when the principal dies or becomes legally competent again and revokes it.

3. Springing power of attorney. This is designed for a principal who wants to retain control until he becomes incompetent or otherwise unable to make decisions. It takes effect only when a specified event—mental incompetence, for example—occurs. A springing power of attorney can be general or for something specific, such as health care, so that the attorney-in-fact can make health-care decisions if the principal cannot.

THE ADVANTAGES OF A LIVING TRUST

Another way for your parents to maintain control over their financial affairs while still keeping the future in mind is to establish a "living trust." A living trust allows them to transfer the legal title of their property to a trustee, who manages the property on their behalf. When they die, their assets belong to the trust and are not subject to probate. If your parents wish, they can name themselves as trustees and name you as a cotrustee. If the trust is revocable, your parents may be able to cancel or amend it at any time.

Living trusts are complicated and should not be created without serious consideration and the advice of a lawyer and financial adviser. Such trusts mainly benefit people who have large estates and wish to minimize probate costs and delays. Also, a living trust does not eliminate the need for a will.

PREPARING FOR POSSIBLE INCOMPETENCE

Protecting the distribution of assets is essential but may not be enough. If your parent becomes incompetent and neither you nor he has made advance preparation for such a situation, you may have to go to court to get conservatorship or guardianship to take control of his affairs. (See also "Declaring a Parent Incompetent," page 153.) To avoid such problems, many people establish some form of power of attorney to maintain control over the way their affairs are handled—and by whom—should they become physically or mentally incapacitated. (See "Three Types of Power of Attorney," at left.)

To establish a power of attorney or health-care proxy, your parent must be legally capable of understanding the power that he or she is turning over. The law varies in each province as to whether witnesses or a notary is required to make a power of attorney or health-care proxy legal. The participation of witnesses, as well as a lawyer's counsel, can help ensure the validity of the document.

Your parents may also want to inform banks, insurance companies, investment firms, doctors, and other institutions that a designated attorney-in-fact will be dealing with their affairs. Some institutions, such as the bank, may ask your parents to sign a form, including a clause holding the bank blameless for any act performed at the request of the attorney-in-fact if the power of attorney is later revoked. Your parents can revoke or change the power of attorney or health-care proxy at any time.

LIVING WILLS

Even if your parents are reluctant to give up control of their assets or decision-making power, they may be open to creating a living will. A living will is a document that informs family, friends, and doctors of a person's wishes concerning health

care in the event that he or she become incapacitated by serious illness. For example, a living will might state that a person does not want to be kept alive by artificial means if she is suffering from a terminal condition and death is imminent. Unlike a health-care proxy or power of attorney for health care, a living will specifically states a person's wishes instead of naming a person to carry them out.

Although statutes vary from province to province, most explicitly provide civil and criminal immunity for physicians who follow a valid living will's directions. Moreover, these laws establish that a decision not to prolong life does not constitute suicide and, therefore, insurance is not affected. To be valid, the document must be signed and witnessed. All provinces allow a person who has made a living will to revoke it. (See also YOUR HEALTH CARE, pages 221–222.)

Financing Eldercare

For millions of elderly Canadians, who spent their lives working for small companies and received modest incomes, the Old Age Social Security Pension and its Surviving Spouses and Guaranteed Income Supplement (GIS) provide the backbone of their retirement plan. The GIS is also available to Old Age Security pensioners who have little other income. Unlike the old age pension, where payments continue automatically year after year, the GIS must be applied for annually. A spouse's allowance may also be available from the age of 60 to 64, provided the other spouse is 65 years of age and already collecting the old age pension. This benefit must also be applied for annually.

Contributors to the Canada (Quebec) Pension Plan (CPP) also receive monthly benefits on retirement (or if disabled), and spouses of deceased contributors may qualify for survivor benefits. Payments ordinarily begin at 65 years—at the time of writing, the amount payable is in the order of $700 per month, indexed quarterly—and continue until death. However, if the contributor so wishes, benefits may start as early as 60 years or as late as 70. Those who opt for payments from age 60 receive only 70 percent of the amount payable at age 65, whereas those who postpone payments until they are 70 years old get 130 percent of the amount payable at 65.

There has been much talk lately of both increasing the age at which the old age pension is payable, and decreasing the amount of benefits. Some economists doubt that the old age pension as we now know it will survive much longer, and say it would be unwise for those in their thirties or forties to count on an old age pension in their future retirement plans.

Declaring a Parent Incompetent

One of the hardest things an adult child may have to do is to declare her parent incompetent. It may happen that you have no choice, however, and you should know the proper steps to take.

Courts have the power to appoint one or several persons to take over responsibility for your parent's care. This power, known as "parens patriae," or parentage of the state, allows the government to protect people who cannot take care of themselves by appointing a guardian or conservator, even against the allegedly incompetent person's wishes.

Before the court can appoint a guardian or a conservator, however, a hearing must be held to prove that the person has a specific disabling condition and that as a result he cannot take care of his personal or financial affairs.

An allegedly incompetent person has the right to challenge allegations against him. Doctors, friends, business associates, relatives, and others may testify at the hearing. By and large, any concerned person can petition the court to hold such a hearing.

If you decide to take such measures on behalf of an older relative, hire a lawyer to guide you through the legal labyrinth.

Paying for Nursing-Home Care

Nursing homes costs vary widely depending on whether the institution is government subsidized, totally private but not for profit, or if it is an upscale private-for-profit home. Some nonprofit and government-subsidized or government-run nursing homes accept the amount you receive from your Canada Pension Plan together with your old age pension and Guaranteed Income Supplement, if your are eligible for the latter, as full payment. Usually residents are allowed to keep a small amount of their pension benefits for personal use.

If you are planning to move to any home of this kind, or if you are thinking about placing one of your parents there, here are some things you should investigate:

- The conditions of the building and the grounds. Is there a sprinkler system in place?
- The attitude of the staff. Are they pleasant and friendly? Do they respect the resident's privacy, including her right to unopened mail and private telephone communication?
- Is there a lounge for socializing and receiving guests?
- Are there planned activities, such as arts and crafts, and movies, for the residents? Are there arrangements for residents to visit parks, zoos, and special community events?
- Do the other residents appear comfortable and sociable?
- Is the room size satisfactory? Do residents have private rooms or must they share accommodations? Do they have TVs, radios, hot plates, and air conditioning in their living quarters? If not can residents buy these things and have them installed in their rooms?
- Is storage place available as well as a safe-deposit box for valuable or personal papers?
- Is light cooking, making toast and coffee, for example, allowed in the resident's room?
- Do residents have the right to get up and go to sleep when they desire?
- Is the food adequate, nutritious, and tasty?
- Are there refrigerators available for residents to keep their own perishables, such as milk or cold-cuts?
- Are menus posted? Is there a choice of food, and is there more than one sitting for a meal? Is room service available?
- In the case of residents who must take prescribed medicines, are medications monitored?
- Who is on duty at night, and what services can the night staff provide?
- Are religious services held in the facility?

Choosing Long-Term Care Insurance

It is extremely rare for a private insurer to provide care in a nursing home for long-term patients, but if you find a company that will insure these needs it will certainly be very expensive. Some questions to be clarified in such an insurance contract are:

✔ *Is the policy renewable for life?* Some policies expire at a certain age, possibly before the policyholder can even benefit from them.

✔ *What kinds of care does the policy cover?* It may cover only skilled care and not intermediate, or custodial care, such as rehabilitation centers and nursing homes.

✔ *What conditions are covered?* Some policies will not cover Alzheimer's disease, senility, and similar conditions.

✔ *Where will I be covered?* Some policies will only provide for care at home, until the patient reaches a certain age, or only provide for part of the costs of a nursing home that has been licensed by the province.

✔ *What is the daily benefit rate?* Find out if it compares to the actual charges where you live to determine if coverage is cost-effective. Find out if there is a clause that increases benefits with inflation.

Home Care for the Elderly

Whether your parents live in their own home or in yours, they may at some point require full-time care. While nursing homes can provide a viable option, a network of home health-care providers for the elderly—volunteer, nonprofit, and for-profit—has now appeared, offering in-home alternatives. The result: greater independence for the elderly, less guilt for family members, and less expense for all.

One relatively recent development is the emergence of eldercare specialists, also called "geriatric care managers." Usually nurses or social workers by training, they act as consultants and can help develop a comprehensive plan for care, based on an elderly person's needs, finances, and insurance coverage. Knowledgeable about in-home and community services available, they can help organize care, evaluate the quality and costs, and then monitor the services. These managers can help ease

A Senior's Guide to Planning Ahead

Although you trust your children to carry out your wishes after you die or if you become incompetent, it is up to you to make sure they handle your affairs the way you want them to. Here is a brief review of the elements you need to keep track of to make your survivors' job easier:

• **Will.** The need for a will may seem obvious, but many people neglect to write one. Speak to a lawyer and decide how you want your assets divided after you are gone. It is far better to have a will that you may change later than not to have one at all. Don't keep a will in a safe-deposit box that will be hard to open after your death.

• **Power of attorney.** You need not give up immediate power over your assets in order to create a power of attorney. A "springing" power of attorney allows you to name someone at will to act on your behalf after you become incapable of making your own decisions. You can appoint a springing power of attorney for a specific function, such as health-care decisions. A durable power of attorney allows you to choose someone to act on your behalf even after you become unable to do so on your own. You can change the attorney or the terms of a power of attorney at any time.

• **Living trust.** If you have a large estate, you may want to set up a trust while you are still alive. This way you can determine how your property and money will be managed after your death, giving written instructions. You can name yourself the trustee, naming a successor who will take over only after your death or disability.

• **Health-care proxy.** This document, now recognized by statute in Ontario, Manitoba, and Quebec, is also usually recognized by most other provinces. Do-it-yourself kits are available in stationers and department stores. They allow you to designate someone to have the legal authority to make decisions regarding your health-care treatment. The proxy can be specific, detailing exact treatments, or it can give broad decision-making power and can be revoked or changed at any time.

• **Living will.** This document sets out your preferences for medical care in the event of a terminal illness. You can specify exactly how far you want physicians to go in providing care when death is imminent.

• **Funeral arrangements.** You can buy a plot, pay for funeral arrangements, and even set up a trust payable to a specific funeral home after your death. (See also "Death in the Family," page 162.) If you have special desires about your funeral arrangements, write a letter of instruction.

the emotional strain, particularly if the older person lives at a distance from her family, but they can be expensive. Contact your province's health ministry or department on aging, or your local senior citizen center for information on finding an elder-care specialist in your area.

MAKING YOUR OWN PLAN

You and your elderly parent can organize a plan for services on your own, using the guidance of local or national referral agencies and researching health-care providers in your area. You may be able to hire individuals to assist you and your parent, or you can seek out a home-care agency. (See also "Services for the Elderly," page 157.) Services usually include nursing care; physical, speech, or occupational therapy; personal assistance; meal preparation; and even companionship. Home-care agencies are listed in the Yellow Pages, and your local department on aging may be able to refer you to an agency in your area that will meet your particular needs.

Although you may wish to hire the person who takes care of your parent, her source of financing (such as insurance) may require you to use a particular kind of agency. Some nonprofit agencies will waive their fees if you cannot afford to pay for their services, whereas most for-profit private agencies ask for payment, which is often covered by private insurance policies.

FINDING A LICENSED AGENCY

Contact the provincial or city department of health or your local office of consumer affairs to find out whether the home-care agency you have in mind is licensed, certified, accredited, or bonded? Your local Better Business Bureau will know if there have been any complaints logged against the agency.

Nearly every province requires licensing for agencies that provide more than minimal personal-care services (such as bathing and grooming). Exceptions include some agencies that provide only single services or highly specialized ones.

Bonded agencies, which must put aside money in case of lawsuits, provide a further level of security should your parent be mistreated or should another problem arise. But remember: determining an agency's legal status is no substitute for a personal check of its references, range of services, and personnel.

Foster-home care is another option for someone who can no longer live alone. Some provinces offer foster-care programs in which families or individuals are paid to take in elderly adults, and provide them with a safe and comfortable home, meals, a bed, and companionship. Since costs average well below the cost of nursing-home care, such an arrangement may turn out to be just the solution you have been looking for.

WHEN YOU CONTRIBUTE TO A PARENT'S CARE

You may be one of the growing number of Canadian families providing financial support to a parent. If so, you may be eligible for a dependency deduction when filing your federal income-tax return. Five criteria must be met:

1. Parent's income. Your parent's annual income (excluding welfare benefits and tax-exempt Social Security benefits) cannot be more than a specified amount set annually by Revenue Canada.

2. Provide support. You must be paying the substantial part of your parent's support. This includes housing, utilities, food, clothing, medical care, and transportation.

3. Resident status. Your parent must be either a citizen or permanent resident of Canada.

4. Marital facts. Your parent must file a tax return. If you are supporting both parents, each must file a separate tax return.

5. Blood ties. Your dependent must be your parent or another close relative. The parent or relative does not, however, have to be living with you for you to claim a deduction.

HELPING FROM A DISTANCE

Your mother may no longer be able to live on her own, but she refuses to leave her familiar home. If you live far away, how can you help her from where you are?

Get information. Ask your provincial seniors' directorate or office for senior citizens' affairs, offices usually administered by provincial health or social affairs ministries, what in-home and community services are available for your parent.

Recruit helpers. List the phone numbers of people who are important to your mother and to her business affairs—friends, neighbors, doctors, lawyer, banker, and insurance agent. They can advise you, help you make decisions, or make a home visit in an emergency.

Arrange your mother's finances. Have all Old Age Pension and Canada Pension Plan cheques deposited directly into your mother's chequing account. If possible, have companies deduct their monthly charges from her account, so that services such as telephone, heating, and hydro will never be interrupted due to unpaid bills.

Services for the Elderly

Many programs are available to provide support for elderly adults and to connect them to their local communities, whether they are housebound or out and about. Call your local department on aging and ask about the following:

• **Senior centers.** At one time senior centers primarily provided recreational and social activities, but many now offer a wide range of information and referral services to help older people manage their affairs. Centers may offer meals, educational programs, health services, tax-return advice, as well as social and recreational activities. Most are free or charge only nominal fees

• **Adult day care.** These centers often provide physical therapy, nursing care, meals, and counseling, in addition to other services generally found at senior centers. Services, quality, and fees vary widely. Many of the adult day-care or seniors centers are supported by local charities and private donations so fees for services such as art and crafts, lectures, movies, or outings to local places of interest are usually nominal at most.

• **Local agencies for the aging.** This national system of agencies is funded by federal, provincial, and local governments as well as private contributions. Agencies provide services to those over 60, including adult day care, legal advice, tax advice, job training, meal delivery, referrals, health-insurance information and counseling, protection services, and much more. Contact your provincial department on aging to find out what is available in your area. Many services are free or offered at low cost.

• **Companionship and reassurance.** Local religious and social service groups provide volunteers to make regular visits to the homes of older adults, to help with chores or just to sit and talk. Many organizations also provide daily checkup telephone calls to make sure the person is safe.

• **Meals on wheels.** This delivery service provides hot meals to housebound people either free or for a small fee. Originally a volunteer program, the service is now supported by a combination of private, community, and government funding.

• **Transportation services.** Many communities have some kind of transportation available for the elderly, often sponsored by churches or other social service groups, using volunteers' private cars, vans, or small buses. The services also may have special buses or vans with ramps for wheelchairs and walkers. Many communities provide discounts on public transportation.

FAMILY PETS

Animals are often beloved members of a family, but they may not be so beloved by everyone else. Knowing the law will help keep you and your pets out of trouble.

Taking Legal Care of Your Pet

As every parent tells his child, owning a pet means taking responsibility for its care. It also means recognizing your legal obligations. These may include getting licenses and vaccinations, abiding by local ordinances, and making sure that your pet does not cause trouble in the neighborhood.

Almost every municipality requires dog (and sometimes cat) owners to obtain a license for their pet and make sure that the animal wears it at all times. Without a license it is often difficult to locate the owner of a lost animal, so your straying pet could be adopted by someone else or, worse, be put to sleep at the local animal pound.

Licenses also serve the public health because it is a way that owners must show proof they have had their pets vaccinated for rabies. Check your telephone directory for the city or county licensing office, or call your city hall to find out the regulations in your area. Usually you must reregister your pet annually and when you move to a different locale.

You may be subject to a number of other pet laws in addition to licenses and vaccinations, depending on where you live. Some jurisdictions set restrictions on the number of dogs or cats you can keep in your house or apartment, and in an effort to minimize pet problems outdoors, many cities have leash laws and "pooper-scooper" statutes. In addition to municipal laws, many apartment buildings and homeowners' associations have their own strict rules about pets.

When the Vet Treats Your Pet

Like the family doctor, your pet's veterinarian should be a trusted health adviser, and you are entitled to expect quality care from her. Veterinarians must have received a doctor of veterinary medicine (DVM) degree, passed the province's written test for veterinary medicine, and secured a proper provincial license to treat animals.

As part of their duties, vets are required to prevent or relieve the suffering of animals, to offer proper medical attention to all animals, and to treat animal medical emergencies as well as they are able.

PROBLEMS WITH THE VET

Laws in several provinces permit a veterinarian to keep your pet as collateral until outstanding bills have been paid. But veterinarians are not liable for keeping animals indefinitely if owners fail to pick them up and pay for them. Many provinces have guidelines on how many days vets must keep a pet before seeking a new owner or having the pet sent to the local animal pound. So if you have a dispute with a vet over a bill, your best option is to pay it first and file a suit in small claims court later.

If you have a serious complaint about a vet, you can notify the provincial veterinarian licensing board. Whether or not the matter is investigated, your complaint will be recorded and may help others avoid problems. If your pet was injured or died under veterinary care, and you believe your veterinarian acted incompetently, you may have a legal claim.

The Negligent Veterinarian

PROBLEM
Tina and Russ Bloom's dog, Scout, was hit by a slow-moving car. Although Scout did not seem to have any injuries, he was yelping continuously and so Russ and Tina rushed him to the nearest veterinarian. After examining the dog, the vet told Russ and Tina that Scout had suffered no more than a few bruises. The Blooms paid $50 and went home. Later that night when Scout still had not stopped whining, Russ and Tina took him to another vet, who found that the dog was bleeding internally and required surgery. Sadly, Scout died before the operation began.

ACTION
Russ and Tina were crushed by their dog's death, and upset that a timely diagnosis might have saved him. They talked to a third veterinarian, who agreed to testify in court that he believed that a veterinarian of ordinary competence should have recognized that Scout was bleeding internally and that the first vet made a negligent diagnosis. The veterinarian also said that, had surgery been performed in a timely manner, Scout probably would have lived. Russ and Tina wrote a letter to the first veterinarian, explaining the malpractice case they were building and asked for a settlement for the cost of their dog as well as for both veterinarians' bills. The vet agreed and paid them $350. Tina then called the veterinarian licensing board in her province to report the malpractice.

You can try to settle your differences directly with the vet, or you may have to turn to a mediator or file suit for reimbursement of costs incurred, for negligence, or for malpractice. Usually, however, the legal costs of such a case may exceed what you can reasonably expect to recover, unless you plead the case yourself in small claims court.

123...
WHEN A PET IS BEING MISTREATED

The Criminal Code, as well as many provincial laws (usually legislation dealing with agriculture), makes it illegal to mistreat animals. Some laws are vague, restricting "needlessly cruel" or "inhumane" treatment, while others are more specific—for example, making it illegal to use animals as lures on a dog racetrack. Your local animal-control office will know the exact laws in your case. In general, you can expect the following:

1. You are responsible for taking care of your pet. You must make sure your animal receives adequate food, water, exercise, and shelter, and does not suffer from abandonment or unnecessarily cruel confinement. Cruelty to animals can be reported to the local police.

2. If an animal is tortured or used to provoke a fight with other animals, criminal charges, fines, and imprisonment may result. Pets that are mistreated can be taken from their owners.

3. To determine negligence, evidence that actions were intentionally cruel is not required. Usually it is sufficient to prove that a person knowingly neglected an animal.

4. Acts of malicious cruelty, which are presumed to be intentional, are treated the most severely.

Keeping Wild or Exotic Pets

You might not consider your pet ferret or your baby boa constrictor a threat to anyone, but most municipalities prohibit what they call "dangerous animals," such as wolves, alligators, and poisonous snakes. Some cities allow only dogs, cats, certain birds, rabbits, hamsters, gerbils, and mice to be kept as pets and may even prohibit certain breeds of dog, such as rottweilers, pit bulls, or wolf hybrids, without a special permit.

Generally, the law recognizes two categories of animals: wild animals that cannot be tamed, such as lions, tigers, bears, wolves, snakes, and alligators; and domestic animals that may be tamed by humans or are naturally docile, such as dogs and cats, but also including horses, chickens, goats, and rabbits.

Under the law, wild and domestic animals are subject to different regulations. Owners of wild or exotic animals are subject to a higher duty of care to protect others from harm from their animals. In most areas, particularly urban ones, you need a special permit to keep a wild animal and are responsible for any injuries or damage it causes, whether or not the animal is provoked.

If your domestic-animal pet bites someone, you may or may not be responsible, depending upon the animal's history and your knowledge of its behavior. If your golden retriever, for example, has been a kind, placid dog but suddenly nips a child who pulled its tail, you may not be liable for its actions. On the other hand, if your pit bull jumps the back fence and attacks a toddler, chances are you will be held accountable.

Although farm animals such as horses, cows, sheep, and goats are considered domestic, local zoning laws often prohibit keeping them in residential neighborhoods or, if they are allowed, limit their numbers.

Pet Misdeeds and the Law

It is up to you to see that your pet does not cause injury or damage property. If your rabbit escapes from its hutch and ruins your neighbor's rosebushes, or if your dachshund strays next door and bites your neighbor's ankle, you will be responsible for paying for the damages. Most provinces have strict liability laws and "dog bite" statutes, which make an owner financially responsible for any injury or damage caused by his pet, unless provocation can be proven.

If your pet was provoked, had no history of biting or attacking, or if someone came onto your property despite Beware-

---

Your Dog and Your Neighbor's Rights

Your dog Wellington wanders off your property and down the street, attracted by a little boy playing in his front yard. The child's father gets nervous when he sees your big dog approaching his child. If Wellington stops across the street and merely watches the boy, your neighbor has no right to harm the dog. If your dog barks and growls, but in no way threatens attack, your neighbor has no right to harm the dog either.

However, if Wellington growls at the child, lunges, and bares his teeth in attack, your neighbor can take appropriate action to stop the animal (such as causing it physical harm) in order to protect the child. In extreme circumstances, a person may be justified in killing a known vicious or dangerous animal that is on the attack. In such cases, you would be unlikely to win a suit for injury to your pet.

On the other hand, your neighbor cannot harm your pet for digging in his yard or destroying his property. You may be financially responsible for your pet's actions, but if your neighbor harms your pet when the animal presents no danger of injuring a person, you may be able to recover the costs of veterinary bills or compensation for damages.

of-Dog warning signs, you would probably not be at fault, but provincial laws vary. When someone is injured by another person's pet, the dispute is often settled out of court by the victim and the pet owner. Still, if you are the injured party, you should immediately obtain the name and telephone number of the pet owner and find out if the animal has had its rabies shots. You should also make note of any witnesses. If you get medical attention, save copies of bills and records related to treatment.

Some homeowners insurance policies cover injury or damages caused by pets. If you have been attacked by someone's pet and the owner has no such insurance coverage, or you and he cannot agree to a settlement, you may seek resolution through mediation, arbitration, or small claims court. If the damages you are seeking exceed the small claims limit because your injury is severe, contact a lawyer for advice. You should also report the incident to the local animal control board. If there have been any previously reported cases involving the same animal, or if it has already been determined to be "vicious," the owner may face fines or have to put it to sleep.

The greatness of a nation and its moral progress can be judged by the way its animals are treated.

MAHATMA GANDHI

A Roundup of Dog Laws

Every province and municipality has laws or ordinances dealing with dogs as pets. These rules set limits on owners and protect the public's health, safety, and property—in other words, they define the dog's place in human society. Here is a distillation of the laws:

• **Dog-bite statutes.** Laws in some provinces hold owners liable for any injury caused by their dogs. They are called dog-bite statutes but usually cover any injuries caused by canine misbehavior.

• **Pooper-scooper statutes.** These laws require that the owner immediately remove and properly discard any excrement his dog deposits in any public or private place other than his own property. These laws, essential in large crowded cities such as Toronto, are also in place in other centers.

• **Leash laws.** These regulations require owners to keep their dogs on leashes or face a fine. Dogs need not be leashed on their owner's property, and some cities have set aside certain parks or fields on which dogs can be unleashed.

• **Guide dogs.** Guide dogs for the blind or other specially trained dogs that provide assistance to the disabled are typically exempted from the restrictions placed on other dogs. Such animals have access to public places and private workplaces, the right to travel on public transportation, are exempt from pooper-scooper statutes, and may live in rental housing that forbids pets. Most municipalities will provide an identification tag and license for these dogs without charge.

• **Dog fighting.** Provoking a dog to fight is prohibited by the Criminal Code. Using an animal for organized dog fighting, or even training it to fight, is a crime, punishable by large fines and imprisonment.

• **Vicious dogs.** Many communities have laws restricting dogs that are deemed dangerous or potentially so. In recent years, for instance, many communities have singled out pit bulls for their viciousness and banned them outright. Laws regarding dangerous dogs usually require someone who has been injured or threatened to file a formal complaint. A judge can then decide whether the dog is vicious and needs to be constrained. In an extreme case the judge can rule that the dog be removed or put to sleep.

• **Barking dogs.** A dog does not have to be dangerous to be a nuisance. If a neighbor complains about your pet's barking, you can be forced by law to pay a fine, or be subjected to a civil claim by a neighbor, or you may have to get rid of the dog.

DEATH IN THE FAMILY

No family is ever fully prepared emotionally for death, but you can lessen the stress by knowing what tasks have to be done and how to do them.

⟨123⟩

WHAT TO DO RIGHT AWAY

When someone dies, members of the family need to take certain actions right away:

1. Find, and sign, any documents relating to the wishes of the deceased regarding the disposal of his body, including the donation of his organs or tissue or the body itself.

2. Get the death certificate from the doctor or medical facility where he died.

3. If the deceased belonged to a burial or memorial society, notify the society.

4. Pick a funeral home and make arrangements to transfer the body.

5. Buy a burial plot if the deceased had not already made arrangements for one.

6. Contact a clergy member who can provide spiritual support and assist in decisions about a funeral.

7. Make final arrangements for the funeral and burial or for cremation.

8. Place an obituary notice in the local newspapers.

9. Notify relatives and friends of the place, date, and time of the funeral.

When a Family Member Dies

At a time of great emotional and psychological stress, family members are called upon to make a number of difficult decisions and arrangements. The most immediate decisions concern the funeral and disposition of the body of the loved one; later, survivors may have to take steps to claim benefits to which they are entitled.

In every province, surviving spouses are granted the authority to make these decisions unless they are incompetent or refuse to accept the legal and financial responsibility. If that happens or if there is no living spouse, provinces typically rely on kinship or bloodlines to determine the right of control. This begins with children, then parents, siblings, and other relatives. When the next in line is a minor, the authority will be passed on to the next relationship.

DECISIONS ABOUT THE REMAINS

The deceased may already have established an executor for his estate with instructions about how to handle the costs of his funeral and burial. Even in such instances, the spouse generally retains control over the disposition of the body—that is, she can decide where the burial should be, whether to have a funeral, and where. (If the dead person was indigent, and if no one takes responsibility for the burial or cremation, city or county governments must deal with the remains.)

When a person dies, his spouse or other close family member in effect inherits and is responsible for the body. The survivor then has the right to consent to an autopsy, which involves an examination of the body to help learn the cause and time of death, or to withhold consent for religious or other reasons. Even if the survivor refuses consent, the coroner or medical examiner may order an autopsy in certain circumstances, especially cases of suspected wrongful death.

AUTHORIZING ORGAN DONATIONS

An individual can agree that when he dies his tissue or organs will be donated to be used for transplants, or he can give his body for medical research. Under the Federal Uniform Human Tissues Act, such a donation is legally binding on the survivors if the individual signed a Donor Card. However, such donations are unlikely to be accepted by medical professionals if the surviving kin does not approve of the deceased person's wishes. (See also YOUR HEALTH CARE, page 224.)

APPROVAL FOR ORGAN TRANSPLANTS

If, on the other hand, the surviving relative wants to donate the organs for transplants or research, she can authorize removal. Assuming that the organs are medically acceptable and there is appropriate personnel to perform the operation, they will be removed and then the body will be returned to the place indicated for final disposition. This can be done without delaying the funeral or disfiguring the body.

The deceased person may have specified a final resting place before death. The legally responsible kin must then decide whether or not to carry out the deceased's expressed desires. If these were unreasonable or wasteful, as might be the case if the deceased wished to be buried with his favorite horse, the spouse or next of kin could disregard this wish. In some cases, the deceased person may have already arranged and paid for the funeral, but the decision of how and when to bury, cremate, or entomb rests with the surviving kin, as long as they comply with provincial law.

Arranging the Funeral

Disposition of the body is only one of many decisions grieving survivors will be called upon to make. Among the others are: Where will the funeral be held? Who will conduct the service? Will there be an open casket? What clothes should the deceased wear? Will he be embalmed? Who will carry the casket? Will transportation have to be provided? Who will arrange for the obituary notice? Who will pay for all of this?

You may decide to purchase a complete funeral package from a funeral home. This typically includes transfer of the body to the home; embalming, restoration, and dressing of the body; the cost of a coffin; the use of a hearse and limousine; staff services; and the use of funeral-home facilities. Other services include providing pallbearers, ordering flowers, and providing a guest register.

A funeral home may also organize the service, take care of the burial permit, obtain copies of the death certificate, and place the obituary in the newspaper. Music, flowers, a clergyman's honorarium, and additional limousines are extra. So are burial costs, including the opening and closing of the grave and, in some cases, the purchase of a cemetery plot. All told,

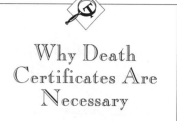

Why Death Certificates Are Necessary

When somebody dies, every province requires that a death certificate be issued, stating the time, place, and cause of death. This is filled out by the attending physician, a medical examiner, or a coroner, and provides legal proof of the death.

If the death was from natural causes, as most deaths are, a certificate should be filed within a few days. If the cause of death is unknown or suspicious, an autopsy may be performed before the death certificate is issued.

If you are the surviving relative taking care of such matters, you should obtain several certified copies of the document. If you need additional copies later, they will be available at your provincial or local health department or vital statistics registry.

With the certificate, you can file for probate of the deceased person's will and seek any government benefits, life insurance, and pension benefits to which you are entitled. You also will need a certified copy of the death certificate to gain access to a safe-deposit box.

Make sure the death certificate states the exact cause of death, which may affect survivors' benefits and, in cases such as suicide, insurance.

funeral costs add up. The average exceeds $3,500, but even an unelaborate funeral can cost many thousands more. The price of the coffin alone can range from $1,000 to more than $4,000.

Although funeral homes are granted authority by the province to embalm bodies and conduct funerals, as well as to perform burials, cremations, and entombments, no one is required to use their services. Some provinces have mortuary companies that perform only burials and cremations at minimum cost, but all provinces have laws to ensure that all burials or cremations, whoever performs them, will be carried out in a way that is consistent with local health and safety standards. Call your Department of Health for more information.

PROTECTING THE VULNERABLE

Occasionally, unscrupulous funeral operators will take advantage of the vulnerability of the survivors when someone dies. By pressuring them into using unwanted or unnecessary services, raising prices, or billing for goods not provided, these crooks add to the survivors' distress, inflate the costs—and reflect badly on all funeral homes.

If you were induced into paying much more for a funeral than you wanted to, as a result of the seller exploiting your inexperience and state of mental stress, the contract may be reduced or even set aside by the courts, acting on various consumer protection laws.

Planning Your Own Funeral

You may decide to ease the financial and emotional pressures on your family by planning and paying for your funeral in advance. One way to do this is join a memorial or burial society. Such societies do not sell goods or services themselves, but for a small, one-time fee they will organize agreements based on your wishes with low-cost funeral providers who will take care of things when you die.

Pre-need funeral plans are another method for protecting your survivors from hard-sell tactics at the time of death. Generally such plans have two components: an agreement for specific funeral goods and services, and a prepayment method.

There are various ways to prepay your funeral. Make your arrangements carefully to reduce the risks of fraud or other problems. In almost all cases, provincial laws, as well as funeral director associations, require that all funeral prepayments are placed in a trust account. This money is returned to the payer if he decides to move to another city or otherwise changes his mind. In some cases, a certain penalty can be charged by the funeral home.

Finding the Right Cemetery Plot

Although cemeteries vary widely as to quality, price, and care, all are regulated and supervised by a local or provincial government agency. Before buying a cemetery plot, consider these points:

✔ *Who owns the cemetery?* Cemeteries can be owned by religious groups, fraternal or charitable organizations, profit-making companies, or public agencies that get tax money. The choice is yours, provided you qualify. A Catholic wife might not be allowed to bury her Jewish husband in a Catholic cemetery.

✔ *Second thoughts.* You may change your mind later. Be sure that you can resell the plot. Find out whether the cemetery will buy it back and for what price.

✔ *Size.* You may buy a plot for yourself, for you and your spouse, or for your whole family. Some cemeteries permit one casket to be buried above another, which uses less space and costs less.

✔ *Maintenance.* Visit the cemetery before you buy to see whether the grounds are well maintained. The cemetery may require you to pay a one-time fee for perpetual care. Or you may have to pay an annual upkeep fee. If so, make sure that your survivors can afford the fee, or make arrangements for the annual payments.

One way to avoid problems is to open a regular interest-earning savings account at your local bank with money to cover the costs of the funeral, earmarked as payable to the funeral home upon your death. Or you might open a joint savings account with a family member and grant that relative the right of survivorship to pay for the funeral. This joint tenant will not be obliged to use the funds for the funeral, so make sure he knows what the funds are for and can be trusted.

Insurance policies are a popular way of prepaying one's funeral. You sign the agreement, buy enough life insurance to cover costs of the funeral of your choice, and designate the funeral home as the beneficiary. In some cases, you may designate the money to an independent agency or a special trust that is responsible for paying the funeral home.

ANTICIPATE FUTURE PROBLEMS

You should be careful to ensure that whatever prepayment mechanism you choose is inflation-adjusted or otherwise rises in value. Otherwise it may fall short of funeral costs at the time of your death. This is particularly true if you organize your pre-need plan while you are relatively young and in good health. The dollar amount you settle on now may not be enough to cover expenses even a decade from now.

You also should find out what happens to any money in excess of the funds needed to cover the inflation-adjusted cost of the funeral. Does the funeral home keep such interest, or does your estate get a share of those excess earnings?

There is no cure for birth and death save to enjoy the interval.

GEORGE SANTAYANA
Soliloquies in England

Regulating Funeral Parlors

To protect consumers who may be emotionally vulnerable after a death in the family, various consumer protection acts and laws dealing with funeral homes set strict standards for what undertakers and others in the funeral industry can and cannot do when dealing with the public.

• Funeral homes must allow customers to buy their products and services individually rather than only as a package deal. Packages, however, can be offered.

• Funeral homes must reveal the prices of their goods and services over the telephone. When inquiries are made in person, they must detail the prices in writing.

• Unless it is required by provincial law, embalming, which is very expensive, cannot be done without authorization, and customers must be informed in writing if embalming is not legally required. (If the casket is to be open, embalming is usually a practical necessity.)

• Funeral homes must provide itemized statements for all goods and services ordered by the customer. The statement must include the individual costs and total cost as well as a listing of the laws or provisions that require customers to buy certain goods and services. Even if a funeral director tries to convince them otherwise, customers are not obliged to pay for a casket for use in cremation,

• Funeral homes must detail in writing any fees being added to the price of an item purchased or service hired on the consumer's behalf. If the customer asks for a simple funeral service, he must be informed if the costs of flowers, an organist, burial clothes, or limousines are going to be extra.

Find out if the plan you select can be canceled or transferred should you later change your mind or move. Provincial laws vary regarding cancellations. Finally, do your homework before choosing an agency or funeral home to manage your funds. If the firm goes bankrupt, you may be left with nothing.

Survivor Benefits

After the funeral, the survivor may have a number of other responsibilities, such as contacting the deceased's lawyer, arranging for a tombstone or marker, notifying insurance companies with which the deceased had policies, and claiming a number of survivor benefits. (See also "Eight Tax-Free Death Benefits," at left.)

Government pensions and Veterans Administration benefits are the most significant sources of help for survivors faced with funeral and burial costs. The Canada (Quebec) Pension Plan pays a one-time, lump-sum death benefit of up to $3,600 to the surviving spouse, or to the surviving eligible child or children of the deceased if there is no surviving spouse.

Under Workers Compensation, a spouse or child under 18 may also be entitled to survivor benefits if the deceased died because of a work-related injury. Each province has its own rules regarding the amount and eligibility requirements.

Veterans' families may get help with funeral costs from the Department of Veterans' Affairs. The Lost Post Fund may also pay part or all funeral costs of a veteran or former serviceman. This fund can be reached by contacting the Canadian Legion Office in your area or the Department of Veterans Affairs.

TRACKING DOWN A MISSING INSURANCE POLICY

You know your late mother had a life insurance policy, but you cannot find it among her papers. How can you track it down? Check her canceled cheques or call her insurance agent. If you do not know who that was, try a local agent whom she or other family members might have used.

Contact her employer. Or, if your mother was in a union or a professional association, contact them. She might have been insured under one of their group policies. Contact her banker, mortgage broker, or automobile club. She may have been insured under a policy related to their services.

The Insurance Bureau of Canada which has offices across the country may be able to check whether or not an insurance policy was issued to a particular person. They only can make a search among about 80 of the larger insurers in Canada, and policies taken out with foreign insurers or small insurance companies may not be traced.

EIGHT TAX-FREE DEATH BENEFITS

After a family member dies, it is easy for survivors to overlook possible sources of income. Here is a list of death-related benefits. Some are obvious, some are not, but none counts as income for federal income-tax purposes.

1. CPP/QPP. The Canada (Quebec) Pension Plan pays survivors a lump-sum death benefit.

2. Veterans' benefits. The Department of Veterans Affairs pays various funeral-related benefits to veterans' survivors.

3. Life insurance. For many survivors, the deceased's life insurance becomes a major source of support.

4. Workers' compensation. Almost all employers are required to carry workers' compensation insurance that pays off for work-related deaths.

5. Health insurance. Medicare and private health insurance policies help pay medical expenses during the last hospital stay.

6. Personal injury awards. Court settlements awarded as compensation in death-related legal actions are not taxable.

7. Employer's death gratuity. Some companies offer payments to their employees' survivors. Up to $5,000 is tax-free.

8. Gifts in memorium. Money given as a gift to survivors in memory of the deceased is tax-free for the recipients.

PROTECTING YOUR FAMILY

No one can say when trouble will strike, but you must be aware that it might, and be prepared if it does. Different modes of defense are available.

Financial Considerations

One way to help insulate yourself from some of life's grievous surprises is through insurance. The law does not require you to be insured—except for a certain minimum amount of automobile insurance—but you can protect yourself, your home, your car, and your health from disaster by making sure you are properly insured. These safeguards can make the difference between coping and devastation if a tragedy occurs.

In addition, life insurance can be both a protection and an investment tool. Indeed, life insurance accounts for much of the estate many middle-class Canadians leave their families when they die, particularly if they die prematurely. By underestimating your life insurance needs, you could leave your survivors without the necessary income to live. (For more information about life insurance, see YOUR MONEY, page 304.)

HOW THE GOVERNMENT HELPS

Insurance, however, is expensive, and many families cannot afford enough of it to protect themselves from disaster. Government support programs have come under serious scrutiny in recent years and undoubtedly will change through the years ahead, but if you are unemployed, disabled, or otherwise unable to provide for your family's daily expenses, many federal and provincial programs provide a safety net.

The Old Age Security (OAS) pension is paid monthly to all persons 65 and over, who are citizens or legal residents of Canada, and who meet certain residency requirements. A monthly Guaranteed Income Supplement (GIS) is also available to OAS pensioners who have little other income. Low-income 60- to 64-year-old spouses, widows, and widowers of OAS pensioners may qualify for a spouse's allowance.

The Canada (Quebec) Pension Plan (CPP/QPP) is financed from mandatory contributions by employees and employers. Retirement benefits ordinarily begin when the contributor reaches 65 years, but can begin as early as 60 years, or as late as 70, with the monthly payout adjusted accordingly. The plan also provides disability pensions and survivor benefits for spouses and children.

123...
IF YOUR APPLICATION IS DENIED

What happens if you apply for public assistance, such as welfare, and are found ineligible or awarded smaller benefits than you feel you are entitled to? Provincial law allows you to appeal such decisions. Here's how:

1. You should have received notice of an agency decision, describing its reasons and explaining your appeal rights.

2. From the date of notice, you have a "reasonable" time, usually 30 to 90 days, to appeal the decision and seek a hearing, which may be at a local or a higher level. Benefits already being received should not be stopped or changed during this period.

3. Before the hearing, you are entitled to examine the case record and all documents the agency may have used to make its decisions.

4. At the hearing, you have the right to be legally represented, to provide evidence, and to question and cross-examine witnesses.

5. If funding was cut off, the agency must comply with the hearing decision within 10 days of the date the hearing was requested, and within 90 days in cases where funding was reduced.

The Unreasonable Use of Deadly Force in Self-Defense

Using a gun or other deadly weapon to defend yourself or your home from a burglar may seem like an effective way of protecting your family. But be careful: emotionally, you may be right; legally, you are probably wrong.

It is not legal to use a deadly weapon solely for the purpose of protecting your property. To do so would be considered excessive or unreasonable use of force. Unless the intruder clearly threatens your life, attacks you, or otherwise places you or a family member in grave bodily danger, you will have a hard time proving in a court of law that you acted in self-defense.

In fact, if you fire your weapon and kill an unarmed burglar, or if you jump on and kill the burglar with a knife, you could be charged with the homicide. Even if you were subsequently found innocent, the slain intruder's family might sue you in civil court for damages.

The prohibition against using unreasonable force applies even more strongly outside of the home. You are permitted to use whatever force is necessary to defend yourself, but it must not be deadly force—a gun, for instance—unless you can prove that you were in mortal danger.

Disability pensions are also provided for persons under age 65, who are suffering from severe and prolonged mental or physical disability. Workers Compensation pays survivor benefits to children of workers who have died, and disability benefits to injured workers who are too disabled to work.

Among other programs are the child tax benefit, a Goods and Services Tax (GST) rebate, which poor families may receive, and, in some provinces, rental assistance and provincial family allowances. If a child (even one over 18) is disabled and dependent, the caregivers of that child may also be entitled to extra support and financial aid. Contact your provincial health department or departement of social services for free pamphlets outlining these programs.

THE WILL AS FINANCIAL PROTECTION

Regardless of your age and financial circumstances, the importance of executing a will cannot be stressed enough. If you were to die intestate (without a will), your assets will be distributed according to provincial law rather than your personal wishes. Do-it-yourself kits are available at stationers, but if you have significant income, it is wise to consult a lawyer.

You should consider carefully who should be the beneficiaries of your will, your life insurance, and any other investment vehicles you own, such as a Registered Retirement Savings Plan (RRSP). If you do not designate a beneficiary, the money may be subject to taxes, especially RRSPs, whereas if you have designated beneficiaries, the money will not be included in the estate and will not be subject to such costs. (See also YOUR MONEY, page 342.) In the case of RRSPs, these should be directly rolled over to your spouse's RRSP. If, at your death, the RRSP is cashed in by your spouse, she will have to pay substantial taxes on it while the money is in her hands, even if she reinvests it into her own RRSP within days.

Gun "Protection"

Some people think a gun would ensure their safety and well-being, but this may not be the case. To acquire a firearm (a rifle, shotgun, and any handgun), you will need a federal firearm acquisition certificate and (after Jan. 1, 1988) will have to register the weapon within five years. Some provinces license firearms for purposes such as hunting. Under new federal legislation, most automatic assault weapons (guns such as AK-47s that fire a stream of bullets with a touch of the trigger) are banned. Present owners of such weapons may keep them, but may not sell or trade them.

YOUR HEALTH CARE

The problems of health care—who receives it, how much it costs, and who pays—are complicated. Knowing your rights can keep you healthy—both physically and financially.

THE HEART OF HEALTH CARE ■ YOU AND YOUR DOCTOR ■ YOUR RIGHTS AS A PATIENT ■ DEALING WITH A HOSPITAL ■ ALTERNATIVE HEALTH CARE ■ SUPPLEMENTING MEDICARE ■ LONG-TERM CARE ■ NURSING HOMES ■ DYING WITH DIGNITY

THE HEART OF HEALTH CARE

Health care practices are increasingly under scrutiny. Understanding the impact of proposed changes is essential if you are to protect your rights.

The Right to Quality Care

Health care in Canada is a provincial responsibility, and the system in place, commonly called Medicare, consists of 10 provincial and 2 territorial health insurance plans that are supported substantially by the federal government. This federal support, a provision of the Canada Health Act (1984), finances 45 to 50 percent of Medicare, and is the underpinning of our national health care system. By making federal subsidies to the provinces dependent on certain core services, Ottawa can guarantee every citizen, or resident, hospital and physician services, including the right to choose one's own doctor and have access to state-of-the-art medical technology. Outside the services specified by the Canada Health Act, the provinces themselves determine the levels of coverage. Accordingly, dental care, physiotherapy, certain medications, hearing aids, artificial limbs, and wheelchairs may be covered by Medicare in some provinces, but not in others.

SPIRALING COSTS

Ever-increasing Medicare expenses cost governments as much as $52 billion or more (augmented by up to $20 billion from private insurers) a year. One reason is the prevalence of chronic, long-term illnesses such as heart disease, cancer, and AIDS and the fact that technological and medical advances enable doctors to prolong the lives of these patients. Many new treatments also involve specialized procedures administered by highly trained physicians and technicians. Another factor is that because Canadians are living longer, large numbers of elderly people are seeking treatment. The result is that treating more patients for longer periods, using more specialized procedures and experts, has inflated health care costs exponentially.

Many people fear that Medicare will fall victim to deficit-chopping by federal and provincial governments. Since 25 percent of health care monies go to physician services, there is some talk of paying doctors an annual salary, regardless of the number of patients they see or how many procedures they carry out. Most doctors reject this idea, which they say would reduce their autonomy and prestige.

"Extra billing"and "opting out" have also been much discussed. Extra billing would enable doctors to bill their clients for services over and above the fees claimed from Medicare. Doctors in most provinces are free to opt out of Medicare and, overall, some 10 percent have done so. They set their own fees, but may not claim any fees from Medicare. Many people fear a two-tiered system will result if too many doctors opt out in this manner. Thus quality health care will become a prerogative of the rich. Nevertheless, the present trend seems to be toward private-for-profit clinics and doctors' services.

ILLNESS OR ACCIDENT ABROAD

If you are injured or become ill abroad, Medicare may only pay health care costs equivalent to what treatment would cost at home. This sum may be substantially lower than your total bill, especially if you were treated in the United States or Western Europe. When traveling, therefore, take out travel-accident-illness insurance. Many companies offer up to $1 million insurance for medical treatment, as well as paying for a spouse or relative to visit you, or to have your auto returned to Canada, and even to fly you home. (Certain restrictions may apply to preexisting medical conditions.) This type of out-of-country insurance is often supplied for a nominal amount to people who hold certain "gold" credit cards.

Some Facts About Medicare

The Canada Health Act, the cornerstone of our national health care system, gives the 10 provinces and 2 territories considerable leeway in financing and administering their own plans. However, each must meet the five criteria below in order to qualify for federal subsidies:

• Comprehensiveness. Each provincial health insurance plan must offer comprehensive coverage, paying for all medically necessary hospital and physician services. There can be no dollar limit or exclusion to these services, except those that are not medically required (as would be the case with physical examinations for life insurance, for example).

• Universality. All residents of the province must be covered under equal terms and conditions, regardless of previous health records, age, or income. (The medical expenses of certain groups, such as aboriginal peoples, members of the Canadian Armed Forces and the Royal Canadian Mounted Police, and inmates of federal prisons, are covered directly by the federal government.)

• Accessibility. The Canada Health Act permits the federal government to make dollar-for-dollar deductions from subsidies to a province that includes user fees or permits extra billing. By thus discouraging the provinces from extra billing and/or user fees, Ottawa ensures reasonable access to insured services.

• Each plan must be run on a nonprofit basis by a public authority accountable to the province for its financial transactions. Some provinces administer their plans through provincial departments; others do so through public agencies that are accountable to the provincial minister of health.

• Portability. A person from one province must be covered while temporarily in another province, or out of the country, and for three months (the usual waiting period when changing plans) after moving to another province.

YOU AND YOUR DOCTOR

Since the relationship with your doctor is one of the most important professional associations you will ever have, be sure that it works for you.

Finding Your Doctor

The best time to look for a doctor is before you need one. Here are some tips to help you find one that is right for you:

✔ **Get recommendations.** Ask family members, friends, neighbors, your present doctor, or your doctor's nurse for names of doctors they trust and respect.

✔ **Call your insurance company.** Ask your insurance company for a list of doctors, especially if you need a specialist for a second opinion.

✔ **Investigate hospitals.** Most hospitals have referral services. They usually recommend doctors who are on staff or otherwise have admitting privileges at their facility.

✔ **Try public-education or advocacy groups.** These organizations can provide you with educational materials as well as the names of respected doctors in your area.

✔ **Call the Canadian Medical Association (CMA).** Ask the CMA or a similar provincial body for a list of doctors who specialize in the field of medicine you think you may require.

How to Choose a Doctor

Remember Marcus Welby, M.D., the smiling, affable doctor on television, who always had time to chat and listen sympathetically. Whatever your idea of the perfect doctor, it is difficult for the average person to choose one who fulfills their every need. The best way to find what you are looking for is to shop around (see left, "Finding Your Doctor"). *The Canadian Medical Directory,* which should be in your local public library, lists virtually all the doctors in Canada together with their complete credentials. Doctors who are recent graduates, interns and residents, for example, may not be included.

Once you have the name of a prospective doctor, schedule a consultation. Prepare a list of questions about any symptoms you have, medications you are taking, or treatments you are receiving. Try describing any pain on a scale of 1 (comfort) to 10 (unbearable). How long does it last? What triggers it?

Let your doctor know your expectations and the kind of treatment you want. Make sure she has copies of your past medical records before your visit. Do not be shy about discussing events in your life that could be affecting your physical or emotional health. The smallest aches and pains could be clues to a larger medical problem. And be honest—if you are a smoker, for instance, don't try to hide it.

Feel free to ask relevant questions, such as whether or not your doctor has hospital privileges and at what hospital. Will you be seen by her at all visits, or will she have colleagues, nurses, or assistants do some procedures? If you do not like the way she treats you, you have the right to complain or to request that you be treated by another doctor.

THE FAMILY PHYSICIAN

Doctors pursue dozens of specialties within the medical profession, and having a general idea of who does what will help you find the best care. Unless you have an acute problem, you should probably start with someone who will coordinate your medical care, from monitoring a chronic disease to referring you to the appropriate specialist. In other words, you need a general practitioner, commonly known as a family physician.

Think of a family physician as an orchestra conductor. He does not play each instrument, but he knows how each should be played to create a symphony. Your family physician conducts your health care. He considers all aspects of your personal and medical history when making a diagnosis. He is trained to meet the special needs of women and children, deliver babies, handle emergencies, and perform minor surgery. Ideally, he should be able to teach you about diet, exercise, and other illness-preventing habits.

If you are chronically ill, your family physician will monitor your condition. If you need a specialist, he will make the referral. A good family doctor will not forget about you after he sends you to a specialist. He will confer with that specialist and monitor your progress.

When You Need a Specialist

Your family doctor is concerned with your overall health, but if he thinks you need a test or procedure he cannot provide, or if he wants a second opinion on a diagnosis, he will probably refer you to a specialist. You have the right to search out a specialist on your own, but your best bet is first to follow the recommendation of your family doctor. By and large, patients see a specialist only on referral, and some specialists will only see patients referred by another doctor. The specialist seen on a referral gets a much higher fee than one sought out by the patient.

Specialists deal with specific body systems, diseases, or age groups. They focus on the part of the body that is presenting problems, rather than concerning themselves with the complete medical condition and history of the patient.

BE YOUR OWN JUDGE

While it makes sense to take your doctor's advice in the matter of a specialist, you are nevertheless entitled to question a recommendation. Before acting on your doctor's referral, find out why he has chosen that physician—and what that specialist's reputation and credentials are.

A specialist should be board certified in the treatment area you need. Board certification represents a minimum standard of excellence. It means that in addition to graduating from medical school and one year of internship, a specialist has completed two to six years of supervised specialty training or residency and has passed a written and oral exam given by a board of professionals in that field. Each specialty has its own board. Doctors who earn the title "Fellow" have met the full requirements for membership in their specialty society and are con-

---

QUESTIONS TO ASK YOUR DOCTOR

Your first visit to a doctor will help you assess whether or not you will have a good relationship. You have the right to ask these questions:

1. Education. Where did you attend medical school and serve your residency?

2. Specialization. What, if any, is your area of specialty?

3. Medical philosophy. What is your medical or treatment philosophy? Do you tend to spend much time with patients? Will you discuss test results and other issues?

4. Hospital affiliation. At what hospital do you have admitting privileges?

5. Availability. Are you available 24 hours a day for emergencies? If not, who covers for you? How long does it take to get an appointment? What is your policy regarding telephone consultations?

6. Fees. Are the fees covered by Medicare or will there be extra billing charges. What medicines or other kinds of treatment or diagnostic procedures will I have to pay for myself?

sidered qualified to practice that specialty due to their education, training, and experience. Some specialists, internists for example, are broadly trained to provide comprehensive medical care, and may provide nonsurgical general care in a family practice. Most people encounter one or more of the following specialists at some point in their lives:

- **Allergist.** A doctor with this specialty identifies and treats allergies.
- **Anesthetist.** As well as administering the anesthetic before surgery, this specialist monitors the patient during and immediately after the operation.
- **Cardiologist.** This specialist treats diseases of the heart and blood vessels.
- **Endocrinologist.** A doctor with this specialty treats glandular and hormonal disorders, such as diabetes.
- **Gastroenterologist.** Gastroenterologists treat digestive system disorders, including the liver, gallbladder, and pancreas.
- **Hematologist.** This specialist treats disorders affecting blood and bone marrow.
- **Internist.** Specialists in internal medicine study the interconnections of body systems and provide nonsurgical general care for adults.
- **Nephrologist.** Kidney and urinary problems are treated by a nephrologist.
- **Neurologist** and **neurosurgeon.** Neurologists treat disorders of the nervous system. Neurosurgeons operate on the nervous system such as the brain and spinal cord.
- **Obstetrician-gynecologist.** These specialists treat the female reproductive system. Their care includes regular examinations; preventive tests such as Pap smears for cancer detection; the surgical removal of cysts or tumors; and the prescription of medications, such as hormones or birth control devices; the treatment of infertility; and the management of menopause. Obstetricians care for women during pregnancy and delivery and immediately after. Many women use their gynecologist as their general practitioner.
- **Oncologist.** Physicians specializing in the study and treatment of cancer are known as oncologists.
- **Ophthalmologist.** These are doctors who specialize in the diagnosis and treatment of vision problems and eye diseases. They prescribe medicines and perform eye surgery, as well as prescribing corrective lenses.
- **Orthopedic surgeon.** This specialist treats and operates on joints and bones.
- **Otolaryngologist.** This specialist, a head and neck surgeon, treats patients with ear, nose, and throat disorders medically and surgically.

- **Pediatrician.** Child development and diseases fall under this specialty which provides general care for children from infancy through adolescence. Pediatricians may subspecialize in particular areas, such as the care of newborn and premature babies and their mothers (neonatal-perinatal medicine), or the treatment of children with cardiovascular problems (pediatric cardiology).
- **Psychiatrist.** Doctors specializing in this branch of medicine treat patients suffering from emotional, behavioral, and mental disorders.
- **Radiologist.** X-ray, ultrasound, and scanning equipment are used by this specialist in diagnosing and treating various disorders.
- **Rheumatologist.** Patients suffering from arthritis and other diseases of the joints, muscles, and tendons may be referred to a rheumatologist.
- **Urologists.** Urologists provide medical and surgical care to patients of both sexes with urinary problems and to male patients with disorders of the reproductive system.

Doctors of osteopathy who have graduated from one of 16 U.S. colleges that graduate osteopathic physicians are licensed by the College of Physicians and Surgeons in British Columbia, Alberta, Ontario, and Quebec. Like medical physicians, osteopathic physicians diagnose diseases, prescribe drugs, refer patients to hospital, perform surgery, and use accepted medical diagnostic techniques and therapies. Osteopathic physicians focus on the musculoskeletal system (muscles, bones, and joints) and stress the body's unity and ability to heal itself. Their specialties include surgery, neurology, gynecology, obstetrics, and psychiatry. If you visit an osteopath, make sure that he is an osteopathic physician. A license to practice medicine issued by your province's College of Physicians and Surgeons will guarantee his professional standing. If he is not accredited, your visits will not be covered by Medicare.

Working With Your Surgeon

When surgery is done on an emergency basis, making choices about doctors, hospitals, and procedures is out of your hands. Most surgery, however, is elective, which gives you time to arrange it according to your best interest.

Before you agree to surgery, make sure you understand exactly why it is recommended. Your doctor has the duty to explain the benefits and the risks to you and whether you can avoid surgery altogether by undergoing alternative treatment.

Mental-Health Experts

Before looking for a mental-health professional, you should understand the different disciplines that treat mental or emotional disorders.

Psychiatrists are physicians licensed to practice medicine and prescribe medications as well as provide psychotherapeutic help. After medical school, they complete a year internship and three years of psychiatric training. They can determine when emotional disorders are medically related and require drug intervention. They can also provide psychotherapy. They are the only mental-health professionals who can write prescriptions.

Unlike psychiatry, psychology is concerned with normal mental processes and behavior. Psychologists are not physicians, but can provide psychotherapy. They usually hold a master's or Ph.D. degree from a university program and have passed a licensing examination. They can counsel individuals, groups, or families.

Psychiatric or clinical social workers usually have a master's or Ph.D. degree in social work. They are licensed in social work and some form of psychotherapeutic counseling.

Beware, however, that the term psychotherapist has no specific meaning and is not a discipline subject to regulation. A psychotherapist who does not have a Ph.D. in psychology from a recognized university should be avoided.

You have the right to get a second opinion on any medical issue, but this is especially relevant when surgery is the issue. For a second opinion, choose a surgeon who is not affiliated with the surgeon who wants to operate: coworkers may tend to agree with each other. Make sure the second-opinion surgeon has seen all your medical records and test results. If you remain unsure, get a third or even a fourth opinion.

YOUR SURGICAL TEAM

Where your surgery takes place will depend on your surgeon's hospital affiliation, the type of procedure, and your overall health. Simple procedures that require only local anesthetics may be done right in the doctor's office or on an outpatient basis in the hospital. If your operation requires general anesthesia, you will need close, constant monitoring, or complications may develop. As a result, you will probably be safest in a hospital.

In choosing a surgeon, get one or more referrals from your family doctor. Investigate their credentials. Are they fellows of the Canadian College of Physicians and Surgeons or other appropriate board. When you decide on a surgeon, find out which hospitals he is affiliated with, and to which one he plans to send you. Find out exactly what will happen during surgery. You are entitled to know what to expect, from the time you get to the hospital to the time you leave. You also should be informed about how you may feel afterward, how long it will take you to recuperate, and how you can make yourself more comfortable.

You can request that specific doctors, including the anesthetist, be part of the surgical team, but your request need not be granted. For one thing, most anesthetists have contracts with hospitals, which make the surgical assignments. Still, you may ask your surgeon to request the anesthetist most appropriate for your operation. Discuss with the anesthetist the type of anesthetic to be used and the associated risks and side effects.

When You Are Dissatisfied

If you are lucky, the treatment you receive from your doctor or other health care professional will always be satisfactory. Unfortunately, many people become unhappy or dissatisfied with their doctor for any number of reasons. Your problem with your doctor may be personal; you may feel she is treating you in a less than professional manner, perhaps by keeping you waiting too long before appointments. Your complaint could be more serious: you may suspect your doc-

Spotting a Quack

The following warning signs could be evidence that the person you are consulting is practicing quackery, not medicine:

✔ *Dodging questions.* He will not tell you where he attended medical school, where he trained, or how much experience he has had with specific procedures and treatments.

✔ *Making serious errors.* He prescribes antibiotics when you have a cold, for instance, even though antibiotics do not work on colds. Or, for a young child with flu he prescribes aspirin instead of acetaminophen.

✔ *Cutting corners.* He writes a new prescription without examining you first.

✔ *Refusing to translate.* He uses pseudo-medical phrases, such as "strengthen your system," "detoxify," or "rejuvenate your body" and will not explain them.

✔ *Shunning second opinions.* He will not refer you to other doctors to confirm his findings and will discourage you from seeking second opinions.

✔ *Blaming your diet.* No matter what ails you, he links most diseases with poor nutrition and relies on vitamin supplements as remedies.

✔ *Offering vague diagnoses.* Be cautious of catchall, indefinite diagnostic terms given without a comprehensive diagnosis, such as "environmental illness."

tor is under the influence of alcohol while she is treating you, or that she is incompetent. Doctors are licensed by provincial medical agencies, and there is no federal legislation that protects you from unethical or unsatisfactory medical conduct. If you are not actually harmed by your doctor's behavior and do not have grounds for a malpractice case, your recourse lies within your provincial College of Physicians and Surgeons, or medical board.

NONMEDICAL COMPLAINTS

Doctor-patient problems that are not directly related to improper medical conduct but to personality or other conflict are best dealt with directly. If you are unhappy about your treatment, speak up and make your concerns known. Tell your doctor exactly why you are dissatisfied. For example, she never fully explains why she is prescribing a particular medication. If you do not speak up, she has no reason to change her customary procedure and she is not likely to do so. However, if your doctor does not change her practices after you have talked to her, you may want to look for a new physician. If the problems are serious, you may also want to complain to local medical associations and hospitals where your doctor is on staff.

WHAT ARE UNETHICAL OR ILLEGAL PRACTICES?

The following are practices your provincial medical regulatory board may consider unethical, or, in some cases, even illegal:

- Incompetence;
- Gross negligence or repeated negligent acts;
- Falsifying medical records or hospital bills;
- Evidence of mental or physical illness that impairs the doctor's ability to practice medicine;
- Prescribing drugs without giving a proper examination;
- Abuse of drugs or alcohol or being under the influence of either while attending a patient;
- Sexual harassment—unwelcome sexual advances toward a client or patient.

If you suspect your doctor is guilty of unethical or illegal practices such as negligent behavior or falsifying records, inform the hospital director and your provincial College of Physicians and Surgeons or provincial minister of health. Every province has agencies that investigate and sanction medical personnel and facilities, and you may want to make a report to such an agency. Call your local health department to find out which one to contact. If you are not satisfied with the response from your local medical board, contact a lawyer specializing in medical malpractice or your crown prosecutor's office.

123

BEFORE YOU SAY YES TO SURGERY

Surgery is risky and often traumatic. If your doctor recommends it, make sure you understand what is at stake—and do not feel obliged to consent until you get every question answered. For example:

1. Your illness or injury. Has your doctor explained to you precisely what is wrong and how surgery will help?

2. The operation. What is the nature of the operation and how will it be performed, step by step? How long will the operation take?

3. Risks. What are the risks and how serious are they? Will there be side effects, residual or permanent damage, or extreme pain? If you will experience pain, how long will it last?

4. Your doctor's experience. How many times has your surgeon performed this procedure? What is his success rate? Has he ever failed?

5. Costs. Will Medicare cover all surgical and hospital costs?

6. Recurrence. Might the condition recur after you have had surgery? What are your options if this happens?

7. Alternatives. What will happen if you choose not to have surgery? Are there alternative ways to treat your condition that you could try first?

Understanding Malpractice

Since medical science is not precise, and because each illness and situation is different, doctors can never be certain that what they prescribe will be successful or that complications and unanticipated side effects will not develop. The law therefore recognizes that physicians cannot always be held responsible if a treatment is not successful. Consequently, failing to cure you is not necessarily grounds for malpractice.

You have the right to sue for malpractice, however, if you suffer injury and disability because a doctor, nurse, or other health provider was negligent in treating you. You may also have a valid malpractice claim if your condition worsens because your doctor has been negligent in that he failed to treat you according to the minimum standards of skill and care that have been established by his specialty and that would be observed by other practitioners under the same circumstances.

If your doctor prescribes medication to which you have a known allergy and you suffer harm as a result, he may be liable due to his negligence. Similarly, if you are hurt because he injects a drug in the wrong area of your body, improperly sets a broken bone, or misdiagnoses a fracture as a sprain, he may be liable for damage caused by his negligence.

However, a doctor is not being negligent if he abides by standard medical practice, even if his treatment fails to help you. For instance, you do not have grounds for suing your doctor if he refuses to make a house call, prescribes an unsuccessful treatment for an incurable disease, or if he orders exploratory tests that come out negative. Not making house calls is considered standard medical practice, as is ordering exploratory procedures.

Doctors and all health providers are required to inform patients about their illness, the proposed treatments, the chances of success, and any risks involved. They are then required to obtain a patient's consent to begin treatment. If a health provider begins a treatment without consent, he may be liable for negligence.

HOW TO GUARD AGAINST MALPRACTICE

Being your own advocate is the best way to protect yourself against malpractice. Before committing yourself to a doctor's care, exercise your right to research his credentials and record. You can ask the Canadian Medical Protective Association (CMPA) if a particular medical practitioner has been sued for malpractice, but the association is not obliged to release this information to the public. You can also check at your local

Know What Your Province Covers

Since Medicare coverage varies from one province to another, make sure your treatment will be covered by your provincial plan. Ontario residents, for example, are entitled to physicians' services at home, office, hospital or institution (if the doctor has not opted out of Medicare); surgery (aside from specific exceptions) and anesthetics; diagnosis and treatment of illness and injury; service of specialists certified by the Royal College of Physicians and Surgeons of Canada; most laboratory services; use of operating and delivery rooms and surgical supplies; X-rays for diagnosis and treatment; nursing while in hospital; pre- and post-natal care; standard ward accommodation; most drugs prescribed by a physician; treatment of fractures and dislocations, but aside from basic hospital and physician services, the package of services offered may vary slightly from province to province.

Some provinces pay for wheelchairs and hearing aids, and cover ambulance costs: others do not. Face lifts and other such esthetic surgery, varicose vein treatment when the condition poses no danger to your health, and most dental work are rarely covered by Medicare.

county or district courthouse for any lawsuit filed against your physician, but even this is not foolproof. Your local courthouse will not list actions filed in another district. If your research proves your prospective doctor has been sued before, you might think about choosing a different one or finding out why.

If you already have a doctor, but have doubts about his competence, you can protect yourself against possible malpractice by looking for certain clues. For example, a misdiagnosis or an improperly prescribed medication is a sign of incompetence. Your doubts would be strengthened if your doctor shrugged off your complaints or avoided your repeated phone calls.

Be alert for signs of physical decline—if the doctor appears ill, unkempt, or intoxicated. Look for the qualities you once admired about him. Have they changed? If so, his professional skills and standards could be slipping. Obviously, such a scenario is not common, but being mindful of such subtleties might help keep you out of trouble if it turns out your doctor has indeed lost his grip.

SEEKING REDRESS

You may believe that you have suffered significant damage due to a negligent doctor, but to win a malpractice suit, you will have to convince a court that your injury is directly related to the doctor's failure to provide appropriate treatment. To do this you will need expert testimony or other medical evidence.

Your first step therefore should be to get your medical records from the doctor. A lawyer or another doctor will need

When a doctor does go wrong, he is the first of criminals. He has nerve and he has knowledge.

ARTHUR CONAN DOYLE
The Adventures of Sherlock Holmes

Filing a Complaint Against a Doctor

Whether you feel that your doctor is not giving you the attention and time you deserve or that your doctor is acting unethically, you have a right to speak out and let your concerns be known. If you have a complaint against a doctor, keep the following in mind:

• If you suspect your doctor of unethical conduct, merely speaking to him may not be enough. If you suffer physically, mentally, or financially because of your doctor's incompetence, you may have a malpractice case against him. Contact a lawyer immediately if you think you do.

• If you have not suffered any real harm, but still suspect your doctor is incompetent, is too mentally or physically impaired to practice medicine safely, or is committing fraud, take your complaint to your provincial health department.

• Making a formal complaint can be time-consuming and complicated. Call your local health department to find out where to register your complaint. You can also file a written complaint with the provincial licensing board that pertains to your physician.

• When you file your complaint, make sure you include the name of the doctor or other health provider; a complete description of the incident or incidents on which you are basing your complaint, including dates and locations; and any witnesses who can support your position.

• Make sure you have all the documents that relate to your complaint: medical or hospital records, lab reports, and bills. Always keep the originals, making copies if necessary. If you do not have these, indicate where they can be found.

these in order to evaluate the treatment you received and determine if you have a claim. Next, ask another doctor for a second opinion. Keep careful records of any incidence of pain, conversations you have with any doctor, appointments, diagnosis, treatment plans, or anything relevant to your condition.

If you still feel you have been mistreated and want to file a claim, consult an experienced malpractice lawyer to make sure you have a case. Take along your medical records, any notes you have made, and any other documents that relate to your care or injury. If your lawyer thinks you have a strong case, you can bring a malpractice claim.

Damages in medical malpractice may be awarded for medical expenses, partial or permanent impairment, pain and suffering, lost wages, and other costs related to the malpractice. Additional punitive damages may be awarded if the physician was intentionally reckless or incompetent. Each province has a statute of limitations for filing medical malpractice claims. This is to ensure that a claim is made while relevant information is still available. In the case of a minor, the statute of limitations may not begin until the minor turns 18.

What to Expect From Your Dentist

A dentist, like a doctor, should be licensed and board-certified, and qualified to treat your particular needs. While it is important to have a good rapport with your dentist, every detail of his practice counts. Here are some things to look for when you are choosing a dentist:

• You should be able to talk comfortably and candidly with your dentist, and he should be willing to explain what your dental problems are and how he will go about fixing them.

• The dentist's office should be scrupulously clean. All of the dentist's equipment should be completely heat-sterilized. To reduce the possibility of transmitting germs, the dentist should use disposable items, such as the needles to administer anesthetics. Similarly, rubber gloves and protective face masks should be worn during every procedure.

• You also have the right to know if the dental assistants on staff are specially trained to take X-rays and final impressions, and clean and polish teeth.

• Ask your dentist how often he recommends X-rays. If your dentist is cautious, he will take the minimum amount of X-rays necessary. Because of the possible danger of radiation, some experts suggest that full-mouth X-rays should not be taken more often than every five years and that children under 16 should not have them at all unless problems are suspected.

• When your dentist or his assistants take X-rays, they should take every safety precaution. For example, they should cover your chest and lap with a lead apron. They should always check with you that it is safe to take an X-ray; do not allow X-rays to be taken if you are pregnant.

• A good dentist is prevention-oriented. The dentist should carefully explain during each visit the best home-care techniques and put you on a regular schedule of office visits.

• If your dentist treats your children, make sure he instructs them how to take care of their teeth, teaches them about cavity-causing foods and eating habits, and sees that they are sent home with a new toothbrush. It is also a good sign if the dentist specializes in treating children, has other children as patients or, at the very least, is thoughtful about family health care.

VISITING THE DENTIST

Most dentists are general practitioners, qualified to perform all phases of dental care. They clean and extract teeth, fill cavities, fit crowns, bridges, and dentures, treat gum disease, and instruct patients in good oral hygiene. Only those dentists with advanced training who are duly certified may perform surgery.

Dental treatment is rarely covered by Medicare except where the dental service is required because of some other medical cause. Regular cleanings, fillings, and dental surgery must be paid for by the patient unless he has some private dental care plan. Like other professionals, dentists are liable for malpractice. For certain problems, your dentist may refer you to one of the following specialists.

A Doctor's Carelessness

PROBLEM
Ed was new in town and did not have a family doctor. After pulling a muscle in his back, he called a doctor whose name he found in the Yellow Pages under "Back Specialists." The doctor prescribed extra-strength aspirin, since Ed did not want anything that would make him drowsy. The physician did not tell Ed to come in for an examination; nor did he ask Ed if he was taking any other medications. Ed took notes as the doctor spoke and followed his advice. As it happens, Ed was taking a drug called Coumadin, which prevents blood clots from forming. After a few days of taking both drugs, Ed began experiencing severe stomach pain. He noticed blood in his urine and stool. Alarmed and unable to reach the doctor, he went to the emergency room.

ACTION
The emergency-room doctors explained to Ed that his stomach lining had become irritated and had started bleeding due to the combination of aspirin, which is known to cause stomach bleeding, and Coumadin, which prevents blood from clotting. According to standard medical practice, the doctor should have insisted on examining Ed before prescribing anything over the phone. Then he should have asked Ed if he was taking any other medications. Ed sued the doctor for malpractice and was able to prove that he suffered harm due to the doctor's negligence. He collected damages for pain and suffering and was reimbursed for the hospital expenses that Medicare did not cover, such as his television, phone, and private nurse.

- **Oral and maxillofacial surgeon.** Dentists with this specialty treat diseases and injuries of the mouth and jaw and correct cosmetic problems.
- **Orthodontist.** This specialist treats teeth that are crooked, badly spaced, or projecting too much, often with orthodontic appliances such as braces. The straightening process usually takes about two years, followed by checkups.
- **Periodontist.** This dental specialist treats gum diseases and disorders of the bones surrounding the gums.

Do You Have a Malpractice Claim?

To win a malpractice suit, you must prove the following:

✔ *The doctor owed you a duty.* The doctor's duty is to fulfill the doctor-patient relationship, providing medical treatment that meets an acceptable standard of care. When your doctor agrees to treat you, he makes a professional commitment to provide appropriate care.

✔ *You were given substandard care.* When a doctor provides care that does not meet the standards upheld by the medical community, he commits a breach of duty. If he does not use the degree of knowledge and skill that a "reasonable physician" in the same specialty would have used under the same circumstances, he is similarly at fault. You must prove this point to win a malpractice claim.

✔ *You suffered harm.* You must prove that you suffered an injury or damage to your health, your financial well-being, or both.

✔ *The doctor's negligence was the cause of harm.* This is perhaps the most difficult point to prove. You must show that your injury or harm was a direct result of having received substandard care from your doctor. Unless you or your lawyer can establish a link between your injury and your doctor's failure to provide proper care, you will have a difficult time winning a malpractice claim.

Your Rights as a Patient

When you are ill or injured, you feel especially vulnerable. But as a patient, you have many rights available to you, and you should not hesitate to use them.

1₂3... ELEMENTS OF INFORMED CONSENT

Make a point of learning all you can about any medical procedure proposed by your doctor. Before signing a consent form, be sure that you:

1. Understand the nature of your medical condition, the proposed treatment, the chances of success, the risks involved, and the expected recovery time.

2. Know the risks and benefits of alternative treatments.

3. Realize what the risks would be if you did not have the treatment.

4. Understand the meanings of all the words on the form.

5. Agree to everything in the consent form—without pressure or harassment—and cross out or change things you do not agree with and show them to your doctor.

6. Know who will be performing the procedure and what his qualifications are.

7. Believe the possible benefits of treatment will outweigh the risks.

Know What You Are Signing

To make the best decisions about your health care, you need to be fully informed about your condition and understand how any medical or surgical treatments will affect you. Every competent adult has the right to this information. Without it, you cannot give your informed consent, which health care professionals must, by law, obtain before treating you. Accordingly, your doctor has a duty to explain any treatment, medication, or procedure to you beforehand and get your permission to proceed with it.

This obligation would not apply, however, if you need life-saving medical treatment, cannot give your consent, and there is no time to find someone to consent for you. Also, in psychiatric cases, if your doctor has evidence that informing you about your condition or a treatment might harm you or prevent you from making a rational decision, he may withhold the information or give it to someone designated by you.

The concept of informed consent means that you agree to treatment based on your understanding of its benefits and risks. If you consent to a treatment when your doctor did not fully inform you of its risks and you are harmed as a result, your doctor may be liable for a claim of negligence.

HOW BINDING IS A CONSENT FORM?

On admission to hospital, you will be asked to read and sign certain consent forms. Usually, such written consent is not legally required when you visit your doctor. Your verbal consent is legally valid. Should you and your doctor disagree about whether your consent was obtained for a specific procedure, however, a written form is most likely to hold up in court.

A consent form must contain all the elements required for informed consent, plus any other relevant information you have discussed with your doctor. If you disagree with something on the form, it is your right to delete or change it. Even so, not all consent forms are legally binding. Blanket consent forms, which seek to authorize a physician to perform any procedure he deems advisable, are the least binding. This is the kind of form that hospital admitting staff generally ask patients to sign when they check in.

Patient's Bill of Rights

The Patient's Bill of Rights is a set of guidelines describing the level of care you are entitled to in most hospitals and centers dispensing health care. Although there is no legislation setting out what is referred to as a Patient's Bill of Rights, most versions state that you have a right to:

• Receive proper medical care regardless of your race, color, religion, national origin, or source of payment for your care.

• Receive prompt emergency services without any prior formalities.

• Receive considerate and respectful care in a clean and safe environment, including reasonable responses to reasonable requests for service.

• Receive complete, relevant, and understandable information about your medical condition, the course of your treatment, and the prospects for your recovery.

• Know the name and position of the doctor who is in charge of your care in a hospital and be able to talk with that physician.

• Know the names, positions, and functions of any members of a hospital staff involved in your care, including medical students, residents, or other trainees.

• Have an interpreter if you do not speak English or if you are hearing impaired.

• Receive as much information as you need about a proposed treatment—including risks, benefits, alternatives, and the name of the person administering the treatment—in order to be able to give informed consent or refuse the treatment.

• Make decisions about the course of your care, including the right to seek additional consultations, before and during treatment, and make decisions about your discharge from the hospital.

• Be notified of your impending discharge at least one day in advance, as well as have a consultation with your attending physician on the reason or reasons for the discharge. You are also entitled to have a person of your choice notified in advance regarding your discharge.

• Refuse treatment and be told how your refusal may affect your health. (If you are not conscious or competent and there is no evidence of your treatment wishes, a doctor or hospital would have the right to provide treatment in cases where your life is in danger.)

• Refuse transfer to another facility unless you have received a complete explanation of the need and benefits of the transfer, the other facility has accepted your transfer, and you have agreed to it.

• Be given every consideration of privacy and confidentiality regarding all information, discussions, and records pertaining to your care. You have the right to know why anyone not directly involved with your care is present.

• Have an advance directive, such as a living will, health care proxy, or durable power of attorney for health care that clearly states your treatment wishes or designates a surrogate to make decisions for you. You also have the right to know a hospital's policy on advance directives.

• Review all records of your care and have them explained, as necessary, except when restricted by law. You also have the right to a copy of your medical record for a reasonable charge.

• You have the right to choose your own doctor (except in emergency situations). For example, if you have a work accident, you have the right to refuse treatment by a doctor chosen by your employer.

• Agree or refuse to participate in research studies or human experimentation that might affect your treatment and care and to have those studies fully explained before consenting.

• Be informed of hospital policies and practices that relate to patient care, treatment, and responsibilities. You have the right to be informed of available resources, such as ethics committees or patient advocates, and be informed of any charges for such services.

• Leave the hospital, even against the advice of doctors. You will be asked to sign a "Discharge Against Medical Advice" form, relieving the hospital of any responsibility for harm you suffer by leaving.

• Receive an itemized bill, together with an explanation of all extra expenses, such as private nurses, upgrade of room, and television and telephone charges.

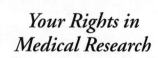

Your Rights in Medical Research

If you participate in any special medical research project, you have a right to:

✔ *Understand the research.* Obtain an explanation of its purpose, procedures, and experimental components.

✔ *A time frame.* Know how long your participation is expected to last.

✔ *Understand the risks.* Ask for an explanation of possible consequences, including risks, discomforts, and benefits.

✔ *Privacy.* Find out how confidential your identity and your records will be.

✔ *Potential compensation.* If you are taking a risk, find out if you will receive payment and what compensation you will get should you suffer injury.

✔ *Hospital approval.* Make sure the research project or use of experimental drugs have been approved by the hospital's ethics committee. Ask the ethics committee if the Research Council of Canada has approved the undertaking.

✔ *Meet the director.* Insist on knowing who is in charge of the research project and whom you can call for answers to your questions.

✔ *Withdraw.* It is your right to refuse to continue at any time without being subject to a penalty.

Detailed consent forms are more binding. They specify your medical condition; the proposed treatment or procedure; and its risks, benefits, and alternatives. You might be asked to sign a surgery consent form, an anesthesia consent form, and so on.

Remember, you do not sign away your rights with a consent form. Your doctor or hospital still may be held accountable for malpractice; and even after you have signed a form you may withdraw your consent.

Medications and Devices

You have the right to refuse any medication, and the right to question your doctor about medication he prescribes. Your doctor is legally obliged to tell you the name of the drug and what it is supposed to do, when it should be taken, and in what dosage. He also should explain what to do if you forget to take the medication or if you want to stop taking it altogether.

If you have ever experienced an allergic reaction to any medications, inform your doctor immediately. Also, tell him if you smoke or drink caffeinated or alcoholic beverages. Any of these substances may mix badly with certain medicines. Should you get a serious or unexpected reaction from a drug, you should immediately report it to your doctor. If the drug proves particularly toxic, you also may want to report it to the drug directorate of the health protection branch of Health Canada, the federal agency responsible for monitoring drug safety.

KNOW THE RISKS OF MEDICAL DEVICES

Under existing legislation, the Health Protection Branch of Health Canada can order manufacturers to stop distributing harmful devices and recall them if necessary. Health Canada would also like to see all medical devices classified by risk levels. Slings and bandages, for example, might be described as relatively harmless; wheelchairs and home pregnancy tests might be considered potentially harmful; and breast implants, pacemakers, IUD's, and other body implants might be said to pose a serious risk.

Health Canada is also considering a proposal that all hospitals, nursing homes, and medical device manufacturers be legally required to report deaths and serious injuries caused by medical devices, and that manufacturers of certain high-risk devices implement a tracking mechanism, so that anyone fitted with such devices can be contacted should problems arise.

If a medical device makes you ill or causes injury, you should first inform your doctor. You may also file a product-liability lawsuit against the manufacturer of the device and anyone involved in its sale. To win, however, you must prove that the product's defective manufacture or design led to danger, that you were not informed of the product's risks, or that the instructions were inadequate or unsafe. Most cases against the medical device manufacturers cost vast sums of money. Your best bet is to see if others have also been hurt by the device, in which case you might participate in a class action suit.

Getting Your Records

The information in your medical records can be characterized as your property, but the records themselves generally belong to the doctor or medical facility that holds them. According to the federal Privacy Act and similar provincial statutes, medical records generally must be made available to patients. Sometimes your doctor or the medical records department of your hospital will honor your request by phone. More often you will be asked to make a written request, possibly in person, and you may have to pay a small retrieval or copying fee.

Medical record access is more limited in cases involving mental illness. A doctor may even have a responsibility to withhold information that might pose a danger to a patient's health and well-being. However, the person denied access is entitled to a written explanation from the doctor or hospital concerned. Anyone refused access to his medical records can appeal to his provincial privacy commission, which can hold a hearing and rule on the request.

If the records are being withheld by a hospital, the patient might appeal to the institution's administrator, patients' representative, or ethics committee before contacting the privacy commission. In a dispute with a doctor, the patient might simply seek out another doctor willing to show him his records, and have the file transferred to the new doctor. Physicians and hospitals generally honor requests for patient records if they come from other medical professionals.

Your Right to Privacy

You are guaranteed a right to privacy in most health-care settings. Doctors, nurses, hospital personnel, and other health care providers involved with your care are legally and ethically bound to protect information about your medical condition. But if you are hospitalized, dozens of staff members are likely to be involved with

123

YOUR MEDICAL RECORDS

If you request and receive a copy of your medical records from your doctor, here is what you should find:

1. Information that identifies you, including your name, address, height, weight, and other physical descriptions.

2. An account of your medical history, including family illnesses, surgeries, hospitalizations, and medications that have been prescribed.

3. Results from your most recent physical examination, including laboratory reports and X-ray results.

4. A copy of your written informed consent for any recommended medical or surgical procedures, or a written note explaining why you have withheld informed consent.

5. A description of your medical condition and its progress, as well as recommendations for treatment made by your doctor, and the results of your treatment.

6. Reports of all tests or procedures that have been performed and their results.

7. Your doctor's findings and suggestions at the end of treatment or hospitalization.

8. Findings and correspondence from other doctors regarding your medical condition and treatment.

your care, and any of those who have a legitimate reason for consulting your file may do so. That in itself is one good reason why you might want to know what it contains.

The right to confidentiality may also be impossible in matters involving public health. For example, doctors must report births; deaths; infectious, contagious, or communicable diseases; child abuse; and violent injuries such as gunshot wounds. Health professionals may be required by law to inform public health officials when patients have sexually transmitted diseases. Doctors may ask HIV-positive patients for permission to notify the patient's sexual partners that they risk contracting the disease. Compliance, however, depends on the patient's cooperation. No one can be forced to identify his or her partners.

PRIVACY AND INSURANCE COMPANIES

Technically, insurance companies are permitted only limited access to your medical records and may see only the parts that pertain to a particular condition or treatment. If an insurance company learns of a preexisting medical or psychiatric condition, it could deny you coverage. You may want to ask your doctor or hospital to give an insurance company only those records that pertain to the coverage you are seeking.

Protecting your privacy from insurance companies is getting trickier, however, now that more and more medical files are computerized. By encoding your Social Insurance Number, a doctor in Calgary may be able to find out that you have

> *The patient must combat the disease along with the physician.*
>
> **HIPPOCRATES**
> *Aphorisms*

Keeping Your Own Medical Records

An up-to-date medical file is an excellent way to keep track of your health care, and to help your doctors plan necessary treatment. A medical record is especially important if you move, change doctors, travel frequently, or become incapacitated. Your records should include:

• **Overall medical history.** Write down your name, date, and place of birth, your insurance-company name and identification number, and your Medicare and Social Insurance numbers. List any medical conditions, acute or chronic, that you have suffered. If certain conditions run in your family, like diabetes or cancer, record them.

• **Office visits to physicians.** List each visit to a doctor, with the date, the reason for the visit, the condition that was diagnosed, and the treatment prescribed.

• **Medications.** List every medication you take or have taken, including prescription drugs, vitamins, and over-the-counter drugs; the name of the doc-

tor who prescribed them; the pharmacy where you bought them; and any side effects you may have experienced.

• **Major hospitalizations.** List the date, the hospital name, the doctor overseeing your care, and the reason for your hospitalization. Record laboratory tests, dates, and results.

• **Eye examinations.** Record the results of each examination, and include a copy of your prescription for eyeglasses.

• **Dental examinations.** List the name of your dentist, the dates of visits, any unusual problems you have suffered, and all treatments.

been treated previously in Halifax with certain medications purchased from Dartmouth and Halifax pharmacies. Computer access within some hospital is so easy that any doctor or nurse may access your file.

The positive aspect to this loss of confidentiality is that you are less likely to be prescribed a medication to which you are allergic or which has proven useless. The negative side is that employers and insurance companies might be able to access your confidential files at will.

Children's Medical Rights

Usually parents have the right and responsibility to make all health decisions on behalf of their minor children. Doctors cannot treat a child without parents' informed consent except in an emergency. Barring certain emergencies, parents have the right to stay with their child, whether in the doctor's office or in the hospital.

Your child has a right to be immunized against certain infectious diseases, such as diphtheria, pertussis (whooping cough), tetanus, measles, mumps, rubella, poliomyelitis, and hemophilus influenza type B, for all of which vaccines exist. Due to supportive legislation, and the persistent efforts of physicians and public health authorities down the years, the majority of Canadian children are immunized. As a result, incidences of these killer diseases are now rare.

Provincial requirements vary somewhat as to when immunization should or must take place, and whether parents can prevent this happening. Some parents oppose immunization on religious grounds. Others refuse to have their children vaccinated because of severe, though rare, reactions following immunization, particularly in the case of pertussis. In general, however, your child must be immunized before entering school. (See also "Must Children Be Immunized?" page 188.)

CAUGHT BETWEEN PARENT AND CHILD

Unfortunately, there is no standard protocol for doctors or parents to follow when a child and parents disagree over the child's medical treatment. Policies regarding children's medical rights vary according to circumstances.

In general, doctors prefer to act according to children's best interests, but children by no means have the final word. A doctor who believes that a teenager's health would be threatened by parental involvement may treat her without notifying her parents. In the case of an older child, a doctor is not likely to give tests or treatment without obtaining that child's explicit permission, regardless of parents' requests. Courts also recog-

Hospital Privacy

Privacy is one of your most important rights as a hospital patient. Be aware that you have the right to:

✔ *Refuse visits.* You may turn away family, friends, or anyone not officially connected with the hospital. You also may refuse to see anyone from the hospital not involved with your care, including interns or medical students.

✔ *Safeguard your records.* You may forbid anyone not directly involved with your care to look at your records, including hospital personnel.

✔ *Wear your own clothes.* You can wear your own pajamas, slippers, and robes, if they do not interfere with your treatment.

✔ *Have an attendant of the same sex.* You have the right to have a person of your own gender present during examinations by a medical professional of the opposite sex.

✔ *Remain robed.* After an examination is completed, you have the right to put your clothes back on immediately.

✔ *Expect confidentiality.* Medical personnel are bound to treat information about your condition as confidential and are not permitted to discuss it openly in the hospital.

✔ *Change rooms.* If you are disturbed by someone sharing your room, you are entitled to ask for a bed in another room.

nize that children have the same rights as adults to refuse medical treatment, as long as they are considered competent and mature enough to understand the consequences of their decisions. However, there is no legal consensus about what age or what mental state signifies maturity.

WHEN CHILDREN'S RIGHTS PREVAIL

As a child approaches adolescence, she may be able to seek or refuse certain types of medical care without parental consent, acting as an "emancipated minor." Depending on provincial law, the child must show that she is self-supporting, manages her own financial affairs, and does not live with her parents.

In some provinces, children over 14 may be considered "mature minors" and, as such, be permitted to give informed consent to medical care. The care must be considered medically necessary but not high risk. There is no blanket rule governing the care and treatment of minors and each must be assessed on its own merits.

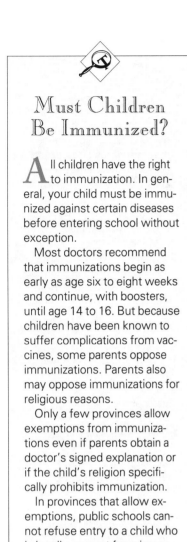

Must Children Be Immunized?

All children have the right to immunization. In general, your child must be immunized against certain diseases before entering school without exception.

Most doctors recommend that immunizations begin as early as age six to eight weeks and continue, with boosters, until age 14 to 16. But because children have been known to suffer complications from vaccines, some parents oppose immunizations. Parents also may oppose immunizations for religious reasons.

Only a few provinces allow exemptions from immunizations even if parents obtain a doctor's signed explanation or if the child's religion specifically prohibits immunization.

In provinces that allow exemptions, public schools cannot refuse entry to a child who is legally exempt from immunization, but private schools and day care facilities may.

If you have questions about immunization laws, contact your provincial health department to clarify your rights.

A Question of Confidentiality

PROBLEM
Sara, a 16-year-old, went to a gynecologist for testing and treatment of a sexually transmitted disease. She asked her doctor to keep her visit confidential, but when a laboratory report arrived in the mail, her parents discovered that she had sought treatment. They called the doctor and demanded to know what was wrong with Sara, claiming that because she was underage, they had a right to know the details of her condition.

ACTION
The gynecologist refused Sara's parents' request. He had a legal obligation to keep Sara's diagnosis confidential despite her age, because she was seeking treatment for a situation related to her sexuality, and his obligation was based on the theory of privacy regarding sexual activity. Many provinces have laws specifically permitting a doctor to treat a minor for a sexually transmitted disease without parental notification. (If her condition had been unrelated to sexual activity—for instance if she had broken her hand, or had leukemia—her parents might have been entitled to information.) The doctor decided to ask Sara if he could tell her parents that she had no threatening condition. When she agreed in writing, he informed her parents that she was all right.

In some situations, a child will seek treatment for a sexually transmitted disease or some other sensitive condition only if she is guaranteed confidentiality. In such instances, which also include seeking substance-abuse treatment or pregnancy-related services, the doctor is free to oblige the child's wish except in some provinces which require either parental notification or judicial permission when a minor seeks an abortion or if the child's life is in danger.

DEALING WITH A HOSPITAL

Checking out hospitals when you are healthy will give you a head start on knowing what to expect if you have to check into one.

Choosing a Hospital

Ideally, a patient should be able to choose the hospital where he would like to be treated. Unfortunately, in an emergency, or when your doctor is only associated with one facility, you are not in a position to do so. If you are lucky enough to be choosing—if your doctor has privileges at a number of facilities for example—you will want to consider a hospital's quality of care, the credentials of its staff, and its location. If you need specific services, such as magnetic resonance imaging (MRI), a hospital's technical capabilities will also be a factor in your decision. But by and large, you will have limited choices, especially now that a number of hospitals have been closed down, and budgets and resources of those still operating are pushed to the limit.

All hospitals must be licensed by the appropriate provincial health licensing authority, which oversees how hospital monies are spent and how the institution is administered. Usually the licensing board is concerned with patients' rights, food, medical records, and quality of care.

DISTINGUISHING TYPES OF HOSPITALS

Different kinds of hospitals have different strengths. General and community hospitals are run by provincial governments and their corresponding health departments. The hospitals may have anywhere from 30 to 300 beds and offer all types of diagnostic services and medical and surgical treatments to people of all ages and both sexes for all types of illnesses.

A handful of specialty hospitals focus on specific illnesses and procedures, and an even smaller number of rehabilitation hospitals serve patients requiring long-term rehabilitative or convalescent care.

Canada has fewer than 100 teaching hospitals, all affiliated with medical schools, and they provide a training ground for medical students and graduates doing their residencies. The hospital's full-fledged doctors and attending physicians are usually highly knowledgeable and experienced specialists who have access to the best technical resources and offer the latest treatments. Patient care is usually handled by resident physicians, supervised by attending physicians or specialists.

123...

SIZING UP A HOSPITAL

Before checking into a hospital you may want to gather some facts about it. For instance, you may want to:

1. Ask for a nurse count. Since nurses are the major caregivers in hospitals, find out how many patients each nurse sees, and how much attention you can expect.

2. Get a mortality rate. If you are about to undergo a risky procedure, find out how many people with the same illness have been through the same procedure and have died as a result. If you can't get information from the hospital, check with your provincial health department to compare information from area hospitals.

3. Ask about infections. It is common for hospitalized patients to pick up infections when their resistance is low. Check with the health department and find out how many patients got infections after being admitted to the hospital and compare the numbers with other hospitals.

4. Check accreditation. Has the hospital received top rating from the Canadian Council on Health Facilities Accreditation?

A teaching hospital can be invaluable if your condition is difficult to diagnose or treat and needs the best possible care. Nevertheless, patients in such hospitals can refuse to be examined by medical students and have the right to know exactly the qualifications of those who are proposing treatment. If you do not want to participate in the education of medical professionals, a teaching hospital is not your best option.

Some hospitals, such as veterans' hospitals and those in federal institutions—penitentiaries, for example—are owned and run by the federal government.

Private hospitals are rare in Canada but there is a movement in Alberta to allow private clinics to bill some of their costs to Medicare. If you use a private clinic's services, make sure you have private health insurance in addition to Medicare, or that you can otherwise afford the costs.

> *It may seem a strange principle to enunciate as the very first requirement in a hospital that it should do the sick no harm.*
>
> FLORENCE NIGHTINGALE
> British nurse
> 1820–1910

Admission and Discharge

Plan ahead if you know you are to be hospitalized. Call the admitting office to arrange a time when you can stop by and do all the preliminary paperwork. Bring your driver's license, Medicare and private health insurance cards, a hospital card if you were issued one previously, and any other documents the office requests. You will also be asked for your Social Insurance Number, and possibly your mother's maiden name.

Advance Directives: Giving the Doctors Orders

An "advance directive" is a document such as a living will, health care proxy, or power of attorney that stipulates your medical-treatment preferences before you become seriously ill. Here are some things you should know before creating an advance directive:

• Only Quebec, Ontario, Manitoba, and Nova Scotia recognize a person's right to state by "living will" or "durable power of attorney" what kind of treatment he would want (or not want) if he falls victim to a terminal illness and has neither a reasonable hope of a cure nor a treatment to slow the body's degeneration. Nonetheless, it is a good idea to complete such a document, which may help relatives and caregivers make decisions in accordance with your wishes.

• If you choose to draw up a living will stating, for example, that, in the event you are terminally ill and near death, you do not wish to be kept alive by artificial means, your caregivers have your written and witnessed instructions. If instead you choose a durable power of attorney, the decision whether or not to maintain life-support equipment is made by someone named by you.

• There is a difference between disconnecting life support in accordance with a patient's wishes and carrying out a deliberate act to end a life, no matter how painful and undignified that life. In the 1991 case of Nancy B, the court held a doctor committed no crime in disconnecting her life-support system. In 1995, an Alberta court sentenced a father to 10 years in prison for ending the life of his young daughter, despite his motive of ending the child's suffering. The Supreme Court later overturned the conviction and ordered a new trial because of doubts regarding jury selection.

CAN YOU BE REFUSED ADMISSION?

If you are not an emergency patient, a hospital can turn you away if it has no free beds or if it cannot deal with your condition. But no hospital may refuse to admit you because of your race, religion, national origin, or lack of financial resources.

As long as you are mentally competent, you cannot be prevented from leaving a hospital to which you have been admitted. If you have not been formally discharged, and the hospital staff thinks you are too ill or physically incapacitated to leave, you will likely be asked to sign a "discharge against medical advice" form. You cannot be made sign, however, as you are within your rights in refusing to do so.

Emergency-Room Rights

You have a legal right to emergency-room care as long as you truly have a medical emergency. If a hospital cannot treat you in an emergency, it must refer you to one that can—after the staff has determined that you do indeed require immediate care. Some examples of true emergency conditions are heavy bleeding from major blood vessels, heart attack, stopped breathing, deep shock, ingestion or exposure to fast-acting poison, a penetrating wound to the heart or lungs, severe head injury, or an acute psychotic state.

Try to have a friend or relative accompany you to the emergency room to help you make decisions. Make sure you understand and approve all tests and treatments that are ordered. You have the right to refuse proposed emergency care, provided you are mentally competent to make that decision.

How to Control Your Care

Unless you enter the hospital on an emergency basis, you have the right to ask that specific doctors care for you. Do not hesitate to ask about the experience of an intern or resident who is assigned to administer treatment or perform medical procedures, or to request a more experienced practitioner. You have the right to refuse care or treatment from any medical staff.

Bear in mind, however, that hospital staff may not have to comply with every single one of your wishes. Remember, too, that even the most junior doctor has years of study and training under his belt and may be more than professionally adequate to care for you. You might also want to reconsider why you are in the hospital at all if you reject every treatment the hospital staff recommends.

Patients' Representatives

If you have questions, problems, or needs concerning your hospital care, a useful person to talk to is the patients' representative. Her job is to act as a mediator between you and the hospital organization to ensure that your needs are met. The patients' representative's primary duties are to:

✔ *Tell you what your rights are.* If you are unsure of your rights in any situation, a patients' representative should be able to clarify things for you.

✔ *Voice your complaints.* She should be able to take your problems to appropriate department heads and get a quick response.

✔ *Steer you in the right direction.* If she cannot help you directly, a patients' representative should be able to refer you to someone who can. For example, she can tell you how to set about getting a second opinion or hiring a private nurse.

✔ *Work with the hospital staff.* A good patients' representative will keep increasingly harried hospital staff aware that a patient's comfort is vital.

GETTING HELP TO GET YOUR RIGHTS

Sometimes, when hospitalized, you may need help asserting your rights. Several sources may be available:

- **Patients' rights advocates.** The job of a patients' rights advocate is to communicate your complaints to the hospital administration and bring the responses back to you while you are in the hospital. A patients' rights advocate might work for the hospital, an insurance company, a consumer group, or directly for you. His role is to help you understand, exercise, and protect the rights contained in your hospital's Patient's Bill of Rights. Although not legally enforceable, these rights are often part of hospital policy. If the hospital staff notifies you of your discharge when you do not feel well enough to go home, you can call on a patients' rights advocate to intervene for you.

- **Patients' representatives.** Unlike patients' rights advocates, most patients' representatives work for the hospital. Rather than championing your cause, a patients' representative will work to ease trouble between you and the hospital. He may be able to help you secure a room change, or ease tensions between you and a staff member.

- **Ombudsmen.** An ombudsman does not help with direct problem resolution. He instead identifies broad problem areas in the hospital, researches them, and offers solutions to the hospital administration. If you were unhappy with a hospital policy, whether you had a problem with treatment, admission procedures, or visiting hours, you could complain to the hospital's ombudsman.

- **Ethics committees.** An ethics committee is a hospital group that helps develop hospital policy and deals with issues regarding difficult ethical dilemmas, such as right-to-die cases. The committee usually includes doctors, a lawyer, a nurse, a social worker, and a member of the clergy. If a relative was being kept alive by life-support systems, and you and the doctor disagreed over whether or not to discontinue their use, the ethics committee could be asked to review the case and make a recommendation.

OTHER WAYS TO COMPLAIN

All hospitals must be licensed by the province, so any complaints about the facilities should be made to the provincial health ministry. Complaints about the conduct of professional personnel should be directed to the board that oversees the particular profession. In the case of doctors, for instance, address your comments to the College of Physicians and Surgeons; in matters to do with nursing staff, contact the provincial College of Nurses, and so on.

123..

DON'T PAY FOR THINGS YOU DON'T WANT OR NEED

Your Medicare coverage does not include such amenities as private rooms and television. If these items are offered and you must pay for them out of your pocket, you have the right to refuse:

1. A private room. If you need a private room for medical reasons, you should be assigned one. But be aware that if you ask for private or semi-private accommodation, such rooms cost more than regular accommodation, and you will have to pay the difference, unless you have private insurance with this coverage.

2. A telephone. Even if you do not use your telephone, the hospital may charge you for calls others make to you. If you do not want a telephone, say so. Cellular phones are usually prohibited, as they may interfere with medical equipment.

3. A television set. The charge for a TV can often be steep. If you do not think you will use it, ask that it not be connected.

4. Personal items. Bring personal items such as a toothbrush from home. Hospitals may charge you more than you would pay in the store.

5. Special meals. If your doctor permits you to eat food not usually available at hospital, arrange for a friend to bring it. Special requests for meals may be charged to you and are not covered by Medicare.

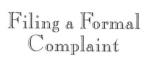

Nurses and the Law

Although doctors have the highest status in the medical profession, nurses actually provide the most care and have the most contact with the patient. Nursing is one of the more demanding occupations and usually attracts people with a high degree of commitment, compassion, and good humor.

Until the last few decades nursing was considered a woman's job and consequently the pay was often low. With changing times, other concerns have beset the profession, not least of which are the loss of jobs through hospital closings, and the fact that less skilled and less demanding occupations offer better pay and working conditions.

Every province and territory has a law dealing with the nursing profession. Depending on the jurisdiction, this is known as the Nursing Professions Act, the Nurses Act, or the Nursing Profession Ordinance. In most cases, these statutes delegate responsibility for ensuring quality care, ethical behavior, and discipline to provincial nursing associations, such as the provincial colleges of nursing. The Canadian Nurses Association, the national federation of provincial and territorial associations, also works at maintaining and improving professional and ethical standards, education, and services.

In order to practice nursing, one must be licensed by the Provincial Nursing Association after graduation from university or college and completing training in a teaching hospital. A license must be obtained from each province in which one wishes to practice. The profession, of course, is open to both men and women.

CONDUCT SUBJECT TO DISCIPLINE

A nurse is subject to discipline for any of the following acts or omissions:

- Abusing a patient verbally or physically.
- Misappropriating a patient's personal property.
- Abandoning a patient.
- Influencing a patient to change his or her will.
- Failing to report a fellow nurse's incompetency which may have a negative effect on the patient.
- Falsifying a patient's record.
- Failing to exercise discretion in disclosing confidential information about a patient.
- Failing to inform a superior that the tasks assigned to her are beyond her competence or require a degree of special training which she does not possess.

Filing a Formal Complaint

If you feel that a doctor, nurse or other health professional is guilty of unbecoming, unprofessional, or improper conduct toward you—which may include being drunk or under the influence of drugs, disregarding your wishes as to medical treatment, sexual assault, or performing a professional service that is not justified on reasonable grounds—there are several ways to proceed.

Each province has a Health Discipline Board where you may file your complaint. In some provinces, the discipline board can suspend or revoke a practitioner's license to practice; in others, the board refers the matter to the Provincial College of Physicians and Surgeons, the Provincial College of Nurses, or other appropriate organization. The process for handling complaints is set out in the various provincial medical and health discipline acts.

A medical practitioner who is found guilty of misconduct or unprofessional behavior may be subject to a reprimand, to a fine, or to a loss of his license. A medical practitioner who has been found guilty of incompetence or misconduct may apply for a formal hearing with a right of appeal.

- Participating in behavior that would reasonably be regarded by other nursing professionals as being disgraceful, dishonorable, or unprofessional.

When a hospital patient suffers injury, there is a tendency to think that only the doctor or the hospital is liable for damages. People feel a nurse's liability is limited by the fact that she is working under doctor's orders and so should not be held accountable. This, however, is not true. Like a doctor, a nurse is a health professional, and as such is liable for injuries to a patient if it can be shown that she was negligent, breached her duty of care, or failed to do something that could have prevented the patient's injury. Most nurses have insurance to cover accidents that happen to patients while in their nursing care.

PERSONAL LIABILITY

Some nursing concerns involve the question of consent. Nurses worry, for example, that when they ask a patient's consent to treatment, the permission may extend only to the doctor and hospital, not to them. Are consents given by common law spouses valid, and would the patient's consent be valid if given while he was drunk or otherwise impaired? What legal consequences are involved if a nurse counsels a minor on the use of contraceptive devices or birth control pills, or assists the physician performing abortions on minors, or implanting intrauterine devices in minors, without parental consent? What is the liability of a nurse who by error gives a patient a wrong dosage, or judges him fit to get out of bed, but because he is weak, he falls and injures himself? What if the nurse forgets to put up the side of the bed and the patient falls out and breaks his hip?

In any of the above scenarios, the nurse may or may not be held liable, since each case is decided on its own merits and circumstances. Such cases revolve around the nurse's duty of care (did she breach her duty of care?) and foreseeability (could the accident have been foreseen by a "reasonable person"?).

If a patient could prove a breach of the duty of care and the reasonable foreseeability of the result, and could prove the existence of a material injury caused directly by the nurse's act or omission, the nurse would probably be found responsible and have to pay damages. If the nurse's assets or insurance coverage are insufficient to compensate the patient fully, the hospital employing the nurse could also be liable to pay damages.

In negligence cases, a nurse's defense may be that her decision was an error of judgment rather than negligence. In nursing, decisions have to be made on a continuing basis, and if the nurse made an honest error in judgment rather than having been negligent, then, based on all the pertinent circumstances, she may be exonerated.

There are no such things as incurables, there are only things for which man has not found a cure.

BERNARD M. BARUCH

Address to the President's Committee on Employment and the Physically Handicapped 1954

ALTERNATIVE HEALTH CARE

Certain remedies practiced outside of the medical mainstream may be helpful to you, but don't jeopardize your safety or your rights when you use them.

Types of Alternative Care

Mainstream medicine is not your only health care option. Alternative approaches to healing are gaining increasing numbers of disciples among those dissatisfied with established procedures. In some instances, traditional caregivers such as midwives are enjoying renewed popularity. Different though they may be, many alternative therapies share a belief in the body's ability to heal itself and in the principle of holistic medicine—in treating a person physically, mentally, and spiritually. This holistic approach has been the attraction for many people who have been put off by the increasingly impersonal and technological approach of modern medicine. Indeed many people feel much of the success of some alternative practitioners may result from the sympathetic hearing they give their patients.

MIDWIFERY

Midwives care for and assist mothers and their babies during pregnancy, labor, delivery, and the period immediately afterward. Many of their deliveries take place in hospital. Some midwives are registered nurses who have taken additional training in obstetrics, gynecology, and newborn care. Lay midwives have been trained in midwifery, but are not registered nurses.

Midwives may employ massage or relaxation techniques during delivery; they monitor the progress of labor, including the presence or absence of fetal distress; and they determine if a doctor is needed. They also assist in the delivery and examination of the newborn. Midwives are restricted to caring for women with normal, uncomplicated pregnancies. They must work in association with a physician, and usually a hospital, in order to obtain assistance if complications develop.

Midwives are now accredited in Ontario and Quebec, but other provincial governments have been slow to establish certification requirements.

CHIROPRACTORS

According to chiropractors, the key to good health is a balanced spine and nervous system. They believe that without that balance, the spine and its related nerve roots become irritated and

---

Recognizing Fraudulent Cures

While many alternative remedies are effective and many practitioners are on the up and up, fraudulent cures and dishonest practitioners are numerous too. Here are some "red flags" to look out for:

✔ *Not enough information.* Find out if an alternative remedy is harmful and what the potential side effects are. If a product does not list its ingredients on the label, it may be because they are harmful.

✔ *Exclusive therapies.* Think twice if a practitioner advises you to stop using therapy or medication your doctor prescribed.

✔ *Miracle cures.* Beware of a seller who claims that a product or therapy works for all kinds of conditions, including yours. There are no cure-alls.

✔ *No proof.* Testimonials that the cure is a success are not enough; the number of dissatisfied customers may outweigh the happy ones. Call the Drug Directorate of Health Canada to find out if the product has been tested.

WATCH OUT FOR FAD DIET PLANS

Dieting is never easy. Warning bells should ring if any plan or weight loss center tells you it is. Here are some basic truths about dieting:

1. Weight loss should be slow. Avoid any diet or clinic that promises fast weight loss. Shedding weight too fast can be dangerous, and the weight usually returns.

2. A good diet includes variety. Diet plans that restrict you to a few foods will bore you and put you at risk for nutritional deficiency. The healthiest way to lose weight is to change your eating habits so that you eat nutritionally balanced, low-fat meals that allow for your individual tastes.

3. Diets should be proven. No plan should be based on a secret formula. The credibility of a regimen is based on the number of people it has helped—the more the better. You are safest choosing a plan that has been shown in controlled studies to be effective and that has been published in a respected scientific or medical journal.

4. A diet should make sense. You should be able to adapt it to your family situation and to restaurants. If you cannot live with it, you are not likely to stick with it and probably will regain any weight you lose.

5. No diet can change your life. Any diet or food plan that promises life-changing miracles is misleading and bogus.

make the body vulnerable to disease. People use chiropractors for relief from ailments such as backaches, spastic colon, and headaches. Chiropractors' training includes course work in anatomy, physiology, neurophysiology, and kinesiology. They are licensed in all provinces, but cannot prescribe drugs or perform invasive procedures. In addition, they may not hospitalize patients and must refer them to a physician for a condition that they cannot treat. Before signing a contract for a course of treatment, check with your private insurer to see if your treatment will be covered by them or by Medicare.

ACUPUNCTURE

The ancient Chinese practice of acupuncture involves the use of very fine needles inserted at various points on the body to treat numerous symptoms and illnesses. Stimulating these points by inserting and twirling needles is believed to send impulses throughout the nervous system that, in turn, sends healing signals to the organs and restores the body's balance.

Acupuncture has been promoted as a cure for obesity, hypertension, ulcers, headaches, back pain, drug addiction, and many other ailments. In some provinces, acupuncturists must be licensed physicians; in others, they are licensed as nonmedical practitioners; and in still others, no licensing is required. Acupuncture is generally not covered by Medicare unless the treatment is done by a qualified physician. Find out if your private insurer will cover the costs, and for how many sessions.

HOMEOPATHY

The theory behind homeopathy is that "like cures like"—the cause of an illness is similar to its cure. Homeopathic doctors treat illness by prescribing a small, highly diluted dose of a natural substance that in a larger, more concentrated dose would reproduce the patient's symptoms. A tiny amount of a laxative, for example, would be used to treat diarrhea. Homeopathic remedies are given in the smallest dose possible, are designed to complement natural body processes, are not dangerous, and have few or no side effect. Although some homeopaths are medical doctors, most mainstream physicians remain skeptical of homeopathy and attribute its successes to a placebo effect.

NATUROPATHY

Naturopathic doctors believe firmly in the body's ability to heal itself and claim health is maintained by avoiding anything unnatural or artificial in the diet or environment. Naturopathic doctors who have completed four years postgraduate study are licensed in British Columbia, Saskatchewan, Manitoba, and Ontario. Some people who claim to be naturopaths are not properly accredited.

HERBAL MEDICINES—WHAT TO KNOW

Despite the resistance of Western doctors to folk therapies, herbalism's natural, holistic orientation has a wide appeal. The Canadian market for herbal remedies is estimated to be about $560 million and growing at a rate of 10 to 15 percent a year. Herbal medicines are now found in health food stores, and pharmacies as well as through natural practitioners. Many are also sold through newspaper and magazine advertisements and are widely available to the public without prescription. Only products carrying the drug identification number (DIN) have been cleared by Health Canada.

Even though the effects of most herbal preparations are quite mild, such remedies can cause allergic reactions in some people, and if taken excessively, or in the wrong combinations, can be toxic. Do not take herbs if you are pregnant and do not give herbal remedies to babies or young children. Fetuses and babies may not have the liver enzymes to properly detoxify some harmful chemicals found in herbs.

BEWARE OF PRACTITIONERS PROMISING "CURES"

Fear and desperation sometimes compel terminally ill patients to seek special diets, experimental drugs, vaccines, salves, even psychological approaches outside regular medical practice. Some promised "cures" do real harm, according to mainstream doctors. For example, some salves said to burn away surface skin cancers may contain corrosive agents that damage the skin and are useless against the cancer. Many physicians believe the biggest danger in alternative therapies is lost time. By the time a treatment is found to be ineffective, the disease may have progressed too far for standard medical treatments to be effective. However, many organizations and professionals, including the Canadian Cancer Society, do not discourage patients from using alternative therapies, provided they are used in conjunction with traditional medicine.

If in doubt about a recommended treatment, ask Health Canada's Health Protection Branch for information on the substance. But even though Canada has stringent drug-testing procedures, some herbal treatments, and many potions, pills, and compounds sold in Chinese medicines reach the public without Drug Directorate approval. The manufacturers feel testing is unnecessary since the medicines, often made of tree bark, roots and plants, are "natural." But even natural ingredients can prove harmful, as anyone who has come in contact with poison ivy or ate a poisonous mushroom can attest. If you are harmed by a natural potion or exploited financially, if for instance you paid a large sum of money for a substance that proves to be nothing more than powderized orange peel, contact the Drug Directorate, and the local police fraud squad.

A miracle drug is any drug that will do what the label says it will do.

ERIC HODGINS
Episode

SUPPLEMENTING MEDICARE

Unless you have supplementary health insurance, you will have to pay out of pocket for any medical procedures, equipment, or prostheses not covered by Medicare.

The Medicare Crisis

Medical costs have continued to rise in recent years, at a time when governments have been increasingly strapped to pay down interest on their debt loads. The outcome has been severe cutbacks in Medicare coverage, and a growing list of procedures, equipment, and prostheses that must be paid for by the patient or his private insurance plan. With more cuts likely, private insurance to augment the benefits presently dispensed by Medicare is a wise investment.

OTHER INSURANCE SOURCES

Group health insurance is attractive financially in that premiums usually cost less than what you would pay for individual coverage. For many years, a group health insurance plan covering employees, their spouses, and children was among standard benefits that governments and large corporations offered their employees. Generally the employer paid all or most of the premiums and, not surprisingly, most employees joined the plan. Nowadays, increased medical costs and a tougher business environment has led some companies to cut back on the quality of their insurance plans or cancel them altogether. But even if your employer does not offer group insurance, you may still be able to qualify if you belong to a fraternal, professional, or service organization. If you cannot get group insurance through your employer or a professional or service association, however, your only other recourse is private health insurance, which is quite costly and sometimes difficult to obtain.

GROUP VS INDIVIDUAL INSURANCE

Group insurance generally requires at least 25 members, and for many the group plan's financial benefits are secondary to the fact that medical examinations may not be a prerequisite. Preexisting medical conditions are usually covered in group insurance of 200 or more people: in setting premiums, insurers take into account that some members most likely suffer from certain medical problems that are likely to require medical attention in the near future. Some plans, however, do call for a medical exam before joining, and employees with certain health problems may be denied coverage.

If you leave a group plan, you usually have 31 days to convert to an individual insurance policy without taking a medical examination. However, this may be limited to people under 65 years of age, and the premium charged would be that charged to a person of your age group. Premiums, which are usually considerably higher than the group rate, must be paid during the conversion period.

INDIVIDUAL INSURANCE

When taking out individual insurance (other than converting from a group to an individual policy), you may be refused coverage because of your age, or because you have a high-risk job or a serious, preexisting health condition. If you pass these first hurdles, you will have to pass a medical exam and complete a questionnaire.

Failure to answer the questions fully and truthfully can return to haunt you. If, for example, you do not mention that you were hospitalized in the last two years, even for a minor problem, you may find your insurance canceled when you present your first claim. Insurance is a special type of contract and requires the applicant to exercise the "utmost good faith" when contracting; even by disclosing certain material facts that were not asked by the insurer.

Some private health insurance plans provide for salary insurance during illness. If this is included in your plan, your premiums for this benefit are tax deductible.

Health insurance plans usually have a certain life span, say five years or until age 65.

HEALTH INSURANCE COMPANIES

If you are shopping for health insurance to supplement your Medicare coverage, you must choose from a limited number of providers. Health insurance is not offered by many large life insurance companies nor by those dealing in home and car insurance. Deal only with reputable, well-established companies such as Liberty Health and the nonprofit Blue Cross, which are licensed by your provincial insurance board.

Since Medicare covers the major health care expenses such as hospitalization, surgery, medical consultation, anesthesia, hospital drugs, services supplied by specialists, as well as X-rays and most laboratory tests, you might want supplementary health insurance for semiprivate or private hospital room accommodation, nursing or homecare services, dental, vision, chiropractic, or physiotherapy services, or prescription drugs. Blue Cross, for example, covers such expenses as:

■ The cost of upgrading a hospital room from public (three or more beds) to semiprivate (two beds).

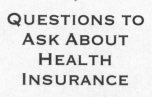

QUESTIONS TO ASK ABOUT HEALTH INSURANCE

Since health insurance plans vary from one insurer to another, study your policy carefully. Here are some questions to ask:

1. Does your plan include private room coverage in the event you are hospitalized? What is the maximum hospital stay covered—the duration of your illness or only up to a stated amount?

2. Are ambulance costs covered? What about out-of-hospital costs such as a wheelchair, or drugs prescribed after discharge?

3. Does your policy pay for medical treatments you receive in other than a hospital, a clinic for example? Does it pay the entire cost of your care, or a percentage, or flat fee per day?

4. Does your insurance cover lost wages? If so, what percentage of your salary and for how long?

5. Are dental expenses caused by accident or illness covered?

6. Will your insurance pay for consultation with a doctor of your choice or are you bound by the diagnosis and treatment prescribed by the insurance company doctors? What options have you if you disagree with the insurance doctor's diagnosis and prognosis, or judgments on other matters relating to your health?

7. What is the deductible?

Insurance You May Not Need

Soaring health care costs might scare you into thinking you need every kind of health insurance policy you can find. Evaluate the cost of coverage versus your risks, and how complete the coverage actually is, and look out for the following:

✔ *Hospital indemnity.* There is a danger of getting little pay-off with this kind of policy. In exchange for your premium, you are reimbursed a set fee for each day you spend in the hospital.

✔ *"Dread disease."* These policies cover specific diseases, such as cancer. Their benefits are limited, however, and many of the services covered are already included in more comprehensive plans.

✔ *Accident insurance.* The components in an accident insurance policy are generally offered in a traditional, comprehensive health insurance package. Most specialty accident insurance policies do not come close to covering the cost of serious injuries.

- Convalescent care for up to 90 days per year providing the insured received convalescent care within 14 days of discharge from hospital.
- Laboratory charges for diagnostic tests and treatments of an illness or injury not covered by Medicare.
- Ambulance services from the site of the illness or accident and back to the place of residence after hospital discharge.
- Expenses for a registered nurse at the insured's home when medically required up to an annual maximum of 20 eight-hour shifts.
- Up to $1,000 in dental work when healthy teeth are damaged by illness or accident.
- Up to 80 percent of the cost of renting crutches, walkers, canes, manually operated wheelchairs, and equipment for administering oxygen.
- A rate of $15 per visit (for up to 20 visits a year) in fees to a chiropractor, a podiatrist, a physiotherapist or rehabilitation therapist, or an occupational therapist.
- $100 per 24-month period for eyeglasses or contact lenses.
- From $100 to $250 per year for prostheses such as elastic stockings, orthopedic shoes, podiatric ortheses, or mammary prostheses following a mastectomy.

Even though the coverage you receive will vary somewhat from one provider to another, the following exclusions are common to most insurers:

- Growth hormones.
- Detoxification program charges.
- Expenses for experimental treatment or the use of medical procedures not in common use.
- Expenses incurred in the case of suicide, attempted suicide or intentional injury.
- Expenses for care, treatment, services, or products other than those specifically declared necessary by a treating physician to treat illness or injury.
- Treatment, prosthesis, or surgery for cosmetic reasons.
- Expenses related to fertilization techniques.

If you carry supplementary health care insurance, but are planning a trip out of the province or the country, check that your coverage includes emergency travel insurance. If not, you would be wise to purchase a separate travel insurance policy. Without such coverage, most supplementary health care providers will not cover charges incurred outside Canada, nor, apart from emergency situations, care given outside your home province if such care is available at home. Before departure, familiarize yourself with the policy's terms and conditions.

PREEXISTING CONDITIONS

One of the loopholes that most insurance companies put into individual (and sometimes group) policies is a clause dealing with preexisting conditions. This can be any health problem, ranging from chronic back pain to a heart condition, that existed before you bought the policy. Some policies exclude coverage not only for the preexisting conditions but for any related illness or injury—even if that related illness or injury occurred after the policy was bought. If you have suffered from high blood pressure, for example, you may not be covered for any future related illness, such as heart attack.

Some policies stipulate a period, say six months after a policy goes into effect, during which costs pertaining to a preexisting condition will not be covered. Coverage begins once the waiting period is over.

Do not let your feelings about the fairness or otherwise of a "preexisting condition" get in the way of your honesty when applying for insurance. Chances are that if you are not truthful, and later make a claim related to that condition, the company's investigators will find out that you lied, your policy will most likely be canceled, and the coverage you sought denied.

Usually an insurance company which is brought to court for denying coverage under these circumstances will argue that it would either have denied coverage in the first place, or else it would have exacted a much higher premium had it known of the preexisting condition.

The Act of God designation on all insurance policies means, roughly, that you cannot be insured for the accidents that are most likely to happen to you.

ALAN COREN
British humorist
1993

Keeping a Lid on Insurance Costs

Securing the right health insurance plan means finding the most comprehensive package you can afford. If you are shopping for complete protection, here are several tips that will help you save money:

• **Avoid duplication.** Do not duplicate your coverage. Buying more than one policy may make you feel more secure, but it will probably not bring you any more cash or savings. Most policies do not allow you to collect from two companies for the same claim. Also, try to find a policy that covers your spouse and children without increasing your premium too drastically.

• **Pay annually.** If you can afford it, arrange to pay your premium annually rather than monthly. Many companies offer a discount for lump-sum payments of annual premiums.

• **Take the highest deductible.** Elect the highest deductible you think you could afford if you were to get seriously ill. You will have to pay for most or all treatment for minor health problems and may face a hefty initial payment if you face more serious illness or injury, but you will pay substantially lower premiums while you are healthy.

• **Consider managed care.** Make sure that your insurer pays the hospital, health care provider, and provider of equipment directly, to avoid out-of-pocket expenses and perhaps disagreements about the bill.

• **Invest in a major health issues provider.** Make sure you deal with a financially secure company licensed by your provincial government insurance board and not a fly-by-night organization.

LONG-TERM CARE

With chronic or terminal illness, you need the strongest, most reliable health care safety net your money can buy.

What Is Long-Term Care and Who Needs It?

Long-term care has many meanings. In general, it includes a broad spectrum of medical, personal, and social support services ranging from home meal delivery to skilled nursing care. Such assistance is provided over an extended period for people who are severely disabled, terminally ill, or have a chronic mental illness.

Long-term care is usually associated with old age. But the elderly represent only part of the long-term care population. People with cancer or AIDS, as well as large numbers of people suffering from chronic, debilitating diseases such as multiple sclerosis, constitute a substantial portion of those who receive long-term care.

Long-term care is not limited to the sick. It may also be essential for someone who is physically disabled, a person with spinal cord injury, for example, or anyone born with muscular dystrophy or spina bifida. The mentally retarded and the mentally ill—individuals suffering from schizophrenia or severe manic-depressive (bipolar) disorder—also may need long-term care. Blind or deaf people may also need long-term assistance, whether they are able to receive it at home or at a specially designed facility.

Caring for the Chronically Ill

There are essentially three types of long-term care: in-home services, community-based services, and institutional care. In-home services assist people who live at home with a certain degree of independence but who need regular assistance with the activities of daily living. Community programs are geared toward people who need constant care and observation, especially during the day when those who normally take care of them are at work or simply need a rest from caregiving. People who require extended around-the-clock care but not hospitalization may need institutional care. Varying levels of institutional care are provided in nursing homes, convalescent homes, and rehabilitation hospitals. The scope and nature of the services depend on the condition and needs of the individual. In some instances, services in different categories may overlap.

IN-HOME SERVICES

Persons who are recovering from surgery or a heart attack commonly need home care, as do people who are in the early stages of a terminal illness or progressive neurological disease. Home care might also benefit someone who is suffering from a chronic illness or condition or who is physically disabled.

In-home services for the terminally ill may include medical care provided by a nurse or therapist, as well as personal support services, such as help with grooming, dressing, and daily household chores. Social support services, such as home-delivered meals, friendly visitor services, and telephone reassurance to the elderly who live alone, are also in-home services.

Members of the Victorian Order of Nurses have been providing wide-ranging home health care for Canadians for more than a century. With services ranging from palliative care to foot care, visiting nurses help individuals and families cope at home with health problems. The organization's headquarters is in Ottawa.

Nursing care and counseling in the home on a visiting basis is also provided by the Toronto-based Saint Elizabeth Visiting Nurses' Association of Ontario. Specialty programs include palliative care, enterostomal therapy, foot care, gerontology, and psychiatric patient monitoring. Another Toronto-based

Exercise and temperance can preserve something of our early strength even in old age.

CICERO
On Old Age

Continuing-Care Retirement Communities

A continuing-care retirement community integrates housing, social activities, and health care services for older adults. If you or someone you care about is considering moving to a retirement community, keep the following in mind:

• **Know what you want.** Some communities allow residents to live independently; some offer assisted living, providing help with bathing, dressing, or other daily activities; others provide full-time nursing care; some provide all these services in one apartment building or other housing complex. Decide which type of assistance you need before considering actual communities.

• **Licensing.** All provinces have assessment procedures that will help you find the proper continuing care unit best suited for you, but no uniform level of protection exists. Licensing indicates that a community meets certain standards for financial stability, management, and resident care. To find out if the continuing-care retirement community you have in mind is licensed, contact your provincial health department or department of aging.

• **Check finances.** Before making a commitment, check that the community you are considering is financially sound. Find out if your monthly fee includes the cost of nursing care should you need it. And see if the community will guarantee you a nursing home bed when you need one.

• **Changing your mind.** Make sure you know the community's refund policy. You also should know if the facility can cancel your contract or if it will require you to purchase long-term-care insurance.

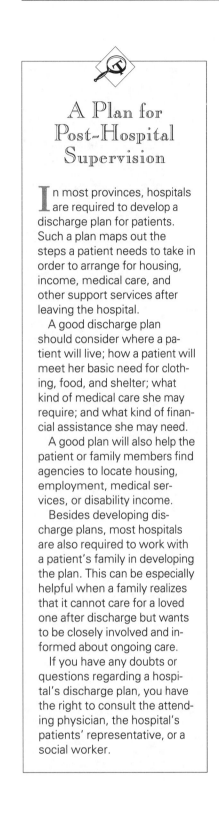

A Plan for Post-Hospital Supervision

In most provinces, hospitals are required to develop a discharge plan for patients. Such a plan maps out the steps a patient needs to take in order to arrange for housing, income, medical care, and other support services after leaving the hospital.

A good discharge plan should consider where a patient will live; how a patient will meet her basic need for clothing, food, and shelter; what kind of medical care she may require; and what kind of financial assistance she may need.

A good plan will also help the patient or family members find agencies to locate housing, employment, medical services, or disability income.

Besides developing discharge plans, most hospitals are also required to work with a patient's family in developing the plan. This can be especially helpful when a family realizes that it cannot care for a loved one after discharge but wants to be closely involved and informed about ongoing care.

If you have any doubts or questions regarding a hospital's discharge plan, you have the right to consult the attending physician, the hospital's patients' representative, or a social worker.

organization, the Visiting Homemakers Association, also assists the elderly, handicapped, and others in crisis. Its trained homemakers work under social worker supervision.

COMMUNITY-BASED SERVICES

Senior centers and adult day-care centers that provide social and recreational programs for older individuals are examples of community-based services. These centers commonly offer meals, counseling, legal, financial, and (sometimes) health care. Some community-based programs provide seniors with inexpensive meals along with opportunities to socialize. These "nutrition sites" are often located in senior citizen centers, housing projects, churches or synagogues, or schools.

Some communities offer alternative living arrangements for the elderly or the mentally or physically disabled, who can no longer live at home. These special-care homes provide people with a room; three meals a day; help with bathing, dressing, and other daily activities; and transportation. These homes may house anywhere from 15 to 100 residents and generally are privately owned and managed. Not all special-care homes are licensed, however, and quality standards vary considerably.

House sharing is another type of community-based program where two or more people live together. Each person has a private bedroom but shares all common living areas. Household chores and expenses are also shared. Similarly, some communities have adult-foster-care programs, placing elderly and disabled adults in private homes.

Respite care offers hours or days of relief to family members caring for frail, ill, or disabled loved ones. This care is generally provided by volunteers who work with churches, synagogues, nursing homes, community health clinics, and volunteer agencies. The volunteers visit a person at home, in an institution, or an adult day-care center. To find respite care, check with your local hospital, department on aging, a social worker, or churches in your community.

Palliative care provides care and counseling for the terminally ill and their families. Workers help patients and families cope with the dying process and provide physical, psychological, social, and emotional support. The care may be provided in a designated palliative care unit or hospice facility or in the patient's home.

INSTITUTIONAL CARE

There are three basic types of skilled institutional care:

- **Skilled nursing care** is designed for people who need intensive, 24-hour-a-day medical care. The patient might be recovering from a serious accident or illness, such as a heart attack, stroke, or spinal cord injury. Skilled nursing facilities are staffed by registered nurses who work under the supervision of a doctor.

- **Intermediate nursing care** is designed for patients recovering from less-serious medical problems. They may be somewhat independent but still need some nursing assistance and supervision that is neither intensive nor full-time.
- **Custodial care** is the least intensive level of institutional care. It is geared toward people who need room and board and some help with personal services but do not require health care services.

Financing Long-Term Care

Not all long-term care poses a financial dilemma. Cost depends on many factors, including the level, location, and duration of care. Some social services are free or provided at a low fee by nonprofit organizations. On the other hand, nursing-home costs can be so high, many wonder if they can even afford it.

Some people buy extensive long-term-care insurance, but this can be quite expensive. As well, very few companies in Canada offer this insurance. Blue Cross, for example, does not cover long-term care. Other consumers choose a policy that merely covers some long-term-care costs. Either way, the policy must be bought when you are still in good health and the premiums will vary according to how old you are at the time of purchase. When applying, do not withhold any information about any preexisting or recently diagnosed medical problem.

PURCHASING LONG-TERM-CARE INSURANCE
Medicare pays for very little short-term, skilled nursing-home care after hospitalization. It also pays for only a small portion of short-term, skilled at-home care. But investing in long-term-care insurance, because you anticipate spending part of your old age in a nursing home, may not be a wise move financially. This is especially true if you have relatively limited income and assets.

In most nonprofit homes you will be charged a flat daily rate (more for a private room than for a shared room). If you need long-term care, many nonprofit homes will charge you the amount you receive from your old age pension and supplement, less a small sum allowed you for personal expenses.

For-profit facilities are more costly and the services, rooms, meals and caregiver-to-patient ratio are usually of higher quality. Costs may exceed $30,000 per year, and considerably more if you request the services of a private nurse or attendant.

Getting Help to Make Your Home Accessible

Physically disabled people often need to modify their homes to accommodate wheelchairs. Government funds to pay for alterations are scarce, but here are some alternative source ideas, depending on the province and status of the disabled individual:

✔ *Disabled vets.* If you are a veteran who was disabled on duty, you may qualify for the Veteran Independence Program or a war veteran's disability pension administered by the Pension Commission of Canada pensions.

✔ *Vocational rehabilitation.* Some provinces will provide financial or other assistance if you can prove that modifying your home will enable you to work and keep you from being hospitalized.

✔ *Insurance.* If you need specific items, such as a chair lift, and your doctor testifies to this in writing, your private health insurance, or Medicare, might cover the costs.

✔ *Loans.* Canada Mortgage and Housing Corporation administers the Residential Rehabilitation Assistance Program, which provides funds for making a disabled person's home more accessible. This program is often run by the provincial housing authority which may also grant low-interest loans.

If you decide on long-term-care insurance, and can find a company willing to issue a long-term-care policy, make sure your policy comes with inflation protection. Nursing-home costs climb every year, but the protection offered by long-term-care policies may not. And such protection does not come cheap. The better your protection, in most cases, the more expensive the policy, and inflation protection will add from 25 to 40 percent to a long-term-care policy premium.

POOR HEALTH MAY EXCLUDE COVERAGE

Before you even consider the costs of long-term-care insurance, check with your doctor and the insurance company to make sure you qualify for coverage. Insurance companies are in business to make money, and they do not like to sell policies to people with preexisting illnesses such as diabetes, multiple sclerosis, asthma, macular degeneration (an eye disease), severe high blood pressure, or who are 60 years and older.

You are a bad risk as well if you are recovering from a stroke, recent cancer surgery, or even if you have undergone a hip-replacement operation within the last 18 months. If you already have a physical disability that keeps you from doing basic activities such as dressing, bathing, and eating, acquiring long-term insurance is probably impossible. Most insurers will insure long-term care only in the case of physical injury, and exclude long-term care due to mental or nervous disorder.

All human beings are born free and equal in dignity and rights.

STEVEN MITCHELL SACK

Attorney at law
New York City

Guardianship of a Mentally Disabled Child

If your child is mentally retarded, mentally ill, or in some other way developmentally disabled and cannot make decisions for himself, you may want to apply for plenary legal guardianship once he becomes an adult. If you are considering this, here are some things you should know:

• You do not have to be a parent to become a legal guardian; you can be a relative or a close friend.

• Guardianship is not a lifelong commitment. You can terminate your legal guardianship at any time after following appropriate legal procedures.

• As a parent applying for guardianship, you must show a court that your child cannot manage his affairs due to mental incompetence. But it is not easy to declare someone—even your own child—incompetent, because the law vigorously protects the civil liberties of the mentally disabled. Courts generally require certification from two doctors: a psychologist or some other mental-health specialist, and a psychiatrist

• Legally, a guardian is responsible for such duties as paying the debts of her ward, entering into contracts for him, and managing his financial affairs.

• Attaining legal guardianship can be an important form of protection for a mentally ill child. Mental illness may be controlled with medication, enabling a person to function independently at least some of the time. Becoming his guardian assures you of having the legal authority to make decisions on his behalf when he is incapacitated.

• If a guardian fails to put her ward's best interest first when conducting the ward's business, the courts can take the responsibility away.

• A guardian may be held personally responsible for the acts of the protected minor, if a lack of proper supervision can be shown.

Policies that cover people with preexisting health problems often cost more and offer fewer benefits than standard policies. Even so, it is worth finding a policy that does not exclude pre-existing Alzheimer's or Parkinson's diseases or stroke-induced dementia, since these are major causes of nursing-home stays.

If you compare premium costs, what is excluded from the policy, and the duration of the policy, it may be cheaper to find a private or public low-cost facility and pay the required costs.

EVALUATING DIFFERENT POLICIES

A policy for long-term insurance generally promises to pay benefits when care is considered "medically necessary." That means care must have been prescribed by a doctor or is needed because a person can no longer take care of herself. Most policies cover skilled, intermediate, and custodial nursing care in provincially licensed nursing homes. Policies may also cover home-care services, including physical therapists, homemakers, and home-health aides from provincially licensed or certified home-health agencies.

Long-term-care policies are either "disability based" or "service based." Disability-based policies cover any type of long-term care, so long as the insured has become disabled. Service-based policies, which are more common—and less advantageous for the consumer—pay only for services that meet insurance-company standards. A service-based policy may pay only for custodial care in a skilled or intermediate nursing facility or in a facility that has at least 25 residents. A disability-based policy does not impose such restrictions.

Most policies pay for at least one year of nursing-home care. You will be hard-pressed to find any policy that covers costs of care for the rest of a person's life. Find out if your policy requires a hospital stay before it covers nursing-home benefits, or if it requires you to be under constant medical supervision.

LONG-TERM-POLICY WRINKLES

Some policies come with a "waiver of premiums," which means that you do not have to pay your premiums during nursing home stays, but most do not waive premiums when nursing care is given at home. Some policies also provide "nonforfeiture benefits," which means that the insurance company will return some of the money you have paid if you forfeit, or discontinue, your policy. An insurer may cancel your long-term-care policy and return your premiums if the company learns that you have not honestly disclosed information about your health. (On the other hand, it may give you a price break for being in good health.) In some provinces, insurers offer a 30-day "free look" period. If, in that time, you decide against the policy, you are entitled to cancel it and get a full refund.

123...

LIMITS ON LONG-TERM CARE

Long-term-care policies use guidelines to determine if a claim is medically necessary. Some restrictions are:

1. Some policies consider care "medically necessary" only if it is related to an acute illness or injury.

2. Some insurance companies insist that their doctors or "benefit advisers" determine customers' health needs and overrule a diagnosis from a patient's doctor. This may be contested since you have the right to consult your own doctor.

3. Some policies stipulate that patients must be unable to accomplish certain activities of daily living, such as bathing or dressing, to be covered. This restriction excludes many patients who are very ill or severely injured, but can still take care of their daily necessities.

4. Some policies pay for only "skilled" care provided by a doctor or a registered nurse, and will not cover costs for a caregiver who might not be professionally trained, but is essential to the patient.

5. Some policies require the insured to be hospitalized before receiving benefits for nursing home stays, excluding those patients whose abilities or health deteriorates gradually until a nursing home is the only alternative.

6. Some policies do not go into effect for three to six months after they are issued.

Be wary of insurance companies that promise you long-term-care coverage beginning within a day or two of purchase. Such companies often attempt to determine your eligibility only after you have filed a claim. As a result, you might be in for a disastrous surprise after it is too late to do anything about it.

Rights of Long-Term Caregivers

Suppose your elderly mother, who lives with you, suffers from Alzheimer's disease. She often forgets to take her medicine and sometimes gets disoriented; you are afraid that she might wander off and come to harm. You worry about her, but you also worry about whether you would be at fault if she caused injury or damage. You think about putting her in a nursing home, but are concerned that you would be forsaking your responsibility. These dilemmas are facing more and more Canadians as the elderly live longer and taking care of them gets more complicated.

Until confronted with the problem, most people never realize what is involved in providing constant, long-term care for someone. When the situation arises, the caregiver may find the burden too heavy, question if they have the right to stop providing care, and want to know who will provide it in their stead.

Caregivers' rights and responsibilities are governed by various provincial laws and by the Criminal Code, which prohibits anyone from abandoning a person who is wholly or substantially dependent upon him or her and by the condition of the person receiving care. All patients have the right to be fully informed about the nature of their illness, proposed treatments, and possible risks or benefits. When they lack the mental capacity to defend their rights or make competent decisions about treatment, they are entitled to the protection of a caregiver who can and will defend their rights. That protector can be a relative, a loving friend, or a court-appointed guardian. It is the caretaker's duty to make treatment decisions that uphold a patient's rights and best interests.

LIABILITY FOR THE MENTALLY ILL

Most people with mental illness are not violent. Nevertheless, some mentally ill individuals, when not treated, may pose a threat to themselves or others. Under such a circumstance, can a caregiver be held responsible?

There is no easy or single answer to that question. Each circumstance depends on a patient's condition and on provincial law. If a person suffering from some form of mental illness causes property damage, for example, the caregiver may or may not be held financially responsible.

Involuntary Hospitalization

Strong legal protections defend the mentally ill from being committed to a long-term care or treatment facility against their wills. Provinces and mental-health facilities generally insist on a clear diagnosis of a person's mental illness and evidence that he poses a danger to himself or others. Before admitting such patients, hospitals usually require reports from two psychiatrists saying the person needs to be hospitalized.

Saying someone is dangerous to himself or others, however, means different things in different provinces. In some, it may mean that a person is suicidal or homicidal. In others, it simply means he cannot care for basic needs, such as feeding or dressing. Courts also vary on interpreting the immediacy of the danger posed by the mentally ill person.

Anyone who refuses commitment is entitled to a court hearing. If he is still hospitalized, he may appeal the court's decision, but his chances for success are not great due to the prior reports by two psychiatrists.

While these restrictions against involuntary committal protect the mentally ill from many abuses, the safeguards often make it difficult for family members to get desperately needed hospital care for a loved one.

If a guardian of a minor or an adult had some way of predicting that he was going to harm a person and negligently failed to supervise or otherwise prevent the harm, then the guardian might be held liable for his actions. But foreseeing potential injury by the actions of another individual is difficult to prove; therefore, a guardian is rarely held responsible.

Some provinces have laws that tailor and limit a caregiver's responsibility to a patient's specific needs. For instance, a caregiver might be assigned to help a patient do his laundry. If he allows the patient to go to the laundromat alone, the caregiver has breached his duty of care in a negligent way and might be responsible if the patient intentionally damages one of the washers or dryers.

Battling a Loved One's Addiction

PROBLEM
George became aware that Rita had a problem with drugs when he discovered that she was sipping brandy and taking sleeping pills during the day. When he suggested she go into treatment, she refused. Feeling frustrated and frightened, he told her that if she did not sign herself into a substance-abuse treatment center, he would do it for her.

ACTION
George made an empty threat. The only way he could force Rita into a treatment center would be to prove to the court that she is incompetent or a danger to herself and others. He could, however, ask family members and friends to join him in directly confronting Rita—when she is sober—about her growing, excessive dependence on sleeping pills and alcohol, a process known as an "intervention." George opted for such a "tough love" confrontation. Shaken by the concern her family and friends showed, Rita acknowledged her problem, and agreed to try treatment.

CAN YOU COMMIT SOMEONE?

It is difficult to commit someone against his will to a long-term-care facility, be it a nursing home, a drug treatment center, or a psychiatric hospital. A person who refuses commitment is entitled to a court hearing. In most cases, caregivers, doctors, and anyone else involved with the person's care must prove to a judge that an individual poses a substantial physical danger to himself and others or that he requires some form of institutionalized long-term care for his own well-being. If the problem is acute, and you think someone is in immediate danger of harming himself or others, dial 911 and request assistance from the police or an ambulance. In most cases, a person delivered to a hospital by police or ambulance can be kept for 48 hours. In that time, he will be examined by two psychiatrists who may decide to keep him in treatment for a longer period.

Substance-Abuse and Alcohol Treatment

Provincial and federal laws state that people in rehabilitation programs for alcoholism and substance abuse have a right to confidentiality. But there are certain exceptions:

✔ *Child and elder abuse.* Programs and their staff are required to report suspected child or elder abuse.

✔ *Criminal threat.* A court order may require a treatment center to confirm or deny that they are treating a particular client who is suspected of being a criminal and a threat to the public. A person enrolled in a substance-abuse program who commits a crime is not protected by confidentiality.

✔ *Acute medical hospitalization.* Laws that protect confidentiality may not apply if, during the course of regular hospitalization, a patient is found to be chemically dependent. That information becomes part of the patient's general medical record, which may then be shared with hospital staff or anyone else involved with his care, as well as with insurance companies.

✔ *Employment applications.* A person applying for employment with the armed forces, federal or provincial agencies, and some companies dealing with public safety may be asked if they have ever participated in a treatment program and may be requested to release their treatment records.

Usually, the caregiver's dilemma about whether to commit someone, and how to go about it, develops slowly and does not involve mental illness or violent behavior. After years of caring for a relative with Alzheimer's disease, for example, a caregiver simply may be too exhausted or financially drained to continue the job. Moreover, if the patient becomes incompetent, the home care and supervision may no longer be adequate.

In such a case, a long-term-care facility will have to affirm that the patient indeed has Alzheimer's and is incompetent. After accepting a patient, the facility will design a treatment plan. It must also inform both the patient and the caregiver of its policies regarding discharge and transfer to another facility.

MEDICATION DILEMMAS

Just as you cannot commit someone against his will, you also cannot force him to submit to any form of medical treatment. To make a patient take medication, you or the hospital staff have to prove that the patient is in medical danger by not taking it. Or a judge has to determine that a patient is incompetent and does not understand the need for medication. In that case, the judge could appoint a legal guardian to make sure a patient takes the medication.

HOW LONG IS LONG-TERM CARE?

The duration of long-term care depends on where the care is given, the severity of a patient's condition, and the financial resources and emotional stamina of the caregiver. For a patient with Alzheimer's, care can last until the patient dies. For a person who is addicted to drugs or alcohol, the length of care may last only as long as the rehabilitation process.

In some circumstances, a caregiver's role depends on legal guardianship. Depending on the province, most legal guardianships have time limits and are subject to regular court reviews.

WHEN CAREGIVERS STOP GIVING CARE

Sometimes families can no longer care for their loved ones and must find alternative settings. If a caregiver dies without making provisions for care and support, and a patient has no other family, the patient may be declared a ward of the province, which must arrange for the patient's care. The province will use any money the patient has to pay for this care. If the patient has no financial resources, Medicare or the provincial health ministry will pay the bill. If you are a caregiver, make sure you investigate alternative arrangements for providing for those under your care in case of your death. A caregiver who feels unable to continue providing care can always ask the court for help in finding either an alternative caregiver or a new care setting, such as a group home, adult foster care, or a hospital.

NURSING HOMES

As the population ages, more and more people will spend time in a nursing home before they die. Be sure you know what you or a loved one can expect.

Three Levels of Care

Some 3,000 long-term-care facilities operate in Canada, many of them nursing homes, and the service they provide has become an essential part of the social fabric. As more Canadians survive into old age and fewer families are able to take care of their elderly relatives at home, the prevalence of nursing-home care will continue to grow. It is important to learn what to expect if the time comes when you or a loved one needs to take this difficult step.

Nursing homes are known by different names in different areas. Such institutions are called personal-care homes in Manitoba and reception centers (*centres d'accueil*) in Quebec. Their organization and regulation also vary from province to province. Generally, they can be divided into three categories:

- **Skilled-care facilities** provide intensive care—such as intravenous and respiratory therapy and tube feedings—to patients who are bedridden and unable to help themselves.
- **Intermediate-care nursing homes** are for patients who need help with bathing, meals, and other daily functions and with health-related activities, such as taking medications and managing their diets.
- **Custodial-care facilities** serve those who can function independently but need some assistance getting out of bed, walking, and bathing.

As a rule, Medicare does not cover your stay in a nursing home, but some government aid may be available if you need nursing-home care but cannot afford it. In some cases, your old age pension and supplement, or your Canada (Quebec) Pension Plan benefits (less a small sum for personal use), will cover your costs in a nonprofit nursing home. Costs for care in a nonprofit institution begin at about $15,000 per year. Private homes are considerably more expensive. In general, both skilled- and intermediate-care nursing homes must have a registered nurse on duty eight hours a day, seven days a week, and a registered (or certified) nursing assistant on duty at all times. Annual inspections are required, and inspection reports must be made available. If it is not posted, ask for it.

---

1 2 3...

IS IT TIME FOR A NURSING HOME?

If you are unsure when it is time for you or a family member to enter a nursing home, you may want to consider the following questions:

1. Can the prospective nursing home resident cook for herself and manage her household? If not, it may be time for residential care.

2. Is there another family member who can help with caregiving? If there is not, you may be able to hire a home health aide to assist with meals and daily living.

3. Is there another family member who depends on this person for care? Although assistance in the home may be helpful, there may come a time when married couples can no longer look after each other.

4. Is the prospective patient planning to undergo surgery that will disable her for a period of time? If so, a temporary arrangement will have to be made, either in a residential facility or in the patient's home.

5. Does the patient need a new living arrangement, or does she merely need a place to stay during convalescence? There are facilities that specialize in convalescence.

Choosing a Nursing Home

To get a true picture of a nursing home you or a family member are interested in, plan to make both announced and unannounced visits. First, make an appointment with the nursing-home administrator or admissions director. Ask for a guided tour and arrange to speak with staff and residents.

Make your second visit unannounced. Stop by during evening or weekend hours, when administrative heads are least likely to be around. Or visit during the late morning or midday to see if residents are out of bed, groomed, and dressed. A visit during and after mealtimes will give you a sense of the quality of the food and how well the dining area is cleaned.

If after careful consideration, you like what you see, it is time to discuss costs and availability of space. A patient or resident in a nursing home will have to sign a contract before being admitted. If someone is not mentally competent, then a guardian or other legal representative must sign. Review the contract before signing it and see that it sets out the resident's rights and responsibilities. It should indicate how much you are obliged to pay each month, including prices for items not included in the basic charge. The contract should also explain the home's grievance procedures and its policy on holding a bed, should a patient leave temporarily. Before signing, ask about the home's policy on advance directives or living wills.

Nursing Home or Home Care?

Nursing-home residents are often people who need 24-hour nursing care and supervision. Nursing homes are expensive. You may want to look at home-care services instead. Consider the following:

• If 24-hour medical care and supervision is not necessary, you might consider home care. Services, provided by a variety of professionals such as nurses, nurse's aides, physical therapists, and volunteers, are available in most communities.

• Home care is significantly less expensive than nursing-home care and in many cases provides similar services. For a reasonable fee, a nurse may come to the home, for instance, to administer intravenous medication, change a dressing on a wound, or take blood for testing.

• Home care can be highly specialized and tailored to a patient's needs. For instance, someone who has suffered a stroke may be visited regularly by a speech therapist. She may also benefit from the assistance of a nurse's aide who can help her bathe, dress, and prepare meals.

• For those who need minimal assistance, your provincial department on aging may be able to put you in contact with organizations that send volunteers to help with chores such as housekeeping and shopping.

• For a senior who needs companionship more than medical care, an adult day-care center or an assisted-living arrangement might suit her better and cost less than a nursing home. Some of these programs offer recreational and health services as well as community living.

Nursing homes do not have the authority to carry out a resident's advance directive about withholding medication or detaching a life-sustaining medical device. In such cases, the person who is requesting an end to life should be transferred to a hospital where doctors and the ethics committee are better able to handle these problems.

Is the nursing home's administration prepared to see that this takes place?

Financial Considerations

If the future nursing-home resident is mentally competent, be sure that only that person signs the contract. If you, as a concerned son or daughter or friend, sign, or even co-sign, the contract for nursing-home care, you may find yourself personally liable for all the costs. If the future resident is mentally incompetent, make sure that you take the necessary steps to have this confirmed by a court and to have you appointed legal guardian. When you sign the contract, make clear that you are signing in your capacity as legal guardian without personal responsibility for payment. You will probably have to add this clause to the contract, but this small effort may save you thousands of dollars.

Monitoring Care

Although the law varies greatly from province to province, nursing homes should develop individual care plans for all residents. A care plan specifies how the staff will deal with a resident's medical and non-medical needs. You, as the resident or as a friend or relative of a resident, have the right to be involved in the process. The nursing-home staff must first complete an evaluation of a resident's functional abilities, including how well he can walk, talk, eat, dress, bathe, see, hear, understand, and remember. An assessment should be completed within 14 days of admission and at least once a year after that. It should be reviewed every three months and anytime a resident's condition changes.

SAFEGUARDING A RELATIVE'S CARE

You are entitled to ask the staff to schedule a care-planning conference when you, the patient in your family, and other interested family members can attend. It is helpful to involve the nursing-home resident in developing the care plan.

After the care-plan meeting, follow up on what was discussed. Make sure the plan is being followed. If it is not, take

---

Creating a Nursing-Home Care Plan

Care plans for nursing-home residents ensure that they get the treatment they need. As a friend or relative of a nursing-home patient or as a resident, you should take an active role in drawing up these blueprints for care. The information in the assessment should include:

✔ **Medical information.** The plan should include a record of the patient's medical history, current conditions and medical status, dental condition, any drugs currently being taken, and any sensory or physical impairments.

✔ **Mental status.** The plan should include comments about the patient's current cognitive abilities and an analysis of his general psychological and emotional state.

✔ **Nutritional status.** The plan should detail the patient's diet, eating habits, and any special requirements, deficiencies, or requests.

✔ **A strategy.** The plan should take into account the patient's needs and requests regarding food, activities, personal care, and mobility. It should also outline longer-term strategies.

✔ **Potential.** The plan should outline the doctors' opinions regarding the potential for both rehabilitation and discharge. This analysis should be updated whenever the patient's condition changes.

your concerns or complaints to nurses, the doctor, or the nursing-home administrator. Some nursing-home personnel may resent your involvement, but remember that you have the right to protect your relative's welfare.

A man ought to handle his body like the sail of a ship, and neither lower or reduce it much when no cloud is in sight, nor be slack and careless in managing it when he comes to suspect something is wrong.

PLUTARCH
Moralia

Patients' Rights

You are guaranteed certain rights in most nursing homes, no matter how you pay for care. Those rights will vary, depending on whether the home is licensed by the province and whether it is a private or publicly run enterprise. Tragically, those rights are not always respected, and horrific tales of treatment in some privately run, unlicensed homes are exposed in the media from time to time. It is possible, even probable, that some cases of brutality, substandard food, crowding, and general disrespect for residents, may also go unreported.

All provinces require that licensed nursing homes respect certain rights of their residents. The most important of these rights are:

■ **Medical care:** To know your medical condition and to be given an opportunity to participate in any decision regarding your treatment. All mentally competent nursing-home residents have the right to accept or refuse medical treatment and to be told how that decision will affect their health. They are also entitled to be kept fully informed on their

Beware of Nursing Homes' Hidden Costs

The monthly or daily costs of nursing care may not include everything you think it does. Nursing homes may add on a number of extra charges. Obtain in writing a list of exactly what is, and is not, covered by the contract. Look out for the following:

• **Special meals.** Some nursing homes may charge different rates for people who require no-salt, vegetarian, or other special dishes, or meals with larger portions than are usually served.

• **Telephone and outings.** There may be costs for the use of telephone or charges for various outings offered to residents of the home.

• **Room size, location, and utilities.** Check the size and location of the room specified in your contract. Extra charges may apply for a single room, a front-facing room, or one of the institution's larger rooms. Are you responsible for the costs of electricity, heating, and air-conditioning?

• **Personal expenses.** Do you have to pay for use of a television? What about cable costs? You may also be charged extra for telephone service and visits to the beauty parlor and barber shop. Are you expected to "tip" the attendants?

• **Supply charges.** Does the nursing home charge extra for laundry service and dry cleaning? You may also be charged for items you assume are covered, such as soaps, shampoo, facial tissues, toilet paper, wheelchair cushions, or enema bags. Is there any charge for attendant services such as helping you to bathe or to dress? These questions should be clearly answered before signing the contract.

health status, to have complete access to their medical records, and to be guaranteed that their records will be kept confidential.

- **Choice of doctor:** Nursing-home patients also have the right to choose their own doctor, to be seen by a doctor whenever they need one, and to participate in planning their care.
- **Clean and comfortable surroundings:** Residents are entitled to a safe, clean and comfortable environment.
- **Restraints should not be commonplace:** Nursing-home patients should be protected from unnecessary physical restraints, tranquilizers or other drugs not medically prescribed, and from forced seclusion.
- **Spousal considerations:** If you and your spouse are residents in the same facility, you have the right to visit privately and share the same room, barring any medical risks.
- **Personal possessions:** A nursing-home patient is entitled to use certain personal possessions, such as clothing and furnishings.
- **Proper nutrition:** You have the right to adequate and nutritious food.
- **Privacy:** You are free to send and receive unopened letters and private telephone conversations, and to communicate with visitors privately.
- **Money:** You are entitled to control your own finances if you are competent to do so, or to have a friend or relative or a designated third party do so on your behalf if you are not capable of handling money or financial matters on your own.
- **Social and religious observance:** You have the right to participate in social activities and religious services available at the nursing home.
- **Respect for your person:** You are entitled to be respected at all time, and never to be abused physically, verbally, or in any other way.
- **Advance notice:** You have a right to advance notice if you are to be moved to another room or health care facility, or if you are to receive a new roommate.

THE RIGHT NOT TO BE TRANSFERRED

A nursing home is permitted to transfer or discharge a resident only if it cannot provide proper care, if a resident no longer needs nursing-home care, or if the resident poses a danger to others. It can also discharge a patient who has refused notices to pay a bill.

Before it transfers or discharges a patient, however, a nursing home should provide a written explanation for its decision. It should also give the patient a reasonable period of time—30 days might be appropriate—in which to find alternative accommodation and move.

ALTERNATIVES TO NURSING HOMES

For patients who need extra care, but cannot afford or do not want to move into a nursing home, one or more of the following may be appropriate:

1. Consider adult day care. An alternative to nursing home care, adult day care often offers the best of both worlds. It provides daytime supervision, meals, and recreational activities, while allowing an infirm person to live at home.

2. Hire a visiting-nurse service. This form of skilled home care is significantly cheaper than a nursing home and may be appropriate for people who do not need constant monitoring. Check your Yellow Pages for a visiting-nurse association in your area, such as the Victorian Order of Nurses, or the Toronto-based Saint Elizabeth Visiting Nurses' Association.

3. Call meals-on-wheels. If the infirm person cannot cook nutritious meals for herself, consider this service, which delivers balanced meals to the home. Check the Yellow Pages for the nearest branch.

4. Use palliative care. Palliative care for the terminally ill is available in homelike hospital units or hospice facilities or in the family home. It does not provide life-prolonging medical treatment but does offer basic medical care, counseling, and pain management. Most palliative-care facilities require a doctor's prognosis stating that a patient probably has less than six months to live. Ask your doctor for guidance.

Can Emergency Treatment Be Refused?

Nursing-home residents have the same right to self-determination as any patient, as long as they are judged to be competent.

This includes the right to refuse emergency medical treatment, whether it is given in the nursing home or requires transfer to a hospital. The only stipulation is that the patient understands the consequences of his decision.

You do not need to have an advance directive defining your end-of-life treatment to refuse emergency medical treatment. Nor, although it might help, do you need to have signed a "Do Not Resuscitate" order or living will.

A living will is a document a patient can make if he does not want his life needlessly prolonged, directing that all forms of resuscitation, such as cardiopulmonary resuscitation (CPR), be withheld in the event of a medical emergency. A patient can execute a living will at any time during a nursing-home stay. To make it effective, however, it should be signed by the patient's doctor before two witnesses and it should be posted on the patient's chart, where nurses and nurses' aides can see it easily.

A living will can be revoked at any time. Even in the middle of a medical crisis, if a patient suddenly decides to change his mind and accept lifesaving medical treatment, he may, by verbally requesting the treatment, overrule the living will he wrote.

If you or a family member is being discharged without good reason, ask your provincial department on aging for advice. You may also be able to seek help from your local community health center or provincial health ministry. As a last resort, lawsuits can also be filed against nursing homes that fail to provide adequate care or whose services do not meet customary health standards and, in the case of public nursing homes, when charges exceed those permitted by law. Contact a lawyer for advice.

IF YOU BECOME INCOMPETENT

If you are suffering from a disease such as Alzheimer's, which progressively leads to a decline in all areas of mental ability, you would be wise to prepare a living will or advance directive while the disease is still in its early stages. This way you can name a trusted friend or relative to be an alternative decision-maker for you when the disease has rendered you mentally incapable.

If you are a Jehovah's Witness, or you belong to another group or religion that prohibits blood transfusions, your advance directive should state that you do not want to be transfused, even if your health or life depends on this.

If a nursing-home resident who has no advance directive becomes incompetent, the facility must contact the next of kin for guidance on medical decision-making. If the patient has no family or relatives, the facility or its doctor will make medical decisions on a person's behalf until the courts can appoint a legal guardian to assume decision-making responsibility.

Dealing With Problems

If you have a complaint about a nursing home, and the staff does not respond according to your wishes, you may need outside help. Your first recourse might be your provincial health department. In addition to licensing nursing homes and conducting annual inspections to evaluate their quality of care, health departments also handle consumer complaints.

Try to bring your particular problem to the attention of the department inspectors who periodically survey nursing homes. They regularly set time aside for meeting with residents and sometimes with residents' families. This gives the the home's an opportunity to air any concerns they have with the home's services. It also gives the inspectors a chance to discover how the users view the facility overall. Find out when the next inspection is scheduled, and be prepared to talk with inspectors at that time.

Your provincial seniors' secretariat or your provincial department of social services may also have advice or solutions for nursing-home-related problems.

In some cases, your best recourse may be your ombudsman, an independent public protector found in every province except Prince Edward Island. Generally, the ombudsman can intervene when you get the runaround from government agencies, or when you feel a government body has treated you unfairly. The ombudsman's office can investigate your complaints and make recommendations, but it cannot force an agency to act on its recommendations. If you live in Prince Edward Island, call the Office of Consumer Services, a division of the provincial affairs ministry, for advice on who can best deal with your problem.

In all these cases, check your telephone directory for the appropriate number. The Blue Pages will either direct you to the department you need or a general information number, from where an operator can point you in the right direction.

What If You Suspect Abuse?

Abuse can take many forms: physical, emotional, or even financial. The nursing-home patients' bill of rights specifically prohibits all kinds of abuse, and all provinces have laws forbidding abuse of hospital or nursing-home patients and of the elderly.

Abuse happens nonetheless, so do not ignore obvious signs that all is not well. You should be concerned if an incontinent patient is not cleaned and changed regularly, or if you see signs of developing bedsores, or find the person restrained needlessly or for unnecessarily long periods.

Even if there are no such obvious signs of abuse, but you suspect from the patient's frightened demeanor that he is being victimized in some way, broach the subject. Ask him directly if he is being mistreated. If his response confirms your hunch, ask him to tell you specifically what has taken place, and which staff member is responsible. After you have compiled detailed information, take your concerns and the supporting facts to the nursing-home administrator and ask for an investigation.

If the nursing home's management and staff ignore your complaint, contact the ombudsman, as well as your provincial ministries on aging and health, and your province's attorney general. For extreme cases of abuse that present an immediate threat to the patient's safety or well-being, call your local police department. If abuse or battery has taken place, criminal charges may be laid against the nursing home.

Nursing-Home Warning Signs

As a friend or relative of a nursing-home patient, you will want to be assured that she is getting good care. Here are some indicators of neglect:

✔ *Unanswered call bells.* A call bell may be a patient's only link to the nursing staff, so observe for yourself and ask the patient whether her call bell is answered promptly.

✔ *Overuse of restraints.* Physical or chemical restraints may be used to keep patients from harming themselves. Bed rails and wrist restraints may be legitimate preventive measures for some patients, and sedatives may help patients sleep. But drugs and wheelchair harnesses have sometimes been used only to make life easier for the nursing-home staff. Be sure the patient is not needlessly tied into a chair or unduly lethargic as a result of too much medication.

✔ *Bedsores.* Bedsores are a clear sign that a person is not being moved often enough and also may be suffering from malnutrition, dehydration, or lack of bathing.

✔ *Toilet distress.* The elderly often need help going to the bathroom and may have to be taken as often as every two hours. Neglect can lead to incontinence, urinary-tract infections, or other problems.

DYING WITH DIGNITY

Ultimately, we cannot overrule death, but by making informed decisions about how we want to die, we can assert our right to a dignified end.

Life-Prolonging Treatments

Before exercising your right to accept or refuse certain life-sustaining medical measures, make sure you understand your condition and the risks associated with the following:

✔ *CPR.* Cardiopulmonary resuscitation involves restarting the heart manually, mechanically, or with injectable drugs. If begun too late, CPR may restart the heart after the brain and other vital organs have been permanently damaged.

✔ *Respirator.* Mechanical respirators help people who cannot breathe on their own by providing oxygen through a tube that is inserted into the windpipe. If breathing cannot be restored, a person might become dependent on the respirator.

✔ *Feeding tube.* This is given to people who cannot swallow food or fluids. A tube, placed through the nose or the wall of the abdomen, delivers liquids and nutrients. It can permanently sustain unconscious or severely brain-damaged people for many years.

Final Treatment Decisions

In this age of life-sustaining medical technology, it is vital to decide—while you can—how much treatment you want at the end of life. Making such predictions with finality is almost impossible. Today you may feel certain that you want no heroic measures to prolong your life. Tomorrow you may want every effort made to keep you alive.

DECIDING FOR YOURSELF

As long as you are mentally sound, you will be able to make your own treatment decisions—and to reverse them. If you become incompetent, the people closest to you will probably face the task of making those decisions for you. Therefore you should inform family, friends, and your doctor of your end-of-life treatment wishes, especially as those wishes change. It is the medical community's standard to sustain life any time there is no clear and convincing evidence that a patient would have wished otherwise.

You can express your wishes verbally. Some doctors and hospitals recognize verbal statements as evidence of a person's wishes. In fact, some provinces have laws authorizing families to make medical decisions for loved ones who cannot decide for themselves and have not made advanced directives. Of course it is best (and may be required in some provinces) to put your wishes in writing and to give copies to family, friends, and your doctor.

Try to choose more than one person to make treatment decisions for you, in the event that someone will not be available when needed. Also, specify under what circumstances you do or do not want life-sustaining treatment, how long you want to be treated, and the particular kinds of treatment you will not accept.

DECIDING FOR SOMEONE ELSE

Being appointed as a "surrogate," or substitute decision-maker, gives you the authority to make treatment decisions on someone's behalf. You are entitled to know everything about a person's medical condition in order to make well-informed decisions. If that person never wrote down her wishes, you will have to recall the most recent conversations in which she discussed the kinds of treatment she would have wanted. Your request to stop a loved one's medical treatment is appropriate, as long as it is what she requested of a medical practitioner, friend, or family member. If she never expressed her desires not to be kept alive on life support, a doctor cannot legally terminate such treatment.

EUTHANASIA AND ASSISTED SUICIDE

Since modern medical measures permit life to be prolonged, but not necessarily improved and sometimes worsened, euthanasia—sometimes described as mercy killing—has become an increasingly controversial topic among medical and legal experts in recent years.

There is, of course, a fundamental difference between ending medical treatment that is prolonging life and ending life itself. Disconnecting a respirator that is breathing for an individual who otherwise would not survive is a form of passive euthanasia. Giving someone a lethal injection to hasten their inevitable death is active euthanasia.

Active euthanasia is illegal in Canada. However, passive euthanasia—allowing a terminally ill person to die by withholding or withdrawing medical treatment—is a patient's legal right. So, while a doctor may not administer a lethal dose of drugs with the specific intent of causing death, she may legally turn off a respirator if the patient had asked that she not be kept alive artificially.

Between the idea
And the reality
Between the motion
And the act
Falls the shadow

T. S. ELIOT
The Hollow Men

The Definition of Death

In earlier times, people were declared dead when their hearts stopped beating. But since the 1960s, medicine has been able to restart the heart with CPR and sustain life with artificial respirators. As a result, death is currently defined by a number of other criteria, including:

• **Medical criteria.** The medical community has not formulated a precise definition of death. Most doctors and scientists agree that definition is important since medical science has created so many life-support vehicles to sustain life, and also, the success of organ transplants depends upon the organs being taken from the donor as soon as possible after death.

• **Legal criteria.** Death is usually defined as the cessation of all brain activity resulting in the cessation of the individual's respiratory and circulatory functions. In other words, the patient's brain has stopped giving orders to the autonomic nervous system and therefore the patient stops breathing and his heart stops beating, thus stopping blood circulation. Although the law does not define death, it does accept a doctor's report that death has occurred.

• **Other criteria.** Some doctors determine death by a complete state of permanent unconsciousness. Doctors also consider the patient's total unreceptivity to external stimuli and complete absence of movement of the body's muscle system to be additional signs. Particularly, doctors look for absence of reflex in the eyes, including lack of dilation of the pupils and blinking.

• **Elapsed time.** The protocol of declaring death varies from hospital to hospital, but must include a combination of the above criteria.

The Legacy of Nancy B

In 1989, 23-year-old Nancy B of Quebec was diagnosed as having Guillain-Barré Syndrome, a disease that eventually left her permanently bed-ridden, unable to feed or care for herself in any way, and unable to breathe without a respirator. By 1991 doctors had declared her condition incurable.

Taking into account her grim future, Nancy, once a very active person, petitioned the court to cut off her life-support system. The court was told that Nancy could never come to terms with her condition and that she had desired death for a long time. Evidence also showed that she was mentally capable of making rational decisions, and understood the consequences of her request to have the medical equipment turned off.

In rendering his decision, the Hon. Mr. Justice Jacques Dufour noted that the Criminal Code does not prohibit a doctor from following the informed consent of his patient. The judge also pointed out that both provincial law and the provincial Code of Medical Ethics require a doctor to respect his patient's wishes.

Nancy wanted to spend one last Christmas with her family. Shortly after the 1992 Christmas holidays, she was allowed to die.

As regards suicide, it is a criminal offense to suggest to someone else that he kill himself, or to help someone kill himself. In fact, if you counsel someone to commit suicide, and he attempts to do so and fails, you can still be convicted of a criminal offense. In a five-to-four decision in 1993, the Supreme Court of Canada ruled that assisted suicide, even where a person is terminally ill and in a vegetative state is illegal.

Formalizing Your Wishes

Protecting your right to die with dignity may involve a number of actions on your part, such as verbally expressing your end-of-life treatment wishes, informally writing them down, or creating a formal advance directive or living will. You can even do all three.

The two kinds of advance directives most commonly recognized are living wills and durable powers of attorney for health care. (See also YOUR FAMILY, page 152.)

An advance directive is a legal document in which you explain what kind of medical care you want at the end of your life. You may not need a lawyer to prepare an advance directive, although you should consult one for advice. You may need witnesses to sign the document, depending on your province's legislation in this regard.

Most provinces honor advance directives, but each one regulates them differently. Some provinces may require you to update your living will every few years to ensure it reflects your current thinking, or to register it with the public trustee or other public body. If you move to a new province, remake any such directive you have already prepared to ensure it complies with the law in your new province. Give copies of your living will to your doctor, lawyer, and any family members and friends who may be caring for you.

WILL YOUR WISHES BE HONORED?

Even if living wills are not yet legally recognized in your province, it is still a good idea to have one. Living wills are currently covered by legislation in Ontario, Quebec, Manitoba, and Nova Scotia. Health care workers in these provinces are legally required to respect an individual's wishes. Other provinces are moving in the direction of respecting living wills, so it is possible that a document you prepare now will receive legal approval in your province in coming years.

Even when there is no legal obligation on others to follow your written instructions, a written document makes your wishes known and helps doctors and hospital staff make difficult decisions. Even more important, a living will relieves families of the burden of making a decision about continuing care if a patient is incompetent or otherwise unable to communicate his wishes.

A durable power of attorney for health care may be preferable to a living will, which cannot make adequate provision for all future circumstances. A power of attorney for health care gives another person authority to make decisions for you respecting life-prolonging treatments, but not until you become incompetent. This form of power of attorney is recognized in Ontario, Quebec, and Nova Scotia.

Even though these documents are not included in the legislation of all provinces, no province has laws specifically declaring living wills or durable powers of attorney for health care illegal. Remember, too, that many doctors will follow the patient's directives in cases of extreme impairment or extreme pain when there is no possibility of an effective treatment.

Be aware, however, that in an emergency situation your advance directive may not be honored, because emergency medical technicians are charged with stabilizing you and getting you to a hospital where your condition can be evaluated. Indeed, the first obligation of all medical practitioners is to keep the patient alive. That is why it is so important to make your end-of-life wishes known while you are still able to do so.

Dying at Home

Every person who wishes to do so, and who can call on family members who are mentally and physically able to provide whatever nursing and other care is needed, has the right to die at home. There, the patient can be enfolded in the close, supportive love and quality of care that only family can provide.

Yet dying at home is an emotional strain for patients and caregivers, especially when it comes to pain management. Although patients have the right to as much pain medication as they need to stay comfortable, getting enough medication for a patient at home can be difficult. Doctors and nurses are not always present to monitor a person's pain level and authorize the administration of medication. Doctors may also underprescribe pain medications for fear of hastening death.

Therefore it is important to develop a cooperative relationship with a doctor or other health care provider who can prescribe pain medication for the person dying at home. Specify in your living will that you want enough pain medication to keep you as comfortable as possible. Make sure your doctor is willing to provide the amount of medication necessary to keep you pain-free.

Living-Will Terms

If you are writing an advance directive or have a parent or someone else whose life may be in your hands, you should understand these terms:

✔ *Extraordinary measures.* Also called "heroic measures," these are life-sustaining treatments considered "above and beyond" ordinary care.

✔ *Guardian.* A person authorized by the court to make decisions for another person who cannot make decisions.

✔ *Surrogate decision-maker.* A person authorized to make decisions for an incompetent patient who has no advance directive.

✔ *Incompetent.* Lacking the mental capacity to make decisions or to understand the implications of them.

✔ *Life support.* The use of machines to take over bodily functions and keep a patient alive, usually while attempts are made at cure.

✔ *Natural death.* Death that occurs when the body's basic functions are permitted to stop on their own.

✔ *Terminal illness.* A hopeless condition that shows no promise of recovery.

✔ *Immunity clause.* A provision in a living will that relieves health care providers and others of any liability for honoring a patient's end-of-life wishes.

Living Will

1 To my family, doctors, and all those concerned with my care:

I,_____, being of sound mind, willfully and voluntarily make known my desire that my dying shall not be artificially prolonged under the circumstances set forth below:

2 If at any time I should have an incurable injury, disease or illness, or be in a continual profound comatose state with no reasonable chance of recovery, where the application of life-sustaining procedures would serve only to prolong artificially the dying process, I direct that such procedures be withheld or withdrawn.

To arrive at this conclusion, I direct that my condition be certified to be terminal and irreversible by two physicians who have personally examined me, and have determined that my death will occur whether or not life-sustaining procedures are utilized. Specifically, I do not want **3** cardiac pulmonary resuscitation (CPR), mechanical respiration, or artificial nutrition or fluids administered by tube. **4** I wish to be permitted to die naturally with only the administration of medication or the performance of any medical procedure deemed necessary to provide me with comfort and relieve pain. If time and opportunity permits, I would prefer to die at home.

5 In the absence of my ability to give directions regarding the use of such life-sustaining procedures, it is my intention that this declaration shall be honored by my family, my physicians, and anyone else concerned with my care. This is my final expression of my legal right to refuse medical or surgical treatment, and I accept the consequences from such refusal. In so doing, I free anyone who carries out these directives of any legal liability.

I understand the full import of this declaration, and I am emotionally and mentally competent to make this declaration.

6

Declaration made this day of 1997.

_____
Signed

_____
City, County, and Province of Residence

The declarant has been personally known to me and I believe him or her to be of sound mind.

_____
Witness name

_____
Address

7

_____
Witness name

_____
Address

Preparing a Living Will

To ensure that your end-of-life wishes are followed, it is wise to prepare a living will. Since statutes vary by province, write down your wishes using these general guidelines, then ask a lawyer to check that it abides by your province's laws. **1.** Address those who will most likely be making decisions regarding your care should you become incompetent; **2.** Make a simple directive that medical treatment be withheld at a particular time (or, you can express your wish to have every effort made to prolong your life); **3.** List specific treatments you do not want; **4.** Add instructions about the care you desire; **5.** Indicate whom you wish to carry out these wishes if you are unable, and, if necessary, relieve them of liability; **6.** Sign and date your living will; **7.** Have the will witnessed by two witnesses or according to the laws of your province.

WHEN TO CHOOSE PALLIATIVE CARE

Palliative care can be given in a patient's home, in a hospital, or in a hospice. Aimed at easing pain and giving comfort, not curing disease, it also provides supportive, social, emotional, and spiritual services to both the terminally ill and their families. It may include nursing care from registered nurses, social services, physician services, spiritual support and counseling, and homemaker services, as well as respite care and bereavement support for caregivers. Some palliative-care units permit family members to be with a patient full-time. Patients admitted to such units are generally considered to have no more than six months to live. They must not be on curative radiation or chemotherapy, since palliative care focuses on peaceful, natural dying. Drugs are usually given only to ease pain.

What Would Roger Have Wanted?

PROBLEM

Roger was a lifeguard, too young and healthy, he thought, to worry about illness, death, or anything like an advance directive. One day Roger suffered a heart attack while swimming underwater. Emergency medical personnel who pulled him from the pool gave him cardiopulmonary resuscitation to restart his heart. In the hospital, doctors put him on a ventilator so that they could evaluate his chances of fully recovering. When it became apparent that Roger was permanently comatose, his doctors refused to turn off the respirator, having no idea of what he would have wanted.

ACTION

Fortunately for Roger's family, they lived in a province that allowed family members to make "substituted judgment" end-of-life decisions for a relative when he is unable to do so. Although Roger left no living will, he had repeatedly told his parents and fellow lifeguards that he would never want his life to be artificially prolonged. He took great pride in his physique and athletic prowess, and could not bear the thought of being "totally out of it," as he had put it. His family told the doctors what they knew, and persuaded the doctors to talk to Roger's fellow lifeguards as well. The doctors then asked Roger's family to go to the hospital ethics committee and explain the situation. After a hearing, the committee decided that there was "clear and convincing evidence" of Roger's final treatment wishes. The doctors agreed to disconnect Roger's life-support equipment.

Are Autopsies Mandatory?

Autopsy is the dissection of a body to determine cause or circumstances of death. Generally, autopsies are ordered in cases of suspicious death, such as when someone who appeared to be in good health dies suddenly. Some provinces may require a coroner to perform an autopsy in all cases of infant deaths or in deaths of

The Heroin Controversy

It is generally established that the terminally ill are entitled to receive as much pain medication as they need to be comfortable. It is also recognized that doctors may underprescribe medication for fear of causing drug addiction or hastening death.

To encourage doctors to give patients sufficient amounts of pain medication, some provinces have enacted "intractable pain measures." These laws codify the well-established medical practice of giving terminally ill patients pain medication in doses needed to relieve pain, even if the doses might themselves hasten death.

Although its pain-killing effects are well known, heroin, a highly addictive drug associated with comas, respiratory failure, and heart attacks, and whose nonmedical use is prohibited under the Narcotic Control Act (Narcotics—Specialized), is almost never prescribed. Doctors prefer to use analgesics such as morphine, which also relieve severe unrelenting pain. Nonetheless, some people feel doctors should be able to prescribe heroin for terminal cancer patients who are in intractable pain. This movement has a considerable following in the United States, where federal legislation to permit it, a bill known as the Compassionate Pain Relief Act, has been introduced in Congress every year since 1984. But despite some support from the politicians, the measure has been strongly opposed by the medical establishment, and has repeatedly "died in committee."

those under age 40 where no obvious cause of death is present. In some cases a medical examiner or coroner may perform a "death investigation," a process to determine whether or not a full-scale autopsy will be necessary.

If an autopsy is not required by law, a hospital must obtain permission from the deceased's next of kin to perform one. You may be able to sue a hospital for mental anguish for performing an unauthorized or unordered autopsy. However, if the law calls for an autopsy, it will be performed even if you have serious religious reasons for refusing your consent.

Organ Donation

As medical technology gets ever more sophisticated, and the concept of donating organs for transplant into someone else's body gains widening support, all provinces have enacted human tissues acts, which allow you to donate your organs or your entire body for transplantation or research. The medical need for organs is so great that provinces even encourage donation by including organ-donation permission panels on drivers' licenses.

To become an organ donor, you must be 18 years or older (19 years in some provinces) and understand the consequences of your actions. You may make a specific provision in your will, or you may sign an organ-donor card in the presence of two witnesses. You may name an individual or an institution to whom you want your donation to be made, and you also may specify which organs you want donated. Even if you have not filled out a donor card, on your death, your relatives or next of kin may consent to have your organs donated.

All provinces specify that your decision to donate your organs can be revoked. The revocation need not be in writing—you may simply destroy your card or verbally withdraw your wishes in front of two witnesses. When families oppose the donation wishes of a person who has died, hospitals tend to honor the family's wishes.

ORGAN DONATION IS VOLUNTARY

Organ donation is a completely voluntary, altruistic act. You cannot be coerced into it. Nor can you be offered money or gifts for donating your organs or those of a loved one. Moreover, a hospital cannot refuse to release your body to your relatives if they refuse to consent to organ donation. All provinces except Quebec have "required request" legislation: someone on the hospital staff must ask the next of kin of every potential organ donor if he or she wants to donate. If they refuse, doctors must release the body for burial.

FACTS ABOUT ORGAN DONATION

Here are some things you should know about organ donation for transplantation or research:

1. Under the federal Uniform Human Tissue Act, most people may consent to donate organs. Consent may even be given where the donor will survive the transplant (*inter vivos* donations) but this applies only to regenerative tissues such as skin or bone, or bone marrow. The kidney is the only non-regenerative organ that may be donated *inter vivos* (while alive).

2. The kidneys, heart, liver, lungs, intestinal organs, and pancreas are the solid organs generally considered for donation. "Solid" organs have a major blood flow through them.

3. Tissues, which include heart valves, corneas, skin and bone, are not considered solid organs, but still can be transplanted successfully.

4. You are ineligible to donate organs if you have some types of systemic or malignant cancer, or if you have the HIV virus, leukemia, or hepatitis B. However, your organs may be useful to research.

5. If you donate only part of your body, the rest will be returned to your surviving relatives for burial.

6. Some provinces, Manitoba for example, permit minors to donate their organs to close relatives, but only if they are at least 16 years of age and fully understand what is involved.

YOUR JOB

From your first job search to retirement, a complex legal network protects you from discrimination, dangerous conditions, and unscrupulous practices in the workplace.

THE CHANGING WORKPLACE

New laws as well as new economic and social realities make the place where you work far different from what it used to be.

New Terms for the New Workplace

Today's increasingly complex job market is developing a new vocabulary. Here is a glossary of some new words:

✔ **Downsizing.** A company downsizes when it makes staff reductions (often on a large scale) to cut costs and remain competitive. A refinement of the term is "rightsizing," which describes the more precise policy of consolidating jobs and responsibilities.

✔ **Restructuring.** Changing the corporate organization. The chain of command shortens, with fewer managers and more low-level employees.

✔ **Lean and mean.** A description of the new corporation that has to produce more with fewer assets and that may care less about its employees.

✔ **Global economy.** The meshing of economies around the world that has led to dislocations of traditional jobs and market alignments.

✔ **Telecommuting.** This is when an employee works primarily at home and communicates with the office by way of computer, electronic mail, modem, and fax.

A Harsher Job Market

For a number of years after World War II, many Canadians became accustomed to a high degree of job security as a healthy, growing economy promised plenty of steady work and a solid future for anyone who buckled down and stuck it out. But such job security is no longer guaranteed.

Foreign competition, a larger work force, and a fluctuating economy have forced Canadian companies to change, and the impact of these changes has been felt from the assembly line to the executive suite. The traditional social contract which rewarded corporate loyalty with job security has seen its force and application diminished. Today, workers cannot always look to a large corporation to provide a career path. Instead of working for one or two companies in your lifetime, you may very well work for seven or eight. You may even find yourself switching careers in response to an increasingly unstable job market.

New Ways of Working

Technology has also contributed to the changing face of the workplace, where whole job categories have been eliminated. If you are not computer literate, you may have a hard time getting and holding a job. On the other hand, if your computer skills are top-notch, you may find you are quite marketable. As computers and other modern technologies reshape the workday, many more employees work at home, communicating with the office or with clients via phone, electronic mail ("E-mail"), computers, and facsimile, or "fax," machines.

Legislation, too, has affected the modern workplace. Although government once took a hands-off approach to employer-employee relations and you were offered relatively little legal protection, today's laws, in conjunction with court decisions, specifically define what your employer can and cannot do, and what your recourse is should laws be broken. (See also "Glossary of Federal Job Laws," opposite.) Knowing your workplace rights is your best defense against having them violated.

Glossary of Federal Job Laws

Over the years the federal government has created many laws to protect the rights of citizens in the workplace. Most federal legislation of this nature applies only to federal government jobs and to industries that are regulated by the federal government, such as maritime and inter-provincial shipping and transport, railways, telecommunications, aviation, broadcasting, and banking. Most provinces have also adopted laws that resemble the federal legislation. Here is a glossary of the most important federal laws affecting the workplace:

• **Canada Industrial Relations Regulations:** These provide guidelines for collective bargaining, dispute and conciliation assistance, and the appointment of arbitrators. In 1992, the federal government created the Canadian Artists and Producers Professional Relations Tribunal to enable self-employed cultural workers, such as artists and writers, to benefit from the regulations. The tribunal, a quasi-judicial agency, oversees relations between self-employed artists and federal producers. About 25 percent of Canada's cultural workers are self-employed.

• **Canada Labour Code:** The code provides guidelines for industrial relations, and regulates the collective bargaining of employees of the federal government or industries under federal jurisdiction. It protects the right of employees to join the union of their choice, and requires the employer to bargain in good faith with the union chosen as the bargaining agent by a majority of employees. It also regulates occupational health and safety, and such things as minimum wages, standard hours, overtime, statutory holidays, vacations and vacation pay, time off to vote, maternity leave, equal pay for men and women, employment termination and unjust dismissal. The federal government enforces the Canada Labour Code and investigates any violations. An employee who believes the code rules have been broken should complain to the nearest office of Human Resources Development Canada, formerly known as Labour Canada.

• **Canada Labour Standards Regulations:** These regulations govern hours of work, wages, vacations, holidays, group and individual employment terminations, and severance pay. The regulations provide that whenever 50 or more employees are to be terminated within a four-week period, the employer must give a 16-week notice of termination. In addition, the employer must give severance pay of two days for each year worked, with a minimum of five days' severance pay.

• **Canada Occupational Safety and Health Regulations:** These regulations provide minimum workplace standards in terms of building safety, housekeeping and maintenance, elevating devices, boilers and vessels, lighting, levels of sound, sanitation, and hazardous substances (additional Safety and Health Regulations exist specific to the aviation, mining, marine, and oil and gas industries). Workers who refuse some duties, when there is a reasonable chance that such work could be dangerous because of defective equipment, or because the required procedures would expose them to unacceptable risk, are protected under these regulations. Because of their special nature, separate federal laws may apply in such industries as aeronautics, petroleum exploration and production, public hospitals, railways and shipping, and highway transportation.

• **Department of Labour Act:** This act requires investigations into conditions of labor. Investigators have large powers, and employee complaints may be kept confidential to avoid retribution by the employer. An employee wishing confidentiality, however, should specifically ask that his comments be treated in this manner.

• **Motor Vehicle Operators Hours of Work Regulations:** These set a work limit for bus drivers on interprovincial routes of 8 hours a day and 40 hours a week, after which overtime must be paid. The regulations also stipulate that overtime be paid to city truck drivers working more than 9 hours a day and 45 hours a week, and highway drivers working more than 60 hours a week. Despite these restrictions, studies show that, to stay competitive, many highway truckers drive long distances without breaks, and sometimes take artificial stimulants to stay awake.

• **Trade Unions Act:** This act regulates the constitution and registration of federally regulated trade unions, annual statements, accounting duties, trade union rules, and fees. It also enumerates infractions and penalties. Despite the protection the act gives to organized labor, the power of unions has begun to wane in recent years. This is partly due to the pressure put on unions by treaties such as the North American Free Trade Agreement, whereby an employer can readily relocate in Mexico, where wages and benefits are lower than in Canada, and where there are few unions to protect workers.

FINDING A JOB

Being out of work is tough; the frustrations of the job hunt can be tougher. But you have rights from the moment you start looking. Make them work for you.

Choosing an Employment Agency

Finding an employment agency you are comfortable with is worth the effort it takes. Here are some tips to help you:

✔ *Experience.* Find out how long the agency has been in business and whether it has a good track record. In many provinces, agencies must be licensed, so you can check with the local licensing bureau.

✔ *Specialties.* Agencies often specialize in certain types of employment. Ask people in the field you are interested in whether they know of any specialized agencies.

✔ *Assistance.* Look for an agency that offers facilities for improving your on-the-job skills. This amenity can be critical for learning modern office skills such as word processing and desktop publishing.

✔ *Contract.* Before you commit yourself to the agency, find out what its terms are. Ask to see a copy of the contract. If there is anything in it you do not like, keep looking for an agency that is right for you.

Putting Agencies to Work

Sooner or later you will be looking for a job—either your first one or a new one—and one of your options will be to get in touch with an employment agency to help you find the right spot. Employment agencies provide referral and counseling services and help employers in locating and screening job candidates.

Most employment agencies have a contract with the employees, and contract out workers to employers. Such agencies are regarded as employers and are subject to the same laws as any other employer. Another type of agency refers clients to prospective employers for a fee. In the eyes of the law, such agencies are not considered "employers."

Before signing any contract, find out what fees you will be required to pay, and what services you can expect in return. Several provinces limit what an employment agency may charge a prospective employee. In many other provinces, agencies are prohibited from charging prospective employees any fee at all.

Federal Job Banks

Anyone legally entitled to work in Canada, whether currently employed or out of work, can get free job-search assistance at one of some 300 federal Human Resources Development Centres across the country. About 100 of these are full-service centers where a staff member will meet with the job applicant, establish the client's needs, and see what services the center might offer.

If you are "job-ready"—you are not in need of any special training—you will be introduced to "job banks," user-friendly computerized kiosks listing job openings and their pay rates. All human resource centers now have these job banks, and another 400 kiosks are located in public buildings and shopping malls throughout the country.

Job seekers can also get help writing or updating resumes, and those who need to brush up on job-search techniques can get tips on organizing a work search or, if they are getting employment insurance benefits, may be referred for three weeks' intensive training in a job-search club. Clients who are not "job ready," or who want to try some other line of work, may be referred to the center's employment counselors, who can offer services ranging from job training to psychological counseling.

Working as a Temp

If you are not looking for a permanent job, but need work for only a limited time, you should consider employment agencies that specialize in short-term assignments. The most common jobs handled by temporary agencies fall under the category of general office work, such as word processing, data entry, typing, filing, and reception.

In most cases, the temporary worker, or "temp," is paid by the temporary agency. Although the worker may report to several different job sites, the agency is the employer, and has the same responsibilities under the law as any other employer. The agency must pay you punctually for the work you do, and supply you with equipment and a safe place to work. The agency must obey all federal employment provisions, such as withholding income tax, and wage and hour laws.

The Interview and the Law

Stringent restrictions limit the kinds of questions an employer may ask in an application form or when interviewing a potential employee. The Canadian Charter of Rights and Freedoms, provincial human rights laws, and unfair labor practices legislation prohibit discriminating against job applicants (and employees) on the basis of sex, race, age, religion, disability, or national origin.

Acceptable questions include your name and address, previous work experience, education (but only if it is relevant to the job), and citizenship (but not national origin). Asking questions that have nothing to do with job performance can lead to charges of discrimination, unfair hiring practices, or invasion of privacy.

An employer is entitled to ask if you belong to a union (and must do so if his collective agreement restricts hirings to trade union members), but should not ask your age (unless the law requires you be a certain age to perform the job—to serve alcohol, or to work in factories, mines, or construction), your maiden name or your spouse's, your sexual orientation, whether you own or rent your home, whether you are pregnant or plan to be, or with whom you live.

IF YOU NEED TO HIRE A TEMP

Once you get a job and find yourself sitting on the other side of the employment desk, you may end up hiring someone yourself. If you are looking for a temporary worker, keep the following points in mind:

1. Find out if your company already has an account with a temporary agency. If not, ask colleagues and friends to recommend one they have used.

2. Give the agency as much notice as possible and clearly communicate the duties of the temp position you need to fill.

3. Get the name of the temp from the agency before he arrives. Write it down. If you work with someone you like, let the agency know. You may be able to get the same worker back in the future. If you are unhappy with a temp, inform the agency as well.

4. Take pains to inform the temp of all workplace rules and policies, especially those regarding safety and smoking.

5. Usually the temp will ask you to sign a time card at week's end. Keep a copy, and check it against the agency's bill when it arrives.

6. Some temporary agencies will charge you a fee if you hire a temp they have placed in your firm. Be sure to consult your contract or the agency before offering a temp a permanent job.

Questions about your nationality, ancestry, religion, and race are forbidden; even questions about height and weight are off-limits in most cases.

However, to satisfy employment insurance, pension, tax and immigration legislation, as well as labor standards and safety legislation, employers are required to obtain certain information after you are hired. If you do not have a Social Insurance Number, he may be entitled to ask about your nationality or place of origin to ensure you are legally able to work in Canada. To determine how much tax to withhold, he may ask you to fill out a TD-1 form, where you must state your marital status, number of dependents, and the salary earned by your spouse.

Most provinces let employers ask about past criminal activity if this is relevant to the job. However, you do not have to disclose information about a criminal charge which resulted in an acquittal or an unconditional discharge.

If you are asked a question you believe is discriminatory, try to document it. If it is part of a written application, ask for a copy. If it is asked during an interview, ask your interviewer to repeat it, or to elaborate, so that you are absolutely certain of what you are being asked.

Take detailed notes after the interview. If you believe you did

Employment Tests and Your Rights

If your present or future employer asks you to take any kind of test, make sure it is a legal request and that the test is given under the proper conditions. You may be reluctant to challenge an employer in this way, but it is important because skewed test results can hurt your job prospects. Here are some common tests and your rights regarding them:

• **Lie detector tests.** New Brunswick and Ontario are the only provinces with legislation prohibiting employers from asking employees to undergo lie detector tests. Legislation in both provinces also forbids the results of lie detector tests that preceded the legislation from being divulged to prospective employers or employment agencies.

• **Medical.** The courts have recognized the employer's right to have an employee undergo a medical examination, including a blood test, as a condition of employment. The law also stipulates certain circumstances in which an employee *must* submit to a medical exam. For instance, the Canadian Safety and Health Act requires medical exams of any employees exposed to hazardous substances. An employer could probably insist that an employee who has been ill have a medical exam before returning to the workplace, especially if the illness is contagious.

• **Drugs.** In many provinces, drug testing by employers is not regulated by law, although there may be legislation guaranteeing the right to privacy. The courts have often allowed employers to require prospective employees to undergo a drug test, especially when testing is in the public interest, as it is for pilots, for instance. Taxicab companies may require their employees to submit to periodic tests for drug or alcohol use.

• **IQ, personality, and physical ability.** An employer can ask you to take a written, verbal, or physical exam to measure skills and knowledge required to perform a job. Such tests must be given to all applicants under the same conditions and cannot discriminate against a "protected group," such as women, minorities, or older applicants. The test must measure a bona fide occupational qualification and may not adversely affect the hiring of women or minorities.

not get a job because of the way you answered, or refused to answer, a discriminatory question, you may have a legal claim for damages or compensation.

PREEMPLOYMENT INVESTIGATIONS

A prospective employer may ask you to take a preemployment test to help determine whether you are qualified for a particular job. In certain cases, employers can use tests to measure your intelligence, determine your physical strength, or evaluate your personality.

The test should measure some asset needed for the job, such as a typing test for word processing. If you believe a test you were given was biased and you were denied employment because of it, file a complaint with your provincial human rights commissioner.

Manitoba's Personal Investigations Act, legislation which applies only to positions paying less than $12,000 a year, permits employers to investigate potential or newly hired employees who give written consent. Investigated individuals are entitled to examine their files and have errors corrected.

Problems With References

Your former employer need not provide a reference unless she agreed to do so in your employment contract. Any reference given, however, should not make false statements about your performance, job skills, or offer an opinion about you which is not relevant to the job requirements.

You may have a legal claim against a reference giver if a reference contains particularly defamatory information. For example, if a former employer tells your prospective boss that you were let go for insubordination when in fact you were laid off for economic reasons, you may be able to sue for defamation. You will have to prove, however, that the statement was false and that as a result your reputation or credibility suffered—to the point that you were denied a job.

Contract or No Contract

Even if you have no written contract, as is the case in most employment situations, your rights will be protected under the Canada Labour Code and your province's labor standard laws. If you have a signed contract, and your employer dismisses you prematurely without just cause, you are entitled to all the wages you would have

---

Keeping References Fair

A good reference can give a job searcher a boost, while a bad one can be devastating. Therefore, if you are the one giving a reference, you need to be cautious. Here are some general guidelines regarding references:

✔ *Authority.* No one who does not have explicit authority to do so, should ever give a job reference.

✔ *Honesty.* Comments in a reference should be fair, objective, and true. An employer can make a subjective, negative statement as long as she believes it to be true and relevant to job performance.

✔ *Relevance.* Information should be limited to the purpose of the inquiry and appropriate to job-skills evaluation. If the reference giver is asked whether someone can operate a cash register, she should not answer the question and then volunteer, ". . . but he has an unprofessional phone manner."

✔ *Neutrality.* Opinions and personal feelings should be kept to a minimum or avoided whenever possible, especially if they are not directly related to job performance. A reference should give only the information requested.

earned if the term of the contract had been respected. You may also be entitled to damages.

If, however, you are dismissed for just cause, you will not be entitled to prior notice or compensation for lost wages.

Just what comprises "just cause" may be hard to determine, beyond the obvious—incompetence, insubordination, theft, or criminal activity on the job.

Resolving a Breach of Contract

PROBLEM
Monica Smith was hired by Susan and Todd Lawson to run their small knitwear company. The Lawsons offered Monica a fair salary and an employment contract. The contract, which was to be in effect for two years, stipulated that Monica could not be fired without cause. In exchange, Monica would run all day-to-day operations of their company. But at the end of the first year, the Lawsons told Monica that although she was doing a great job, they would no longer be needing her services. When she asked why she was being fired, she was told that the Lawsons' niece was moving to town, and they wanted her to run the company.

ACTION
Monica showed a copy of her contract to a lawyer, who immediately sent a letter to the Lawsons pointing out that they had dismissed Monica without cause during the term of her contract. He asked the Lawsons for a settlement to compensate Monica for breach of contract, and provide her with money to live on while she looked for another job. The Lawsons, now aware of their legal obligation, and convinced that Monica would probably win a case against them in court, agreed to her terms.

IMPLIED CONTRACTS

An implied contract is one that is not in writing, but which can be recognized legally because of a verbal agreement or other acceptance of employment conditions. Minimum notice requirements apply equally to implied or written contracts, although the prescribed time periods vary from province to province.

In Ontario, for instance, if you have been employed for three months or more, you must get one week's notice, two weeks' notice if you have been employed from one to three years, and so on, up to a maximum of eight weeks if you have been employed for eight or more years.

No matter how long his employment, a worker in Prince Edward Island is only entitled to one week's notice. In Manitoba, the notice period is based on the length of the employee's pay period.

An employer's obligation to give notice is also satisfied when, upon dismissal, he pays his employee an amount equivalent to the salary that employee would have earned had he remained in the job during the requisite notice period.

EMPLOYEE BENEFITS

Some employee benefits are federally or provincially mandated rights; others are privileges your employer may—or may not—offer. Be sure you know the difference.

Government-Mandated Benefits

A s a Canadian worker, you are entitled to a number of government-prescribed benefits, not least of which is an annual vacation with pay. (See "Minimum Vacation Legislation," below.) Vacation entitlements for employees of the federal government and federally regulated institutions are guaranteed by the Canada Labour

MINIMUM VACATION LEGISLATION

Under the Canada Labour Code, all federal government and Crown Corporation employees are entitled to two weeks' annual vacation with pay for each completed year of work. This chart shows what all other workers are guaranteed under provincial employment standards laws.

Jurisdiction	Length of Annual Vacation	Vacation Pay
Federal	2 weeks after one year's service; 3 weeks after six years	4% of annual earnings; 6% after six years
Alberta	2 weeks after one year's service; 3 weeks after five years	4% of annual earnings; 6% after five years
British Columbia	2 weeks after one year's service; 3 weeks after five years	4% of annual earnings; 6% after five years
Manitoba	2 weeks after one year; 3 weeks after four years of service (completed within 10 years)	regular pay during vacation period
New Brunswick	2 weeks after one year	4% of annual earnings
Newfoundland	2 weeks after one year	4% of annual earnings
Nova Scotia	2 weeks after one year	4% of annual earnings
Ontario	2 weeks after one year	4% of annual earnings
Prince Edward Island	2 weeks after one year	4% of annual earnings
Quebec	2 weeks after one year; 3 weeks after five years	4% of gross wages; 6% after five years
Saskatchewan	3 weeks after one year; 4 weeks after 10 or more years	3/52 of annual earnings after one year; 4/52 after 10 years
Northwest Territories	2 weeks after one year; 3 weeks after five years of service (completed within 10 years)	4% of annual earnings; 6% after five years
Yukon Territory	2 weeks	4% of annual earnings

Code, while those of other workers fall under provincial employment standards legislation. These provincial laws regulate hours of work, overtime pay, maternity leave (see "Leaves of Absence for Parents," below), sick leave, severance pay, and vacation entitlements. Many provinces also have legislation providing for bereavement leave, in the event of the death of a spouse or relative, sick leave, and even education leave, paid or unpaid, after a predetermined period of employment.

LEAVES OF ABSENCE FOR PARENTS

Once you have been working for a designated period of time, you may be entitled to maternity leave, paternity leave, or child care leave. All provinces have legislation regarding maternity leave, and most also provide for paternity or child care leave. Maternal/paternal leave schedules are shown below.

Jurisdiction	Qualifying Period	Length of Leave	Extension
Federal			
(pregnancy)	6 months	17 weeks	not specified
(parental)	6 months	24 weeks	not specified
Alberta (pregnancy)	12 months	18 weeks	6 weeks
British Columbia			
(pregnancy)	Not specified	18 weeks	6 weeks
(parental)	Not specified	12 weeks	5 weeks
Manitoba			
(pregnancy)	12 months	17 weeks	not specified
(parental)	12 months	17 weeks	not specified
New Brunswick			
(pregnancy)	not specified	17 weeks	not specified
(child care)	not specified	12 weeks	5 weeks
Newfoundland			
(pregnancy)	20 weeks	17 weeks	6 weeks
(parental)	20 weeks	12 weeks	not specified
Nova Scotia			
(pregnancy)	1 year	17 weeks	one week
(parental)	1 year	17 weeks	not specified
Ontario			
(pregnancy)	13 weeks	17 weeks	6 weeks
(parental)	13 weeks	18 weeks	not specified
Prince Edward Island			
(maternity)	20 weeks	17 weeks	6 weeks
(parental)	20 weeks	17 weeks	not specified
Quebec			
(pregnancy)	none	18 weeks	6 weeks
(parental)	none	34 weeks	not specified
Saskatchewan			
(pregnancy)	20 weeks in 52 weeks preceding leave	18 weeks	6 weeks
(parental)	20 weeks	12 weeks	not specified
Northwest Territories			
(pregnancy)	12 months	17 weeks	6 weeks
(parental)	12 months	12 weeks	5 weeks
Yukon (pregnancy)	12 months	17 weeks (only 6 weeks without prior notice)	not specified

Working Canadians also derive retirement and disability benefits from the Canada Pension Plan (CPP), and those who lose their jobs through no fault of their own have a safety net in Employment Insurance (EI), formerly Unemployment Insurance. The CPP is available to employees and the self-employed in all provinces except Quebec, which has an almost identical Quebec Pension Plan (QPP). (The major difference is that QPP investment funds are controlled by Quebec.)

Both employers and employees are legally bound to contribute to the CPP/QPP. With certain exceptions, the employer must deduct a specified amount from his employees' wages, and remit them to the government. These contributions finance a monthly pension for retired workers, who have earned enough credits in their working life.

On retirement at 65, you are entitled to 25 percent of your average monthly pensionable earnings, but you can apply anytime between 60 and 70, and receive benefits prorated accordingly. Benefits are also payable should you become disabled, and your surviving spouse and/or children are also eligible for benefits under the Plan.

SURVIVOR AND SPOUSAL BENEFITS

In Alberta, New Brunswick, Nova Scotia, and Prince Edward Island, survivors are entitled to a pension of at least 60 percent of the benefits vested at the time of their spouse's or parent's death. Federal government employees, and residents of British Columbia, Manitoba, Ontario, Quebec, and Saskatchewan may only be entitled to the discounted value of the pension, unless the spouse or parent dies after retirement, in which case the survivors would be entitled to 50 percent or more of the pension.

EMPLOYMENT INSURANCE

Over the years, the eligibility requirements for unemployment insurance (UI) benefits gradually became stricter, although allowances for maternity and adoption leave, including the father's right to benefits in certain circumstances, improved. (See "Leaves of Absence for Parents," at left.) Under UI, eligibility was largely determined by the number of weeks worked in the previous year. This changed in January 1997, when UI was replaced by employment insurance (EI), and is based on hours, rather than weeks, worked.

This is intended to reflect current work patterns, such as the disappearance of the traditional, 40-hour, Monday-to-Friday work week. Since every hour worked is insurable, those who work 15-hour weeks, or hold down two or more part-time jobs, can qualify equally with those in seasonal occupations who may work 50 or more hours a week in high season. As was the case

---

CLAIMING EMPLOYMENT INSURANCE BENEFITS

Should you find yourself unemployed, or wish to collect employment insurance benefits while on sick, maternity or parental leave, keep the following in mind:

1. You must get a record of employment from your employer: otherwise, you will not qualify for EI.

2. You must also complete certain forms at your nearest EI office. Be prepared to explain in writing why you are unemployed, how long you foresee yourself unemployed, and what kind of work you are willing to accept.

3. At least two weeks will elapse before you receive your first payment.

4. Claimants receiving less than $200 a week in payments can earn an additional $50 a week, or 25 percent of their benefits, whichever is higher, without any loss of benefits.

5. At most, you will only receive about 55 percent of your average wage up to a maximum of $413 a week for 36 to 45 weeks. You can get benefits for up to 15 weeks for sick or maternity leave and up to 10 weeks for parental leave. You may be eligible for higher payments if you have dependent children.

6. You have the right to appeal any assessment you believe is unfair.

DIFFERENT TYPES OF DISABILITY PAYMENTS

Suppose you slip and injure yourself at work. If this injury makes you unable to work permanently (or even for more than one week), you may be entitled to benefits from one of two sources:

1. Private insurance. Often, large and medium size companies have group plans that cover disability for short or long absences from work because of injury. Under these plans, the insurance company would pay you about 75 percent of your salary. Anyone who is self-employed, can also buy private disability insurance. Such policies sometimes cover you for sickness as well as accidents.

2. Workers compensation. All provinces and territories provide compensation for workers who are injured on the job or even at company-sponsored events, such as company soft ball games. If you are eligible, you will be paid 50 to 75 percent of your salary. Your job will also be available to you when you are able to return to work.

under UI, the qualifying period for EI varies according to employment rates. In regions where 13 percent or more of the population is unemployed, you will need 420 hours of work to qualify for benefits; where unemployment is as low as 6 percent, 700 work hours is the minimum requirement.

How "Workers' Comp" Works

Under workers' compensation, employees are entitled to monetary compensation for job-related injury and disease. If you are a construction worker and suffer a severe back injury, or a maintenance worker who slips and falls on the job, workers' compensation insurance will probably pay certain medical bills and a portion of your salary for any work missed because of the injury.

WHO IS COVERED?

Although workers' compensation is compulsory in many industries, as well as for federal employees, students, and even prisoners in some instances, coverage varies from province to province. Illnesses and injuries that might qualify for compensation range from chicken pox (in British Columbia) to writer's cramp (in Quebec). Entertainers, dentists, lawyers, doctors, accountants, and the self-employed are exempt from compulsory participation but, in most provinces, may voluntarily join the scheme. Farm laborers, domestic help, and casual workers are also exempt, but private employers can choose to cover such workers. Many provinces also exclude volunteers and employees of nonprofit organizations but, by and large, most people who are employed by a company at the time of an on-the-job accident are eligible for workers' compensation benefits.

WHAT IS COVERED?

To be eligible for compensation, your illness or injuries must be directly related to your job. Depending on your province, these might include allergic reactions, hearing loss, contagious diseases, osteoarthritis, or disabilities resulting from exposure to vibrations or absorption of chemicals through the skin.

Coverage depends on whether you are injured or become ill while performing your normal duties. Most provinces will cover you even if you are in the employee lunchroom, say, but not if the injury occurs when you are traveling to or from work. However, a salesperson injured while traveling on the job probably would be covered. Mental and psychological disorders, sexual dysfunction, and death might be other medical conditions deemed to result from the nature of the job, and so entitling you to benefits. An Ontario seaman was awarded workers' compensation for emotional shock suffered during a winter storm when he discovered a corpse on board his freighter.

You will probably forfeit your eligibility if you deliberately hurt yourself, or knowingly violate a safety rule. A welder who knows safety goggles must be worn on the job but who removes his anyway probably will not be covered for injuries sustained as a result.

However, if he is injured because of mere carelessness—he wears his goggles but unknowingly fastens them incorrectly—he will probably qualify for compensation, even though the injuries suffered were due to his mistake.

How to File a Claim

Any time you are injured at work, even slightly, you should notify your employer or supervisor immediately. If necessary, ask for a claim form, which will cover the basic information—the where, when, and how of the accident or the illness. In some provinces, your employer will require that you be examined by a doctor.

You should start receiving benefits as soon as your claim is accepted. Should your claim be denied, either in part or totally, you can call the workers' compensation board in your province to find out the procedures for initiating an appeal or review. You will probably want to contact a lawyer who specializes in workers' compensation claims.

Permissible Wage Deductions

If you are a federal employee, your employer can deduct any portion of your wages authorized by a court order (a garnishee, for example), as well as the standard deductions for employment insurance and Canada (Quebec) pension plans. Your employer can also deduct union dues and any overpayment of wages. Most other deductions require your written authorization. Your employer cannot deduct from your wages anything for lost money or lost or damaged property if any other person has access to the money or the property.

Most provinces have similar wage-deduction legislation that applies to workers who are not federal employees. In Alberta, for example, your employer must notify you before he reduces your wages for a pay period. In British Columbia, Nova Scotia and New Brunswick, if you sign an authorization allowing deductions from your wages to pay back a debt to a third party, your employer is not necessarily required to do so.

If You Quit Your Job

You are not entitled to employment insurance benefits if you are fired for misconduct, or if you quit without "just cause." With proof, any of the following would be considered "just cause":

✔ *Harassment.* This could be sexual, or otherwise.

✔ *Family reasons.* You have to accompany a spouse or dependent child to another residence, or you must care for your child or other immediate family member.

✔ *Discrimination.* You are being discriminated against because you belong to an employee organization, or for any other unlawful reason.

✔ *Health or safety.* Working conditions are hazardous to your health or safety.

✔ *Constructive dismissal.* Your employer has cut your salary, demoted you, or modified your duties drastically for the sole purpose of encouraging you to quit.

✔ *Career change fails.* You leave your job for a definite offer of employment only to have the job fall through.

✔ *Illegalities.* Your employer's practices are against the law. (This and the two following items are very difficult to prove, and the employer can always appeal the claim.)

✔ *Antagonism.* Your supervisor is antagonistic toward you.

✔ *Pressure to quit.* Your employer or other employees are pressuring you to quit.

In Manitoba and Quebec, employers are not allowed to make deductions for uniforms and the like if you are receiving less than minimum wage as a result of the deductions. In Newfoundland, employers are not allowed to make you pay for anything supplied by your employer.

BANKRUPTCY

If your employer is declared bankrupt, the federal Bankruptcy Act will apply, and you will only be able to claim a maximum of $2,000 for your unpaid wages earned in the six months preceding the bankruptcy.

In Alberta, Manitoba, Nova Scotia, Prince Edward Island, Saskatchewan, and Ontario, vacation pay is supposed to be set aside by the employer and you may have a special priority claim against the bankrupt company's assets. Alberta, Manitoba, and Saskatchewan also require that wages be set aside and kept "in trust" for the employees.

ADDITIONAL RECOURSES

In addition to your recourses under the Bankruptcy Act, some provinces offer additional measures for recovering lost wages. In Manitoba, you can be entitled to as much as $1,200 for unpaid wages. Employees in the construction industry in Quebec are entitled to be paid in full. In Ontario, you can file a complaint with the Employment Standards Branch, which may compensate you for up to $5,000 under the Employee Wage Protection Program. Finally, the directors of an incorporated company can be sued personally for unpaid wages for a period not exceeding six months.

Recovery of Unpaid Wages

What can you do to recover your wages if your employer refuses to pay them? In most provinces, you have two options if your employer will not pay you what you are owed.

• Your best option is to file a complaint at the employment standards branch nearest you. You normally have about a year in which to do this. A government officer will meet with you and examine your records. If he finds your claim justified, he will most likely begin recovery proceedings by asking the employer to pay the amount owed, and if the employer pays immediately, the matter is settled at once. Alternatively, the inspector may negotiate a written agreement on a sum you are willing to accept and the employer is willing to pay. An employer who refuses a verbal request to pay up will, in all likelihood, receive a demand letter calling upon him to pay. If all else fails, the employer can be prosecuted, have his assets seized, and could be liable for a fine of up to $10,000. But criminal prosecution, followed by fine and imprisonment, is rare. An employer who disputes the inspector's findings has a right to appeal and so most cases are resolved long before prosecution becomes necessary.

• In most provinces, employees are entitled to recover all pay owing, including commissions, overtime, vacation and severance pay. If your employer refuses to pay any of your entitlements, you may choose to institute a law suit. You can do this yourself in small claims court.

DISCRIMINATION

Discrimination in the workplace can take many ugly forms. A comprehensive package of laws aims specifically at protecting you from the worst of them.

Legislation to Protect Your Rights

The Canadian Charter of Rights and Freedoms prohibits discrimination in the workplace by employers, by other employees, by unions, and by employment agencies. Similar prohibitions are found in human rights legislation enacted by all provinces, although the grounds of discrimination may vary from province to province.

All provinces forbid discrimination on the basis of race, nationality, ethnicity, place of origin, color, religion, creed, marital status, physical or mental disability, and sex. British Columbia, Saskatchewan, Manitoba, Ontario, Quebec, New Brunswick, Nova Scotia, and Yukon forbid discrimination on the basis of sexual orientation.

Some provinces prohibit discrimination based on a criminal conviction, unless the offense is related to the employment sought. A bank, for instance, might have the right to refuse to hire a teller previously convicted of embezzlement or theft.

DISPARATE TREATMENT

If you are treated differently from other employees primarily because of your race, religion, sex, or national origin, you may be a victim of discrimination and protected by the human rights laws. Such behavior is called "disparate treatment," and it is prohibited in hiring, firing, promotions, discipline, compensation, and any other employment decisions. Say, for example, that you are from a visible minority, and were reprimanded by your employer because you took four sick days in one month. However, a white coworker in the same situation was not disciplined at all. If your employer's only reason for treating you as he did was your ethnicity, you are the victim of disparate treatment—but you must show that your employer purposely discriminated against you. If your employer has another legitimate reason for punishing you, such as your history of calling in sick, he is probably not in violation of the law.

ADVERSE IMPACT

"Adverse impact" takes place when the effect of a company policy or rule has a disproportionately negative effect on a protected group. Whereas disparate treatment refers to deliber-

Every individual is equal before and under the law and has the right to the equal protection and equal benefit of the law without discrimination and, in particular, without discrimination based on race, national or ethnic origin, colour, religion, sex, age or mental or physical disability.

CANADIAN CHARTER OF RIGHTS AND FREEDOMS

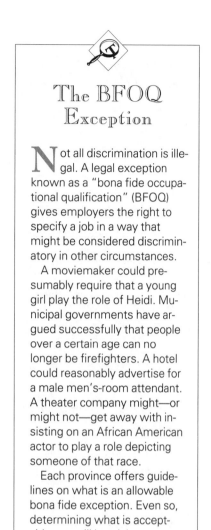

The BFOQ Exception

Not all discrimination is illegal. A legal exception known as a "bona fide occupational qualification" (BFOQ) gives employers the right to specify a job in a way that might be considered discriminatory in other circumstances.

A moviemaker could presumably require that a young girl play the role of Heidi. Municipal governments have argued successfully that people over a certain age can no longer be firefighters. A hotel could reasonably advertise for a male men's-room attendant. A theater company might—or might not—get away with insisting on an African American actor to play a role depicting someone of that race.

Each province offers guidelines on what is an allowable bona fide exception. Even so, determining what is acceptable can still be tricky.

An employer has to prove that the limiting requirement is necessary to business operations, and that the requirement, say as to age or height, applies equally to all those in the excepted category.

Thus, an airline might impose an age limit on its pilots, the BFOQ being that their vision would be impaired by age; yet if some of those pilots over the limiting age still have perfect vision, they could plead discrimination without reasonable cause.

ate discrimination because of your membership in a minority group, adverse impact can be more subtle and is often unintentional. For instance, requiring that police officers meet certain height and weight requirements when job duties do not necessitate it may be discriminatory. Such requirements may have an adverse impact on women, who are generally shorter and weigh less than men.

It is legal for an employer to be discriminatory in hiring in some instances. If the employer can show that a certain criterion is a "bona fide occupational qualification" (BFOQ) for a job, he can refuse to hire those who do not meet that criteria. An example of a BFOQ would be requiring a woman for a specific acting role or hiring someone over a certain legal age to serve alcohol.

Building an adverse-impact case is not easy. If an employer places male workers in certain jobs and females in other, lower-paying jobs, claiming that the men's jobs require heavy lifting, you will have to show that the requirement is actually a pretext for discrimination, that some women are capable of doing the men's jobs, and that your employer is placing females at a disadvantage by not giving them the same opportunities.

OTHER KINDS OF DISCRIMINATION

An employer may be perpetuating past discrimination if a seemingly neutral policy continues to reinforce workplace bias. For example, if an employer generally asks employees to recommend friends for open positions and the workplace is predominantly made up of white males, he may be guilty of discrimination if white males continue to be hired, and minorities and women do not have an opportunity to be employed.

Laws also offer recourse if you are subject to a hostile environment because of your membership in a minority group. Ethnic slurs or racially based jokes that continue even after you have voiced an objection can be judged discriminatory, whether or not your employer is actually participating in the behavior himself. If an employer is aware of discrimination, or even if it is judged that an employer should be aware of it, and does nothing to stop it, he can be held accountable for it.

Anytime you feel you are being discriminated against, try to document the behavior that gave rise to this impression. If it occurs during a job interview, take notes if you can. If possible, keep a copy of an application or an employment test that asks discriminatory questions.

If the suspected discrimination is happening while you are on the job, save memos, written reprimands, performance reviews, forms, or any policy statements that you think are discriminatory. If you are the victim of a verbal attack, find out if anyone else heard it.

Keep detailed notes of anything you were told that may be grounds for a discrimination suit. Include names, dates, and any other pertinent information, even your feelings at the time. If you file a complaint with a human rights commission, documentation may be essential in proving your claim.

MAKING A COMPLAINT

An individual or a group can make a complaint to the Canadian Human Rights Commission or a provincial human rights commission. Procedures vary from province to province, but generally the matter will first be investigated by the commission receiving the complaint. If it finds a valid grievance, it can order that the situation be corrected and, depending on the case, can order that the aggrieved individual be compensated for lost wages or benefits, humiliation, or indignity. The commission can also impose fines or penalties on the wrongdoer.

Age Discrimination

Even though the federal and provincial governments have anti-age discrimination, and that mandatory retirement, with certain exceptions, has been abolished in the public service, British Columbia, Saskatchewan, Ontario, and Newfoundland permit mandatory retirement at age 65. The Supreme Court of Canada has ruled that although compulsory retirement-age policies may be discriminatory, they can be justified by the labor market and the need to provide work opportunities to others. But all court rulings are not consistent. Judges in some provinces have also declared that a compulsory retirement age violates their province's human rights legislation.

Gender Discrimination

Job discrimination on the basis of sex, including discrimination because of pregnancy, is prohibited by federal and provincial human rights statutes. If an employer refuses to hire you because you are pregnant, or fires or demotes you because you would like to have a baby, he may be violating the law. Gender discrimination can take on many forms and is prohibited by a number of laws.

EQUAL PAY FOR EQUAL WORK

All provinces have laws addressing equal pay for men and women, and the Canadian Human Rights Commission especially encourages the following:

Forced Retirement: Discrimination?

Unless the employer can show that an employee's age may affect the health and safety of the public, age may not be a factor in hiring an employee, or in establishing a younger-than-average retirement age for certain occupations.

Two Ontario firefighters are among those who have challenged such policies and won. When the firemen charged that the Borough of Etobicoke discriminated against them by forcing them to retire at age 60, the Ontario Human Rights Commission agreed. The ruling was then reversed by the Court of Appeal, which found the policy was in the best interests of the employees and the public. But the Supreme Court of Canada disagreed with the appeal court and maintained the commission's original decision. In the Supreme Court's view, the mandatory retirement policy in this particular instance was discriminatory since the employer could not prove that the age requirement was a bona fide occupational qualification exception.

- Equal pay for equal work, where men and women are performing identical tasks;
- Equal pay for substantially similar work (for example, a cleaning woman is entitled to the same wages as a janitor);
- Equal pay for work of equal value, where men and women, although performing completely different tasks, are equally valuable in the contribution they make;
- Pay equity, which obliges employers to take positive steps to eliminate wage discrimination in all areas of employment.

Complaints regarding wage discrimination can be brought before federal and provincial human rights commissions, which can order that the situation be corrected, and in some cases, can impose fines and penalties on the employer.

SEXUAL HARASSMENT

Sexual harassment can be defined as unwanted sexual advances or conduct of a sexual nature. It includes graphic or negative comments about an employee's appearance or anatomy, unwelcome sexual advances or propositions, unwelcome descriptions of personal sexual experiences, questions about an employee's sex life, the display of pornographic materials in the workplace, and threatening to fire or demote an employee for rejecting

Making the Human Rights Commissions Work for You

The federal government and all provincial governments have established human rights commissions to help you fight discrimination in the workplace. All these commissions have tribunals which will formally adjudicate your complaint and take appropriate action.

• If you work for the federal government or in a federally regulated institution, such as a bank or Crown Corporation, you should address your complaint to the federal human rights commission. Race, national or ethnic origin, color, religion, age, sex and sexual orientation, marital or family status, disability, and conviction of an offense for which a pardon was granted are all prohibited grounds of discrimination under the Charter of Rights and Freedoms and the federal Bill of Rights and Human Rights Act.

• The following are prohibited grounds of discrimination according to provincial legislation: race, national or ethnic origin, color, religion, age (not all provinces), sex, sexual orientation (not all provinces), marital or family status, disability, and conviction of an offense for which a pardon was granted. Before filing a complaint with your provin-

cial commission, check your province's equal-opportunity procedures and antidiscrimination legislation. There may be some limits to what you can file, and these may vary from province to province.

• Once the human rights commission receives your complaint, it will contact your employer and investigate your case. If you can prove your discrimination claim, the commission may order your employer to do one or more of the following: cease the discrimination; hire, rehire, or promote you; award back pay; establish an affirmative action program.

• If the problem cannot be resolved amicably, you are entitled to a hearing before the human rights commission tribunal, and you are also entitled to be represented by a lawyer at these hearings.

sexual advances. The harassing party may be the victim's co-worker, supervisor, or associate, and can be of either gender.

The courts recognize two general types of sexual harassment: "quid pro quo" (something received in exchange for something given) and "hostile environment." A classic quid pro quo situation is when a supervisor tells a female subordinate that unless she complies with his sexual advances, she will be fired. Such harassment is usually clear-cut. If the victim has any proof, she will most likely win a lawsuit. Some forms of quid pro quo are more subtle. They might be promises of advancement, of better working conditions, of better pay, coupled with threats of retaliation if the employee does not submit to the harassing party's demands or threatens to complain to coworkers, a supervisor, or the human rights commission.

HOSTILE ENVIRONMENT

Conduct that interferes with a person's work performance or creates an "intimidating, hostile, or offensive working environment" is also considered sexual harassment. An individual may be a victim of sexual harassment even when she does not lose her job or get passed up for a promotion. In the courts, conduct is considered sexual harassment if it is conduct that a "reasonable person" would find hostile, abusive, or detrimental to a comparatively normal and effective work environment. No two cases of sexual harassment are exactly alike. In some cases, such as a quid pro quo situation, you may want to take immediate legal action at even a hint of harassment. If you are being subjected to conduct that makes you uncomfortable, do not hesitate to file a complaint—call the human rights commission, or consult a lawyer.

Affirmative Action

In affirming that "every individual is equal before and under the law," the Charter of Rights and Freedoms also notes that such guarantees do not preclude measures that promote the hiring of individuals or groups "disadvantaged because of race, national or ethnic origin, color, religion, sex, age or mental or physical disability," in an effort to improve their job opportunities. Such affirmative action programs are usually instituted by the federal and provincial governments. Private employers are generally not required to implement affirmative action plans, unless a pattern of discrimination has been noted by the courts. Of course, some employers may do so voluntarily or because of stipulations in a union contract.

Affirmative action plans can involve recruitment, hiring, promotions, transfers, and other conditions of employment. Local,

---

A MODEL POLICY AGAINST SEXUAL HARASSMENT

In today's workplace, companies must make it clear that sexual harassment will not be tolerated, and they must let employees know how it will be dealt with. An effective sexual harassment policy should do the following:

1. Be published. The policy should be in writing, be posted, and given to all employees when they are hired.

2. Educate. All employees should know how to recognize sexual harassment. Seminars or workshops may work better than a written statement.

3. Encourage participation. Employees should be encouraged to report any and all behavior they feel uncomfortable with or offended by.

4. Promise results. Victims should be assured that a speedy investigation will take place after charges are made.

5. Discipline violators. Quick action against violators sends a clear message. Punishments must be carried out.

6. Assure job security. Victims need to know that their job security and prospects for advancement will not be jeopardized if they participate in an investigation.

7. Designate policy administrators. Employees should know exactly whom to report abuse to. It is best to have more than one administrator.

provincial, or federal government employers may be required to publicize job openings where women and minorities are likely to see them. The objective is that underrepresented groups will thus be encouraged to apply for positions and help balance the workforce.

Under one such affirmative action plan, Canadian National (CN) began hiring women for jobs such as welding that had previously been open exclusively to men. This happened when the Canadian Human Rights Commission, having learned that less than one percent of CN's blue collar employees were women, ruled that one of every four such employees hired by CN be female until women made up 13 percent of CN's workforce. An appeal court later held that the human rights tribunal could not institute such measures, but another court ruled that the tribunal could order the adoption of special programs to remedy and prevent discriminatory practices.

An affirmative action plan cannot, however, automatically exclude nonminorities, lest it become "reverse discrimination." For example, the courts would not approve of a minority employee being favored by an affirmative action plan if he was not qualified for his position. The courts also do not look favorably upon strict quotas that ignore the number of qualified minorities in the workforce. But if two candidates are equally qualified for a position, the plan may call upon the employer to give the job to a minority or female candidate if they are underrepresented in that position in the workplace.

Religion in the Workplace

The religious beliefs of every Canadian worker are protected by law. Freedom of religion is specifically named as a right in all provinces and territories, except Ontario and the Northwest Territories. But even though discrimination on religious grounds is illegal, there are legal limits to your right to practice your religion in all circumstances. Your religious practice may not interfere with laws that are in the public interest, as was the case with a Sikh railway employee who refused to wear a hard hat since his religion did not permit him to remove his turban. Since the hard hat was compulsory to ensure employee safety, the Supreme Court of Canada held that the hard hat rule was a bona fide occupational requirement, and so the practice was not discriminatory.

In most cases the law says employers should make "reasonable accommodation" to their employees' religious beliefs and practices. If work interferes with an employee's Saturday Sabbath for example, an employer should, if possible, find somebody else to work a Saturday shift, reschedule work, or make

---

What If Religion Interferes With Work?

Employers are entitled to ban certain religious activities from their premises. Here are some practices that can be legally forbidden:

✔ *Proselytizing.* You cannot proselytize for your religion at work without your employer's consent. However, the company may not bar one religion from seeking converts and give free rein to another.

✔ *Daily prayers.* You cannot organize prayers, meditation, a religious sing-along, or a Bible reading without employer consent. Some employers will allow such activity if it does not interfere with the orderly flow of work.

✔ *Wearing religious costumes.* Your employer may prohibit religious dress such as turbans, yarmulkes, long hair, or beards in the workplace if it interferes with job performance. But beyond that restriction, the employer cannot prohibit some workers from wearing religious garb while permitting others to dress however they want.

other changes. Not every religious accommodation is reasonable, however. A large company can juggle schedules more easily than a small company. When the economic toll becomes too high, employers are justified in refusing to make special accommodations or give time off for religious reasons.

The Disabled

Disability, as defined in human rights legislation, often includes mental disabilities, such as depression and mental retardation, as well as physical disabilities, such as epilepsy, confinement to a wheelchair, reliance on a guide dog, and visual or hearing impairment. In some cases, alcoholism, drug addiction, and contagious and noncontagious illnesses have also been recognized as disabilities that deserve protection under the law.

In Alberta, for example, the drummer of a band hired to entertain at a hotel was found to have AIDS. The band leader, who was sharing living quarters with the drummer, whose cut hand he had once bandaged, dismissed the drummer. Declaring the dismissal discriminatory, the Alberta Human Rights Commission awarded the drummer his lost earnings.

On the other hand, certain policies or practices which at first seem discriminatory may nonetheless be upheld if the employer can justify their use. For instance, an airline may refuse to hire a pilot who is color blind, since it is reasonable for an airline to require that pilots have color vision.

"Reasonable Accommodation" for the Disabled

To make the workplace more accessible to the disabled, employers must make "reasonable accommodations." It is the employer's responsibility to:

• Modify the application procedure so that a disabled person can be considered for the position. This would include reading a written application to a blind person, or altering a preemployment test as necessary.

• Adjust the work environment or job duties so that a disabled person can perform the essential function of the position. For example, if a clerk-typist spends 20 percent of her time filing, it is not an essential function of the job and can be performed by someone else.

• Meet the job-related needs of the disabled individual. The employer does not need to come up with the ideal accommodation, just a reasonable one. If raising the height of a workstation to accommodate a wheelchair enables the employee to do the job, the employer need not buy other specialized equipment at the employee's request.

• In general, make all accommodations that are reasonably affordable to facilitate a disabled person's job performance. The employer may not need to make an accommodation, however, if it would be too expensive, difficult, or disruptive to the point of creating an "undue burden" on the business. Such undue hardship must be specifically proven by the employer, and cannot be a result of fear or prejudice.

BASIC RIGHTS ON THE JOB

Every employee enjoys fundamental rights at work. You must know what they are and how to make sure you get them.

123..

CHILD LABOR LAWS

Most provinces have child labor laws specifying that a child cannot be employed before a certain age and in certain occupations.

1. Government. No one under age 17 can work for the federal government, unless he or she does not have to be in school, and the job will not endanger the child's health or safety.

2. At sea. A child must be at least 15 before being employed at sea.

3. Construction. In most provinces, children under 16 are not allowed to work in the construction industry. (The Northwest Territories sets the minimum at 17.)

4. Mining. You have to be 18 to work in the mines in most provinces, although you may be able to work aboveground at a younger age.

5. Entertainment industry. Many provinces regulate the employment of children in the entertainment industry. In Alberta, a 12-year-old may be employed in the entertainment field if the provincial Child Welfare Commission approves.

Wages and Hours

Each province has legislation regulating hours and wages, but some of these laws are more specific than others. Some laws only indicate when an employee must be paid overtime. According to others, employees can refuse overtime once they have worked a certain number of hours a week, or when they haven't been given enough notice, or if they face a personal emergency. But in most provinces, you may be required to work more hours than would normally be allowed by law if you work in an essential service industry, and the work is urgent to ensure the health and safety of the public.

In Ontario, employees must be paid time and a half their regular wages after 44 hours of work, but are not allowed to work more than 48 hours a week, or 8 hours a day. However, there are exceptions. Workers repairing roads and bridges and those in the tourist industry may be required to work 50 hours a week before they are entitled to overtime rates. In Nova Scotia, employees are entitled to overtime (at a rate of time and a half the minimum wage) after 48 hours of work in a week, but there is no fixed maximum number of hours that an employee can be required to work.

Certain industries may be excepted from labor standards legislation. Manitoba and Quebec, for instance, have specific laws which regulate the construction industry. Ontario and Quebec have specific laws regarding hours of work in the garment industry.

MINIMUM WAGES

Some provinces set different minimum wage rates for certain industries. In Ontario, Nova Scotia, and Newfoundland, for instance, minimum wage rates for garment and textiles workers are different from rates for workers in other industries; British Columbia has special minimum wage rates for farm workers; New Brunswick, for camp counselors; and Ontario, for those who serve alcoholic beverages.

Alberta, Manitoba, and Saskatchewan permit employers to set lower than average minimum wage rates for the disabled, but this is rarely done.

OVERTIME

In New Brunswick, Newfoundland and Nova Scotia, overtime pay is only one and a half times minimum wage, whereas in most other provinces, you are entitled to one and a half times your regular pay. In British Columbia, you are entitled time and a half after 40 hours of work, and twice your regular pay if you work more than 11 hours a day or 48 hours a week.

In some provinces, you may arrange to take paid leave for the equivalent of the overtime hours that you work.

Under federal legislation and Saskatchewan labor laws, an employer may average your working hours over two or more weeks, in which case you may not be entitled to overtime. With government approval, Quebec employers may calculate hours over a period longer than two weeks. In the case of four-day work weeks, Alberta, British Columbia, Manitoba, Saskatchewan, and Yukon employers can insist employees work more hours a day than would normally be allowed.

Overtime Must Be Compensated

PROBLEM
Adam Parker worked in a retail electronics store in British Columbia. His regular schedule was from 9:00 A.M. to 6:00 P.M. every day with an hour for lunch: a 40-hour week. The week before a big sale, his employer, Mark Tanner, told him to go home an hour early each day that week. When Adam asked if he would be docked pay, his employer replied, "No, I need you to stay late every day next week. It will even out."

ACTION
It would not even out. Adam called his employment standards branch, and learned that under British Columbia's Employment Standards Act, Adam's employer must pay him overtime if he works more than 40 hours in a week. It was legal for Mark to pay Adam for only 35 hours the first week, but he had to pay the time-and-a-half overtime rate for the extra five hours in the second week. For those two weeks, Adam earned an extra two-and-a-half-hours pay.

Occupational Health and Safety

Safety conditions in the workplace are governed primarily by provincial and territorial legislation, with occupational safety and health provisions of the Canada Labour Code regulating the federal public service; Crown corporations and agencies; ships, trains, and aircraft; petroleum exploration on federal lands; and such interprovincial and international industries as pipelines, ferries, radio and television, and banks. By and large, the federal law does not regulate the mining, retailing, construction, and bottling industries.

EMPLOYEES' RIGHTS

Your rights as an employee will vary depending on the province where you live and the terms and conditions of your contract, or verbal agreement. Those below are fairly common rights.

1. Sunday work. In most provinces, you must be given one full day's rest per week, preferably Sunday. Alberta, British Columbia, and Quebec do not recommend a particular day. Sunday shopping is now legal in several provinces.

2. Coffee and meal breaks. Most provinces insist workers get a half-hour's break (an hour's break in Newfoundland and Manitoba) after every five hours of work.

3. Paid breaks. In Ontario, Quebec, and Saskatchewan, employees must be paid while on their breaks.

4. Statutory holidays. Employees, with certain exceptions, are entitled to a day off on New Year's Day, Good Friday, Labour Day, and Christmas Day. Canada Day is also a statutory holiday everywhere except Newfoundland, and Victoria Day, Thanksgiving Day, and Remembrance Day are statutory holidays in some provinces. By and large, only those employees who have been working for the employer for at least 90 days are entitled to paid statutory holidays. In many provinces, the employer can require you to work on a statutory holiday, provided you get another day off with pay, or are paid overtime for the hours you work on the holiday.

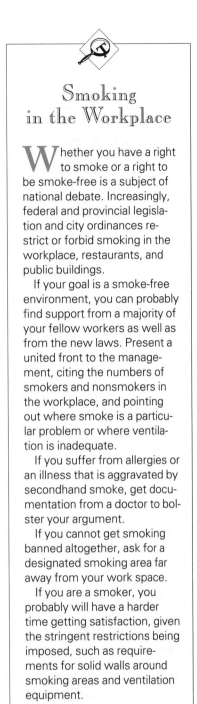

Smoking in the Workplace

Whether you have a right to smoke or a right to be smoke-free is a subject of national debate. Increasingly, federal and provincial legislation and city ordinances restrict or forbid smoking in the workplace, restaurants, and public buildings.

If your goal is a smoke-free environment, you can probably find support from a majority of your fellow workers as well as from the new laws. Present a united front to the management, citing the numbers of smokers and nonsmokers in the workplace, and pointing out where smoke is a particular problem or where ventilation is inadequate.

If you suffer from allergies or an illness that is aggravated by secondhand smoke, get documentation from a doctor to bolster your argument.

If you cannot get smoking banned altogether, ask for a designated smoking area far away from your work space.

If you are a smoker, you probably will have a harder time getting satisfaction, given the stringent restrictions being imposed, such as requirements for solid walls around smoking areas and ventilation equipment.

If you can rally enough fellow smokers to your cause, however, you may be able to convince your employer to create smoking areas that comply with the restrictions.

Most provinces have general health and safety regulations requiring employers to ensure the welfare of employees in the workplace. Many provinces stipulate that employers and employees report any conditions that may endanger employees' health and safety. The names of the statutes setting out health and safety rules, and the agencies responsible for implementing them, vary from one province to another. Ontario, for example, has enacted its own comprehensive safety and health act, but safety and health issues in British Columbia are regulated by the workers' compensation board.

Some provinces regulate such matters on an industry by industry basis.

In recent years, British Columbia and Saskatchewan broadened their health and safety legislation, forcing employers to implement policies designed to minimize violence and harassment in the workplace. Employers are now obliged to have internal complaint procedures for reporting and investigating such incidents.

Self-employed individuals, companies with fewer than 10 employees, and family-owned and operated farms may be exempt from health and safety laws in some jurisdictions. But generally, the relevant legislation requires a workplace free from hazards likely to cause death or severe physical harm. Some of the basic standards require that:

- Workplaces be kept clean and orderly;
- Medical and first aid treatment are readily available;
- Emergency exits and fire protection plans are implemented;
- Temperatures are maintained at a comfortable level;
- Workers receive proper training on machinery and equipment;
- Suitable drinking water is available;
- Adequate lighting is available;
- Noise levels do not exceed a certain level (unless protective gear is provided);
- Smoking is not permitted in elevators.

In determining how well employers meet these specific standards, governments largely rely on random inspections and alerts from employees and other observers about conditions that might endanger the health and safety of workers.

RIGHT TO REFUSE UNSAFE WORK

As long as the refusal does not put another employee at risk, and provided the perceived danger is not a normal condition of the job, employees governed by the Canada Labour Code can refuse to do work that may endanger their health or safety, without any risk to their jobs or wages. In most provinces, if your refusal to work is well founded, you are entitled to be paid even for the period in which you refuse to work. An employer who violates health and safety laws could be prosecuted and, depending on the jurisdiction, imprisoned, or fined from $2,000 to $500,000.

All governments, federal, provincial, and territorial, rigorously control the use of toxic agents, their storage, and handling. Where such substances are in use, your employer must follow certain precautions, such as monitoring your exposure to the substance, and requiring you to submit to medical examinations. In Quebec and Ontario, companies must report if they are using new biological or chemical agents. In most other provinces, the workplace must be tested for toxic substances.

INSPECTIONS

Inspectors or "safety and health officers" may enter any workplace at any time to inspect the premises. This includes testing equipment and monitoring the presence of certain substances. The officer can order whatever may be necessary to correct any problems which may endanger the health and safety of the employees.

COMPLAINT PROCEDURE

When you suspect a health or safety problem at work, it is best to go to a union or management representative first. Management is usually concerned with safety and health issues, and in many cases will respond to a valid complaint. If the employer does not correct the situation, however, employees of federally

In order that people may be happy in their work, these three things are needed: They must be fit for it; they must not do too much of it; and they must have a sense of success in it.

JOHN RUSKIN
Pre-Raphaelitism
1851

AIDS in the Workplace: Promoting Awareness

When an employee has AIDS, many of his coworkers' concerns may be unfounded, because they lack knowledge of the disease and how it is transmitted. Under such circumstances, employers should ensure the workforce is informed on what medical experts and the law says:

• The risk of contracting AIDS in most circumstances is minimal. Medical experts generally agree that an employee cannot contract AIDS by working alongside someone with the disease, by shaking hands, or by sharing the same water glass. AIDS can only be contracted through the exchange of bodily fluids.

• As a general rule you cannot be required to divulge that you are HIV positive, or be required to submit to an HIV test, unless there are other interests at stake that are more important than your right to privacy. In most provinces, you may have to submit to an HIV test if there is an increased risk of transmitting the virus in light of the kind of work you are doing.

• There are a limited number of situations where an employee infected with the AIDS virus may put other individuals at risk. A dental surgeon or health care worker with the AIDS virus, for instance, may expose a patient to a greater risk of contracting AIDS because of the nature of the work involved.

• The Canadian Human Rights Commission has ruled that employees cannot be required to take HIV tests, except when the employee must perform invasive procedures, such as surgery; when the employee must travel to countries which do not admit people infected with AIDS; and when the employee has duties which might compromise the public's safety if he or she is HIV positive.

regulated workplaces can complain to the safety and health representative or committee, which must be in place wherever there are five or more employees, and workers in other jurisdictions can make their case to whoever is charged with occupational health and safety in their province. If the investigating inspector finds little or no hazards, you will be required to return to your job. If the inspector finds that employees' health or safety are at risk, however, the employer will be ordered to correct the problem before work is resumed.

Working Part-Time

When you work part-time or in a temporary position, you may not have much job security. Part-time and temporary workers are often hired for specific assignments and let go when the assignments are done. But when it comes to health and safety at work and freedom from discrimination and sexual harassment, part-time employees have the same rights as full-time employees.

In some provinces, minimum wage laws do not apply to part-time workers, or part-timers in certain occupations, who may only be entitled to a lower part-time wage. You may not be covered by the company's health, life or disability insurance if, for instance, you work less than 20 or 30 hours a week.

Privacy on the Job

The right to privacy is not specifically protected by human rights legislation, but it can be implied that you are entitled to protection against unreasonable invasions of your privacy. Some provinces have laws that give employees the right to view their personnel files; others limit the release of records to third parties. Some provinces also have laws regarding workplace communications, such as telephone calls, correspondence, and electronic mail.

Still, your private life may not be immune to employer scrutiny. Companies can sometimes insist on moral codes whose violation, on or off the job, can lead to discipline or dismissal. Employers have been allowed to fire people involved in illicit activities or who were moonlighting at another job.

Your employer may also be entitled to know if you abuse alcohol or use illegal drugs, although drug testing crosses a fine legal line. Federal testing guidelines exist for the transportation industry, people who carry weapons, and people with classified information. Truckers, pilots, and train engineers may be subject to random testing. Few others are.

When the Boss Can Invade Your Privacy

However much you treasure your privacy, you may not be able to protect it fully from your employer.

✔ *Searches.* A private sector employer may search your desk, locker, workstation, or computer as long as you have no legitimate expectation of privacy and he has a reasonable suspicion of illegal behavior and has notified you in advance that a search is likely.

✔ *Telephone calls.* Private sector employers may monitor telephone calls if you consent to being monitored, or if listening to your phone conversations is considered part of the "ordinary course of business." If it is clear that a call is personal, however, the listener is supposed to hang up.

✔ *Surveillance.* Employers can observe employees in the workplace with video cameras, but cannot create an unnecessary invasion of privacy by installing cameras in areas such as employee rest rooms.

✔ *Electronic mail.* The courts are still setting precedents in this relatively new area, but in general, if your employer tells you that all communications or computer data are subject to monitoring, he can read your electronic mail, since he has removed your expectation of privacy in this area. If he owns the computer, he may be able to monitor your data even if he has not notified you.

PERFORMANCE REVIEWS

Many companies have made performance reviews an integral part of their employee relations. What was once an employer privilege has now come under court scrutiny, and the courts have held that reviews must be fair, unbiased, objective, and professional. If they are not, employees may be entitled to sue for reinstatement or back pay should they be fired, and they may be able to protest reviews that smack of personal bias or do not live up to the company's own policies.

If your employer fires you after one bad review, you may have a negligent-job-evaluation suit. You will need to prove that you were fired for a reason other than the negative review, and that the review was only a last-minute cover-up.

In many cases, your review may be the only documentation of your job performance your employer has. Save all copies of reviews you receive as well as your notes. They can offer protection further down the line. If you feel you have been reviewed unfairly, it is important to put your thoughts in writing and pass them on to your employer. You may also wish to consult a lawyer.

MANAGEMENT AUTHORITY

Employers have a right to discipline you for cause. Use of abusive language, shoddy work performance, habitual tardiness, refusal to obey lawful instructions, use of drugs or alcohol, dishonesty, and breach of trust all qualify as legitimate reasons for discipline. What your employer may not do is impose what the courts have called "outrageous" discipline.

Making an example of you in front of other employees, forcing you to stay on the premises against your will, docking your pay for time you have worked, and any physical abuse or harassment inflicted on you are all examples of what might be deemed "outrageous" discipline, and give you a legal claim against the employer.

COMPLAINING

Grievance procedures, known as "corporate due process," can take many different forms. Some firms use committees to consider both sides of a dispute and then hand down a decision. Other companies assign the task to an objective investigator. Under a union contract, filing a grievance is a strictly defined procedure.

Before taking action, find out all you can about your company's grievance procedure. Prepare all documentation detailing dates, circumstances, and any witnesses or other parties involved with your complaint. Write down everything you are told regarding your complaint. If you suspect that your job is in jeopardy, consult a lawyer.

123...

PERFORMANCE REVIEWS

If you are asked to review an employee, you owe it to the employee to conduct a fair and constructive interview by following the suggestions below. If you are on the receiving end of a review, be aware of these guidelines as indicators of how an interview should go. Make sure to let your reviewer know if you feel you were not treated fairly.

1. Be candid. Identify weaknesses and strengths, and give clear, specific suggestions as to how the employee can improve on-the-job performance.

2. Document it. Put the review in writing and sign it.

3. Be prepared. Keep written notes of the employee's performance throughout the review period.

4. Listen. Make a special effort to hear what the employee has to say, and take it seriously. If you disagree with anything, offer your own opinion, backing it up with examples from your notes.

5. Note disparities. If the review contains information that the employee feels is false, briefly note the objection on the document before having the employee sign it. This can be a peaceful way for the employee to voice disagreement without causing a scene or an argument.

TERMINATION

Whether you resign from your job, are laid off, or get fired, you have certain rights, and your employer has certain responsibilities to you. Insist on them.

Resigning Gracefully

An employee's resignation is not governed by law in British Columbia, Saskatchewan, Ontario, New Brunswick, and the Northwest Territories, although courtesy suggests employees should give an employer reasonable notice before leaving a job. Notice would certainly be mutually advantageous for employees planning to give the employer's name as a reference.

In all other provinces you must give your employer advance notice if you plan to leave. Whether the notice be for one or two weeks depends on how long you have been employed.

It is both courteous and practical to write a formal letter of resignation, stating why you are leaving, and confirming the verbal agreements you have made concerning your departure date and the financial details that remain outstanding. (See "A Termination Letter That Does the Job," page 255.)

Regardless of whether your province requires employees to give advance notice when quitting their jobs, your employer has certain legal obligations when you resign. He must give you your separations papers, for example, together with any other benefits, such as vacation pay, due to you.

Termination and the Law

Whatever the province, if you are an "at-will" employee (that is, you are not protected by an employee contract or other agreement), your employer is legally obliged to give you notice of termination if you have been working for a certain period of time. If you are not given such notice, you are entitled to severance pay. In most provinces, you are entitled to one week's notice after working three months, and up to eight weeks' notice if you have been employed for 8 to 10 years. If several employees are being laid off at the same time, employers might be required to give more notice than what is specified for a single employee. In New Brunswick, for example, six weeks' notice must be given to groups of employees if they have been working for six weeks.

If you are protected by a union agreement, employee contract, provincial law, or if illegal discrimination is suspected, your employer may need "just cause" to fire you. Many reasons can be "just cause" for dismissal: lying on your job application; excessive absences or latenesses; sleeping, drinking, fighting, gambling, or taking drugs on the job; stealing from your employer; harassing coworkers; or being physically, mentally, or emotionally incapable of doing your job.

Just cause does not simply refer to unacceptable behavior, insubordination, or poor job performance. Just cause also can involve legitimate business issues: bad economic conditions can force a business to trim its staff; or reorganization or technological changes may render some jobs obsolete. Despite the broad parameters defining just cause, several strong laws protect employees from being fired unfairly or "discharged wrongfully." You are protected by law if your employer:

- **Violates provincial or federal laws.** This would be the case if you have been discriminated against because of your gen-

---

When You Have to Do the Firing

If you are an owner, manager, or supervisor, you will probably at some time have to fire an employee. The process can be painful for both parties—and it can also lead to legal hot water. To protect yourself and your employer against possible claims, follow these guidelines:

• **Be aware of protected groups.** Many groups are protected by law: racial and ethnic minorities; females; workers over age 40; the handicapped. Members of these groups can be fired for just cause, but you must do it with extra awareness of the employer's responsibility, the possible impact of the firing on that particular worker, and your company's past history of hiring and firing. (See "Discrimination," page 239.)

• **Use progressive discipline.** If you have an employee who needs discipline, plan a system of steps that has the primary goal of improving his performance, and not getting him fired. (See also "Progressive Discipline," page 254.)

• **Document performance.** Keep a written record of the employee's wrongdoings. For example, if chronic lateness is the problem, keep a file of attendance records, warnings, and any written policy regarding excessive tardiness.

• **Know the regulations.** Read your company's rules regarding discipline and termination policy. If you work in a union shop, stay informed about grievance procedures and union regulations. Know and understand the current laws in your province regarding discharge.

• **Use the chain of command.** If you think you will have to fire an employee, be sure to get the approval of your own supervisor. Never discuss the matter with any other employees.

• **Consult a lawyer.** Seek the advice of legal counsel, particularly if you are experiencing problems with a member of a protected group. Be aware that if a member of a nonprotected group is fired to retain a protected-group member you may be in legal trouble.

• **Prepare for the termination.** If you must fire the employee, clearly and calmly communicate the reasons for the dismissal. Inform him of when he will receive his outstanding pay, his rights with regard to his health benefits, the rules regarding employment compensation, and the company's proposed severance pay, if any. Prepare a dismissal letter, and have it reviewed in advance by your superiors, the personnel director, and legal counsel. Be aware that the terminated employee has the right to refuse to cosign the letter.

PROGRESSIVE DISCIPLINE

If an employer or a manager has a serious discipline problem with a subordinate, he may exercise a system known as "progressive discipline."

1. A verbal warning. This should be a clear and straightforward discussion of the problematic behavior, not an "off-the-cuff" remark. The employee should be in no doubt that he has been reprimanded. A note about the warning then goes in his personnel file.

2. A written warning. If the verbal warning has not been heeded, the employee should receive a memo outlining the problem and the appropriate solution. Again, a copy of the memo is usually put in the employee's file.

3. Probation. If the problem persists, the next step is to put the employee "on notice" for a specific length of time—one month, for example—with a written statement that if the problem is not resolved, serious action will be taken.

4. Suspension without pay. For many problems, this step may not be appropriate, but if the employee has a drug or drinking problem, suspension while he seeks rehabilitation may be an effective solution.

5. Termination. If all good-faith efforts have failed to solve the problem, an employer may have no recourse but to fire the employee.

der, age, religion, disability, or national origin, if constitutional rights such as freedom of speech, press, or religion have been breached; or if you have been let go because you participated in union activities.

- **Violates "public policy."** Public policy is what a court would deem activities for the public good. You may be protected from discharge if you are summoned to serve on a jury, if you report your employer for breaking a law or violating safety standards, or if you engage in other activities that a court would deem to be in the public interest.
- **Violates a written employment contract.** Specifically, your employer cannot fail to honor any facet of a legal employment agreement he has with you.
- **Violates implied agreements with you.** "Implied agreement" may apply to rules in an employee handbook; verbal promises made when you were hired; written or verbal reviews or other acknowledgments of good work; or, in some cases, simply having given long, "good faith" service.

CONSTRUCTIVE DISCHARGE

Under certain conditions, you may have a wrongful termination claim, known as "constructive discharge," even if you have quit your job. If you are forced to leave because of intolerable working conditions or harassment, you may be the victim of constructive discharge.

In order to win a constructive discharge case, the intolerable conditions must have been extreme, and you must have had no other recourse but to resign.

Your Rights If You Are Fired

Even employees who are fired for misconduct have certain rights—some legal, others customary. First, you are entitled to receive prompt payment of any wages owed you. Depending upon the law in your province and your company's policy, you may also be entitled to payment for commissions, overtime pay, and unused vacation days, holidays, sick days, or other accrued benefits. (See also "Recovery of Unpaid Wages," page 238.)

Many, but not all, companies provide severance pay, depending upon how long you have been employed and the reasons for your dismissal. Under legislation in most provinces, you are entitled to severance pay if you have not been given the notice required by law, unless of course your employer had just cause to terminate your employment immediately.

If your employer does not offer you severance pay, you should ask for it, especially if you are being fired without notice.

418 Longbeach Parkway • *St. John's, Newfoundland*

August 3, 1996

Mr. John Jones
Vice President, Human Resources
The Ajax Tool Company
Chatsworth, Ont. N0H 1G0

Dear Mr. Jones,

I am writing this letter to confirm the points we agreed on with regard to my termination from Ajax Tools. At our meeting on August 1, 1996, we settled the following:

① Ajax will keep me on the payroll through August 31, 1996, and my last paycheque, due on that date, will reflect my regular salary through that date, as well as five unused vacation days and my annual bonus of $3,000.

② Ajax will also pay me a severance cheque on August 31 reflecting eight weeks' pay or one week for every six months I have been employed at Ajax.

③ Ajax will pay the premiums on my health and dental insurance through September 30, 1996.

④ Ajax will not oppose my claim for employment insurance and will provide me with any help required in completing all the necessary documentation.

⑤ Ajax will give me positive references, explaining to anyone calling for a reference that I was laid off as a result of economic cutbacks, not because of misconduct or inadequacy with regard to my work.

Thank you for your help in this matter.

Very truly yours,

Sylvia Scott

A Termination Letter That Does the Job

When you leave a company, for whatever reason, clarify your termination agreement in writing. If your employer does not write a letter to this end, write your own.

1. Specify when you will receive your final paycheque, how much it will cover, and if it will include any additional payments such as bonuses or unused vacation or sick days.

2. Discuss any severance pay that may have been offered to you, as well as when and how it will be paid.

3. Note any agreement you have about drug plans or medical or dental insurance.

4. Remind the employer that you will be applying for employment insurance benefits, and that you expect the company to support the claim.

5. Explain why you are leaving, and what you expect the employer to say when asked for a reference.

BEFORE YOU BLOW THE WHISTLE

If you are thinking of blowing the whistle on criminal behavior by your employer or other employees, or reporting a workplace hazard to the media or a law-enforcement agency, take the following steps first:

1. Research. Find out if your employer has a previous record of violations of the law and, if possible, what has happened to prior whistle-blowers. You will not be eligible for employment insurance if you are fired for misconduct or if you quit without just cause. If you are refused benefits, you can appeal the decision.

2. Find proof. Be absolutely sure your accusations are well founded. Take detailed notes of illegal behavior and anything said regarding it. Having solid proof of your employer's illegal activity is essential to making a case, and protecting yourself and your job. (It is also vital, after you blow the whistle, to be able to prove any steps taken against you for doing so.)

3. Talk to a lawyer. Discuss your accusations and intentions with a lawyer, who will counsel you on the practical risks involved in blowing the whistle. Your employer may accuse you of defamation or libel if he refutes your charges, so you need to be on firm legal ground.

UNJUST DISMISSAL

If, for instance, you have filed a health and safety complaint against your employer, your wages have been garnished, you are pregnant, or you refuse to work overtime and you are dismissed as a result, you may be able to recover lost wages or be reinstated if you bring the matter before the employment standards branch in your province. If you belong to a union, your recourses are spelled out in the collective agreement or in the provincial or federal labor codes. Find out how provincial labor or health and safety laws, or union agreements will protect you.

WRITTEN CONFIRMATIONS

Confirm your separation agreement by writing a letter to your employer that details your termination terms. Better yet, ask that your employer write the letter to you, and request that it be signed by both you and your former boss. (For a sample of such a letter, see page 255.)

Be wary if your employer asks you to sign a release or any other documents, particularly in the immediate aftermath of being fired. Your employer may be taking advantage of your distress by offering you a severance package in exchange for your relinquishing your right to sue. Carefully read exit agreements, releases, and any other forms that your employer wishes you to sign. If you are in doubt about their meaning, discuss the documents with your lawyer.

Bringing Suit

If you believe you have been discriminated against or that your human rights have been violated, think carefully before taking action against your employer. Do not ask yourself if you "deserved" to be fired; ask yourself if your employer had a "legal right" to fire you. If you think that your discharge was discriminatory or in violation of a written or implied contract, you may have a claim.

If you believe your employer has discriminated against you on the basis of race, national or ethnic origin, color, religion, sex, age or mental or physical disability—in other words, if you believe your employer to be in violation of human rights legislation, you should contact the Human Rights Commission in your area to file a complaint.

The commission will investigate the matter and institute the appropriate action to have you reinstated, recover your wages, and in some cases impose fines and penalties on the employer.

Before going to court, decide if it is worth the expense, the energy, and the emotional stress. Also, clarify your objectives: Do you want your job reinstated? Monetary compensation?

Rectification of a serious problem in your former workplace? If you still want to take your case to court, hire a lawyer immediately. (See also YOUR RIGHTS IN ACTION, page 456.)

If the Firm Fails

Sometimes dismissal is the result of economic problems beyond the worker's and the employer's control. Often, large companies find that they must make large temporary or permanent layoffs. When a number of employees are laid off or dismissed by a company who has shut down operations, it is called a "mass layoff" or "collective dismissal."

There are special federal and provincial laws protecting employees in these circumstances.

In Ontario, if 50 or more employees are going to be laid off over a four-week period, the employer, by and large, must give notice to all the employees. However, there is no need to give notice if the layoff is temporary.

Legislation in Nova Scotia and British Columbia requires employers to give 8 weeks' notice when 50 to 100 employees are to be laid off over a one-month period, 12 weeks' notice if the layoffs affect 100 to 300 employees, and 16 weeks' notice if more than 300 employees are to lose their jobs.

In British Columbia, such layoff notice must be added to the "regular notice" to which workers are entitled. In other words, if you have been working at a company in British Columbia for 10 years, your employer is obliged to give you 8 weeks' notice before dismissal. If you are one of 350 people the company is laying off, you are entitled to 8 weeks' regular notice in addition to the 16 weeks' notice called for by the layoffs.

Making the Best of It

If you are laid off, you will most likely be eligible for employment insurance benefits. Depending upon your company, you may also be entitled to severance pay, retraining programs, job-search assistance, and a number of other optional benefits.

Your reputation does not have to suffer because you lost your job. Layoffs are a sign of the times, an indication of unhealthy economic conditions. Telling a prospective employer that you were laid off is not a shameful admission. Employers know that being laid off is not the fault of the worker and generally do not hold it against job applicants.

Taking Some of the Pain Out of a Layoff

It may not seem to make much difference whether you are laid off or fired—either way you are out of a job. But it does make a difference. Being laid off may not be as bad as you think. Here are some things to keep in mind:

✔ *It's not your fault.* Unlike firings, layoffs are not the result of bad on-the-job performance on your part; they are a function of economic conditions.

✔ *You may get your job back.* You cannot count on it, but sometimes laid-off workers are rehired. Workers may be laid off when sales or profits are down, and if business improves, may be reinstated. Union members who are laid off usually have a contractual right to be called back to work first when a company resumes full production.

✔ *You can collect employment insurance benefits.* Laid-off workers are entitled to employment benefits if they otherwise qualify—for example, if they have been working long enough. As a general rule, employers do not contest the right of laid-off workers to collect employment insurance.

LABOR UNIONS

*Although labor unions do not have the power they once had,
they can still benefit workers in a number of ways.*

Union Laws

The importance of labor unions in the Canadian workplace has declined since their peak of power during the years after World War II, but unions are still a force to be respected. Roughly 20 percent of Canadian workers belong to unions, which use the collective bargaining process to negotiate contracts designed to improve the salaries and working conditions of their members.

Various federal and provincial laws govern union activity, such as picketing, strikes, and lockouts. Unions must represent the interests of all their members, and cannot discriminate on the basis of color, religion, sex, marital status, etc. Employees cannot be coerced or intimidated to become union members, and members cannot be forced to remain in a union. Unions also have "constitutions" in which there are regulations governing the union, as well as guidelines for disciplinary action.

Collective Strength

Once a union is certified, and as long as it represents a majority of the workers, it has the exclusive right to represent its members. If membership drops off, however, other unions can seek to represent the workers. If the collective agreement, the contract a union makes with an employer, is a "closed shop" agreement, the employer may agree to only hire union members. This guarantees unemployed union members priority if the employer needs to employ more workers.

However, while most unions let employers hire workers of their choice, they require that the newly hired workers become union members within a specific period of time. Sometimes new workers have the choice of not joining the union. Under some collective agreements, employers agree not to hire non-unionized workers until all the members of the union are employed.

All provinces require employers to deduct union dues from employees' wages. These dues defray the union's administrative costs, and sometimes pay strike pay to striking members.

You do not have to belong to a union to be covered by a collective bargaining agreement. If you are a forklift operator, and the union was formed to bargain on behalf of forklift operators, you are part of the bargaining agreement, whether or not you are a union member. If your job is not covered by a collective bargaining agreement, however, you do not have union rights, although federal and provincial laws still apply.

STRIKERS' RIGHTS

Unions may organize strikes in order to increase wages, benefits, or working conditions, or in protest of employers engaged in unfair labor practices. Workers may go on strike as long as the strike is legal. (Illegal strikes are either those not authorized by your union or those that violate a no-strike clause in the union contract or do not follow proper legal procedures before striking.) Striking workers do not get paid. If a worker is permanently replaced during a strike, he may become eligible for employment insurance benefits. Unions which are regulated by the Canada Labour Code are not allowed to call a strike or a lockout unless negotiations for the collective agreement fail, and conciliation has failed. If a strike is called illegally, employees may be ordered back to work by the courts.

Similar laws apply in every province. In some cases, strikes are legal only when approved by a majority of union members. Picketing is prohibited in Alberta if there is any attempt at preventing anyone from entering the workplace. It can also be limited or stopped altogether if it presents a danger to people trying to enter the workplace, or if violence seems likely. Similar laws apply in Ontario and Nova Scotia, where strikers or picketers cannot interfere with the operation of the employer's business. In British Columbia and Quebec, employers are not allowed to hire replacement workers during a strike. Firefighters in New Brunswick are not allowed to strike.

When a strike is called, the union usually pays strikers nominal strike benefits comparable to employment insurance benefits. During a strike, you can picket—hold signs and stage organized protests—as long as it is done peacefully and for no longer than 30 days. You may be held personally responsible for any property you destroy while striking. As a union member, you agree not to cross a lawful picket line; and if you do, you can be fined by your union.

BACK TO WORK

Most provinces have laws to ensure striking employees will not lose their jobs if they exercise their right to strike. When the strike or lockout ends, striking employees have preference over any replacement workers who may have been hired during the strike or lockout.

123

MUST YOU JOIN A UNION?

The union's relationship to workers varies from place to place, the main differences being whether or not an employee must join a union or pay dues.

1. Open shop. With this type of union shop, union membership is completely voluntary. The employee will nonetheless be required to pay union dues, and the union must represent all workers, members or not, who are part of the collective agreement.

2. Union shop. In a union shop, all workers must pay dues and join a union within a specified period, usually 30 days after being hired.

3. Modified union shop. Employees cannot be forced to join the union, and members can resign from the union under certain conditions.

4. Closed shop. An employee must be a union member before he can be hired.

WORKING FOR GOVERNMENT

If you work for government—federal, provincial, or local—
you are expected to serve with impartiality and loyalty.

Who Is a Civil Servant?

Employees of national, provincial, and local governments who carry out their day-to-day operations are called "civil" or "public servants." Police officers, firefighters, public-school teachers, administrative assistants to elected officials, hospital employees, and Foreign Affairs employees staffing our embassies and consulates around the world are all part of the civil service. The civil service system refers to the manner in which these government employees are hired, fired, paid, and promoted. Civil service jobs and upgradings to higher classifications within the service are generally decided by competition: applicants qualify by passing certain examinations. Many appointments at the higher level are the prerogative of cabinet ministers.

Because government employees must serve the public impartially, they were once forbidden to participate in political campaigns. In 1988, however, the Supreme Court of Canada ruled that all government employees can both participate in political campaigns and run for political office. Because of public concerns that those who make the law should not also enforce it, the matter of police officers holding public office is not yet fully resolved. In Ontario, for example, police officers cannot perform police work while running for public office.

Your Rights in the Armed Services

Prohibitions on discrimination by reason of sex ensure that membership in the Canadian Armed Forces is open to men and women, and many women are now officers as well as regular members of the military forces. Freedom of expression in the armed services is limited, however. Members may vote, attend political rallies, and even join a political club, but may not wear their uniforms to any such event. They cannot seek election, campaign for a candidate, or speak at political rallies.

The matter of homosexuals' rights are still controversial in the military. In general, however, their rights are less protected by military regulations than by civilian law.

Under military law, armed forces personnel charged with criminal activity or behavior that is not criminal in civilian law, but which violates military regulations, may be subject to a court-martial. A court-martial can impose punishments ranging from imprisonment and dishonorable discharge to reduction in rank. Defendants in a court-martial do not have a right to trial by jury, but rather are judged by a tribunal of five to nine senior officers assisted by a legal officer known as a judge advocate. The person being court-martialed has the right to legal counsel, to call defense witnesses, to cross-examine accusers, and to appeal a conviction right through to the Supreme Court of Canada.

Although capital punishment has been abolished under the Criminal Code, it still exists under the National Defense Act for cowardice, desertion, spying for the enemy, and unlawful surrender.

VETERANS' BENEFITS

Canada's veterans may qualify for dental and prescription coverage, medical travel expenses, and funds for special equipment. They may be entitled to compensatory pensions for disability related to military service, and can obtain assistance to help them live in their homes, and adapt their surroundings to their needs (see below). Funding is available for funeral and burial expenses through the government and the Last Post Fund. Those who gave their lives for Canada are commemorated by the Commonwealth War Graves Commission and in commemorative volumes kept at the Peace Tower in Ottawa.

Your Rights to Veterans' Benefits

The federal Department of Veterans' Affairs administers a wide variety of programs created to meet the special needs of its armed forces veterans. As well as eligible veterans of the Korean and world wars, and eligible veterans of peacekeeping/peacemaking duty in various war zones of the world, beneficiaries may include veterans' spouses and children.

• **Veterans' Independence Program.** The VIP program offers help to veterans who want to remain independent and self-sufficient in their homes and communities rather than move into institutions. The help provided may include counseling and referral services, ambulatory health care services, transportation, home care, and adapting the home to the veteran's particular needs.

• **Disability pensions.** Veterans may be entitled to disability pensions and prisoner of war compensation. Additional provisions may be allotted for disability devices or specially tailored clothes.

• **Allowances.** Veterans with low income may benefit from an allowance paid at the single, married, or orphan rate. Canada also provides financial support for emergency shelter and health care through its assistance fund.

• **Veterans' descendants.** Spouses of deceased pensioners are generally entitled to receive monthly pension payments for one year after their mate dies, and a reduced amount in subsequent years. Dependent children may also be eligible to receive pensions. War veterans' allowances may also be extended to surviving spouses or orphans.

SMALL BUSINESSES

Big corporations dominate the economic skyline, but millions of Canadians work in small businesses, and the law protects their rights in many ways.

Planning Your Own Retirement

If you are operating your own business, you cannot contribute to the Canada (Quebec) Pension Plan, so you would be wise to invest in a Registered Retirement Savings Plan (RRSP). Here are some thoughts to keep in mind.

✔ *Tax deductibility.* Your RRSP contributions are tax deductible, and the investment income is not taxable.

✔ *First-time home buyers.* If you decide to buy a home, you may pay up to 20 percent of the down payment from your RRSP funds. You will have up to 15 years to repay the amount to your RRSP.

✔ *Maximum contributions.* There is a maximum amount that you are allowed to contribute to an RRSP. The amount is based on your gross earnings or your net business income. Check with Revenue Canada.

What Is a "Small Business"?

A small business can run the gamut from a flourishing computer software manufacturer with offices in five countries to a jewelry design firm that has only one employee—the jewelry designer. Another way to define a small business is as an independently owned and operated firm that is not considered a dominant force in its particular area of commerce. However you define the concept, Canadians have been increasingly motivated to start up their own businesses, and government has encouraged such enterprises with tax incentives and funding programs.

EMPLOYEE RIGHTS AND BENEFITS

Even if your company employs only two people—you and your boss—the boss is legally obliged to pay you the minimum wage plus overtime if you work more than 40 hours in a given week; to provide a safe working environment; to refrain from discriminating against you in equality of pay because of your gender, and to permit you to join a union. The Canada (Quebec) Pension Plan, workers' compensation, and employment insurance must also be provided to all employees, however small the company. (See "Employee Benefits," page 233.)

WHEN BENEFITS ARE LIMITED

As much as they might wish, many small-business owners cannot afford to foot the bill for fringe benefits, such as life insurance, pension plans, profit sharing, paid vacation, sick days, and dental and disability insurance, benefits that are commonplace in large companies. Yet, considerations such as the higher odds for promotion in a small company, greater flexibility, a more-relaxed atmosphere, and congenial working conditions may more than make up for lesser monetary rewards. As an employee, you certainly have the right to suggest that your employer look into group health insurance plans that may be offered by professional societies with which your business is affiliated. (See YOUR HEALTH CARE, page 198.) As an employer, you should explore the options carefully. You may discover that providing fringe benefits for your workers produces rewards that more than justify the cost.

STARTING A BUSINESS

If the entrepreneurial spirit spurs you to set up your own business, you will need to know how the law affects you, and when to seek professional help.

Becoming an Entrepreneur

Becoming your own boss may be part of the North American dream, but running a business can also keep you awake nights. Your efforts as a small-business owner may be highly rewarded, but along the way, major decisions, petty details, money worries, and, all too often, legal problems may plunge you in over your head.

Even before you devise your creative and marketing plans for a new business, you need to consider some personal issues. For example, are you a risk-taker or a conservative? Do you have personal funds to support you while your business grows or to lose if your business fails? Are you a workaholic, prepared to spend most of your days and nights working? Do you have family obligations that may limit the time you can allocate to your business? And, finally, how much experience do you have, particularly in this business?

The answers to these questions should clarify your goals, and give you an idea of how much money you will need to borrow, for instance, and, indeed, how much you may be able to borrow, given your experience and credit. Your responses will also tell you how fast and how far you can expect to take your fledgling venture.

FORMING A PROFESSIONAL TEAM

Every business presents a different set of considerations for legal interpretation. What's more, laws vary from province to province and locality to locality. Despite some initial expense, it will save you time, stress, and probably money if you form a "professional team" to provide advice: a banker, an insurance broker, an accountant, and a lawyer. In fact, some experts believe that if you cannot afford such professional help, you cannot afford to go into business at all!

You can finance your business in many ways—from getting a simple personal loan from a bank or other financial institution, a family member, or a friend; to selling ownership in your business (equity financing), or securing a business loan (debt financing). You might check with your local branch of the Federal Business Development Bank to see if it will finance your project. There are other government programs, too, that are

The Legal Entity of Your Business

When setting up your own business, you must carefully consider the sort of entity you wish to establish. Three types of business organizations are legally viable—a sole proprietorship, a partnership, and a corporation. Choose the one that best meets your resources and aspirations.

Sole proprietorship
• **Description.** This is a business with one owner who makes all business decisions. Few legal formalities are required. Some localities require a license for certain businesses (such as a liquor license) or registration if you are doing business in a name other than your own. Some localities also charge an unincorporated business tax. You must make periodic estimated tax payments on income from your business. All income or losses, which include deductions for business expenses, belongs to you.

• **Employees.** You will have to deduct federal and provincial taxes, employment insurance contributions, and Canada (Quebec) Pension Plan payments from your employees and remit them to the federal or provincial government. You will also have to make contributions to the workers' compensation fund for your employees.

• **Liability.** The sole proprietor is personally liable for all the debts of the business, including loans, defective products, and employee accidents.

Partnership
• **Description.** A general partnership is an association of two or more persons as co-owners who contribute money or property to form a business for profit. No legal contractual agreement is required by law, but certain provincial laws establish rules for partnerships when its members do not have a written agreement. Each partner has an equal say in managing the business unless authority is given, in writing, to one particular partner.

• **Employees.** You will have to deduct federal and provincial taxes, employment insurance contributions and Canada (Quebec) Pension Plan.contributions from your employees and remit them to the federal or provincial government. You will also have to contribute to the workers' compensation fund for your employees.

• **Liability.** Whatever property each partner contributes to the partnership becomes the property of the partnership as a whole, and is used to pay the costs of the business. If the partnership assets are exhausted, each partner is liable for the debts incurred by the business. In a "limited partnership," a limited or silent partner's liability is limited to the amount of money or property he contributed to the partnership, but he has no rights regarding corporate management. The silent partner is entitled to a share of the profits according to whatever terms have been agreed on, and he has the right to be informed of the activities of the general partners. If he begins making decisions concerning the partnership, he may lose his special status and be liable to third parties.

Corporation
• **Description.** A corporation, the most complex business organization, is formed by a group of investors and has rights and liabilities separate from the individuals involved. A corporation is created legally through a government charter, and those who hold shares are stockholders. The investment in shares is used to buy property and equipment to conduct business. If the corporation makes money, the profits are paid to the stockholders, either in dividends or in reinvestment in the company, making the stockholders' original stock more valuable. If the company loses money, the stock of the owners becomes less valuable, but the personal assets of the owners/investors are protected from failure of the venture. A corporation must pay taxes on its income and must file its own tax returns. Stockholders are individually taxed on their corporate dividends or profits.

• **Employees.** You will have to deduct federal and provincial taxes, unemployment insurance contributions and Canada (Quebec) Pension Plan contributions from your employees and remit them to the federal or provincial government. You will also have to contribute to the workers' compensation fund for your employees.

• **Liability.** There is a significant amount of legislation imposing liability on corporation directors and officers. A chief characteristic of the corporation is that assets of the stockholders are distinct from those of the corporation. Stockholders in the corporation are not personally liable for the corporation's debt; creditors cannot go after stockholders in ordinary circumstances. If a corporation has trouble securing a loan, however, stockholders may be asked by a lender to guarantee the corporation's loans and accounts payable, and in some cases, the directors may be personally liable for unpaid wages of employees, or for gross misconduct.

specifically designed to help businesses that are just starting out. However you get the necessary start-up funds, all methods have legal ramifications, particularly equity financing and debt financing, which are subject to complex laws and regulations. Work closely with a lawyer who understands financial and corporate law.

You may decide to buy an existing business. An established enterprise can be less risky than one you build from scratch, as it has a track record you can judge. A franchise is another possibility. A strong franchise can reduce the impact of sole financial responsibility.

Finally, how you decide to fund your business will have a direct impact on the sort of entity you wish to create: a sole proprietorship, a partnership, or a corporation. (See also "The Legal Entity of Your Business," page 264.)

STARTING UP

In the early days of getting your business going, you will be concerned with a host of matters, including setting up bank accounts, getting insurance, hiring employees, and planning how to market your product or service. You must check federal, provincial, and local requirements for all licenses, permits, and tax issues.

In most provinces, you can register your business for a nominal fee. Make sure the location of your business is in line with municipal zoning laws. In some areas you will not be able to set up a business in a residential area.

Have enough liability insurance to cover any damage caused by you or one of your employees. Unless you are incorporated, you could be personally liable if someone is injured on your premises and for the acts of your employees.

If you are your own boss, you cannot benefit from employment insurance or the Canada (Quebec) Pension Plan, so consider investing in disability insurance to cover you in the event that you should become ill or unable to work. At the outset, you should have enough savings to cushion you in the event that the business does not generate a lot of revenue in the beginning, or that it fails altogether.

The list of your company's needs depends upon the kind of business you are starting, where you are launching it, and how large it is. You will need to establish company policy with regard to personnel, and decide what salaries and benefits to offer your employees. Depending upon the nature of your business, you will be concerned with labor legislation, tax law, environmental concerns, consumer protection, credit law, commercial practices and international trade laws, and the intricacies of finance. Your lawyer or accountant will be able to advise you on these matters.

Work keeps at bay three great evils: Boredom, Vice, and Need.

VOLTAIRE
Candide

Buying a Franchise

A franchise is a license or permit that allows you to operate a business that sells a particular product or service, such as a retail clothing outlet, a fast-food restaurant, a gas station, or a temporary employment agency. The basic franchise business is created and developed by the franchiser, and you, the franchisee, are permitted to sell the product or service for a fee or royalties, and sometimes additional costs such as rent and equipment leasing fees.

A franchise allows you to start and run your business with less risk than if you started from scratch, but it also reduces your potential profit, since you will have to share it with the franchiser. It also reduces your autonomy and therefore your ability to develop the business in ways you might like.

WHAT KIND OF FRANCHISE?

There are three basic types of franchises, which vary according to the amount of control exerted by the franchiser:

- **A turnkey operation.** The franchiser exerts full control over the business. In other words, all you do is "turn the key and open the door" of your new business. With a turnkey operation, the franchiser builds the outlet, furnishes it, hires the employees, and dictates all sales and marketing decisions.
- **Trade-name franchise.** The franchiser permits the franchisee the exclusive right to sell a product manufactured by the franchiser in a particular area. The franchisee operates according to specified guidelines.
- **Business-format franchise.** The franchiser dictates quality and sometimes marketing techniques, but the franchisee produces an outlet and manufactures (or cooks, as with a fast-food chain) and sells the goods.

Franchises are not risk-free business. Just because a franchise works well in one location does not guarantee it will be successful everywhere. Even well-known fast-food and retail franchises have been known to fail. Also, buying a franchise can be costly and complicated. Despite stringent laws, fast-buck artists can con the unwary. If the franchiser fails to keep its end of the bargain, you may have to sue for breach of contract. If the franchiser is bankrupt, you may not get all your money back. Be wary also of business opportunities called "distributorships" or "dealerships." They may not be as advantageous as franchises and may even be illegal, as would be the case in "pyramid" style operations where you must constantly recruit new members to realize a profit.

A Franchisee's Checklist

If you are thinking about buying a franchise, the first thing to do is see a lawyer. Here are some other useful steps:

✔ *Study the disclosure document.* Will the franchiser provide training programs, help with the selection of the ideal location, and other marketing and accounting assistance, and if so must you pay extra for this help? Will other franchises be able to open in your area, or will you have exclusive rights there? Must you buy all supplies and inventory from the franchiser?

✔ *Shop around.* If other franchises in your area deal in the kind of product or service you are interested in, ask them for disclosure documents and compare offerings.

✔ *Talk to current owners.* The disclosure document must list others who currently operate the franchise. Interview them and try to verify the franchiser's earnings claims.

✔ *Check on sale and inheritance rights.* Do you have the right to sell the franchise, or is this subject to the franchiser's approval. If your spouse has worked in the place and is well qualified to run it, can she take over if you should die?

✔ *Get professional advice.* Examine franchiser's royalty fees: If a franchiser requires 10 percent of your profits for royalty fees, it could be difficult to turn a profit. Check that any lease you have with the franchiser is not for a longer period than your franchise agreement.

WORKING AT HOME

Corporate downsizing and technological developments have combined to place many working Canadians in a new venue: their homes.

On Someone Else's Payroll

More and more employers are discovering that having some employees work at home is good business. Eliminating a worker's daily commute not only saves time, but it can also increase productivity and improve morale (to say nothing of reducing pollution and traffic congestion).

"Telecommuting," a term recently introduced into the workplace vocabulary, refers to employees who work somewhere other than the employer's workplace and communicate via cellular telephones, computers and modems, pagers, and fax machines. These devices can move information virtually instantaneously, thereby cutting office expenses and in many cases helping meet the changing needs of an employee's lifestyle.

If your employer gives you the option of working at home, ask whether it is really the best option for you. If you have children at home, you may want to be near them. On the other hand, you may be subject to a number of distractions at home that you would not be at the office. You may be the kind of person who works best with direct supervision or who needs constant contact with coworkers or customers on a daily basis. Although working at home may give you a great deal of flexibility, it can be isolating as well.

Be aware of the fact that if you are an employee (rather than an independent contractor), you are permitted to deduct the cost of a home office only if the office itself is created or used for your employer's benefit. If you are working at home solely for your own convenience, your home-office costs are not deductible.

Independent Contractors

Independent contractors, or freelance workers, constitute one of the fastest-growing segments of the economy. They are people who own their own businesses and who contract to do specific jobs for other individuals or companies. This kind of arrangement, while freeing you from the constraints of the 9-to-5 routine, also entails responsibilities.

---

1 2 3 ...

FREELANCERS MAY FIND THAT FREEDOM HAS A PRICE

Freedom from regular hours and office routines may seem very attractive if your employer suggests you do the job from your home. Before making a final decision, consider the following:

1. Freedom. Do you really have the freedom you would not have at the office? Once you have "logged on," you can be monitored continuously by computer operators. You may have frequent phone calls or visits from your supervisor.

2. Assessing your work. If you are doing piece work, for example, will you be able to assess your output without seeing how others perform? Also, without other employees around you, you may not know when your employer's demands are unreasonable.

3. Lost benefits. Employment standards legislation in Manitoba and Ontario excludes homeworkers from regulations governing hours of work, overtime, holiday and health and safety laws.

123...

EMPLOYEE OR INDEPENDENT CONTRACTOR?

The difference between an employee and an independent contractor can be a fine line. If you work odd hours or not full time, your employer might try to classify you as a freelancer rather than as an employee in order to avoid paying for your benefits, employment insurance, Canada (Quebec) Pension Plan, and workers' compensation insurance. But if you answer yes to more than one or two of the following questions, chances are you are an employee, not a freelancer.

1. Are you trained or instructed how to do your job by the employer?

2. Do you have to perform the job in person, on the company premises, at certain hours?

3. Do you have an ongoing work relationship, rather than being hired on a job-by-job basis, as needed?

4. Do you work for one company only?

5. Are you paid hourly or weekly instead of by the job?

6. Are you reimbursed for business expenses instead of paying for them yourself?

7. Does the company provide the tools necessary to complete the job?

Some types of work lend themselves to independent contracting. Writers, translators, graphic designers, craftspeople, and other professionals often prefer the flexibility of freelance work. As an independent contractor, you must set your own work hours and arrange for a place to work that is properly insured, licensed, and zoned for the work you are doing. You will have to keep careful records, bill your clients, file taxes for your business, and be very careful about paying quarterly income tax on the money you earn.

Other distinguishing marks identify you as an independent contractor as opposed to a full employee. (See "Employee or Independent Contractor?" at left.) These distinctions are important, because it is not uncommon for an employer to try to hire independent contractors to do work that a regular employee used to do.

Firms do not have to pay freelancers such benefits as Canada (Quebec) Pension Plan, employment insurance, workers' compensation, or deduct income tax. Nor are they bound by long-term agreements. Therefore the temptation to call an employee an independent contractor is great, but Revenue Canada takes a dim view of this practice. An employer who falsely characterizes employees as independent contractors can be subject to heavy fines.

ARE YOU DEDUCTIBLE?

The most important distinction, however, is that you, as an independent contractor, are in charge of the work you do and are responsible for its content. That can have wide-ranging legal ramifications.

When an employee makes a mistake, the company is responsible and pays the penalty or the compensation. The employee may get fired for the mistake, but he is rarely held legally responsible for it. Independent contractors, however, can be named as codefendants in a damage suit if they are responsible for a shoddy product. This is why a carefully drawn contract can be so important in safeguarding your work.

Independent contractors usually work at home or at a location away from the employer's workplace. In recent years, Revenue Canada has become stricter in what it allows independent contractors to deduct for home offices on their tax returns. Today a home office must be a legitimate place of business and must be a separate room that is your principal place of business, and it must be used only for that purpose.

RETIREMENT PLANS

Regardless of where you work, if you are self-employed you must remember that you are responsible for putting aside money for your retirement. (See YOUR MONEY, page 334.)

YOUR MONEY

Handling your income, credit, investments, and estate affects every aspect of your life—so it pays to know your rights

BANKING ■ BORROWING MONEY ■ CREDIT CARDS ■ CREDIT BUREAUS ■ DEALING WITH DEBT ■ LIFE INSURANCE ■ INVESTING YOUR MONEY ■ INCOME TAXES ■ INCOME SECURITY PLANS ■ SAVING FOR RETIREMENT ■ WILLS AND ESTATES

BANKING

The basics of banking are changing daily—and you need to know how to use these services to your best advantage.

1 2 3

BEFORE YOU STOP PAYMENT

A stop-payment order allows you to cancel a cheque you have already written before it is cashed or deposited. If you place a stop payment on a cheque, be aware that:

1. Under banking law you are entitled to request a stop payment on a cheque by telephone or in writing. If done by phone, you must go to the bank in question as soon as possible, preferably the same day, to have your request properly documented.

2. Your bank will charge you a fee—usually $15 and sometimes more—to stop payment on a cheque.

3. If a cheque is not returned to you, you should place a stop-payment order, in writing, on that cheque every six months until it is returned.

4. You cannot place a stop payment on a certified or cashier's cheque because the bank withdraws the money from your account when the cheque is issued.

Choosing the Best Bank Account

What services do you need from a bank? For most people, the answer is simple. You need a chequing account to pay bills and a savings account where your money can grow, however slowly, or be kept safe for a rainy day. But finding the best deal in a bank account is no longer a simple process. Today both chequing and savings accounts come laden with an array of fees, maintenance charges, and minimum-balance requirements. In this confusing environment, be prepared to shop around for the best arrangement for your needs. Because of competition between the various financial institutions, consumers have a wide variety of options. These include:

- **Commercial banks.** All are chartered by the federal government, and have long offered a wide range of services, including savings and chequing accounts, mortgages, registered retirement savings plans, and credit cards.
- **Trust companies.** These offer many of the same services as chartered banks—chequing and savings accounts, mortgages, registered retirement savings plans—and they also issue their own credit cards.
- **Credit unions.** These nonprofit financial cooperatives also offer many of the services of a commercial bank. However, credit unions do not carry Canadian Deposit Insurance Corporation (CDIC) insurance, although they may have similar protection through a provincial insurance plan. Check before depositing large amounts of money. (See "Credit Unions: A Good Banking Alternative," page 276.)

THE RIGHT CHEQUING ACCOUNT

Though the chequing accounts that banks offer go by many different names, they can be divided into two main types: those that pay interest and those that do not. The best type for you will probably depend on your answer to this question: What is the lowest average balance you are going to be able to leave on deposit every month?

To earn interest, banks usually require a minimum balance of at least $1,000, and if your balance falls below that amount, you must pay a fee. Thus, if your balance is usually below $1,000, you should choose a chequing account that pays no interest. However, even if you are able to keep a balance that meets the minimum for an interest-bearing chequing account, find out how that minimum balance is figured.

The most attractive option for consumers is the "average-daily-balance" method, by which the bank takes the amount you have in your account each day and averages it across the entire month. Less favorable to you is the "low-balance" method, by which a bank considers only your lowest balance for the month. So if you kept $2,500 on deposit for 30 days, but withdrew the full amount on the 31st, the bank would figure your interest based on a zero balance for the month. Not only would you earn no interest, you would pay a fee for falling below the minimum balance.

SMART BANKING STRATEGIES

Banking experts predict that bank fees will only continue to escalate. To hold down your chequing account costs, adopt "defensive-banking" strategies.

If you risk overdrawing your account more than three times a year, a $5 monthly overdraft protection fee may be a sound investment. Overdraft protection is actually a line of credit that lets you write cheques for more than you have in your account. Should you not have this protection and just one cheque bounces because you have insufficient funds in your account, your bank could charge you $20. As well, the person to whom you wrote the cheque might insist that the replacement cheque be certified, thus increasing your costs even more.

Bankers are just like anybody else, except richer.

OGDEN NASH
"I Have It on Good Authority"

Specials for Seniors

In their ongoing battle for customers, most of the chartered banks offer special deals to older people. These privileges apply to anyone 59 years and older at The Bank of Nova Scotia, and to those 60 years and over at other chartered banks. Among these benefits are:

- **Free chequing privileges.** The bank issues cheques to seniors without charge.

- **Safe-deposit boxes.** At a certain age (it varies somewhat from bank to bank), you can obtain a safe-deposit box at half the standard rate.

- **Service charges.** In the case of seniors, most banks waive the service charges ordinarily applied to such things as using automatic banking machines and certifying cheques.

- **Free bill paying.** Banks charge most depositors a $1 fee for paying telephone, hydro, or other such bills through the bank. These charges are dropped for the older depositor.

- **Travelers cheques.** Banks issue free travelers cheques (usually Visa or Mastercard travellers cheques) to older depositors. The one percent fee saved could add up to $30 for a senior requesting $3,000 in travelers cheques.

- **Reduced loan interest.** Older people can often receive a reduction of one-half to one percent on loans.

If you do not routinely need your canceled cheques, you may want to ask your bank to "truncate" your account. This way, you will receive only a monthly statement listing the amounts of the cheques you wrote, not the canceled cheques. Because truncated accounts are cheaper to administer, banks will sometimes waive or reduce the monthly fee requirements. If you want the lower fees of a truncated account, but like to have an accurate record of your transactions, you can get chequebooks that retain photocopies of each cheque you write.

The High Cost of Saving

A bank savings account may seem like a good place to keep your money, but it may not be the most profitable. Although you have ready access to your cash, you will earn a low rate of interest. Meantime, inflation combined with an array of fees and penalties can eat into any money you accumulate. It can be a good idea to keep some money in conventional savings accounts, so that you have some cash readily available in an emergency. Also, if you link your savings account to your chequing account, you may be able to avoid many expensive bank fees.

Bear in mind, too, that banks are now allowed to offer services such as investment counseling and portfolio management. You may want to take advantage of these services to maximize the return on your savings.

Depending on when and how you need to use your money, you should consider the following savings vehicles:

- **Service packages.** Many banks offer special service packages for about $10 monthly. One such package might include automated banking transactions, cheques, overdraft protection, money orders, foreign currency exchange, stop payments, travelers cheques, and bill payments. Some packages also include rebates on various other charges, such as annual credit card fees. These packages can be worthwhile even if you do not need all the services offered, and some banks offer them free to senior citizens and students. Most banks also offer a variety of chequing and savings account packages, but interest rates rarely exceed one percent no matter how much you have in your account. If you have $500 or more sitting in a savings account, your money could be earning a great deal more in an alternative plan.

- **Investment savings accounts.** These accounts are ideal for those who maintain a balance of $5,000 or more, who want their money to be accessible, and who want to track their funds by statement or passbook. If you maintain a balance of $5,000 to $10,000 in such an account, the interest rate will be about 5 percent, a great deal more than it would be earning in a standard savings account. There may be a limit on how many transactions you can have, and service charges may be higher than with a regular savings account.

- **Guaranteed Investment Certificates (GICs).** By placing your money in a GIC, you could earn a great deal more interest than you would from an investment savings account. Some banks will let you place as little as $500 in a GIC for as little as 30 days. Interest rates will vary depending on the term you choose, and whether the GIC is redeemable or non-redeemable, but are usually similar to the current prime lending rate. Some banks pay seniors their GIC interest monthly, where ordinarily this is paid only at the end of the term. Banks also vary in their penalties for premature withdrawal of funds. Some banks also compound interest annually, others semiannually.

Electronic Banking

By now most consumers take for granted the computer technology that enables banks to offer a variety of automated services, known as the electronic funds transfer (EFT) system. Whenever you use an automated banking machine (ABM) or arrange for a paycheque to be directly deposited into your account, you are tapping into the EFT system. The EFT system offers consumers convenience and quick access to their money. But when errors occur, they can wreak havoc—as some 100,000 Americans discovered in 1994, when a U.S. bank mistakenly deducted a total of $15 million from its customers' accounts in a single night.

When they receive their debit cards, customers often sign an agreement which exonerates the bank from liability for any sums deposited through an automatic teller. Basically, the customer must use the machine at his or her own risk. The exoneration clause might be challenged, but in any case it will fall to the customer to prove that the deposit was made or that he did not receive the funds he was trying to withdraw, even though his account was debited. Other errors too may be hard to prove and may have serious consequences. For example, if you expect a loan payment to be automatically deducted from your account but the EFT system fails to make the transfer, you could be charged a late fee; worse still, your credit rating could be damaged.

When you bank electronically, your best defense is to keep accurate transaction records and to reconcile your figures with your account statement within days of its receipt. Quick action

Code of Practice for Debit Cards

The Canadian Payments Association has established a code of practice for debit cards, such as bank cards, which use personal identification numbers (PINs) to access automatic banking machines (ABMs).

The code requires the card issuer to inform the consumer of any fees associated with the card; to ensure that only the consumer knows his PIN number; and to see that cardholder agreements be clear and precise, and that the cardholder be issued a copy of such agreements.

Other terms are that transaction records contain enough information for the cardholder to check account entries; that cardholders be informed of whatever card dispute resolution mechanisms are in place; and that, in the event of a dispute, cardholders not be unreasonably restricted from use of funds that are the subject of the dispute.

Compliance with the code is voluntary, but it has been endorsed by provincial consumer affairs ministers, the Canadian Bankers Association, the Trust Companies Association of Canada, the Credit Union Central of Canada, and the Consumers' Association of Canada.

The code does not apply to transactions made outside of Canada or transfers of funds between Canada and other countries.

improves your chances of having errors corrected. Delay will make it harder to reclaim any lost interest, avoid bad-cheque charges, or rectify other mistakes. Be aware of the following and follow the appropriate procedures:

- If you notice an error on your bank statement or on an ABM receipt, notify the bank orally or in writing without delay.
- If the bank asks you to put your complaint in writing and you refuse, the bank does not have to recredit your account.
- If you do not report an unauthorized transfer immediately on receiving your statement, you are completely liable for the amount withdrawn.
- The bank must cover unauthorized transfers made with an ABM card you never received; you are not liable.
- When the bank investigates your complaint about an ABM transaction, it must notify you in writing of the results. If you disagree with the decision, you can appeal to higher authorities within the bank, or to the Canadian Bankers Association or to the Canadian Payments Association.

If Your Bank Makes a Mistake

It will probably happen to you someday: Your bank will make an error. Most errors are detected when you reconcile your monthly bank statement (the bank's version of your monthly transactions) with your chequebook (your own version of events). If you discover an error, double-check to make sure the error is not your own, then be prepared to take action:

• It is the policy at most banks to allow 30 to 60 days for customers to correct errors in their accounts. However, even if it has taken you longer than 60 days to discover and report your problem, you still maintain the right to insist that your bank resolve the error. In general, banks will respond positively to your demand.

• Call or visit the bank, find out the name of the bank's branch manager or customer service representative, and register your complaint with that person. Make a dated notation of your call or visit; record the branch manager's name and telephone number together with comments about the content of the conversation.

• Follow up in writing, addressing the letter to the branch manager or service representative with whom you dealt. Describe the problem, and state how and when you want it resolved. For example, if the bank sent you an overdraft notice when you still had plenty of funds in your chequing account, make it clear you want the overdraft penalties revoked and letters of apology sent to those to whom you wrote cheques that were returned due

to the bank's mistake. Include names, addresses, and telephone numbers of all the people involved.

• Send the letter to the bank by certified mail, return receipt requested. Keep a copy.

• Under the Bank Act, a bank must designate one or more employees to handle complaints regarding their accounts, credit cards, debit cards, or loans. When you file a complaint, a copy of the report must be filed with the office of the Superintendent of Financial Institutions.

• If you are not satisfied with the bank's response, write to the Federal Superintendent of Financial Institutions. If the problem is outside his jurisdiction, he will refer you to the appropriate agency.

• There are no specific laws governing the banks' liability in the event that they make an error. They do, however, have a contractual obligation to their customers as well as an obligation to be diligent in their operations. They must act with integrity and in good faith, and must abide by your instructions.

When you open an account of less than $100,000 with any of Canada's chartered banks, the bank must disclose the interest rate applicable to your account, and how that interest will be paid. It must also explain how your account balance or other factors may affect your rate of interest, list all applicable service charges, and tell you how you will be notified of any new or increased charges.

A Bank's Liability

PROBLEM
When Sheila tried to pay for a store purchase, she discovered her wallet was missing. She immediately called the police and also informed her bank that her ABM card had been stolen. Meantime, the thief had withdrawn $500 from her account using the ABM card. Because Sheila had written her personal identification number (PIN) on her ABM card, the bank insisted that she was liable for the $500.

ACTION
Sheila wrote to her bank's branch manager, but he pointed out that no matter how an unauthorized user obtains the PIN, Sheila was responsible for all withdrawals made with her card up to the time the bank was notified it was stolen. By that time the disputed sum had been withdrawn, so Sheila was liable for the $500. It was an expensive way to learn she should not write her PIN on the card. When she received her new card, she memorized her PIN for her future protection.

Similarly, when you take out a loan, the bank must specify what the loan will actually cost you—how much you will have to pay back once borrowing costs are factored in. Banks cannot impose extra charges or penalties if you do repay the loan over the specified term, but they can demand interest on the overdue balance and reimbursement of any legal fees incurred in collecting it.

Except for student loans and loans that exceed $250,000, your agreement must indicate if you are allowed to repay the loan before the maturity date and stipulate the effect of early repayment. (Banks are not allowed to prohibit prepayment except in the case of a mortgage, or a loan that exceeds $100,000.) Depending on the agreement, prepayment can net an interest rebate or a penalty charge.

By law, a bank's promotional handouts must contain information on fees, minimum balances, and other conditions imposed on savings vehicles. Those that fail to provide these facts can be penalized. If a consumer suffers financial loss because of a bank's lack of disclosure, he can sue the institution for damages.

USING ABMs SAFELY

Automated teller machines are a great convenience. They can also be a great nuisance if a crook discovers your PIN and cleans out your account, or worse still, withdraws more than you have in your account. This he can do by making a phony deposit, then withdrawing funds to match. But above all else, ABMs can sometimes be downright dangerous. Here's how to avoid trouble:

1. Memorize the personal identification number (PIN) for your ABM debit card. Keep a written record of it at home. Report the loss or theft of your cards to the bank immediately.

2. Record ABM withdrawals in your chequebook, including the service fee, if applicable.

3. Avoid depositing cash in an ABM. The burden of proof is with the depositor if a cash deposit is lost or stolen; you are better off depositing cash with a teller.

4. Don't discard your ABM receipts at the bank. Not only may you need them to verify deposits, but high-tech bandits can use receipts to raid accounts.

5. Avoid using ABMs at night (when most ABM crimes take place), in isolated places, or when you are the only person in the "chamber."

6. Many insurance companies offer coverage up to a fixed amount for funds stolen from bank cards as a standard part of tenant or housing insurance.

Credit Unions: A Good Banking Alternative

In annual surveys of consumer satisfaction with banking institutions, credit unions rank consistently at the top. A credit union is a not-for-profit financial cooperative that is both owned and operated by its members. Most people join through their place of employment, but you may also be eligible through some other affiliation.

Most credit unions offer both chequing and savings accounts, and many of the larger ones also handle credit cards, payroll deductions, and loans. Because credit unions have lower operating costs, they are able to offer lower-cost loans and pay slightly higher rates for savings. Most deal only with loans to individuals and rarely make business loans. Credit unions return part of their profits to members at the end of the fiscal year, usually in the form of a small dividend or as a rebate of loan interest.

Determine in advance all the rates, fees, and penalties that would apply if you join a credit union. Some offer only limited banking services. Will the one you are considering be able to handle all your needs? For example, smaller credit unions may not be equipped to handle electronic fund transfers or may send out statements quarterly instead of monthly.

Is Your Money Safe?

As "safe as money in the bank" has long been a popular phrase but consumers still need to know precisely how their deposits can be affected if their financial institution fails and what they can do to protect their assets. Although the Canadian Bankers Association issues ratings of banks' solvencies, it is very difficult for the average consumer to tell if a bank is in trouble. The simplest solution for most people is to bank with a federally insured institution such as one of the chartered banks.

The Bank Act requires all banks that accept cash deposits to belong to the Canada Deposit Insurance Corporation (CDIC). As a result, deposits in all chartered banks are insured by the CDIC for up to $60,000 per institution (not per branch). This insurance covers funds in savings accounts, chequing accounts, guaranteed investment certificates, and term deposits. If you have a savings account, a Registered Retirement Savings Plan (RRSP), and a joint account with your spouse, all with the same bank, each of your three accounts will be covered by the CDIC for up to $60,000. In effect, you have a total guarantee of $180,000. However, certain bank-controlled investments may not be protected by the CDIC. For example, mutual funds bought through a bank are not insured and neither are the contents of your safe-deposit box.

Should your bank or trust company fail and not be taken over by another buyer, the CDIC will step in, and pay off all deposits in full (or to the maximum insurable amount), with interest, to the day of closing. Usually this process should take no more than three days after the bank's official closing. If you have an outstanding loan, the CDIC will inform you where to send your future payments. If you have a loan that is delinquent and a chequing or savings account at the same failed institution, the CDIC has the right to deduct the overdue amount from your accounts before returning your deposit.

Although federal insurance programs guarantee the safety of deposits, they do not necessarily guarantee that you will be able to withdraw your money on demand. If a bank had kept incomplete or inaccurate records, you would be required to provide proof of your own deposits. As a precaution, keep all recent bank statements and savings books in an accessible file.

PLAN AHEAD

If, despite choosing a CDIC member institution, you still feel insecure, consider one of these options:

- Place an emergency cash fund at a second bank;
- Take out a credit card that allows cash advances from another institution;
- Buy a savings bond that can be cashed at any savings institution.

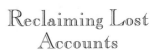

Reclaiming Lost Accounts

Banks must notify you in writing, at the address they have on file, when you have money in an account, or an unpaid instrument, and the account has been inactive for two years.

Notices must be sent out in January, the first after the account has been inactive for two years, a second after five years. If after 10 years, the account remains inactive, the deposit and its interest are turned over to the Bank of Canada. You then have 10 more years to present your claim to the Bank of Canada.

The names and amounts of unclaimed balances are reported in the Canada Gazette.

Federal Protection for Your Money

Federal deposit insurance is the consumer's main defense against bank failure. The following guidelines will help keep your money as safe as possible:

- Select a banking institution that belongs to the Canada Deposit Insurance Corporation (CDIC), which protects commercial banks and trust companies. Credit unions are usually covered by a provincially guaranteed fund.

- To find out whether an institution is protected by the CDIC or a provincial insurance fund, look for prominently displayed advertising in the institution's lobby or ask the institution's customer service representative.

- Bear in mind that your accounts in a federally insured institution are covered up to a maximum of $60,000 per person, per bank. If your balance exceeds $60,000, the best protection is to open accounts in several banks insured by the CDIC, or to place funds in increments of less than $60,000 in the name of different family members.

- Remember that mutual funds and various other investment products sold by banks are not covered by the CDIC.

BORROWING MONEY

Most of us need a loan occasionally—but since it costs money to borrow money, be sure you know how to get the best loan for the lowest price.

Choosing the Right Kind of Loan

Borrowing money can be a sensible way to achieve important life goals. Yet it is important to borrow for the right reasons, to make sure that the cost of a loan does not bog you down with a debt you cannot afford. The best reasons for taking out a loan are to buy something you truly need right away and could not otherwise afford, such as a house or a car, or to buy something that will profit you in the future, like a college education. If you consistently borrow money to pay for nonessentials like vacation trips or holiday gifts, you may put yourself in constant financial jeopardy without getting any lasting benefits.

When you take out a loan, you are, in effect, buying money from the lender. So you need to shop around for the loan as carefully as you would for any other major consumer item.

FINDING THE RIGHT LENDER

Many different kinds of establishments are in the business of lending money. Banks probably come first to mind. If you have dealt with a particular bank for at least five years, you probably should start your loan search there. Banks are more willing to offer preferred rates on loans to long-standing customers.

Do you belong to a credit union? These not-for-profit financial cooperatives consistently offer their members loans that are two to three percentage points cheaper than the average rates of national banks and trust companies. Furthermore, while banks typically want to loan a minimum of at least several thousand dollars, credit unions will allow you to borrow a much smaller amount—sometimes as little as $100. (For more information, see "Credit Unions: A Good Banking Alternative" and "How to Join a Credit Union," page 276.)

Consumers with credit-rating problems often turn to finance companies, which are solely in the business of lending money to individuals or institutions. Finance companies usually charge higher interest rates than other lenders, and often penalize you if you pay off the loan early. Also, because finance companies do business with higher-risk borrowers, credit bureaus may look askance at anyone who has ever dealt with one.

BORROWING FROM YOURSELF

Borrowing against your own resources can be a quick and convenient loan source. Often, the cheapest loans are of the home-equity variety, when you borrow against the equity built up in your house. In effect, you take out a second or third mortgage. If your plan permits loans, your own retirement plan can be another good loan source. Some defined-contribution plans and company profit-sharing plans allow participants to borrow from them. But the loans usually must be repaid within a designated period, or repaid immediately if you leave your job.

Your savings account offers still another loan option. You pledge your savings account or Guaranteed Investment Certificate as collateral, and the bank lends you money at a rate pegged to what your savings are earning. But be forewarned: The rate banks charge for loans secured by savings is often two to four percentage points higher than the rate they pay on your savings.

Most people do not think of the overdraft privileges on their chequing account as a loan source, but every time you over-

---

A Glossary for Borrowers

Loans come in many different forms with a wide variety of terms and conditions that are described in a specific language full of unfamiliar words and phrases. Here are some common terms you are likely to encounter when negotiating a loan.

- **Adjustable rate.** The interest rate, also called a variable rate, that is raised or lowered periodically on the basis of a specified index (see below).

- **Annual percentage rate (APR).** The actual rate you pay on a loan over the course of a year. The APR is higher than the actual interest charged because it also factors in service fees as well as other changes. The annual percentage rate is also known as the effective rate to distinguish it from the nominal rate, which is the stated rate of interest which does not take into account loan application fees and other charges.

- **Collateral.** Assets or property, such as a car, home, or guaranteed investment certificates, that you offer as security to back up a loan.

- **Finance charge.** The total cost of borrowing, including interest and service fees. Most consumer legislation requires this disclosure.

- **Index.** A set standard, such as the prime rate given to banks, or the rate on one-year Treasury bills, against which interest rates for variable-rate loans are adjusted.

- **Points.** An up-front fee charged by a lender, separate from interest. A point equals one percent of the principal borrowed. On a $100,000 mortgage loan, a charge of three points would equal $3,000.

- **Prime rate.** The interest rate banks charge their most creditworthy, income-producing customers, such as other banks and blue-chip corporations.

- **Principal.** This is the amount of money you have actually borrowed. What you owe the lender will be considerably more, depending on the interest charged, service fees, and other expenses.

- **Secured loan.** A loan guaranteed by collateral such as property or other assets. Mortgage loans and automobile loans are two common types. The lender can take back the collateral—the house or the car—if the borrower does pay on time.

- **Unsecured loan.** Instead of collateral, the borrower pledges "full faith and credit" to repay the loan. If payments are not made, the lender can take legal action against the borrower. Credit card purchases and cash advances are common types of unsecured loans.

draw your account and trigger the credit option, you are taking out a loan. Since banks often charge more than 16 percent on these overdrafts, this kind of loan is very expensive for you. Avoid the temptation to overdraw your account for routine bill paying; overdraft credit is best used for emergencies and protection against the occasional bounced cheque.

FIRST-TIME HOME BUYERS

If you are borrowing to buy a house, you may want to consider the federal Home Buyers' Plan. It allows Canadian residents to withdraw up to $20,000 from their RRSPs to purchase their first home. A married couple or a couple who has been in a common-law relationship for one year can borrow $40,000, $20,000 per person. The amount borrowed however must be paid back over 15 years in equal annual payments.

If you miss a payment, or if your annual payment is less than one-fifteenth of the amount borrowed, any sum owing for that year is taxable. If you borrowed $15,000 from your RRSP, for example, your annual repayments should be $1,000. If you only pay $500 in one year, you must pay tax on the $500 still owed to your RRSP plan.

Most homes are eligible under this plan, and include mobile homes, condominiums or houses under construction. The home however must be situated in Canada and serve as your principal residence.

The positive aspect of this type of loan is that it allows a couple to put a down payment on a house they might not otherwise be able to afford. The downside is that borrowing from your RRSP could drastically cut down on your retirement income since you lose the advantage of compound interest accruing on your tax-free RRSP.

INSURANCE AS COLLATERAL

Most cash-value life insurance provides a savings and investment feature (the cash value) as well as a death benefit. (See also "Safety Net or Savings Plan?," page 304.) Your policy will have a loan provision. You can usually borrow most of the "cash value" of your policy at a very low rate of interest. After all, you are borrowing your own money. The flaw with whole life insurance is that the money you paid into the policy that forms the cash value bears a very low rate of interest and in the case of death, your beneficiary receives only the stated death benefit, not the cash value.

Ask your insurance agent how your policy works. Typically, you are not required to pay back a life insurance loan. The main drawback of borrowing against a life insurance policy and failing to repay is that if you die with the loan outstanding, the policy's death benefit will be reduced by what you owe.

Consumer Rip-off: Credit Insurance

Would you willingly overpay for a product you do not need? Consumers spend millions of dollars a year on credit life and disability insurance policies, but few people actually need them.

The policies cover loan payments to the lender should you die or become totally disabled. Lenders often try to bully borrowers who are getting substantial loans—such as a car or mortgage loan—into buying credit insurance from them instead of from an insurance company. (They are often motivated by the hefty commissions they get for selling it.) But their credit insurance is almost always overpriced. And if you are already adequately insured with life insurance and disability policies, credit insurance is unnecessary.

If you must buy it, go through a legitimate insurance agent; and buy term insurance for the term amount of your loan. It will cost much less. After you have paid off about half the loan and have demonstrated reliability, ask the lender to allow you to drop it.

Be sure to ask potential lenders in advance whether they require credit insurance. If an institution really wants your business, it may well drop the requirement for you.

LOAN OPTIONS CHART

If you want to buy a house, you go looking for a mortgage loan. For other borrowing needs, however, you can easily become confused by the number of possible options. This chart describes eight common varieties of loans, where you can get them, what to use them for, and their relative merits. It will help you decide what kind is best for your financial situation.

Type of Loan	Source	Best Used For	Advantages	Disadvantages
Chequing-account overdraft privileges	Banks, trust companies, credit unions	Emergencies	Easily accessible	Expensive; easy to over-access
Home equity line of credit	Banks, trust companies, credit unions, mortgage brokers	When you need to make large payments over an extended period	Good rates, usually variable; tax deductible if used for investment purposes	Variable-rate risk; requires discipline to repay promptly; home is collateral
Home equity loan	Banks, trust companies, credit unions, mortgage brokers	When you have a large, onetime expense	Good fixed rates; also tax deductible	No flexibility in repayment schedule; home is collateral
Life insurance	Life insurance policy	Most borrowing needs	Good rates; interest payments go into your own account	Potentially diminished death benefit
Personal line of credit	Banks, trust companies	Short term of credit companies needs	Easily accessible, sometimes only interest need be paid for long periods of time	High interest, easy to over-access, eligibility usually checked annually
Retirement plans	Employer	Housing, tuition, emergencies	Can allow your savings to remain intact	Usually must be repaid within five years; job changers must repay immediately
Secured loans (by stocks, savings account, etc.)	Banks, trust companies, credit unions	Short-term needs; improving your credit rating; emergencies	Can be a better alternative than credit cards and other high-interest sources	Assets used as security may be tied up until loan is repaid
Unsecured personal loans	Banks, credit unions, friends, family, credit cards	Short-term needs; emergencies	When from family or friends may not require credit check; interest rates are usually good except on credit cards	When from banks, usually have very high interest rates; much higher than your savings earn

Negotiating Mortgage Loans

Mortgage loans are the biggest loans most consumers will ever assume, so even a small difference in interest rates and other costs will add up to a large amount of money. Many consumers believe they have to accept the first terms, rates, and closing costs that a lender stipulates. This is not true. Especially if you have a good credit history, lenders may be willing to bargain with you to get your business.

To negotiate effectively, you need to do your homework. Start by making calls to several lenders to get an idea of what mortgage-loan deals are available in your community. Once you know the cost range, you are in a better position to ask for changes in rates or fees that a lender would find reasonable. When you talk to a loan officer, be firm and specific about what terms you expect. Make it clear you know what the competition is offering and that you are resolute about shopping around until you find the best deal.

Above all, read the small print of the mortgage agreement, and don't hesitate to ask someone you trust to explain anything that is not clear to you. A mortgage is likely to be a 15- or 30-year business commitment. Know what you are getting into before signing anything. For a full discussion on mortgage loans, see also YOUR HOME AND COMMUNITY, page 25.

Mortgages in a Nutshell

There are typically two types of mortgages, conventional or high ratio. In a conventional mortgage you must make a down payment of 25 percent whereas in a high-ratio mortgage, one guaranteed by the Canada Mortgage and Housing Corporation, the down payment need only be 5 percent.

Mortgage payments are either fixed rate or variable. Fixed rate mortgage payments stay the same regardless of how interest rates vary during the mortgage term. Variable rate mortgage payments on the other hand vary in keeping with the fluctuations of the prime rate of interest charged by banks.

Amortization is the time it takes—usually 15 to 30 years—to repay the entire mortgage. The longer the amortization period, the smaller the monthly payments and the more interest you pay in the long run. Amortization should not be confused with the "term" of your mortgage. The term is the period of time, usually one to five years, that your mortgage agreement with the lender remains in force.

Mortgages can be open or closed. In an open mortgage you can repay the loan without penalty. You would be wise to negotiate a mortgage that allows you to make extra payments annually (13 instead of 12 for example) or negotiate a deal where payments are made weekly or monthly instead of twice a year. The savings in interest are dramatic when you shorten the amortization period of the mortgage. Take, for example, an $80,000 mortgage amortized over 25 years with monthly payments set at $715.59. If interest rates are 10 percent, total interest would amount to $134,677. If payments were made weekly, however, the weekly payment would be $178.90 and the term would be cut to 18.7 years. Total interest paid then would be $93,566, a saving of more than $41,000 in interest over the life of the mortgage.

Home Equity Borrowing

A loan against your home equity is among the best—and potentially the most dangerous—loans you can get. These loans come in two forms. With the home equity loan, also called a *second mortgage*, you borrow a fixed amount in one lump and repay it in monthly installments over a set period, such as 10 years. With a home equity line of credit, you arrange for a fixed amount of money to be available to you; then you are able to give yourself a loan whenever you choose by drawing against that amount. You pay interest on the balance due, just as you would with a credit card.

But unlike the interest on credit cards, the interest rate on home equity loans is usually lower. These benefits, coupled with easy availability, make home equity loans very appealing to consumers. Most lenders limit borrowing to 75 percent of a home's current value, minus any existing mortgage debt.

So what is it that makes this good deal dangerous? If you cannot make the payments, the lender can foreclose on your home, just as the primary lender could if you defaulted on the mortgage loan. So be certain you can carry this extra debt before you succumb to the tempting notion of having another source of cash available.

WHY DO YOU NEED THE MONEY?

Before deciding between an outright loan and a line of credit, be very clear how you plan to use the money. Will you be using it for expenses that are due periodically, such as tuition or a home-improvement project that will be done in several phases? That is when the flexibility of a line of credit works best. Or do you have a major onetime expense that you must pay in a lump sum, such as paying for a wedding? In such situations,

---

Don't Gamble Your Home to Consolidate Debt

It sounds like a good idea: You are swamped with high-interest credit card or overdraft chequing account debt. Home equity loans are cheaper, and relatively easy to get. Why not take out a home equity loan to pay off all of those other debts hanging over you? What could possibly go wrong?

Plenty, if you do not change the spending pattern that got you into heavy debt in the first place. Remember that you are not getting that loan for nothing—your house is at stake.

So before deciding that a home equity loan is the cure-all for your debt problems, resolve to curb your appetite for credit. It would be foolish to create new debt while still paying off the loan you got to clear up your old debt. You might even consider seeking credit counseling before taking out that loan.

For additional ways to help consolidate your debts, see "Dealing With Debt," page 297.

WHEN SOMEONE OWES YOU MONEY

If a person to whom you have lent money has not repaid it, you can pursue three legitimate options for getting it back:

1. Start by contacting the borrower directly—by letter, telephone, or personal visit—and try to work out a repayment arrangement. To avoid charges of harassment, you should *not* make such contact in an abusive way or at inappropriate times or places.

2. If you get no satisfaction with a personal approach, and if the loan is relatively small, you can go to small claims court. Each province has its own definition of a "small claim," and procedures vary. (See YOUR RIGHTS IN ACTION, page 452.)

3. If a large sum is involved, you may want to consult a lawyer about filing a claim in a court. You could request a judgment authorizing a garnishment, which in some circumstances may permit you to collect the debt from an outside source, such as the borrower's bank account or paycheque. Your chance of success is best if you have a written document, such as a promissory note, to prove you did indeed lend the money. But even oral promises can stand up if the loan and its terms can be proved with clear evidence and credible witnesses, especially if the amount is less than $1,000.

you may prefer the home equity loan with fixed rates. Be certain, however, that you borrow an adequate amount in the first place—if you go back to borrow more, you will have to pay a new set of fees.

Banks and trust companies dominate home equity lending, but some credit unions, finance companies, and mortgage brokerage houses offer such loans as well. Whatever lender you settle on, use these guidelines when negotiating the loan:

- Base the size of your loan on your ability to repay.
- Understand the repayment terms of your loan or line of credit.
- Confirm how your interest rate is set.
- Don't be fooled by "teaser" rates that start you off with a low interest rate and then jump up later.
- If you are getting a credit line, ask about the interest rate "cap," or limit.
- Find out what costs and fees you will have to pay in the process of getting your loan.

Just because the lender allows you to borrow a certain percentage of your equity does not mean you should take the full amount. Begin at the other side of the question—instead of asking "How big a loan can I get?" ask "How much can I afford to pay for it?" Financial experts believe your mortgage loan and home equity loan payments, together with your taxes and energy bills, should not exceed 30 percent of your gross monthly income.

Different lenders have different rules for repayment of a loan or line of credit. Many lenders, for instance, require you to pay only the monthly interest each month. Although that makes the loan seem more affordable, you could be unpleasantly surprised by the whopping balance—called a "balloon payment"—that you will be required to pay when the loan finally comes due.

Most credit lines have variable rates tied to an "index," the base for rate changes that the lender uses to decide whether and how much the annual percentage rate will change. Some variable-rate loans are tied to the prime rate plus three or more percentage points. Other indexes that lenders use include the 90-day Treasury bill rate and the average 30-day "jumbo" ($300,000) guaranteed investment certificate rate.

Home equity lines of credit are among those often advertised with "teaser rates." Don't be fooled by very low interest rates offered in the first six months or year on a line of credit. These rates could jump later on and surprise you with substantially increased payments, even on funds you have already borrowed.

Closing a home equity loan, or second mortgage, can involve a host of incidental expenses. Various up-front charges such as the property appraisal and credit investigation can cost hundreds of dollars. Home equity lines of credit have annual fees, which can range from $25 to more than $100.

THINKING OF RENTING OR SELLING?

If your short-term plans include renting or selling your house, think twice about taking out a home equity loan. Some home equity agreements prohibit you from leasing your home, or even renovating it.

Finally, if you decided to sell your house, you probably would be required to pay off your home equity line or second mortgage in full. Ask yourself whether it really makes sense to take on the trouble and the substantial costs of acquiring such loans for a short-term benefit.

Debt is a kind of household tool. It's like a rope. You can use it for lifting or many other tasks. Or you can use it to hang yourself.

JAMES GRANT
Grant's Interest Rate Observer

Lending Money to Others

Not all loans have to involve institutional lenders. Suppose you have a friend who needs money to buy a car, and you have some money in a savings account that you will not need for a while. You can offer your friend a loan on terms that will benefit both of you. You might suggest an interest rate of, say, 7 percent, which is probably more interest than your money is earning in your savings account, but still cheaper than the 15 percent your friend might have to pay to get an unsecured loan at a bank. This stratagem is perfectly legal and is a good arrangement all around: it makes you some extra money and saves her some.

Be aware, however, that loans between friends or family members can go sour if you are not careful about the details. Even friends and family should spell out the terms of their agreement, write them down, and sign the document, thus guarding against problems later on. If the loan is not properly handled, the lender may suffer significant tax consequences. (See "A Gift of a Loan," page 286.) To ensure financial peace of mind—and to avoid losing a friend or the goodwill of a family member—consider the following guidelines:

- **Draw up the right papers.** A simple "promissory note" will specify the full amount, spell out the interest terms and the repayment schedule, and identify any collateral offered. You may want to consult a lawyer for the proper wording.
- **Choose a reasonable interest rate.** Remember that it is illegal to charge anyone 60 percent or other exorbitant interest. Remember, too, that if you do not charge any interest,

and the loan is not repaid and no repayment term is arranged, Revenue Canada may deem the loan a disguised form of income and subject to tax.

- **Structure the loan as either a demand loan or a term loan.** A "demand loan" sets no timetable for repayment, but the loan can be recalled at any time. A "term loan" has a set repayment schedule.
- **Observe the necessary formalities.** If you are making a mortgage loan, for instance, you must include in the promissory note the information that the debt is secured by your borrower's residence.

A Mother's Dilemma

PROBLEM
Marian's son Jeff did not make enough money at his part-time job to qualify for a car loan, so he asked his mother to co-sign a loan at a local bank. By co-signing, she would become responsible for Jeff's debt if he did not meet his payments. Marian was happy to help Jeff but wanted to limit her liability as much as possible. At the same time, she also wanted Jeff to learn how to handle his debts maturely.

ACTION
Marian consulted with the loan officer at the bank. From him, she learned that according to the terms of the loan agreement she would be responsible for paying only the principal balance on Jeff's loan if he defaulted—but not any late charges, court expenses, lawyer's fees, or other costs that could be generated. The lender included a statement in the contract: "This cosigner will be responsible only for the principal balance on this loan at the time of default." Marian also asked the lender to notify her if Jeff missed a payment, so that she could address the problem with Jeff before he actually defaulted. As a final step, Marian called her provincial consumer protection office to see if any other laws applied to her rights as a cosigner.

A GIFT OF A LOAN

Sometimes people want to extend a large loan to a family member or close friend but wish to charge only minimal interest. A parent may want to lend a child a down payment on a house or contribute toward his college education and charge little or no interest.

If the loan is confirmed by a promissory note or other written document, the lender has a limited period of time, usually three to five years, in which to collect the loan once the repayment period has ended.

In another scenario, if someone tries to avoid paying income tax by having relatives or friends pay her for work performed by way of monthly or bimonthly "loans," Revenue Canada may see through this scheme and consider the loans to be revenue, taxable in the hands of the recipient.

Gail L. Mathews • 201 Coolbreeze Avenue • Meaford, Ont. N0H 1Y0

Promissory Note

For value received, I, Gail L. Mathews, of Meaford, Ont., ① promise to pay to Robert H. Mathews, of 277 Iroquois Road, Barrie, Ont., or any subsequent holder of this Note, ② the sum of six thousand dollars ($6,000), with annual interest at 10 percent on the unpaid balance.

Payments shall be made in 24 installments of $278 each, with a first payment due on April 1, 1997, and the same amount due on the first day of each month thereafter until the entire principal amount of this note and earned interest are ③ fully paid. All payments shall be applied first to earned interest, and the balance to principal. I may prepay this note in whole or in part without penalty.

The full unpaid principal and any earned interest shall be fully due and immediately payable upon demand of the holder of this note in the event that the borrower shall default in making any payments due under this note within 60 days of the payment due date, or upon the death, bankruptcy, or insolvency of the borrower. ④

I waive presentment, demand, protest, and all notices thereto, and agree to remain fully bound to this note notwithstanding any extension, indulgence, or modification under this note, unless personally released or discharged in writing or having fulfilled its terms. ⑤

Signed this 25 day of March, 1996.

Borrower: Gail L. Mathews
Payment schedule attached

Witness: Karin Martin ⑥

An Installment Promissory Note

An installment promissory note expresses the terms of a loan to be repaid in equal payments of principal and interest, in this case by a daughter to her father. **1.** The name and place where the note (contract) was drawn up with must be included; **2.** If the lender dies before the loan is repaid, the borrower is obligated to his heirs and estate; **3.** The sum of the loan, the interest rate, the number of installments, the amount of each payment including interest, and the payment due dates are clearly specified; **4.** If the borrower defaults, the lender can demand immediate payment; this note works in the lender's favor because he is not required to follow certain procedures for repayment; **5.** Indulgences (like chronic late payment) may be condoned but will not negate the agreement; **6.** Witnesses are not required but can be present for protection.

CREDIT CARDS

Credit cards affect the way Canadians spend their money—and the way people go into debt. The right knowledge will help keep your debt under control.

Finding the Best Deal in a Credit Card

Thousands of offers for easy-to-get credit cards flood Canadians' mailboxes every year. Banks, nonprofit organizations, department stores, travel-and-entertainment companies, oil companies, and a host of other enterprises dazzle us with their versions of buy-now-and-pay-later convenience. How can you make your way through the maze of offers?

Bank cards, the most common type of credit card, offer you access to small personal loans, which the bank gives you each time you buy something with the card, and which you repay with interest over time. The card may be called MasterCard or Visa, for example, but it is issued by a particular bank that sets its own terms for the use of the card. Policies about interest rates, annual fees, billing practices, and other costs vary widely from issuer to issuer—which makes it essential to shop around and compare terms. Obviously the lower the interest rate and the less onerous the fees, the more desirable the card.

The general terms that banks typically offer cardholders are a credit limit of at least $500 and the option of making small monthly payments in lieu of paying the entire amount charged. Interest is charged on what is left over. Most bank cards also offer loans in the form of cash advances, almost always at very high interest rates.

"T&E" AND DEBIT CARDS

The term "credit card" is applied somewhat casually to all the pieces of plastic that allow you to buy without using cash or a cheque. But two kinds of cards differ from most of the others. The so-called T&E card (issued by travel-and-entertainment companies such as American Express and enRoute) is more accurately defined as a "charge card," since it does not offer credit on a month-to-month basis. In other words, you cannot carry an ongoing balance but must pay in full each month whatever you charged to the card that month.

The other kind of "plastic" that is not a true credit card is the debit card, which is basically an electronic cheque: what-

CREDIT CARD TYPES

Credit is issued by thousands of different financial entities: banks, oil companies, retail establishments, as well as travel-and-entertainment enterprises (such as American Express and enRoute), whose cards are not really credit cards, but a form of charge card. Debit cards, such as automated bank machine cards, are another type. A well-informed public coupled with competition between card issuers has been responsible for some slight reductions in credit card charges in recent years as well as such new products as "air miles" and points which can be used to obtain gifts. Bank cards, such as Visa and MasterCard, dominate the field with more than 24 million cards in circulation and accounting for about 75 percent of outstanding credit. According to a government survey, there are now 2.3 cards for every adult Canadian over 18 years of age.

Even among the true credit cards, there are many important differences as this chart shows.

Type	Terms	Advantages	Disadvantages
Affinity cards	Like bank credit cards, but sponsored by professional associations and charities that promise to donate part of the annual fee (often more than $20) or part of each purchase to the sponsoring organization	Convenient way to donate money	Usually high costs
Bank credit cards	Can include annual fees, credit limits, interest rates ranging from 12 percent to 22 percent; minimum monthly payments	Convenience and wide acceptance	Often high interest rates, and high fees for cash advances
Debit cards	Do not offer credit; a charge is electronically deducted from a bank account linked to the card	Easier than writing cheques; you can't spend more money than you have in your account	May be harder to keep track of account activity without a cheque register or passbook on hand when using
Gasoline cards	Balance must be paid in full every month	Easy to obtain; may offer such benefits as travel clubs and credit card registration	Can cost more to use than paying cash; use limited to car- and travel-related expenditures
Retail cards	Issued for use in specific retail establishments; interest rates from 18 to 26 percent are charged on unpaid balances	Easy to obtain; no annual fees; often provide access to special sales and discounts	Extremely high interest rates make carrying a balance very expensive
Travel-and-entertainment cards	Do not offer month-to-month credit; bill must be paid in full every month; no preset charge limit	Convenient for travelers who might quickly reach their limit on a bank card; offer financial services geared toward travelers and executives	Accepted at fewer locations than bank cards; high annual fees

Getting Students Started on Credit

Many of today's college students carry some kind of credit card. Used wisely, it can be a great convenience and can help the student build a good credit history. If a student's income is too low to qualify for a credit card, she has a few other options for obtaining one.

✔ *Co-signed card.* A parent or other adult co-signs, and the payment history is reported in both names. If neither co-signer pays the bills, that negative information will likely be reported to a credit bureau under both names.

✔ *Special programs.* Many large credit card issuers have special application procedures for college students. Usually the cards have a smaller credit line than conventional cards, and the applicant must have proof of college acceptance. Most major banks and college admissions offices have information on these programs.

ever sum you charge on your debit card is taken directly out of your bank account. An automated banking machine (ABM) card is a kind of debit card—the machine gives you some cash, and that amount is instantly deducted from your bank account. Since T&E and debit cards do not offer you ongoing credit, interest rates are not a factor. Annual fees, late-payment charges, and many other kinds of fees add up, however, as they do with any other type of card.

LEARN THE LANGUAGE

Before applying for a bank credit card, you should be familiar with the following terms: "interest rates," "grace periods," and "balance calculation methods."

Provincial consumer law requires that banks state their "annual percentage rate" (APR) in credit card offerings. The banks express this rate as simple interest charged on purchases not paid in full each month. But the cost to you may be more than you realize, because most card issuers in fact compound the interest you pay on new purchases *and* interest charges carried forward each month. Card issuers may change the interest rate at will if they give consumers 15 days' written notice.

Some cards allow a 25- or 30-day grace period during which you do not pay interest on expenses charged to your card. Usually, however, you are guaranteed a grace period *only* when you do not carry a balance forward from the previous month. The small print explains that if you carry any balance forward, your grace period is forfeited on all new purchases, which means that interest will accrue not only on the carry-over balance but also on new charges from the date of purchase.

The balance calculation method most favorable to consumers is the "adjusted balance method." With this method, the interest is applied to the amount you owe after your monthly payments are made.

The most widely used method, however, is the "average daily balance method," which averages the amount of debt you had in your account each day during the month and charges interest on that amount.

The least advantageous method for consumers is the "previous balance method"; you are charged interest on the balance you owe on your account at the end of the previous month, with no credit at all for payments made since then.

A general guideline for choosing a credit card is that if you are in the habit of paying your whole bill every month, you need a card with no annual fee and with a grace period; since you do not carry a balance from month to month, the interest rate is less important to you. If most months you do carry a balance, however, you should look for a card with the lowest interest rate and the most favorable billing method.

Hidden Credit Card Costs

By law, credit card costs—interest (and how it is calculated) plus all fees—must be displayed in an easy-to-read box format on most applications and solicitations. But some credit card costs are harder to figure out. For example, card issuers usually charge interest on purchases from the date the charge slip reaches the issuer and is placed on your account. But many issuers "backdate" interest to the date of purchase, which adds anything from one day's interest to as much as several weeks' worth of interest to your bill.

You should also be aware that when you charge a cash advance against your card, interest is always charged from the first day.

Dealing With Credit Rejection

PROBLEM
Although Barry had been steadily employed for a number of years, his application for a credit card was rejected. As reasons for its action the bank noted that Barry had been at his present job for less than a year and that he already held six other credit card accounts.

ACTION
Barry called the bank's credit manager. He pointed out that although his present job was new, he had been in the same field for several years and his present employer had hired him away from his former job. He offered to close some of his existing credit card accounts, but the credit manager refused to reconsider. Barry took action by canceling a few of his other cards, and then applying to another card company, which accepted his application. (Barry could also have waited until he had been at his current job for a year and reapplied to the original bank.)

Many cardholders believe a credit card repayment schedule that requires the lowest minimum monthly payments is the best deal. Nothing could be further from the truth. True, the payments may seem easier when you sit down to pay the bills, but low monthly payments can mean shockingly high costs in the long run. Most card issuers require payment of 5 percent on the outstanding balance each month, with a minimum payment of $10, whatever is larger. By paying only the minimum payment it takes many months or years to pay off a credit card debit with most of the payments going to cover interest charges.

Even a balance of $1,000 or $2,000 at an annual percentage rate of 13 percent would take several years to pay off at a minimum payment of only 5 percent, not counting any new charges.

Credit Card Travel Troubles

Hotels, motels, and car-rental companies sometimes use an irksome but legal tactic that can put a big dent in your travel or vacation plans, and may even severely inhibit your travel enjoyment.

When you check in to a motel room or rent a car that you have reserved with a credit card, the clerk may put a hold on your card account for the estimated amount of the rental or the hotel bill. This ploy ensures the merchant's payment, but it can create serious problems for you.

For example, if you book a hotel for eight days and the room costs $150 per day, the hotelier can put a hold of $1,200 on your card. If the cost of the auto rental is $400 for the same period of time, plus insurance of, say, $100, you may have used up $1,700 in credit before your vacation even begins. This may put you close to the credit limit on your card, and the hold can remain on your card for as long as two weeks, even if you pay your hotel or auto-rental bill in cash or by cheque before you leave on your trip.

Perhaps the best way you can handle this irritating situation—except for finding a hotel or car rental agency that will help you out—is to use two cards. Put lodgings and car rentals on one card, and use the other for restaurants, shopping, and other incidentals.

Using Your Card Wisely

The convenience of credit cards makes it tempting to use them indiscriminately. Indeed, studies show that people who shop with credit cards spend more than those who pay by cash or cheque—which is one reason retailers such as department stores urge their customers to sign up for the stores' credit cards. Common sense and a little discipline are the best remedies for overspending, of course, but there are also some strategies in both using the card and paying your bills that will help keep a rein on expenses.

Some merchants prompt consumers to spend more by requiring a minimum dollar-amount purchase for the use of the card. Minimum-purchase requirements are legal, but the major credit card companies do not allow them. Other card issuers may have their own policies; so call your card issuer's customer service department to find out. If a merchant insists on a minimum-purchase in violation of the credit card company's policy, inform the company as well as the local Better Business Bureau.

Usually, it is best to own no more than two credit cards. Keep one card that has a low (or no) annual fee and a grace period, and use it when you expect to pay off your balance on time. Keep another that has a low interest rate for occasions when you won't be able to pay the entire amount when due. Canceling all your other cards will save money and simplify your record keeping.

Whatever cards you have, you can save money when it is time to pay your bills by observing these tips:

- Try to pay off your entire credit card bill every month. You will spare yourself the finance charges.
- If you cannot manage to pay in full, pay what you can the moment you get your bill. The sooner the bank gets your payment, the less interest you will usually pay that month, and in the long run.
- Never accept a card issuer's enticing offer to skip a payment for a month. Although you would not be paying, interest charges would be accruing. That means you would just be adding to the amount you owe.
- Pay as much as you can on the highest-rate cards first. Then make minimum payments on your other ones. This reduces your debt more quickly than if you spread partial payments evenly among all your cards.
- If you are a good, longtime customer, try asking your card issuer to waive your annual fee. Many will do so, but you must initiate the request.

Keeping Private Information Out of the Wrong Hands

Often when you pay for a retail purchase with a personal cheque, the store clerk asks to see your driver's license and a major credit card to validate your payment. He then writes those numbers on your cheque and may even ask for your telephone number, too. But this form of "validation" exposes you to fraud, invades your privacy, does nothing to protect the merchant from bad cheques—and may be illegal besides.

How does it put you at risk of being defrauded? Many eyes see your cheque between the time it is written and when the bank returns it to you. If the cheque has your name, address, telephone number, and credit card number on it, anyone can use that information to buy merchandise by telephone or from mail-order catalogs. One crime ring specialized in mail-order fraud by paying dishonest store clerks for credit card information.

You have the right to refuse to allow a merchant to write your credit card number on your cheque. If you wish, you can suggest that instead of your credit card number, the merchant use your driver's license or social insurance number.

In credit card transactions, too, some merchants ask customers to write their telephone numbers on the credit card sales slips. Most people comply, not realizing that, again, the major card issuers prohibit this practice.

Remember that the more information you divulge about yourself, the easier it is for someone to defraud you. Recent privacy legislation protects the consumer from being required to divulge personal information unless such information is directly related to the transaction at hand.

Coping With Billing Errors and Disputes

Skirmishes with credit card companies over billing errors have become almost as inevitable as death and taxes: a bank incorrectly totals your charges; you get charged for something you did not buy; or a mail-order merchant delivers items different from those you ordered. The liability of the consumer who uses a credit card is contained in the contract one gets when a card is issued, called the master agreement. In almost all cases, the terms are written in favor of the card issuer and require that payment be

---

Tactics for Protecting Your Privacy

To limit the chance of being victimized by credit card fraud, do not allow a salesclerk to write your credit card number on your personal cheque or your phone number on a credit card sales slip. If the clerk insists even after you have explained your position, take these steps:

✔ *Speak to the manager.* Ask to speak to the store owner, or manager, or someone who has the authority to alter store policy if necessary.

✔ *Clarify your position.* Inform the merchant that Visa, MasterCard, and American Express prohibit stores from refusing sales to customers who decline to provide personal information such as telephone numbers.

✔ *Verify with a credit card.* If you are trying to pay by cheque, allow the merchant to verify that you hold a major credit card, but do not let him write the account number on your cheque.

✔ *Refuse the purchase.* If the merchant insists on recording personal information on your cheque or on the bank card sales slip, take your business elsewhere.

✔ *Complain to the credit card company.* Be sure to inform your card issuer of the name and address of the intractable merchant.

YOUR RIGHTS IF YOUR CARD IS STOLEN

Credit card crooks and con artists cause credit card companies massive losses every year. Your liability for unauthorized charges is strictly limited by law. Specifically, these are your rights if you:

1. Report the loss quickly. If you report the loss or theft of a credit card before it is used fraudulently, you have no liability for any charges.

2. Report the loss after illegal use. If you report the loss of cards that have already been used, you must pay the first $50 charged on each card. (The $50 limitation of liability does not apply to withdrawals made from an automated banking machine (ABM) in which case you could be liable for all amounts withdrawn until the issuing company was informed of the loss of your card.)

3. Are the victim of a mail-order scam. If a lost or stolen card is used for a mail-order purchase and has not been presented directly to the merchant, you are not liable for any amount, whether or not you have reported the loss of the card.

4. Are offered insurance. If your credit card company offers you "credit card protection" insurance, think twice before signing up. After a few years, the fees you pay would probably exceed the $50 a loss or theft can cost.

made according to the terms of the contract while the dispute is being investigated. Withholding payment could adversely affect your credit rating. The following steps will improve your chances of having a billing error resolved satisfactorily:

- Respond in writing within 60 days of the date the credit card bill was sent to you. In some cases involving relatively small amounts, a telephone call to the card issuer may resolve the problem, but to be safe follow up with a letter, always keeping a copy for your records. (The address for billing problems should be printed on your monthly statement. Usually it is different from the address to which you mail your monthly payments.)
- Give clear details of the disputed transaction. Your letter to the creditor must contain your name, address, account number, the dollar amount of the erroneous billing, and a description of what you believe the error to be. Send photocopies of the relevant receipts or other documents, and keep the originals as well as a copy of your letter.
- Send your complaint by certified mail, return receipt requested, so that you can prove the card issuer received it.
- Pay your bill as usual to avoid a bad credit rating. Include a note stating that your payment is made without prejudice to your rights and recourses. If the dispute is settled in your favor, the card company will credit your account.

If you are not satisfied with the way your complaint was handled, and the card is issued by a federally regulated financial institution, write to the Office of the Superintendent of Financial Institutions. If the issuing institution is provincially chartered, address your complaint to your provincial consumer protection office.

Within 90 days, the creditor must make a "reasonable investigation" of the error, and may, if necessary, send documentation on the disputed charge back to the merchant. If the investigation shows you are correct, you will not have to pay either the charge or interest accrued on it. If the card issuer decides against you, it must give you a written explanation and a statement of the amount you owe. If you are still convinced the company is in error, seek legal advice or contact your local consumer protection agency.

If you decide to withhold payment, you must immediately inform the issuer in writing. Be aware that this option could damage your credit history. The card issuer can report you to a credit bureau for not paying the disputed charge. Should you finally win the dispute, the credit card issuer must promptly clear your record with anyone who received that version of your credit report.

CREDIT BUREAUS

These electronic warehouses bulge with details of your credit history—and some of them are wrong. It is up to you to make sure your credit record tells the truth.

Your Rights to Accuracy and Confidentiality

Whether you are looking for a loan, an insurance policy, or an apartment, chances are that your interviewer will ask a credit bureau to run a check on you. Credit bureaus are private companies that collect information on people—their employment, revenue, and debts, and how good a risk a particular individual may be. Their reports will reveal such details as who has extended credit to you, whether you pay your bills on time, whether you have ever defaulted on a loan, even how much you owe each of your present creditors. Credit companies compile this data from many sources—financial institutions where you have car loans or charge cards, department stores, municipal tax lists —and boil it down into a credit report. Usually these credit bureaus are members of the Associated Credit Bureaus of Canada. The country's largest credit bureau, Equifax Corporation, has offices in every major city and region.

Credit bureaus do not need your permission to show your credit file. If a company or an individual has a *bona fide* reason to check your credit, the bureau will be happy to oblige. However, credit bureaus are prohibited from giving information about you to nosy neighbors, friends, or others, who do not have a direct financial interest in your credit history.

Various provincial credit-reporting and consumer laws govern how credit bureaus gather and give information and what type of information your credit file may contain. Reference to your race, religion, country of origin, health, or other facts not directly linked to credit is forbidden. Provincial privacy legislation also limits the type of information that can be obtained and disclosed. These laws may require a bureau to notify a consumer either prior or after a credit check, and to name the person or company that made the request.

In most loan applications or large credit sales, the consumer usually authorizes the prospective lender or seller to obtain a credit report. Sometimes the cost of the check is included in your borrowing costs. Anyone applying for a loan or planning a major credit purchase should review his credit rating beforehand to ensure any errors or omissions are corrected.

123.

HOW TO CORRECT A BLEMISHED CREDIT REPORT

A credit bureau is legally required to investigate and correct wrong information on a credit report. But it is usually up to you to discover the error and see that it is corrected. Here is how to go about it:

1. Write a letter describing the error and requesting a prompt investigation. Cite your rights under the appropriate consumer or credit collection law. Include your full name, address, social insurance number, and phone number.

2. Send the letter by certified mail (return receipt requested), so you will have proof that the credit bureau got your letter.

3. If the investigation shows that one of your creditors incorrectly reported the disputed information, contact the creditor directly and explain the error. Ask the creditor to send a written correction to all its credit bureaus.

4. If you disagree with the results of the credit bureau's investigation, you can insist that your version of the dispute be included with its report.

5. After you have set the bureau straight, always request a copy of the revised report to ensure that it is now correct.

When Your Credit History Will Dog You

In most cases, credit bureaus must remove from your record any negative information that is more than seven years old. Under some circumstances, however, potential creditors, insurers, or employers may legally request negative data that goes back further. Here are examples of times when a blemished credit history can cause you trouble:

✔ *A history of bankruptcy.* If you have been through a bankruptcy, the negative information stays on your record for up to 10 years.

✔ *A large loan application.* If you try to borrow $50,000 or more for any reason, including a mortgage loan or home equity loan, the financial institution has the right to be appraised of your credit history.

✔ *A life insurance application.* If you apply for a life insurance policy with a benefit amount of $50,000 or more, the insurer has the right to know your complete credit history.

✔ *An employment search.* If you are applying for a job, your potential employer has the right to information about your credit history if this information is pertinent to the position you are seeking.

✔ *An apartment application.* If you are renting an expensive apartment or home, the lessor usually has a right to check your credit rating to insure that you can afford the rent and are a good risk.

SUMMARY OF CONSUMER RIGHTS

- The right to review your credit report. You may do this in person, by phone, or by mail.
- The right to have investigated within a reasonable period (generally within 30 days) any information in your credit report that you dispute.
- The right to have the erroneous information deleted from your record if the investigation finds that the information was, in fact, wrong.
- The right to have negative credit-related entries such as late payments deleted from your record after seven years and a bankruptcy report deleted after 10 years.
- The right to have the credit bureau notify—at no expense to you—those creditors you name who previously received the incorrect information.
- The right to know who has received a copy of your report for employment purposes, and for credit-granting purposes.
- The right, if a credit bureau investigates and insists its information is correct, to include a statement expressing your version of the dispute.

WHAT IS NOT ON THE REPORT

You may be surprised that your credit report does not describe your bank accounts, including either your chequing or savings accounts, your mortgage loans, or any other major assets. Furthermore, unless a debt collection has been launched against you, you probably will not be cited for owing money on oil and gas credit cards, utility bills, or lawyer's fees. A credit bureau's report is not, strictly speaking, a financial rating. Basically, your potential creditors usually evaluate the report and decide for themselves how much of a potential risk you may be. However, some credit bureaus now use scoring systems to help creditors evaluate your creditworthiness. They instruct lenders to identify credit-related factors, such as income, length of employment, and payment history, and assign various "point values" to each characteristic, resulting in a score that either meets or does not meet the lender's requirements.

Many people overestimate the value of a good credit rating and fear a bad one will adversely affect their whole lives. In fact creditors usually assess potential borrowers individually, using the credit bureau rating as only one of several criteria. The hundreds of responsible people who found themselves in default on loans and other debts because of the recent recession and subsequent "downsizing" by many companies should bear that in mind. In a few months or years, when they are back in the work force, they can explain the prior defaults and many creditors will still regard them as good risks. They can then rapidly reestablish a good credit rating.

DEALING WITH DEBT

Millions of Canadians live permanently in debt. For most it is a manageable problem, but when it gets out of control, it could cause serious trouble.

Practical Steps to Take When You Are in Trouble

Mortgage payments, car loans, credit card charges —these are debts that most of us manage to cope with. Being in a serious financial crisis, however, can be a frightening and crippling experience. Some fiscal emergencies, such as getting laid off or becoming seriously sick, are beyond our control. Other acute debt problems are caused by poor financial management. Whatever the cause, it is important to face up to such a problem, and take steps to resolve it, so as to avoid the serious legal problems caused by unpaid debts.

Most financial experts believe that consumers who spend more than 20 percent of their after-tax income on non-mortgage debt are dangerously overburdened. Non-mortgage debt includes all your other borrowed money, such as car loans and credit card debt. For example, John and Jane together earn $60,000 a year, with a net income after taxes of $3,500 per

A fool and his money are soon parted.

Anonymous
English proverb

Debt Danger Signals

You can often detect the warning signs of overindebtedness long before the collection notices from creditors arrive. If more than two or three of these danger signs apply to you, you need help to develop a budget and debt repayment plan.

• You have begun charging to a credit card such essentials as food or daily expenses that you used to buy with cash.

• You make only the minimum payments on your charge accounts each month and perhaps do not pay one or two at all, even though it will mean additional finance charges on your next bills.

• You take a cash advance from a credit card to make the minimum payment on another or to use for incidental expenses.

• You no longer contribute to a savings or retirement account or, worse, have closed your savings account altogether.

• You put off all maintenance activities—from visiting your dentist to painting your house—because you cannot afford them "right now."

• You consistently have to work overtime, or are holding down a second job, just to make enough money to pay your creditors.

• You are at or near the limit on the line of credit on all of your credit cards. In fact, you have too many credit cards.

• You are unsure of how much you owe creditors, are unwilling to admit to yourself or anyone else just how big your debt might be, and avoid actually adding up the total debt.

month. They have a car loan of $250 a month, and they owe $5,000 to credit card companies on which they must pay a minimum of $800 per month. The result is that they are paying 30 percent of their income to cover non-mortgage debts—a very dangerous position indeed.

To find your ratio, add all your monthly non-mortgage loans or credit card payments and then divide the total by your monthly net income. If your debt-to-income ratio, like Jane and John's, is above 20 percent, you should take immediate action to get your debt under control.

First, find out where you stand. Summarize all your debts, including the total amount due, the amount overdue, and the minimum monthly payment requirements. Figure out what you can afford to pay each creditor; it is best to pay at least something on all your bills. If you ignore a creditor, the account may be sent to a collection agency.

If you cannot keep up to date with your payments, contact your creditors. Your position will be stronger if you are the one to initiate contact and you have a clear idea of what you can afford to offer. Speak to the credit manager or whoever can approve a repayment plan. Most creditors prefer negotiating a new repayment schedule to taking costly and time-consuming legal measures. (This renegotiation will appear on your credit record, however.)

Explain your situation and offer a modified payment plan, such as paying 75 percent of the normal amount for four months, then resuming the normal payments. Even small, consistent payments prove to your creditor that you are a responsible customer experiencing temporary difficulties, and not a deadbeat. In some cases he may agree to waive or reduce interest while you respect the repayment arrangement. Be sure to follow up with a letter that restates your agreement, and send it certified mail, return receipt requested, so that you have proof it was received.

AVOID BACKSLIDING

Resolve to stick with your revised payment plan. This is especially important if your debt is secured by collateral that a creditor can seize if you fail to pay your bill. The bills that should have priority include: your rent, utility bills (if your service is disconnected, you will probably have to pay larger security deposits for future services), and credit cards (late payments are reported to credit bureaus, which will make it difficult for you to get credit in the future). Some creditors write off accounts to "profit and loss" if they are delinquent for 90 days or more. If you put off paying any bill for more than 90 days, the possible profit-and-loss mark on your credit file is an extremely negative entry.

A Respected Source of Help

Every year, thousands of debt-burdened Canadians turn for free or low-cost help to various government or private debt-counseling services. For example, British Columbia's Ministry of Labour and Consumer Services has a Debtor Assistance Branch. Alberta's Ministry of Consumer and Corporate Affairs offers a similar service through its Family Financial Counselling Department. Saskatchewan's Ministry of Justice provides the Mediation Board. Ontario debtors can turn to the Association of Credit Counselling Services.

Depending on your needs, a counselor will work out a budget for you or advise you to enrol in a debt-management program. If you enrol, the counselor works out a repayment schedule with your creditors. From then on, your creditors are asked to contact your counselor, relieving you of collection calls. If you go into the debt-management program, any of your creditors may report that fact to a credit bureau, and a future creditor could hold it against you. But credit experts point out that the fact you have been through debt counseling is preferable to a credit report that you have not paid your bills or that you filed for bankruptcy.

For help in finding the nearest debt counseling office in your area, check the Yellow Pages of your telephone directory, or see Resources, page 469.

You will have somewhat more leeway in delaying payments to lawyers and dentists, who generally do not report to credit bureaus and rarely charge interest or late fees, although they may send your bills to a collection agency. The local business-people you deal with regularly, such as appliance repairmen and dry cleaners, do not generally report late bill paying to credit bureaus. Rather than taking advantage of them, however, you should overcome your embarrassment and tell them you are in temporary financial trouble; if you have been a good customer, they may agree to take reduced payments until you are back on your feet. If you feel unable to resolve matters on your own, credit counseling is available. Many banks and credit unions offer formal or informal debt counseling for their customers or members, and valuable advice is available from non-profit credit-counseling services nationwide.

Coping With the Bill Collector

Creditors are quick to act when payments are late. If you miss more than a few payments, creditors will often ask for the balance of the loan or debt to be paid immediately. The creditor has the right to do this if your loan agreement contains an "acceleration clause." If you immediately bring the payments up to date, the creditor may decide not to insist that you pay the balance at once.

But when you do not respond with a payment, the creditor may threaten to turn the matter over to a debt collection agency. Often collection agencies work on commission, collecting between one-third and two-thirds of the amount they bring in. You can expect debt collectors to use high-pressure tactics to collect a debt, although provincial collection agency laws protect consumers from unnecessary harassment and offensive strong-arm tactics. These laws—which apply only to debt collectors, not creditors—make very clear what a collection agency may not do in its efforts to get you to pay.

Most collection agency laws prohibit the following practices. A bill collector may not contact any third parties about your debt except your lawyer, credit bureaus, and those who might help the agency locate you. If a collector contacts someone else in an effort to locate you, he or she cannot indicate that debt collection, or your debt, is the reason for the call.

Contact can be made only during normal hours. You cannot be called before 8:00 a.m. and after 9:00 p.m. Nor can a collector call you repeatedly simply to annoy or intimidate you. You have the right to demand that the debt collector stop calling you at work. If you have indicated that you are represented by a lawyer, a bill collector may not call you in person at all.

How to Stop Bothersome Bill Collectors

Various provincial acts protect consumers from bullying tactics that were once the stock-in-trade of collection agencies. If you feel you are harassed or unduly pressured by a bill collector, these laws often offer a simple way to put a stop to it.

In some provinces, a collection agent is obliged to stop communicating with you once you, or your lawyer or financial adviser, send him a letter telling him to communicate only with your representative. The letter should be sent by registered or certified mail (return receipt requested), so you can later prove that the agency received it. (Remember that the legislation applies to collection agencies only, so your dentist, lawyer, or other private party to whom you owe money would be within their rights to call you.) Once the collection agency gets your letter, it may not contact you again, except to say that collection efforts have ended or that some legal action is being taken against you. (Your letter has not absolved you of your debt; you may still be taken to court for it.)

If a collection agency continues to badger you after you have sent the letter, keep notes about the offending contacts, and notify the provincial government office that licenses and regulates collection agencies. You may well have a legal case against the collection agency.

HOW SAFE IS YOUR PAYCHEQUE?

If the courts permit a creditor to garnishee your wages, your employer may be required to withhold part of each paycheque and send it to the creditor until your debt is satisfied.

1. Besides straight wages, your commissions, bonuses, retirement program payments, and vacation pay can be garnisheed.

2. Each province specifies what percentage of your pay may be garnisheed. Alberta, for example, allows a single person to keep $525 per month plus $140 a month for each dependent; a married person may retain $700 plus $140 per dependent child. Most provinces prohibit garnishment of welfare payments, old age pensions, employment insurance benefits, disability pensions, and Canada (Quebec) Pension Plan benefits.

3. If the debt is for spousal or child support, the creditor can have the debtor's income tax rebate or other monies paid by the federal government seized. Some provinces, Ontario and Manitoba, for example, automatically deduct the support payments on default by the debtor.

4. If your wages are garnisheed for one debt, you cannot be fired; if other debtors sue you, they must share the amount of salary garnisheed by the first creditor.

5. If you receive notice of wage garnishment, you may want to seek legal advice.

No one can use false or deceptive collection methods, such as threatening you with arrest if you do not pay the debt, using a false name, or pretending to be a law enforcement officer or government official when calling to collect the debt.

Neither may these agencies make frequent telephone calls, discuss the debt with your employer, or otherwise harass you.

If you believe a collection agency has been acting illegally, you can take any of the following steps: notify the collection agency in writing that you do not wish to be harassed; write to the government agency that regulates the collection industry. In the case of federally governed creditors such as chartered banks, contact Consumer and Corporate Affairs.

COMING TO TERMS

The protection that the various debt collection laws offer you does not prevent debt collectors from exercising *their* rights. These will vary from province to province but may include the right to sue you in court. To keep matters from going that far, consider some tips for dealing with bill collectors:

- As you would with the actual creditor, be honest about your financial problems. If you are being pressured to pay more than you can afford, you may want to draw up a statement of your income and expenses to show what you can afford to pay.
- Resist pressure to agree to a repayment schedule you cannot afford or to pay with a postdated cheque. Ask for more time, and call back with a reasonable counteroffer. Often debt collectors have a great deal of flexibility both in terms of time and in negotiating the amount of the payments. However, if the collector's agreement with the creditor specifies a minimum acceptable amount, you will be unable to negotiate an alternative.
- Get the name of the person you spoke to. Record when and where you were contacted and any agreements you made with the bill collector. Keep copies of all correspondence pertaining to the debt. If you agree on payment terms, spell them out in a letter to the collector.
- If you agree to settle a debt for less than the total amount, take two precautions. First, write a disclaimer on the cheque that states "cashing this cheque constitutes payment in full." In some cases, this will prevent the collector or creditor from suing you for the difference between the cheque and the total amount of the debt. Then send a certified letter that spells out your agreement and asserts that if the debt collector cashes the cheque you have enclosed, it will satisfy the debt in full. Check with a lawyer to make sure that this practice is legal in your province.

Is Bankruptcy the Answer?

At first glance, bankruptcy may seem like an easy way to get rid of debts and make a fresh start. Indeed, this country's bankruptcy law is designed not as punishment but as a stepping-stone to rehabilitation. Still, declaring bankruptcy can have a devastating effect on your life, and it should be pursued only as a last resort.

A bankruptcy filing generally stays on your credit report for six years, but the impact can last much longer. With a bankruptcy on your record, you could have trouble getting a job or renting an apartment, because of the black mark on your credit reports. You will also find it almost impossible to take out a loan, obtain a credit card, or be granted a mortgage. Most mortgage applications ask if you have ever declared bankruptcy—your "yes" will count strongly against you.

Why then did so many Canadians choose to file for bankruptcy in recent years? Because despite its ruinous effect on a credit record, bankruptcy can be a flexible and humane alternative for people who are so far into debt that there is no other hope of recovering. This is why federal law protects your right to file for bankruptcy—you cannot be fired from your job, for

Annual income twenty pounds, annual expenditure nineteen pounds nineteen and six, result happiness. Annual income twenty pounds, annual expenditure twenty pounds ought and six, result misery.

CHARLES DICKENS
David Copperfield

Two Ways to Go Bankrupt, One Way to Avoid It

Canada's Bankruptcy Act was modified in 1992 to reflect the realities of the nineties. Among the changes were the right of a consumer to file a consumer proposal with his creditors, which, contrary to the old law, does not automatically result in bankruptcy if the proposal is refused. Another change is that in consumer bankruptcy financial counseling is offered prior to and after declaring bankruptcy.

• You can file for bankruptcy if you owe at least $1,000 and are unable to meet regular payments as they come due, or you own insufficient property to cover your debts. Once your petition is filed with the courts, all property you own, other than property exempted by provincial or federal law, is turned over to a bankruptcy trustee whose job is to sell your property for as much as possible in order to satisfy your creditors' claims.

• You can be forced into bankruptcy if a creditor to whom you owe at least $1,000 petitions the court for payment, and his petition is upheld, but you are unable to pay. Once you are bankrupt, the proceedings for settling the debts is similar to what happens when you petition for bankruptcy: you must meet with your creditors; file income and expense reports; and attend financial counseling sessions. You will be prohibited from using credit cards or obtaining goods by credit (except in certain cases) while your bankruptcy is undischarged. In the case of most simple noncommercial bankruptcies, where the amount owed is $75,000 or less, a first bankruptcy can be discharged in about nine months.

• For debtors who do not have an overwhelming amount of debt or complicated financial affairs, the Bankruptcy and Insolvency Act allows the debtor to make a consumer proposal. In a proposal you can ask your creditors to accept reduced payment, say 65 percent of the debt, or you may request additional time (but not longer than five years) in which to pay. If your proposal is accepted you make payments to the trustee and your creditors cannot sue so long as you respect the terms. To present a proposal, you should get advice from a trustee in bankruptcy.

example. The law offers two types of personal bankruptcy: one by which you file a petition for bankruptcy; the other when a creditor petitions you into bankruptcy.

As an alternative to bankruptcy, you can make a consumer proposal (see "Two Ways to Go Bankrupt, One Way to Avoid It," page 301).

WHEN NOT TO CHOOSE BANKRUPTCY

Before seriously considering bankruptcy, ask yourself the following questions, which will help reveal whether your situation really requires that fateful step.

- **Do I have much property to protect?** For consumers who have little money or property and no joint debts, a creditor who chooses to sue would have little chance of ever collecting the debt. In that case, filing for bankruptcy would mean unnecessary time and expense.
- **Will I lose property I need to keep?** Laws vary from province to province on what property is exempt from seizure by the trustee. If you are concerned you may lose essential property, avoid filing for bankruptcy and clarify any questions with your lawyer.
- **Could someone else get saddled with my debt?** If you had a cosigner on a loan, or if you have joint accounts, the lender can require the cosigner to make the payments once you have declared bankruptcy.
- **Will I need to borrow again soon?** Getting credit after declaring bankruptcy is a difficult undertaking. Though most people considering bankruptcy have already severely compromised their credit reports, actually filing for bankruptcy is the worst mark you can put on your credit file.

If the answers to these questions are no and you still favor bankruptcy, most experts suggest you should get professional advice. Bankruptcy laws are extremely complex. Legal fees range from around $500 to more than $1,000 for a consumer bankruptcy and much more for a commercial bankruptcy.

Refurbishing Your Credit Image

Often people who have been through a major economic setback such as bankruptcy fear they will never get credit again. Because negative information remains on your credit report for six or even 10 years, it may seem as though only time will take care of a bad credit report. No doubt about it: cleaning up a blemished credit history will take time, but with persistence and a focused strategy, within a few years you can reestablish your credit to the point where lenders will start talking to you again.

Your first step should be to review your credit report for any outdated or inaccurate information. (See also "Credit Bureaus," page 295.) If accounts you have paid in full are still listed as unpaid on the report, immediately notify the credit bureau. Try to pay off any accounts that are in arrears. Before you send a cheque, ask the creditor to remove all negative information from your credit file in exchange for your taking care of the outstanding balance. Although under no obligation to agree, the creditor may be willing to remove at least some of the negative information. For example, if you overextended yourself to a department store, it may be eager to keep your business and may remove a problematic notation.

ACCENTUATING THE POSITIVE

You will also need to get positive information in your credit file as soon as possible. This is where strategy counts. If you have just been discharged from a bankruptcy send a copy of the discharge order to the credit bureau so that your record can be brought up to date.

A good next step is to take out a savings passbook loan at a bank that will report this loan to a credit bureau. For passbook loans, you deposit a certain sum and ask the bank to give you a loan against the money in your account. In exchange, you turn your passbook over to the bank. Banks are willing to do this because they incur no risk: If you do not pay back the loan, the bank simply takes the money out of your account. As you repay the loan, month by month, you steadily rebuild your credit standing.

Holding a major bank credit card is usually considered a stronger reference than any other type of account, even a mortgage. If you had a credit card that was canceled, try to reopen the account. Often, paying what you owe will enable you to get your card back.

KEEP YOUR EYE ON THE GOAL

Not all credit accounts will enhance your creditworthiness. Some creditors, such as furniture stores and most gasoline card issuers, do not report accounts unless they become delinquent, so that kind of credit activity will not bolster your credit standing. Until your credit standing is restored, avoid opening any accounts that will not help you achieve that goal, so that you do not further overextend your ability to pay.

Finally, don't think you can get away from your bad credit record by moving. The major credit bureaus operate nationwide, and they will find you. Only by rebuilding good credit can you set the record straight.

123..

BEWARE CREDIT-REPAIR SCAMS

Credit-repair companies that promise to "clean up credit reports" prey on debtors looking for a quick fix for their credit problems. Most of these companies charge hefty fees for advice but do nothing to improve credit ratings that the average consumer could not do alone. If, nevertheless, you decide to pay a credit-repair company to deal with your creditors and credit bureaus, protect yourself by following these guidelines:

1. Contact your provincial consumer affairs office or local Better Business Bureau to see if any complaints have been lodged against the company.

2. Make sure that the company is licensed or bonded in your province.

3. Avoid firms claiming that accurate negative data can be changed or erased. Such claims are false.

4. Avoid firms that offer quick-fix solutions to your indebtedness. Often these firms do nothing more than refer you to a trustee in bankruptcy.

5. Be wary if you are asked for a large fee up front. Choose a company that charges only if it succeeds in getting information removed or corrected.

6. Ask whether you will receive a refund if the negative or incorrect information reappears on your file. Use only credit companies that offer this guarantee in writing.

LIFE INSURANCE

Two out of three Canadians buy life insurance, but almost everyone is confused by it. To protect your money, get all the information you can.

How Much Life Insurance Do You Need?

If anyone besides yourself is dependent on your income, you should have life insurance. But how much should you buy? Enough to fill the gap between the amount of income your dependents would have at your death, and the amount they would need to live on.

Before consulting an insurance agent or broker, make your own estimate based on an honest assessment of your present financial situation. Here is one useful rule of thumb: Buy life insurance worth five to seven times your gross annual salary. That figure is your starting point. From it, subtract the resources that will be available at your death, such as income from investments and savings, your spouse's earnings, death benefits from your company insurance policy, government and private pension benefits.

Armed with this estimate of how much extra income your family will need, you can better judge the figure that an insurance agent will suggest. The money your family will need changes with time, so every year or two, review your financial picture and compare it with the coverage you have.

Safety Net or Savings Plan?

When you buy life insurance, you are buying protection for your dependents from a loss of income if you die prematurely. But life insurance can also be a savings program, an investment opportunity, a source of collateral—or perhaps a waste of money. One thing life insurance is not, is simple. Buying it presents one of the most perplexing financial decisions consumers face: whether to buy, how much to buy, what type to buy, and from whom?

Although Canadians spend billions of dollars annually on various forms of life insurance, few people really understand it. Consumer experts report that buyers of life insurance are less knowledgeable about the product than are the consumers of almost any other product in the country. One reason is that life insurance comes in a baffling array of forms. To find one that matches your needs and your ability to pay, you should begin by learning the vocabulary of life insurance. (See "Basic Life Insurance Language," on the next page.) Then start asking questions about how life insurance can work best for you.

The first consideration is whether you need it at all. Does anyone besides you depend on your income? If not, life insurance is probably the wrong way for you to spend your money. If you have dependents who would not otherwise have enough money to live on should you die, then you probably do need some kind of coverage.

TERM LIFE INSURANCE

Life insurance goes by many names, but comes in two basic varieties: "term insurance" and "cash-value insurance." Term insurance provides protection in much the same way that auto or homeowners insurance policies do: you pay premiums, and in exchange the policy pays a sum of money to your beneficiaries if you die. As the name implies, a term policy is for a set period of time, usually one or five years. When the term ends, so does your coverage unless you renew. You get back nothing—neither your money nor any interest—from the policy. However, for people with average incomes and family responsibilities, term insurance is appropriate.

Basic Life Insurance Language

Almost as many different life insurance policies are available to confused consumers as different kinds of loans. Life insurance is a major financial commitment for most families, so before you start shopping for a policy, familiarize yourself with the basic types, their advantages, and their drawbacks.

Policy type	Features	Advantages	Disadvantages
Term (includes yearly renewable term; decreased term; and level premium term)	Offers protection for a specified period of time. A physical exam is usually required. The insurance premium buys you simple risk coverage. Term insurance is almost always cheaper than whole life or universal life insurance, sometimes about seven or eight times cheaper. Yearly renewable policies cover you for a fixed period of years or until a specified age. With "level term," the annual premium stays the same for a designated period, such as 5 or 20 years, and so does the amount of coverage. Yearly premiums for "decreasing term" are always the same but the amount of coverage decreases annually	Most affordable and simplest form of insurance protection when you are young; easiest to comparison shop. A yearly renewable policy is the cheapest and best type for someone who requires insurance for a short period, With level term policies, you can select the term you want. Level term is best for those who need long-term coverage. Decreasing term insurance is recommended for people who need short-term insurance and whose liabilities such as outstanding loans decrease with time	Premiums increase periodically as you become older; after age 55, term becomes very expensive. In the case of yearly renewable policies, the premium is higher each year. Although decreasing term yearly premiums remain the same, the amount of coverage decreases annually
Whole life	A cash-value policy that covers you for your entire life and offers a guaranteed sum payable to your beneficiaries when you die. Part of your premium pays the actual cost of the insurance risk, part pays the insurer's expenses, and part goes into the reserve fund known as the cash value. The cash value builds up annually but usually at a very low rate of interest	You can borrow against the cash value at favorable rates; you pay the same premium into old age; simplest type of cash-value insurance	Premiums start and remain high because some of the money goes toward cash value; not all policies offer dividends; even if they do, the amount of the dividend is not guaranteed
Universal life	A variation of whole-life insurance that allows flexible premium payments. The premium is first used to pay for insurance protection and expenses. Any excess (the cash-value portion) is put into an interest-bearing account. When money has accumulated, you can increase or decrease the premium—or even skip a year or two—without affecting your coverage	Flexibility in amount of coverage and the amount of premium; you can see how your premium is divided	The return on your cash value is tied to an interest-rate index, and your return will vary; flexibility feature means you may have to put extra money aside each year in premium payments to make sure the death benefit remains at the desired amount

Illustrations of Dubious Worth

A convincing sales tool for insurance agents pitching cash-value life insurance is the so-called policy illustration. This is a computer printout with impressive columns of figures that are supposed to show how much you can expect to pay for a particular policy and what any investment account that comes with it might earn in interest. Can you trust these figures?

Unfortunately, no. In drawing up the illustration, an insurance company can make whatever assumptions it wants about such variables as the interest rates it will be paying 20 years from now. Often such projections are not realistic. The illustration may also be embellished with intimations of premium bonuses that in fact are not guaranteed.

Furthermore, the illustration may fail to show the true costs of your policy—the amount the insurance company takes from your earnings to cover the cost of administering the policy and its investments. And, should you borrow against your cash-value policy in the future, that, too, might darken the rosy picture painted by the illustration.

How can you protect yourself? Be skeptical of optimistic speculation and ask your agent to point out and confirm those factors that are guaranteed in your contract: the premium, the actual cash value, and the death benefit.

CASH-VALUE INSURANCE

"Cash-value insurance" (also known as whole-life or universal insurance) is more complicated because it is essentially a combination of a life insurance coverage and a savings plan. You pay periodic premiums, and the insurer pays a specified death benefit when you die. But the policy, in addition to covering your life, also builds a savings account or a "cash value" that is worth something even before you die. You can borrow against it, cash it in, or, with some policies, invest it. This kind of dual-purpose policy costs more—about eight times the cost of term insurance for a comparable death benefit.

Cash-value insurance seems to offer some advantages: it is forced savings; it can be fully paid after a number of years; you can borrow against the cash value at relatively low interest rates; and the cash value grows at a tax-deferred rate. As life insurance benefits are not considered to be revenue, your policy's beneficiary will not have to pay tax on it.

However, these advantages may not be as glowing as they first appear. For example, you can usually earn more money faster investing it in other ways. Cash-value insurance is sold on the basis of a "policy illustration." Illustrations estimate how much the cash value of your policy will grow and how much interest this money will generate over a period of years. These illustrations are not guaranteed, and, in fact, the interest rates proposed are often overestimated.

Moreover, if you borrow against the cash value, your death benefit is reduced by the amount you borrow. If you die while the loan is outstanding, your heirs will receive less than the policy's face value. Also, although you may be borrowing at a relatively modest rate (usually 5 to 7 percent), bear in mind that you are actually borrowing from yourself. Depending on your situation, it may be more advantageous to borrow from another institution such as a bank or a credit union. You should also find out whether or not you can cash in your cash-value policy. Usually you can, after an initial three-year period.

How to Work With an Agent

Most prospective buyers need help in choosing the right insurance policy. Can you count on an insurance agent to help you understand which is the best one for you? Yes—but only if you do your homework first. When you have come to at least a basic understanding of how much coverage you need and can afford, you are ready to ask for help with filling in the details.

Start with an agent (who is a representative of one particular company) or broker (an agent who represents several insurance companies) who has at least one or two clients you know. Ask the agent how long she has been with the agency she is representing. You will want to establish how long this agent will be available to help you. When you make a major purchase such as life insurance, you obviously want an agent who will be around to service it.

All provinces require that agents be licensed to sell life insurance. Before receiving a license, an agent must follow a course of study (usually given by the insurance company) that covers the elements of contract, personal-risk management and ethics. Complaints about an agent should be taken up with his supervisor, failing that with the Canadian Association of Life Insurance Companies, and as a final step before legal action, communicate with the superintendent of insurance for your province or with the federal superintendent.

Consider also if you want to buy from a "captive" agent, who sells only one company's products, or from an independent broker. Although captive agents can sometimes offer better prices, they must try to sell you their company's policies even if another firm's might suit you better. Independent brokers may sell for six or eight different insurers. You may pay more in insurance costs for their services, but they can pick the best of what each company has to offer.

Insurance agents sell on commission, and that can work against the consumer. Here is why: the cheapest life insurance is term, which pays agents a commission of about 60 percent of your first-year premium. Cash-value (or whole life) insurance is more expensive for the consumer, and therefore more difficult to sell. But for a cash-value insurance policy, an agent may receive a commission as high as 90 percent of your first-year premium.

With that kind of incentive, agents tend to push cash-value policies. If you drop your policy within five years—as about 40 percent of buyers do—"surrender" charges (such as an agent's commission) will absorb most if not all of the money you put in.

HOW AN AGENT HELPS

Nevertheless, an agent can be a big help to you in your search for the right policy. Always ask the agent for a sample policy form to read and request clarification about anything you do not understand. Be sure to ask these questions:

■ What is the financial strength of the insurance company? Has it received top rating from one or more organizations that rate insurance companies?

■ What assumptions are used to calculate the potential value in the savings component of a cash-value policy? These so-

---

Other Routes for Finding Life Insurance

Calling an insurance agent is not the only way to find the right life insurance policy. Here are some other sources to consider:

✔ *Your employer.* Your employer may already provide some insurance as part of your compensation package. If so, you may have the option of purchasing additional life insurance through your employer. Talk with your director of human resources or your corporate agent.

✔ *Non-agented policies.* Some companies now offer both term and cash-value insurance directly to the public. Their policies have lower fees because no sales commission is involved. For a list of such insurance companies, ask your provincial superintendent of insurance.

INSURANCE TO AVOID

About 10 percent of the money Canadians spend on life insurance is unnecessary, say the insurance experts. To keep your coverage cost-effective, avoid policies such as:

1. **Life insurance for children.** Insurance agents sometimes encourage new parents to purchase cash-value insurance for their children as a way of building up a long-term savings account or a college fund. But you do not need to insure your child's life, and you can find better ways to save for her college education.

2. **Travel insurance.** Policies covering death or loss of limbs are often sold through credit cards and even at airport vending machines. The cost is low —less than $20 for a half-million dollar policy—and for good reason. You are far less likely to be killed in a plane than in a car. This insurance is lucrative for the insurer but rarely pays off for you.

3. **"Final expense" policies.** These "low-value" life insurance policies are often pitched to the elderly as a way of paying for funeral costs. However, these policies often do not pay full benefits for the first two years if the policyholder dies from an illness, as most old people do.

called policy illustrations are not guaranteed. (See also "Illustrations of Dubious Worth," page 306.)

- If you are buying a term policy, how often must it be renewed? Can you renew it automatically, or will you have to go through a medical exam again?
- Will the premiums of a term policy go up? If so, by how much? And are those figures merely projected or are they guaranteed?
- If you bought whole-life or other cash-value insurance, how long must you wait to cash it in if you decide to purchase another type of insurance or just need the money?

If after buying a policy you decide you were pressured or misled into buying it—or even if you simply have second thoughts—you may have 2 to 10 days in which to cancel the policy if you signed the contract in your home or somewhere other than the insurance company office. This "grace period" varies from province to province. Anything the agent tells you about the policy should be written into the policy and signed by the agent. If the agent refuses to put it in writing, it is probably because what he told you is inaccurate.

Making Sure Your Policy Keeps Up With You

As your life changes, so should your life insurance. It is important to review your insurance periodically to make sure it reflects your new circumstances. Have you had another child? Have your children all graduated from college? Has your health improved dramatically? Have you been divorced or remarried? These are all milestones that can affect your insurance criteria.

If, for example, you named "my husband" as a beneficiary in the original policy and have since been divorced and remarried, you may want to make it clear that you mean your current spouse, and name him. If you were a smoker and have since given it up, you may be able to get your premiums lowered by as much as one-third. A diabetic who has brought the disease under control, an avid scuba diver who has given up that risky avocation, an alcoholic who has quit drinking—all may be able to show that they have become less of a risk to the insurer, and so get their rates reduced.

If you have a cash-value policy and want to know the effect of rising or falling interest rates on your life insurance investment, you can receive information by sending for an "in-force ledger statement." This is an updated version of the policy illustration you were shown when you first purchased your policy, and it will show exactly how much cash you have built up in

the policy. The company's policyholder service department can also draw up ledger statements to show any changes that would occur if interest on your cash value should drop further or move higher. Thus, there are many reasons why you should check your life insurance policy every year or two to make sure it remains appropriate to your needs. Reading your policy carefully is the only way to be certain what your coverage is and how it might be changed to your advantage.

WHERE TO FIND HELP

Because life insurance is such a complex financial instrument, and because no standardized forms exist for the many different types of life insurance policies, you may need help figuring out what changes you can make to keep your policy timely. The Toronto-based Canadian Association of Life Insurance Companies, the Federal Superintendent of Insurance in Ottawa, or the Canadian Consumers Association, also in Ottawa, may be of help to you. (See RESOURCES, page 469.)

Are You Insurable?

To decide whether to insure you and how much to charge for doing so, an insurance company goes through a process called underwriting. An underwriter tries to estimate how much it will cost the company to insure your life by learning as much as possible about your background, your present state of health, and your habits. For example, an underwriter may want to know if you told the truth about your smoking habits or if you have a spotty driving record. Statistics tell the underwriter that these two habits can shorten your life—and thus increase the company's costs for insuring it.

Your insurance application includes a waiver that allows the insurer to check your background. The more insurance you apply for, the more extensive the checking process will be. Usually the waiver states that information can be passed on to the Medical Information Bureau (MIB), a giant clearinghouse of information for the insurance industry.

SEARCHING FOR FLAWS

The MIB is usually the first stop in an underwriter's background check. The bureau, a consortium of about 750 of the largest life insurance companies in the United States and Canada, keeps records on some 15 million people who have medical conditions or other factors that could affect their longevity. The MIB then sells this data to insurance companies, which use it to discover false or incomplete information on insurance applications.

Coming Clean On Your Insurance Application

Much is at stake, for both you and the insurer, when you fill out an application for life insurance. How you answer the questions about your health, previous medical conditions, and lifestyle will affect whether your application is accepted and what rates you will be charged. Giving untrue or incomplete answers—even slightly understating your age, for example—can have serious consequences.

If you lied or deliberately omitted important information—such as whether or not you smoke—and if you then die, the insurer can deny all or part of your claim. Your survivors will get back the premiums you paid but will not get the substantial sum you wanted them to have.

Your application will probably have a provision authorizing the insurer to check into your background. If you had a substantial amount of insurance, the insurance company will most likely make an investigation to determine if all the information you gave on your application was true before making payment. It should be noted that even in the case of suicide, however, a company must pay the death benefit, if the suicide happened more than two years after the policy went into effect.

Insurers cast a wide net to fish for information about applicants. Insurers hire investigators to get records from doctors, hospitals, financial institutions, medical labs, employers, and motor vehicle licensing bureaus. If the underwriter discovers a condition that bears on your health or longevity, he sends a report to the MIB.

What are the chances of your being in the MIB files? The bureau says that out of 10 applicants, it will have a record on only one or two. It also claims that fewer than one percent of consumers who send for their MIB records find them to be inaccurate or incomplete. (The MIB's policy is to eliminate any reports more than seven years old.)

Insurers who uncover a potential medical problem in an MIB search are prohibited by the MIB's rules from making eligibility decisions that are based only on that information. The insurer must then conduct its own independent investigation to confirm the report.

As with credit bureaus, the MIB is required by law to either verify or remove information that you dispute. To receive a free copy of your file, call or write to the MIB. (For the address and telephone number, see RESOURCES, page 469.)

When You Think You Want to Switch Insurance Policies

Whether or not to change life insurers after you have been with a firm for several years is a thorny question. Whatever your reasons for thinking of switching—you are worried about your company's financial stability, for example, or you want a different type of policy—you should proceed with caution, because switching can be costly. Here are some guidelines:

• Consult the agent who sold you your current policy, or another agent from the same company. With their help, you may find a way to modify your present policy to achieve the coverage you want and need.

• Before committing yourself, discuss your plans with at least two insurance agents and let them review each other's advice. That way you can avoid making a bad decision based solely on sales pitches or unrealistic policy projections.

• Be wary of agents who approach you to suggest a switch from your old policy to a new one. First of all, you may have to pay a new sales commission. Agents do much of their most lucrative commission business this way.

• Insurance experts caution that you will probably take a loss if you switch a whole-life insurance policy that you have held for less than 10 years to a new company. To assess the costs of making the switch, your calculations should include how much you have already paid in, the cash value of the policy, and the insurer's surrender charges. Don't forget that if your cash value is more than the cost of all the premiums you paid in, you will owe income taxes on the difference.

• You can usually transfer the cash value from your old policy to a new policy tax free if the transfer is made directly by one company to another without the cash value ever being in your hands.

• Switching to cheaper term insurance may well be a sensible move. If you find a lower-priced policy that suits your needs, consider it seriously.

• Never cash in your current policy until you get a new one. If your health has deteriorated over the years, you may not pass the medical exam a new insurer is likely to require.

If Your Insurer Fails

The peace of mind that life insurance is supposed to buy can disappear quickly if your life insurer gets into financial trouble. Many people were stunned when one of Canada's oldest insurance companies, Confederation Life, failed in August 1994. Unfortunately, when such a catastrophe happens, a policyholder has few rights and can face long delays in getting both money and information.

Although most of the country's 150 life insurance companies are in no danger of going under, every policyholder should understand what can happen if an insurer fails. One possibility is that another company will buy the failed company's policies. In that case, the insured's death benefit would be protected, since insurers and regulators make paying death benefits in full a top priority.

But the new company could raise premiums or lower the interest rates used to build up savings in a cash-value policy. Options to withdraw your cash value may be limited or suspended.

If no other company steps in, a backup system called a guaranty fund that all insurance companies participate in may come to the rescue. Through the fund, licensed insurers promise that if one of them fails, the others will put up money to reimburse the failed insurer's customers.

These funds usually have no assets, however; they must collect from other insurers to cover the policyholders of the failed company, a process which can take years. In addition, some guaranty funds have limits to their coverage, typically $100,000 for individual cash-value policies, $200,000 for death benefits, and $200,000 for all claims combined.

The 214-member Canadian Life and Health Insurance Corporation (CompCorp) guarantees policyholders up to $200,000 repayment. Many policyholders of failed insurance companies have discovered that the guaranty funds fell far short of the amounts they expected their policies to deliver.

WHAT IF TROUBLE LOOMS?

If you see trouble looming, you will find no easy solutions. Changing to another insurance company can be time-consuming and expensive. (See also "When You Think You Want to Switch Insurance Policies," page 310.)

One possible alternative is to take out a loan against your policy (if it is a cash-value policy) and put the money into a safer investment. Of course you will have to pay interest to the insurer, but at least the money will be where you can get it if the company fails.

Rating the Raters of Insurers

How can you be sure your insurance company is financially sound? Consumer experts advise you to check with an organization such as Standard & Poor's, A.M. Best Co., Moody's, or Duff and Phelps that rates the financial health of individual insurers. Here is how the major insurance raters operate: Each assigns a letter ranking to a company based on its estimate of the firm's financial stability. But the rating services vary in how they interpret financial data the insurers supply to them. One rater gave an A+ to a major insurer just 10 days before the company failed. Also confusing is the different grading system each rater uses; an A– from one service may not mean the same as A– from another.

In order to make the best-informed choice, stick to insurers that have received a top rating from at least two of the major insurance raters. Also, avoid companies rated less than A+ and triple-A by any of the rating agencies. Even with no guarantees, high marks are still better than low ones.

Remember, too, that the Federal Superintendent of Insurance supervises federally registered insurance companies, which most insurance companies are. To conduct business in Canada, insurance companies must comply with certain solvency standards and submit to systematic inspection of their books by the superintendent's staff. Provincial superintendents of insurance operate in similar fashion with provincially registered insurance companies.

INVESTING YOUR MONEY

You have worked hard, borrowed wisely, and saved a bit. Now it is time to make that extra money grow. Learn how to protect yourself from the pitfalls of investing.

Investment Basics

Like cash stashed under the mattress, money in the bank is safe—but earns very little. If you want greater reward from your savings, you will have to invest elsewhere. The financial world offers a daunting variety of investment prospects, and the law provides a number of consumer safeguards. One of the most basic of these is that any firm or individual who accepts investment funds from the public has an obligation to manage the money responsibly. The law cannot, however, protect you from yourself. Understanding the basic types of financial investments and their degrees of risk will help you avoid mistakes. (Other investment opportunities also abound, ranging from real estate to collectibles; here we will consider the chief financial instruments that are available.)

Financial investments fall into one of two categories: bonds or stocks. The difference between them is the difference between being a lender and being an owner. When you invest in bonds, you are really lending your money to a business or a government. The borrower pays you interest on the money you lend until a specific date, when you expect to get your money back. By investing in stocks, you become an owner of shares in a business. The value of your investment depends on the company's success. You share in the profits of a company in the form of dividends as well as any future increase in the stock price. Stocks are traditionally a riskier investment than bonds, but over time, stocks have offered greater monetary rewards.

TYPES OF INVESTMENTS AND THEIR RISKS

Here are brief descriptions of some common investment vehicles, their relative benefits and risks:

Treasury bills (T-Bills) are short-term notes of a year or less (often 91 + 182 days) that are auctioned every Tuesday by the Bank of Canada. Because they are backed by the Canadian government, they are very secure and are usually bought by banks, investment dealers, and other financial institutions. The average yield of the 91-day T-Bill determines the bank rate—the interest rate the Bank of Canada charges the chartered banks for money they borrow. The chartered banks usually add another one percent to establish the prime rate, the rate the banks charge their best customers. Instead of offering interest, T-Bills are sold at a discount. This discount is in effect an interest rate and is treated as interest for tax purposes. For example, if you buy a one-year T-Bill with a face value of $1,000, you would pay perhaps $925: when it matures one year later, you would get $1,000, in effect an interest rate of 7.5 percent or $75 profit. Treasury bills are easily bought and sold by banks, trust companies, and securities brokers.

Government of Canada bonds (not to be confused with Canada Savings Bonds) are both a sound investment and a money-raising method for the government. Underwritten by investment dealers, who sell them to other financial institutions and to the public, these bonds take a long time to mature—sometimes 5 to 20 years. However, they are easily traded. These bonds may be retractable or extendible. Retractable bonds can be cashed in before maturity, a good move if interest rates are rising. With an extendible bond, you can lock in the interest rate, say 7 percent for an extended period, even if interest rates drop.

Canada Savings Bonds (CSBs), perhaps the most popular investment for Canadians, are issued every November by the federal government. Cashable after three months, they have fixed rates of interest. When interest rates rise above what certain CSBs are earning, however, the government often increases the interest on these bonds so that bondholders will not cash them in to buy more lucrative investments. CSBs are issued in many denominations from $100 to $10,000 and are only available to individuals or estates. The amount a person may purchase from one series is usually limited to about $100,000. CSBs are nontransferable; they cannot be sold by one buyer to another. They can often be purchased by way of a payroll deduction plan, whereby every payday a certain amount is deducted from your pay to purchase the bond.

Provincial and municipal bonds are offered from time to time to institutions and individuals by various provinces and municipalities. Somewhat riskier than Canada Savings Bonds, they offer higher interest, but may not be as readily redeemable as CSBs, and are more difficult to trade on the bank market. Bond issues by government utilities such as Ontario Hydro are guaranteed by the provincial government. Unlike provincial bonds, municipal bonds are not always safe investments. Interest earned on municipal bonds is taxable as is interest on all other types of bonds.

Corporate bonds are issued by private corporations as a way to raise large sums of money, usually for capital expansion or for diversifying debt. If the corporation is highly rated by agen-

Tips for Fighting Investment Fraud

Canadians lose millions of dollars annually to con men who talk them into investing in ventures that do not live up to the advertising or are simply nonexistent. The swindlers mimic the approaches of legitimate firms, but they usually tip their hands in one way or another:

✔ *Large-profit expectations.* A swindler might convince you that buying stock in a local cable company will be profitable since cable companies are hot. However, he then exaggerates its value and encourages you to buy more than you should by suggesting the potential profit is far greater than he could possibly guarantee.

✔ *Low risk.* The con man becomes impatient or angry if you question the risk involved in an investment that he insists is safe. Visionary Cable is so hot, he insists, that your investment risk is virtually nil.

✔ *Urgency.* The swindler pushes you to rush into the investment. Unless you invest in Visionary Cable now, he says, the opportunity to buy at a good price will be gone. If you ask for a prospectus, he ridicules you, saying you will only lose out on a good deal if you take time to do research.

✔ *Confidence.* To secure your trust, the swindler conveys the notion that he is doing you a favor by offering you this investment opportunity, often warning that other people will be interested if you are not.

cies such as Standard & Poor's or Moody's, they usually pay slightly more interest than do Government of Canada Bonds, at relatively low risk. Low-rated corporations offer even higher rates but usually carry higher risk. If interest rates drop, a corporation may call in its bonds and give you the cash amount ("call price") promised when issued.

Corporate debentures are issued by companies, pay annual fixed interest, and are tradable, but they are guaranteed by the company's securities and accounts receivable instead of its fixed assets, as is the case with corporate bonds. Companies may also offer **corporate convertible debentures** as well as **corporate convertible bonds.** These often interest investors because the purchaser has a stated period within which to buy a stated number of the company's common shares. If the shares go up in value, the value of the bond or debenture does too, and you have the option of converting the bond or debenture into company shares. If the value of the shares drops, you are still guaranteed the stated annual interest rate.

Stocks represent shares of ownership in a company. Many high-quality stocks pay owners dividends—cash returns on their investments. Stocks may be common or preferred. A common stock carries the most risk and the greatest potential for profit. The holder of each common stock usually has one vote at annual meetings. Preferred stocks or shares do not usually confer voting rights, but they guarantee a fixed dividend. Dividends on shares, even preferred shares, are paid on the company's after-tax income.

Buy an annuity cheap, and make your life interesting to yourself and everybody else that watches the speculation.

CHARLES DICKENS

Martin Chuzzlewit

Three Rules on Risk

The point of investing rather than saving money is to make a bigger profit. But that means taking risks, and in general, the amount of money you can make is relative to the amount of risk you take. Here are some basic ground rules about risk:

• **Never risk money you cannot afford to lose.** For example, if you are retired and depend on your old age pension and Canada Pension Plan benefits to break even, it may be unwise to take risks with whatever extra money you have saved over the years. Or, if you have accumulated a nest egg to pay for a major expense, such as a child's college tuition, you may want to switch that money out of riskier investments, such as stocks, into a federally guaranteed savings bond so that you can be sure it is there when the college bills come due.

• **Never invest in anything you don't understand.** In order to invest sensibly, you do not need to understand all the intricacies of the stock market's operation, but you should certainly understand how *your* money is being put to work. If the salesperson cannot explain the terms of the investment (the relative riskiness of a particular stock, for example) to you clearly and briefly, don't buy it.

• **Never exceed your tolerance for risk.** Some people are temperamentally capable of riding the ups and downs of the stock market, while others find themselves unable to sleep at night because they worry that their investments might take a dive on the next day's market. Only you can determine how much risk you can handle—but it is the responsibility of your stockbroker to explain clearly how much risk is likely to be involved in a particular transaction.

The People's Choice—Mutual Funds

Mutual funds are investment vehicles: mutual fund companies pool your money with that of thousands of other individuals and invest it in an assortment of stocks, bonds, and other securities. The numbers and diversity result in a considerable amount of safety, but mutual funds are not guaranteed and, like the securities in which they invest, the funds will fluctuate in value with changing conditions in the financial markets. For investors accustomed to watching their savings grow, however modestly, in a bank account, this factor can be unsettling.

HOW TO CHOOSE A FUND

With some 600 funds to choose from, you may decide you need help. One way to get it is to pay a broker or financial planner an up-front sales commission or "load" to do the selecting for you. Loads range from 2 to 9 percent, depending on the investment. If you invest less than $10,000, the load or commission would be about 9 percent, but would drop to 2 percent if you invest $300,000 or more. As a general rule you should not pay more than about 5 percent commission when buying shares in a mutual fund, and if you deal with a discount broker such as Green Line Investor Services (available through any Toronto Dominion bank branch), the commission is about 2½ percent.

Mutual funds offer "front-end" and "back-end" loads. When you choose a front-end load fund, the commission is deducted from your investment at the outset. So if you invest $1,000 in a 9 percent frontload fund and the fund returns a 10 percent performance that year, you will indeed earn 10 percent, but not on your full $1,000. You will earn 10 percent on only $910, because the sales load gets taken out before your money is invested. Back-end or deferred loads are taken out of the value of your shares when you sell them. Since all your money gets invested, a back-end load fund is usually preferable to the front-end variety.

Typically mutual fund commissions are charged on a sliding scale, decreasing the longer you keep your money invested. There are also mutual funds that do not charge any commission to buy or sell your shares but these no-load funds come with little broker services. As a result, you may not be told that your fund is underperforming, or that your money should be transferred to another fund that is outperforming the market.

Bear in mind, too, that some no-load funds charge management fees that are much higher than those for managing load funds, and these management fees may even be higher than the load or commission charged by no-load funds.

More Facts About Mutual Funds

Mutual funds may be purchased from banks, as well as from trust, insurance, and private companies. However, banks and private companies will not usually sell each other's mutual funds, since each institution is competing for your money. If you want to sell your shares, and no outside buyer is available, the fund itself will buy them back. Here are some other points:

✔ ***Investing is easy.*** Most funds allow people to invest as little as $50 or $100. As well, investments may be through pre-authorized debits from your bank account or automatic payroll deductions.

✔ ***No FDIC guarantee.*** Mutual funds are not guaranteed by the Federal Deposit Insurance Corporation.

✔ ***Diverse portfolio.*** Aside from an historic high return, the main advantage of mutual funds is that your money is placed in a variety of investments and this diversity of investment is managed by skilled and knowledgeable financial managers.

✔ ***International equities.*** Since other economies often grow faster than Canada's, some financial advisers recommend that you put 10 to 20 percent of your investment in international equity funds.

Because of the success of mutual funds in Canada in recent years—investments such as The Trimark Fund, Templeton Growth Fund, and the Altamira Equity Fund have had average annual gains in the 15 percent range—mutual fund investments have exploded from less than $5 billion in 1980 to some $130 billions by the mid-nineties and a projected $200 billion by the year 2000.

If you wish to keep track of how various mutual funds are performing, the *Financial Post, The Globe and Mail* and other newspapers and periodicals publish extensive mutual fund listings as well as monthly comparative surveys.

MONITORING YOUR FUND

To calculate exactly how much you have made or lost on your mutual fund investment, compare the value of your holdings in the fund today against the dollar amount you originally invested, plus dollars reinvested, if any, minus any loans. First, consult your most recent fund statement to see how many

Unraveling Mutual Funds

Mutual funds are one of the most popular investment instruments on the market today, but they present a mystifying assortment of choices. Some invest in bonds and mortgage funds, others in company shares (equity funds) and others in real estate, and resources such as oil, gas and gold. Since funds can be conservative, moderate, or aggressive, many people opt for a balanced portfolio—a mixture of investments in resource-based shares, money market plans, bonds, and Canadian and international equities.

• **Labor-sponsored funds.** These relatively new funds came about through tax legislation aimed at promoting Canadian business ventures. They provide enormous tax savings for people in high-tax brackets, but there is a negative side. Your money is tied up for a specified period (usually five years) and it is invested in new companies, which always have a high failure risk. The largest labor-sponsored fund currently available is the Working Ventures Canadian Fund, sponsored by the Canadian Federation of Labour; similar funds are sponsored by provincial labor groups.

• **Equity funds.** Such funds invest in common shares of Canadian and/or Canadian, U.S., and international companies. Growth is the primary objective. You can make large profits with equity funds but you also risk losing a large part of your investment.

• **Dividend funds.** Dividend funds invest in preferred shares and high-quality common stocks. They provide good after-tax income (the issuing company has already paid tax prior to issuing the dividend so the dividend is taxed at a lower rate

in your hands) and you can expect moderate growth.

• **Mortgage market funds.** These funds invest in a range of real estate properties with a view to offering attractive income and moderate growth as real estate values increase. Declining property values in many regions of Canada have made these a somewhat risky investment in recent years but such funds may prove profitable in the long run.

• **Sector equity or speciality funds.** These funds invest in specific commodities such as gold or precious metals, or specific industries such as telecommunications or computers. Investments may also be in oil or gas or forest products. Such investments are volatile, allowing for large profits but also large losses.

• **International funds.** Investments are made in companies and industries in the Far East and in developing countries. Historically, these funds have provided rapid growth but they can also be quite risky.

shares you now own. Then, look up the fund's net asset value (sometimes called the "sell" or "bid" price) in the financial section of a major newspaper, or, if you are computer-savvy, through one of the popular on-line tracking services. You might also call the fund's 800 number.

Multiply the net asset value by the number of shares you own to figure out the present value of your investment. It is important to keep track and to record how much you invest, particularly if you don't buy fund shares at one time.

You and Your Stockbroker

Until the advent of mutual funds, the only way to invest in securities was to buy individual stocks and bonds, which is still done by millions of investors. Stocks, bonds, and certain mutual funds are purchased through a stockbroker, whose basic job is to place orders to buy and sell on the various exchanges where they are traded. A broker, however, is also expected to advise customers on the general state of the market and to make specific investment suggestions. It is here that misunderstandings with, or incompetence on the part of, the broker can cause trouble for the client. You can minimize such problems by choosing your stockbroker carefully in the first place. If worse comes to worst, there are regulations and legal mechanisms in place to help resolve disputes between you and your broker.

MAKE YOUR GOALS CLEAR

Every investor should understand that the traditional broker, known as a full-service stockbroker, faces an inherent conflict of interest in advising clients because her livelihood depends on the commissions earned by buying and selling. That can be an incentive for brokers to push high-commission financial products, such as limited partnerships, which invest in real estate or gas and oil holdings—and are often highly risky. To protect yourself, make sure your broker understands your long-term investment goals, as well as how much risk you want to take. Confirm in a letter how you and your broker have agreed to handle your account, and have your broker initial it.

Pay special attention to the account form, which must be filled out by either you or your broker before you can open an account with an investment firm. Aside from your name, address, occupation, net worth, and annual revenue, there will be a description of what type of account you want. In a cash account all purchases are paid in cash, whereas in a margin account the broker buys your securities partly with your money and the rest with the broker's money which bears interest as does any loan. Other parts of the agreement set out your objectives, such as income, long-term growth, or speculation, or a mixture of the three. The agreement should also indicate how the broker will transact business on your behalf—by telephone order, by written orders, or at the broker's discretion.

You will also be asked questions about your past experience with investments. Never exaggerate your income or experience on the account form. Unless a broker knows these things about you, she cannot suggest investments that are appropriate to your situation. If there is a dispute about an investment you feel was wrong for you—if, for example, your broker puts you into risky junk bonds (bonds with a low investment grade from the rating agencies) when what you needed was something safe and steady for your imminent retirement—you would have compelling evidence in the account form, as well as the letter of agreement, that the broker did not act in your best interest.

For any recommendation your broker makes, ask how it will meet your investment goals. Ask for research material, and read it before you decide. Let your broker know you are keeping dated notes of every conversation. Be aware that orders are taken according to the number of shares, not the monetary amount. Thus an order for 500 Bell Canada refers to 500 shares, not a $500 investment in Bell Canada shares. After the transaction you will receive a confirmation slip and then a monthly statement. Review both to make sure the price and quantity of all transactions are listed correctly.

SETTLING DISPUTES ABOUT YOUR ACCOUNT

If any dispute arises about your account, try to resolve it promptly and in writing. Say your broker did not sell the shares on the day you asked they be traded, but the next day. First, take the matter to the broker or her manager. If no help is forthcoming, the next step might be arbitration. When you opened your account, you were probably required to sign a form agreeing to submit any disputes to arbitration instead of filing a lawsuit. In arbitration, a panel of one to five people—usually lawyers, accountants, brokers, or businesspeople—reviews the evidence and decides the case. Arbitration is usually a much quicker and less expensive way to resolve a dispute than going into litigation. However, arbitration awards are final. If you are dissatisfied, you cannot pursue the matter through the courts.

DISCOUNT BROKERS

Until the industry was deregulated, all brokerage firms were required to charge the same fixed-rate commission. Today, each firm can determine what commission schedules to use, and this competition in fees has resulted in the rise of discount brokerage firms. Like traditional brokerages, many discount firms do business nationwide and have 800 numbers as well as local offices. Discount brokerage services are now offered by all the major chartered banks and most trust companies, and the largest Canadian discount broker is Green Line, a subsidiary of the Toronto Dominion Bank.

Discount brokerage firms pay their brokers a straight salary, not commissions, and fees are substantially lower than what full-service brokers charge—often 50 to 80 percent less. Discount brokers do not offer investment advice; however, some may provide research reports on securities for an additional fee. If you are willing to do your own research and be responsible for decisions on what securities to buy or sell, your most economical choice would be a discount broker. To find one, contact the Investment Dealers Association, which requires members to meet strict financial criteria.

Do You Need a Financial Planner?

Financial planning is a relatively new profession, and its standards of ethics and conduct are not well regulated or defined. So the consumer must be both aware and wary: regulators estimate that financial planners have caused consumers to lose millions of dollars. Still, many investors feel more secure having an individual professional adviser planning the best financial strategies. A good planner is trained to devise a campaign to help you achieve

If Trouble Brews in Your Brokerage Account

If you discover an error in your statement, find that your broker bought a stock without asking you, or suffer unexplained losses, you must take action quickly. A delay can weaken the credibility of your claim. Here are steps to take to resolve the problem:

• **Contact your broker.** Often an error may be caused by a computer glitch or miscommunication between you and your broker. Whatever the cause, call your broker immediately. Ask for an explanation of the transaction or for a correction to be made. Follow up with a letter stating clearly what you want the broker to do; for example, "Please sell the 100 shares of XYZ Corporation, and restore my money to my account."

• **Inform the manager.** If the broker's response is unsatisfactory, write a letter to the branch manager outlining your complaint and include a copy of the letter you sent to your broker, along with copies of any records that support your claim. Request a written explanation.

• **Contact your provincial securities commission.** If the brokerage firm does not respond, or if it rejects your complaint, write to your province's securities commission. Include copies of all your correspondence with the broker and the brokerage firm as well as copies of any records that prove your claim. The commission may be able to solve the problem within a few weeks. You can also contact the Investment Dealers Association which works together with the various stock exchanges and securities commissions.

• **Try arbitration or take legal action.** If these measures bring no success, but you still think you have a case, you might consider taking it to arbitration. (See YOUR RIGHTS IN ACTION, page 450.)

QUESTIONS FOR A PROSPECTIVE PLANNER

Many financial planners offer a free consultation. That is the time to evaluate your candidate and judge whether you will be able to work together. Don't be bashful—after all, it is your money at stake. Here are some direct questions to ask:

1. What is your educational and professional background, and what training for financial planning have you had?

2. Are you a Certified Financial Planner, a member of the Canadian Order of Chartered Accountants, or a member of any other professional groups dealing with finance?

3. What types of services do you provide, and what kind of financial products do you recommend?

4. Will you disclose in advance of the presentation any commissions you receive for selling particular products, as well as your general fees? If no fee is charged you can bet that this "planner" works for an insurance company or mutual fund and will try to sell his company's products.

5. Will you give as references three clients you have counseled for at least two years?

6. May I see some sample plans you have made for other investors?

your immediate or future financial goals and can be a great help in piloting you through unfamiliar waters. Many accountants and tax lawyers may act as financial planners as do some officers in trust companies or banks. Just be prepared to do a thorough background check before hiring a planner.

In most provinces, anyone can be a financial planner—no tests are required. But a planner who charges fees for securities investment advice must register as an investment adviser with the Securities Commission. The Investment Dealers Association also works with stock exchanges and securities commissions to ensure high standards of conduct from its members.

Financial advisers charge for their services either on an hourly rate or a percentage of the funds under their management or a set fee for preparing a personalized financial plan. Most planners are compensated through fees, commissions, or a combination of both. A fee-only planner is paid on an hourly or retainer basis, and sometimes charges a fee per job. A commissioned planner is paid through sales that generate commissions. The more financial products you purchase, the more money your planner will make. For that reason, you should be especially wary of stockbrokers and insurance salespeople who call themselves financial consultants or financial planners.

A Planner's Risky Advice

PROBLEM
For advice on supplementing a pension from their savings, James and Laura consulted a certified planner at a local brokerage firm. Although the couple requested low-risk investments that would provide steady income, the planner instead put most of their funds into high-risk limited partnerships, telling them they needed the extra income the partnerships would provide. The partnerships failed, and James and Laura were left with less than half their original investment.

ACTION
Because the planner took unsuitable risks for retirees who needed conservative investments, he violated his role as a "fiduciary," a person legally obliged to act in the best interest of a client. James and Laura had a fair claim for restitution. They wrote to the brokerage's branch manager, explaining the situation and emphasizing their lack of knowledge about investing and their reliance on the planner to explain the risks and rewards. The manager, who had had similar though less serious complaints about the broker, arranged for the firm to reimburse James and Laura, and the planner was fired. Had James and Laura not received a satisfactory solution, they could have filed a claim for arbitration with the stock exchange of which their brokerage is a member. They could also have filed a complaint on the planner with their provincial securities commission and with the Investment Dealers Association. As a last resort they could have sued the planner and his employer for negligence and breach of fiduciary duty.

INCOME TAXES

Taxpaying time can be less painful if you understand the rules of the game and know your rights when dealing with the tax collector.

What Revenue Canada Owes You

The taxes levied on corporations and individuals are the major source of federal government revenues. All Canadian residents who have spent 183 or more days here in the previous year, as well as Canadian military personnel and diplomatic staff stationed overseas, must file an income tax return for that year.

Most citizens are all too well aware of their annual duty to file a tax return, which reports all taxable income as well as deductions and certain nontaxable income. But not everyone knows that the government also has certain responsibilities toward you, the taxpayer.

- **Free help in preparing returns.** You have the right to information about the tax laws and guidance in filling out your tax forms. Revenue Canada offers free publications and walk-in tax help at many of its offices.
- **Privacy and confidentiality.** You have the right to privacy; in other words, Revenue Canada must keep your personal and financial information confidential.
- **Payment of only the required tax.** You have the right to plan your personal finances so that you will pay the least amount of tax due under the law.
- **Fair collection of tax.** If you disagree with the amount Revenue Canada claims, you have the right to dispute the assessment.
- **Representation.** In dealings with Revenue Canada, you have the right to represent yourself, have someone accompany you or, with Revenue Canada approval, have someone represent you in your absence at an audit.

If questioned by Revenue Canada, you have the right to know why it wants the information, how it will be used, and what might happen if you do not divulge it. The employees of Revenue Canada are required to explain and protect these taxpayer rights at all times. If you have a complaint about your treatment by Revenue Canada representatives, write to the district director for your area. You will find the number in the government pages of your telephone directory.

Be Your Own Tax Preparer

No one likes preparing tax returns, and some people cannot cope with the intricacies of their tax situation. That is why so many people turn to a professional for help. But there are real advantages to doing the return yourself. If you have a straightforward return—one without complicated deductions, for example —you can both save money and learn helpful ins and outs of the tax code by filling it out yourself. If you operate a computer, there is software available to help you complete your return.

The comprehensive tax guide sent with your tax form has most of the information you need. Revenue Canada also publishes some 25 other booklets, available at no charge, on topics such as "Canadian Residents Going Down South," "Northern Resident Deductions," and "Preparing Returns for Deceased Persons." Some of these may be precisely what you need to file your income tax return. You can obtain a list of all the booklets and order those you need by calling your district office of Revenue Canada.

Getting a Helping Hand

Although some taxpayers are undaunted by the chore of filing their own returns, you may be among the many who need both the expertise and reassurance of a professional. Reliance on a tax preparer may be even more necessary if Revenue Canada decides your return needs to be examined or audited. (See also "How to Survive an Audit," page 325.) No matter who prepares your return, Revenue Canada still holds you responsible for its accuracy. Thus it is vital that you hire someone who is both trustworthy and competent. Tax practitioners fall into four main categories:

■ **Preparers** generally have the least amount of training, and many of them work part-time for the major tax preparation firms. If you have an uncomplicated return but do not want to prepare it yourself, a preparer can be the least costly alternative. But although the average tax-return preparer is per-

Types of Audits

Every tax return is scored by a Revenue Canada computer program that compares it with the typical return: the more it deviates from the norm, the higher its score. Returns that score too high get marked for further examination, which usually involves one of the three conventional noncriminal audits: correspondence, office, or field. Revenue Canada also makes random audits.

• **Correspondence audits.** Audits by mail generally involve fairly straightforward problems, such as verifying itemized deductions and real estate sales. Revenue Canada will mail you a letter explaining the problem and citing the recalculated tax. You may be asked to pay more, or to complete additional forms. You may also be requested to send copies of receipts or other documentation to substantiate certain statements and figures in your return. Remember that Revenue Canada is capable of human error, and frequently makes them. Don't be alarmed if you receive a request for substantiation on your return. If you have the evidence to support your figures, the chances are that will be the end of it.

• **Office audits.** You are summoned by a form letter requesting you to call your local Revenue Canada district office for an appointment for an audit. At this stage, an agent has gone over your return and has compiled a portfolio of questionable items that he wants to examine more closely. Often the notification letter notes the sections of your return that are under scrutiny, and the letter may also include a list of documents you are requested to take with you to the audit, such as receipts and canceled checks, to substantiate your return.

• **Field audits.** If your return has complex problems, particularly business assessments, a Revenue Canada field agent will handle the case. Again, questions will have been generated from the Revenue Canada service center and passed on to the field agent for review. The agent will notify you by mail that you are being audited and will inform you of topics being challenged. The field agent will arrange a time to visit you at home or your business. The agent will address a list of items that Revenue Canada wants to look at, but the audit is by no means limited to that list; the agent can examine any area of your tax return.

• **Random selection.** Revenue Canada selects unfortunate taxpayers at random every three years for this program, designed to develop profiles of "typical" returns for various levels of income in Canada. A random selection audit is painstakingly thorough and requires you to provide documentation of every line of your tax return.

mitted to accompany you in responding to a Revenue Canada inquiry to explain how your return was prepared, she cannot represent you. In other words, she cannot present substantive legal arguments on your behalf.

- **Chartered accountants (CAs)** must go through lengthy training and exams to receive the CA credential. Continuing education is also required. CA fees can be high—as much as $300 an hour or more in larger firms or for the services of a partner—so consider them only if you have a fairly complex return or when you need advice on other accounting and financial matters beyond your taxes.
- **Tax lawyers** do various types of tax-related work, including tax planning and resolving disputes with Revenue Canada. In view of the high fees charged by tax lawyers, consider this option only if you have more than $10,000 at stake in your tax problem.

To simplify your preparer's job and to save money, keep your records organized throughout the year. Make sure the figures you supplied to your tax preparer match those on the return. Never sign a completed form without checking it over first. If the return gets lost, you could be charged a late-filing penalty if you owe money, so file your tax return by certified mail. A certified or registered mail receipt is the only proof of filing that is accepted by Revenue Canada. You can also file electronically in some instances. Nevertheless, Revenue Canada will usually accept a reasonable explanation for tardiness.

Penalties and Interest

One of the most frightening aspects of tax filing is the prospect of penalties and fines Revenue Canada can impose for late filing or underpayment of taxes. Suppose you go to the hospital in early April for a serious emergency operation. A few months later you discover that Revenue Canada has branded you a delinquent taxpayer and is not only charging interest on your unpaid income tax but is also demanding a penalty for failing to file on time. You know you have to pay your taxes, but what about the penalties and interest that have accrued because you neglected to file on time?

The bad news is that if you owe money, you will probably have to pay interest for late payment—Revenue Canada is usually quite firm about this. The penalty for late filing is steep: $25 per day of default up to $2,500 plus 7 percent of the tax owing per month, although the $25 per day penalty is rarely used. The good news is that if Revenue Canada owes you a

---

123
FINDING HELP FOR YOUR RETURNS

Be sure to get answers to these questions before hiring a tax preparer:

1. Are you available year-round? A preparer who is available only at tax time may be unable to answer questions when you need to ask them. Also, if you hire a preparer who works alone, make sure she has a backup.

2. What is your fee? The charge for completing a tax return ranges from $30 to $200 an hour, depending on the qualifications of the preparer. But the amount you pay should never exceed the value to you of the service in terms of reduced taxes, refunded taxes, or in relation to the time and tax knowledge required.

3. What is your professional education and experience? Determine whether the preparer is a chartered accountant or has a degree in accountancy. Ask also about his experience.

4. Will you go with me to Revenue Canada if I am audited? Anyone who prepares your return should be willing to go with you to an audit. (However, an uncertified preparer cannot legally represent you.) You will probably be charged a standard hourly rate for this service. Request that the preparer repay you for any Revenue Canada charges due to the preparer's error. A reputable chartered accountant will do this—but it would not hurt to get the promise in writing.

refund, you will not be charged a penalty; and even if you owe taxes, you may not have to pay the interest. Revenue Canada may reduce or eliminate a penalty if you show that you had a "reasonable cause" for failing to observe the tax law. Some examples of reasonable cause are:

■ If you or an immediate family member is seriously ill, or dies.
■ If you are unavoidably out of the country.
■ If your place of business or records are destroyed by fire or other disaster.
■ If you could not determine the amount of tax due for reasons beyond your control, such as loss of your T4 form.
■ If your ability to pay was seriously impaired by civil disturbances—the business was looted during a riot.
■ If you, despite ordinary business care and prudence, have insufficient funds to pay the taxes.

REQUESTING A PENALTY ABATEMENT

Upon rising from your sickbed, you should immediately file your income taxes. If you anticipate that you will be late filing, you may ask for an extension and pay an estimated amount due. (See also "If You Cannot Pay What You Owe," page 327.) If you have received a notice that you are being charged a penalty for late payment, contact the Revenue Canada service center that sent the notice and ask for an abatement.

Include copies of any documents that help prove your claim, such as a doctor's statement or, depending upon the reason for your delay, a fire department report, an insurance claim, or the death certificate of a family member. This written proof will help ensure that your request receives serious consideration. You might also enclose payment for the underlying taxes, and be sure to indicate that the payment does not include the penalty. In the lower left-hand corner of your cheque or money order, write your social insurance number and the tax year for which you are paying. This at least will stop the accrual of interest on the amount you owe. If you get another penalty notice, write another letter and include a copy of your first letter.

UNDOING INTEREST

Interest on overdue tax or a late-filed return is rarely reduced. However, if a tax or penalty is canceled, then interest on the tax or on the penalty should be canceled as well. (The Revenue Canada computer is supposed to do this automatically, but check your bills to make sure.) A few other circumstances in which you might get an abatement of interest include:

■ Revenue Canada was wrong to charge interest, because you did not owe any tax on which interest could be charged.

- Revenue Canada wrongfully sent you a refund and now wants not only its money back but interest as well.
- The interest resulted from Revenue Canada's delay in performing "ministerial acts"—that is, its job.

If you get a Revenue Canada notice that wrongfully states you owe more tax, any interest assessed while you resolve this matter should be canceled. If you do owe more money, however, Revenue Canada can charge interest from the moment it requests the money until you pay. As for interest charged on a refund you did not deserve, you are entitled to an interest abatement as long as your actions and return preparation did not cause the refund.

How to Survive an Audit

Revenue Canada accepts most tax returns without question. But each year it plucks from the pile slightly more than one out of 100 personal tax returns to be subjected to an audit. The purpose of the dreaded audit is to find out if you reported your income properly, whether the deductions, exemptions, and credits you claimed are allowable, and whether you calculated the tax correctly.

Tax law gives Revenue Canada wide powers to inspect your papers and financial records during an audit and to ask you and others about your financial affairs. For example, an auditor can issue a summons to get information from your bank, employer, or business associates. And the fact is that Revenue Canada usually finds what it is looking for: most people who are audited end up owing more taxes.

Nevertheless, can you protect yourself during an audit? The easy answer is to do your utmost to avoid being audited in the first place. (See also "Watch Those Deductions," page 327.) In any case, your first line of defense is to be honest and to keep good financial records. The law places the burden on you to demonstrate that the information you provided is correct. Being able to verify the information on your return is the key to prevailing in an audit. Revenue Canada auditors confirm that the biggest reason taxpayers cannot verify tax-return information is not dishonesty but poor record-keeping. Failure to keep proper records and to supply them to the auditor when requested could result in a fine of $200 to $10,000.

When you receive an audit notice, do three things right away: (1) write down what parts of your return are being questioned; (2) make copies of any documents that support your case; (3) decide whether you need an adviser to help you. The

A Temporary Measure

Income tax legislation, first enacted in 1917 as a temporary measure to raise money during World War I, is now a permanent fixture. The law is constantly changing to meet new social realities and public policy goals. Often the changes coincide with every new budget.

All income is taxable no matter what the source. Thus old age pensioners and recipients of employment insurance benefits must file returns as long as they are Canadian residents (defined as someone who spends 183 days or more a year in Canada).

Quebec is the only province to collect its own income tax from individuals. For all other provinces, the federal government collects provincial income tax in the form of a surtax on your federal income tax. Alberta, Ontario, and Quebec collect their own corporate tax.

audit notice will say how Revenue Canada wants the information delivered. The simplest audits are by mail: you send in the requested documentation and the matter is resolved. Most taxpayers can handle such requests without professional assistance.

Much rarer is the field audit, when a Revenue Canada agent visits your home or business to sift through records, perhaps to see if your standard of living matches the picture suggested by your return. This is a serious business. Consult a chartered accountant or tax lawyer.

Most audits, however, are conducted in a Revenue Canada office. You are asked to appear at a specified time (you can request a more convenient date) armed with documents that support your return. Normally, Revenue Canada notifies you in writing and indicates the data desired. If someone else prepared your return, ask him to accompany you.

GOING IT ALONE

If you decide to handle the audit yourself, thoroughly review the return so that you understand how you, or your tax preparer, arrived at its figures. Organize all the records you will need to substantiate your return. The more evidence you present, and the more clearly you can present it, the more likely you are to prevail. But take only materials that relate to the areas identified by Revenue Canada so as to limit the scope of the audit. Never volunteer any unasked-for information.

If you disagree with an auditor's decision, you may want to

Audit Readiness

Income tax payments are based on self-assessment in that each taxpayer prepares his own return and the information provided is considered by law to be true and accurate. Revenue Canada may nonetheless request an audit, and has four years in which to do so. That limit can be extended in cases involving fraud. About one percent of tax returns are audited each year. These guidelines will work in your favor if you should find yourself among that one percent:

• Private advance rulings may be obtained from the tax authorities. If you have a financial transaction, request by letter an advance ruling that will outline the tax consequences of your transaction. Revenue Canada will also supply you with a circular setting out the procedure to be followed in order to get an advanced ruling.

• A taxpayer can get a technical interpretation from Revenue Canada, explaining how the law would be applied to a specific transaction.

• If your return is other than a simple short form, have your income tax return prepared by an accountant or other professional who may represent you at an audit and who is familiar with the tax laws.

• Revenue Canada publishes many interpretive bulletins, pamphlets, guides, information circulars and booklets. Its staff will also give you information by phone about tax legislation and regulations. Take advantage of these sources of information.

• Keep your records and bills in good order and save them for at least four years.

• Always be polite and co-operative with the auditor. If however you find him rude or abusive, you have the right to request that another auditor be called in to replace him.

ask to see her supervisor. Supervisors have more experience than auditors and also have wider authority to make compromises. Often you can make this informal type of appeal immediately. Do so, however, only if the amount of money in question is significant.

If you do not accept the supervisor's finding, you have 90 days in which to file a "notice of objection." The 90-day limit may be extended if you can show cause why the delay is too short. (Illness or an imminent business trip might justify an extension.) Unresolved objections are usually referred to a regional income tax appeal office for consideration at a senior level, but you can also ask for a hearing before the Tax Review Board or either the Federal Tax Court or the Federal Court (trial division).

If You Cannot Pay What You Owe

Like any business, Revenue Canada would prefer to collect its payments immediately and in full. But in recent years it has become more flexible about taking payments in installments and even forgiving some debts. If you cannot pay all your income taxes, you should still file a return and pay what you can. The penalty for not filing or filing late is quite steep—$25 per day of default up to 100 days. But for not paying in full, the penalty can be 9 to 14 percent of what you owe. Any amount you can include with your return will reduce the penalty amount.

If you do not have the funds to pay your taxes and cannot take out a loan to make up the full amount, Revenue Canada will let you pay by installments. Interest at a rate set by regulation is added to the amount of tax owing. If you do not honor the installment plan, Revenue Canada can garnish your wages and/or your personal effects, furniture, or home.

Help for Nonfilers

Technically, you are guilty of a summary conviction offence if you fail to file a tax return when you owe taxes. You could be fined not less than 25 percent of the tax owed or up to 200 percent of the tax you tried to evade, as well as sentenced to two years in jail.

If charged by way of indictment, and convicted, you could be sent to prison for not less than two months or for a maximum of five years.

However, the purpose of the Income Tax Act is to collect

Watch Those Deductions

Anything that makes your return stand out increases your chances of an audit. If you take any substantial deduction, such as those listed below, consider attaching relevant documents with an explanatory note. Although this will not stop Revenue Canada's computer from flagging your return, the classifier who screens computer-picked returns for potential audits may pass yours over if the additional documents are convincing.

✔ *Casualty losses.* If you claim significant losses due to natural disasters such as earthquake, flood, or fire, make sure you have sales receipts (in the case of jewelry, for instance), repair receipts, insurance reports, and pictures of property damage.

✔ *Cash contributions.* Taking a sizable deduction for cash contributions to charities can be a red flag to Revenue Canada. Deductions must be substantiated by a receipt from the charity for amounts of $20 or more. A returned cheque is not acceptable proof.

✔ *Child care.* Many people pay their child-care providers in cash and cannot substantiate the amounts they have paid. Revenue Canada will not allow a tax credit unless all child-care payments are documented by an employee social insurance number.

taxes rather than to punish taxpayers who filed late, or not at all, so Revenue Canada rarely lays criminal charges against the average nonfiler. It assumes most nonfilers are in that situation due to ignorance, fear, or an inability to pay. It will work out a payment schedule with the individual once the nonfiler voluntarily comes forth to file returns for the missing years.

Keep Records for Six Years

Keep all your tax records—bills, receipts, T4 and T5 forms—for at least six years. Although your tax return ordinarily cannot be audited more than four years after its original filing date, there are some important exceptions to this statute of limitations. For example, any of the following would constitute an exception:

■ If you understated your gross income by 25 percent or more on your tax return, the deadline for tax assessment (and possible audit) is six years after the return was first filed.

■ If you are accused of filing a fraudulent return, the four-year limit does not apply, since fraud is a criminal offense. If the government suspects fraud, it can demand your tax returns from any year.

■ The statute of limitations applies only if you have filed a tax return. In any tax year that you do not file, your tax status is always open to assessment by Revenue Canada—until you file a return for that year. Once you file the return, the four-year statute of limitations begins.

■ The four-year statute of limitations applies to refunds as well as audits. Thus, if you discover that you made a mistake on a previous tax return and overpaid your tax, you cannot demand the refund if more than four years have passed from the tax due date or the date filed, whichever is later.

Tax-Time Volunteers

About 12,000 Canadians volunteer their time each year to help New Canadians, students, seniors, and people with certain disabilities complete their income tax statements. The program is intended for those who have difficulty completing their returns but cannot afford professional help. Volunteers are recruited from community groups by Revenue Canada and the Quebec revenue ministry. (Quebec is the only province to collect its own income tax from individuals.) While they do not become tax experts, the volunteers do learn the basics of completing tax returns.

INCOME SECURITY PLANS

When the time comes to get your share of Canada's Income Security programs, be sure you know what you are entitled to, and how to get it.

Facts About the Benefits

Canada offers two types of retirement benefits: the universal Old Age Security (OAS) pension and the earnings-related Canada Pension Plan (CPP). The legislation governing old age pensions also grants a spouse's allowance, plus a Guaranteed Income Supplement (GIS) to pensioners who have little other income.

In Quebec, the CPP is replaced by the more-or-less identical Quebec Pension Plan (QPP). Every payday workers across the country contribute either to the CPP or the QPP fund.

OLD AGE SECURITY PENSION

Although there is talk of replacing the OAS pension with an income-qualifying senior's benefit in 2001, under present legislation every citizen and legal resident who has lived 10 years in Canada is entitled to a monthly pension at age 65. Payments do not begin automatically: you, or your legal guardian, must complete an application. To avoid delay, file your application six months before your 65th birthday. To get the form or other pension information, call your nearest Human Resources Development Canada office.

OAS benefits are taxable but are payable regardless of whether you are retired, or ever worked outside the home, or paid taxes. You are entitled to them even if you are receiving payments from CPP or QPP.

Since the pension is indexed quarterly to the cost of living, the monthly rate varies. (In October 1996, the full monthly pension was $399.91.) Whether you get the full amount depends on how long you have lived in Canada. Anyone who has lived here for 40 years after age 18 is entitled to a full pension. You will also get a full pension if you were 25 years of age, or older, on July 1, 1977, and either you were a legal resident at that time or had lived here at some time between age 18 and that date, *and* you lived in Canada for the 10 years immediately preceding your application. Absences during this 10-year period may be offset by certain conditions. Check with Human Resources Development Canada for details.

You will receive a partial pension if you live in Canada and have lived here for at least 10 years since age 18 or, if you no

International Agreements

Canada has reciprocal social security agreements with several other countries. According to these agreements, if you lived and worked in Canada as well as one of these countries, you may qualify for social security benefits from both, or your residence in Canada or the other country may be taken into account to meet either country's residency requirements for pension benefits.

Reciprocal agreements are currently in force between Canada and Antigua and Barbuda, Australia, Austria, Barbados, Belgium, Cyprus, Denmark, Dominica, Finland, France, Germany, Greece, Guernsey, Iceland, Ireland, Italy, Jamaica, Jersey, Luxembourg, Malta, Mexico, Netherlands, Norway, Portugal, Saint Kitts-Nevis, Saint Lucia, Spain, Sweden, Switzerland, and the United States.

longer reside here, you did live in Canada for at least 20 years after age 18. Partial pensions are paid at the rate of 1/40 of the full amount for each complete year you lived in Canada since your 18th birthday. A person who resided here for 10 years after age 18, for example, would be entitled to 10/40 of the full pension. A partial pension, once approved, will not be increased to reflect subsequent years of residence.

Once your right to OAS benefits are established, your pension will be paid in Canadian dollars anywhere in the world, provided you lived in Canada for 20 years after age 18. If your time here was less than 20 years, but more than 10, your pension will cease six months after you leave Canada.

Even if you do not meet the residency requirements, you may still qualify for a full or partial pension if you have lived in one of some 30 countries with which Canada has reciprocal social security agreements. (See "International Agreements," page 329, or check with Human Resources Development Canada: more names are added as new agreements are concluded.) Your years abroad could be added to your years in Canada to make up the residency limits for Canadian benefits, or conversely, your Canadian years might enable you to qualify for benefits elsewhere.

OTHER BENEFITS

If you are an old age pensioner with little or no other income, you may receive the nontaxable GIS. Unlike the taxable OAS

There are people who have money and people who are rich.

COCO CHANEL

Keeping an Eye on Your Nest Egg

For many people, government pension plans provide a substantial portion of their retirement income. Thus it is important that contributions be recorded accurately and errors corrected as soon as possible. It is difficult to correct a 20-year-old mistake. Keep these points in mind.

• Your record of earnings, kept by the CPP and QPP managers, is filed under your name and social insurance number, and updated with information supplied by Revenue Canada. If you change your name, you should inform the CPP (QPP) as soon as possible.

• Once a year, ask for a statement of participation—a list of payments made and benefits accumulated. Check this statement carefully.

• If there is an error in your statement and the CPP (QPP) refuses to correct it, you can appeal the matter to the Revenue Minister. If the matter is still not resolved to your satisfaction, within 90 days of receiving the minister's decision, you can file an appeal with the Tax Court of Canada, or an inde-

pendent QPP commission. The court's (or commission's) decision is binding: further appeals or judicial review by the Federal Court of Canada are rarely granted.

• If the amount of your CPP benefits is the issue, write to the Minister of Human Resources Development. If still not satisfied with his decision, you may within 90 days file an appeal with the Review Tribunal. A further appeal can be made to the Pension Appeals Board whose decision is final except for a rare request to the Federal Court for a judicial review if the proceedings before the Pension Appeals Board were irregular.

• Despite what creditors may tell you, pension benefits are unseizable.

pension for which you need only apply once, you must apply annually for GIS benefits. Your income and that of your legal or common-law spouse—but not your assets—are taken into account in assessing eligibility. GIS payments are adjusted quarterly. In October 1996, the top monthly payout was $475.25 for a single recipient, or $309.56 for each spouse if both were receiving OAS and GIS benefits.

A GIS pensioner's 60- to 64-year-old, legal or common-law spouse, or a widowed person aged 60 to 64, may also qualify for a nontaxable spouse's allowance (SPA) if they have lived here for at least 10 years after age 18. Annual application is also required to receive the SPA, which like the GIS ceases if you are out of the country for more than six months.

CHANGES PENDING

If proposed legislative changes are enacted, a combination OAS/GIS known as a senior's benefit will replace the OAS program in 2001. Unlike the universal OAS, the senior's benefit will be based on income. Present suggestions are that everyone who is 60 and over on December 31, 1995, as well as their spouses, can choose either the senior's benefit or OAS.

CANADA PENSION PLAN

The CPP, designed as a mandatory social insurance program to provide retirement benefits for working Canadians, now pays benefits to contributors' survivors and orphans and to some disabled contributors and their dependent children. In Quebec, the CPP is replaced by the relatively similar QPP, the investment funds for which are controlled by the province. Depending on where you have worked over the years, you may have paid into both plans. If you have paid into only one plan, you apply to that plan for your pension or benefits. If you have contributed to both, you apply to the QPP if you are living in Quebec at the time of your application, to the CPP if you are living anywhere else in Canada.

Although the CPP/QPP was never meant to be a person's only retirement support, it has become a cornerstone of many retirees' incomes. There is widespread concern that the system may need a major overhaul if it is to continue paying benefits into the next century and there is a good likelihood that the first step will be increased contributions.

Both plans are currently funded by mandatory contributions from employees and employers, including the self-employed. Contributions are paid equally by you and your employer. If you are self-employed, you pay both shares. Both the contributions and the benefits are relative to the earnings of the individual employee. As well, payments are not based on one's entire income, but rather on that portion of one's salary that is

How to Claim Your Benefits

When you apply for CPP (QPP) benefits, you will need some of the documents listed below. But do not delay making your claim even if you do not have everything you need; Human Resources Development Canada often can help you get them. The Quebec Pension Plan does not ask for birth, marriage, or death certificates.

✔ *Social insurance number.* You must know your own number; if you are applying for spousal benefits, you will need your spouse's number as well.

✔ *Proof of your date of birth.* You will need a legal document such as a birth or baptismal certificate, passport, or driver's license.

✔ *Proof of name change.* In order to get a pension from the CPP (QPP) your name must match that on your social insurance number kept by the pension fund. If you have changed your name, bring your marriage certificate or other proof of the name change.

✔ *Marriage certificate.* To get spousal benefits, you must have proof of marriage.

✔ *Death certificate.* If you are applying for spousal or child-support benefits from a spouse who has died, you must show proof of death.

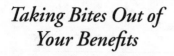

Taking Bites Out of Your Benefits

Whether you belong to the Canada Pension Plan or its Quebec counterpart, your plan's nearest client service center can tell you what your monthly payments will be after you retire. Whether you can hold on to the full benefit, or indeed whether or not you ever get the full amount into your hands is another matter.

✔ *When benefits begin.* Keep in mind that if you retire or substantially stop working at 60 your CPP/QPP pension benefits will be reduced by 30 percent. On the other hand, if you choose not to collect your benefits until you are 70, your monthly payments will be 130 percent of what you would otherwise receive at age 65.

✔ *Taxes on benefits.* The law is still in flux, but if your total income after retirement exceeds a certain limit, the government will tax part of your pension benefits. If you continue working after age 65, you no longer have to contribute to the CPP, but all workers aged 18 to 70 must contribute to the QPP. Persons receiving a retirement or disability pension can no longer contribute, however.

comparable to the average Canadian wage. So even if you are earning $60,000 annually, contributions (in 1996) are based on the first $35,400 of your income.

Because of the paperwork involved, you should apply for your pension about six months before you decide to retire. You can find out how much you will get by completing a form available from Income Security Programs of Human Resources Development Canada. The maximum CPP/QPP benefits payable at age 65 in 1996 were $727.08 per month.

Divorced and Worried

PROBLEM
Clara, a 63-year-old homemaker, was married to Phil, age 65, for 35 years. They were divorced two years ago, and Phil has since moved to another city, where he has remarried but not retired. Clara, who has never worked outside the home, is not eligible for CPP benefits in her own right and fears she will not be entitled to any of Phil's benefits, either.

ACTION
As the divorced spouse of a retired worker, Clara is eligible to claim part of Phil's CPP credits. Even though Phil himself has not retired (and even without a court-ordered support agreement), Clara can still draw against Phil's account. Her share will equal 50 percent of Phil's credits from the CPP to which he contributed during the 35-year marriage. To initiate her payments, Clara should go to her local CPP office. She will still be entitled to half of Phil's credits even if she also remarries.

Benefits are fully portable and can be paid outside Canada. The amount of your benefit is based on your earnings and contributions. Your contributions cease at age 65, if you apply for a retirement pension. Benefits however can begin as early as age 60 and as late as age 70 and the payments will be adjusted to reflect the age at which the pension begins. If you decide to ask for CPP/QPP benefits at age 60, for example, you will get only 70 percent of what you would receive if you wait till 65 and, other than yearly adjustments to reflect Consumer Price Index increases, there will be no pension adjustment when you reach 65. If you elect to begin collecting at age 70, your pension will be 130 percent of that payable at age 65.

Spouses in an ongoing relationship may share their CPP retirement pensions, as can married spouses under QPP. If both are CPP/QPP beneficiaries, each can receive a percentage of the other's pension corresponding to their contributions during their marriage. For example, if their lives together represent 20 percent of their contributory periods, they will each keep 80 percent of their individual pensions and they will split the remaining 20 percent with each other.

In cases of divorce, marriage annulment, or when common-law partners cease to cohabit in the case of the CPP, the CPP and QPP allow credit splitting. (Your credits or earnings are based on what you contributed to the plan while you were in the labor force.) Again, not all credits are split, only that portion of the contributory period corresponding to the length of the marriage (or cohabitation, in the case of the CPP). If Robert paid into his CPP for 25 years, for example, but was only married to Janet for 10 years, Janet is only entitled to one-half of the credits that Robert made to the CPP during their 10-year marriage.

Pension credits are split automatically in the case of a divorce, legal separation, or civil annulment that took place on or after January 1, 1987, in the case of CPP, and on or after June 30, 1989, in the case of QPP. Some spousal agreements signed before June 1986 had clauses specifying that CPP benefits would not be split. Under legislation enacted in 1991, however, the Human Resources Development Minister can approve benefit splitting even when this was excluded in agreements signed before June 1986.

SURVIVOR, ORPHAN, AND DISABILITY BENEFITS

Aside from retirement benefits the CPP/QPP also pays survivor benefits to deceased contributors' spouses (including common-law spouses) and dependent children. When a contributor dies, the estate is entitled to a death benefit of up to $3,540. The amount of the spouse's monthly benefits depends on the survivor's age and whether there are dependent children. Spouses under 35 years of age are not eligible for CPP-survivor benefits, unless they are disabled and have dependent children. A 65-year-old survivor receives benefits equal to 60 percent of what the deceased spouse would be entitled to at age 65. In between these ages, monthly payments vary considerably. In 1996, the maximum payable to a surviving spouse under age 65 was $399.70, and the maximum payable to a surviving spouse over age 65 was $436.25.

Up to the 1980s, the surviving spouse's pension was cut off in the event of remarriage. This is no longer the case.

Dependent children of deceased contributors get a flat-rate monthly orphan's benefit to age 18, and in the case of the CPP, up to age 25 if attending school or university. If both parents are disabled, or deceased, and both were contributors, the child may receive two benefits. In 1996, the CPP monthly child's benefit was $164.17, the QPP benefit was $52.12.

A CPP/QPP contributor between the ages of 18 and 65, who suffers a severe, prolonged mental or physical impairment, may also qualify for disability benefits. Dependent children of a disabled contributor receive a flat-rate monthly sum.

Several Programs Exist to Assist the Disabled

Usually your application for CPP/QPP disability benefits should be made as soon as possible after an impairment occurs. If you do not apply in time, you may not qualify. If you are under 65, you must have contributed to the fund in two of the last three years, or five of the last 10 of your contributory period, in order to be eligible for benefits.

Keep in mind also that you may be entitled to disability benefits from other federal departments such as Veterans Affairs (where the Canadian Pension Commission administers disability pensions), or the Merchant Seaman's Compensation Board, or Human Resources Development Canada.

Short-term sickness benefits may be available through Employment Insurance programs. Every province and territory has Workers Compensation programs that provide assistance for low-income recipients of disability pensions.

Consult the source most likely to apply to your case for more information. You may not qualify for some benefits if you are already getting a CPP/QPP pension. Keep in mind also that your disability pension will be replaced by a retirement pension at age 65.

SAVING FOR RETIREMENT

Guaranteed company pension plans used to be taken for granted, but now more and more people are taking on the job of providing for their retirement years.

123.

KEY QUESTIONS ABOUT YOUR PENSION PLAN

Your retirement may be a long way away, but it is never too soon to learn the details of your pension plan. For answers to these questions consult your firm's "Summary Plan Description," or ask your plan administrator:

1. How are benefits calculated? Find out if bonuses and overtime are counted, and if the payout is based on all earnings or just your peak years.

2. When can I join? Ask how long you have to be employed to start in the plan, and how long after that to benefit fully.

3. Does the promised benefit include Canada (Quebec) Pension Plans and the Old Age Security pensions? Many defined-benefit plans call for "integrated benefits." This means that your pension cheques will be reduced by a certain percentage depending on how much you get from the government.

4. What happens if I retire before age 65? If early retirement is allowed, how much will your benefits be reduced?

5. Is the plan insured and if so by what agency or insurance company? Is the insurer a stable company and has it been around for a long time?

How Pension Plans Work

Although employers are under no legal obligation to provide pension plans, most large and medium-size companies do so anyway. A pension is any plan fund or program that an employer or union establishes to provide retirement income for its workers. The pension may be noncontributory—the plan is funded entirely by the company—or contributory—it is financed by both the employer and employee. Since pensions are such an important source of retirement income for working Canadians, you should learn all you can about your plan and how it works for you. Although plans may vary from one employer to another, most follow certain legislated rules designed for your protection. All will have defined rights, benefits, eligibility standards, and predetermined formulas to calculate benefits.

Basically, there are two types of company pensions, those with "defined benefits" and those with "defined contribution." With a defined-benefit plan, upon reaching a certain age, you receive a fixed income (usually monthly) which continues until your death. The amount you receive depends on how long you were employed and the amount of your salary. The better plans are indexed for inflation.

Funds in a defined-benefit plan are managed by the employer but regardless of how the investments do, you should be entitled to a fixed monthly payment.

A defined-contribution pension plan does not promise you specific benefits at retirement. Usually both employer and employees contribute into this kind of plan, and retirement benefits depend on the amount paid in and how the investment has performed over the years.

BASIC PROVISIONS

Generally, company pension plans require that you be at least 18 years of age and have worked for the company for a stated period of time before you can join the plan. Provincial human rights legislation prohibits companies from discriminating against older workers by excluding them from pension plans on grounds that they are "too old." Even workers who are aged 60 to 65 must be accepted into the pension plan.

Under employment pension acts in most provinces, part-time workers are also eligible to participate in company pension plans.

Most pension programs require the plan managers to issue a summary plan description booklet that describes how the plan works, its eligibility requirements, and the method used to calculate your benefits. You are also entitled to a summary annual report containing information on your pension plan's investments.

How to Monitor Your Plan

You are the best watchdog of your own pension plan. Billions of dollars are invested in thousands of company and union pension plans, and government investigators can review fewer than one percent of these plans each year. Fortunately, you have some important rights to help you get the information you need to monitor your plan yourself.

Start by getting familiar with the rules that those managing private pensions (defined-benefit plans) must follow. Provincial law requires that pension funds be invested prudently. One important provision in the "prudence rule" limits a fund's investment in securities of its own firm to no more than 10 percent of the fund's assets. The law also prohibits loaning *significant* portions of the fund to the corporation. The "Summary Annual Report," which outlines the financial activities of your plan, can give you a sense of how well your pension money has been invested, but you as a worker are fairly well removed from the fund's operation.

Participants in defined-contribution plans have somewhat more active roles. This fastest-growing type of pension plan encourages members to choose wisely and educate themselves about available options. In the case of self-directed plans, employers may let you select an investment for your contributions from a family of several mutual funds or Registered Retirement Savings Plans (RRSPs) and guaranteed investment contracts. You agree to put a certain amount of your salary into the plan regularly (your company may add some too); your contribution offers tax-deductible savings whose growth, tax-deferred, depends on the success of the investments chosen. If your plan permits, you may be able to change investment options, and, depending on company policy, borrow against the value of your account.

As a participant in a defined-contribution plan, you should get, and scrutinize, a written performance report from your company at least once a year. If you do not like the plan, you

ARE YOUR PENSION BENEFITS VULNERABLE?

You don't want chunks of your retirement nest egg to slip away because you weren't forewarned. To familiarize yourself with your pension rights, you should have answers to the following questions:

1. Is my pension indexed? Is it indexed to the inflation rate or the cost of living?

2. If my employer offers a deferred-profit sharing plan instead of a pension plan, what will happen if I leave the company before retirement?

3. If I leave the company, can I transfer my pension credits to my new employer's pension fund? Am I entitled to my former employer's contributions?

4. Will my spouse be entitled to my pension if I should die? (Pension benefit legislation in most provinces insists on this entitlement.)

5. If I divorce, or separate from my common-law partner, does the ex-spouse have any rights to part of my pension?

6. What penalties apply to early retirement, and what is the earliest date I can retire and receive benefits? Also, how would early retirement affect my spouse? Will my common- law spouse be treated the same as a legally married spouse?

7. What company benefits will exist after retirement? For example, will I still have dental and life insurance?

can initiate action by discussing it with the human resources division of the company. Don't expect to move mountains, however. Firms are not liable for poorly performing investments if their plans satisfy rules about the number and variety of investing options and employees' opportunities to switch investments.

Still, the plan administrator must follow the rules laid down and enforced by Revenue Canada, which monitors the plan's tax aspects, by Labour Canada, and by your provincial pension commission, which monitors fund management. If you

A Glossary of Pension Terms

Private pension plans have grown in both number and complexity in recent years. Their purpose is to encourage saving for retirement, and to make sure those savings will be there when you need them. Here are some basic terms:

• **Annuity.** A monthly payment made for the lifetime of the retired worker or for the lifetime of the worker's spouse after the death of the worker.

• **Combined pension plan.** A defined-contribution, profit-sharing plan permits employees to make automatic tax-deferred contributions in investment vehicles provided by the company.

• **Defined-benefit plan.** A type of pension plan that offers a fixed, lifetime income, provided by your employer and based on how long you worked for the employer and how much you earned.

• **Defined-contribution plan.** A type of pension plan based on the sums your company and you contribute to it and how well it is invested. These plans may include profit-sharing plans and employee stock ownership plans.

• **Employee stock ownership plan (esop).** A pension plan that encourages workers to buy their employer's stock, typically at a reduced price. Because the value of your benefit is directly related to the value of your company's stock, esops offer no guarantees and can be risky.

• **Forward averaging.** A tax-saving device that lets those whose lump-sum payout benefit is less than a specified amount pay income tax on that benefit as if they had received the money over 5 or 10 years.

• **Guaranteed investment contract.** A contract between an insurance company and a corporate savings or pension plan that offers a fixed rate of return on the capital invested over the life of the contract, usually one year.

• **Lump-sum distribution.** The payment of all the money in a worker's retirement account at once, instead of in installments; usually done when the worker leaves a job.

• **Pension surplus.** The money that is held in a pension plan after the pension has enough funds to pay full benefits to all its employees.

• **Profit-sharing plan.** An agreement by which the company makes annual contributions out of profits to an account for each worker or to a collective account for the workers. This money may be invested in stocks, bonds, or money market securities. The funds are tax-deferred.

• **Qualified plan.** An employer-sponsored retirement plan that meets various requirements of Revenue Canada.

• **Registered Retirement Savings Plan (RRSP).** A government-approved plan which allows you to accumulate tax-sheltered savings.

• **RRSP rollover.** A technique by which funds can be transferred from one RRSP to another without being taxed.

• **Termination.** With reference to a defined-benefit plan, the ending of a pension plan. In a "standard termination," the plan has enough assets to pay off all its obligations.

• **Vesting.** Completion by a participant of a pension plan's "years of service" requirement. Vesting entitles you to a permanent legal right to your pension benefits, whether or not you continue to work for the company.

think the plan's fees are excessive, that its investments are not prudent, or that any requirements have been violated, contact the nearest Revenue Canada field office, your provincial pension commission, or your union.

You can get additional advice from several nonprofit consumer groups that publish helpful guides on pension law and consumer rights. The Canadian Association of Retired Persons (CARP) also offers several publications on pensions. (For its address, see RESOURCES, page 469.)

When—and How—to Cash In

At retirement, and long before then for some workers, most people will have to decide how they want to receive the retirement money from their pension plans. Whether you are actually retiring, have been laid off, or are simply changing jobs, you will need to evaluate your options carefully since some choices can trigger stiff penalties. In the case of most private pension plans, if you have been at your job long enough to earn a pension (usually two years), your provincial pension commission specifies that the plan administrator must give you your "Individual Benefit Statement" before you leave the job. This statement will tell you how much money you have earned in benefits and (taking the company's years-of-service requirements into account) what percentage of your accumulated benefits you are actually entitled to receive.

Review this information carefully before you leave your job. Remember it may be decades before you actually claim your benefits. If you disagree with the information you receive, or do not understand any statements in the document about your pension plan, now is the time to resolve any problems. See your plan administrator. Ideally, you should do this several months before you plan to retire or resign so that you have as much information as possible about claiming your benefits.

TAKING IT WITH YOU

When you leave, you may receive some or all of the funds in your pension account as a lump sum. But be warned that if you do not reinvest this payout by transferring the money directly from your former account into an RRSP or other qualified retirement plan, Revenue Canada will withhold a hefty chunk of it. To transfer the money directly, establish an appropriate retirement account. This could be an RRSP or your new employer's plan. Inform your previous employer's benefits department in writing where you want your money transferred.

If you get a lump sum and put it into another registered pen-

---

Warning Signals in Your Pension's Annual Report

Every year, your employer must file a pension report with Revenue Canada, detailing your defined-benefit plan's liabilities and assets. Ask your plan administrator for a copy and review it carefully for clues as to how your plan is doing. Scrutinize the following areas, and if you have questions, ask the administrator or your union representative for answers or explanations. Should you still be concerned, review the document with your accountant:

✔ *Asset amounts.* Compare the plan's assets over the last 1-year, 5-year, and 10-year periods. Although every fund will have bad years, a well-managed fund should show at least an 8 percent annual growth rate over the last 10 years.

✔ *Types of assets.* All of the pension money should not be placed in one type of investment. The fund should have a variety of investments, such as stocks, bonds, and secure holdings.

✔ *Employer contributions.* Compare employer contribution on the current statement with those for the previous year. A significant drop could mean that the plan has piled up more funds than it needs to achieve its goals—or it could mean that the company has money problems. If you suspect this, seek financial advice.

As a participant in a private employee benefit plan, you have certain rights. If your claim for benefits is denied or you disagree with the amount coming to you, your plan administrator should notify you in writing, explaining why your benefits were denied or reduced. Your rights should you choose to appeal the ruling against you are outlined below:

1. You have at least 60 days to file an appeal. Your plan administrator must tell you how to submit your denied claim for a full and fair review.

2. A decision on your appeal generally must be made within 60 days of your filing it. You must be informed of the decision and also of the specific reasons for it.

3. If your appeal is denied, you have the additional right to bring a lawsuit against your pension plan.

4. You cannot be fined, discharged, suspended, or discriminated against for exercising these rights. The use of violence or intimidation to interfere with your rights under a pension plan is against the law.

sion plan or if you buy an RRSP, you can defer taxes. The money you transfer need not be included as income on your tax return. However, Revenue Canada limits how much of your lump sum can be put into an RRSP. If your payout exceeds the amount permitted, report the excess transfer as pension income on a T4A slip, then claim the excess contribution over the next few years. Revenue Canada can advise you on how best to proceed and give you whatever forms you need to fill out as well as several informative pamphlets on this matter.

Your retirement money may well be the largest sum of money you will ever have in one place, so be prudent about managing it. By all means consult a financial professional if necessary, but be as well informed as possible before doing so.

If Your Plan Is Terminated

An employer has the legal right to close down a pension plan if the plan is in serious financial trouble or if the company shows that it cannot afford to continue it. However, the company must disperse funds in the account to everyone who is enrolled. How that is done depends on how the plan is terminated.

In a "standard termination," the plan has enough assets to pay all the pension benefits it owes. Often the plan administrator will transfer the plan money to an insurance company that will then pay your monthly benefits when you retire. If you get a notice informing you that you will be receiving this type of benefit, called an "annuity," be sure that you receive a certificate from the insurance company issuing the annuity. The annuity will be based on credits you have earned as of the date of the plan's termination.

A "distress termination" occurs when the company is in serious financial difficulty. In this case, all or part of your pension may be protected by a government's pension insurance program or private insurance companies. They will also notify you of your guaranteed benefit and of your right to appeal this decision. But the government pension commission and the company's insurance company cover only certain kinds of pension plans, and even those may not be fully protected. You also should be aware that a pension plan's rules can change over the years. For example, a company may alter the formula for calculating your pension or end special early retirement benefits. Whenever changes occur, your plan administrator must notify you in writing. Under most provincial benefit laws and regulations, pension funds are kept quite safe as the pension managers are often restricted to investing in the same types of investments as insurance companies.

Self-Directed Plans

Financial experts are unanimous in urging workers who are not part of an employer's pension plan to set up personal retirement plans as soon as they start earning money. Otherwise the retirement years may be bleak indeed. Even if you are employed by a company with a plan and work part-time for yourself, you are eligible to set up your own retirement plan. You will have to take the initiative in choosing and starting the plan, but you will have great flexibility in choosing one tailored to your needs.

Three of the most popular individual plans are discussed here. The plans' tax incentives are designed to help you save; if you withdraw your money before you have retired, you must pay a steep penalty plus the taxes due. At age 71, you must begin to withdraw your funds.

RRSPs

Registered Retirement Savings Plans (RRSPs) are tax deferral plans registered with Revenue Canada. You pay no taxes on money placed in an RRSP and any interest and capital gains

---

KEEPING TABS ON YOUR FUND WHEN YOU CHANGE JOBS

If you change jobs, you may need to find a new home for the money in your profit-sharing or other defined-contribution retirement plan. (A defined-benefit pension normally remains with your former employer until you apply for benefits.) Your action could trigger penalties and taxes, so be aware of the options below:

If you decide to:	This will happen:
Leave money in a former employer's plan	Your funds will continue to grow tax-deferred. You have the option of moving the money later on to an RRSP or a new retirement plan.
Have your employer transfer the money directly into an RRSP or other qualified retirement plan	Your money will continue to grow tax-deferred until you withdraw it.
Withdraw the money as a lump sum	Federal law requires that a certain percentage be withheld for income taxes from the money you take out. Depending on your tax bracket, you may owe additional taxes at tax time or be due a refund on what was withheld.
Receive a lump-sum cash payment and put the money into an RRSP or other qualified plan	You can defer taxes by putting the money into another registered pension plan or an RRSP. If the amount exceeds what you are permitted to put in an RRSP for that year, check with Revenue Canada for procedures on reporting excess pension income.

Some More Facts on Registered Retirement Plans

Registered Retirement Savings Plans (RRSPs) and Registered Retirement Income Funds (RRIFs) are among the best ways of saving for retirement. To cut down on poverty among the elderly, the government gives excellent tax breaks to people who invest in those plans. Some highlights about RRSPs and RRIFs follow:

✔ *Book and market value.* You may come across the terms "book value" and "market value" when dealing with RRSPs. Book value refers to the amount of money you have invested, whereas market value is what you would get if you sold your RRSP. In other words, it includes the capital gain and the compound interest earned.

✔ *18 percent.* You can currently invest up to 18 percent of your income in RRSPs up to maximum $13,500. This figure will increase each year until 1999, when the amount will be $15,000. However, the amount you contribute to a pension plan reduces the amount you may contribute to an RRSP.

✔ *Handsome deduction.* You can claim a deduction on your income tax for your RRSP contribution. If you are in a 50 percent tax bracket, your contribution saves you 50 percent in taxes: if you put $10,000 into an RRSP, you get a $5,000 deduction.

that accrue are tax-free until you withdraw that money. Your RRSP investment must be earned income, whether from employment, net rental from real estate property, taxable alimony or maintenance payments, net research grants, even royalties from your writing or inventions.

RRSPs may be purchased through banks, trust companies, insurance companies, and other financial institutions, and may contain Guaranteed Income Certificates, Canada Savings Bonds, shares and bonds in Canadian companies listed on certain Canadian exchanges, such as the Toronto, Alberta, and Montreal stock exchanges, and certain U.S. and European exchanges, mortgages of property situated in Canada (including your own mortgage), mutual funds registered with Revenue Canada and other financial instruments such as cashable term deposits. Up to 20 percent of your RRSP contributions may be in eligible foreign investments, although you may circumvent this limit by investing in a Canadian mutual fund that has most of its portfolio in Canadian assets, but a large portion in foreign stocks, bonds, or other assets.

To avoid taxes on your RRSP when you die, name as beneficiary either your spouse or a dependent child under 18, and arrange that your RRSP be "rolled over" to your spouse's RRSP or used to purchase an RRSP for your dependent child.

Bear in mind that you are not limited to one RRSP, and that all are guaranteed for up to $60,000 each, provided they are held by different financial institutions.

If you are a first-time home buyer, you may invest $20,000 of your RRSP in purchasing a home—new or old. In the case of a married couple, each spouse may invest $20,000, for a total $40,000 tax-free investment.

TYPES OF RRSPs

There are two basic categories of RRSP: those offering a guaranteed rate of return, and those whose rate depends on the value of assets held by the plan. With guaranteed plans, you also choose either a fixed or variable rate of return. The interest in a fixed plan stays the same for from one to five years; with a variable plan, interest fluctuates with the prime lending rate.

Whichever category you choose, your RRSP may be managed by a financial institution or be self-directed. Self-directed RRSPs are mainly for people who are able to spend time managing their portfolio and are investment-minded. You can choose your investments such as stocks, bonds, or your own mortgage, and you can transfer from one investment to another. You will pay from $100 to $250 in annual fees, but you can claim them as a deduction on your income tax. There will be additional costs if you change investments, so you may want to consult a discount broker for this transaction.

Some couples choose to have a spousal RRSP among their investments. Its main advantage is that if you must cash an RRSP, you can save substantially on taxes by cashing a spousal RRSP. With spousal RRSPs, one spouse (usually the higher income earner) contributes to the other's RRSP. The paying spouse receives the tax deduction but the assets belong to the other spouse. If she cashes the RRSP, and she has little or no income, the RRSP is taxed accordingly.

Funds withdrawn within certain time limits may be taxed to the contributing spouse and special rules may apply to those receiving retirement income.

Spousal RRSPs may be purchased for a common-law spouse with whom one has a child or has cohabited for at least one year, as well as for a legal spouse.

ANNUITIES, RRIFs, AND LIFs

Your RRSP matures the year of your 69th birthday, so you must stop paying into it that year and begin receiving retirement income from it instead. To do this, you must buy either an annuity, or a Registered Retirement Income Fund (RRIF), or a Life Income Fund (LIF) with the proceeds of your RRSP. However, if your spouse is not yet 69 years of age, you may still pay into her RRSP and claim the resulting tax deduction.

An annuity is a contract, usually with a bank, trust company or insurance company, by which you pay a certain amount of money and in return receive a set amount of income on a specific date—monthly or quarterly—for a set period. Some annuities are paid until age 90, others for the remainder of your life. Either way, the payments represent what you have invested with the insurance company or bank, plus the interest on that investment. Your contract might even specify that any balance remaining after your death be paid to someone you name as beneficiary.

An RRIF is an extention of an RRSP in that funds transferred into an RRIF remain tax deferred and can earn tax-free income until the funds are withdrawn. You may buy an RRIF at any age, but since a certain amount must be withdrawn every year, it hardly makes a good investment for a 30-year-old. Ideally an RRIF should be structured in such a way that it provide income for the entire life of the holder.

A LIF is an alternative to an annuity and in fact a LIF must be rolled into an annuity at age 80. With a LIF, the big advantage is that you control how your money is invested, although you must withdraw a set minimum amount each year, based on a term-certain annuity, to age 90.

Legislation on LIFs varies from province to province, however; in Alberta, for example, a LIF does not have to be cashed in at age 80.

Which Fund Should You Fund First?

Many people have access to more than one type of retirement account. For example, you could have mutual fund at work and an RRSP for income earned doing freelance work. How should you decide which accounts to contribute to first?

Begin with the plan that returns the most to you. For example, your first contributions should be to an employer-based plan in which your company matches what you put in. That way you double your money, free. Next in line should be any other employer or self-employed plan that enables you to make tax-deductible contributions.

When you have put the maximum allowed into tax-deductible plans—or do not have access to any—contribute to an RRSP. If you are not eligible for an RRSP because you are not earning an income, or have already reached your annual limit on contributions to the RRSP, consider an annuity, an investment product sold by life insurance companies.

Annuities, like RRSP, allow your money to grow and compound without being taxed until withdrawal. And you can deposit as much as you want each year into an annuity. On the other hand, you get no tax deduction when you set it up.

WILLS AND ESTATES

Since death is even more certain than taxes, you and your heirs should take pains to make sure that your worldly goods are distributed the way you want them to be.

Estate Plans Are for You

The phrase "estate planning" sounds like something that goes on behind high gates at the end of a long driveway. But estate plans are not just for the very rich. If you own any more property than a minivan and a pair of running shoes, you should have a plan for making sure that your property will go to those to whom you want it to go as quickly and economically as possible.

An estate plan is simply a legal, written document—or set of documents—that provides for the distribution of your estate when you die. Your estate comprises everything you own at the time of your death: house, car, furniture, jewelry, savings accounts, insurance policies, stocks, and bonds.

Some of this property, such as insurance policies, will pass automatically to named beneficiaries. Some of it, such as your home, may belong to a person named as the joint owner. But only in a will, the most essential estate-planning document for most people, can you distribute the rest of your assets in the way you wish.

In most circumstances, every adult needs a will. Your lawyer can draw one up for you for $150 and up, depending on its complexity. If you have minor children, a will is the only way to name a guardian for them. If you and your spouse should both die "intestate"—without a will—the courts and social service agencies decide who will raise your children. That in itself is a compelling reason to have a will. Even though the clause naming a person to take care of your children could be contested if, for example, you didn't name your surviving spouse, the courts and social service agencies will seriously consider your request.

Besides taking charge of your children if you should die intestate, provincial succession laws also set the rules for distributing your money and property. Even though inheritance laws differ from one province to another, in nearly every case, the province in question will distribute the largest portion of your assets to your surviving legal spouse. Next in line are your children, your parents, and other relatives, starting with those who are closest blood relations. If no heirs are found after a reasonable search, the property "escheats"—passes to the state.

PREPARING A WILL

Whether simple or complex, a will must follow the requisite legal forms. There are three types: the formal witnessed will, also called an English form will, the holographic (handwritten) will, and in Quebec, a notarial will. Of the three, only the formal witnessed will and the notarial will are valid in all situations. Holographic wills are valid only in Alberta, Ontario, Manitoba, Saskatchewan, and Quebec.

The basic requirements for a valid will are not complicated:

- You must be a legal adult—at least 18 years old in most provinces, 19 in British Columbia, Nova Scotia, New Brunswick, and the Northwest Territories.
- You must be of "sound mind": you must possess a general understanding of the purpose of the will, know what property you own, and name those whom you wish to inherit.
- Your will must meet the requirements of your province's will-drafting law.

Most provinces have similar rules regarding wills. They involve requirements such as dating the will and appointing an executor, the person who sees that the provisions of your will are carried out. You must also sign the will in front of two witnesses, who will not receive anything under your will. In most provinces, if your will is executed properly and notarized upon execution, your witnesses will not need to appear in court when your will is probated after your death. Such a will is known as

Money begets money.

JOHN RAY

English proverb

How to Guard Against Challenges to Your Will

Anyone who might gain from contesting your will may try to do so. The two most common grounds for such a move are that the testator, or will maker, was not of sound mind and that someone used coercion to unduly influence her. Here are some safeguards:

• Use an experienced lawyer (ideally one who specializes in estate planning) to draw up your will. Your local bar association can provide you with necessary referrals.

• Use respectable witnesses who can vouch for your mental state when you sign the will. Choose witnesses who are not personal friends or beneficiaries so that if the will is challenged, they cannot be charged with bias.

• Videotape the signing and have the will read aloud. This may seem extreme, but especially in cases where a person's health or memory is failing, it is a sensible precaution to record the will being approved by the testator.

• Keep the will clear and unambiguous, and be sure it says exactly what you mean. Do not erase passages, cross out lines, or write new provisions in the margins. Any handwritten alterations could raise suspicions that the changes were made without your knowledge. Be sure you and your witnesses sign or initial each page of the document.

• Consider putting your property into a revocable living trust. You control the living trust during your lifetime; the assets pass to your beneficiaries when you die, avoiding probate entirely. Unlike a will, a trust is private, and courts must be persuaded to make the document public. Only rarely have living trusts been invalidated in court. (See also "When to Trust a Trust," page 347.)

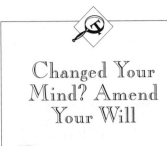

Changed Your Mind? Amend Your Will

Do you have to write a whole new will if you change your mind about who should inherit your grandmother's ring to? Probably not. For a relatively small and straightforward change such as that, the traditional procedure is to make a "codicil" to your existing will.

A codicil, a formal legal method for making changes to an already drafted will, must be prepared, signed, and witnessed with all the formalities of a will. You should sign and date it in the presence of two witnesses, who are told it is your will and who then sign their names. The witnesses do not have to be the same as those for your original will, but you should use them if they are available.

If, on the other hand, you have changed your mind about a lot of things in your will, it is better to make a new one to prevent confusion when the time comes to probate the will. In fact, computers and fast printers have made it so much quicker to prepare a document for witnessing and signing that it is becoming almost as easy to make a whole new will as to write a codicil.

a "self-proving" will. Some lawyers suggest having one more witness than is required by law so that the will would not be nullified should one witness later be deemed unqualified.

Although you can designate whether or not you want your children to receive an inheritance under your will, in all provinces you must use the correct language if you want to specifically disinherit a child. If a child is simply omitted, probate court later might treat it as an oversight. All provinces, however, prohibit you from disinheriting a spouse, although some may allow you to reestablish such an arrangement with a legal document such as a valid premarital agreement. If you try to disinherit a spouse, the spouse can "contest" your will after you die, and could inherit a portion of your estate.

Forgiving Debts

PROBLEM
Caroline, a divorced mother, loaned her son, James, and daughter-in-law, Cathy, $15,000 for a down payment on a house. Caroline was concerned that the couple should not be obligated to her estate for this loan if she should die before the loan was repaid. She decided that she wanted to forgive the debt as a bequest in her will.

SOLUTION
Caroline called her lawyer, and her lawyer advised her to revise her will with a provision that explicitly stated that she forgave whatever remained outstanding on her loan of $15,000 to James and Cathy. Since Caroline was divorced from James's father when she made the loan, she was free to deal with the debt in her will as she chose. However, if Caroline had made the loan while still married, she might have had the right to forgive only half the debt unless her husband agreed in writing to allow her to forgive his share of the debt as well.

The old rule, where the testator had complete discretion in disposing of his goods in a will, has been replaced by legislation on family relief and matrimonial property, which gives rights to widows, widowers, and dependent children. As a result, it is almost impossible to disinherit your spouse or dependents. In Ontario, for example, the Succession Law Reform Act and the Family Law Act grant rights to surviving spouses which override the provisions of a will. Under the Family Law Act, a surviving spouse can claim up to half the deceased's net property, and the court has discretion to award even more than half in some cases. Where there is no will, the surviving spouse is entitled to half the deceased's property.

In most wills, however, each spouse names the other as beneficiary. But what happens if both die together in an accident? One solution is a "30-day clause" stating that to inherit under your will, your spouse must outlive you by 30 days (three or six months if you like), and should he or she not do so, your estate should go to another named beneficiary. Without such a clause, the estate usually goes to the younger spouse, and then to the younger spouse's parents or other relatives, and perhaps creating great hurt and animosity among the other spouse's family members.

By law, you have the right to draft your own will; forms and kits can be found in stationery, card, and book stores. But having a lawyer advise you offers several advantages. For example, a lawyer can tell you if there are laws that will affect your bequests.

She can also suggest the most advantageous ways for you to hold title to your property and can ensure that your will is unambiguous and complies with your province's laws. The point is to craft a foolproof document so that when it goes through "probate"—the legal process that proves your will is valid—no one will contest it successfully.

Transferring Property: Other Ways Besides Wills

Making out a proper will and keeping it up to date is by far the most accepted way of making sure that your money and property pass in an orderly way to those you leave behind. Yet wills have some significant drawbacks. The chief one is that assets left in a will must go through probate court (sometimes called surrogate court), where your will is authenticated, your assets are ascertained, and your debts are paid. After any fees owed to lawyers, appraisers, and accountants are paid, the remaining property is distributed to your heirs.

The average probate proceedings often take a year or more. Furthermore, probate takes place not only in the province where you live but in every province where you own real estate property. (Although you do not need to file a will in every province, your will should account for all property and reflect the laws in provinces or foreign countries where you own property.) The legal fees for taking your estate through the probate process can add up to as much as 10 percent of the value of your estate in complicated cases.

For those who want to spare their heirs some of these costly delays, other legal and surprisingly simple strategies are available to help executors avoid the probate process altogether. (Also note that in some provinces, simple estates can skip the most onerous part of probate. An individual can file independently using form documents and paying small fees. Probate court can often help.) These strategies should not be thought

When You Want to Leave Property to a Minor Child

In general, you have the right to leave property to anyone you want. But the law says that minor children cannot own property outright, free of supervision, beyond a limited amount—in the $2,500 to $5,000 range, depending on the province where you live. So if you want to leave a significant sum to a minor, you may have to appoint a guardian to hold title to the property until the child reaches adulthood under provincial law, usually age 18 or 19.

If the value of the property will be more than $25,000, you should consider a child's trust. This allows you to name a person you can rely on to manage property for your child until he or she reaches an age you have designated (it does not have to be 18). In the meantime, your successor trustee can spend any of that child's trust income or property for the child's health, education, or living needs.

You can set up a child's trust in your will, but using a will means that the property must go through probate before it is turned over to the child's trust. So it is worth considering setting up a child's trust as part of a living trust.

You should not try to set up a trust alone, unless you have specialized knowledge. Consult a chartered accountant or a tax or estate lawyer.

of as substitutes for a will but as supplements to your plan for passing on specific parts of your estate.

- Joint ownership. Joint owners with a right of survivorship, sometimes known as joint tenants, co-own property. When one tenant dies, ownership transfers to the surviving joint tenant (or tenants) without probate.
- Life insurance proceeds. Life insurance proceeds normally will avoid probate because you name your beneficiary in the policy instead of in a will.
- Annuities and pension plans. Like life insurance benefits, those paid to your beneficiaries under a pension or profit-sharing plan normally do not go through probate.
- Living trusts. You can set up a living trust so that when you die, all or part of your property will go directly to your named beneficiary. (For more on trusts, see also "When to Trust a Trust," page 347.)

Joint tenancy with a right of survivorship is usually applied to real estate, but any type of property can be owned this way, including bank accounts and cars. You should be aware that you cannot leave your share of a joint-tenancy property to anyone but the other joint tenants. Each joint tenant has rights to ownership. A potential risk of owning a joint-tenancy bank account is that another joint tenant could withdraw your money before you die (although real estate cannot be sold without the agreement of the other or all other owners).

GIVING AWAY POWER

Transferring money or assets is the main purpose of estate planning, but good estate planning also involves provisions for transferring your "power"—that is, authorizing another person to make decisions in your place in case you are unable to do so. The legal document by which you do this is called a power of attorney.

There are different types of powers of attorney. Some grant limited rights, such as allowing another person to pay your bills while you are traveling abroad. This type expires if you become mentally disabled, a time when you most need it. But by setting up in advance a document called a "durable power of attorney," you can authorize someone to make medical and financial decisions for you if you become incapacitated. Should you become unable to manage your affairs without having signed a power of attorney, a judge might appoint someone, called a conservator or guardian (depending on the province), to make the decisions for you.

The person who holds this durable power of attorney has the right to exercise it at any time, even if you are of sound

---

IF YOU ARE NAMED AN EXECUTOR

An executor is appointed in a will to see that the wishes of the will maker, legally known as the testator, are carried out. If you are named an executor, be prepared to spend a considerable amount of time on the job. For your efforts you may receive a court-appointed fee set by the province, usually according to the value of the estate. Here is what you are expected to do:

1. Present the will to probate court, and receive legal control of the deceased's property. You may want to hire a lawyer.

2. Open an estate chequing account to receive and disburse all funds. File claims for any life insurance and Social Insurance benefits.

3. File an estate tax return within nine months of the death; and file a final income tax return on behalf of the deceased.

4. Deal with all personal financial business, such as informing banks, brokerages, and creditors about the death, and attend to all outstanding debts.

5. Make an accounting of the estate's assets to the heirs and distribute the assets as the will directs.

6. Submit an accounting of your activities to the probate court. Petition the court for discharge when your duties have been completed.

mind, so choose someone you trust entirely. Or you can ask your lawyer to set up a "springing" durable power of attorney, which takes effect only if you become mentally incapacitated. Whatever kind of power of attorney you set up, it can be revoked at any time, and it ends when you die.

When to Trust a Trust

Trusts, like the concept of estate planning, are often considered to be a trademark of the very rich. But today, people of widely varying incomes find that the versatility of trusts makes them useful estate-planning tools. Although trusts are more complicated and more costly than drafting a will (you or your heirs may have to pay annual fees of 1 to 2 percent of the trust's assets to a professional trustee), they offer several advantages.

Broadly, there are two kinds of trusts: the "testamentary trust" and the "living trust." The testamentary trust is set up by a will and takes effect after the will is probated. A living trust, sometimes known as an *inter vivos* trust, takes effect as soon as it is established. It is a legal device designed to hold property of an individual, called the settlor, for the sake of one or more beneficiaries. A living trust can be revocable—the settlor can revoke or change it at any time—or it can be made irrevocable, in which case the settlor cannot change it, regardless of mistakes, altered circumstances, or a simple change of mind.

The trust document will specify a trustee to manage the trust's assets; usually that is the same person who established the trust—that is, the settlor. The trust document will also name a "successor trustee," who takes over after the settlor dies and becomes responsible for distributing the remaining assets to the beneficiaries. If the settlor has young children, the successor trustee can manage their assets until they are whatever age the settlor specifies. In addition, a clause can be written into the trust document that protects an estate plan from attacks by its beneficiaries.

One advantage of a trust is that the assets go directly to its beneficiaries, bypassing the probate fees. This is possible since the title is already in the name of a living entity (the trust) and is not part of the deceased's estate.

WHY BOTHER WITH A TRUST?

Probate costs can be high. Lawyers' and executors' fees vary widely, as do court costs. In some provinces the cost of probate is a percentage of the estate's gross value. If you live in one of these provinces, a living trust is an effective way to sidestep the high probate costs.

123...

DON'T SEND AN EXECUTOR ON A TREASURE HUNT

Your will provides for the orderly distribution of your assets after you die, but you also have to make sure your heirs and executors know where to find all those worldly goods. You can help by keeping an updated inventory of your assets—and don't forget to tell your executor where you keep the list, which should include:

1. Your social insurance number.

2. The number and location of all bank accounts and safe-deposit boxes; the location of stock, bond, and mutual fund accounts; and the name and number of insurance policies.

3. The name and address of your lawyer, accountant, broker, and insurance agent.

4. Where your jewelry and other valuables are kept, and the location of any other property you own, such as real estate or a boat.

5. Location of your will and other estate-planning documents, as well as your birth, marriage, and military discharge certificates.

6. Credit card accounts, with account numbers.

7. The details of any outstanding debts that you owe or that are owed you.

Another advantage of a living trust is the matter of privacy. Once a will is admitted to probate, anyone can read it at the courthouse. A trust document, however, remains secret even after the assets are distributed. If, for any reason, you do not want the world to know about your estate after you have died, the living trust is the answer. A living trust also enables you to avoid a conservatorship; that is, being placed under a court-appointed guardian should you become unable to manage your own affairs. When setting up the trust, you can provide for a successor trustee to manage your assets if you are incapacitated.

Granted, these benefits come with a price. Trusts, depending on their complexity, can cost from $600 to several thousand dollars to establish. You will also have to go through the process of retitling all your assets that you plan to put into the trust. Finally, a living trust will probably not take care of your whole estate. You will most likely still need a will to deal with any assets that you do not transfer to the trust.

Trusts are complex, so you would be wise to consult a chartered accountant or lawyer when dealing with a trust.

When You Inherit

Between 1996 and the year 2000, it is estimated that billions of dollars will be passed on to the middle-aged generation by their elders. If you are likely to receive a lump-sum inheritance, large or small, it is smart to figure out ahead of time what you will do with it. To avoid making hasty and costly decisions, take the following steps before spending or investing your inheritance:

• Understand your tax liability. For instance, your inheritance itself is not subject to estate taxes or inheritance taxes. Since the Income Tax Act considers that all of the deceased's assets were distributed at his death, the estate may have to pay capital gains taxes and recaptured depreciation which could reduce the amount inherited.

• Cash your inheritance cheque and put the money into an interest-earning account immediately—even if you later decide to do something else with it. A good place to store your money until you decide what to use is to buy a redeemable Guaranteed Investment Certificate or mutual fund that invests in bonds and debentures.

• Determine how much of your inheritance you will spend, and in what way. One recommendation: pay off all nondeductible debt first, such as credit card bills.

• Understand the "cost basis" of the property you inherit. The cost basis is the value used to measure the capital gains tax owed when you sell inherited assets. It is fixed at the time of death.

Suppose you wish to sell some stocks that you inherited from a parent who bought them at $30 a share and that, at your parent's death, are worth $40, but when you finally sell them, you get $50 a share. You pay tax only on the difference between the $40 (the "stepped-up cost basis" at the time of the testator's death) and $50. By contrast, the cost basis of assets you are given while the donor is alive is fixed at the asset's purchase price. If your parents give you the $40 stock they bought at $30 a share and you sell it at $50, you pay tax on the difference between $30 and $50 per share.

• Use this opportunity to set aside an emergency fund for yourself and your family. Financial experts recommend setting aside three months' living expenses as a cushion against an unexpected loss of income or sudden major expenditure.

• If the inheritance is large enough to change the nature of your own estate, get professional advice from an experienced estate planner to help you review or create your own estate-planning documents.

YOUR CAR

Whether you are buying, selling, maintaining, or driving an automobile, knowledge of the law enables you to avoid trouble.

BUYING A NEW CAR ■ BUYING A USED CAR ■ MAINTAINING YOUR CAR ■ INSURING YOUR CAR ■ AUTOMOBILE ACCIDENTS ■ MOTOR VEHICLE LAWS

Buying a New Car

Homework takes the guesswork out of shopping for a new automobile.
Do plenty of research to make sure you get the best deal.

Information Sources for Car Buyers

These reliable sources for car data can be found at libraries, bookstores, and newsstands.

✔ **Consumer Reports.** Published by the nonprofit Consumers Union, this magazine annually rates all new cars and compares prices for many models and their options.

✔ **Consumer Reports Used Car Buying Guide.** Also published by Consumers Union, this book rates used cars that are less than six years old.

✔ **AAA Auto Test.** This annual publication rates all new auto models by overall value, fuel economy, important options, repair costs, and more.

✔ **Chilton's Road Report.** This publication evaluates imported cars, adapting prices for Canadian readers.

✔ **The Canadian Red Book.** This gives the relative value of new and used cars, citing prices for many models and options. (Car dealers use **The Canadian Black Book**, a trade publication that rates the dollar value of used cars.)

✔ **Lemon Aid.** Best and worst ratings of new and used vehicles are standard in this annual report by the nonprofit Canadian Automobile Protection Association. There are two editions, one for new cars, another for used vehicles.

Research, Research, Research

A new car is one of the most expensive items most consumers will ever buy. Knowing your rights as a consumer, doing your homework on car values, and understanding auto-selling techniques will put you in the driver's seat when you go out to shop. In the auto industry there is something known as the 80/20 rule: 80 percent of a dealer's profit comes from 20 percent of buyers.

First, determine exactly what kind of car you need. Are you a single person who commutes to work; a parent who needs plenty of space for kids and gear; or a retiree who values a comfortable automobile? Must your car be practical or can you go for something sporty? Do you want two doors or four? Do you frequently drive long distances, or do you need your car only to run in-town errands?

Then, figure precisely how much you can afford to spend per month on a car. Bear in mind that the cost of a car covers more than simply the price of the vehicle. It also includes insurance, various fees and taxes, operating costs such as gas and oil, and even the price of depreciation. (See "Calculating the Real Cost of a Car," page 351.) Once you have a firm ceiling price, you will be better able to withstand a salesperson's pitch.

COMPARISON SHOPPING

Next, research available choices in the styles you want and the range you can afford. A variety of books and journals readily available in your local bookstore and library provide unbiased new car ratings, best-buy recommendations, and other useful information. (See also box at left.)

Compare the cars in your price category for reliability, repair records, cost of maintenance, owner satisfaction, and safety. Note which cars have the most comprehensive warranties and the best fuel economy ratings. Take the resale value of different models into account.

You may be able to get the kind of car you want for less if you buy a clone—a similar model sold under another name. For instance, a basic General Motors body may be available with slight modifications as a Pontiac or Oldsmobile. Ford and Mercury share several clones, as do Dodge, Plymouth, and Chrysler.

Generally, a clone has the same auto body as the more expensive car, but perhaps a less powerful engine, fewer mechanical amenities such as cruise control, and fewer optional luxuries such as leather seats. However, these clones can provide the basic car you need for hundreds of dollars less.

ALL ABOUT INVOICE PRICES

After you have decided on a model, research the "invoice price" of the car—that is, the amount the dealer actually paid for the basic car. It will also be useful to know the invoice prices for various add-on options such as power steering, air-conditioning, central locking system, and radio. You can get this information from auto-pricing services or auto books and magazines and, if you are a member of the Canadian Automobile Association, from counselors at the CAA.

If you plan to trade in your old car, find out its cash value by consulting used-car pricing guides such as the *Canadian Red Book*. Also, get at least one bid from a used-car dealer. If the new-car dealer's trade-in offer is low, it may pay to sell your old car yourself or through a used-car dealer.

Calculating the Real Cost of a Car

Loan or lease payments are only the start of the many factors that go into the cost of driving an automobile. Use this checklist to compare estimated first-year ownership costs for subcompact, compact, midsize, and large model cars.

• **Financing a loan or lease.** Multiply monthly payments by 12 to calculate the total annual cost of your loan or lease.

• **Depreciation.** The value of a car goes down from the moment it is driven out of the showroom. Depreciation takes into account normal wear and tear as well as the fact that newer models may offer more advanced features. You should figure an average depreciation of 35 percent of the price of the car in the first year.

• **Insurance.** Car buyers are often unaware that sportier and costlier models are more expensive to insure. Calculate the difference in rates before deciding what kind of car you can afford.

• **Registration and license fees.** Most provinces have annual fees for auto registration and periodic fees for renewing a driver's license. Divide each total fee by the number of years the fee covers to arrive at an average annual fee.

• **Taxes.** Your provincial Motor Vehicle Bureau can tell you what is required locally in sales tax on the vehicle and its accessories.

• **Gasoline.** Use this example to estimate your annual costs. Suppose you drive 20,000 kilometres a year in a vehicle that averages about 9 litres of gas per 100 kilometres: divide 20,000 by 100 and multiply by 9. The result is 1,800 litres. At about 65 cents a litre, your annual gasoline outlay will be around $1,170.

• **Maintenance and repair.** For the first year, major costs should be covered by the warranty, but there will be ordinary maintenance costs such as oil or filter changes. Ask your service station how much these will cost you.

• **Parking and tolls.** Calculate what you spend on these per week, then multiply by 52. The result may surprise you.

• **Total cost.** The total cost is the sum of all of the above. To calculate the cost per kilometre, divide the total cost by the distance driven.

Finally, before you venture into a showroom, check out the latest information on factory rebates, which are discounts and incentives provided by the manufacturer. These deals vary by season, manufacturer, and dealer, but are often advertised in the local media. A legitimate rebate can save you money—as long as it does not tempt you to buy a more expensive car!

Figuring the Financing

With the high prices of even modest automobiles, most car buyers find that they must secure outside financing. The most obvious source of financing is the car dealer, and many dealers offer seemingly sound incentives like no down payment, lower prices, and low interest rates in order to draw buyers. However, just as you must shop intelligently for the car, you should also shop carefully for its financing.

Financing with the dealer is convenient, but the dealer is not a financial institution. He must get the financing from another party, either a bank or the manufacturer, and may add on a small percentage for his service. You may save money by going directly to a bank or credit union. You might even consider taking out a home equity loan, since the lower interest on such a loan may be advantageous. (See also YOUR MONEY, page 283.) If you own whole life insurance with a cash value, you may be able to borrow from your policy at relatively low interest while maintaining your full insurance coverage.

Research several institutions to compare terms on auto loans; even banks within the same community may offer substantially different terms. Lenders are required by law to provide detailed information regarding loans, so don't hesitate to ask for clarification of any points you don't understand. Compare total payments for 12-, 24-, 36-, 48-, and 60-month terms. Your monthly payments will be smaller for longer-term loans, but your total payment will be greater. The extra cost of a longer loan can add up to a significant expense.

Don't buy credit insurance from a lender if you already have either a life insurance policy or disability insurance. Credit insurance is not required for a loan, and even if you need the protection, you can often purchase it for much less from an insurance broker.

Of course, the cheapest way to buy a car is to pay with cash. If you make regular payments to yourself, the cost of "borrowing from yourself" will be only the interest that money would have earned in your savings account, or, if you take a loan from your whole life insurance policy, the interest you pay will be the interest paid on the cash value of your policy.

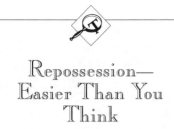

Repossession— Easier Than You Think

Until you have made the last payment on your car, it does not belong to you. In some provinces, the creditor can repossess your car if you fail to make timely payments on a secured loan with the car as collateral. This will not happen if you finance the car through a bank or other financial institution rather than through the dealer's finance company, and expressly exclude the car as collateral. Should you default on such a loan, the lender may sue only for the money owed, but cannot touch your car until he has obtained a final judgment against you for his debt.

The law varies when the vendor is also the lender. In British Columbia and Ontario, the creditor must have a court order to repossess when two-thirds of the debt has been paid. In Quebec, the lender must obtain court authorization to repossess if the consumer has paid 50 percent of the sale price. Alberta, British Columbia, Manitoba, Quebec, Yukon, and the Northwest Territories consider the contract canceled —the borrower owes no more money—once repossession occurs. In other provinces, an unpaid vendor may sell the repossessed vehicle. If the sale brings in less than is owed, he can sue you for the difference. Unless your contract specifies otherwise, you are usually entitled to any surplus.

Defaulting on one or more payments may never become an issue if you have insurance to cover payments in the event of illness or nonvoluntary unemployment.

Leasing Versus Buying

With car prices rising, leasing has become a popular way to afford a new car. You can lease a car from a leasing company, the leasing division of a car rental firm, or a new-car dealer. Some banks offer leasing packages: the Royal Bank of Canada's "buy back loan option" is one example. Leasing a car means paying a monthly fee for a set period of time in exchange for its use.

Basically, leasing firms offer two types of contracts.

With a "closed-end (fixed-cost) lease," you agree to return the car at the end of a specified length of time. You may have a buy-out option, which is the right to buy the car at a price that was set when you entered the lease.

With an "open-end lease," you negotiate a "purchase option," that is, an agreement to buy the car at its "estimated residual value," at the end of the lease. You, the lessee, are responsible for any difference between the "estimated resid-

---

Negotiating a Leasing Agreement

A leasing agreement is a legal contract: you will be bound by its terms once you sign. Therefore be clear about your commitment. Ask the dealer to explain all of the terms in detail and pay special attention to the following:

• **Up-front charges.** The lessor, or dealer putting up the auto for lease, must disclose in writing all payments that are due upon delivery of the car. The first month's payment, plus one month's payment as security, is standard.

• **Options.** The contract should specify the options you, the lessee, ordered. You are not required to pay for options you did not request.

• **Taxes and fees.** All taxes and title and license fees must be spelled out, along with the precise penalties for late payments.

• **Capitalized cost reduction.** This is a fancy term for down payment, which may be negotiable.

• **Warranty.** Ideally, the manufacturer's warranty should cover the entire term of the lease. If not, try to negotiate this coverage with the lessor.

• **Metreage limit.** Metreage allowances, the number of kilometres covered by the lease, can range from 16,000 to 30,000 per year. You will be charged for every extra kilometre. The metreage allowed is also often open for negotiation.

• **Early termination.** Be clear about the penalties charged if you want to get out of the lease early or if you miss a payment.

• **Gap insurance.** This guarantees the difference between what you, the lessee, collect from the insurance company in case of theft or accident and what you may owe the lessor. Some leases include gap-insurance protection free of charge.

• **Estimated residual value.** This is what the lessor anticipates the car will be worth at the end of the lease. The lessor is obliged to disclose this price to the lessee, and it should also be written into the lease.

• **Purchase option.** Your buy-out price should be written into the contract. On a closed-end lease, it should be the same as the estimated residual value. On an open-end lease, both the estimated residual value and the formula that will be used to determine the final price should be stated.

• **Final costs.** Excess metreage charges, fees for late payment, wear and tear charges, and any other end-of-lease payments must be defined.

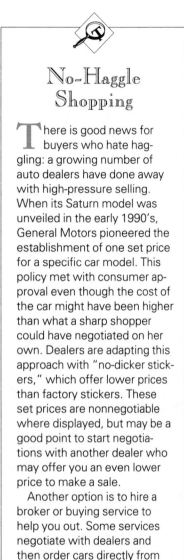

No-Haggle Shopping

There is good news for buyers who hate haggling: a growing number of auto dealers have done away with high-pressure selling. When its Saturn model was unveiled in the early 1990's, General Motors pioneered the establishment of one set price for a specific car model. This policy met with consumer approval even though the cost of the car might have been higher than what a sharp shopper could have negotiated on her own. Dealers are adapting this approach with "no-dicker stickers," which offer lower prices than factory stickers. These set prices are nonnegotiable where displayed, but may be a good point to start negotiations with another dealer who may offer you an even lower price to make a sale.

Another option is to hire a broker or buying service to help you out. Some services negotiate with dealers and then order cars directly from the manufacturer for you. Others search local dealerships for the car you want and then negotiate a price. If you want to do the negotiating on your own, some services will send you four or five different quotes on the model that interests you.

Most services usually charge less than $200. Sometimes such services are a free benefit of membership in a credit union or automobile club. Your employer may offer services as well, but be wary of brokers that require you to go through a particular lender or dealer. Car-buying services are also listed in the Yellow Pages under Automobile Brokers or Automobile Purchasing Services.

ual value" of the car and its actual value when the lease ends. If the final resale value is less than the estimated residual value, you owe the lessor the difference. (You might want your lease to specify that any direct consumer rebate will be deducted from the selling price.) If the resale value is greater than the estimated residual value, you may choose to sell and make a profit. Since the lessee assumes more financial responsibility with an open-end lease, monthly rates are usually lower.

PROS AND CONS OF LEASING

For many drivers, leasing offers several advantages. Since the cost of the lease is based on the car's estimated residual, or depreciated, value, the down payment and monthly payments will be lower than if you were buying a new car. Therefore, you may be able to afford a more luxurious model than if you were buying. Since the typical lease term is from 24 to 48 months, you can always be driving a fairly new car. Leasing may also be a good choice for those who want short-term use of a car. Finally, depending on the model and prevailing interest rates, by leasing first, you may save thousands of dollars on the purchase price if you choose to buy at lease end.

On the downside, you are responsible for all the costs of ownership, including insurance, repairs, and maintenance, but you do not own the car. You may be charged a hefty fee if you exceed a metreage limit, and you may be subjected to expensive penalties if you terminate the lease early. Some lessors also charge fees to cover wear and tear when the car is returned.

Visiting the Showroom

After you have decided on the makes and models that interest you, how much you can afford to spend, and whether you want to buy or lease, you are ready to visit some showrooms.

Limit preliminary activity to checking out the cars firsthand and taking test-drives. Resist pressure from salespersons to close a deal immediately. Visit at least three dealers and do not talk price until you have decided exactly which car you want to buy. If you do not plan to finance with the dealer, do not discuss your intentions until after you have settled on a firm price. Dealers may raise their prices if they know they will not be receiving the profitable interest payments from a loan.

STICKER PRICES

Consumer law requires dealers to post a sticker on each new vehicle showing the manufacturer's suggested retail price for the base model and for all factory-installed optional equipment.

By law, the dealer's transportation charges and the litres per 100 kilometres estimate from Transport Canada must be included. The "sticker price" on a new car is usually 10 to 15 percent higher than what the dealer actually expects.

Watch out for supplemental stickers marked ADM (additional dealer markup) or ADP (additional dealer profit). These items price expensive dealer-installed extras such as undercoating, and you have the right to refuse to buy any of them.

NEGOTIATING THE PRICE

Start from the invoice price (see page 351) and work up; don't begin with the sticker price and come down. Draw up a worksheet listing the exact make and model you plan to buy. List each option you want by name and invoice number (which you got from the sticker or your research). Though dealers are anxious to sell the models on hand, there is no reason you should pay for options you don't want just because they are on the floor model. Order precisely the car you want from the factory, or negotiate hard with the dealer for cars on the floor that have options you don't need. Be aware that delivery of a "custom made" car may take up to three months.

Negotiating a Trade-In

PROBLEM
Richard visited three showrooms and asked for competing bids on a new car. With the invoice price in mind, he negotiated a fair price for the car he wanted, but when he asked about trading in his old car, he was quoted $400 less than the used-car guides said his car was worth. The salesman complained that Richard's car had too many kilometres on it, was not in perfect condition, and therefore was not worth the book value.

ACTION
Because Richard had done his homework he was not taken in by this common ploy used to jack up the overall cost of a car. He knew he had a desirable trade-in model that offered potential profit to the dealer. He also had a quote $200 higher from a used-car dealer across town. As a result, he decided to sell the car on his own for an even better profit.

One of the best techniques is to introduce competition. Tell each dealer that you are getting several bids and will take the best offer. Ask what is the least acceptable amount over the invoice price. Don't settle for a promise to beat any other offer; insist on an exact quote. If the dealer refuses to cooperate, go elsewhere.

A fair price gives the dealer $300 to $500 over the invoice cost, sometimes more on popular models. Often the dealer makes more because the manufacturer has provided discounts.

Beware of Add-Ons

Dealers try hard to sell expensive extras to new-car buyers. Beware, for many are not worth the money, and you should not pay for any options you do not want. Here are some add-ons to avoid:

✔ *Rustproofing, paint sealant, and fabric protection.* These protect the dealer's profit; most cars are treated by the manufacturer.

✔ *Factory- or dealer-supplied sound systems.* You will get a better buy at a company specializing in car stereos. If you take the dealer's upgraded equipment, be sure that the price of the standard radio is deducted from the cost.

✔ *Extended warranties.* With the protection plans common with most new cars, these are not worth the money.

✔ *Credit insurance.* If you need it, you will get it for less from an insurance broker.

✔ *Advertising fee.* Don't agree to accept this cost. You should not have to pay for the dealer's promotions.

✔ *Options packages.* Often added equipment is sold as a package. This can be an advantage if you want everything; if not, you will save by ordering options individually.

✔ *Dealer preparation.* Before you pay extra to have your car made ready to drive, check the sticker; often the price includes dealer preparation.

123

SAVVY CAR-SHOPPERS' CALENDAR

You will have more negotiating power if you shop for a car when dealers are most anxious to sell. Four prime times for best buys are:

1. Late summer and early fall. The end of the model year is peak season for rebates from both dealers and manufacturers who are trying to clear inventory to make way for next year's models.

2. The Christmas season. Business slows down in December, so dealers are very happy to see you just before and after Christmas.

3. Other holidays. Thematic holiday promotions are often held to boost business during other slow holiday periods such as Canada Day, or Easter. When you see advertising for these special sales, you know dealers need to sell a lot of cars to offset their promotional costs.

4. The end of the month. When salespeople are striving to meet their sales goals, they are eager to negotiate and may give up some of their commission in order to make a sale.

These discounts, also known as holdbacks, average about 3 percent. Thus if a dealer sells you a car for the dealer's invoice price, he still makes a $450 profit on a $15,000 car. The only way to know for sure whether or not you are getting a good deal is to check the competition.

Beware if the salesperson who has just offered you a good price leaves to have the deal "approved" by his manager. This is known as "low balling." Having whetted your interest, the manager or another salesperson may tell you that the original salesperson made a mistake and will try to renegotiate—for a higher price, of course. Your best response is to walk out the door. You can be fairly sure that you will get a phone call the next day hoping to get you back in the showroom.

As with financing, do not discuss trading in your old car until you have a firm quote. Having checked competitive rates in advance, you know that you can get financing elsewhere and can sell your old car yourself.

THE PURCHASE AGREEMENT

When the sale is complete, read the purchase agreement carefully. It should specify the make, model, and year of the car, the engine type, and the vehicle identification number, so that you can be sure you get the car you have paid for. Make sure that all of the prices match those quoted by the salesperson and that all the agreed-upon options are listed. The amount and receipt of the down payment should be noted, and any additional charges should be specified, including relevant taxes, and charges for title and registration.

The purchase order should clearly state the conditions under which a refund of the down payment will be made. If you have accepted dealer financing, insist that the interest rate and monthly payments be specified, as well as your right to cancel and get a refund if the dealer fails to obtain financing on those terms within a specified period of time. If the contract is for future delivery, it should guarantee full return of the deposit if delivery is not made by a specified date, or if you reject the car because it is defective or lacks equipment you ordered. Be sure an officer of the dealership signs the agreement, because the salesperson's name alone may not be sufficiently binding.

TAKING DELIVERY

Before you drive out of the showroom, make sure your new car is free of scratches or dents, and that all the specified options have been installed. If you asked for air-conditioning, do not drive the car off the lot without it. Have any problems corrected before you leave with the car or, if you cannot wait, make sure the dealer agrees in writing to correct the problem at a later date, and make sure to hold him to his promise.

Buying a Used Car

Used cars are thrifty but risky. Before you buy, be sure you know your dealer's or the seller's reputation—and your rights.

Buyer Beware

Many good reasons exist for buying a used car, the most obvious being savings. The steepest depreciation on a car is in the first two years of its life. If you find a late-model car in good condition, you may drive away with most of the life of the car ahead of you and pay much less than the cost of a new car.

Although you pay less, you also assume more risk with a used car. For one thing, repairs can be costly. Fortunately, many sources of help are available for used-car buyers.

As with new cars, start with references that rate used-car models by year on the basis of reliability, repair records, and recall history, and that provide pricing guides. (See "Information Sources for Car Buyers," page 350.) Make a list of four or five recommended models that fit your budget.

GOING SHOPPING

With your data in hand, shop around. Try new-car dealers; you may pay more, but they have the widest selection and the greatest accountability for their used cars. Used-car dealers may offer better prices, but their stock and follow-up service can be less reliable. Work only with a dealer who has been in business for a long time and check the Better Business Bureau about dealers with whom you are considering doing business.

When car-rental agencies update their fleets, they often sell off their older cars. These vehicles usually have had regular maintenance, and most come with a warranty. Call a car-rental office to locate the nearest company used-car lot. Auctions also offer bargains, but they also carry risk, since the cars have often been repossessed by lenders and come without guarantees.

Private sellers may be the least expensive source because they have no overhead. However, you may have limited recourse if problems arise once the sale is complete. To survey the options, check local ads. The more ads you see for the model you want, the better your bargaining leverage.

Wherever you find a car that interests you, ask questions like: How many owners has the car had? Who was the last owner? Why is the car being sold? Has it been in any accidents? What is needed to put the car in top condition?

Inspecting a Used Car

Be sure to check these items when you inspect a used car:

✔ **The odometer.** For signs of illegal tampering, check the dashboard for missing screws, and be sure the odometer numbers line up properly.

✔ **Pedals and seats.** Look for signs of age on clutch, brake, and accelerator pedals, and a saggy driver's seat.

✔ **Fenders and trim.** Look for ripples in the metal or patches, indicating rust or body damage.

✔ **Doors and windows.** Look for rust on the bottom of the door; make sure all doors and windows close easily and completely.

✔ **Trunk.** Check inside the trunk for rust. Look under the mat for stains.

✔ **Spare tire.** Make sure the spare is usable and insist on a replacement if it is not.

✔ **Undercoating.** Check for fresh undercoating in the wheel wells or under the carriage, indicating rust.

✔ **Glass and plastic surfaces.** Make sure these are intact.

✔ **Heating and cooling systems.** In winter check the air-conditioning system; check the heater in summer.

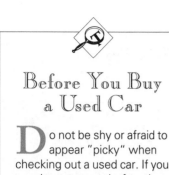

Before You Buy a Used Car

Do not be shy or afraid to appear "picky" when checking out a used car. If you are about to spend a few thousand dollars, you have the right to answers to your questions. Operate from the premise that a used vehicle will have some problems or at least some signs of "wear and tear."
In setting a purchase price, take into account imminent expenses for such things as new brakes or a new exhaust system.

Ask the dealer for the name and telephone number of the previous owner. Telephone to see if there were any problems with the car and ask what the odometer reading was when the car was traded.

Have a trusted mechanic check out the car and provide a written estimate of needed repairs. His fee (about $50) may save you hundreds of dollars. The repairs list alone may convince the seller to lower his price.

Test-drive the car for at least 30 minutes in traffic and on highways. Some problems do not appear in a quick ride around the block. If the vendor will not let you test-drive the car or have it checked by a mechanic, walk away: he obviously has something to hide.

Any warranty or promise by the seller—to make certain repairs or add new tires, for example—should be in writing, and should specify exactly what is covered and what repairs will be done.

When you find a car you like, test-drive and inspect it carefully in bright daylight. Unscrupulous sellers may have buried body rust or accident damage under layers of paint. Dishonest sellers may also turn back the odometer to make an older vehicle appear more attractive.

Follow your own examination with an inspection by a mechanic, with particular attention given to transmission or engine problems. Do not deal with a seller who will not allow you to have the car inspected. If defects are found, they should be corrected by an agreed-upon mechanic, or the price of the car should be reduced.

Making the Deal

The price of a used car is based on its condition and metreage, or mileage as it is commonly called. The bargaining process is similar to new-car negotiations. The best tactic is to ignore the sticker price and make an offer slightly above the listed wholesale price, which you know from your research. Used-car warranties are negotiable and can vary widely.

Get the vendor to put the warranty in writing before you sign the contract. A full warranty means that service will be provided free of charge on the specified parts and systems during the warranty period. A limited warranty usually means that you pay some of the repair costs. Try to negotiate a full warranty. Bear in mind, also, that you have the legal right to read the warranty before you buy.

Find out if the dealer uses a third party to provide repair service. If so, make sure the company supplying the service is responsible and insured.

Unless a car is being sold for scrap, it comes with an "implied warranty" given by law, even if the dealer sells the car without a written warranty. This legal "implied warranty" guarantees the buyer that the car will be roadworthy for a "reasonable period of time." Bear in mind that a "reasonable period" can vary from 30 days to six months depending on the price paid, and the vehicle's age and condition.

Often the dealer will try to sell you a service contract in addition to the warranty. There is no point in buying such a contract if it covers the same repairs offered by the warranty. It may be worthwhile investing in it, however, if it extends beyond the warranty and the potential cost of repairs seems more than the cost of the contract. Make sure the service contract you sign includes towing charges and the cost of a rental car for use while your car is undergoing repairs. Watch out for any extra cancellation costs that may be included.

How to Sell Your Own Car

If your old car is in good condition and you are willing to invest some time, you will get more money for it if you sell it yourself. Since savvy buyers will have researched values, it is important to handle your sale in a professional manner. Here are tips for successful marketing:

• **Set a realistic price.** Find out what the car is worth by checking reference guides and ads for similar cars, and getting quotes from used-car dealers. Decide on the most you can realistically get, and the least you will accept. Your sale price will probably be between these two figures.

• **Compose an advertisement.** State the year, make, and model, and list desirable equipment, such as air-conditioning or a tape deck. List any strong points such as low metreage or good condition, but if work is needed, say so; if you misrepresent the car, you could face a legal claim if a buyer has problems. Name a price to deter bargain hunters, or say "best offer" to garner the most responses. List only your phone number. Leaving your address out of the ad allows you to screen buyers before they come to your home.

• **Spread the word.** Begin by advertising in less expensive outlets, such as small neighborhood papers. If you do not get enough responses, move up to the local newspaper with the largest circulation. Don't forget free advertising. Put a "For Sale" sign with your telephone number in the car's rear side window. Post an ad on bulletin boards at your office, schools, churches, and shopping centers in the area.

• **Put the car into top shape.** Clean the car inside and out, wax the exterior, repair torn upholstery, and replace worn floor mats. Shine up the chrome, but don't have the car painted; prospects may assume the new coat is covering body work. If you replace worn gas or brake pedals, do it well in advance of when you try to sell the car so that they will not look brand-new.

• **Be sure everything works.** Check the air conditioner and heater, the clock, the defroster, the window controls, the windshield wipers and washers, the lights, and the fluid levels for the automatic transmission and brakes. If the tires are worn, either replace them or take the replacement cost into account when you price the car.

• **Have the car serviced.** Do whatever you can to ensure that it will perform well in a test-drive. Check the battery so that the car will start smoothly.

• **Have your documents ready.** Your title and registration, warranties, and the owner's manual should be ready for inspection. Maintenance receipts should be available to prove the service record.

• **Protect yourself.** A serious customer must be allowed to test-drive the car and have it inspected. Go along on the test-drive and allow the prospect to take the car for inspection, but only after leaving a valuable deposit with you, such as her car registration, or a passport. Accept payment only in cash, by certified cheque, or by money order; never take a personal cheque.

• **Transfer the title.** Procedures for transferring a title vary. In all provinces you will be required to fill out an odometer statement, and may be required to sign a statement assigning the title, and to fill out a sales-tax form. The buyer will take these forms to the motor vehicle bureau, get a new registration and license plates, and notify the bureau that you no longer hold title to the car. Call your motor vehicle bureau for local rules.

• **Pay off any loans.** If your title had a lien on the car from a lender, it is your responsibility to give the purchaser proof of the release of the lien.

• **Remove the license plates.** You and the purchaser should meet at the motor vehicle bureau, where you will turn in the car plates. You will have to make this trip even if you are transferring your plates to another car. In some cases you may get a rebate if you return the license plates before the expiry date. Inform your insurance company of the sale, but do not cancel your insurance until the ownership transfer is completed.

• **Create a bill of sale that protects.** The bill of sale is an important legal document that can be used against you in small claims court if you fail to word it in such a way as to protect yourself. It should state clearly that the car is being sold "as is," with no guarantees. A bill of sale should also state that the seller is the sole legal owner of the car, that the vehicle meets all applicable federal and provincial safety requirements, and that the emission control equipment is fully operational. It should also state the odometer reading, that the buyer has had the opportunity to drive the car and have it inspected by a mechanic of his choice, and that the seller makes no further claims, either verbally or in writing, as to the condition of the car.

MAINTAINING YOUR CAR

To keep your car in top shape, be sure you understand the basic warranties required by law from the auto manufacturer.

Understanding Your Warranty

Carmakers have a legal responsibility to ensure that the autos they sell have no defects. The so-called warranty is a package of guarantees that spells out their responsibility and define your rights.

The "basic warranty" promises that the manufacturer will make any repair necessary because of defects in materials or manufacture, without charge, for a specified period, which can range from one year or 20,000 kilometres (whichever comes first) to six years or 100,000 kilometres.

In addition to the basic warranty, new cars are protected by the "power-train warranty," which covers important parts of the engine, including the transmission, the drive train, and other specified systems. The power-train warranty may last beyond the basic warranty. A separate rust or corrosion warranty is usually included in any sale. Various parts of the emission control system must be warranted by provincial law. Most manufacturers include an emission control system warranty on new cars for five years or 80,000 kilometres.

Parts that are routinely replaced because of normal wear—filters, brake pads, fuses, and lubricants such as oil and coolant—are not covered, nor are costs for routine maintenance. Tires and batteries come with their own warranties.

To ensure the manufacturer-provided warranties remain in effect, the driver must follow the maintenance schedule in the instruction manual. The warranties will not cover problems caused by misuse, neglect, or damage from an accident.

FULL AND LIMITED WARRANTIES

The best warranty is a full warranty. It provides free repair within the stated period and permits the owner to elect a refund or replacement if the car contains a defect that cannot be repaired after a reasonable number of attempts. However, most cars come with limited warranties. In either case, you must be clear from the start as to what is covered and for what length of time.

In addition to the manufacturer's warranties, two warranties are guaranteed by law on every dealer-sold car: a "warranty of merchantability," which promises that the car will perform

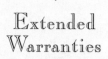

properly, and a "warranty of fitness," which assures that the car can be used for the specific purpose for which it was designed. (See also YOUR CONSUMER RIGHTS, page 381.)

Finally, any claims made to you by a salesperson are "express warranties." If you are misled, you may have a legal case against the seller; make sure you have express claims put into writing so that you have proof of any promises.

THE SERVICE CONTRACT

A service contract, which is offered by the dealer rather than the manufacturer, is sometimes referred to as an "extended warranty." Like the basic warranty, the service contract creates a promise to perform certain repairs or services, but it comes with a price—sometimes a high price. It usually includes a deductible—a specified sum that the car owner must pay toward repairs before free service begins.

Before you agree to a service contract, compare it carefully with the manufacturer's free warranty to make sure that you are not paying for duplicate coverage. Many service contracts will not offer any more protection than the original warranty does. Also note carefully anything that is not included. If the contract specifies only "mechanical breakdowns," you will not be reimbursed for problems related to normal wear and tear—having to replace your brakes, for example.

You should also know whether repairs will be done by the dealer or if you will be sent to other service centers. Find out whether you will be covered if your car breaks down out of town. Are towing charges included? Will parts be replaced with new or reconditioned parts? If you wish to cancel the service, will you be entitled to a full or partial refund?

Cars That Defy Repair

All car owners dread the thought of buying a "lemon," a new car that continually breaks down. If you discover that you bought a lemon and have submitted the car for repair a reasonable number of times, your first recourse is to ask for a refund or replacement from the dealer or manufacturer. If necessary, go straight to the head of the company.

If neither dealer nor manufacturer is responsive to your request, you should contact a lawyer, especially if a defect in the car has caused bodily injury or property damage. Manufacturers' liability has grown dramatically in recent decades and there is abundant jurisprudence that holds a manufacturer liable for the safety of his wares. Ruling on *Kravitz* v. *General Motors of Canada* in 1979, the Supreme Court of Canada held that the

Extended Warranties

Add-ons, such as extended warranties—coverage that goes into effect once the manufacturer's warranty ends—are a potential source of profit for car dealers. Depending on what they cover, such warranties can range from $500 to $2,000, a figure that is always negotiable. If interested, offer about 50 percent of the price asked.

Extended warranties were worthwhile when cars were warranted for one year or 20,000 kilometres, but are less attractive now that warranties run for 36 months or 60,000 kilometres. Car owners may enjoy trouble-free motoring for extended periods simply by having their cars checked and any problems corrected in the weeks before the manufacturer's warranty expires.

Before buying an extended warranty, ask yourself how long you intend to keep the car and how many kilometres you will put on. If you intend to keep the vehicle for just three to four years, you may be better off pocketing the money an extended warranty would cost, and dealing with repair costs yourself should they arise.

If you do invest, however, buy only a factory-backed warranty. Too often, third party warrantors go out of business or declare bankruptcy leaving you with a worthless contract. Make sure also that your warranty is transferable if you decide to sell or trade your car.

Jack Brown
1552 Wagar Avenue
Calgary, Alberta T2J 1J5

March 31, 1996

Mr. Robert J. Thomas, President ①
Belchfire Motor Company
Oshawa, Ontario

Dear Mr. Thomas:

On August 5 last year, I purchased a Belchfire Nebula, serial number JK745839278, from Greenboro Auto, an authorized Belchfire dealership at 7 Oak Boulevard in Calgary. I have put 9,500 kilometres on the car, have fulfilled all the requirements in the warranty, and have enclosed copies of receipts documenting these visits. ②

I have had repeated problems with the transmission, which locks and prevents the car from being driven. The car has been in the dealer's repair shop four times in the last six months; August 25, September 28, November 25, and February 10. Each time I was told the problem was corrected, and each time it recurred. I have been without the use of my car for over four weeks in the last seven months—a major inconvenience and expense. ③

I feel this car can never be properly repaired and request that I be given a new car. ④ I count on you as president to demonstrate the reliability of the Belchfire Motor Company.

If you do not respond favorably to this request, I will have no choice but to take whatever legal action is necessary. I hope that the company will act responsibly, making further action unnecessary. I look forward to hearing from you within the next 10 business days. ⑤

Sincerely,

Squeezing a Lemon

If your attempts to resolve car problems with the dealership are unsuccessful, you may choose to approach the manufacturer with a letter that carefully documents your claim. 1. Address your letter to the company's top official. 2. Give the vital statistics concerning the auto, including date of purchase, style of car, serial number, place of purchase, current condition indicated by the number of kilometres driven, and the fact that you have fulfilled all maintenance requirements in the warranty. 3. Spell out the problem in detail. State the number of times you have had the car repaired and any contingent problems. 4. State clearly how you want the problem resolved. 5. State how and when you will proceed if the problem is not resolved. Enclose copies of all bills and invoices, and send the material by certified mail, return receipt requested.

manufacturer as well as the dealer can be sued by the consumer, even though the manufacturer never directly contracted with the consumer.

When no injuries are involved, consumers may choose to settle disputes with automobile dealers or manufacturers through arbitration. Owner's manuals usually identify impartial arbitration programs that can be used. (See also YOUR RIGHTS IN ACTION, page 448.)

The Canadian automobile industry advocates a national arbitration plan similar to those in place in British Columbia and Ontario, and has outlined a proposed framework to all provinces. This proposal is modeled on the Ontario Motor Vehicle Arbitration Plan (OMVAP), which has existed since 1986. The Ontario program is financed by the car companies and is free to the consumers. Its arbitrators are independent of the industry, and can render binding decisions, usually within four to six weeks of hearing the evidence.

Some arbitration boards require personal appearances by those involved; others will accept written evidence alone. Either way, to present your case successfully you must have written documentation of your attempts to have the car repaired, and the failure or inability of the dealer or manufacturer to remedy the defects. Keep a careful file with all records, copies of all correspondence with the repair shop, the dealer, and the manufacturer, and a log of all related phone calls.

In most cases, arbitration decisions are binding on the manufacturer, but buyers may pursue further legal action if they feel they have not received fair treatment. Civil suits allow the purchaser to sue the manufacturer or dealer or both for either a replacement vehicle or restitution, and to ask for payment of any lawyer's fees and other costs incurred.

Car Repair Without Headaches

While most auto mechanics are trustworthy, some dishonest repairmen will diagnose work far beyond what is actually needed to correct a particular problem. Wise drivers look for a reliable mechanic *before* they need one. Word of mouth from satisfied friends and relatives is usually the best method of finding an honest, reliable, and competent mechanic.

When you visit the shop, look for a current operating license and recent certifications, such as certification from an approved Canadian Automobile Association repair facility or an attestation from the Better Business Bureau. Be sure the shop has the modern diagnostic equipment necessary to identify problems in computer-controlled late-model cars.

HOW AUTO CLUBS HELP MOTORISTS

Auto clubs are worthwhile investments for many motorists. The Canadian Automobile Association is the largest; others include the Esso Auto Club, Sears Auto Club, and some clubs operated by banking institutions. Exact offerings vary, but for a yearly fee members are usually entitled to the following:

1. Rescue on the road. If you have trouble, clubs will provide necessary help without charge, even for towing.

2. Bed and board. If a trip is interrupted because an auto is disabled, you may receive a refund for meals and lodging.

3. Legal aid. In case of arrest for a traffic violation, some club's members are guaranteed up to $5,000 for legal expenses (including bail bond, as might be required in the U.S.A.). The motorist will reimburse the club when billed on his return.

4. Travel aids. Maps, guides, discounts on car rentals and hotel rates are benefits.

5. Cheque cashing. Members may be able to cash personal cheques at participating service stations or at local club offices.

6. Personal insurance. Members may receive accidental death and dismemberment coverage in case of travel-related accidents.

7. Convenience. Some clubs provide license plates, registration, and other vehicle documentation services.

Beware of Auto Repair Scams

Most mechanics are honest, but occasionally you may run into an unscrupulous person bent on taking advantage of your lack of knowledge of auto repairs. Here are some classic scams:

✔ *New problems.* Your car is in the shop for a new muffler, and the garage calls to say that the oil pump is broken, too. "Discovering" new problems is a common ploy used to con customers into spending more.

✔ *Instant leaks.* Using a concealed can to squirt oil or gasoline on parts, a mechanic may convince you that he has found a leak. Ask to have the part wiped clean so you can see whether the leak reappears as you drive the car.

✔ *Phony parts.* Sneaky shops may charge for a new part, but install a reconditioned used one. Be sure the work order specifies new parts and ask for the box in which they came.

✔ *Illegible work orders.* If you cannot read the work order, you won't know if you are being overcharged. Ask to have your order rewritten clearly.

✔ *Upping the ante.* The mechanic says he will try to save you money with a cheap repair, but if it does not work, a more costly one will be needed. The car goes into the shop, the small repair is never made, and when the problem recurs, you are stuck with the expensive alternative.

GETTING THE MOST FROM A MECHANIC

Most disputes over car repairs arise because of poor communication between the repairman and the customer. Prevent misunderstandings or rip-offs by following these guidelines:

- **Put your problems in writing.** Don't expect your mechanic to recall your directives. Before visiting the garage, make a note of the problems, listing the things you want checked or repaired.
- **Be specific.** Describe the problem as clearly and as accurately as you can—where the sound comes from, for example, when it appears, and under what conditions.
- **Get a written estimate.** Before you sign any work order, get a written estimate for the job. The estimate should specify work to be done, charges for parts and labor, whether replacement parts will be new or used, and that no work will begin without your approval. Most garages give you estimates free of charge.
- **Sign only a detailed work order.** The work order should describe the problem and the repairs exactly as they are stated on the estimate. Never sign an open-ended order, or you could be charged for work you did not authorize.
- **Ask for an itemized bill.** Check it against the work order to ensure you have been charged only for work you authorized.
- **Get a written guarantee.** Make sure that all work is guaranteed in writing. A reputable shop will stand behind its work with a guarantee of 30 to 90 days.
- **Keep records.** Your estimate, work order, and guarantee are contracts. Make sure they are dated, signed, and identify your vehicle and its metreage (mileage).
- **Take the car for a test-drive.** Test-drive your car the moment you pick it up. If the problem remains, report it immediately. If you have dealt with it fairly, an honest garage will respond to you in the same manner.

IF YOU MUST COMPLAIN

If you are not happy with the work, complain in person to the shop owner or service manager. If the problem is not resolved, write a letter to the service manager explaining why you are displeased and stating what action you will take, such as reporting the shop to the provincial department of consumer affairs. If the problem concerns a new car under warranty, write the general manager or owner of the dealership and include a copy of your first letter. If you still fail to get satisfaction, you may sue the repair shop in small claims court.

You will probably have to pay for your repair in order to take your car out of the shop, since the law usually gives the mechanic a lien on the car until the bill has been paid in full.

INSURING YOUR CAR

Insurance is a necessity for car owners. Learning how to compare companies and choose wisely cuts the cost of owning a car.

How Much Insurance Do You Need?

An auto insurance policy can consist of several types of coverage, liability and collision among them. Each option is priced separately. As a car owner, your goal is to define and obtain the protection you need, and eliminate unnecessary options.

Before buying a policy, check what your provincial insurance laws require. All provinces insist on liability insurance, which protects other people from damage you cause. Each province sets its own minimums, which range from $50,000 in Quebec (where bodily injury is covered by that province's "no fault" insurance plan) to $200,000 in Ontario.

If you are sued for amounts above your policy limit, you will be responsible for the additional amount. Because costs can run high in a serious accident, those who can afford to upgrade their coverage should do so. This is especially true for anyone who drives in the United States, where awards are often higher than those in Canada. An umbrella policy covers liability costs in excess of car and homeowners insurance policies. The extra premium is worthwhile since the premium difference between $200,000 and $500,000 coverage is usually quite reasonable.

ADDITIONAL COVERAGE

Collision/comprehensive insurance, usually bought as a package, not only covers the repair of your car after an accident regardless of who is at fault, but also protects you if you drive another person's car, or if someone else drives your car. The comprehensive portion covers theft or damage from causes other than an accident, including fire, flood, and vandalism. If you must rent a car as a result of a theft or accident, the policy may also pay part of the cost. These policies have deductibles that the policyholder must absorb before the insurance company pays. Although collision/comprehensive insurance is optional by law, lenders may insist that it be carried until a car loan is paid off.

Uninsured and underinsured motorist coverage, medical payments insurance, and personal-injury protection are

---

Insurance Buyers Guide

Here is a checklist of various auto insurance options:

✔ *Liability.* Covers damage or injury you cause to others and pays for your legal defense.

✔ *Umbrella.* Pays costs beyond the limits of both auto and homeowners policies. Most insurers require you to have both policies with the same company and to buy a minimum amount of coverage.

✔ *Collision.* Covers damage to your car or another car if you are in an accident.

✔ *Comprehensive.* Protects against auto theft or damage not resulting from a collision.

✔ *Uninsured motorist.* Pays costs in case of a collision with a driver who is not insured.

✔ *Personal injury.* Usually optional, but required in some provinces with no-fault laws; pays for certain medical costs and income lost if you are unable to work due to an accident. This type of insurance is automatic in Quebec under its no-fault law. Vehicle owners must pay up when registering their vehicles.

✔ *Medical payments.* Available in provinces without no-fault laws; pays for injuries to you or your passengers in an accident, no matter who is at fault.

designed to pay for costs of personal injury to you or passengers in your car. They may or may not be necessary, depending on the coverage you and your passengers already have through other policies. Before you sign up, carefully read through your other insurance policies.

Shopping for the Best Deal

Auto insurance companies base their rates on many factors: a driver's age, gender and driving record, the ages of others who will drive the car, the make of the car, where the driver lives, and how many kilometres the car is driven regularly. Cars that are less attractive to thieves and cost less to repair will cost less to insure.

Auto insurance is a highly competitive field so shop around to get the most coverage for the smallest premium. Compare rates by checking with two or more agents who represent one insurer, independent agents who represent several companies, and "direct writers"—companies that deal directly with the consumer. If you belong to a professional group, teachers for example, see if there is a reduced rate for members of your group.

In addition to reasonable rates, be sure to consider reliability, financial stability, and speed in processing claims. To make sure that a company is financially sound, check Moody's Investor Service and Standard & Poor's Corporation, both of which evaluate insurance companies for financial stability. Your provincial insurance bureau, the federal or provincial superintendent of insurance, and the Insurance Bureau of Canada may also be of some help in this regard. (For the addresses and telephone numbers for these firms, see RESOURCES, page 469.) Find out whether your provincial insurance department or local Better Business Bureau has had complaints about an agent or company with which you are considering doing business.

After you determine financial stability, get quotes from three insurers on the same amount of coverage—such as collision/comprehensive rates for a range of deductibles from $50 to $1,000. Make up a chart comparing rates. You will quickly see the best deals.

Here are other ways you can save on auto insurance:

- **Raise your deductible.** The biggest way to cut your insurance bill is to assume some risk yourself.
- **Buy multiple policies with the same company.** If you use the same insurer for both homeowner's and auto insurance or for insurance for two or more cars, you may be entitled to volume discounts.

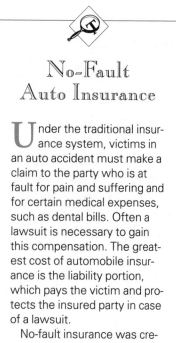

No-Fault Auto Insurance

Under the traditional insurance system, victims in an auto accident must make a claim to the party who is at fault for pain and suffering and for certain medical expenses, such as dental bills. Often a lawsuit is necessary to gain this compensation. The greatest cost of automobile insurance is the liability portion, which pays the victim and protects the insured party in case of a lawsuit.

No-fault insurance was created specifically to cut down on costly and lengthy lawsuits. Government-backed no-fault plans are now in place in most provinces. These plans entitle anyone—drivers, passengers, and even pedestrians—injured in motor vehicle accidents to compensatory damages up to a certain limit, no matter who was at fault. In turn the injured parties cannot sue the party at fault except in extreme cases—those involving severe injury or death, for example— or when the money damages exceed the no-fault limit.

Quebec's plan prohibits anyone from ever suing another for bodily injuries suffered in an auto accident. British Columbia and Ontario plans limit recourse to the courts to cases where the injury results in serious permanent disfigurement or permanent serious impairment of an important physical or psychological function.

- **Limit coverage on older cars.** Consider dropping collision/comprehensive insurance after five years, since the book value that insurance companies will pay if the car is damaged may be less than the cost of insurance.
- **Pay up front.** You will save interest charges if you pay for the policy all at once rather than in installments.
- **Limit teen insurance.** Indicate which car teenagers will drive (and do not allow them to drive another) so that the higher rate for teenage drivers applies only to one car.
- **Take advantage of discounts.** Take advantage of any carrier discounts (see below) for which you qualify.
- **Drive carefully.** Rates go up if you are in an accident or get a ticket for a serious violation, such as speeding.

If you are underinsured or don't have insurance at all, you could be courting disaster if you suffer a loss and have no financial net to catch you.

RALPH NADER
The Frugal Shopper

How to File a Claim

Notify your insurance company immediately after an accident so that an investigation can be made while events are still fresh in everyone's mind. In provinces with no-fault insurance, each driver is paid by his own insurance company for accident damages, regardless of who was at fault. In other provinces, when the other driver is at fault, your insurer has the right to sue the other driver's insurance company for compensation. If the company collects, you may receive a refund on your deductible, or you may sue for the deductible in small claims court.

Discounts on Auto Insurance

Automobile insurance companies have determined factors that lower accident rates, and offer discounts to drivers who take advantage of these findings. Discounts vary from company to company, so comparison shopping pays. Here are ways to cash in on discounts:

• **Install safety devices.** Factory-installed antilock brakes, antitheft devices, automatic seat belts, and passive restraints such as air bags may reduce your premium payments.

• **Take a defensive driving course.** Some provinces require these courses for learners, teenagers, and drivers 70 years and over, and some insurance companies give discounts to anyone who takes them.

• **Enroll your teenager in a driver training course.** You may be eligible for a discount if a teenager on your policy takes a driver training course either privately or in school. Notify your insurance company when a child moves out of your home or goes away to college. Your rates could go down considerably.

• **Join a car pool.** Rates may be cut for those who cut their driving distances. Discounts are available for any driver who logs less than the average number of kilometres per year.

• **Check your claims status.** Insurance companies rate clients according to their claims records. If you fall into a group that has favorable claims records, you may qualify for discounts. Among these categories are drivers over age 50, females who are the sole drivers of their cars, and drivers who have not had a moving violation or an accident in the past two to five years.

Do Rental Cars Need Extra Insurance?

Collision-damage waiver insurance and loss-damage waiver insurance offered by rental car companies are the most expensive kinds of auto insurance you can buy. Moreover, they are protections that most drivers do not need. If you are renting a car within the United States or Canada, your own auto insurance policy will most likely protect you when you are driving another car, including one you have rented.

However, be sure to confirm your policy's regulations. Most companies limit the number of rental days they will cover (although you can get around this stipulation by returning one car and renting another) or will not insure car rentals for business purposes.

If you rent frequently for business and your employer does not pick up the cost, you may find it cheaper to extend your personal car insurance to cover business rentals than to pay out high rental premiums.

Another way to be covered, especially if you do not have auto insurance, is to use a credit card that includes collision or theft coverage for rentals charged with the card. Most premium "gold cards," such as those offered by American Express, Visa and Mastercard, include this feature.

Bear in mind that credit card insurance is secondary coverage, meaning it pays only what your own insurance policy does not cover. Credit card terms for rental insurance may also be limited.

Send your insurance company a detailed written account of the accident, and keep a copy. This file will be valuable if you later find yourself in a dispute with the other driver or with your insurance company. Keep a record of expenses such as towing or car rentals that you incur as a result of the accident, in case they are reimbursable.

If your car has been damaged, the insurer will send an appraiser to inspect it soon after the accident. Appraisers assess the cost of repairing damages and report their findings to an adjuster at the company. The adjuster authorizes payment. It can help to be present when the appraiser arrives. By pointing out features that might be overlooked, you may be able to increase the amount of the settlement.

If the car has been taken to a repair shop, the appraiser usually negotiates directly with the shop. Don't authorize any repairs until the appraiser has done his inspection. Only he can decide what repairs the company will pay for. If the mechanic finds other problems later, he will contact the insurer directly to arrange additional payment.

If you cannot find a garage willing to repair your car for the price the insurance company agreed to pay, notify the company and ask for a higher settlement. Do not accept an inadequate amount or sign away your right to additional claims by cashing a cheque that says "in full settlement." Get an independent estimate from a reputable repair shop and submit it to the adjuster as a model for a reasonable settlement. If you do not get satisfaction, go to the claims supervisor. If you still cannot reach agreement, the settlement you are offered is unsatisfactory, or your claim is denied, contact the provincial insurance board or consult a lawyer.

You can seek recourse in the arbitration procedures provided for in some automobile insurance policies. To cut down on expensive, lengthy lawsuits, some insurance companies have instituted arbitration procedures for cases in which one driver's insurance company files a liability claim against another driver's insurance company. Under the provisions of some policies, arbitration is mandatory, although the right to a trial sometimes remains if either party is dissatisfied with the decision of the arbitrators.

FAILURE TO REPORT AN ACCIDENT

Many drivers hesitate to report minor "fender benders" for fear of an increase in their insurance premiums. You may well be tempted to settle small accidents directly with the other driver, paying for minor repairs yourself or accepting payment from the driver. However, if the other driver later files a claim against you, your insurer can drop you or refuse to cover you because you failed to report the accident initially.

AUTOMOBILE ACCIDENTS

Accidents can lead to potentially costly lawsuits. Doing the right things after the accident will protect you whether you are suing or being sued.

The Meaning of Negligence

Some automobile accidents are nobody's fault, but most prove to be somebody's fault, and in court that fault is known as "negligence." Legally, negligent driving refers to an individual's omission of any reasonable precaution, concern, or action while driving an automobile. Failing to signal a turn or stop at a red light is one example of negligent driving. When a driver is reckless or drunk and is clearly at fault in an accident, he may even be charged with "gross negligence."

Often both drivers are partially at fault. Suppose you failed to come to a full halt at a stop sign, and a speeding car rushed into the intersection and hit your car. In some provinces the compensation you or the other driver would receive depends on the degree of fault, or "comparative negligence." There are no set rules to determine degrees of fault; it is up to the court to decide where the blame lies.

Sometimes neither driver is to blame. Potholes, misplaced barriers, or nonfunctioning lights are the culprit, and the city or the provincial highways department is at fault. If a car malfunctions and causes damage or injury because of faulty parts or improper repairs, the owner and anyone injured may have a legitimate lawsuit against the manufacturer or the repair shop.

PROTECTING YOURSELF LEGALLY

Legal action is a possibility anytime an injured party is dissatisfied with the settlement offered by the other driver's insurance company. So know your province's laws and respond properly after an accident. The police must always be notified if anyone is injured or if damage exceeds a specified amount: in Ontario, for example, this is $700. If you hit a parked car and the owner is not around, leave a note with your name and telephone number and notify the police.

Failure to report an accident and failure to remain at the scene are two separate offenses. You can be fined from $60 to $500 for not reporting an accident, and you may also lose up to three demerit points. But failing to remain at the scene may net fines ranging from $200 to $1,000; imprisonment of up to six months, in some cases; and loss of up to seven demerit

---

Safety First

Installing the best safety devices and equipment in your car will help prevent serious problems in case of accident or theft. For extra assurance, consider:

✔ *All safety features.* Buy a car with dual air bags, antilock brakes, three-point lap-and-shoulder seat belts, shatter-proof window glass, a padded dashboard, rear window defoggers, childproof locks, and head restraints.

✔ *Infant seats.* If you have children, purchase the best seats. Also, position infants facing the rear in a semi-reclined position; seat older children facing forward in the back seat.

✔ *Locked doors.* Secured doors are more likely to stay closed in case of a crash, and they can also discourage carjackers.

✔ *Antitheft devices.* Install an alarm, and place an alarm sticker in the car window. Also, install hood and trunk locks and a disabling device for the ignition.

✔ *Careful identification.* Etch or paint your car registration number under the hood, inside the trunk, and on the battery and other parts so that the car and its parts can be identified quickly.

points. If you hit a parked car, telephone pole or other inanimate object, get out of the car, assess damages, and report to the police and your insurance company without delay.

If you are contacted by the lawyer of someone you have injured, refer the party to your insurance company. Any statements you make could jeopardize your liability coverage. Your insurer will assign a lawyer to your case, but if the other party is asking for sums higher than your policy coverage, you will probably need your own lawyer as well.

If you are hurt in an accident, don't rush to settle claims. Many injuries don't develop fully for months. Some claims must be filed within 100 days, but the statute of limitations in most provinces is one or two years from the date of the accident.

Keep a diary of all doctor visits, hospital stays, and medicines prescribed, and retain copies of all drug bills. Keep track of any work hours lost because of incapacity, or outpatient treatment. Sometimes several years can pass before a case comes up for trial; your diary will help you remember accurately and your receipts will serve as proof of your expenses.

If You Are in an Accident

Even the most minor "fender benders" can lead to costly lawsuits if you do not handle the situation properly. To protect yourself from a lawsuit following even a minor accident, carefully follow these procedures:

• **Stop.** Failure to stop at the scene of an accident where property damage or injuries occur can be considered a "hit and run" crime. Always wait until the extent of the damage has been determined.

• **Call the police.** Report the accident as soon as possible. If the accident is serious, wait at the scene until the police arrive, and do not move the car. Get the names and badge numbers of the police officers who come to the scene and the address of the police station where the report will be filed.

• **Seek necessary medical attention.** If anyone is injured, don't try to move him. Cover him with a blanket or coat to help prevent chills or shock; then call an ambulance or emergency care. If you have been injured, even only slightly, see a doctor promptly and get the diagnosis in writing.

• **Get information from the other driver.** Exchange names, addresses, telephone numbers, license plate numbers, driver's license numbers, year and make of car, and names of insurance agents and companies. Don't discuss coverage; let the insurance agents negotiate those details.

• **Do not discuss fault.** You may be upset, injured, and not completely clear about what happened. Anything you say may fog the issues and can be used against you later.

• **Secure witnesses.** Get the names, addresses, and telephone numbers of any witnesses. Ask them to stay until the police arrive. If they refuse, ask them to describe what they saw, write it down, and ask them to sign the statement.

• **Take notes.** Make notes about the road and weather conditions. If possible, take photographs of both cars at the scene of the accident or make a sketch.

• **Notify your insurance agent immediately.** Call your insurance company as soon as possible. You may be violating the terms of your policy if you avoid filing a claim for fear of higher premiums.

• **Get a copy of the police report.** Read it carefully. If you find errors, send a certified letter, return receipt requested, to the police, correcting the information. Ask that your letter be attached to the report.

MOTOR VEHICLE LAWS

Drivers must abide by the rules of the road of their province and town. These regulations protect the rights of other drivers—and your own.

Your License and Registration

Every province has regulations designed to ensure safety for motorists and all other citizens, and as a source of provincial revenue. Although each province sets its own rules, all the relevant laws are devised to assure the public that drivers are competent and vehicles are protected. Speed limits guard against reckless drivers, and parking limitations are intended to ease traffic congestion and open up parking spaces at regular intervals.

DRIVER'S LICENSE REGULATIONS

Before you can drive legally, you must demonstrate your ability and your knowledge of the rules of the road. To apply for a license, you must be a provincial resident and above the minimum age, which ranges nationally from 16 to 18 years of age.

Some provinces issue a learner's permit to minors before they are old enough for a regular license. This permits them limited driving, ordinarily when accompanied by a licensed driver. Other provinces require drivers under 18 to take a safe-driving course, such as the driver education classes offered in many high schools.

In addition to a road test, new drivers must pass a written test with questions on local and provincial laws and regulations. In some provinces, prospective drivers must show they have no physical or mental disability that would impair their ability to drive. Other provinces require a vision test. If you need glasses to see properly, that fact will be noted on your license, and you will be obliged to wear glasses while driving.

Prompted by statistics that showed Canadian drivers ages 16 to 24—a mere 17 percent of the driving population—caused almost 30 percent of injury-causing collisions, British Columbia, Nova Scotia, Ontario, and Quebec have introduced a graduated license for new drivers. With this type of license, the learning period is six months, the number of passengers is limited, the new driver must be accompanied by a licensed driver, a zero-alcohol blood level is the rule, and some provinces even impose a driving curfew between midnight and 6 a.m. Before graduating to a full license, the new driver has to pass a driver improvement course and a written test.

1,2,3...

A DRIVER'S DOCUMENTS

To drive legally, you must possess certain documentation. You will be asked to produce these documents if you are involved in an accident, so it is important to keep them safe and current. Here are a few tips to keep in mind:

1. You must have a current driver's license, a valid registration, license plates or tags, and proof of valid insurance.

2. In all provinces you must certify that you have the minimum liability insurance required by law, usually about $200,000. Your driver's license can be revoked for driving without insurance.

3. Failure to produce legally required documentation could result in a ticket and fine ranging from $60 to $500; you may be allowed 24 hours to produce the documents or may be able to appeal the ticket in court.

4. Ask for duplicates of your registration, license and proof of insurance, and keep these copies in a safe place at home, in case you lose the ones you carry with you.

5. When your car is in the garage or parked somewhere, keep your license (or license renewal stub) and car title in a safe place at home—not in the car.

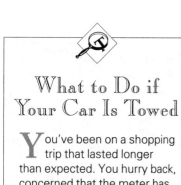

What to Do if Your Car Is Towed

You've been on a shopping trip that lasted longer than expected. You hurry back, concerned that the meter has run out, but the car has disappeared. Perhaps it has been stolen—or towed.

Your car can be towed if you park overtime, park in an illegal space, or if you have ignored parking tickets. (Computer systems identify license plate numbers of scofflaws who owe money for past tickets.) Some cities use a "Denver Boot," a device placed on a wheel to prevent the car from being moved. The car will not be "unbooted" until all fines are paid.

When your car is missing, call the police or local parking violations bureau to find out if it has been towed. If so, ask for the location of the pound and the cost of retrieval. Inquire whether you have outstanding fines since you cannot get your car back until you pay up. Reclaiming your car may cost up to $150. Be prepared to pay with cash, a certified cheque, or a money order. You must show your driver's license, registration, and proof of insurance. Act promptly or you may also be charged a storage fee. After a specified period, anywhere from 20 to 40 days, unclaimed cars are sold at auction.

If your car was damaged in towing, the tow truck company is responsible, but you must file a claim, and it may be hard to prove that the company is at fault. Some cities videotape cars being seized. If the tape shows that damage occurred in towing, the car will be repaired.

Licenses must be renewed periodically. A number of provinces will allow you to do this by mail, but some with photo identification on the license require you to appear in person to have a new photograph taken. A vision test may be required for a license renewal as well.

If you move to a new province, you usually must apply for a new license within 30 days. All provinces automatically accept license transfers from other provinces without a test.

AUTO REGISTRATION

Every vehicle must be registered, a process that ensures that owners are identified and certain requirements are met before a car can be driven on public roads. To register, you must show a title to prove that you own the vehicle, present a receipt showing that sales taxes on the car's purchase have been paid, and provide written proof that the car is insured. If you buy a car from an individual, you usually pay the sales tax at a motor vehicle bureau when you register the car.

After submitting all the necessary documents and paying a registration fee, you are issued license plates and a temporary registration. The permanent registration follows by mail. If you are transferring registration from one car to another, you usually will receive credit for the unused portion of the current registration, and you can move the same license plates to your new car. When you buy from a dealer who is registered with the provincial department of motor vehicles, the dealership is authorized to register the car for you and give you a temporary registration and new license plates, if needed.

Most registrations must be renewed every two years. Generally, a reminder arrives in the mail about 60 days before the expiration date, and you pay the new fee and registration by mail. When your registration is renewed, you will receive a tag on your license or a sticker for the windshield showing that the registration is up to date. If you let it lapse, you are likely to be stopped by the police and fined.

MOTOR VEHICLE INSPECTION

To ensure that automobiles on the road are safe to drive, police sometimes "pull over" drivers of older vehicles that look like they might be in "dangerous driving condition." The police usually give you a type of ticket that allows you to avoid paying a fine if the repairs are done in a stated period of time and proof is made to the police. Among the features checked in an inspection are brakes, lights, wipers, horn, mirrors, seat belts, steering, and tires. The car may also be checked to see if it meets emission control standards.

Cars bought from a dealer come with a valid inspection sticker.

Parking Regulations

The most common driving violation is illegal parking, either by using a prohibited space or by staying beyond the time allowed by a meter or sign. You may return a parking ticket by mail with payment of the specified fine, which is equivalent to pleading guilty to the violation, or you may plead not guilty and take the case before a judge or justice of the peace. Many areas have a separate court to handle parking tickets, since they are not as serious as other violations.

Though pleading your case is time-consuming, in certain instances you are right to defend yourself. Some valid reasons to contest a ticket are:

- **A defective ticket.** "Defective" means that some required information is missing, such as the nature of the offense, or the description of the car and license.
- **A broken meter.** Usually the back of the summons tells where claims of a defective meter should be sent. An inspection is made to verify that the meter is broken.
- **A disabled car.** If your car could not be moved, you may have a legal defense—but only if you have written proof.

Driving Regulations

More serious than parking tickets are "moving violations," certain offenses committed while you are behind the wheel. These violations cover a wide range of infractions including speeding, careless driving, tailgating, failing to obey a stop sign, and driving the wrong way on a one-way street.

If you are stopped by a police officer for one of these violations, you will be given a ticket indicating a fine. Many provinces give you the choice of pleading guilty by paying the fine, or taking your case to court. The Crown may require a court appearance if you plead guilty to charges that can result in your license or registration being suspended or revoked.

Since single offenses where no injury results usually involve minor fines and no jail time, most provinces and cities have a separate traffic court to handle them. Generally you do not need a lawyer to plead your case, but you will need evidence to support a not-guilty plea, and you may present witnesses to back up your statements. A Crown prosecutor has the right to cross-examine your witnesses, and, in turn, you may examine any witnesses testifying against you.

Fight That Traffic Ticket

A traffic ticket on your record can send insurance premiums soaring and can blemish your record for three or more years. So you should fight tickets whenever you believe you are not guilty. Here's what to do:

✔ *Read your ticket carefully.* Is the information correct? If the police officer made mistakes, the ticket may be invalid.

✔ *Know the law.* Unless the offense is serious, you can defend yourself without a lawyer. Learn the details of the law you are accused of violating. Ask your local librarian for help with this research. In some provinces, paralegals can represent you in traffic court.

✔ *Ask for a hearing.* Insist on a formal hearing with the arresting officer present. If he does not show up, your case may be dismissed.

✔ *Question the officer.* If he claims you were speeding, ask what time of day it was, and what weather and road conditions were like. Did he calibrate the radar equipment before checking your speed?

✔ *Bring witnesses.* If you have witnesses to back up your story, bring them to court.

✔ *Appeal the verdict.* If you think the verdict is unfair, you can appeal, although you may want to hire a lawyer.

✔ *Call a lawyer.* In serious cases, such as when an accident has occurred or when your license or liberty is at stake, consult a lawyer.

Sobriety Tests

Driving a motor vehicle when your blood-alcohol concentration (BAC) exceeds 0.08—you have 80 milligrams of alcohol per 100 millilitres of blood—is one of several drunk driving offenses governed by the Criminal Code. During periodic, publicly announced crackdowns on impaired drivers, or when police have reasonable grounds to suspect intoxication, they may ask a motorist to take a roadside Breathalyzer test, such as the Drager Alcotest or the Alcohol Level Evaluation Roadside Test (ALERT). Depending on the outcome, you may be asked to take a more formal test at the police station. The roadside breath sample cannot be used against you as proof that you have more than 0.08 alcohol in your blood, but failure to take the test is an offense. Penalties are similar to driving while intoxicated. You do not have the right to a lawyer for a roadside test but you do have that right before submitting to a Breathalyzer test at the police station.

Although most drunk driving convictions are based on excessive BACs, you can be within the legal limits, at 0.05 for example, and still be convicted of impaired driving. Some people become impaired even with a minimal amount of alcohol in their blood, and so police may ask a suspected drunk driver to take a sobriety test—walking a straight line heel to toe, or picking up coins from the floor. Although no one is legally obliged to take a sobriety test, often it is best to cooperate with police who otherwise may lay charges.

You can also plead guilty but with mitigating circumstances, meaning that you are asking the judge to consider the reason for your infraction. If you swerved out of your lane to avoid hitting a deer on the highway, for example, the judge might reduce your fine and waive court costs.

If you are found guilty, you will be asked to pay court costs in addition to the fine. The judge also has the power to suspend your license. If you do not agree with the decision or penalty given by the judge, you have the right to file an appeal.

Appearing Careless

PROBLEM
Ann was driving home late one Saturday night from a party along a busy two-lane highway. The couple in the car in front of Ann were deep in conversation and, as a result, the driver was weaving all over the road. Ann wanted to pass, but she could not see around the other car in order to make sure the oncoming lane was safe. To her chagrin, the police stopped her and accused her of "careless driving," saying her car, not the car in front of her, was weaving. They also asked her to take a Breathalyzer test, indicating that not only did they think Ann was a careless driver, they thought she was drunk. Ann was furious—especially since she had deliberately drunk only nonalcoholic beverages at the party because she knew she would be driving herself home.

ACTION
Ann was stopped on suspicion of drunken driving, a potentially serious moving violation. She complied calmly and took a Breathalyzer test, since she knew that the fact that one has a license implied consent to all motor vehicle laws. Of course, the test indicated that Ann had not been drinking. She then explained why it appeared that she was weaving. If she had nevertheless been arrested for careless driving, she should have taken detailed notes and appealed her ticket in court.

A single violation normally will not bring suspension, but chalking up a number of violations in a short amount of time will. Most provinces use a demerit point system to deter frequent offenders. Points are charged against a driver's record according to the seriousness of the infraction. A driver going less than 20 kilometres per hour above the posted speed limit might have three points deducted; driving 30 to 50 kilometres over the limit could net six points. High-point infractions other than speeding usually include careless driving and failure to stop for a school bus.

By law, information regarding the status of your license is available to your insurance company, and if points mount up, your insurance rates may go up accordingly. If you accumulate too many points within a specified period, say 12 months, your license may be suspended or revoked. Conversely, you can clear your record with safer driving. Usually a three-year period with no convictions and no accidents will remove points from your record and may make you eligible for lower rates.

DRINKING, DRUGS, AND DRIVING

The most harmful motor vehicle violations involve driving under the influence of alcohol or drugs. Both substances impair judgment, vision, and reflexes, making it almost impossible to drive safely. Because impaired driving is so potentially dangerous, charges are often laid under the Criminal Code and penalties are severe. If convicted, your license will be suspended, you may go to jail, and you are liable for a steep fine. If you repeat the violation, your license may be revoked.

A police officer who spots erratic driving may ask the driver to take a field test, such as walking a straight line, to determine whether reflexes have been impaired. If a driver fails this test, he may be asked to take a medical test to measure the level of alcohol in his bloodstream. This may be done on the spot, or at a police station or hospital, where blood, urine, or Breathalyzer tests can be administered.

If Your Driver's License Is Taken Away

A driver's license is a privilege, not a right, and if you fail to obey the law, your license can be suspended for a specified period, or revoked—meaning it will be canceled for a certain period and you will be required to apply to get it back.

SUSPENSION

• In most provinces causes for suspension include driving under the influence of alcohol or drugs, speeding, careless driving, driving without liability insurance, refusing to take a blood-alcohol test, leaving the scene of an accident in which someone was injured or killed, certain medical reasons or failure to answer a traffic summons, pay a fine, or file an accident report. In provinces that have a demerit point system for moving violations, accumulating too many points within a specified period can also lead to suspension.

• When a suspension expires, you are free to drive again, although some provinces impose a fee to have the suspension terminated. In many provinces, having an accident while you are not insured or refusing to take a blood-alcohol test carries a fine as well as suspension.

REVOCATION

• Your license can be revoked for criminal negligence resulting in death, or on a second conviction for drunken driving involving personal injury. It may also be revoked if you give false statements when applying for a license or registration.

• You may apply for a new license when the revocation period ends. In some cases, you must pay a fine as well as a fee to reapply. If you have a poor driving record or refuse to meet provincial requirements, to pass a test or take a driving course, for example, your application may be denied.

TRAFFIC COURT

• In many localities, traffic violations other than parking tickets are heard by a special traffic violations court. You are considered innocent of the charge until proven guilty at the hearing. If you are found guilty, you will pay a fine and court costs, and may have your license revoked or suspended. At this point you may want to hire a lawyer and take your case before an appeals judge or a traffic appeals board. To appeal, however, you must prove "manifest error" by the first judge.

VIOLATING SUSPENSION OR REVOCATION

• If you drive while your license is suspended or revoked, you can be fined or jailed, or both. Penalties for driving with a suspended license range from $500 to $5,000. Subsequent convictions can result in a fine of $5,000 plus six months in jail and two years' probation.

If you are arrested for driving under the influence of drugs or alcohol, you have the right to call a lawyer, relative, or friend as soon as possible to arrange for your release from custody. It is best not to make statements to the police or discuss the incident before you have consulted a lawyer. Whatever you say can be held against you in court. If you feel that you have been wrongly charged, your lawyer can present your side of the case in court.

Laws Governing Other Vehicles

Vehicles that share the road with automobiles have their own regulations. Truck drivers must qualify for a special license certifying that they have passed a road test handling a large vehicle. Commercial vehicles also have special registration requirements. For instance, additional lighting and reflectors may be required. Certain highways also have weight restrictions on trucks.

Recreation vehicles (RVs) also must meet provincial regulations. They must be registered and meet certain specifications for electrical, plumbing, heating, fire and light safety set by provincial transport departments. Depending on the vehicle's size, you may be restricted from certain tunnels or low bridges. Keep in mind, too, that although passengers may ride in a van or motor home, they may not ride in a trailer.

MOTORCYCLES AND BICYCLES

Motorcycle riders also must pass written and driving tests. In most provinces they are required to use extra safeguards. Front lights must be on at all times to improve their machine's visibility to other drivers, and motorcyclists may be required to wear helmets. A motorcyclist generally has the right to the full use of a lane, and two cyclists may ride side by side in one, but they may not share a lane with a car and may not drive between lanes. In most provinces licenses are also required for mopeds, lighter motorcycles that travel at lower speeds.

Bicyclists have the right to share most roads except highways, parkways, and expressways. Most municipalities require bicycle riders to travel in the same direction as auto traffic and obey all traffic signs and signals. Bicyclists are advised to ride in designated lanes. Some municipalities require bicyclists to have licenses, which generally cost $10 to $15. All municipalities require them to observe safety regulations, and insist that their machines be equipped with adequate brakes, a horn or bell, and visible reflectors. Recently, many provinces and city and town councils enacted laws requiring bicyclists to wear helmets.

YOUR CONSUMER RIGHTS

In today's complex marketplace, getting a fair deal can be a challenge. But help is available for consumers who know their rights.

THE WISE CONSUMER ■ CONSUMER CONTRACTS AND WARRANTIES ■ PROBLEMS WITH PURCHASES ■ ADVERTISING AND MARKETING ■ DECEPTIVE SALES PRACTICES ■ BASIC SHOPPERS' RIGHTS ■ BUYING BIG-TICKET ITEMS ■ BUYING ELECTRONIC EQUIPMENT ■ BUYING CLOTHING ■ BUYING FOR CHILDREN ■ SMART SUPERMARKET SHOPPING ■ SHOPPING FOR HEALTH AND BEAUTY PRODUCTS ■ BARGAIN SHOPPING ■ SHOPPING FROM HOME ■ SERVICE PROVIDERS ■ YOUR RIGHTS AS A TRAVELER

THE WISE CONSUMER

As marketing techniques get slicker, consumers become more vulnerable.
Knowing your rights can give you power in the marketplace.

123...

CONSUMER RIGHTS

Canada's federal and provincial consumer protection laws are designed to protect consumers from harmful goods and products and from harmful, unfair and deceptive sales practices. In effect, they give consumers the following basic rights:

1. Choice. Consumers have the right to make an intelligent choice among diverse products and services.

2. Information. Consumers have the right to accurate and complete information about the products they buy.

3. Remedies. Most provinces have remedies in place which will allow you to cancel the contract under certain circumstances, or to claim damages from the seller.

Caveat Emptor

Once upon a time, shopping was a simple matter. Storekeepers were part of the community and knew their customers personally. If you were not happy with your purchase, you knew exactly where to go with your complaint. Of course, unscrupulous people who try to cheat or get away with selling inferior products have always been around, but the motto *caveat emptor* ("Let the buyer beware") is far more relevant today than it used to be.

As buying opportunities have expanded, so have the challenges for the consumer. Plastic-wrapped products deny consumers a close look at what they want. Electric and electronic appliances are offered in such profusion that consumers may not understand what they are buying. Con artists can operate invisibly from behind telephones, televisions, computers, mail-order scams, and advertisements.

MINE-STREWN MARKETPLACE

To protect consumers in such a mine-strewn marketplace, almost every province has adopted laws to guard against nefarious practices and provide recourses for victims. Some laws are aimed at defective or harmful merchandise, others at misleading, unfair or deceptive sales practices or instances where the seller misrepresents his product or service. These laws place special emphasis on requiring full disclosure by the seller about the products offered and the financial terms of the sale.

Many provincial laws prohibit such things as selling second-hand merchandise as "new"; telling the consumer a product can be used for something it can't; saying the product price is cheaper than a competitor's when it isn't; misrepresenting the authority of company representatives or employees; advertising that a product will be available when the seller knows that it won't; lying about the ingredients of a product, or claiming it is "fat-free," when it really isn't; grossly exaggerating or lying about an important feature, such as telling the consumer that a computer has sufficient memory to operate any computer program when, in fact, it doesn't; or informing a customer that his appliance or automobile is in need of repair, when this is not the case.

Certain purchases are treated by specific legislation. For instance, Ontario, British Columbia, Quebec, and Alberta all have legislation dealing specifically with automobile purchases.

The federal government also has a number of measures in place to protect the health and safety of Canadians, and to ensure consumers are properly informed about the products they buy and their use. Failure to respect the guidelines may be punishable by fines and sometimes imprisonment.

- **The Competition Act.** This act protects consumers from such unfair trade practices as price-fixing. It prohibits a company from requiring retailers to sell a product at a set price.
- **The Consumer Packaging and Labelling Act.** This act regulates packaging, importation, labeling, and advertising of a number of consumer products and foods.
- **The Hazardous Products Act.** Advertising and sale of poisonous, toxic, corrosive, explosive, or unstable products are regulated by this act, which also sets minimum standards for toys, cribs, and certain potentially flammable or toxic materials.
- **The Food and Drugs Act.** This act regulates the production and use of foods, drugs, cosmetics, and medical devices as well as their packaging and labeling. The act also limits the advertising of certain medications, prohibiting, for instance, advertisements for medicine said to prevent, treat, or cure certain diseases, such as arthritis, bladder disease, epilepsy, and impotence.
- **The Narcotic Control Act.** All prescription and over-the-counter drugs, as well as all restricted substances, are regulated by this act.

What a Consumer Should Know

You should be especially cautious when buying used articles or items reduced greatly in price. Depending on where you live, the law may not protect you if you had an opportunity to inspect the merchandise and did not so. Below are some other points you should know:

• If a product is faulty or does not perform as you were led to believe, return it immediately. In many provinces, you are entitled to a refund or repairs only if you act within a fixed period of time.

• Not all penalty clauses or cancellation fees are valid.

• A merchant cannot repossess an item if you have already paid a certain percentage of the purchase price—the percentage varies from province to province.

• If you finance an item on a payment plan, the merchant must disclose all interest rates, penalty fees, and handling costs at the time you sign the contract.

• Exoneration clauses in contracts or on receipts which limit the merchant's liability are not always valid, even if they bear your signature.

Consumer Contracts and Warranties

Two basic agreements protect both buyers and sellers.

Understanding Purchase Contracts

Good things cost less than bad things.

Italian proverb

In simplest terms, a contract of purchase or sale is formed when one party offers to buy a product or service for a certain price or "consideration" and the other party accepts. Once the offer is accepted, two binding obligations are created: the seller must deliver the product or service and the buyer must pay for it.

Conventionally, we think of contracts as lengthy legal documents, but any agreement—written or verbal—between a seller and a buyer that involves money or some other form of payment is, legally speaking, a "contract." For example, if you redeem a $5-off-on-any-item coupon in a grocery store, you are performing your part of a contract with the grocer who has made the offer; if you offer to pay the teenager next door $10 to mow your lawn and he agrees, then, here too, a contract has been formed.

Once the contract has been made, it can be altered only if both parties agree to any changes. Unless the coupon has expired, the grocery store must honor it. If your neighbor mows your lawn and then demands $15 for his work, you are not legally obliged to pay him that amount if he has agreed to work for $10.

The law does not necessarily require that the reciprocal obligations of the parties be of equal value. Thus, a buyer will have little recourse if he discovers that his new shirt could have been purchased for $5 less from a competing retailer. The first merchant may decide to meet his competitor's price, but is not legally obliged to do so. (See also "What If You Got a Raw Deal?" page 385.)

The principles outlined here apply whether the contract has to do with buying a car or a major appliance, renting an apartment, or signing a contract to have a book published.

BREACH OF CONTRACT

If one party does not respect the obligations described in a contract, the contract has been broken, or "breached." If a major breach of contract occurs, the other party can demand that the contract be canceled or seek other remedies. For example, if a contract specifies that your new dining room table will be delivered by Thanksgiving and it does not arrive on time, you may have the right to cancel the agreement and have your down payment returned.

A contract may be declared "void"—indicating that no valid agreement was ever made—if essential terms are missing. For example, a contract may be void if one of the parties is a minor or is incompetent, meaning that he is incapable of understanding what he is signing. A contract may also be deemed void if terms were misrepresented, or if some aspect of the agreement is fraudulent or involves an illegal or immoral practice, such as the selling of illegal drugs.

COMMON-LAW PRINCIPLES

Even where provinces have enacted minimum standards for merchandise and so on, some transactions may still be outside the scope of consumer laws, or a contract may not be expressly covered by consumer or trade practice legislation. If you buy a car from a neighbor, for example, the consumer protection legislation might not protect you. However, all provinces except Quebec (where the Civil Code prevails) abide by "common law" principles, and these will apply in addition to whatever consumer or trade practices legislation has been enacted. The common law rules are especially important when you are not protected by specific legislation—as would be the case with the car-purchase example above.

Quebec's Civil Code lays down specific rules affecting the validity and proof of contracts. In that province, oral contracts involving transactions of $1,500 or more are not easily enforced.

Even in transactions of less than $1,500, and regardless of where you live, you are always safer if you put your contractual agreement in writing. This does not have to be a formal legal document. A bill of sale or a letter can serve as a contract as long as it clearly states the obligations of all parties and the payment or other consideration involved.

Be sure that all oral understandings about a transaction are included in the written document. Otherwise, they will be difficult to prove in a court of law.

The primary concern of laws governing contracts is to protect the "reasonable expectations" that are created in the marketplace between buyers and sellers. The laws governing contracts come from three sources:

- Statutes, or the laws and regulations enacted by the federal and provincial governments.
- Common law, or the body of rules and regulations that is established by custom (or the Civil Code in Quebec).
- Case law, or the law created by the decisions of federal or provincial courts that interpret the law.

Key Elements of a Contract

A contract can be anything from an oral agreement to a multi-clause, densely worded document. Whatever its form, a contract, to be legal, must contain several important elements:

✔ *An offer.* This is a promise to do or supply something specific. For example, the baker offers to sell you a loaf of white bread for 89 cents.

✔ *An acceptance.* The contract is made when the offer is accepted. If you think the price is too high and refuse to buy, then there is no sale—and no contract. But if you tell the baker you will take the bread, you are accepting his offer.

✔ *A consideration.* The agreed-upon price for the product or service is called the consideration. The contract is completed when each party actually gives or does something in return for something else: the baker gets your money, and you get the loaf of bread. If you shortchange the baker, you have breached the contract.

✔ *Duration.* Sometimes, a time limit for fulfilling the contract must be stated. If no specific time is spelled out, the law may imply a reasonable time, such as 30 days, for delivery of a household product.

✔ *Nonperformance.* Often, a contract states what action is to be taken if either party does not perform his obligation as stipulated.

BILL OF SALE

Date of sale: March 20, 1996

Acme Bike Shop
710 North Avenue
Kitchener, Ontario M3C 1B5
Telephone: 519-333-4444

Customer: John Newton
51 Lake Drive
Charlottetown, P.E.I. M5H 1E6
Telephone: 111-222-3333

Salesperson: Andy Brown

Merchandise ➊

Johnstone Mountain Bike, model number 8114, red
Easy-lock padlock

Date of delivery: March 25, 1996 ➍

Delivery charge: $50 (Includes assembly)

Total price: $485 ➌

Method of payment: Mastercard #299 40 3577

Signature of customer: _____ ➋ _____ Date _____

WARRANTY: Acme provides no warranty beyond of that provided by the manufacturer. ➎

ACME BIKE SHOP SALES EXCHANGE AND RETURN POLICY: Merchandise may be returned within 10 days of delivery. If exchanged or returned, the merchandise must be accompanied by this bill of sale. All exchanges are subject to a 10% restocking charge.

A Simple Contractual Agreement

A relatively simple bill of sale is as much a contract as a 20-page agreement between an author and a publisher. As with any contract, it must include: **1. The offer.** In this case, the offer is a particular bicycle and lock as described under "Merchandise." **2. The acceptance.** Here the acceptance is confirmed by the customer's signature. **3. A consideration.** This is the agreed-upon price for the service or product. **4. Duration.** Even in a bill of sale, a time limit or delivery date can be stated; in this case, the merchandise will be delivered by March 25, 1996. **5. Performance.** The contract is not complete until each party supplies something. The customer pays the agreed-upon price based on the delivery of the bicycle and lock. If the customer does not receive the bicycle and lock by the date stated, the contract will not be complete.

Understanding Warranties

A warranty may be part of a contract for the sale of a product or service. It is the company's promise to stand behind its products by making repairs or offering replacements if something goes wrong. Just as you compare product prices and features, you should also make the warranty an important consideration when you shop. A warranty may be "express," meaning its terms are explicitly expressed in writing, or "implied," meaning that based on common law, consumers have an implied right to a level of reliability in the product or the service they are buying.

EXPRESS WARRANTIES

Express warranties are written promises from the manufacturer. These warranties commonly come with products such as cars, television sets, and other appliances large and small.

Make sure your warranty includes:

- A description of which parts or components are covered;
- A clear statement of what the warrantor will do in case of a defect or a malfunction, including what items or services the warrantor will pay for and provide;
- A definition of exactly who is covered under the warranty—for example, any owner or only the original buyer;
- A statement of the length of the warranty period and when it comes into effect;
- An explanation of how to obtain service under the warranty.

FULL WARRANTIES

A full warranty states that the manufacturer will repair a defective product within a reasonable time or else he will replace the item with one of equal value or make a full refund. A full warranty need not cover every product part, but it must spell out exactly what is covered. If a warranty is restricted to a certain period of time, the time limit must appear at the top of the warranty. Sometimes this coverage applies to subsequent owners for the life of the warranty.

LIMITED WARRANTIES

Limited warranties may cover only the cost of parts, requiring the customer to pay for labor; or they may cover repairs, but not offer refunds. Customers may have to pay handling or shipping charges when repairs are necessary.

The warranty is generally nontransferable. Once again, the written warranty must detail exactly what the seller will and will not guarantee.

RED FLAGS ON WARRANTIES

Here are some small-print clauses often found in warranties that should be warning signs for consumers:

1. "This warranty is in lieu of any other warranties, express or implied, including any implied warranty of merchantability or fitness." With this, you lose the additional legal protection of implied warranties. Some provinces prohibit this disclaimer.

2. "No responsibility is assumed for incidental or consequential damages of any kind." This clause limits the consumer's right to sue for personal injury due to product defect. In many provinces such a warranty is unenforceable.

3. "Defective parts will be repaired or replaced at our option." Baldly, this means that repair or a replacement is at the whim of the manufacturer.

4. "In the event of a claim, mail your product, properly packaged and insured, to the nearest authorized service dealer; any postage, insurance, or shipping charges must be prepaid by the sender." Returning defective products becomes the buyer's problem—and can be an expensive one.

5. "All products must be shipped in their original cartons or in replacements supplied by us." This is a nuisance, but if the warranty is a limited one and the stipulation is spelled out, it is legal.

Extra Protection on Credit Cards

Consumers have an extra source of warranty protection when they buy products with credit cards that extend the original coverage offered by the manufacturer. Terms of this protection vary, so comparing various card offerings may save you money. Here are some terms to consider:

✔ *How long is the warranty coverage?* Some cards offer an extra year of warranty, others double the original period, and some offer protection for the expected service life of the product up to 12 years.

✔ *How do you qualify for coverage?* With some cards, coverage is automatic; others require you to fill out a form within a specified period.

✔ *What products are excluded?* Purchases that may not be covered include those made outside Canada, cars, and items bought for professional use.

✔ *How easy is it to file a claim?* Look for the least complicated procedure. Find out which forms must be filed and whether you need authorization to make a repair.

✔ *What is the dollar limit on repairs?* Find out if the company will cover you for the original purchase price of the item.

✔ *Is there a dollar limit per year?* Many plans have caps on annual purchases.

IMPLIED WARRANTIES

Most consumers are protected against faulty products even when they come without written guarantees. In fact, every product is protected by an implied warranty unless it is specifically marked "as is" or the seller indicates in writing that no implied warranty is given.

Based on the common-law principle that the consumer is entitled to fair value for money spent, an implied warranty is assumed to exist even though it is not stated. As a result, courts often rule that the consumer is entitled to believe the product he purchased can be used for the purpose for which he bought it, and that the quality of the item will match similarly priced products.

One category of implied warranty is *merchantability*—the consumer is entitled to expect a product to do the job for which it is intended. For example, a lawn mower must cut grass. A second category applies the standard of *fitness for a particular purpose.* This comes into play when the consumer relies on a seller's advice that a product can be used for special purposes for which he has a need. If the seller assures you that the mower you are buying is powerful enough to cut fields of tall weeds, it should be able to do so.

Products should last *a reasonable period of time.* If you buy a bedframe and it breaks shortly after purchase, the manufacturer might be obligated to repair or replace the frame within a reasonable time. How you used the product, however, would be fundamental to such a ruling. The manufacturer might have no need to make repairs or give a refund if the bedframe had been used inappropriately—if, for instance, the frame breaks while your 10-year-old and 10 of her friends are jumping up and down on the mattress at a sleep-over.

WARRANTY VIOLATIONS

Manufacturing or selling faulty merchandise can net significant penalties. Courts can award monetary payments that go beyond the costs of repairing or replacing the product. Under certain circumstances, courts can also require companies to pay a consumer's legal fees when the consumer's suit is successful.

Consumers can make a claim against the manufacturer for any property damage or personal injuries suffered as a result of the seller's negligence. In addition to filing individual suits, Ontario and Quebec consumers can join together to bring class action lawsuits against companies that repeatedly violate warranties. (See also YOUR RIGHTS IN ACTION, page 464.)

Returning a registration card is not necessary to validate a warranty unless the manufacturer specifically states that you must do so to be covered. Often warranty cards are simply sales-promotion tools.

PROBLEMS WITH PURCHASES

When you buy any merchandise, you make a contract. If there is something wrong with what you bought, the law will help you get the contract enforced.

The Purchase Contract

Most problems encountered by buyers concern overpricing, deceptive advertising, poor service, refunds, and delivery issues. All these problems, on a basic level, are "contractual" problems in that they concern an agreement between the buyer and seller that is protected under the law.

Both a buyer and a seller are protected against "breach of contract," or the breaking of an agreement. For example, as a buyer, unless the contract states otherwise, you have no obligation to pay for goods if they are not delivered. Conversely, you have no right to keep goods you order if you do not pay for them: the seller has a right to sue to collect any money you owe, plus any incidental costs such as interest.

Unless goods have been ordered COD, you have the right to inspect them before paying for them. If you discover that the merchandise is not what you ordered or expected, or is broken or damaged, the seller may make suitable replacements within the time specified for delivery in the contract.

If you discover problems after you accept delivery, satisfactory replacement goods must be provided, as long as you notify the seller within a reasonable time. If suitable merchandise is not delivered within an agreed-upon time period, you may cancel the contract and demand your money back. In some cases, you may have the right to ask for any difference between what you agreed to pay and what it would cost you now to buy similar goods elsewhere, as well as any incidental costs, such as the cost of transporting or storing the rejected merchandise.

In fact, most of the problems commonly encountered in day-to-day purchase agreements are covered by federal or provincial contract and warranty law.

WHEN YOU NEED A LAWYER

Breach-of-contract suits involving limited sums of money can be tried in small claims or conciliation court. The limit for claims varies by province and ranges from $3,000 to $10,000. Most of the time, you do not need a lawyer to present a case; in fact, many provinces do not even allow lawyers in small claims court. But if the sum in question is higher than the small

What If You Got a Raw Deal?

Consumer protection legislation in many provinces offers some solace to a buyer who is grossly overcharged for a product. Contracts that are shockingly unfair or that result from unfair pressure are called "unconscionable." A classic example is a salesman who pressures an unsophisticated or elderly person into buying a product at a price many times higher than its worth.

Sometimes contracts are written with a liquidated-damages clause, which limits how much the buyer can collect in case of a breach of contract. Film-processing firms, for example, claim that if they ruin a roll of film and lose your photos, the processor is responsible only for the cost of the film itself. Liquidated-damages clauses, like clauses limiting the buyer's right to demand damages for personal injury, may themselves be declared unconscionable.

While recourse for unconscionability is available under certain consumer protection legislation and recognized in most case law, going to court is a time-consuming and complex process, and those people who need help the most may be the least equipped to know how to get it. For that reason, the best protection against bad bargains, as always, is to avoid them in the first place.

A SAFETY SHIELD FOR CONSUMERS

Various federal laws, including the Consumer Packaging and Labelling Act, Hazardous Products Act, Food and Drugs Act, Narcotic Control Act, and Meat Inspection Act, have guidelines and programs in place designed to:

1. Obtain the recall or repair of products that fail to comply with mandatory standards or that present substantial hazards to consumers.

2. Ban products for which no feasible standard would adequately protect the public.

3. Regulate and enforce important federal safety measures dealing with such things as flammable fabrics, hazardous substances, and poison prevention.

4. Work with industry to develop voluntary safety standards and require warnings or instructions for use to appear where appropriate on all consumer products.

5. Conduct research on products that may potentially be hazardous to consumers.

6. Carry out information and education programs, such as issuing safety alerts with regard to particular products.

claims limit, or if personal injury is involved, your best course is to consult a lawyer.

Make sure to file your claim within a reasonable amount of time following the incident. There is a time limit on filing a breach-of-contract suit. Provinces also have time limits for filing cases in small claims court. Check with the court clerk to find out what the statute of limitations is in your province.

ALTERNATIVE DISPUTE RESOLUTION

Consumer complaints involving amounts greater than amounts the small claims court can handle may have to go to a higher court, but whether your problem is small or large you can avoid the courts altogether by using alternative dispute resolution (ADR). ADR is an umbrella term that encompasses several ways of resolving disputes: negotiation, mediation, arbitration, and administrative hearings. (For a discussion of ADR, see YOUR RIGHTS IN ACTION, page 448.)

ADR is cheaper and much less stressful than litigation, and helps resolve disputes effectively and quickly. It can be used for everything from resolving neighborhood disputes to consumers' battles with manufacturers, doctors, and contractors. Alberta and Ontario have both implemented programs offering arbitration services. Here are four ways to find an ADR practitioner, regardless of where you live:

- Consult the Yellow Pages under "Arbitration" or "Mediation" to find the names of possible companies or lawyers who practice ADR.
- Call the Better Business Bureau for directions to a local mediator or arbitrator.
- Write or call the Canadian Bar Association, or your provincial bar association for the names of lawyers or retired judges in your area who would be prepared to arbitrate your case.
- Ask your business associates if they are familiar with any possible arbitrators.

Suppose It Doesn't Work?

Products can be considered defective for two reasons: they do not perform as promised, or they are unsafe and cause personal injury. If a product does not perform as the manufacturer promised, you are protected by the warranty. (See also "Understanding Warranties," page 383.) If a product causes personal injury or damage, you can sue the manufacturer or seller for product liability.

Product-liability cases have been brought to court involving almost every kind of defective merchandise, from contact lenses to cars. Cases have also been won against manufacturers of products whose dangers have not been discovered until a much later date, such as the drug DES, which was prescribed for pregnant women in the 1940s and 1950s and proved damaging to their adult daughters decades later.

Product-liability claims can be based on injuries caused by defects in design, faulty manufacturing procedures, inadequate packaging or labeling, inadequate warnings or instructions, or misrepresentation of what the product is able to do. For many years, winning a claim meant proving negligence by the manufacturer in one of these areas—a hard thing to do—but the Canadian courts have increasingly recognized that manufacturers have a responsibility to customers regarding the products they sell.

STRICT PRODUCT LIABILITY

When strict liability applies, a manufacturer is held responsible for selling any product that is deemed "unreasonably dangerous" and results in injury to the buyer or other foreseeable

---

Tried-and-True Tips for Returning Goods

Many consumer complaints fall into predictable categories, and problems with "returns" are a major annoyance. The best advice is to take extra care before you make the original purchase, but if you have bought the goods and want to return them, follow these guidelines:

• **Save receipts for 30 days.** Alternatively, you can use the statement from a credit card if you have charged the purchase. If you do not have the receipt, ask to see the manager when you try to return an item.

• **Save packaging.** Some warranties, especially for appliances and electronic equipment, require that merchandise be returned in its original box.

• **Use a credit card.** Charging gives you more leverage when you need to return. If a store is reluctant to accept a return and you have charged it, you have time to negotiate before you must pay (see also YOUR MONEY, page 288).

• **Beware of boutiques.** Many small stores have strict return policies. (In some localities, shops are legally required to post their return policy in an obvious place.) Often a store will not budge. Make sure you really want the item, or shop in department stores, which have more liberal return rules.

• **Try returning at similar stores.** If you receive a best-selling book or CD as a gift, but you would prefer something else, try taking it to a local book or record shop. A store may take back an item if it has not been opened and if the store stocks it. Or, more likely, it may agree to exchange the item.

• **Save warranties.** Warranties protect consumers for months, and sometimes years. But don't lose hope if your warranty has run out. Manufacturers and retailers take pride in their products and in their clientele. If your new food processor breaks down in six months but was covered only by a 90-day warranty, the manufacturer may still be willing to replace it.

• **Complain in writing.** If the store will not accept the return, write to the store and the manufacturer. Address your letters to whoever heads each organization and explain the situation. Include copies of receipts and describe the remedy you are seeking. If you do not get satisfaction, write to the Better Business Bureau and your nearest consumer protections branch, and copy all concerned.

• **Don't be intimidated.** If you have purchased defective or bad merchandise, you have the right to return it. If you have incurred a loss, consider taking your case to small claims court.

users. It is no longer necessary to prove the manufacturer was negligent, only that the product was defective, that it was for sale, and, most crucially, that injuries were caused by the defect.

The doctrine of strict product liability puts merchants on their toes as well. If you buy a stove that blows up because of improper design, causing a fire that injures someone, you can sue not only the manufacturer but the store that sold the item to you and the distributor who supplied the store. They share the responsibility to avoid selling hazardous products, as well as to convey any safety warnings or recall notices.

Generally, with strict liability statutes, you do not need to be the owner or purchaser of a defective item to sue. If you are injured by the flying blade of your neighbor's defective lawn mower, you may have a case against the maker of the mower.

PRODUCT RECALLS

You may be entitled to a refund or a repair of an unsafe product and not even know it. Hundreds of products are recalled each year because either the Product Safety Branch of Industry Canada or the manufacturer has found them defective. When a car is recalled, owners are notified because dealers must keep records of purchases. Large-scale recalls of other products are occasionally reported on the radio and in newspapers, and some provinces require retailers to post prominent notices of recalls on products they carry.

But if you buy a television set or an infant's car seat, it is not likely that the merchant records enough information about his sales to allow him to notify you personally if the product is recalled. Even if the recall is publicized, you may not happen to see announcements in the media or in the store.

Complaining Effectively

If your new toaster will not toast, your new CD player will not play, or your new percolator does not perk, you should not have to resort to a lawsuit to remedy the problem. Too often consumers assume that they will not get satisfaction and do not even voice a complaint. Many buyers do not even try to resolve the problems they have with products, fearing only more frustration. But you can get results if you learn how and where to complain effectively. Here are some basic strategies for asserting your rights:

- **Keep records.** Every time you buy something of value, file the bill of sale, receipt or contract, the credit card draft if the item was charged, any canceled payment cheques, and all instructions and warranties.

Delivery Woes

When you have ordered something, whether it is a book, a sweater, or a new sofa, you may experience delivery problems. Here are some guidelines to follow:

✔ *Delivery of defective merchandise.* If you have ordered something by mail, and it arrives damaged, mail it back immediately. If something is delivered, such as a new piece of furniture, examine it carefully. Don't sign a release stating you are satisfied unless you are.

✔ *Canceling a delivery.* If you decide to cancel a mail-order product, the company must refund your money within a reasonable time. If you purchase by credit card, the company must adjust your statement as soon as possible, ideally within one billing cycle after you notify it of the cancellation.

✔ *Late delivery.* If the company notifies you that it cannot ship your goods on time and you do not respond, the company can assume you will wait. If a delivery date is clearly specified on the bill of sale, you can cancel the order and get your money back.

- **Start at the source.** Read your warranty carefully and follow the directions on it for seeking redress if the product malfunctions. Usually this means contacting the person who sold you the product or the customer-service manager by telephone or, better yet, in person.
- **Put it in writing.** If the retailer agrees to do what you want but cannot do it on the spot, send a letter confirming your understanding of what action will be taken and when.
- **Go to the top.** If you cannot get action from the store or the retail chain to which it belongs, contact the manufacturer directly. Many manufacturers have toll-free numbers for consumer complaints. Or else write directly to the president of the manufacturing company, and send your letter by certified mail with a return receipt requested.

Taking It to the Top

PROBLEM

Warren bought a lawn mower with a one-year limited warranty covering all parts. After six weeks the mower's blades had loosened, so that it no longer cut properly. The seller tried to repair the mower, but the blades loosened again. When Warren asked for a refund or a new mower, the merchant offered to tighten the blades again, saying he was certain the problem could be corrected. The repair did not hold, and Warren demanded a refund. The dealer refused, claiming the mower must have been misused, since it had worked properly when it was originally sold. Warren wrote to the president of the retail outlet that had sold him the mower, but the president accepted his dealer's assessment.

ACTION

Warren decided to approach the manufacturer of the mower. He addressed his complaint to the company's president, stating that he had chosen this mower because of the manufacturer's excellent reputation. He explained his problem, including a mention that loose blades were a safety hazard that might cause injury. Since apparently the mower could not be repaired to function properly, he asked for a refund or a new mower. The manufacturer realized that not only was the company obligated by an implied warranty—that is, that a lawn mower should cut grass—but that it was important to preserve its corporate reputation. Warren was given a new mower.

- **Ask for help.** When you cannot get cooperation from either the maker or the seller of the product, write or call the Better Business Bureau and your nearest consumer-protection agency. If your complaint involves a violation of federal or provincial law, the agency's legal staff will be notified for appropriate action.
- **Go public.** Consumer reporters for local newspapers and television stations perform a valuable service by investigating complaints. The last thing any business wants is to be publicly accused of unfair treatment of its customers.

Using the Better Business Bureau

The Better Business Bureau (BBB) is a private nonprofit organization comprised of a voluntary association of business people who provide free or low-cost services to consumers. You will find a BBB office in a number of Canadian cities. Often it may be able to assist you with a problem.

The organization's function is to collect information that will help buyers make informed decisions. If you are thinking of hiring a service or dealing with a store, the BBB files can tell you how long the party has been in business and provide a summary of any complaints received about it.

If you report a problem, in many locations the BBB will first contact the firm involved to try to settle the matter. Some bureaus may offer mediation or arbitration with both parties to try to work out mutually agreeable solutions. The BBB has no official power, but in extreme cases it may refer its file to a law-enforcement agency to evaluate whether further action is warranted.

The BBB depends on consumers to make its files useful. By reporting unethical companies, you will save others from unhappy experiences.

Jane Jones • 2100 Hill Street • Vegreville, Alberta
March 1, 1996

Mr. John Harrison
Consumer Relations Director
Speedo Vacuum Cleaner Company
333 Third Street
Littlefield, Alberta

Dear Mr. Harrison,

On January 10, 1996, I purchased a Speedo Vacuum Cleaner Model XYZ from The Floor Store, 212 Main Street, Vegreville. **1** (A copy of the receipt is enclosed.) **2** Unfortunately, I have had problems with both the product and the service I have received.

Specifically, I have the following complaints: **3**

First, the vacuum does not work efficiently to pick up dust or dirt on either bare floors or carpets. Even after I have gone over the same area several times, the dirt remains. The power shuts off by itself when the vacuum has been running for several minutes, then comes back on after 30 to 60 seconds.

Second, when I brought this to the attention of The Floor Store, I was told that because the vacuum was on sale, I could not exchange or return it, which I was not told when I made the purchase. I was also treated rudely by the salesman, Robert Rule, and then by the manager, Alfred Adams.

4 I am requesting that you provide me with a new vacuum cleaner, on condition that if this one proves to be unacceptable, I will receive a refund. I also ask that you investigate the business practices of The Floor Store, as they are poor representatives of your company.

I can be reached during the day at (222) 444-5555 or after six in the evening at (222) 555-6666 **5** Kindly respond before July 17 **6**

Yours truly,

Jane Jones

Writing an Effective Complaint Letter

An effective letter of complaint should be polite and free of rancor, but also firm. For best results, include the following points: 1. Address the letter to someone with sufficient authority to handle the problem; describe the product, then tell when, where, and how you purchased it. 2. Include a copy of the purchase receipt. 3. Outline the complaints clearly and concisely, but include all the details. 4. Make clear the remedy you want, whether it is a new product, a refund, or additional damages. 5. Tell where you can be reached during business hours. 6. Set a firm deadline for action. Send the letter by registered mail, return receipt requested.

ADVERTISING AND MARKETING

The wise consumer knows how to sift through sellers' claims and persuasions.

Advertising's Pros and Cons

At its best, advertising helps inform consumers, makes them aware of convenient new products, and helps them to compare similar products. When products are basically alike, however, advertisers must use subtler means to set their brands apart. Their approaches do not come about by accident. Some of Canada's brightest minds are devoted to creating advertising intended to create brand awareness and give products an image or a "personality" that will appeal to consumers. To learn which messages are most effective with their target audience, companies spend millions on market research. They often go beyond questionnaires, using electronic testing devices that measure whether viewers' eyes widen when they watch an ad, indicating interest, or whether they wriggle in their chairs, showing that the ad is not capturing their attention.

The result is commercials that may grab attention but may not tell the reader or viewer much about the product. They may show an actor, who looks like a doctor, recommending a cold remedy or may feature a sports hero wearing a particular brand of shoes, implying that you will be in good company if you do the same. Or, they may play on emotions such as fear, showing the wreckage of a burned-out house in order to sell batteries for smoke detectors or pictures of real people touting the safety features of a make of car.

KEEP YOUR WITS ABOUT YOU

Building brand awareness pays off for the manufacturer, but not necessarily for the consumer. Buyers may be willing to pay more for a brand name they recognize, but comparing products on their merits rather than their advertising appeal can save you a lot of money—similar, cheaper products may be just as good as big-name items.

Some misleading advertising claims actually cause consumers to waste money. One product was advertised as being effective against the second-most-common form of baldness. What the ad neglected to say was that the first cause, heredity, is responsible for nearly all baldness in men. Thus only a tiny fraction of people could possibly be helped by the advertised product.

The Soft Sell of Indirect Advertising

Movies and television often subject viewers to hidden advertising. The heroine says a tearful good-bye to her lover at the airport—with the plane and its logo directly behind. Or the hero orders a beer or a soft drink, and the label is clearly on camera.

Although the message is low-key, this indirect technique is a favorite device for building brand awareness. There are companies that specialize in this kind of exposure for products and services.

One of the most popular techniques is the video news release. Whether promoting a new athletic shoe or Dutch tulip bulbs, these highly professional videotapes are made in the format and length commonly used for items on television news broadcasts. They usually contain a legitimate bit of news about the company or product, perhaps a new way of harvesting grapes for wine or a survey showing how many consumers eat cold cereal for breakfast.

Television stations use these slick presentations as free fillers for their news reports—and consumers are never told they are watching a subtle commercial.

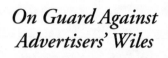

On Guard Against Advertisers' Wiles

The watchful consumer can learn to separate fact from fiction in advertising. Here are ploys to watch for:

✔ *Puffery.* Fact and opinion are not the same thing. Because a paid model or celebrity likes a product does not mean that it is better than its rivals.

✔ *Misplaced emphasis.* Telling you that a loan company is "friendly" does not tell you anything useful about its interest rates or financial stability.

✔ *Empty claims.* Stating that a face cream may make you feel years younger is not promising that it will change the quality of your complexion.

✔ *Emotional appeals.* Words like "stylish," "masculine," or "sexy" do not give you facts. They are merely appealing to your wish to be attractive or up-to-date.

✔ *Ego appeals.* Ads aiming for the ego use words like "exclusive" and "luxurious," implying that you deserve the best—and this product will provide it.

✔ *Guilt appeals.* Busy mothers are often targeted with ads suggesting that a product looks or tastes as though it were homemade.

✔ *Preying on children.* Children are easy targets for cartoon ads. Wise parents watch TV ads with their kids, making a game of spotting exaggerations or deception.

Clever demonstrations can also be misleading. Because a razor can peel peach fuzz does not mean it will do as well on a beard. Both federal and provincial agencies regulate ads that are clearly fraudulent, but it is up to educated consumers to train themselves to be on guard against half-truths and cleverly misleading claims.

Wrapped Up to Sell

Packaging and labeling, like advertising, are used to build brand identity. They are designed so that the buyer will be drawn to a product and can spot it quickly on a shelf crowded with those of competitors. Extensive marketing studies are done to find out which colors and shapes are most appealing to potential buyers.

Competition has led to many kinds of improved packaging, such as unbreakable plastic bottles, smaller boxes, and more convenient toothpaste dispensers. It has also produced less constructive ploys. Knowing that a product's outward appearance can shape the buyer's perception of what is inside, advertisers put foods in crocks to make them seem homemade or in fancy gold paper to make them seem "deluxe"; of course, the consumer pays for these frills.

Packaging can also be downright deceptive. A large box or container may have less inside than the package implies. Often canned coffee comes in containers that appear to be one-pound cans, when in fact they contain only 12 ounces of coffee. It pays to compare a product's cost per ounce or per pound with the competition's product. Don't assume that a bigger box means more for your money.

Packages frequently bear prominent but vague claims to appeal to consumers. "New and improved" does not mean anything unless improvements are explained. Federal law prohibits false claims and requires specific nutritional data, but some claims though legal can still be misleading. "Lite," for example, can sound great but may be meaningless. Buyers must understand that manufacturers—whether they produce food, cosmetics, or TVs—are wrapping their products to sell.

Sales-Promotion Tactics

Sales promotion—ranging from free samples to coupons to rebates—is another way that sellers encourage people to try their products. A smart shopper will take advantage of promotions on products she can use, and will steer clear of seductive come-ons.

When manufacturers spend millions putting out new products, they often willingly take on the cost of mailing out free samples. They hope that once the product is in your house you will try it—and like it enough to switch from your old brand. Bonuses with purchases are another way to induce you to buy and try. Perfume companies often give a set of free samples with a purchase, or for larger purchases they may offer premiums such as umbrellas or carrying cases.

Packaging can be a sales-promotion tool. By banding three bars of soap together and selling them at a savings over buying each separately, the manufacturer moves more merchandise and may interest more buyers. Packages can also offer premiums that lead to repeat business, such as an offer to exchange a free box of cat food for a proof-of-purchase seal.

RESISTING IN-STORE SEDUCTION

In-store marketing is a direct effort to woo customers. Manufacturers frequently set up booths where a representative offers free samples of their products. Cosmetics companies, for example, often provide free "makeovers" or attractive gifts, such as overnight bags, hoping the results of a professional makeup job or the gifts will please the customer enough to persuade her to buy more of their products.

Savvy supermarket owners are particularly creative with subtle techniques to lower your willpower when you shop. When you walk into a supermarket, you are often greeted by displays that look like specials, but often they are seasonal items, such as picnic supplies in summer, positioned to encourage impulse buying. Or, to draw your attention, a certain product may be on sale, but the rest of the barbecue needs—paper plates, hamburger buns, or hot dogs—are sold at regular price. The bakery is usually near the front so the aroma hits you immediately, while milk, an essential on most shopping lists, is deliberately placed at the back of the store so that you must pass through all of the aisles with their shelves of tempting products.

CATCH YOUR EYE, GET YOUR DOLLAR

Product placement is another ploy. Putting an item at eye level increases sales noticeably, so cheaper items are relegated to the top or bottom shelves. Specials are often displayed at the end of the aisles—but right next to the discounted chips you may find high-priced dips. Magazines, candy, and gum are placed to tempt you while you wait in the checkout line.

Department stores are equally canny about placement of goods. Customers must pass the jewelry counter to get to the clothing; cosmetics are also placed up front to appeal to impulse buyers. Knowing the perils from the start, you may be better able to resist temptation and stick to your shopping list.

Is It Really a Bargain?

Sales are effective promotion tools used by merchants to bring in customers. But a sale may not always be what it seems.

An authentic sale means that the seller is offering stock merchandise for less than the normal price for a limited time only. Seasonal specials such as semiannual "white sales" are a good example of a legitimate sale. Regular sheets and towels are commonly marked down in January and August.

But buyers need to beware of merchants who repeatedly advertise the same items as being on sale. Equally tricky are those who raise prices by putting on higher tags than normal so that they can claim a sale when an item in reality has been "marked down" to the regular price.

A price tag that shows the "suggested retail price" of an item beside the store's substantially lower price may be deceptive as well. The suggested price may be inflated in an attempt to make you feel that you are getting a bargain when you are actually paying the store's full price.

Unscrupulous merchants sometimes keep "going out of business" signs posted in their windows for years, especially in tourist areas where potential customers will not be in town long enough to recognize the classic ploy.

In short, buyers need to be certain that they are getting legitimate savings, not cheap merchandise. Low price alone does not mean a good buy.

DECEPTIVE SALES PRACTICES

An informed consumer is the best defense against fraud in the marketplace.

Are Sweepstakes Legitimate?

A sweepstakes is a game of chance offering a prize, usually cash, to a winner who is chosen in a random drawing.

Companies sponsor sweepstakes to increase sales or consumer awareness of their name. Legitimate magazine publishers, charities, fast-food restaurants, and time-share resorts may all use sweepstakes as a promotional effort.

Many people feel they will better their chances of winning if they purchase a product, make a contribution, or subscribe to the magazines sold by the sponsoring company, so they check the "yes" box on the reply envelope.

However, to be legal, sweepstakes cannot require you to buy or pay anything to enter. You can legally enter by submitting your name and address on a plain sheet of paper. Such entries must have the same chance of winning as an entry that includes a proof of purchase or that was obtained, for instance, along with a hamburger or soft drink at a fast-food establishment.

The odds of winning a sweepstakes are slim, perhaps 400 million to one. The law prohibits sponsors from misrepresenting these odds. If you want to know your chances, read the fine print on the promotional materials.

What Constitutes Fraud?

If a seller intentionally deceives you about a product or service and if you suffer a loss as a result, you have been victimized by fraud. Fortunately, a number of laws exist to help you protect yourself against the myriad fraudulent schemes that are constantly being invented—and reinvented—by scam artists everywhere. Federal organizations such as the Consumer Products Branch of Industry Canada and the Bureau of Consumer Affairs are empowered to punish businesses that engage in consumer fraud. These agencies have jurisdiction in cases of false advertising, unfair competition, and unfair or deceptive acts or practices. Although these federal agencies enforce federal law, they do not get involved in resolving claims. As a result, individual consumers are more likely to get satisfaction from provincial laws. Legislation in most provinces protects consumers from fraud and deceptive advertising and sales practices, which may be punishable by fines, imprisonment, or both. These laws may also address matters that are not expressly covered under federal regulations, such as requiring telephone solicitors to register with the province and post a bond, or making it illegal to falsify an odometer when selling a used car. Such laws often provide recourse for victimized consumers, allowing them to go to court or file a lawsuit.

What to Do About It

You have purchased a freezer from an appliance dealer in your town. The dealer delivers and installs the freezer, but after a week it has broken down and all the food it contained is ruined. You strongly suspect that the freezer had been used, but the dealer insists he can repair it and refuses to give you an exchange or refund. You begin to realize that you have been the victim of fraud.

A good place to start researching your rights is your nearest consumer protection branch. Another possibility is your Better Business Bureau. Either of these agencies can tell you how and where to report the fraud.

GOING TO COURT

Often the most effective way to deal with a difficult situation is to take the seller to small claims court, possibly on the grounds of violation of your province's deceptive-practices law. (See also YOUR RIGHTS IN ACTION, page 452.) In general, to prove fraud, you must convince the judge or jury that the seller's misrepresentation was intentional; for example, the seller told you that a freezer was new when he knew it was used.

The misrepresentation must be of a "material" fact, or one that is important and relevant. If the freezer had only one basket for loose goods rather than the two you were promised, that probably would not have changed your decision to buy and would not constitute a material fact that would provide grounds for a lawsuit. In court, you must also prove "reliance"—that is, that you could not have known from your own inspection that the product was not as represented.

DAMAGES

If the seller is found to have committed fraud, victims may be able to collect money for three kinds of damages:

- **Direct damages.** These repay you for what you lost. For example, if you bought a freezer that you believed to be new and able to keep your food frozen and it broke down, you would expect to receive a new freezer or be repaid your costs.
- **Consequential damages.** These cover the cost of foreseeable losses suffered as a result of the fraud, such as frozen foods spoiled by a nonfunctioning freezer.
- **Punitive damages.** Also known as exemplary damages, punitive damages are permitted in some provinces, where they may be added on to direct and consequential damages. They are intended to punish the person who committed the fraud, and they can run into thousands of dollars if a judge rules the fraud cruel or excessive. For example, if you purchased a faulty freezer for a nursing home, and the elderly, sick people were forced to go without food, you might be able to collect punitive damages. (Awards for punitive damages in Canada are much less than those awarded in many American states.)

To obtain punitive damages, it is usually necessary to show that the seller of the goods or services intended to defraud or otherwise cheat the buyer. In a Waterloo, Ont., case involving a $200,000 contract, the court ordered a vendor to pay $20,000 punitive damages for falsifying invoices and financial statements relating to a restaurant he was selling. The buyer's decision to purchase was based on the falsified documents, which made the deal look better that it really was.

FOUR QUACK CURES TO AVOID

1. Magic weight loss. Ads for pills and potions guaranteed to produce rapid weight loss make many claims—that they curb your appetite, or block the absorption of fat or calories, or flush fat out of the body. Some of these products are diuretics that merely rid the body of excess water. Despite "before" and "after" photos of models, none of these products produce permanent weight loss.

2. Beauty miracles. "Shed cellulite without exercise." "Make wrinkles disappear." Any quick, painless cure or special formulas available only by mail and from only one supplier are suspect. Ask to see copies of research studies.

3. Wonder cures. "Magic bracelet cures arthritis," boasts the ad, with a photo of a woman who claims to have obtained relief from the product. When testimonials or case histories are the only evidence, the buyer should be wary. Be sure to check with your doctor before trying a product that may affect your health.

4. Nutritionists. Diploma mills selling certificates for a correspondence course turn out unqualified nutritionists, who may prescribe useless pills for "effortless weight loss" or "fat-burning vitamins." Look for real credentials. Legitimate dietitians have undergraduate or graduate degrees from accredited universities. Registered dietitians have served internship and passed certification exams.

COMMON SCAMS
AND HOW TO AVOID THEM

Frauds are as varied as the con artists who commit them, but they often fall into predictable patterns. Here are some of the most common scams and ways to avoid or remedy them. Always check any questionable offers with the Better Business Bureau, your local consumer protection agency, and the attorney general's office. Report violations to these agencies to save others from dishonest dealers.

The Scam	What It Is	How to Avoid Being Taken
Dishonest advertising	A rug-sale ad claims prices are slashed because the company is going out of business next week. You think you got a bargain but spot the same ad three months later with the same prices.	Don't shop in an unfamiliar store without getting references and doing comparison shopping. When you spot false or misleading advertising, report it. The store is breaking the law.
Mislabeling	The label on the coat says cashmere, but the store owner knows better. It is actually camel hair marked up to an unrealistic price.	When you discover the scam, demand a refund and report the merchant. If you cannot avoid deceptions, at least stop them from happening again.
Bait and switch	The VCR was advertised at a bargain price, but it looks like an outdated model. The salesman says they have had many complaints about it—and recommends a more expensive machine instead.	Bait and switch is a ruse to get customers into the store. When someone tries to pull this all-too-common scam, the best remedy is to leave. Report the store's tactics and do your buying elsewhere.
Inflated appraisals	The jewelry clerk assures you that the ring has a fine one-carat stone, well priced at $1,500. He urges you to have it appraised, even recommends a nearby appraiser—one who will get a bonus for affirming the store's evaluation.	Check jewelers' references carefully in advance. You are at the mercy of their expertise and honesty. Use an appraiser other than one recommended by the store. If you get cheated, you may be able to sue, claiming an unconscionable sale.
Failing to give full disclosure	The art school contract promises weekly painting lessons for $50 per month. It does not say that you have to buy an easel and other materials for $350—far more than an art store would charge.	You can cancel your contract and get a refund, since the agreement you signed did not fully disclose the terms of lessons.
Phony prizes	An official-looking letter or postcard arrives announcing you have won a prize—a diamond, a deluxe vacation, or a food processor. To collect, all you have to do is attend an informational meeting about a new vacation community.	Pass up any "free" offer that requires you to attend a sales presentation. The prize may be worth little—the diamond is a tiny chip, the food processor a hand chopper. And you may be asked to pay a handling charge worth more than the prize.
Sweepstake swindle	"Congratulations," says the official-looking letter. "You have won a consolation prize in the $10 million Pie-in-the-Sky Sweepstakes. The attached voucher for $220 is yours as a consolation winner and may be applied toward your choice of one of the following products. . ."	You do not have to pay anything to win a legitimate sweepstakes. These letters are simply selling schemes. The products are probably not worth what you will pay even after your $220 credit. Phony sweepstakes offers should be reported to Canada Post Corporation.
900-telephone numbers	A card promises a prize. Just call a 900-number to find out what you have won. You listen to a long message—and learn that you are only a finalist, not a winner.	Don't make the call. The caller pays for 900-number calls. If you have children, ask your phone company to block access to 900-numbers. There is a nominal fee.

The Scam	What It Is	How to Avoid Being Taken
Pyramid sales scheme	The right to distribute a product, such as a line of cosmetics, is offered to four people. Each buyer pays $2,000 and, in turn, may sell four dealerships, making a profit of $6,000. Money is made from selling the dealership, not a product, and finding new prospects gets tougher and tougher as the pyramid grows.	Only the promoter and those who get in at the top of a pyramid make money. The later you enter, the less your chances. Often, you are not told the size of the pyramid when you join, only that you need to find a few other people. Pyramid schemes are illegal. They should be avoided and reported to the authorities.
Art frauds	The gallery owner offers you a "fabulous investment," a signed print by a famous artist like Picasso, costing anywhere from $500 to $10,000. In fact, the prints are counterfeit, reproduced without authorization and bearing a forged signature. "Certificates of authenticity" are probably worthless.	Before buying an important piece of art, check out the gallery's credentials with an expert art appraiser or a museum curator. Make the sale conditional on an appraisal by an expert of your choice. Be sure the sales slip states in writing that you are entitled to your money back, not just an exchange for another print.
Bogus charity	A policeman is killed in the line of duty. The day following the newspaper headlines, you get a call asking for a contribution to his family. The cheque should be made out to the family friend who is heading the collection.	Never make out a cheque to an individual who is a stranger to you. Ask for the name, address, and telephone number of anyone asking for money by phone. Don't feel pressured to give on the spot. Check out any charity before you give.
Travel scams	The phone call promises you a free vacation—all you have to pay is the airfare. The fare turns out to be much higher, more than twice the price of an economy ticket. The "luxury hotel" is a cheap, run-down resort. You could have bought a better trip for less.	Don't succumb to scam artists who try to tempt you with the idea of a bargain vacation. Strangers are not likely to call out of the blue with a real windfall. Remember the old adage: If it sounds too good to be true, it probably is.
Credit card fraud	The caller says your credit card company has a gift for all cardholders—a $50 credit. She wants to verify your card number. The credit never appears on your bill, but many other unauthorized charges do.	Never give credit card or bank information on the phone unless you have initiated the call. Also, because con artists can get numbers from discarded carbons of sales slips, be sure to destroy the carbons.
The long lost relative scam	Someone contacts you by mail or telephone claiming you are the only living relative of someone who recently died in a faraway place. You are asked for a fee of $50 to cover the investigation and necessary paperwork to ensure your claim on the relative's estate is protected.	You will likely be asked to send the money to a post office box and will never hear from the con artist again. You should report the incident to the local authorities, or, if you were contacted by mail, to Canada Post Corporation.
Time-share schemes	The salesman shows handsome drawings of a new resort on a Florida beach, and offers you a "time share," a week's vacation at the resort every year, for only $2,000. You pay the money—but the resort is never built.	Never buy until you can inspect an actual building. Never buy without checking fully the builder's track record and his financial stability.
Phony inspector	An inspector in an official-looking uniform comes to the door to say that your home needs immediate repairs to meet city safety standards. He recommends a "reliable" repair service.	Don't let fear tactics make you panic. Get another opinion, and if repairs are actually necessary, get at least three legitimate estimates from licensed repair firms.

BASIC SHOPPERS' RIGHTS

Every time you walk into a store to buy something, you are entitled to expect fair treatment and good value.

Protecting the Consumer

In day-to-day dealings with merchants, shoppers have many rights that are guaranteed by local laws. You are entitled to a safe, clean environment. In most areas, stores must meet sanitary requirements determined by the local department of health. The posting of store policies concerning returns and refunds is usually enforced by your province's consumer affairs department. In many cities, all businesses must be licensed, and companies that violate the rules risk losing their licenses.

The local human rights commission generally handles complaints concerning discrimination against buyers due to race—for example, overcharging in certain neighborhoods or refusing service to certain customers. If you have been a victim of discrimination, you may also want to speak to a lawyer.

COMMON SALES PRACTICES

In addition to the federal Goods and Services Tax (GST), all provinces except Alberta impose sales tax. However, the amount of the tax as well as the items taxed varies from one place to another. Some provinces have no clothing tax so a shopping excursion might yield big savings if clothes are taxed where you live.

Receipts are an important part of the sales transaction and should always be kept in case of problems. Receipts should state refund policies clearly. If a store closes down or goes into bankruptcy with paid-for but undelivered merchandise, government agencies generally cannot help you collect a refund. Your recourse in these cases is filing a claim with the trustee of the bankruptcy.

Perils of Installment Buying

The cost of appliances tempts many consumers to pay on an installment plan. Ads that promise "Only $49 per month" make it seem easy to afford a new dishwasher or air conditioner. But think twice before you sign on the dotted line. While installment buying is tempting, you are actually taking out a loan from the dealer. Financing with the dealer is convenient—but you may pay dearly for it. High interest can increase the total price of the item anywhere from 50 to 100 percent, far more than if you took out a small bank loan or paid with a lower-interest credit card. Many credit cards also automatically extend your warranty. (See also "Extra Protection on Credit Cards," page 384.)

By law, creditors must disclose the total of all payments required to pay off the amount financed and the annual percentage rate you are being charged. However, some canny merchants manage to hide this total in very small print or in the loan agreement, which you should always read carefully before you sign. Look closely, too, at penalty fees or repossession rights for late payment, and be clear about what happens if you miss payments. (For additional information about credit cards and loans, see also YOUR MONEY, page 288.)

COLLECTION AGENCIES

Sometimes retailers turn their unpaid debts over to bill-collection agencies, which get a percentage of the debt they collect—sometimes as much as 50 percent. As a result, these agencies try to collect as much money as possible as quickly as possible and some will resort to any means to do so. In many cases the agency succeeds, given that most consumers are unaware of their rights and are frightened by the agency's threats and abusive behavior.

Many provinces have laws regulating collection of debt practices and these laws protect you against unethical operators. Collection agencies can lose their licenses for repeated violations of such practices as communicating with your neighbors, employer, or anyone else for any reason except to ask where you live; telling anyone they are trying to collect a bad debt from you; phoning you before 8 a.m. or after 9 p.m.; using court documents or pretending to be a police officer, lawyer, or government official in order to intimidate you; phoning you at work if your employer objects to you receiving calls there; adding collection charges to the amount of your debt; using obscene, profane, or threatening language.

If you think a collection agency is acting illegally, take the following steps:

- Notify the collection agency by certified or registered mail that you do not wish to hear from it anymore (its next step must be to take you to court);
- If the collection agencies threatens you or uses foul language, record the conversation;
- Contact your local consumer protection office and/or the attorney general's office.

"No Interest" Financing

Many stores have adopted a sales come-on that encourages customers to buy merchandise—usually expensive furniture or appliances—with a store credit card and not pay interest for a period of, say, 90 to 180 days. Consumers sometimes do not realize that unless they pay the bill in full when it comes due, they will have to pay interest on it from the day of purchase, at rates which may be higher than for many bank cards—sometimes as high as 28 percent. Before succumbing to this pitch, check:

✔ *Price.* Shop around to be sure you are getting the best possible price, including interest, for the item in question.

✔ *Due dates.* Find out the exact date when full payment is due, and ask if you must make any installment payments during the interest-free period.

✔ *Interest and penalties.* Know precisely what the interest rate will be on the bill if you fail to pay it in full by the due date. Also ask if a penalty will be imposed in addition.

✔ *Restrictions.* Ask if other conditions or restrictions are part of the deal.

✔ *Other financial obligations.* Scrutinize the application carefully. Consumer protection legislation usually requires that terms of special financing offers be included in advertising, sales contract, or store credit card agreements.

BUYING BIG-TICKET ITEMS

Consumers faced with baffling choices and clamorous advertising need solid information to make smart decisions and avoid buying traps.

The Real Cost of an Appliance

An appliance represents a sizable investment, and the temptation is to look for the best price when you buy. However, the real cost of an appliance over the years depends on how much energy it will consume. An energy-efficient appliance will save money in the long run by cutting down on your electricity or gas bill.

The government has determined that consumers have a right to know the energy cost of an appliance before they buy. Federal law now requires that enerGuide labels be placed on all new refrigerators, freezers, water heaters, dishwashers, washing machines, room and central air conditioners, and heat pumps. (Since all dryers use approximately the same amount of energy, they are not required to carry a label.) The cost information from these enerGuides will help you calculate not only the energy cost for one year but how much an appliance will cost over its lifetime.

New federal efficiency standards have also aided the consumer. Refrigerators account for about 20 percent of the home electric bill because they run around the clock, so energy cost is a major factor. Refrigerators must meet new federal energy-efficiency standards, using less than 1,000 kilowatt-hours per year compared with 1,500 to 2,500 kilowatts on models of 10 or 15 years ago. Some models use as little as 650 kilowatts. These newer units can save as much as $15 per month on utility bills. Similar improvements have also been made on dishwashers.

Delivery and Installation Woes

Having an appliance installed properly is as important as choosing the right one. When you buy an appliance, be sure to find out whether the store will deliver and install it for you, whether there is a charge for this service, and whether the retailer guarantees the work. Ask for a sales contract that specifies delivery terms. Excessive delivery and installation charges can turn a bargain into a bad deal. Ask whether the store has insurance that will cover any damage that may be done to your home during delivery or installation.

If you buy from a store that does not provide installation, you will most likely have to hire someone to do it. It is equally important to be sure that an independent plumber or electrician has liability insurance. If a problem, such as a plumbing leak, is caused by improper installation, the product warranty may not be valid and turning to the installer is your only recourse. Ask the service provider for the name of his insurance company, call to make sure he is covered, and call the Better Business Bureau to find out if any complaints have been filed on him or his company. (See also YOUR HOME AND COMMUNITY, page 44.)

Headaches arise when purchases do not arrive on the promised date or arrive damaged. You may have the right to cancel the contract if goods are not delivered by the date specified on the bill of sale. You also have the right to refuse delivery if merchandise does not arrive in perfect condition. Therefore, be sure to be at home to inspect goods when they arrive. Insist that the delivery people stay until you have made your inspection. (See also "Delivery Woes," page 388.)

OTHER PROBLEMS WITH APPLIANCES

If you have major problems with a faulty appliance, describe what is wrong in a letter and send it to a top-level executive at the retailer or manufacturer. Be specific about the nature of the problem and indicate what remedy you have in mind—repairs, replacement, or a refund. Ask for a reply by a certain date. If you get no reply, or the response is not to your satisfaction, contact your local consumer protection branch. As a last resort you may file a claim in small claims court.

Appliance Shopping Guidelines

Because appliances come with an ever-widening array of features, finding the best product for your needs at the best price requires research. You will find a number of publications in every public library that give unbiased ratings, and that compare and rank almost every type of product for cost, performance, ease of using, and so on. Some include repair records, an important point for you to consider before you buy. Still, appliances can put a big dent in your budget, and even after you have done your homework, you should proceed prudently. Here are some suggestions:

■ **Recheck your space.** Be sure the appliance will fit into the available space with clearance for ventilation and servicing.

Service Contracts: a Good Buy?

When you buy an appliance, many stores will try to sell you a service contract. Often this is a waste of money because it duplicates much of the warranty coverage. Read the warranty carefully to see how long it lasts and exactly what it covers. Is it likely that the appliance will need repairs during the period covered? If so, how much will they cost? You may be better off paying for small repairs than buying a contract you will seldom use. Ask the following questions before purchasing a service contract:

✔ *The basics.* What is the cost and length of the term offered in the contract, and what services and parts does it cover?

✔ *The terms.* Is the cost of labor as well as necessary parts included in the contract? Is the repair service "in home" or must you bring the appliance to the store for repairs?

✔ *The service provider.* Who provides service if needed, the dealer or an independent repair shop? If it is a repair shop, is it reliable? (Check the Better Business Bureau for any complaints.)

✔ *Transportation.* What are the provisions for getting large appliances to the repair shop? Who pays the cost of transporting a refrigerator, for instance?

✔ *Cancellation.* Do you get anything back if you cancel the contract? Is there a penalty?

✔ *Transferability.* Can you transfer the contract if you sell the item?

- **Reconsider convenience features.** Will a feature save you enough time or trouble to be worth the extra cost?
- **Compare warranties.** What is the duration of the warranty? Is the coverage full or limited? Is service provided in your home or at a service center? If the appliance needs servicing, who pays for pickup and delivery or shipping?
- **Choose a reliable dealer.** Lower prices may be false savings if the dealer does not stand behind his products.

Buying Furniture and Carpets

When you select furniture, you are creating surroundings that you will live with for many years. The old cliché is true: It pays to buy the best you can afford, since higher-quality products will look better and last longer than poorly made items, saving you money in the long run.

Furniture and rugs are major purchases, and you should plan carefully. Begin by making a floor plan of your room to scale on a piece of graph paper, then make paper cutouts of furniture—sofa, coffee table, chairs, dining room set—using the same scale. Try various arrangements and sizes in the available space. When you decide on dimensions—say, for a new coffee table—that seem right for the room, use them when you shop. Bring a ruler or a tape measure. If you see a piece of furniture you like, write down the measurements and check them out at home before you pull out your wallet.

When you compare prices, include credit terms and delivery charges, which can be substantial. If you find that you like a particular manufacturer, look in the Yellow Pages or in the back pages of home-decorating magazines to see if you can order directly from the manufacturer. Check the manufacturer's prices against those of local retailers to make sure you are getting a fair deal.

When shopping for wood furniture, these terms will help you define better pieces:

- **Hardwood** refers to mahogany, walnut, maple, oak, cherry, birch, teak, and other high-quality, long-lasting woods. Less expensive softwoods, such as pine, cedar, and redwood, show dents and scratches more readily.
- **Veneer** means a thin layer of good hardwood has been bonded to a softwood base. Veneer is not as good as a solid wood piece.
- **Bonding** is the composition of several layers of low-quality inexpensive wood, such as plywood, and may be used under veneer in cheaper furniture.

■ **Finish** determines the look of the wood. It may be clear, allowing natural color and grain to show through, or tinted to change the color or to resemble another wood.

When choosing upholstered furniture, check for good construction before considering fabric. Lift one end of the frame to see that it does not creak or wobble. Sit down and bounce a bit. If you hear creaks, the springs may be hitting the frame, a sign of cheap construction. Check the upholstery fabric label for cleaning instructions and information on whether it has been treated to resist stains.

Choosing Carpeting

Whatever style of carpeting you prefer, the most important factor in carpet quality is the density of the weave. The most expensive carpeting is made of wool, but more carpets today are created from synthetic fibers, many of which are attractive, durable, and economical.

To determine your carpeting needs in square metres, measure the room's longest and widest walls (include doorways and alcoves in the measurement), adding 7.5 centimetres to each wall for good measure. (If you're working in imperial, multiply the length of the room in feet by its width in feet, and divide that figure by nine to get the square yardage.) Add 10 percent for room irregularities. To get the price, multiply your square metre total by the carpeting price per metre (or the square yardage by the per-yard price). When you calculate price, don't forget to include the cost of padding and installation. By the way, don't skimp on the padding. Good padding can add years of wear to your rug or carpet.

DELIVERY PROBLEMS

The problems associated with the delivery of furniture and carpeting are legion. Special orders can arrive months late, wood pieces are delivered with scratches. The new armoire won't fit through your front door. Delivery men are shocked when you ask who will lay the 4–5-metre rug. To avoid these problems, make sure you shop at stores that stand behind their merchandise. (If you have doubt about a shop's reliability, check with the Better Business Bureau.) Anticipate delivery and installation, and get solutions in writing. Make sure a specific delivery date appears on the bill and do not accept a delivery until you have inspected it carefully. You should also clarify in advance who installs a rug or puts together an article of furniture as well as who will pay for this service.

TIPS FOR BUYING ORIENTAL RUGS

Buying Oriental carpets can be not only a bewildering experience, but a risky one. The "rug world" is full of hucksters ready to take your money and unload a fake or inferior rug on you. If you want to buy an Oriental rug, here are some tips:

1. Do your homework. Don't buy an expensive rug without learning something about rugs. Read a book, go to museums, and ask rug dealers lots of questions. (Most dealers are reputable and enjoy talking about their carpets.)

2. Know carpet quality. Be able to identify the tightest weaves, the best wools, the relative values of various styles, the signs of good color, and other indicators of quality.

3. Avoid shady venues. Oriental rugs are often sold at "going out of business" shops, warehouse outlets, and trunk sales. These rugs are inferior. Don't buy them.

4. Learn how to bargain. As with home or car purchases, rug dealers expect you to make a counteroffer.

5. Understand the market. Just because a rug is an antique does not mean necessarily that it is valuable. Just because it is new does not mean it is worthless.

6. Be wary of auctions. Buyers who bid at legitimate auctions are usually experts. Don't compete against the experts.

BUYING ELECTRONIC EQUIPMENT

Technological change and dealer competition force shoppers to learn before buying.

123...

DISCOUNT OR RETAIL—WHERE TO SHOP?

Is it better to shop for electronic equipment in a retail specialty store or a discount store? In years past, consumers tended to view discount stores warily and to put their trust in their local retail dealers. Today, the lines are not so clear. Some discount chains hire experienced clerks, have liberal return policies, and offer strong servicing capabilities, while some high-priced retailers cannot afford to permit returns. Here are subjects you should explore wherever you decide to shop:

1. Delivery. Will the store deliver? How long will it take? Is there a delivery charge? What if the delivery is out of province?

2. Installation. Will the store install this equipment? Will you be charged for installation?

3. Returns. Will you be able to return products? Must merchandise be returned unopened or in its original box? Must it be returned within a certain time period?

4. Servicing. Does the store or chain provide servicing? Is servicing factory-guaranteed?

5. Warranty. How long is the warranty? Is it a full, limited, or extended warranty?

Making the Right Choices

When it comes to home entertainment, consumers have more choices than ever before. The selection of television sets, VCRs, stereo equipment, telephones, and computers can be confusing. Unfortunately, the selling climate in some stores makes things even more difficult. Many electronics and camera dealers are extremely competitive in their advertised prices but may give you a hard sell to upgrade to more expensive models once you are in the store. If you do not know what you need, you are an easy mark for a salesman hoping to increase his commission with a bigger sale.

It can be worth paying more if you can find a knowledgeable, reliable merchant who can guide you through the maze of multiplying options and technical terms and can help you to make sensible choices. Or, you can avoid paying for extras you do not need by doing some homework. Analyze how you will use your equipment and which of the available features will be valuable to you. For example, if you use a VCR mostly to show movies and only occasionally for taping, it makes little sense to pay more for a machine that can record many different programs over several weeks. Nor do you need a camera with an expensive set of lenses to take occasional snapshots.

GETTING THE BEST BUY

Once you are sure of the model and features you want, shop hard for the best price, comparing local advertising as well as discount mail-order catalogs and advertising in big-city newspapers. In many cases, electronics prices are negotiable. Some stores advertise that they will beat any price. If you present the competing ad, the merchant must make good on this claim as long as the advertised item is the same model with the same features as the one he stocks.

Repair records should be a serious consideration in deciding which brands to buy; these records can be found in consumer rating guides. Because electronic equipment is usually complicated to repair, good warranties are doubly important, and a dealer who stands behind his products should they not perform can be vital if you have a warranty problem. Choose

a company that has been around for some time and is likely to stay around.

It is generally true that reputable electronics manufacturers make remarkably similar products in the same price categories. If the TV sets, VCRs, or stereos are of equal quality, the only remaining basis for choice is the convenience of using the various features and controls.

BEWARE OF THE "GRAY MARKET"

"Gray market" merchandise is imported into the country by someone other than the manufacturer's authorized distributor. There may not be anything wrong with the goods, but they come without the usual manufacturer's warranty. Sometimes there is an "international" warranty, which offers little help if you need local service. The retailer may tell you that your sales slip is your warranty—meaning that the shop, not the manufacturer, assumes responsibility for repairs—but if the store goes out of business, you are out of luck.

Prices are generally lower on gray-market goods because they have not come through regular channels, but they are a risky way to save, particularly if you are buying an expensive camera or electronic equipment. If you see prices that seem too good to be true, always ask whether the product comes with a warranty.

Repairing Electronic Gear

The availability of reliable repair service is a key consideration when you choose an electrical-appliance brand, particularly now that so many products are made in other countries, making it impractical to send items back to the manufacturer for repair.

Occasionally, manufacturers operate their own service repair centers. More commonly, they authorize independent repair shops to service their products, using approved test equipment and replacement parts. Technicians in these shops sometimes have had special training by the manufacturer; sometimes they have not. Usually, buyers are required to use an authorized center during the warranty period.

Addresses of authorized service centers are generally included in the warranty, product instructions, or service contract. If not, call the dealer or the manufacturer directly for names. If you have a choice between a product whose manufacturer uses a local repair service and one that requires mailing the product to the manufacturer at your own expense, the product with a local service center is a better choice.

Service-center ads in the Yellow Pages showing the logo or

Interactive Electronics

Interactive technology, which is technology that allows the user to communicate directly with a screen or other piece of equipment, is opening up new ways of seeing, hearing, learning—and buying.

In the past, for example, to order goods advertised on television or to see a pay-per-view movie, you needed to make a phone call. Soon you will be able to make such choices simply by using television controls or touching the screen.

A type of interactive technology that is fast becoming essential in schools, libraries, and homes is the CD-ROM. This is a compact disc—similar to the familiar audio discs—on which have been stored huge amounts of information in a "read-only memory" mode, which means, in brief, that the information on it can be read but not changed.

A CD-ROM disc may contain an entire encyclopedia or dictionary, and the user need only type a few letters or numbers to call up a selection on a screen. Since CD-ROMs have audio as well as video capability, the information you access can have several dimensions. For example, if you look up "Beethoven" on a CD-ROM encyclopedia, you may be able not only to read about the composer but to also see and hear orchestras playing his music.

If you are buying a new computer, it would be smart to get one with a CD-ROM drive, or one with enough expansion room to allow for its addition.

Buying Home-Entertainment Electronics

When you buy audio and visual equipment, it makes sense to select products that can be upgraded to incorporate the latest—or the next—round of improvements. Here are tips and facts to consider when you are buying home-entertainment equipment:

TELEVISION SETS
• **Sound.** Stereo models generally produce good picture and sound quality.

• **Inputs and outputs.** If you want to use a stereo, VCR, cable, laser disc player, or video camera, be sure your TV has video and audio input jacks, an audio output jack, and a coaxial cable jack.

• **Size of screen.** A set with a 19- or 20-inch screen (measured diagonally) is large enough for the family to watch without dominating the room. If you are buying a 35- to 40-inch set, note that the recommended viewing distance (about four times screen height) may be up to 13 feet.

VCRs
• **Heads.** The most basic videocassette recorder (VCR) has a two-head player and monophonic sound, which will be fine for occasional recording. Four-head models with high-fidelity stereos improve both picture and sound quality. ("Heads" contain sensing devices used in recording.)

• **Other features.** Ease of recording is a key factor in comparing VCRs. Some recorders now have VCR Plus—which is a recording system by which you enter a code found next to the television listings and the VCR is automatically set.

• **Tapes.** Little difference in quality has been found between brand-name or high-grade licensed tapes and ordinary licensed tapes. To be safe, however, don't buy unlicensed tapes; the quality may be poor and they may damage the VCR.

STEREOS
• **Receiver.** This is the heart of the system. Price depends on the power it can deliver to provide sound. The power is expressed in watts; the higher the number, the stronger the signal, and hence the louder the sound without forgoing quality. Twenty to 30 watts per channel is generally adequate, but go higher if you like your music loud or you have a large space.

• **Speakers.** The quality of your speakers determines the quality of your sound. The best speakers deliver both deep bass and high notes clearly and distinctly. However, all speakers combine sounds differently. Listen to several to decide which ones you prefer.

• **Walkabout stereos.** For quality sound with portable radios, compact discs, or tape players, a unit with a snug belt clip is preferable to a shoulder strap, which may bounce around.

• **Compact disc (CD) player.** CD players read music by a laser beam that translates digital information stored on a durable plastic disc. Because nearly every model will provide high-quality sound (subject to the quality of the speakers), the choice between models generally comes down to the features offered, such as a remote control, multi-disc play capability, and programmability.

CAMERAS
• **Lenses.** A 35mm lens provides larger negatives and thus better quality enlargements than 110mm models. The greater the versatility of the lens focus, the more expensive the camera. A 35mm to 70mm zoom capability takes quality close-ups and panoramic shots. A 35mm to 105mm lens takes a better-quality distance photo. More expensive cameras can be outfitted with interchangeable lenses, a feature not necessary for a casual photographer.

• **Features.** Cameras today combine many automatic features in increasingly compact models, including autofocus, autoflash, and automatic exposure control and shutter speed. These features enable even beginning photographers to get excellent results.

• **Convenience cameras.** These include Polaroid and disposable cameras. Photo quality may not be as good as with a 35mm camera, but with Polaroids the results are immediate and disposables offer convenience and affordability.

VIDEO CAMERAS
• **Features.** Look for a video camera that has a motorized zoom lens with 6:1 ratio. Preferably, the model should allow for automatic adjustment of the balance of the picture and both automatic and manual adjustment of focus and lens opening. The viewfinder should be designed for use with either automatic or manual adjustment.

• **Size.** Larger models are more cumbersome, but because they rest on the shoulder they are easier to hold steady. Hand-held cameras are more portable, but more difficult to focus.

trademark of an appliance do not necessarily indicate that the service center is authorized by the manufacturer. Even though the repair shop may provide adequate repair service, if you use anything other than an authorized center while the product is under warranty, you will have to pay for service and you may void your warranty.

If you have a serious complaint about a television set, a radio, stereo equipment, or a tape recorder and cannot resolve the problem with the dealer or maker, contact your local consumer protection branch on the Better Business Bureau.

Telephone Equipment

Some years ago, most people rented their phones from the local phone company; today you have the choice of renting or buying. To find out which best meets your needs, compare the cost of buying versus renting over one or two years. Take into account that if a rented phone breaks down, the phone company will usually replace it at no cost, whereas if you own the phone, you pick up the tab. Consider, too, if you are going to be satisfied with a basic phone or will you want to have such services as call display (where the phone number and even the name of the calling party appear on the screen)? If not, you will need a somewhat sophisticated phone and, in terms of purchase and repair, this will be costlier than a basic phone, which is quite inexpensive. Also keep in mind that technological advances in the communications industry are ongoing, so you may wish to "upgrade" your telephone regularly. Telephones are now available in a vast array of styles, and in equally great variations of price and quality. Select a reputable manufacturer who is likely to be in business to take care of problems, and look for the best warranty—two years rather than one. Choose a phone that seems sturdily constructed, and a brand with service and replacement parts available locally. Handy cordless telephones use a special radio channel instead of a cord for transmitting sound between the telephone base and the handset. Phones using only one or two of the frequency range used by cordless phones will not give sound as clear as that of a 10-channel model, which lets you switch among the channels until you find the best static-free connection.

TELEPHONES TO GO

Cellular telephones are more powerful portable phones. Some are called "mobile units" because they can be permanently installed in a car or boat. Others, referred to as "portable models," may be carried around in a pocket, purse, or briefcase.

A Few Facts About Fax Machines

The word *fax* is an abbreviation for "facsimile machine," a device that transmits and reproduces written messages using telephone lines. Fax machines, a virtual necessity for any office, are becoming commonplace in the home as well. Here are some fax features to consider:

✔ *Telephone lines.* If you do not expect to use a fax constantly, you need not install a separate telephone line. Many models can switch from phone to fax with the touch of a button. Others make the switch automatically when the telephone detects a fax signal.

✔ *Paper.* Most home facsimile machines use rolls of heat-sensitive paper, which curls up and may be hard to write on. Machines using plain paper are available at ever lower prices, although their maintenance may be costly.

✔ *Feeder.* An automatic document feeder allows you to stack pages for the machine to send consecutively. This saves you the trouble of feeding each page separately.

✔ *Features.* Many units come with a telephone handset for use as a phone, and some include an answering machine, so that a caller can either leave a message or send a fax. If you are considering one of these combination units, be sure all of the parts do not become unusable if one part fails.

Getting the Best Help With Computer Software

Computer manufacturers' warranties cover only the hardware, and software manufacturers' warranties go into effect only if the software fails to operate at all, which hardly ever happens.

Nevertheless, problems with software are more common than troubles with hardware, usually because of users' lack of expertise. Before you buy a program, make sure the manufacturer has a toll-free customer-support number available, not just during work hours, but also in the evening and on weekends, when you might be using the computer at home.

It is a good idea to ask salespeople, friends, and co-workers about their experiences with various software support lines, since some are more helpful than others. Some manufacturers have a staff of support personnel who will stay on the line with you and give you patient step-by-step instructions for solving your problem. Unfortunately, many software companies are beginning to charge for telephone support, so be sure to ask about what is available.

Also don't fail to send back the registration card to qualify for support service, because the computer support person will ask for your reference number before helping you. (This is one way manufacturers discourage people from copying programs instead of buying them.)

These phones are called "cellular" because geographic areas are divided into "cells" by the telephone company, each with its own mobile-telephone switching office (MTSO). When you dial, your call goes to the nearest MTSO, which routes it into the conventional phone system. As you move from one cell to another, you are switched automatically to the service in the new area.

When you buy a cellular phone, you must also pay an installation fee, an activation fee, a monthly charge, and a usage charge for each minute you use the phone. Often carriers offer free telephones, installation, or activation to encourage people to sign up, because they profit primarily from usage charges, which can be quite high. Compare day rates with evening and weekend rates.

Some companies will request that your payment be automatically charged to your credit card. In the event of a dispute over charges made to your credit card, you can write the cellular phone company and state that the charges are no longer authorized. Notify your credit card company about the withdrawal of your authorization. Be sure to ask about any discounts or special offers when you compare carriers.

The theft of telephone numbers is becoming a major problem in relation to cellular phones. Electronically skilled criminals are able to intercept the code numbers that identify cellular phones belonging to other users, and then make calls that are billed to those owners. Cellular-phone manufacturers hope to develop foolproof digital precautionary devices, or blocks, to prevent this kind of theft. Meantime, telephone companies are trying to crack down on the cellular phone crooks.

TELEPHONE ANSWERING MACHINES

Tape recorders have been the standard way to record outgoing and incoming messages on home answering machines, but newer digital machines use microchips that record messages in their memory, allowing for faster retrieval and less cumbersome operation. Useful features to look for in answering machines include:

- **Unlimited message and announcement lengths.** This feature allows you to record a lengthy greeting and to record the caller's complete message no matter how long it runs.
- **Time and date stamp.** This allows the machine to record the time when each message comes in.
- **Automatic interrupt.** Machines with this feature stop the recorded message when you pick up the phone—handy if you forget to turn off the machine when you come home or if you like to screen your calls.

Buying Computers

You can save a considerable amount of money buying a new computer if you live without the very latest electronic twists. Technological innovations appear so rapidly and regularly that models considered the latest thing only last year can be had for bargain prices this year. In this sense, buying a computer is like buying a car. Even so, a computer is a major purchase, and making a selection can be intimidating. Before you shop, it is a good idea to read a book for beginners, take a class to learn the basics of what a computer can do for you, and develop a clear understanding of why you believe that you need a computer.

HARDWARE AND SOFTWARE

The mechanical parts of a computer are known as the "hardware" and include the drive (which is the heart of the computer), the keyboard, and the screen. In order to operate the computer, you also need to become familiar with computer "software." Software is the information and materials (usually stored digitally on computer disks), or "program," that enable the machine to perform specific tasks. There are programs for word processing, making spread sheets, balancing your chequebook, printing labels, playing games, and much more. Learn which programs will be useful to you, since you need to choose a computer with enough power, RAM (random access memory, or storage), and other capabilities in order to run them. The packaging for each software product should tell you how much hardware memory you need to run it. If it does not, ask the salesperson before you buy.

Be sure that all the hardware inside the computer is under a legitimate warranty. The hard drive, for example, may have a separate warranty if it is not made by the same manufacturer as the rest of the system. An unscrupulous dealer could substitute cheaper parts, and you would not know until it was too late. Ask for the registration serial number for the hard drive. Watch out for ads that say "monitor optional" in tiny print. A computer is useless without a monitor, or screen, which should be figured into all prices. The monitor is already attached to laptop and notebook computers.

Many consumers are chagrined when a newly purchased, software program proves to be impractical or difficult to use. Better to try out the program first by renting: most large centers have stores that rent software with instruction booklets. Of course it is illegal to copy copyrighted programs, and anyone doing so will be unable to obtain upgrades and, without a registered user number, unable to receive support from the software company.

Questions to Ask in a Computer Store

When shopping for a computer, you should be able to ask intelligent questions about the hardware you are looking at—and to understand the answers:

✔ **Power.** Ask if the computer has a powerful microprocessor. For example, a Pentium processor is more powerful than a 486. Will the machine you are looking at suit your needs for the next few years?

✔ **Speed.** How fast is the machine? Computer speed is measured in "MHz," or megahertz. A 50-MHz processor is faster than a 25-MHz processor.

✔ **Hard-disk storage.** How much overall storage for data is available on the hard disk? It is measured in megabytes. How much will you need for your purposes?

✔ **RAM.** "Random access memory," also measured in megabytes, is the storage space available for running software. The minimum for running most new software is four, and if you want to run CD-ROMs you will need eight.

✔ **Expansion.** How many expansion slots are there? Is there room to add more RAM, more storage space to the hard disk, an internal modem, or a CD-ROM player?

✔ **Service.** Is there a responsive service number? Is there a fee? If so, how much is it?

BUYING CLOTHING

Be sure you know a store's policy about giving refunds or taking back merchandise, in case you decide you bought the wrong overcoat.

123...

QUALITY IS IN THE DETAILS

Well-made clothing looks, fits, and wears better than cheap clothing, and so it is worth stretching your budget a bit to get good workmanship. (Conversely, beware of poor-quality merchandise with a high price tag based on a trendy brand name.) When you shop, look for these signs of well-made clothing:

1. Stitching should be small and even, and seams should be smooth, not puckered.

2. Material should lie smooth around the zipper. The fabric should not pull when the zipper is closed.

3. Hems should be generous, and in good proportion to the skirt, sleeve, or trouser leg. Both hems and seams should be finished.

4. Buttonholes should be finished so that they will not fray. Snaps, hook and eyes, and other fasteners should be strong and discreetly placed.

5. The lining must be long enough and wide enough for the garment; it should not cause the fabric to pull.

6. Patterns in the fabric, such as plaids or stripes, should match at the seams, armholes, and collar.

Comparing Stores

Clothing can be bought in many different kinds of stores—from discount outlets to mom-and-pop shops, from large department stores to exclusive boutiques. At times, the same manufacturer's labels might be found in all of those places. But you may also find a substantial difference in the kind of merchandise, service, and refund policies even within the same category of store.

Wherever you shop, you have the right to expect courtesy. Look for the store that gives you the best service as well as the best merchandise for your money. Establishments that take pride in their service are liberal about accepting returns, figuring that they will make up the difference in customer satisfaction. They provide comfortable dressing rooms and have adequate personnel to help you find what you are looking for.

If you are willing to give up service to save money, be sure you are actually getting more value for your dollar. A well-known brand name in a discount store does not always mean a bargain. Many manufacturers have several lines and sell their cheaper lines to one outlet, their quality clothing to another. To compare prices realistically, you must also compare the fabric and workmanship that goes into each garment.

In any store, you have the right to know its policy regarding refunds and exchanges before you buy. In many provinces, the refund policy must be posted. At the very least, it should be explained to you before you pay and should be presented clearly on the sales slip. If it is not, ask the salesperson to put it in writing on your receipt. As a safeguard, save all tags and sales receipts until you have worn and cleaned the garment.

Ways to Save

Canny shoppers can find many ways to save on clothing besides simply keeping an eye on the price tag. First of all, the better a garment is made, the better it will look and the longer it will last, so paying attention to signs of quality construction saves money in the long run. Be sure to read care labels carefully, too, since maintaining clothes that can only be dry-cleaned adds considerably to their overall cost:

- **Take advantage of seasonal sales.** Generally, the earlier in the season you buy, the greater the selection. But to save money, wait for the end-of-season and post-holiday sales. When stores need to make room for the new season's merchandise, the markdowns can be significant. Late summer is the best time to shop for bathing suits or short-sleeved shirts; the biggest price reductions on overcoats come at winter's end.

- **Look for seconds.** Socks, T-shirts, and underwear from major manufacturers are often half price if they have a slight snag or a missewed label that will never be seen.

- **Pay with cash.** If a store accepts credit cards, but you pay with cash, ask for a percentage off the purchase price. Stores pay about 5 percent to credit card companies; some may be willing to pass that savings on to you.

- **Visit clearance centers and once-a-year clearance sales.** Many better department stores have clearance centers or sales where they sell clothing that did not move fast enough in the store. These are not necessarily leftovers—sometimes the buyer simply overordered; sometimes certain sizes did not sell. Clearances may cut prices as much as 75 percent on high-quality merchandise.

- **Never buy something just because it is cheap.** A sale item isn't always a bargain. If you feel that a garment does not suit you, does not quite fit, or does not match anything else in your wardrobe, the chances are you won't wear it. And "bargain" clothing that stays in the closet or is worn only once is never a good buy.

All that glitters is not gold.

WILLIAM SHAKESPEARE
The Merchant of Venice

Be Wary Buying Fine Jewelry and Furs

Consumers are at the mercy of merchants when buying jewelry and furs. Only an experienced eye can judge the quality of gems, or gold jewelry, or the authenticity of furs. Your first rule should be to deal only with reputable merchants. In addition, follow the guidelines below:

• **Get an appraiser.** The only way to be absolutely sure you are getting your money's worth on an expensive purchase is by having it evaluated by an independent appraiser. Don't rely on a recommendation by a jeweler or furrier. If the seller is dishonest, chances are he will send you to a dishonest accomplice.

• **Choose a reputable and licensed appraiser.** There are licensed appraisal boards in most areas, where the members are certified professionals.

• **Get a second opinion.** Even if your appraiser comes well recommended, ask for other references from insurance companies, antique shops, or auction houses that have used her services.

• **If you are misled.** If you discover you have been misled , either by a merchant or an appraiser, you can sue for intentional misrepresentation or fraud. You should file a complaint with the local Better Business Bureau and department of consumer affairs.

BUYING FOR CHILDREN

Safety comes first when shopping for youngsters. Consumers need to check government guidelines and keep up with recalls on toys and equipment.

Buying for Babies

Safety first is always the rule when buying baby equipment. Strict federal regulations apply to manufacturers of cribs, strollers, car seats, high chairs, and other products for infants and small children. Industry Canada's Product Safety Branch monitors children's products such as clothing, sporting equipment, and juvenile furniture for potential safety hazards, issuing recalls, and obtaining corrective action as required. When you shop, look for seals indicating that a product meets the mandatory federal requirements. Then, do some testing on your own:

- Run your hand over any surface that a baby is likely to touch. Is it rough? Will it become too hot if exposed to the sun?
- Inspect all hinges, springs, and moving parts. Is there anything to catch, scratch, or pinch small fingers or toes?
- Check for stability in any product designed to hold a child. Could a baby unlatch or wiggle out of the seat or harness?
- Strollers should be stable and have solid wheels that maneuver easily, comfortable seats, and secure safety belts.

IS THAT CRIB SAFE?

Because baby cribs used to be a major cause of infant accidents, safety rules for these products were added to the Hazardous Products Act in the 1970s. They regulate the space between slats and crib height, so that an infant's legs, arms, or head cannot be caught between slats, and an infant will not fall out because the sides are too low. Even the cheapest cribs must meet certain standards. Because an occasional unsafe crib may slip by, or you may be getting one secondhand, you should know what to look for.

The overall structure must be solid. Toxic finishes are illegal. Slats must not be more than 6 centimetres ($2\frac{3}{8}$ inches) apart. If there is more space than that, a child can wedge his head between the slats. Crib mattresses should be firm and fit tightly, with no spaces where hands or feet could get caught. They should be no more than 15 centimetres (6 inches) thick and fit within 4 centimetres ($1\frac{1}{2}$ inches) of the crib edges. If two adult fingers can fit between the mattress and the frame,

choose another mattress. Fabrics must be flame-resistant. Avoid decorative knobs or corner posts that could catch a garment and entangle a child climbing out of the crib. Cute panel cutouts are potential traps for small limbs. The side release mechanism must require two separate and simultaneous actions. The lowered drop side must be 23 centimetres (9 inches) higher than the mattress.

Selecting Safe Toys

Industry Canada's Product Safety Branch sets minimum safety standards for toys, but this does not guarantee compliance by toy manufacturers and importers. In fact, the department issues hundreds of safety warnings and product recalls every year.

Although most Canadian toy manufacturers comply with the Hazardous Products Act regulations concerning toy safety, and also adhere to voluntary safety standards developed by the industry's trade association, in conjunction with Industry Canada, hazardous products may reach the market before problems are discovered. As a result, hospital emergency rooms treat thousands of children each year for toy-related injuries.

It remains up to parents to be alert when they select toys. Here are guidelines to help you avoid dangerous items:

- Balloons can suffocate young children and babies.
- Watch carefully for toys with small parts that can come off and be swallowed. For example, check for sturdy, securely fastened features on stuffed animals and cloth dolls. Toys with points or sharp edges are also taboo.
- Be sure rubber rattles and teething toys are too large to fit all the way into a baby's mouth, even when compressed.
- Be guided by age recommendations on the labels, which are based on safety considerations as well as age appeal. Toys suitable for older children, games with small pieces, for example, can be hazardous for younger children.
- Don't give toys with long strings, straps, or cords that hang around the neck to infants or very young children.
- Look for the word *nontoxic* on painted toys, *flame-retardant* or *flame-resistant* on fabrics, and *machine-* or *surface-washable* on stuffed and cloth toys.
- Noisy toys placed close to the ears can damage hearing.
- Battery-operated toys may leak acid.
- Electrical toys should have a seal saying "ULC approved," or "CSA approved," indicating certification by the Underwriters Laboratory of Canada or the Canadian Standards Association.

Protecting Your Kids From Their Toys

Government regulation of toys sold in stores cannot entirely prevent accidents at home. These steps will help avoid injuries:

✔ *Avoid strings and cords.* Never hang toys with long strings across cribs or playpens. They are particularly dangerous when infants are learning to pull themselves up.

✔ *Be careful with small objects.* Rattles, squeeze toys, and teethers should be taken out of a crib when a baby is sleeping to prevent choking.

✔ *Teach safety.* When a child is old enough to understand, explain how a toy is to be used and warn the child about any possible dangers from its misuse.

✔ *Be neat.* Teach children to put their toys away on shelves or in a chest to prevent trips and falls.

✔ *Check toy chests.* Children have been seriously hurt when the lids of their toy chests have fallen on their heads or necks. Add a spring-loaded lid support to avoid accidents.

✔ *Examine toys periodically.* Watch out for sharp edges or points that may have developed. Repair broken toys and throw away the ones that cannot be fixed.

Bikes, Blades, and Skis

Bicycles, skates, skis, and other sporting equipment can be dangerous if they are not suited to a child's size. So resist the temptation to buy items that are too large on the assumption the child will grow into them. Doing so may force a youngster to deal with equipment he cannot properly control. Bicycle seats and handlebars can be adjusted as children grow, but the bicycle frame must be appropriate for your child's size. A bicycle that is too big will be hard to mount and dismount. Never buy a bike without taking the child with you. The handlebars and seat must be adjusted according to the rider's height; toes should be able to reach the ground for balance. Remember that safety helmets reduce the risk of head injury by 85 percent. Some city bylaws oblige all bike riders—children and adults—to wear helmets. Look for the CSA seal of approval.

FOR SAFE SKATING

Helmets are equally important for children who wear roller skates, sometimes known as Roller Blades. Protective pads for knees and arms are also a necessary safeguard. Boots that are too large will not give proper ankle support, and the skates will be hard to control. Have your child wear athletic socks when you buy skates to be sure the skates allow enough room to fit over the sock. Other in-line skate recommendations include:

- The brake on the rear of the boot should be made of hard rubber. If it is too soft, the child will not be able to control a quick stop. Also make sure it is not too small or too high.
- The frame attaching the wheels to the boot should be strong and rigid. If you can twist it, it could break.
- Choose softer wheels if the skates will be used on the sidewalk. They rebound from shocks and grip the surface better. Hard wheels are suited for indoor rinks.

CHOOSING SKI EQUIPMENT

Properly fitting ski boots are essential for safe skiing. When trying on boots, the child should wear the insulated socks he will wear on the slopes. Wearing two pairs of socks to fill out the boot is never a safe practice. Skis and poles must also be the proper length. When the skis are held upright, their tips should be no higher than the child's extended arm. Poles must not be too long to plant easily for a turn. Flea markets and garage sales can be an economical source for children's skis and sports gear. Have used equipment inspected and serviced by a reliable dealer.

CHECKING THE FIT OF A BICYCLE HELMET

Whether you are buying a bike helmet for a child or an adult, a snug, proper fit is essential to ensure maximum protection. Bicycle helmets are required by law for cyclists in many localities. Check for a good fit by following these guidelines:

1. Size. Buy the smallest size you can use comfortably. Parents sometimes buy "larger" articles for children hoping clothing will last longer. This thinking should never be applied to safety helmets.

2. Helmet pads. Pads should touch your head at the crown, sides, front, and back. When you put the helmet on, try to push it forward, backward, and to the sides. If it moves enough to create a space between your head and the pads, get thicker pads. If it is still loose, choose a smaller size. Also, helmets with sizing pads can be adjusted for better fit.

3. Chin strap. When the chin strap is buckled, the helmet should not move when you shake your head or push the helmet backward or forward. The chin strap should feel tight when you open your mouth.

4. Back strap. This should lie straight and taut, just below the ears. Straps should meet in front just below the jaw and in front of the ears.

SMART SUPERMARKET SHOPPING

You have the right to true measurements, honest labels, and fair guidance.

Laws at Work in the Supermarket

Canadians visit supermarkets more often than any other kind of retail establishment. It has been estimated that a shopper spends an average of $50 on a typical trip to the supermarket, and the average weekly grocery bill is around $100. That adds up to a lot of money over the year, and enterprising grocers have stocked their stores in a way to tempt you to spend even more.

The "specials" of the week will be arranged throughout the store, forcing you to wheel your cart past almost every shelf. Stores want to tempt you into selecting many items along the way, picking up a carton of ice cream here, soft drinks or pickled onions there. Market research shows that people are loath to reach up or bend down, so stores stock their more expensive, high-profit items at eye level. Related goods, spaghetti and pasta sauce, lettuce and salad dressing, for example, may be displayed side by side in hopes that the purchase of one will induce you to buy the other.

LABELING IN FLUX

Labels can provide much of the information needed for wise choices and Health Canada and Consumer and Corporate Affairs Canada are currently reviewing their food labeling regulations and policies. The goal (a requirement of the Canada–U.S. Free Trade Agreement) is to harmonize Canadian and American labeling methods, though not necessarily to make them identical. Currently, food and drug regulations enforced by Consumer and Corporate Affairs Canada specify that ingredients in most prepackaged products be listed in descending order of amount. If sugar is listed first, you know that the largest percentage (or the primary ingredient) of the food is sugar.

Nutrition information, if included, must relate to a single serving, and the amounts must be given in metric, or common household measures such as 1 cup. The suggested serving size may vary according to food type and brand name, but should be based on amounts an average person ordinarily consumes. Each label must give the amount per serving of energy (in calories or kilojoules) and of protein, fat, and carbohydrates (in

Can You Trust the Scanner?

Most large stores have installed electronic scanners at the cash registers. Prices come from a central database that quickly records weekly price changes on thousands of items in each store. Since the advent of scanners, many stores have stopped putting price tags on individual items, and showing the price by shelf tags instead.

Scanners can and do make mistakes, usually not in your favor. Often the error is an honest one. The new price of an item on special may not have been entered, and you may be charged the regular price. But dishonest merchants can deliberately overcharge through the scanner if you are not careful.

If a store does not put price stickers on items, jot down prices from the shelves as you put items into your basket. At the checkout, make sure to watch as items are put through the scanner. Put the items on special at the front; these are the ones most likely to be incorrect. If you spot an incorrect price at the checkout, your store's policy will probably be to correct the error and give you a refund.

grams). Vitamins and minerals may appear if the amounts are given as percentages of the recommended daily intake in a suggested serving size.

Although nutritional labeling has been voluntary to date, manufacturers increasingly provide this information to stay competitive. Studies by the National Institute of Nutrition show that nutrient content is the main influence on the Canadian shopper's choice of product, when health is a concern.

*The buyer needs a hundred eyes,
the seller not one.*

GEORGE HERBERT

Jacula Prudentum

1651

CANADA MAY FOLLOW SUIT

Newly revised U.S. food labels on the other hand are a good indication of what Canadian shoppers can expect once government officials and representatives of the food industry, health interest groups, and health professionals work out an equivalent labeling system. The United States has now established standard serving sizes for each type of food, regardless of brand, and U.S. food labels must specify what constitutes a serving size, the number of servings in the package, and the calories per serving. Each label lists, in grams, total fat and saturated fat, cholesterol, sodium, carbohydrates, including sugars and dietary fibers, and protein.

In addition to the ingredients (in descending order according to quantity) and storage instructions, the labels also show the name and address of the manufacturer, packager, or distributor, and the packaging date or the last date on which the item can be consumed.

Reading Food Labels

All packaged food sold in Canada must carry a list of ingredients, but nutrition information is optional. This might change when Canada and the United States harmonize their food labeling systems, a condition of their free-trade agreement. A nutrition label is now mandatory on all U.S. packaged foods offered for sale. Whether Canada retains its voluntary system or makes nutrition labels mandatory, the following tips will help you assess the information provided:

• Complete harmonization with the United States offers no competitive edge to Canadian manufacturers, who must produce bilingual and metric labeling for products for sale in Canada and separate labels for goods to be sold in U.S. markets.

• Canadian and U.S. reference standards for vitamins and minerals are markedly different. The reference in Canada is the Recommended Nutrient Intakes (RNIs) established in 1983 by the Nutrition Research Division of Health Canada. The RNIs take into account such factors as age and gender and average heights and weights. The U.S. standard is based on the 1968 Recommended Dietary Allowances of the National Academy of Sciences.

• Proposed Canadian regulations aim to set standards for such terms as "light" (or "lite") and "low fat." A product that derives more than 50 percent of its calories from fat would have to reduce its fat content by at least one-third in order to be marketed as "light." In instances where "light" is used to describe a product's flavor, texture, or color, the label should specify for example, "light in color."

• New Canadian regulations may also insist that health claims be based on evidence accepted by qualified experts. If a manufacturer claims that a product lowers the risk of heart disease, this benefit must have been proven in scientific studies.

Understanding Unit Pricing

Unit pricing is intended to help the consumer compare prices by weight or measure—the cost per 100 grams or 100 millilitres—rather than depending on the size of the container, which may be deceptive. Often, unit-pricing labels become confusing because they are placed on the edge of the shelf just below each product rather than on the package, and they are not always lined up beneath the correct item. If you want to accurately compare two products of different weights, bring a small calculator along when you shop.

To get each unit price, simply divide the product price by the weight in the package. This way you can quickly tell that a 525-gram box of cereal priced at $3.25 is a better buy than a 350-gram box of the same brand selling for $2.88.

Your calculation will look like this: $3.25 \div 525 = 0.00619$; $2.88 \div 350 = 0.00822$. Multiply each result by 100, or simply move the decimal point two places to the right, and you see that the unit price for the larger box is about 62 cents compared to 82 cents for the smaller.

Ways to Save in the Supermarket

You can realize big savings in the supermarket by becoming a more savvy shopper. Stock up when there are sales on nonperishable items such as bottled and canned goods or paper products that can be stored in a closet or basement. Apples, oranges, carrots, potatoes, and onions are generally less expensive when they come already bagged. Use the customers' scale to weigh the bags, and choose the heaviest ones to get the most for your money.

Buy the store's own label instead of brand-name products. Sugar, flour, salt, white vinegar, ammonia, and bleach are identical no matter what name is on the package. Other products vary in taste, but it is always worth your own taste test to decide whether you need to pay more. Store-label ketchup, mayonnaise, sauces, cold cereals, and coffee may be half the price of the name brands. Also worth trying are store-label cat litter, dog food, foil, laundry detergent, and dishwashing liquid.

Don't buy nonfood items in the supermarket. Light bulbs, toothpaste, toiletries, and stationery can usually be found for less elsewhere. A time-tested way to save is using manufacturers' and store coupons. But comparison shop first: sometimes the couponed item's regular price may be double that of comparable products.

Does Your Supermarket Measure Up?

The basic information you need to get the most for your money should be readily available in the supermarket. Check to see how your market compares:

✔ **Scales.** Are scales provided so that you can weigh your fruits and vegetables yourself?

✔ **Prices.** Are unit prices posted under the items they are describing? Can you easily read the name of the product? Are the items themselves marked with price tags?

✔ **Perishables.** Are perishable foods such as milk and juice dated to tell you when they are no longer salable? Are berries and tomatoes packaged so that you can clearly see the bottom layer?

✔ **Eggs.** Are egg cartons marked with grade and size?

✔ **Meat.** Are meat packages clearly labeled? For example, does the label tell you whether the rib bone is included in the weight of a chicken breast?

✔ **Itemization.** Does the sales receipt itemize as well as spell out your purchases so that you can compare each item with the price charged?

✔ **Rain checks.** Does the supermarket give you another chance when the weekly specials are sold out?

SHOPPING FOR HEALTH AND BEAUTY PRODUCTS

Strict labeling rules help protect buyers of drugs and cosmetics.

Over-the-Counter Safety

All drugs, whether sold by prescription or off the shelf, can be dangerous. Most headache pills, antacids, hay fever and cough medicines, and all proprietary (patent) medicines are classified as nonprescription or "over-the-counter": you can buy them without a doctor's authorization. Although many of the products may only cost a few dollars individually, most families spend hundreds of dollars annually on nonprescription medications.

Taken in excess, in the wrong combinations, or under unusual conditions, even the most ordinary medicine can turn deadly. That is why the Food and Drugs Act and the Consumer Packaging and Labelling Act require that all over-the-counter drug labels list all their ingredients. The labels must also specify the recommended dosage, proper storage conditions, the date after which the contents may become spoiled or ineffective, and they must carry extensive warnings about any possible side effects. Manufacturers are legally responsible for any claims about the content of their products and what they can do for or to you. The label can be considered a contract between you and the manufacturer, and if it misstates the facts, you may have a legal claim against the manufacturer.

SAFE SAVINGS

These regulations enable you to safely save on many over-the-counter products, from aspirin to eyedrops, by choosing the store brand over a "name" brand. As long as labels list the same active ingredients in the same amounts, you can feel confident that the products are equally effective. Savings can be dramatic if you choose generic or store brands of nonprescription drugs such as ibuprofen. The same regulations apply to prescription drugs (see also "Generic Prescription Savings," page 419).

Once products are on the shelves, the consumers themselves must sound the alarm on problems that may develop. Any time you suspect that products may be spoiled or unsafe, you should report them immediately to your local consumer protection agency and to the Product Safety Branch of Industry Canada or the Health Protection Branch of Health Canada.

If you suffer an injury from a drug or other product, particularly if there was no clear warning about the danger, you may have a legal claim against the manufacturer or seller. Contact a lawyer for advice.

Buying Cosmetics

The Food and Drugs Act defines a "cosmetic" as "any substance or mixture of substances manufactured, sold or represented for use in cleansing, improving or altering the complexion, skin, hair or teeth, and includes deodorants and perfumes." The long list includes skin-care products, shampoo, deodorants, shaving products, bath oils, baby products—even toothpastes and mouthwashes.

The act forbids the sale of any cosmetic which may compromise the health of a consumer and stipulates that cosmetics that might cause injury if misused carry a warning to ensure proper use. If a safety problem is discovered after a product has been marketed, Health Canada's Health Protection Branch or the Product Safety Branch of Industry Canada will run tests and, if a defect is found, request that the manufacturer recall the product. In serious cases, they will take legal action against offenders. In recent years, hair straighteners, nail hardeners, and sunscreens have been among the targeted products.

While serious injury from beauty products is rare, allergic reactions and skin irritations do occur, most commonly as a reaction to fragrances or preservatives. Some products are

He who will not economize will have to agonize.

CONFUCIUS

Generic Prescription Savings

Prescription drugs sold under their generic names may cost half as much as those sold under a brand name—the name that was given by the company that held the original patent on the medication. After 20 years, others may produce the drug under a generic name:

• Copying a drug is cheaper than producing it originally because there are no development costs. Thus, the price goes down. The shape and color of a generic pill may be different from those of the brand name, but effectiveness is the same.

• Under the terms of the Food and Drugs Act, a generic drug must comply with the standard of the drug being emulated.

• In the interests of economy, most provinces have laws that require pharmacists to substitute lower-priced brands deemed to be interchangeable with the brands prescribed by physicians. Accordingly, the pharmacist may substitute a generic drug without telling you.

• Since different manufacturers may formulate a drug in different ways—even though the active ingredient is the same—two versions of the same drug may not always produce the same actions or take effect in the same amount of time. For these reasons, and in these situations, your doctor may write "No substitution" or "Dispense as written" on the prescription. Cost may be important to you, but it must take second place to the safety and effectiveness of your medication.

• If you are getting a prescription repeated, your new medication could be a different shape or color to the previous one. However don't take chances. Consult the pharmacist to be sure of what you are getting.

labeled "hypoallergenic," implying that they will not cause such reactions. *Hypo* means "less than," and hypoallergenic means only that the manufacturer believes the product is less likely than others to cause an allergic reaction, perhaps because perfume or other problem-causing ingredients have been omitted.

The price of makeup items in department stores can be two or three times what the same items would cost in a drugstore. Comparing labels will tell you if the products have the same main ingredients, but the full formulas will never be identical. Manufacturers guard their formulas as trade secrets. Often the difference in products is purely a matter of packaging—and you can get the same results with products from the drugstore.

The rising awareness of the dangerous effects of too much sun on the skin has produced a flood of sunscreen products, some of which are rated by their "sun protection factor" (SPF). SPF is rated by the numbers, but don't be fooled by extravagant claims: research has shown, for example, that an SPF of 45 is no more effective than one of 30. And be aware that sunscreens do not prevent the serious skin cancer called melanoma.

We shall never be as happy as angels until we are healthy as animals.

BLISS CARMAN
The Friendship of Art

So-called Health Food

Be wary of claims of so-called health-food products that promise everything from cures for the common cold to bulging muscles and eternal youth. Many of the claims are not medically proved and some of the products are exorbitantly priced. At best such products cause no harm even if they confer no great health benefits; at worst they can delay or prevent people from seeking sound medical advice. The manufacturers of such products are careful not to make claims in a manner that would get them into trouble with Health Canada. Advertising a product as as a "muscle-building vitamin" may be misleading, but if the product label does not contain false claims there is nothing the government can do about it. Health Canada will only intervene if the label claims the product can remedy a specific ailment, but not if it says the product will help ensure your overall health. If you read the label on a liquid diet product carefully, for instance, you will find that it usually protects the manufacturer by stating that the liquid is part of a weight-loss plan. It will often advise you to drink adequate water, follow a sensible diet, and exercise regularly. If you followed this good advice, you could probably lose weight without buying the product.

Consult your doctor before experimenting with new health treatments or products. Report suspected health frauds to Consumer and Corporate Affairs Canada or Health Canada.

BARGAIN SHOPPING

Everyone loves a bargain, but before you spend money in stores that promise lower prices, be sure the savings are real.

Outlets, Discount Chains, and Clearance Centers

Stores that promise discounts over standard retail price are tempting, but the words "outlet" and "discount" are not necessarily synonymous with "bargain." They may also mean, simply, "cheap goods." Before you shop the discount stores, check department stores and other traditional retailers for quality and prices so you can recognize true bargains when you find them.

Big savings are possible when department and clothing stores maintain their own clearance centers to move out unsold merchandise. Clearance centers may cut prices as much as 75 percent. Here, as in any discount store, you should examine clothing carefully for flaws or damage and try it on to be sure it is sized correctly.

FACTORY OUTLETS

Factory-owned outlet stores promise savings of 25 to 40 percent off retail. The idea is so popular that giant malls have grown up where dozens of manufacturers sell direct to the consumer. The savings are real, but in many cases the selection and sizes are limited, and you will seldom see the same merchandise that is currently in the stores. In most cases, merchandise cannot be returned even if it doesn't fit or match other items in your wardrobe. Some garments may be mislabeled, or not sized at all.

Discontinued patterns and merchandise that did not sell last season are often offered in factory outlets. The best buys are likely to be found in items like sneakers or jeans that do not tend to change with the season.

OVERSTOCKS AND LEFTOVERS

Several retail chains promise discounts on fashions from a variety of makers. Their best values are overstocks, either directly from a manufacturer or from a larger department store. But operations with retail outlets in many cities must often supplement better clothing with cheap merchandise to fill their racks. Labels are often removed, so you cannot be sure whose brand you are buying. Shopping wisely means learning to rec-

---

1 2 3 ...

IS IT A BARGAIN?

Low prices alone do not add up to a bargain on clothing. Ask yourself these questions before you buy:

1. Who made it? Discounters often cut the names from labels so that you cannot identify the manufacturer. But federal law requires all clothing labels to carry a number assigned to each manufacturer. Savvy buyers can use a directory (found in larger libraries) to look up the numbers of their favorite clothing makers and identify their products by the number on the uncut part of the tag.

2. How much alteration does it need? Unfortunately, tailoring may turn a bargain into a major expenditure.

3. Will it need to be dry-cleaned often? Expensive upkeep may negate savings on the initial price.

4. What goes with it? Do you have the right accessories to go with your find?

5. How often will I wear it? Can you wear it a few times each month? Can you wear it over several seasons of the year, like spring and summer.

6. Does it really fit? If it pulls across the chest or hips, you may never wear it comfortably.

ognize quality merchandise even when labels are removed. (See also "Quality Is in the Details," page 410.)

Stores specializing in odd lots of discontinued merchandise other than clothes can also offer substantial savings. You never know what you will find, and you may not see it again, but if you can use what is available, it will probably be a bargain.

ONE-STOP SHOPPING

The fastest growing retailers in North America are big one-stop marts selling everything from groceries to clothing, home furnishings to auto supplies. Customers at these stores are willing to accept less service and more spartan shopping conditions in return for lower markups.

Compare prices on items like appliances and clothing to be sure the savings are real—and remember that the name brands you see may have been made especially to sell in these chains and may not be the same quality as the same brands sold in other retail stores.

Look-alike Luggage

PROBLEM
Carolyn saved up for several months to buy some designer luggage. Then just two weeks after she made her big purchase, she was shopping with a friend in a discount store and spotted a set of luggage by the same maker that looked the same as the set she had bought, but for $100 less than she paid. She was furious, and convinced that she had been overcharged.

ACTION
Carolyn's first impulse was to return her more-expensive luggage and berate the manager of the store who had sold it to her. However, her friend suggested that she carefully compare the two sets of luggage before doing anything. So she bought one (returnable) piece of luggage at the discount store and took it home. She discovered that the two sets were not alike. Her more expensive set had larger and sturdier wheels, better zippers, and stronger fabric. Her luggage came with a five-year guarantee, while the cheaper set had a one-year guarantee. Carolyn realized that the same manufacturer made different grades of luggage, providing cheaper products for sale in discount stores. She decided to stay with the quality purchase which would give her longer wear, and returned the cheaper bag.

SUPERSTORES

Huge selections of one category of merchandise—books, toys, home appliances, office supplies—are found in the growing category of "superstores." These stores claim to buy in bulk and pass savings on to the consumer. Often they have a worthwhile weekly special to tempt customers into the store. The surest values are found in stores that offer a standard discount, such as 10 or 20 percent off list price.

SHOPPING FROM HOME

By mail, by phone, or from the TV screen, shopping at home is easy and tempting. But before ordering from a distant seller, be sure you know your rights.

Pitfalls of Catalog Shopping

Many busy Canadians use catalogs to buy everything from high-tech computers to regional foods, enjoying the tremendous variety of goods available and the ease of shopping from home. Most mail-order merchandisers are reliable. Some hundreds if not thousands of companies are members of the Canadian Direct Marketing Association and abide by industry guidelines and standards. The association mediates between consumers and member retailers in case of disputes.

Still, shopping by mail from an out-of-town, or even an out-of-country, retailer offers dangers that you do not encounter when you deal face-to-face with a local storekeeper. Potential problems are magnified if you know nothing about the mail-order company, because there are a few fraudulent ones that tempt customers with misleading ads and other shady ploys.

There are some 600 catalog companies doing business in Canada and there are thousands in the United States. With that many to choose from, it is best to do business only with reputable catalog outfits. You might also try starting out with a small order to test the service, or you might ask your Better Business Bureau if it has any information about the company you have in mind.

Shopping From TV

The latest temptations for at-home shoppers are cable-TV networks devoted to shopping. This is already a booming business, and it is growing fast. Television gives a better picture than a catalog, and if you like what you see on the screen, you need only dial a toll-free number to place your order.

Some of the jewelry and private-label fashions sold on TV by celebrity vendors are exclusive designs not available elsewhere. But while some items live up to promises of big savings, shopping networks have been accused of inflating list prices to exaggerate the savings.

As with any discount shopping, it is wise to compare prices in the stores before you buy.

Negative Options

Book and record clubs try to attract members with tempting low-cost introductory offers. The catch is that when you join you must agree to additional purchases under what is known as a "negative option." This means that each future selection will be mailed to you automatically unless you exercise your "negative option" by returning a card stating that you do not want to receive it. If you fail to return the card, you receive the item.

If you receive merchandise you do not want, you usually have at least 10 days in which to return it; the seller is required to take it back, pay the return shipping cost, and give you full credit.

Consumer protection legislation also requires advertisers of these plans to disclose full terms in advance, including how many items you are required to buy in what period of time, how often the company will send you offers, how to inform the seller that you do not want the item offered, and how you can cancel your membership.

These plans often have hidden costs, such as shipping. Before signing up for a club, consider all the costs of the plan, and your ability to operate according to its rules.

COMPUTER SHOPPING

Computer owners with a modem and a subscription to an on-line service can order products while sitting in front of a computer screen. Do not give your credit card number out this way unless you are certain the company you are ordering from employs sophisticated encryption software. The nature of on-line communication transmits information to a number of computers, not just the one you are trying to reach. You can never be certain who will have access to your information.

Owners of computers equipped to read CD-ROM disks can combine the visual appeal of television with the ability to browse as you do with a mail-order catalog. CD-ROM shopping services are already available with some two-dozen catalogs on a single disc. Viewers can print out order forms for the goods they have selected. As you would with any catalog, make sure the catalogs are from well-known, reputable companies so that their selections will be safe.

Never buy what you do not want because it is cheap; it will be dear to you.

THOMAS JEFFERSON
1825

Telemarketing

Telemarketing—sales made by telephone—offers great opportunity for scam artists, who can remain unseen behind the telephone. Although some telemarketers represent honest companies, fraudulent operations swindle Canadians out of considerable amounts of money each year. In 1995, police in Quebec uncovered a scam whereby a

---

Commercial Advertising

The Canadian Advertising Foundation (CAF), a self-regulating association of advertisers, advertising agencies, media organizations, and advertising sector suppliers, promotes industry standards and codes of ethics, and mediates complaints from the public, industry, and government.

• The CAF administers numerous self-regulatory codes and guidelines, such as the *Canadian Code of Advertising Standards*, *Gender Portrayal Guidelines*, and *Broadcast Code for Advertising to Children*.

• The *Canadian Code of Advertising Standards* concerns itself with content, specifying that pertinent details of an advertised offer must be clearly stated, that relevant information may not be omitted in a deceptive manner, that advertisements may not be presented in a format or style which conceals their commercial intent, nor may they exploit superstitions or play upon fears to mislead the consumer. These are just a few of the stipulations by which CAF seeks to maintain standards of honesty, truth, accuracy, fairness, and taste in advertising.

• The rules in *Gender Portrayal Guidelines* are meant to ensure that advertisements reflect equality between the sexes, in terms of their authority, their household roles, and their occupations.

• Advertising aimed at children must not exploit their lack of experience and must not present information or illustrations that might result in their physical, emotional or moral harm.

• If you have complaints about advertising carried by Canadian media, write to the CAF office nearest you. See RESOURCES, page 469.

company promised (for an advance fee) to recover money for consumers who had been defrauded by telemarketers. Of course this company was as fraudulent as the thieves who committed the first offense. Senior citizens are particularly frequent and vulnerable targets. All it takes is rented office space and a bank of telephones for a swindler to be in touch with hundreds of potential victims all over the country.

Con artists usually want to get your credit card number for fraudulent purchases or to use your chequing account number for unauthorized withdrawals. With your account number they can write a "demand draft" on your chequing account. The draft is processed like a cheque but does not require your signature. You will not learn of the illegal transactions until you receive your statement.

Dishonest telemarketers have devised dozens of ingenious approaches to separate you from your money. Beware of the following scams:

- A sales call from a stranger, who might be selling anything from "low-cost" magazine subscriptions (which turn out to be grossly overpriced) to gold mines, to "fabulous" gemstones, to land "bargains" in Florida.
- A letter or postcard announcing that you have won a prize or a free trip. If you return the postcard with the requested information, you will soon be called by a salesperson ready for the kill.
- Broadcast and print advertisements that ask you to phone a 900-number for information, such as how to get a major credit card if you have been having trouble getting one. Charges for 900-calls are high and can be excessive if you are kept on the line for an unnecessarily lengthy call, and you may not even get the information you seek.

AVOIDING TROUBLE

The best way to handle unknown telemarketers is to avoid them. Whatever their approach, never give your credit card, chequing account, or telephone calling-card numbers over the phone unless you know the person you are talking to or know the company to be reputable. Ask to see all offers in writing, so you can check the details, and be wary if no written information is available.

Be leery of prizes if you have not entered a contest and of all promises of free gifts, especially free trips. Do not accept any offer if you have to pay a fee or join a club before you receive the proffered "complimentary" goods or services. Do not respond to any offers that require calling a 900-number.

Before you buy anything, check out telemarketing companies with the Better Business Bureau to see if local complaints

Things You Should Know About Credit Cards and Interest Rates

All the provinces have laws protecting you from unreasonably high interest rates. You have the right to know how much interest you will be charged, as well as what other charges or fees you will have to pay before you enter into a transaction:

✔ *5 percent maximum.* The federal Interest Act stipulates that, if an interest rate is not specified in a contract, the maximum you can be charged is 5 percent per annum.

✔ *Courts can intervene.* If you feel that you are being charged an unreasonably high rate of interest, you can ask a court to lower it.

✔ *Exorbitant rates illegal.* It is a criminal offense to charge more than 60 percent interest.

✔ *Unsolicited cards.* If you are mailed a credit card that you did not request, in most provinces you cannot be held responsible for the credit charges in the event of loss, theft or misuse. Once you use the card once, however, you may be responsible for charges on the card in the event of loss or theft, because the fact that you used it means that you accepted it.

have been lodged against them. Through its publication *CARP News*, the Canadian Association of Retired Persons frequently provides a consumer alert describing various schemes and the legal remedies available to seniors if they have been taken. Contact CARP for information. (See also RESOURCES, page 469.)

AUTOMATIC DIALING–ANNOUNCING DEVICES

Automatic Dialing-Announcing Devices (ADADs) are machines able to dial phone numbers sequentially or randomly, using prerecorded or synthesized voice messages for telemarketing purposes. Following a number of complaints filed by customers of B.C. Tel in the 1980s, a Canadian Radio-Television and Telecommunications Commission (CRTC) investigation decided that, although many people felt their privacy was violated by the automated messages, ADADs are useful for fire and police departments, schools and hospitals for emergency, and for informational and charitable purposes. However, the CRTC also decided that ADADs would be restricted, and any person or company wanting to use one would have to advise the phone company of the kind of device to be used, and the number, duration, and time of day of the call.

If you receive a phone call from an ADAD, you should be aware that the calling party must identify itself and the nature of the call, and advise you of your right to terminate the call at any time. ADADs can also only operate between 9:30 a.m. and 8:00 p.m. on weekdays, from 10:30 a.m. to 5:00 p.m. on Saturdays, and from noon to 5:00 p.m. on Sundays. If a company violates these restrictions, their service may be cut off within five days. In the event that you are harassed by an ADAD, you should file a complaint with your local phone company.

Protecting Your Privacy

You have the right to be free from unwanted intrusions in your home. Yet mail-order vendors daily fill Canada's mailboxes with waves of glossy offerings, universally known as "junk mail," while telemarketers besiege residential phones and fax machines with seductive pitches for everything from rubber boats to retirement plans. By no means are all of these offerings offensive: mail-order catalogs provide major shopping convenience, and phone callers may suggest useful services. Still, most citizens would happily reduce the volume of uninvited solicitations.

No law prohibits someone from sending you mail (except in special cases such as those involving obscene materials), and nothing you do will staunch the flow overnight, but you can begin by writing letters to all the specific companies that have

---

Stemming the Junk Mail Flood

Here are some steps you can take to eliminate some of the intrusive mailings, phone calls, and faxes that come under the general category of junk mail:

✔ Write to the companies sending you junk mail that does not interest you and request that you be removed from their lists.

✔ Obtain a "no flyer" sticker from your local post office to make it clear you do not want to receive junk mail.

✔ The Canadian Direct Marketing Association, a professional association of direct marketers, represents many firms engaged in direct marketing. At your request, they will remove your name from the lists they handle or will ask their clients to do so.

✔ If you are receiving mail which is offensive, such as erotic or sexually explicit material, you can file a complaint directly with the Canada Post Corporation.

targeted your mailbox and asking to be removed from their lists. (See also "Stemming the Junk Mail Flood," page 426.) If you are receiving unsolicited pornographic literature, report the matter to Canada Post.

Door-to-Door and Party Sales

In suburban and rural areas, door-to-door salespeople are familiar figures, offering everything from vacuum cleaners to home-freezer plans to cosmetics to vocational-school courses—even home improvements. Another familiar form of person-to-person selling is the at-home party: a friend or a friend of a friend invites you to a party and tries to get you to buy from a line of cookware, cosmetics, jewelry, or books.

Many of the products sold this way, of course, are legitimate; but there are also unscrupulous vendors peddling overpriced goods and services. Their sales pitches are hard to resist because the successful door-to-door salesperson has been carefully trained in hard sell tactics. The more expensive the product or service, the more aggressive the pitch. It is easy to make a hasty decision that you will regret later.

IF YOU CHANGE YOUR MIND

Many provinces require that door-to-door salespeople be licensed and bonded, and almost all provinces allow you a grace or "cooling off" period of anywhere from 2 to 10 days to cancel any order you place with them. (In Ontario you only have two days, whereas in British Columbia, Newfoundland, Prince Edward Island, and Yukon, you have seven days; in Alberta, you have four days, and 10 days in Quebec.)

These laws apply primarily to door-to-door sales, not those negotiated in a store or regular place of business. In some cases, the law may not apply to sales of $25 or less, or to dealings at auctions, trade sales, and exhibitions.

In some provinces, the door-to-door salespersons and other itinerant vendors must show you identification, must furnish a cancellation form with the contract, and must inform you fully of your rights. If you wish to cancel a contract and you are within the "cooling off" period, do so in writing by registered or certified mail. This way you get a receipt proving the date you mailed the letter. You do not have to give any reason for the return—under the law, you have the right to change your mind. Canceling by phone, especially if the company is unethical, is risky. You may be told that the salesperson is unavailable and all efforts you make to cancel will be stalled until the "cooling off" period has expired.

DOOR-TO-DOOR SALES PLOYS

The salesperson who calls at your door has been carefully trained to make a sale. Knowing some of the common tactics used will help you to resist the sales pitch:

1. The door opener. Salespersons have many ruses to get past your door. A caller says she is taking a community survey, for example, and adds that your neighbor has suggested your name (which she has just read off your mailbox).

2. The sympathy appeal. Salespersons will tell you how far they have traveled to see you, how badly they need just one more sale to meet a target, or, the oldest ploy of all, that they are working their way through college.

3. The guilt approach. Playing on guilt puts the consumer on the defensive. The book salesman asks, "Can't you put away just this small amount each month for your children's education?" Or a seller of vocational-training courses asks, "Don't you owe it to your family to better your skills?"

4. The price deception. Instead of a total price, you are told only the deceptively low weekly or monthly charge; or the salesperson may offer a very small down payment to induce you to sign up.

5. The long spiel. Carefully rehearsed chatter keeps the seller inside the house long enough to wear down the prospective buyer.

Solving Shop-at-Home Problems

1ᵃ3°°

UNORDERED MERCHANDISE

Your mailbox contains a product you never ordered, with a note saying it is yours to try free for 10 days—and a bill. Or you receive a box of greeting cards from a charity asking you for a donation. If this happens to you keep the following points in mind:

1. Canada Post regulations forbid sending unordered merchandise through the mail unless it is a free sample clearly marked as such, or it is sent by a charitable organization asking for, *but not requiring*, a contribution.

2. Any unordered merchandise sent to an individual is considered a gift. Those who send such merchandise are prohibited from demanding payment.

3. If you receive goods in the mail that you did not order, you have the right to keep or dispose of them in any way you see fit.

One of the hazards of order-from-home shopping is that packages may get lost, stolen, or damaged in transit or that when you receive them, the goods are not what you had expected. Even the best companies sometimes make mistakes. They send a blue shirt instead of the red one you ordered. An unexpected rush of orders on a popular item may mean it is out of stock when your order arrives.

But consumers have rights when ordering by mail or telephone, and those who speak up usually get quick satisfaction from reputable companies who want to maintain good customer relations. Reputable businesses, especially major companies with national reputations, are likely to resolve problems quickly, whereas unethical companies have no such stake in customer satisfaction.

Here are some common problems:

- **Wrong merchandise.** A seller may not send you substitute merchandise without your consent. Inspect items you buy by mail as soon as you get them. If goods are not as ordered, the company is responsible for the cost of return postage, whether the substitution was intentional or accidental.
- **Damaged goods.** It is the sender's responsibility to ensure safe delivery of merchandise to customers. If your order arrives damaged, save the packaging material and contact the company immediately. They will want to take the matter up directly with the shipping company. They should also arrange to have the order returned at their expense and send you a replacement immediately.

DEALING WITH HASSLES

If a mail-order company does not comply with these rules, you can ask for help from the Canadian Direct Marketing Association, the professional organization of home marketers. State the problem and enclose copies of a canceled check, money order, or credit card invoice.

If you get bills for merchandise you did not order, or receive items you consider offensive, annoying, or sexual in nature, file a complaint with your local post office. Canada Post can order the offending company to stop. If the company persists in mailing you the material, it could be held both criminally and civilly liable.

Bills for unordered merchandise may constitute mail fraud or misrepresentation, or both. Under the Criminal Code, mail fraud is an indictable offense punishable by a maximum five years imprisonment. Contact your lawyer.

SERVICE PROVIDERS

From the telephone company to the dry cleaner, you depend on service providers every day. It is important to know your rights when things go wrong.

Tackling the Public Utilities

Consumers usually have no choice about the companies that provide electricity, gas, or telephone service for their homes, but because these utilities are monopolies, they are closely regulated by government commissions whose duty is to see that customers receive the services they are paying for.

The commissions set rates, trying to achieve a balance between profit for the company and reasonable cost for the customer. Users have the right to testify when rate increases are being considered. If they come prepared with facts and figures that refute the claims of the utility, they may be able to convince the commission to reduce or deny the increase.

Federal and provincial commissions also prevent utility companies from arbitrarily cutting off service without ample notice to the customer. The customer who is behind on his bill must be given a chance to arrange payments. Some provinces forbid cutting heat service in cold weather even if bills are unpaid. Most gas and electric utilities have plans to even out yearly payments, and some offer free energy audits to help cut energy leaks and costs.

As a utility customer, you have the right to know that your gas and electric meters are working properly and being read accurately. If you think the meter is faulty or a reading was wrong, you can request a field survey to check it. The federal government also provides a free inspection service for electric and gas meters. You can find their telephone number under the Industry Canada section in the Blue Pages of your phone directory.

Choosing Service Providers

Like the protection offered by law when you buy goods, consumer protection legislation governs businesses or individuals who provide services, so when choosing someone to do you a service—whether it is fixing a faucet or shampooing your rugs—dealing with reputable people is key.

Watch Out for 900-Numbers

Telephone numbers starting with *900* are businesses that charge you—often quite a lot—for services that range from astrological predictions to what is sometimes described as adult entertainment. They have an arrangement with a long-distance carrier who collects fees, takes a handling charge, and remits the rest to the business. All 900-number businesses must disclose their prices in all advertising.

To dispute 900-charges, call your phone company. If this does not help, write or call the business within 60 days. The Canadian Radio-Television and Telecommunications Commission (CRTC) makes the rules concerning the proper use of telephones by companies. They can cancel the license of offending companies.

Many scams have been associated with 900-numbers. If you or a member of your family has been a victim, contact the CRTC, your phone company, your consumer protection office, or your provincial attorney general's office. (See RESOURCES, page 469.)

Here is what to look for:

- **References and reputation.** In addition to getting recommendations from friends and acquaintances, you should feel free to ask anyone you are thinking about hiring to provide you with satisfactory references from past customers. The longer an outfit has been in business, the clearer its track record. Your Better Business Bureau or the local department of consumer affairs can tell you of any complaints against the firm you are considering.

- **Up-to-date licenses and inspection certificates.** Many businesses, such as plumbers, electricians, and home contractors, must be licensed by the city or province. Some provinces require businesses to post a bond in order to be licensed, guaranteeing funds to remedy consumer damages. Check also that the company has up-to-date liability insurance covering its employees and any damage they may cause while at work or by faulty workmanship. Establishments such as restaurants, beauty salons, and barbershops must be inspected by the health department to ensure safe and sanitary conditions. A certificate should be on view.

- **Professional affiliations.** Membership in professional organizations, trade associations, and the Better Business Bureau indicates the willingness of a business or individual to abide by acceptable standards.

- **Guarantee of satisfaction.** Choose the contractors, plumbers, electricians and other service providers who guarantee the quality of their work for a reasonable period after the job is completed.

Beware of little expenses, for a small leak will sink a great ship.

BENJAMIN FRANKLIN

Choosing a Long-Distance Carrier

Although local telephone service providers are designated by the Canadian Radio-Television and Telecommunications Commission, each customer has the right to select a primary long-distance carrier. Competition among carriers is fierce and finding the best deal can be difficult. Here are some guidelines:

• Check the quality of service of each carrier. Two important factors in comparing companies are quality connections and easy access to an operator when you need one.

• Make sure errors can be corrected easily. With some carriers, errors cannot be claimed until the bill arrives; others have a number you can call to get immediate credit.

• To compare carrier rates, experiment with other carriers besides your primary carrier. In some cases it may be necessary to "make the rounds" by subscribing to different long-distance callers and comparing the charges for long-distance calls, the quality of service, ease of dialing and access to operators. With so many special deals being provided by different companies it may be the only way to find out which company can give you the best service at the best price.

• Check the cost of using directory assistance. Fees vary among carriers, and if you use the service often, it can make a significant difference.

Recourse for Injuries or Damage

What if a plumber breaks a pipe, causing a flood that damages your furnishings; a beautician burns your scalp; or a carpet cleaner ruins your priceless carpet? Under the law of negligence, consumers may have legal recourse when service providers cause personal injury or property damage. Negligence is defined as failure to act with an accepted reasonable standard of care. Even if the negligence was unintentional, an individual or business can still be responsible for actions that harm others. To win a lawsuit for negligence, you must be able to prove three things (in most provinces, claims for negligence must be initiated within two years of the negligent act):

- That the negligent person failed to meet his duty or standard of care;
- That the injuries are measurable; that is, you suffered financial or personal harm or both;
- That negligence was the cause of the damage. For example, you must prove that a pipe burst because the plumber botched the job, not because it was a faulty pipe.

BREACH OF CONTRACT

In addition to liability for negligence, home-service providers may be subject to legal action for breach of contract if they do not fulfill their obligations and you suffer a monetary loss as a result. If an electrician does not finish an agreed-upon job and you have to hire someone else at a premium rate to complete it, you could sue him for the additional cost of the work.

While a verbal agreement may be considered a contract, secure a written contract from a service provider whenever possible. Include a description of the service to be performed, a proposed completion date, a warranty for any work being done, and a payment schedule. If a service provider has breached a contract with you and you have suffered relatively minimal monetary damages, you may be able to take him to small claims court. (See also YOUR RIGHTS IN ACTION, page 452.)

Protection at Home

When you hire someone who will come into your home, such as a cleaning person, a gardener, a plumber, a carpenter, or an electrician, your best protection is to deal only with individuals or companies that are bonded or that have sufficient liability

What If You Cancel a Caterer?

Suppose you have hired a caterer, but the wedding is called off, or the guest of honor at your scheduled party becomes ill? If you cancel on short notice, you are breaking a contract, and the caterer could ask for the entire amount agreed upon, claiming that she cannot find another party to fill your date on short notice.

First of all, cancellation policies should be discussed well in advance, including what will happen if a snowstorm, tornado, or other act of nature forces a cancellation.

Many factors can limit the amount of damages a caterer may claim in connection with a canceled contract. For example, if the caterer is able to rebook the date, this would reduce the amount of damages the caterer may claim from you.

To check whether the caterer has rebooked, ask a friend to call requesting the same date and room and have the friend document the conversation. If you are charged a cancellation fee, it may or may not be valid, depending upon whether the fee is reasonable and whether you were informed of a cancellation fee.

If you find yourself forced to cancel at the last minute, the best course is to try to work out a fair settlement with the caterer. If you cannot come to an agreement, the caterer has the right to take you to court to present her case.

When Care Labels Mislead

The Textile Labelling Act requires that manufacturers sew a permanent and easily found care label into each garment. It must list at least one method of safe care for the garment and warn about care that could reasonably be expected to harm the garment or other garments being laundered with it. The tag must be sturdy enough to remain legible throughout the useful life of the garment.

If you follow the manufacturer's instructions and the garment is damaged in washing, your first recourse is to go back to the store where you bought it. If the store will not resolve the problem, ask for the manufacturer's name and address and write directly to the company.

In your letter, provide a full description of the garment and when it was bought. State all the information that is given on the labels and tags, and include a detailed description of what was done to the garment and what happened to it. Estimate how many times the garment has been washed or dry-cleaned.

Provide the full name and address of the store where it was purchased. Finally, state what you want done about the problem—for example that you want the garment to be replaced, or your money refunded. Also, send a copy of your complaint letter to the Product Safety Branch of Industry Canada.

insurance to cover any damage that may occur due to their error. Always ask about their insurance coverage before you sign a contract. When you hire cleaning personnel, baby-sitters, or handymen without such coverage, you are assuming a risk, since they may not be able to afford to pay for damages, even if you take them to court.

Just as service providers are expected to use care when working in the home, homeowners have the responsibility to provide safe premises for workers. If a workman slips on a broken step or a toy left on a stairway and breaks a leg, you may be sued for negligence—one good reason to maintain adequate liability coverage on your home. (See also YOUR HOME AND COMMUNITY, page 32.)

Services Outside the Home

When you use outside services—anything from cleaners to health clubs—you have the advantage of seeing the premises before doing any business. You can judge if a place is dirty or poorly run. Look for licenses and membership in industry service organizations, which shows a desire to maintain standards.

THE DRY CLEANER

Among the most frequent sources of consumer complaints are dry cleaners that lose or damage garments. When the cleaner accepts your clothing, you are creating a type of legal contract

A Glittering Responsibility

PROBLEM

Andrea bought an expensive sequined dress to wear to a formal New Year's Eve party. When she sent the dress to the cleaner afterward, it came back ruined, with many of the sequins curled and discolored. She demanded a refund, but the cleaner refused, stating that it was not his fault that the label did not warn about the sequins.

ACTION

The cleaner was a member of the provincial dry cleaners' association, so Andrea asked that the dress be sent to the association's Garment Analysis Laboratory. The lab found the cleaner at fault because he had steam-pressed the garment despite a warning in a bulletin sent out by the organization, advising that many sequins are heat sensitive and recommending testing procedures. A responsible cleaner should first have recognized the potential problem, warned Andrea, and asked for a written release. Then he should have tested the sequins before pressing. Because she still had the receipt proving the dress was brand-new, Andrea was able to recover the full price of the garment.

known as a "bailment." You put your property in his charge for your mutual benefit—you will get clean clothes and the cleaner will receive money for his work. He is responsible for taking reasonable care of your clothing, and by accepting it, he is implying that it can be safely dry-cleaned.

If clothes come back discolored or misshapen after cleaning, they can be sent to a laboratory for analysis to find out whether the dry cleaner is at fault or whether the garment was mislabeled by the manufacturer. The Canadian Textile Testing Laboratories analyze garments cleaned to determine if the damage is due to a manufacturing flaw on improper labeling, or is in fact the fault of the dry cleaner. There are also professional chemists employed by dry cleaners associations that can carry out the same type of tests. If a report shows that a garment was not cleaned properly, you should have little difficulty being reimbursed. If the garment was not new, however, you will probably receive only a portion of the purchase price.

If a garment damaged at a dry cleaner was mislabeled or the fabric was shoddy, you may have to take it back to the store where you bought it with a copy of the report and a request for a refund. If the store refuses to accept responsibility, go directly to the manufacturer. Always keep the sales receipt you get when you purchase a garment of any value.

RESTAURANTS

All provinces and cities have laws requiring restaurants to maintain sanitary conditions and forbidding the serving of contaminated or unwholesome food. If you are served contaminated food, you may be able to sue the restaurant if you suffer harm as a result. Less hazardous restaurant rip-offs are not always easy to spot. Is it really "100 percent pure butter" or part margarine? Is the "chicken salad" made from turkey? If you suspect that a restaurant menu is not truthful, complain to the local restaurant association or city health department.

BEAUTY CARE

When you use the services of a beauty salon, you are relying on the experience and expertise of the operators to use safe products and methods. If you are harmed by a chemical process such as a hair dye and you can prove that the operator did not use reasonable care, you can sue for negligence. If the product is faulty, the manufacturer may be liable as well.

You also have rights if the operator does not follow your instructions. If you ask for a trim and come out with a crew cut, or request red hair color and wind up blond, the operator has, in effect, broken a contract. If someone hired to perform a service deliberately disobeys instructions and performs to your detriment against your will, you do not need to pay.

FINANCIAL HAZARDS OF HEALTH CLUBS

Health clubs are blossoming everywhere, but they also are notorious for going out of business, leaving members with worthless contracts. And some offer contracts that need careful scrutiny. Ask these questions before signing up:

1. How long has the club been in business?

2. Is the club bonded to protect members if it should close? If so, for how much?

3. Is the club well maintained and clean? Are there enough facilities? Visit at a busy time to check for overcrowding.

4. What are the qualifications of staff members? Are they trained in physical education?

5. What are the fee arrangements? Some clubs make you sign a loan contract and pay interest on the unpaid balance.

6. Can you get your money back if you get sick?

7. Does a waiver of liability clause say you cannot sue even if the club's negligence causes your injuries? If so, cross it out.

8. What is the shortest membership available? Since 90 percent of health-club members drop out after three months, it pays to start with a short-term commitment.

YOUR RIGHTS AS A TRAVELER

From missing baggage to lost room reservations, traveling can present challenges. Knowing your rights will smooth the way.

Up in the Air

Airplane tickets are considered legal contracts between the passenger and the carrier, and airlines are required to disclose all terms, including how problems will be handled. Many conditions of the contract are printed on the ticket or the envelope that holds it. Read the small print carefully to learn about check-in deadlines to assure your seat as well as refund restrictions, liability limitations, lost-luggage procedures, overbooking procedures, claim-filing deadlines, and other relevant information.

Lost airline tickets should be reported immediately, since they can be used by anyone. Since you will need proof of purchase for a refund, using a credit card to buy tickets is helpful. Keeping a record of your ticket number will speed your refund and may enable you to get an on-the-spot replacement ticket.

If you have complaints about the way an airline handles your problems, contact the airline's customer service department. If you do not get satisfaction, your next recourse is Transport Canada which regulates the airlines. Foreign airlines are governed by the Warsaw Convention and other international agreements. According to these laws, an action against an airline must be taken within two years of the incident. For more information regarding foreign airlines, contact the International Civil Aviation Organization (ICAO) or the International Air Transport Association (IATA). (See also RESOURCES, page 469.)

WAYS TO SAVE MONEY

You may be able to save if you make one change of planes in an airline's hub city rather than flying nonstop. In cities with more than one airport, rates may be less for less popular airports; it pays to compare. Reserve one to three weeks ahead to qualify for most low fares. Because seats at special fares are limited, the earlier you reserve, the more likely you are to get the dates you want. The cheapest rates are available when the airlines offer sales during slow periods. Refunds on lower fares are "restricted"; you cannot get your money back. But you should be allowed to change the ticket by paying a service charge. Before you buy, check the penalties for canceling or changing your ticket.

Tours and Cruises

Scores of tour operators send parties of travelers on successful jaunts to all corners of the globe, but unfortunately there are those who cancel unfilled trips or, worse, go bankrupt with your money still in the till. To protect yourself, deal only with a reputable tour operation association member, and be sure the operator's membership is current. Members must have been in business at least three years and must post a bond to protect consumers in case of financial problems. If possible deal only with a tour operator recommended by people you trust who have had direct experience with the tour operator.

Read the fine print on the back of tour brochures. Find out what exactly is included in the price. Are meals and tips included? What is the refund policy if the operator cancels the trip or changes the itinerary in an unacceptable way? Are insurance charges and departure taxes part of the deal? If you don't see any of these, ask for detailed information.

The great advantage of a hotel is that it's a refuge from home life.

GEORGE BERNARD SHAW
You Never Can Tell

CANCELLATION INSURANCE

If you cancel because of a last-minute emergency, you stand to lose a substantial sum of money, sometimes the entire cost of

---

How to Deal With Airlines

Airline passengers cannot do much about weather-related problems, but if you have been bumped from your flight despite holding a confirmed reservation, or if you arrive at a beach resort but your suitcase does not, you are entitled to compensation:

• **If you are bumped.** Airlines are allowed by law to overbook. When too many passengers show up, the airlines can ask for volunteers to take a later flight and offer a free ticket as a reward. If you are bumped involuntarily, the airline must indemnify you on the basis of how late you finally get to your destination. To qualify, however, you must have met the carriers' check-in deadline for the original flight.

• **If you miss a connection.** If the airline's dereliction costs you more than it is willing to pay in compensation—if you miss an important connection, for example—you can try to negotiate a higher settlement with the airline. You may also decline a settlement offer, and sue in court for additional compensation.

• **If your luggage is late.** If your bags do not arrive with your flight, airport managers usually are permitted to disburse money for emergency purchases. If you cannot get a cash advance on the spot, you may be able to be reimbursed for necessities after the fact; submit receipts to the airline.

• **If your luggage is lost.** If a bag is permanently lost, the airlines will reimburse you up to an amount that varies for international and domestic flights. Carriers' settlements are based on the depreciated value of the bag and its contents; so, expect to dicker over the value of your goods. Since they are not covered, always carry jewelry and cameras with you on the airplane.

• **Exoneration clauses.** Such clauses or severe limits of liability often printed on the reverse of your airline ticket are not always binding. Some courts have overturned these clauses when they were clearly unreasonable or conflicted with provincial consumer protection legislation.

the trip. So, low-cost trip cancellation insurance is a worthwhile investment anytime you book ahead for an expensive trip. Insurance also includes coverage for any costs that may occur due to travel delays en route.

Your Rights in Hotels

Like airlines, hotels sometimes overbook in case of noshows. If a hotel is full and you have a written confirmation proving that you have a reservation, you are entitled to higher-priced accommodations at no extra charge, if available, or free comparable lodgings at another hotel. If the clerk hesitates, ask for a manager and make it clear that you will take the matter up with local consumer authorities and your travel agent.

If you are sent to an inferior hotel and the first hotel pockets the difference in rates, cancel your credit card payment to the first hotel. Pay the second hotel directly and report this fraud to both the hotel management and to your travel agent.

Innkeeper-liability laws in most provinces require hotels to provide a safe place to store valuables. Hotels that comply may not be liable for theft from guest rooms, and most hotels state clearly that they are responsible only for items put in the safe-deposit vault. However, if you are robbed or injured in a hotel and can prove that the hotel was negligent or that security was lax, you still may be able to win a case in court.

Renting a Car on Vacation

Like other reservations, car rentals may not be ready when you need them. Although they sometimes overbook, car rental companies also run into trouble when customers do not bring cars back at the time promised. Always have the reservation number given to you when you reserve the car. It is your proof that you were promised a car. If the class of car you reserved is not available, you are entitled to a larger model at no extra cost.

Always inspect the car before driving away. The agreement you signed promises that you will bring the car back in the condition you received it. If you find dents, scratches, or a missing spare tire, have that noted on your contract or you may be asked to pay for them later.

The rental agency may offer you a collision-damage waiver, which releases you from liability if the car is stolen or damaged. But chances are that your own auto insurance covers you in a rented car, and your credit card may provide automatic insur-

Should You Use a Travel Agent?

A good travel agent can be a great help in planning a trip and handling all your ticket, hotel, and tour reservations. Although changes may be in the offing, currently these services are free: the agent is paid by the airline, hotel, or tour operator.

An agent can also give you the benefit of other clients' experiences with hotels and tours. In case of problems, an agency will usually have more clout than an individual. An agent can be especially helpful when you travel to countries you have never visited before.

A drawback with agents is that they often prefer dealing with clients who pay them commissions. Airlines and hotels may offer bonuses to encourage agents to recommend them. Smaller hotels and airlines with consolidators who offer cheaper fares may not be on the agency's computer. Nor do agents handle many offbeat tours. If you are a thrifty traveler, it can be worth making calls on your own.

Furthermore, like tour companies, travel agencies can be guilty of false advertising or deceptive practices. Use a well-established agency that is a member of a professional travel agent association. Pay with a credit card so that the card company can cancel charges for undelivered services. Otherwise, if you find on arrival that a hotel never received payment from your agent, you have no recourse but to pay the charge and try to collect through the courts.

ance as well. However, the credit card insurance may not include liability insurance—to pay for damages you cause to other cars and people—so be sure you know what kind of coverage you have before you sign or initial any rental agreement. (See also YOUR CAR, page 368.)

Visas and Vaccinations

Except for travel to Mexico, the United States, and some Caribbean countries, you must have a government-issued passport that identifies you as a Canadian citizen when you leave the country. Some destinations also require a visa, a special stamp placed in the traveler's passport by the nation's embassy or consulate that permits a limited stay in the country.

To find out whether a visa is required and how to apply for one, call the nearest embassy of the country you plan to visit or inquire at a reputable travel agency. Whenever you travel abroad, keep a photocopy of your passport in the bottom of your suitcase for easier replacement in case of loss or theft.

While abroad, you are subject to the laws of the country you are visiting and, if you break these laws, you will be subject to the same court procedures and penalties as local citizens. The Canadian consulate can step in to see that the laws of the country you are visiting are fairly applied and officials may recommend a lawyer or appear on your behalf in court. The consular staff can also lend you money to return to Canada if you lose your funds, or if you are stranded abroad because of civil disruption or a natural disaster.

An International Appendectomy

PROBLEM
Dale was vacationing in France with his wife, Sue, when he was suddenly stricken with appendicitis. Their hotel arranged to get Dale to a hospital, where he had a successful appendectomy. Sue, however, faced problems with all the extra issues that arose out of Dale's emergency. Their Medicare cards were not acceptable as payment in a French hospital, and the delay due to Dale's illness meant they were not be able to use their nonrefundable airline tickets to fly home.

ACTION
Fortunately, Dale had a travel health-insurance policy to guard against medical emergencies during his international holiday. The policy, which cost $150, also paid for the couple's nonrefundable air arrangements. Dale also carried a gold credit card that helped out: by calling an assistance-center number collect, Sue got the names of English-speaking doctors and hospitals and help in arranging for transportation.

LESSONS IN HOTEL SAFETY

While hotel thefts are infrequent, they do occur. A few precautions will help ensure your safety:

1. Ask for a room near the elevator. Don't accept rooms at the end of a long corridor.

2. Use the peephole to identify callers before you open the door to your room. If the caller says he is a hotel employee but looks suspicious to you, ask for a name and verify with the front desk before admitting the person.

3. Never put the "Make up my room" sign on the doorknob, announcing that the room is unoccupied. When you leave your room at the end of the day, leave a light on and close the curtains if you will be returning after dark. The "Do not disturb" sign may discourage uninvited visitors, who cannot be sure the room is empty. Leaving the radio or television on is a deterrent, too.

4. Have your keys handy when returning to your room so you don't have to stand in the hallway searching for them.

5. Don't leave money or jewelry where they can be seen by anyone entering the room. Use the room safe provided in some hotels or the safe-deposit box at the desk.

6. If you enter an elevator and sense trouble, stand next to the floor-button panel so you can call for help if necessary.

The cautious seldom err.

CONFUCIUS

HEALTH AND SAFETY CONCERNS

Under the International Health Regulations adopted by the World Health Organization, countries may require proof of immunizations, such as certificates of vaccination against yellow fever, in order to enter. When you travel abroad, make sure your immunizations against tetanus and polio are up-to-date. Preventive medication for malaria is recommended for travel to some areas of South and Central America, Africa, and Asia. When asking about immunization requirements, mention all the countries on your itinerary. Some may not require vaccination against yellow fever if you go there directly from Canada, for example, but may insist on it if you arrive via another country. Call Health Canada for the latest immunization requirements. Information can also be found at many of the larger hospitals or at clinics that provide vaccinations for travelers.

TO GET COVERED ABROAD

If you become ill overseas, you will probably have to pay the doctors and hospitals that treat you out of your own pocket and recoup the money later from Medicare. Your refund may fall short of what your treatment overseas costs since Medicare may only recompense you at the rate of equivalent services in Canada. You would be wise to take out overseas health insurance, which you can buy from your insurance broker or travel agent for all except preexisting medical conditions. The Canadian consulate or embassy in the country you are visiting may also be able to help in cases of illness abroad.

Protecting Your Money While Traveling

Since pickpockets operate in tourist destinations all over the world, it pays to be careful with cash when you travel. The most common safeguard is to carry your money in traveler's cheques, which can be easily replaced if stolen and to cash only what you need each day.

• **Use your ATM card.** The advent of international banking networks now means you need to carry less cash when you travel. If your bank belongs to a network, you can use your regular automated banking machine (ATM) card in major cities throughout the world to access cash from your account. While you pay a transaction fee when you use a bank card abroad, you receive cash in the local currency based on the bank's exchange rate, which is better than the rate that is charged to individuals.

• **Use your credit cards.** Using credit cards to pay for lodging, meals, and purchases gains the same advantaged exchange rate. You can also get cash advances on major credit cards in many places; but unlike getting cash with a bank card in an automated banking machine, you will pay interest on the credit card advance until it is repaid.

• **Change foreign currency.** Change enough foreign currency before you leave home to cover transportation, tipping, and immediate cash needs when you arrive. This eliminates standing in line at airports, where you often find unfavorable, often exorbitant, exchange rates.

• **Limit your cash.** Carry only whatever cash you need on hand for the day. Keep it zipped or buttoned up in an inside pocket. If you use a fanny pack, wear it in front. Never walk around with an open purse or shoulder bag.

YOUR RIGHTS IN ACTION

Action brings satisfaction. After learning your rights, you need to know how to exercise them effectively. Here are some guidelines.

PREVENTIVE LAW ■ TAKING ACTION ■ RESPONDING EFFECTIVELY ■ ALTERNATIVES TO COURT ■ GOING TO COURT ■ USING A LAWYER ■ REPRESENTING YOURSELF ■ MAKING YOUR VOICE HEARD

PREVENTIVE LAW

When it comes to safeguarding your rights, an ounce of prevention is worth several pounds of cure.

Full Disclosure and Your Rights

Full disclosure refers to certain information—including price, terms, and other factors—manufacturers and suppliers are required to give you about a service or product before you buy it. While the information is supplied for your protection, you should pay close attention to what is being disclosed: If certain limits are imposed, you will have little recourse if you later feel you have been treated unfairly.

Full disclosure can be given in a contract, on a receipt, in bank or investment terms, on an application, or even on a sign posted on a wall reading: "No refunds." Wherever you find it, be wary of certain words and phrases that may put you at a disadvantage.

The phrases "as is," "with all faults," and "no representations" all mean that an item, broken or functioning properly, will be yours to keep.

The words "hold harmless" or "will not hold liable" are also danger signals. If you consent to such clauses, you may give up your right to be compensated or to sue.

Avoid signing anything with the words "waive my rights." You could be giving up legal claims that you might otherwise have, such as the right to the privacy of your credit rating on a loan application.

Protecting Yourself

How many times have you faced a problem and wondered, "How did I get into this mess?" The concept of preventive law, as with preventive medicine, is to take simple measures in advance to forestall potential problems. Of course, not all legal troubles can be avoided, but generally, preventive measures can help keep a bad situation from getting worse.

When you have to make major decisions, whether they relate to health care, schooling, housing, consumer products, or even personal relations, step back and think about them. Arm yourself with facts and information. Get second opinions, not just on medical decisions, but on major purchases and investments.

BE PREPARED

Ask as many questions as you can before entering into an agreement. Don't shy away from a direct query such as: "Have you given me all the facts?" When you are negotiating a major purchase, tell the seller what needs you have. If you make it clear, for example, that you need a riding mower that can cut coarse grass, an "implied warranty of fitness for a particular purpose" may be established, making it more likely that you can hold the seller to that commitment. Be sure that sales pitches or verbal promises are confirmed in writing. Above all, never sign anything you do not understand.

Knowing the relevant laws can be important and helpful. For example, most contracts signed in your home with itinerant or door-to-door vendors can be canceled within 3 to 10 days. Therefore, if you agree to purchase an encyclopedia that you later—within your time limit—realize you do not want, you can legally cancel the contract. In some situations, you may want to have a lawyer go over a matter or review documents before you agree to a contract. If you anticipate a confrontation, consider taking another person along as a witness. Take notes on all conversations relating to the problem, whether in person, over the telephone, or by a mini tape recorder.

Before taking action, ask yourself the questions a judge might ask: "Would a reasonable person do the same in this situation?" If the answer is "no," reconsider your decision.

Keeping Records

Your word may be your bond, but when it comes to a legal conflict, your records are your proof. Whether you deal with a situation in a simple one-on-one negotiation or end up going to court, the best chance of securing your rights lies in your ability to prove that you have the facts, and that they are in your favor.

Get into the habit of maintaining records that are comprehensive, organized, and accessible. You may keep such important documents as insurance policies and armed services discharge papers in a safe-deposit box. Wherever you store your records, you should catalog *all* of them in a master file that is stored in an obvious place so that in an emergency, family members can find important papers quickly.

Maintaining the file will be much easier if you organize it by category. Using a home computer can make the job of creating and updating this essential record much less daunting.

Keeping Track of Your Life

The ever-growing complexities in today's society have created a veritable paper trail of records that you should keep to document your rights. How long you hold on to each document depends on its intended use. And, of course, you need to keep track of where you have put them.

• **Family.** Keep birth certificates and social insurance numbers for each member, as well as marriage license, adoption, prenuptial, divorce, armed services, paternity, and citizenship documents. Keep a signed list of separate property brought into the marriage by each spouse. Have a valid will naming a guardian for children. After a separation or divorce, keep all accounts of child or spousal support payments and child custody conflicts.

• **Home.** While you own your home and, for income tax requirements, five to seven years after you sell it, you should keep your mortgage loan documents, payments, deed, title insurance, escrow account, homeowners insurance policy, renovation contracts and repair receipts, property tax statements, appraisals, and leases with tenants. Renters should keep a copy of their lease, deposit, and letters to the landlord. For insurance purposes keep, at a location away from the home, inventories (including photos and videos) of all personal property, purchase dates, and values.

• **Job.** Keep paycheque stubs until you get a T-4 form from your employer. Retain pension information; your job record for résumés, unemploy-ment insurance, and social security; employee contracts, manuals, and union information.

• **Health.** Keep information on immunizations, allergies, reactions to drugs, blood type, records of disease, health insurance policies, Medicare card numbers, and the names of your doctors. Also create a living will documenting your wishes concerning organ donations and the use of life-saving equipment.

• **Money.** Keep listings of bank accounts, investment advisers, and financial institutions. File loan documents, credit card agreements, wills, trust arrangements, stock and investment certificates, and pension plan information. Keep copies of tax returns and supporting documents for five years in case of audit.

• **Car.** Keep purchase and leasing agreements, warranties, repair log, leases, registration, insurance policy, and any accident records.

• **Major purchases.** Keep cheques and receipts of major purchases, sales slips, warranties, and a complete file on any problems and complaints.

TAKING ACTION

When your rights are at stake, you need not fold your tent and steal away—but instead of getting mad, get a plan.

Getting What You Deserve

Problems are like people: no two are exactly alike. Your predicament could consist of excessive charges for a bounced cheque, a sagging floor in a new house, or a broken appliance. One way to make many problems easier to cope with is to develop an effective problem-solving strategy. Problems that involve time deadlines, such as being served with court papers and home foreclosures, or other serious issues such as an injury or job dismissal, require the advice of a lawyer. However, you can solve many consumer issues on your own.

First, write down everything you know about the problem. Next, focus on the solution you are seeking—do you want your money back, the insurance policy changed, or an apology? Find out what protection is already available to you—a contract, an insurance policy, or a warranty that came with a defective product. List anyone who is in a position to help you, such as your bank manager, the building contractor, or the manufacturer. Make note of any limited claim period or deadlines, such as a 60-day limit on appealing property taxes or the duration of a warranty. Try to analyze your problem calmly. Anger, no matter how justifiable, can reduce your chances for success.

CONTACTING THE OTHER PARTY

Now you are ready to contact the other party directly. The initial complaint is often made over the telephone. Use a calm and reasonable tone and keep your complaint brief and straightforward: "I've got a problem, and I'm hoping you can help me."

Follow up with a short letter explaining your dispute, which will also serve as evidence of your notification to the other party. You can also tape conversations between you and the other party—perhaps statements that can serve your cause will be made by the other party.

GETTING ATTENTION

Don't be discouraged if these overtures do not bring satisfaction. Now is the time to enlist the aid of other organizations or persons to help you. Think about what will get the other side's attention: the threat of publicity? government regulations? Then figure out which federal, provincial, or local agencies may be able to resolve your complaint directly or indirectly by putting pressure on the other side. Keep in mind that while many agencies can order businesses to stop certain practices, they may not resolve individual problems. Still, a letter to the appropriate organization may result in prompt attention to your problem.

For the agency—government or private—most likely to go to bat for you, see "What Will an Agency Do for You?" below, and "Places to Get Help," on page 444. You will find the telephone numbers of the government agencies in the Blue Pages of your phone directory. For addresses and phone numbers of numerous government and private agencies whose programs and services may assist you, see also RESOURCES, page 469.

Sometimes a letter from a lawyer can work wonders. A lawyer's fee for writing such a letter may be less than you think, and pay substantial dividends. A letter is not a lawsuit, although bringing suit may be your next option if no amicable resolution is forthcoming.

What Will an Agency Do for You?

Many government agencies deal with consumers' rights—some are listed below—but only a few actually tackle individual complaints. Check the Blue Pages of your phone book for numbers of these agencies, then call to find out if they can help you resolve your specific problem.

• **Provincial consumer affairs offices.** All provinces have consumer affairs offices that are authorized to investigate consumer complaints and if necessary contact the businesses involved to seek recourse for consumer complaints.

• **Industry commissions.** Certain industries—including insurance, banking, health, environment, hospitals, and nursing homes—are closely watched by specific commissions, some of which will investigate consumer complaints. A letter to the commission often prompts a response from the party in question.

• **Federal and provincial human rights commissions.** These commissions investigate and act on individual complaints of employment bias. Provincial boards may also look into bias relating to housing, public service, or other issues. These commissions have tribunals which act as courts and can settle many complaints involving discrimination.

• **Industry Canada's Consumer Product Division.** This federal agency regulates dangerous products, issues rules, and takes action on decep-

tive advertising, door-to-door sales, warranty claims, and credit practices. In some cases, it may help resolve a problem that affects a large number of people, but otherwise it does not act for individual consumers.

• **Canadian Radio-Television and Telecommunications Commission (CRTC).** This federal agency regulates television and radio, but does not handle individual complaints.

• **Health Canada's Health Protection Directorate.** This is the federal agency that regulates foods, drugs, and cosmetics, tests new drugs, and investigates complaints about existing products. It does not seek recourse for individual consumers.

• **Canada Post.** This federal agency investigates mail fraud and looks into individual complaints.

• **Canadian Direct Marketing Association (CDMA).** A private industry based association, such as the CDMA, will also investigate claims of fraudulent practices by companies using the mail to sell products or services.

Framing a Complaint

The most successful complaint letter does not merely "complain." Instead, it attempts to provoke a solution. Whether the letter is to the person responsible for the problem or to an outside organization from which you seek help, keep your letter factual and straightforward. Be firm, but reasonable.

Briefly describe the situation. Answer the following basic questions: who, what, where, when, and how. Instead of laying blame, make neutral statements such as "the bicycle crashed into . . .," as opposed to "you smashed my greenhouse walls." If a product was involved, give the model and type; when and where you bought it; when and how it stopped working. Finally, if a full account takes more than 15 lines in your letter, include a separate page and inform the reader: "The complete history of this problem is attached." Enclose copies of receipts, warranties, or other documents, but keep the originals.

Specify What Action You Want

The most important part of your letter is the statement of what you want the recipient to do. If you want compensation, the money you seek is referred to as the "damages." Be specific. If a flying ball thrown by a neighbor's child smashed your window, you can seek direct damages for the cost of the broken window and the replacement of rain-soaked furniture.

Make it clear that you expect the recipient of the letter to take action, whether it is to pay for the broken window, correct a safety hazard in an apartment you rent, or finish a contracting job. Describe precisely what you want done, and include dollar amounts if you expect monetary recompense. Before signing off, make a positive statement: "I hope that we can resolve this matter without too much difficulty."

GO TO THE TOP

If you don't get results, send a follow-up letter, stating that you have had no response. Mail this to the highest level person you can locate, such as the president of the company with whom you have a billing dispute, and send it by certified mail, return receipt requested. Keep copies of your letters.

If you need a name or the address of a particular company, consult a corporate directory in your library, or call the company directly. Most large companies have toll-free lines; call 1 (area code) 555-1212 for the listing.

RESPONDING EFFECTIVELY

When problems arise unexpectedly, keep your head—how you respond can make all the difference in securing your rights.

If You Are Sued, Act Fast

Although the judicial system often moves at a snail's pace, some legal actions unfold quickly. If you get a "writ" and "statement of claim" or "declaration"—documents that inform you of a lawsuit against you—you will generally need to respond within 10 to 30 days. Usually, the writ and statement of claim are hand-delivered by a process server or bailiff. Sometimes they are left at a residence or published in a paper. For a case in small claims court they may arrive by mail. No matter how you receive them, don't delay in filing your formal defense, or "answer."

Except in small claims cases involving small sums of money, you should consult a lawyer immediately. You or your lawyer must file your "answer" with the court or with the lawyer for the other party, depending on local rules. (In a small claims case a court clerk can advise you.) Failure to file an answer can have dire consequences: A decision or judgment may be taken against you by "default," whether or not right was on your side.

If you cannot meet the deadline for filing, your lawyer must contact the courthouse or the lawyer for the party that filed the complaint and formally seek an extension of time. If you miss the deadline, your lawyer can request permission from the court to file a late answer and prevent a default judgment.

IF YOU ARE A CRIME VICTIM

Numerous Canadian families are victimized each year by crime. The overall statistics are startling: millions of thefts, millions of burglaries, and thousands of crimes involving physical violence. When crime hits, victims suffer physical injuries, property loss, and emotional trauma. Knowing your rights can help ease the pain.

All provinces and territories have crime victims compensation schemes. What is covered varies greatly from one province to another. As a rule you cannot claim for lost or damaged personal property. Alberta, however, will compensate you for property damaged by police in preventing a crime or apprehending a criminal. Some provinces' criminal injuries compensation schemes may compensate you for pain and suffering from injuries sustained in a crime or wages lost as a result of a crime.

How to Answer a Summons

A process server knocked on your door and handed you a writ and statement of claim. You are being sued. For all but minor amounts claimed before the small claims court, you should contact a lawyer right away.

When you are sued in a civil lawsuit, you are the "defendant" and the person suing you is the "plaintiff."

Your lawyer will prepare a legal document known as an "answer or plea." In it, each point in the "statement of claim" of the plaintiff is "affirmed" or "denied." The document might affirm that your name is correct, but deny that you owe the money claimed by the plaintiff.

Although it may appear simple, an answer to a summons may contain complexities, and you need a lawyer to ensure that your rights are protected. Your lawyer will determine, for example, if you can claim a technical defense, if your answer should include reference to a third party, and other important legal matters.

When you contact a lawyer about representing you, make certain that you mention immediately that you have been served with a summons and complaint and that you are facing a deadline.

Once your compensation is approved, you are paid in one lump sum. Quebec and British Columbia may approve additional payments if you have a relapse and a reevaluation indicates that additional sums are warranted. Claims should be filed as soon as possible, but the delay in which an actual claim must be instituted is usually up to one year from the crime. Coverage for losses varies greatly, but in some provinces you can include dental bills, lost wages, funeral costs, counseling services, and transportation expenses not covered by insurance. Many claims for compensation are reduced by the amount you receive from employer subsidized salary, insurance, or similar compensation plans. Private insurance (where you pay all the premiums) does not usually affect your claim.

Taking the Bite Out of Crime

PROBLEM
Returning from a seniors' picnic, Mary and Bud saw their condominium door ajar. From a neighbor's apartment they called the police. Total disarray greeted Bud and Mary when they entered their unit, and they were badly shaken. The TV, VCR, and a pouch with Bud's hearing aid were gone. A window was smashed. The police made a report and took a silver bowl for fingerprinting.

ACTION
Bud and Mary called their son, Fred, who had been burglarized recently. With his video camera, he documented the damage and discovered other missing items, including a camera and credit cards. They canceled the credit cards and made a new list of stolen property. With the list, they went to the police station, and asked for copies of the police reports, names of the police officers, and a receipt for the silver bowl. This documentation was needed when they made a homeowners insurance claim. At Fred's suggestion, they also called a crime victim assistance center. A counselor arranged for the broken window to be repaired immediately, as part of a special program for seniors. The counselor also told Bud that, under his particular province's crime victim compensation program, he might be eligible for the replacement cost of his hearing aid.

Crime victims have other rights in the criminal justice system besides compensation. Property taken for evidence must be returned as soon as possible. Get a receipt and send a letter to the prosecutor stating that you want the property returned. If a suspect is arrested and charged with a crime, victims have the right to know the progress of the case, including court dates of hearings or a pending plea bargain. Victims are also entitled to be protected from harassment or intimidation for reporting the crime. Victims may also have a civil claim for injuries or loss against a criminal or third party who acted negligently. For example, an apartment owner was found liable when it was discovered that the inside door leading to the apartment lobby had a defective lock, which allowed a crimi-

VICTIM SERVICES

Victim services agencies provide emergency care, counseling, and other services to crime victims. For a referral to a program in your area, call your provincial crime victims' compensation agency, also known as the Victims of Crime Board. Here are the services offered:

1. Crown attorneys' offices often have victim and witness aid service centers and social service departments.

2. Crime victim compensation programs help pay for injuries or in some cases property losses. If you cannot find one near where you live, call directory assistance in your provincial capital.

3. Elderly crime victims resource centers offer special services for seniors.

4. The Red Cross serves emergency needs of crime victims for housing and food.

5. Traveler's Aid assists people who are victimized by crime while traveling.

6. Hospitals and emergency clinics have social workers or counselors who can aid victims of violent crimes.

7. Shelters offer victims of family violence safety and support services.

8. Crisis prevention hotlines offer tips, guidance, and counseling for victims of rape, domestic abuse, or crimes involving discrimination.

nal to enter and attack the tenant. If you have suffered injuries and feel that you have a civil claim, talk to a lawyer.

Dealing With Arrest

Finding yourself on the "wrong side of the law" is no joke, and it is particularly important to know your rights if you should be arrested. According to the Canadian Charter of Rights and Freedoms, if an arresting officer wants to question you, he must inform you that you have the right to remain silent and to have a lawyer at your side during the entire process.

In many cases, particularly minor crimes, you will not be questioned formally by the police. Even if you feel that the arrest is unjustified, do as the officers say. If they are abusive, make a special effort to note everything that happens so that you can report it in detail later on. Be aware, though, that a police officer has the right to use reasonable force to make you comply with his orders, and that resisting arrest is a crime.

After you are taken into custody and booked, the criminal justice process is set in motion for arraignment, a bail hearing, and other court proceedings. Discuss the charges and your options with your lawyer. (If you cannot afford a lawyer, ask that one be appointed for free.) Until your lawyer speaks to you, say nothing and stay calm. You need give only your name, address, and birth date, and decline to discuss anything else.

The law of England is a very strange one; it cannot compel anyone to tell the truth . . . but what the law can do is to give you seven years for not telling the truth.

LORD DARLING

A Child in Custody

You receive a call from a police officer saying that your son has been "picked up" for vandalism and is being held in custody. You are sure your son would not do anything wrong, but you still need to know what is at stake and what you can do about it.

• Detained minors are held in detention centers separate from adult prisoners. Usually they are not arrested, but are served with a notice of charge based on the commission of an act such as vandalism. However, if a child is charged with a serious crime such as murder or arson, he or she can be arrested like an adult.

• Minors are entitled to remain silent and to be represented by a lawyer. It is the duty of the arresting officer to advise them of their rights.

• A minor can be released to the custody of a parent. However, if a minor is charged with a severe crime, he may be held in a detention center until the trial.

• If a child is charged with a crime according to the Criminal Code on the Narcotic Control Act, he will be tried in a nonjury trial in youth court. If the youth is found guilty, the judge may determine him to be a young offender. Or the child may be charged and tried as an adult, and adjudged guilty or innocent.

• If found to be a young offender, a child can be placed under court supervision; ordered to reform school, a detention center, halfway home, or special counseling; or be placed on probation. A minor found guilty as an adult will be sentenced as one.

• Young offender records are sealed to the public. Records can eventually be expunged.

ALTERNATIVES TO COURT

Going to court is not the only solution for legal confrontations—you can try any one of several alternative proceedings to resolve disputes.

Direct Negotiation

Negotiating is a part of daily life. Lawyers, for example, tend to devote most of their time to negotiating settlements with the result that roughly 90 percent of lawsuits are settled out of court. In direct negotiation, persuasive skills are used to engage another party in an exchange of information and proposed solutions to find a mutually acceptable result.

Good negotiating is an art. To start you need a convincing argument. Gather facts and evidence in advance. If you are asking a neighbor to replace a window smashed by his son's baseball, come to the negotiation with the name of a witness, a photo of the damage, and an estimate of the replacement cost.

Know your bottom line before you begin. This gives you a yardstick to measure counterproposals. You can still consider other alternatives. The neighbor might not have cash, for instance, but offers to paint your garage instead. Is this offer equal to your bottom line?

Ask for more than you expect, but stay within reason. People anticipate a back-and-forth process involving offers and counteroffers. If you are asking your absolute limit, say so: "This is my final request and I am unable to change it."

Direct negotiations are not appropriate for every situation. If you are in an emotionally charged state, or if you have been the object of physical abuse, do not try to negotiate. It may not serve your purpose to negotiate if you are in a weak bargaining position in terms of status or power. A cashier at a retail store may not be in a good bargaining position with the president of the firm who has laid off workers. Finally, don't negotiate directly if you know you are not good at it.

Mediating Your Problems

The image of the judge with black robe and red stripes is familiar to all. But people are turning to another authority figure to help resolve disputes: a mediator. Mediators do not make decisions. They work with disputing parties to help them reach a voluntary solution.

Mediation involves person-to-person negotiations, but with a disinterested third party present to listen, identify issues, and propose solutions. Since the 1970s, nonprofit mediation programs have opened in many provincial and locally sponsored community mediation centers. Call your provincial government to find out what services are available in your area. Private mediation services, listed in the Yellow Pages under "Mediation Services," are available in nearly every city.

WHY MEDIATION?

Mediation can be initiated in several ways. In some cases it may be required by the court, as in child custody decisions in divorce proceedings. (See also YOUR MARRIAGE AND FAMILY, page 138.) A mediation clause might be part of an existing agreement, such as a homeowners association membership. Or, one party in a dispute may take the initiative and consult a mediation service. This claimant fills out a "Consent to Mediation" form that describes the problem. The form is sent to the other party to the dispute, the respondent, who can agree or refuse to participate.

The kinds of problems most susceptible to solution by mediation are landlord-tenant problems, disputes between neighbors, family issues such as simple divorces, and certain consumer disputes. The process works best when the parties are on good enough terms that they can come face-to-face without excessive anger, and when both are anxious for a speedy resolution.

Mediators come from all backgrounds, including psychology, law, and business. No single style of mediation prevails, and there is no set of standard rules. Before entering into voluntary mediation, you should know something about the background, training, and approach of the mediator and how sessions are structured, including whether or not your lawyer can be present.

GETTING RESULTS

Mediation is oriented toward compromise rather than vindication. Sessions are set in an office or conference room. To begin, the mediator will give you and the other side an opportunity to present your case, without interruption or objection. The mediator will then lead a discussion, make suggestions, and possibly meet with the parties individually. Rules of evidence do not apply, there is no formal record, and confidentiality is maintained.

Each point to which the parties agree is written down in a document called a "consent agreement" or "memorandum of understanding." The parties are given copies to sign, and it then becomes a contract that the parties are bound to follow.

MAKING MEDIATION WORK

Mediation is a relatively new process, and many people do not know what to expect, even when they agree to use it to solve their particular problem. Although it seems informal, mediation is a serious affair. Keep a clear focus on the purpose and your role in the process.

1. The ultimate goal in mediation is to arrive at a voluntary solution to your problem.

2. Mediation is not concerned with who is right or even what your rights are, but in securing a practical and workable result.

3. The goal of the mediator is to focus on the issues and to get each of you to see the other side.

4. Your goal is to present your case as convincingly as possible, so that the mediator and the other side understand your point of view. No one else can present it for you.

5. In order to be as convincing as possible, bring to the meeting all the evidence that you have to support your argument: photographs, bills, receipts, documents, witnesses, items, and statements.

6. Prepare notes before the session to define the issues, the results you want, and the least you will accept.

7. In the mediation, use your notes to analyze whether proposed solutions are realistic.

Questions to Ask About Arbitration

Before going into arbitration, look carefully at these areas of particular concern: who the arbitrator will be; what rules will apply; and how much it will cost.

Who the arbitrator will be is critical, especially in binding arbitration where the decision is usually final and cannot be appealed. The dispute resolution organization you use should present a short list of suggested arbitrators. You and the other side will then be asked to rank them.

Do as much research as possible. Get the résumés of suggested arbitrators and the types of cases they have decided. Ask for references: your provincial legal society or the Canadian Bar Association can give you a list of arbitrators in your district. Don't select someone about whom you cannot get good information. If necessary, ask for more names to consider, or make your own suggestions.

The rules of the arbitration could shape the outcome. Read the rules as soon as possible. What evidence should you present? Will you need a lawyer? How will the proceeding be handled? Find out if you can observe an arbitration proceeding to get the feel of it.

Expense is another essential ingredient—arbitration can cost more than some court proceedings. How much will it be, and who will pay? Are there ways to limit the costs?

In some jurisdictions, this understanding can be incorporated in a court decision, for example, in a divorce proceeding; it will then have the effect of a court order. In other cases, the memorandum of understanding relies upon voluntary compliance. If one side refuses to follow it, the other will have to bring a lawsuit based on a breach of contract to enforce it.

You cannot ask the mediator to advise you, so you may want to have your lawyer review the agreement before you sign it. Don't sign an agreement if you feel unfairly pressured or do not fully agree to or understand all of its terms.

Arbitration Means Business

Arbitration is a proceeding by which the parties to a dispute, in order to obtain a speedy and somewhat less expensive solution than going to court, voluntarily select arbitrators to settle their problem. In arbitration, a neutral third party, the arbitrator holds a hearing on a dispute, listens to evidence, and makes a decision. The hearing is not in a court; the arbitrator is not a judge. Arbitration is a substitute for—not a step toward—litigation.

Binding arbitration clauses prevent you from going to court; that is, once an award is made, it cannot be appealed if the arbitration agreement so states. In the past, these awards were uniformly upheld as valid, but judges are beginning to question the unfair use of arbitration if it deprives people of their rights. While a mediator guides the parties to come to their own agreement, an arbitrator or arbitration panel issues an actual determination. Arbitration is often used for commercial cases, involving business, construction, or insurance companies, and arbitration clauses may be a part of employment, appliance, home remodeling, and stock brokerage contracts.

RULES OF ARBITRATION

Arbitration is conducted by dispute resolution organizations, and arbitrators are lawyers, business people, or retired judges. Dispute centers are often run by private companies, but are also run by provincial and local governments.

The proceedings in arbitration are less formal than in a trial, but they are more complex than mediation or small claims court. Arbitration is private, and a record of the proceeding is not usually kept. At a hearing, one party presents evidence and witnesses, including experts. Then the other side can cross-examine. Depending on the gravity of the problem, both parties may need lawyers to represent them.

After the hearing, the arbitrator sends out a written decision, or award, within one or two weeks. It may order payment or that a certain action be taken. No reasons have to be stated, although the findings may be put on file with the arbitration service. Under provincial law, the decision can be homologated or certified by the court and enforced as though it were a court decision or judgment.

Demanding Arbitration

PROBLEM
When the Smiths hired a roofer to put a new roof on their home, they agreed to a clause in the contract stating that "any claim arising from the contract shall be settled by arbitration." Later, with water dripping down the walls and the contractor refusing their calls, the Smiths were concerned.

ACTION
The Smiths decided to take advantage of the arbitration clause and contacted the arbitration service named in the contract. They filled out a Demand for Arbitration form, which was sent to the contractor. The Smiths suggested that the arbitration hearing be held in their home, where the leaks could be inspected, and the contractor agreed. Within 60 days they were sitting face-to-face with the contractor and an arbitrator to present their evidence.

Arbitration is often described as an inexpensive alternative to court—but that depends on the case. To limit costs, one can simplify the rules of evidence to be used, write in a clause prohibiting appeals, and use one arbitrator instead of three. The costs of arbitration may be low compared to those for a major lawsuit, but still could be 10 times the cost of taking the case to small claims court.

Administrative Hearings

Myriad regulations by local, provincial and federal government agencies touch our lives daily, and open the way for another type of adjudication process: the administrative hearing. Unlike negotiations, mediation, and arbitration, an administrative hearing is not an alternative to going to court, and neither is it a court case. Instead, it is a quasi-judicial proceeding that can be very useful.

If you disagree with a ruling from a government agency—from a property tax assessment to workers compensation to a pension board claim—you may request a hearing by an agency administrator. The hearing officer will review your case to determine whether the agency decision was correct and fair in your circumstances, and he will approve any compensation, which he deems appropriate by law.

123.

HANDLING AN ADMINISTRATIVE HEARING

When a government agency makes a decision you disagree with, you can seek a review in an administrative hearing. Since it is difficult to successfully appeal the decision made at a hearing (you must prove that you did not get due process or that the agency's regulation does not meet legal standards), it is important to present your case effectively. Here's what to do:

1. Respond promptly. When you receive notice of a government decision that you wish to dispute, you must act in a timely fashion. You usually have 60 days to request an administrative hearing to review the decision.

2. Learn the rules. Ask the agency where to find its rules and decisions; then study those that apply to your case.

3. Collect evidence. Gather documents and other backup material showing why the agency did not apply its rules properly in your case.

4. Know the ropes. Ask for a copy of the hearing process and attend an administrative hearing, if possible, to see how it is conducted.

5. Go to your hearing. You can represent yourself, but you may be wise to hire a lawyer or paralegal to guide you through an agency's complex procedures. If you are not eligible for legal aid, ask the agency if it can provide a lawyer to assist you for a minimal fee.

GOING TO COURT

A judge for your dispute may be exactly what you need. For best results, learn your way around the courts.

Appearing in Court

Testifying as a witness, representing yourself, or simply appearing in court can be a nerve-wracking experience. To make the best impression, keep these hints in mind:

✔ *Appearance.* Dress as for a business meeting or job interview. Sit upright and speak calmly; project your voice and look at the jury (if there is one) when speaking.

✔ *What to say.* Answer all questions truthfully. Don't elaborate; try to use a simple "yes" or "no." If you do not know an answer, say so.

✔ *Correcting errors.* If you realize you have made a mistake, especially if you are a witness, tell the judge you want to correct something.

✔ *Composure.* Don't get involved in arguments or discussion of objections, and don't be upset by impertinent or snide questions if you are cross-examined.

✔ *Speak for yourself.* If you are representing yourself, give a straightforward account of your version of the events. Describe only what you personally saw, and don't make accusatory statements or express opinions.

Choosing Small Claims Court

Size says nothing about the aggravation, or the gravity, of a legal problem—losing $100 is as serious to a person of modest means as is the loss of $100,000 to a millionaire. But comparatively smaller claims have one advantage: they can be resolved within the streamlined procedures of small claims courts, which handle cases involving a limited amount of money. The amount varies as follows from province to province: Nova Scotia, New Brunswick, Newfoundland, Prince Edward Island, and Quebec, $3,000; Alberta, $4,000; Manitoba and Saskatchewan, $5,000; Ontario, $6,000; and British Columbia, $10,000. You can initiate a lawsuit by filling out a form stating your claim. Altercations involving bad cheques, apartment security deposits, and faulty workmanship are typical small claims court cases.

Although the process is made easier, small claims court is still a court, and certain procedures must be followed. In order to file a claim, you must have the exact name and address of the person you are suing—the defendant. The claim must be filed in the court area where the defendant resides, or where a contract under question was made, a product was sold, or an accident involving the defendant occurred. Usually, out-of-province parties cannot be sued in small claims court, unless they do business locally. The papers—summonses and complaints—need to be formally served. In some places, papers can be sent by certified mail; otherwise, a process server must be used to present the papers to the defendant. You can find process servers listed in the Yellow Pages. After receipt, the defendant can make a counterclaim (not just an answer or denial, but an independent suit) against the plaintiff.

TIME TO BE HEARD

Usually within two months, you are granted a hearing before a judge. Hearings are short (10 to 45 minutes) and formal rules of evidence (such as objecting) are eased, making the situation less threatening. A lawyer usually is not needed and in some provinces may not be permitted to participate.

Have your evidence ready to convince the judge why a decision should be made in your favor. A decision may be made on

LEGAL PROCEEDINGS EXPLAINED

Courts interpret and apply the law to the facts of each case in order to bring about justice. Proceedings such as mediation and arbitration are also used to resolve legal matters. Judicial proceedings vary from province to province, but generally those involved with civil cases (noncriminal matters) include:

Types of Proceedings	What They Are/What They Do
Direct Negotiations	An exchange of offers to reach a settlement
Alternative Dispute Resolution (ADR)	Procedures for settling disputes other than litigation
Mediation	A confidential meeting (or meetings) with a neutral third party to obtain a voluntary agreement
Arbitration	A hearing (or hearings) by a neutral arbitrator who will make a binding decision
Administrative hearings	Hear appeals of government agency decisions
Specialized Courts	Hear cases concerning particular areas of civil law
Small claims courts	Hear simple cases seeking damages, to a stipulated maximum, such as $3,000 to $10,000
Family (or matrimonial) courts	Hear divorce, separation, and child custody cases
Probate or surrogate courts	Hear estate, incompetency, guardianships, and adoption cases
Youth courts	Hear cases involving young offenders. Also deal with allegations of child neglect or abuse
Other local courts and tribunals	Depending on the province, landlord-tenant, property claims, traffic violations, and lesser criminal cases
General Courts	Hear lawsuits on civil claims: contracts, injuries, property issues
District or county courts	Trial courts of general jurisdiction that handle larger civil cases of any type
Municipal courts	Trial courts of limited jurisdiction that handle civil cases against the city, the beginning (arraignment) of criminal cases, and municipal bylaw infractions
Appellate Courts	Hear appeals of decisions made in lower courts
Federal Courts	Hear certain areas of law (air and space laws—cases against the Crown)
Bankruptcy courts	Hear corporate and individual bankruptcy cases
Tax courts	Hear appeals of disputes with Revenue Canada
Federal Appeal Courts	Hear appeals from Federal Court of first instance or from federal government agencies
Appellate Courts	Hear appeals of decisions made in lower court
Courts of Appeal	Hear appeals from lower courts and from provincial agencies
Supreme Court of Canada	Hears cases of "national concern" and certain cases with a constitutional component of great importance

YOU STILL NEED TO COLLECT

Before spending the money to file a claim, consider whether the other side has assets from which you can collect if you win. Very poor people and bankrupt companies do not. If you do go to court and win a judgment, and if the defendant then does not pay, you can take these steps:

1. Go back to court to record the judgment and file what is known as a writ of execution.

2. If the defendant owns property, you may be able to get an order instructing a sheriff to seize it for sale.

3. You could start a garnishment suit to collect from the debtor's wages or from his bank account.

4. If assets cannot be found, you can bring the debtor back to court to answer questions about them.

5. You may have to hire a lawyer at this stage. A reasonable cost to cover a lawyer's fees can be added to what you are owed.

6. You might be able to engage a collection agency to assist you. A typical fee is half the money collected.

---

the spot or mailed to you within a week or two. In some provinces, appeals from small claims court are either limited or not permitted. Filing a claim usually costs less than $50. Most provinces try to make small claims court accessible, providing pamphlets and assistance from a clerk or court adviser.

Small claims court is not available for all types of cases. Disputes do not qualify if the remedy sought is not money. Judges in some small claims courts do not have the authority to order someone to act or to refrain from acting—for example, a judge sitting in small claims court in Ontario could not order your neighbor to remove the fence dividing your properties. Nor can a small claims court hear disputes which lie in the exclusive jurisdiction of other courts. Thus, all disputes pertaining to alimony will be heard by a Superior Court.

When You Are Suing

Civil suits that are too large or complicated for small claims court are pursued in provincial courts of general jurisdiction. Some common names for these courts are district, county or superior courts (or supreme courts). Federal courts hear, among other things, disputes involving claims against the Crown or claims involving shipping or immigration matters. To sue, you or your lawyer files a complaint that states the basis for the case—the cause of action—and the remedy being sought. For example, you state that you suffered injuries as the result of an auto accident caused by the other party and seek payment for lost wages and auto repairs. Suits with no cause of action or no remedy will be dismissed.

After filing, information about the claim is exchanged, called the discovery phase. In a deposition, witnesses are questioned in private but under oath about what happened. You may be asked to answer written questions, called "interrogatories"; to produce documents that relate to the case; or to submit to a medical examination. This is the time when settlement proposals are likely to be made. Motions are also made in court to settle sticky or technical legal questions, such as whether or not the time period for suing has expired. At any time during these proceedings and even after the case has gone to trial, it may be settled. Most lawsuits are settled out of court. Should your case be one of the small percentage that go to trial, the person who initiated the suit will try to prove the claim by presenting evidence to a judge or jury or both. In a civil case the burden of proof is a preponderance of proof, much less than "proof beyond a reasonable doubt" required in a criminal case. After the trial, some cases can be appealed to a higher court.

USING A LAWYER

In a complex case or one that is emotionally charged, a lawyer can provide you with vital support, but you should know how to use your attorney wisely.

Do You Need Counsel?

Lawyer, attorney, counsel, member of the bar all mean the same thing: a person who, by law, can represent you in legal matters. Whether you need a lawyer or not depends on how complicated the matter is, how important it is to you, and whether you need an intermediary.

A case can be complicated because of technical legal procedures, as occurs in lawsuits in federal court, provincial trial courts (except in small claims court), or binding arbitration. Or it may be made complex because the facts of the case touch many areas, such as a medical problem that involves a hospital, doctors, and a drug manufacturer; or when the parties to the case are numerous, out-of-province, or difficult to identify. One extra complication: If a lawyer is representing the other side, you should probably have one, too.

The importance of a case depends on how much is at stake—in well-being, money, or civil liberties. Other important situations are cases involving large sums of money or property, such as a home purchase, foreclosure, government benefits, substantial marital assets, or large personal-injury claims. The measure of import also may be personal and subjective, as occurs in discrimination or child custody cases.

Whether or not you need an intermediary to speak on your behalf is a personal decision. But if the conflict is emotionally charged, provokes anger, or is threatening, you should get a lawyer.

WHAT CAN A LAWYER DO FOR YOU?

Other than yourself, only a lawyer can represent you in legal proceedings. With rare exceptions, a lawyer is a law school graduate who, having passed a bar examination, is licensed to practice law in a given province. In most provinces, a paralegal cannot be your advocate because practicing law without a license is illegal. Paralegals who work under the supervision of lawyers may handle minor legal matters. In a few provinces, they are allowed to consult directly in limited areas such as small claims court or traffic court. In some instances, non-lawyers, such as brokers, agents, or bankers, may help you draw up papers.

The difference between the right word and almost right word is the difference between lightning and the lightning bug.

MARK TWAIN

Lawyers offer two particular areas of competence. One is familiarity with legal procedure; the other is informed judgment. A good lawyer will listen to your problem, seek out the facts, and do research. The lawyer will advise you on whether you have a legitimate case, or cause of action; enough evidence; a possible remedy; and a favorable position in view of the likely costs and benefits. The final decision is up to you.

Hiring the Right Lawyer

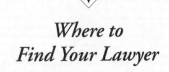

The days when lawyers seldom advertised for clients or when one lawyer could handle all your legal business are virtually gone. In Canada, unlike the United States, a lawyer is not yet allowed to advertise on television or by billboard, but may insert discreet newspaper advertisements which mention his special field of expertise. How do you know which is right for you? Considerations include the individual's availability, specialty, personality, and, of course, fee.

In compiling a list of lawyers to choose from, you will need to focus your search. What type of case do you have? Specialties you are likely to find among lawyers include divorce (also known as family or matrimonial law), bankruptcy, tax, workers compensation, personal injury (accidents), criminal, real estate, product liability, probate (wills), discrimination (equal employment)—the list is long because the law has become so complex that lawyers need special expertise. Even a general practitioner probably works in a limited number of areas. Lawyers also may specialize in particular types of clients such as older persons, or the disabled.

MAKING CONTACT

When you have put together a list of likely candidates, schedule interviews with several on your list, checking first to see if you will be charged for a preliminary interview. Prepare a short written statement about your problem. Ask if the lawyer has had experience with similar cases, and what steps she recommends taking; how she will keep you informed of progress; and how fees are calculated, including all incidental fees. Since it is important not only to trust your lawyer but to work together harmoniously, try to get a sense of her personally as well as professionally. Ask a few informal questions, such as how she got into this specialty area. Initial consultations with a few lawyers will benefit you in the end. You will learn more about your case and how attorneys view it. Because switching lawyers in mid-case can be complicated and expensive, it is worth the extra effort to choose one best suited to your needs in the first place.

Where to Find Your Lawyer

Since a tour of the Yellow Pages reveals a wide array of lawyers, how do you choose the right one? Here are some suggestions of where to find a lawyer who best suits you, your legal problem, and your financial situation:

✔ *Recommendations.* Ask friends, colleagues, and professional contacts for referrals to lawyers they have actually worked with.

✔ *Bar associations.* Local or provincial organizations of lawyers, or bar associations, usually keep a list of recommended lawyers available for referrals.

✔ *Legal advice clinics.* Some bar associations, community centers, or law schools sponsor clinics where volunteer lawyers will meet with a client for a low fee or for free to review a case.

✔ *Legal aid.* People with very little money may qualify for a free or low-cost legal aid lawyer.

✔ *Public defender.* Cases involving poor persons charged with crimes can be assigned to a lawyer serving as a public defender.

✔ *Advertisements.* These can be useful in finding a lawyer who specializes in a given field.

PREPAID LEGAL PLANS

Prepaid legal plans, a newer option in legal services, are offered to members of unions and sometimes through large companies as an employee benefit. You sign up as a member and pay a monthly or yearly fee. In exchange, you get access to a lawyer who will advise you in certain prescribed situations.

Prepaid legal plans are sometimes called legal insurance, but they operate differently from other kinds of insurance. Prepaid legal programs cover the most simple situations for free, but any problems more complex will command an additional fee, which may be discounted.

Services provided in prepaid legal plans vary. Often a plan will pay for telephone consultations, letters from the lawyer to debtors, a review of documents such as leases or contracts (sometimes no longer than six pages), and the preparation of a simple will. But read the literature carefully, and note what kinds of legal help you are not going to get. Going to court, for example, is not covered by most plans.

Flat fees may be available for other services, but with limitations. A flat fee, for example, may be offered for a lawyer to handle a divorce—but only if it is uncontested, if there are no children, if there is no lawyer on the other side, and there is no property agreement to be negotiated.

Plans also vary in format. In one plan called "open panel," you select your lawyer from a list given to you. In "closed panel" plans, you are assigned a lawyer who has been preselected by the administrator of the plan, although you may seek to change lawyers if you are not satisfied. You should know if you can talk to the same lawyer each time you call with questions, or whether lawyers handle calls on a rotating basis.

Be aware that, as for some health insurance, prepaid legal plans will often exclude from coverage problems that began before you joined the plan. Furthermore, if your legal need is immediate, you may not have time to sign up for the prepaid plan and wait for a lawyer to be assigned.

A Client's Bill of Rights

Since you rely so heavily on your lawyer for knowledge and advice in legal matters, it is sometimes hard to remember that he works for you. But lawyers are sworn to follow a code of conduct and ethical standards. You should be aware of what they are and how they affect you.

Virtually all that you say to your lawyer is confidential. This principle is known as the lawyer-client privilege, which can be broken only in the following limited circumstances: if you tell

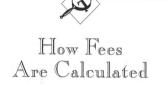

How Fees Are Calculated

Lawyers' fees vary, depending on the lawyer and type of case. Four types of billing are used: flat fee, hourly rate, contingent fee, and percentage fee. Negotiate first; then secure fees in writing.

A flat fee is a set price charged for a routine matter, such as writing a will or lease, drawing up an uncomplicated divorce, or handling minor criminal offenses in court.

Hourly fees are the most common. You are charged for each hour the lawyer spends on the case, at a stated rate per hour. Rates differ by community and firm; larger firms are generally more expensive.

Contingent fees are often applied when you are seeking an award of money: personal injury, collection, discrimination cases. Except for incidental costs such as filing fees, you do not pay unless you recover money, and then the lawyer takes a percentage.

A percentage fee is based on the value of property involved. In probate cases, for example, the lawyer might charge 5 percent of the estate value.

Be aware that additional expenses, such as filing fees, photocopying costs, depositions, expert witness fees, and travel expenses, may be extra.

You may be asked to pay your lawyer a retainer up front. Some lawyers consider such deposits nonrefundable; so confirm the situation in writing.

In some cases, you can recoup your attorney's fees and ancillary costs from the other side, but there is no guarantee.

THINGS YOU CAN DO TO SAVE LEGAL COSTS

By taking certain steps on your own, you may be able to keep your legal fees and costs from skyrocketing. If you are paying your lawyer an hourly fee, you can save time and money by following these tips:

1. Prepare a chronology of events and a written statement of the problem.

2. Make a detailed inventory and listing of the names, addresses, times, and places that relate to the incident. In accident cases, have the date, time, location, witnesses, description of injuries, names of medical personnel, car registration, and insurance information. In family law cases, have names and birth dates of children, a complete list of personal property and real estate, and a history of your marriage and employment.

3. Organize your documents and make photocopies for your lawyer. To each copy attach an index card that explains what it is, when it was signed, and how it fits into your case.

4. Since lawyers usually charge for their time spent on the phone or in meetings, keep phone calls and office visits focused and concise. Prepare a list of questions or subjects, and stick to the issues.

5. Ask your lawyer if there is anything you can do to keep costs down, such as getting police reports on your own, locating title documents, or researching nonlegal points.

your lawyer about a crime that you are planning to commit; if you have a dispute over fees; or if you sue him for malpractice. In some situations, such as criminal cases, documents or evidence that you give your lawyer may be considered "discoverable," which means that the lawyer may be legally bound to turn such evidence over to the Crown prosecutor.

You have the right to a full disclosure of the lawyer's fees, and how they are calculated, and what extra expenses might be added on. Your lawyer should represent you zealously, inform you in writing of any conflicts of interest that arise, and tell you if another lawyer is assisting in your file.

Clear communication is one of your key rights. Your phone calls and letters should be returned. You should be regularly informed about the progress of your case and should get copies of all documents, even if you have to pay a fee for them. You should understand the strengths and weaknesses of your case.

Remember that you make the ultimate decisions on the case. Any settlement offers must be explained to you, and you must respond. Finally, you have the right to be treated with common courtesy and consideration.

How to Help Your Lawyer

The path to resolving your legal problem is one that you and your lawyer travel together. Your lawyer cannot succeed without your help. Maintaining a friendly businesslike relationship is essential and, to a certain extent, is your responsibility.

You will need to educate your lawyer about what happened. Disclose all relevant facts and hold nothing back, even if it is embarrassing. The information will be far more damaging if it comes out later. Moreover, if your lawyer does not have all the facts, he may inadvertently give bad advice or handle the case differently, possibly to your disadvantage. However, this does not mean you should overload your lawyer with meaningless information.

Review documents your lawyer sends to you, and correct errors. Enlighten yourself about the law and court procedures so you will have an idea of what to expect as the case progresses. Be aware that what happened in someone else's case will not necessarily happen in yours. Try to be realistic about outcomes. Keep your lawyer informed of developments that might affect your case or of personal changes—if you change your address, for instance, or your job. If your lawyer asks for a certain piece of information, follow through promptly. Finally, start a written log of contacts with your lawyer and keep files of original documents, legal papers, and correspondence.

Troubles With Your Lawyer

As in any other human relationship, problems can arise with your lawyer. If they do, you should speak up calmly and firmly about what is bothering you. Do it right away. The longer you let resentment simmer, the harder it will be to work out a reasonable solution.

Fees represent the most common problem people have with lawyers, and the best cure for this is prevention. Remember, you are entitled to an itemized bill. If you cannot resolve a money problem with your lawyer, seek fee arbitration through a bar association.

Another common complaint is that a lawyer is not devoting sufficient time or thought to his client's case. Sometimes your lawyer may not have kept you completely informed of progress, but be aware that many delays may be out of his control. Whatever the problem, if it continues, write your lawyer a letter. Letters usually get lawyers' attention because they know you may be building a case against them. If a significant question about the lawyer's work remains, ask another lawyer to advise you.

DISMISS ONLY AS LAST RESORT

If all else fails, remember that you have the right to fire your lawyer. Do so only as a last resort. Unless he did nothing on your behalf or is guilty of malpractice, you will probably have to pay the old lawyer as well as the new one.

If there were no bad people, there would be no good lawyers.

CHARLES DICKENS

Where to Complain About Your Lawyer

Before a problem with your lawyer gets serious, you should have already talked with him or her about what is bothering you. If you are still not satisfied and have thought the matter through, you have several avenues of recourse. Here are some of your options:

• If the lawyer is in a law firm, you can go to the firm's managing lawyer; if you are part of a prepaid legal plan, you can take your complaint to the plan administrator.

• If you are not sure that you have a valid complaint, get an opinion from your provincial bar association's disciplinary board.

• If you think the lawyer's fees are higher than they should be, you can consult a fee arbitration committee of the provincial bar association.

• If the problem is more than a dispute over fees— if a lawyer has stolen money from you or defrauded you, for instance, go the bar association's trustee or disciplinary board. If your charge is justified, all or part of your money may be reimbursed. You should also notify the district attorney or the police.

• If you suspect your lawyer has acted unethically, go to the bar association's disciplinary board. If your lawyer's conduct violates bar association standards, you may want to file a complaint. Your lawyer may then be disciplined, even losing the right to practice law, temporarily or permanently.

• You can sue your lawyer for malpractice and seek reimbursement if he has acted negligently and your rights have been damaged. See a lawyer who handles professional liability cases.

REPRESENTING YOURSELF

In some cases, if you are up to the challenge, you can represent yourself in court—but you'll need to do a lot of homework first.

Attorney Pro Se

Under our legal system, if you are not represented by a lawyer in court proceedings, the only other option is to represent yourself. (Non-lawyer friends may not represent you in court, and unless legally qualified, you may not go to court on behalf of someone else.) When you do so, you are known as an "attorney pro se," or, "attorney pro per." These phrases derive from Latin and simply mean "attorney for oneself."

When you represent yourself, you sign your name on documents in all the places a lawyer would sign. Below your name, you add "attorney pro se" or "attorney pro per."

In addition to alerting the court that you intend to represent yourself, this phrase lets the clerk and the other party know that all documents and communications that would normally go to your lawyer should go to you. If you do not receive proper notification, you could unknowingly fail to file important paperwork, or miss a court appearance.

Failure of the court or the other party to notify you of steps and proceedings in the case could be deemed a denial of your legal right to due process and could give you grounds for a lawsuit. In pleading your case always stick to the point.

Legal Matters You Can Handle Yourself

By law, even if you are not a lawyer, you are permitted to represent yourself in any legal proceeding. You may automatically handle some routine situations on your own, such as making a purchase or taking out a loan. In small claims court and mediation, you may be called upon to represent yourself because lawyers may be excluded. In certain standardized areas, such as executing a simple will, changing your name, and divorcing when money and children are not in dispute, kits and forms are available that can guide you through the legal thicket, especially if you use them with caution.

But when disputes enter more elaborate legal arenas or become more complex, even lawyers hire lawyers to represent them. If important rights or large sums of money are at stake, hiring yourself might be more costly in the long run. So, before tackling a legal problem yourself, consider consulting a lawyer to get a sense of how legally complex the matter will be. Even if you decide to hire a lawyer, your research will help you better understand the process you are about to undertake.

DUAL ASSIGNMENT

A legal matter has two integral components: substance and procedure. Substance involves the legal subject matter, such as whether you are entitled to a reimbursement of costs under a warranty. Procedure has to do with the legal rules and mechanisms by which you achieve your goal—such as how you state your claim and where you file it.

If you act as your own lawyer, you will have to familiarize yourself with both areas. This research involves much effort and can present a challenge even for lawyers. Also, small mistakes can result in great losses; for example, filing the wrong document can result in your forgoing your claim. Judges and clerks are not always sympathetic to the self-helper.

On the other hand, self-representation can have a positive side effect. Whether you win or lose, your efforts may save you hundreds of dollars and result in a feeling of empowerment.

Rules and Regulations

If you are considering representing yourself, your first step should be to research the rules and procedural questions that relate to your case. Are you within the time period for filing? What is the right court or forum? How do you get the other party into court? What types of evidence will you be permitted to present? In courtroom litigation, procedure is complex—in fact, lawyers expend much energy trying to solve procedural issues. Each level of court or administrative tribunal has its own rules, as does each province. In general, there are five types of rules that apply:

- **Statutes and constitutions** define the authority of each court to hear certain types of cases; also defined are statutes of limitations, or the time limits for filing each cause of action.
- **Rules of civil procedure** define what civil court papers should look like, and how and when certain actions such as motions (requests for some action made to the judge) and interrogatories (written questions asked by one party in a lawsuit of the other party) are to be completed. These vary for each type of court.
- **Rules of evidence** describe formalities of introducing documents and witnesses in court.
- **Local court rules** deal with the idiosyncrasies of each court, such as whether a certain type of paper should be used.
- **Protocol,** or customs of the court, deal with matters such as how to address the judge, which can be entirely individual. It is your responsibility to be aware of such fine points.

Ask questions, too. How long will the proceeding last? Will you be allowed to call witnesses? If a witness cannot attend, will you be allowed to present a sworn statement, or affidavit?

Try to get documents from a case similar to yours. Court records are available to the public. To find out how to obtain them, contact a company, such as Butterworths (Canada) Ltd. or Carswell, both in Toronto, that specializes in legal research. In an arbitration or administrative hearing, ask if sample documents are on file.

In mediation, arbitration, small claims court, or an administrative hearing, the rules are usually simplified, and you can ask a court clerk or the agency involved, such as the arbitration association, for a copy of them. You may want to attend a similar proceeding before you file. Regardless of the forum you choose, ask questions of the clerk, the bailiff, and lawyers. Understanding the importance of following the rules will make you a stronger advocate on your own behalf.

Where to Get Legal Forms and Information

Here are several resources available to non-lawyers for help in dealing with legal issues or for information:

✔ *Kits and books.* Do-it-yourself materials, including software, for divorce, simple wills, and other similar legal issues are available at bookstores.

✔ *Tele-law.* You can call your provincial and local bar associations to see if they offer a telephone service with recorded messages that explain common legal questions.

✔ *Legal forms.* Stationery stores carry preprinted documents including wills and leases. Some courts, such as small claims court, also provide preprinted forms.

✔ *Books of "practice forms."* These sample books can be found in law libraries and law school bookstores.

✔ *Law libraries.* Courthouses and law schools often have public law libraries.

✔ *Public case files.* The clerk of courts keeps records of lawsuits open for public review.

✔ *Legal newspapers.* Local legal newspapers carry ads for resources that might be helpful in researching a case.

✔ *Courses.* Seminars are available in some communities for people interested in representing themselves legally.

Strategies for Preparing Your Case

From settlement discussions to arbitration, from small claims court to a jury trial, the key to success in representing yourself is preparation. Since you are going to act as an "attorney pro se," you will have to learn to think like a lawyer. Here are some guidelines, suggestions, and strategies that you can use when representing yourself:

LIST YOUR FACTS

• Using your problem log, documents, or memory, write down a chronology of everything that occurred. In an accident case, include events surrounding the accident, physical injury, medical treatment, property damage, repairs, and contacts with insurers.

• List unknowns—facts that might be known only to the other party or facts that are unknown altogether, such as if a stoplight was working.

STATE WHAT YOU ARE SEEKING

• If you are seeking damages due to injury or property loss, specify the losses you have suffered, such as property damage, physical injury, loss of work. Include the costs involved, such as repair bills, medical expenses, and fines.

• If you want someone to act—to stop making noise or to permit child visitation—write the desired action clearly in a sentence. Then, state the harm that you will suffer if the action does not occur.

• If you have not incurred injury or property loss or do not seek a definite action, rethink your case. A claim based on hurt feelings or speculation is not legitimate.

• Write down your highest expectation—the most you hope to get, and your bottom line—the least you will accept.

CLARIFY WHO THE OPPOSITION IS

• If an individual or small business is responsible, get the correct name and address. If a corporation is your target, you will have to get the name of the company head and the person who can accept the legal papers from Consumer and Corporate Affairs Canada or Industry Canada. Make sure that you sue a company under its legal corporate name. Your local courthouse should have the information you need in this regard. If a government agency is the problem, find out if it is a federal, provincial, or city agency, and the name of the person in charge.

• Determine if additional individuals might be responsible, such as the owner and insurer of a car as well as the driver involved in the crash.

AMASS YOUR PROOF

• Compile as much evidence as possible. Every claim must be verified. Organize each contract, letter, receipt, photograph, bill, videotape, drawing, and the like according to the part of your case it supports, and label it.

• Compile a list of witnesses, including full names and addresses, and describe their direct knowledge of the events. Try to get affidavits or sworn written statements from them.

• Look for holes. Seek additional evidence, such as expert witnesses or relevant documents, that will fill in blanks or further verify your position.

ANTICIPATE THE OPPOSITION

• Write down the reasons you think the other side disagrees with your position, and try to anticipate what they will say.

• Write down the evidence that you think the other side may use to support its position; then, list facts that will contradict the other side's point of view.

CHECK THE LAW

• Check out statutes, decisions, and regulations that apply to your claim. Particularly, make sure that you have a legal cause of action. Look for other cases that support your position.

• Check the rules of evidence for your proceeding to determine if your evidence will be permitted, and how it should be submitted.

• List available places for getting satisfaction or recourse, such as small claims court or mediation. List the pros and cons for each option, including the difficulty of presenting evidence in a particular venue, unavailability of the other party, and expense.

OUTLINE YOUR CASE

• Write a one-sentence statement that sums up your case and the damages you are seeking. The sentence should read: "This case is about . . ., and these are the damages I suffered as a result."

• Make a chart that states your claim, each fact that led to it, each piece of evidence that verifies it, and each legal principle that supports it.

Appearing in Court

Making an appearance in court is the formal term for showing up at a hearing. But the word "appearance" is also appropriate in another way, because personal appearance—your manner of dress and demeanor—is very important in determining how your case is perceived.

In court, wear the type of clothes that you might wear to a business meeting or job interview. Arrive a few minutes early. Even though you may have to wait to be heard, the "calendar call" (a roll call for cases in order of appearance) comes first, and if you are not present, you can be crossed off. If you are late, give your name quietly to the bailiff when you arrive.

REPRESENTING YOURSELF

Have your documents organized and easily accessible. Even in small claims court, you cannot simply show up and tell your story; you must provide documented proof for your case. In major cases, lawyers often prepare a "trial notebook" for themselves, with sections for legal rules, research, evidence, and questions for witnesses.

Whether your appearance is before a judge or a jury, you must show that you are credible, serious-minded, and have done your homework. At all times, be courteous and respectful to the judge, court personnel, and especially to the other side. Speak firmly but without agitation. Stick to the point when you speak, and keep the point short.

If you are the plaintiff, you will be called first. You should know exactly how you are going to present your case. It is not a bad idea to actually memorize one or two sentences to get you going on your opening statement. Then you will call witnesses, testify yourself, and introduce evidence.

TALKING TO THE BENCH

The judge cannot actively help you or the other side. But if you make a reasonable request, the bench might grant it. If the judge rules, for example, that you failed to take proper steps in advance or did not supply necessary information, you might ask for a "continuance" so you will have time to comply. Or if you have forgotten a critical document, you should ask the judge for an "extension" to submit the document later. Or perhaps the bench has just ruled that a piece of your evidence cannot be submitted. You get flustered, and need time to regroup. Address the bench and say: "At this time, your honor, I'd like to request a short recess." More often than not, your request will be granted.

GETTING A COACH

If you decide to represent yourself, you may need help along the way from someone more knowledgeable. A local lawyer might be willing to consult with or coach you, although most lawyers who might agree to help will charge a fee and ask that you sign an agreement stating they are not representing you. You might want to use a coach for help with the following:

1. Ask whether you have a valid claim in the early stages of a dispute.

2. Ask for help in preparing certain forms, such as a subpoena or discovery questions.

3. If you have prepared documents such as a contract, release, or rental agreement, ask the lawyer to review them.

4. If you go into a mediation session, meet with your consulting lawyer in advance to outline the points that you want to make and what your bottom line should be.

5. Have a session with the lawyer before you go into court to go over your evidence, testimony, and outline of the case.

6. Have the lawyer go over a settlement or mediation agreement before you sign it.

7. If you can no longer handle your case, ask your consulting lawyer if he or she is willing to represent you or to recommend another lawyer.

MAKING YOUR VOICE HEARD

Some problems seem too big to handle, but you do not have to be alone. Joining forces with others can get action. Many voices make a loud noise.

What to Do if You Receive a Class-Action Notice

If you receive a notice in the mail, describing a class action that might affect you, or if you see an advertisement in a magazine concerning a suit, what should you do?

These notices indicate that a group of people has already begun a class-action lawsuit, and a court has decided that the group fits certain criteria for a "class," that is, a large group of people with similar claims. A public notice also indicates that a court has "certified" the class, that is, given the group the legal status to conduct their suit. Now, an attempt is being made to notify anyone else who might be in the same situation but who is not part of the original group.

If you think you have a legitimate claim, follow the directions in the notice. At this stage, you have little to lose by investigating further. Usually an address or telephone number will be listed where you can get more information.

At some point you will be asked to submit a proof of your claim, and a court will review it. If you fit into the certified class and the group bringing the lawsuit wins, you should receive a portion of the amount awarded or benefit in some way from its success.

Class Actions Can Help

After analyzing your house payments, you believe that you have been overcharged on a mortgage escrow account. The financial damage is not serious—less than $500—but the bank refuses to cooperate. You know there must be other customers in the same situation.

When many individuals have the same problem, they are sometimes able to join their causes in a "class-action lawsuit." By bringing together several relatively small but similar claims, a group can get the attention of large institutions that might otherwise ignore individual complaints. Class-action lawsuits have been used to pool the claims of groups of 20 to 1,000 people who have been hurt by a particular drug, suffered from pollution, or been excessively penalized for terminating an automobile lease agreement, among other issues.

The requirements for beginning a class-action lawsuit are stiff, and specialized lawyers are needed. If your application for a class action is approved (your application should always be prepared by a lawyer), the provincial government will grant a certain amount of money to cover court costs and other expenses. Your provincial attorney general can tell you who to contact if you wish to start a class action. In addition to getting a refund for all or part of their losses, participants in a class-action lawsuit often succeed in getting an unfair practice changed. However, such suits should be undertaken only after careful consideration. They can be expensive and time-consuming and corporate opposition can be daunting.

Organizing for Action

A class-action suit involves considerable technical legal machinery, but there are other ways to raise a chorus of voices to get something done. When you encounter an issue that affects a large group of people, getting together to achieve social or political change may be more appropriate than trying to force legal action. By organizing others, you can multiply the resources available and draw more attention to your problem.

In organizing, you use all of the skills of individual problem solving, plus several more. You will need to convince others that what is at stake is important and that their efforts have a possibility of getting results.

There are different types of organizations. A broad-issues organization is an alliance of people with common concerns, such as homeowners or cancer victims. They often have a far-reaching agenda for change or may meet for support and education without a particular focus.

A single-issue group forms around a specific concern, such as parents who are concerned about drunk driving. In this case, the organization MADD, or Mothers Against Drunk Driving, was established to promote awareness of, and find solutions to the problem. The single-issue coalition, in turn, is developed when different groups are brought together under one umbrella to find redress for a common problem.

Keeping at It to Get Results

PROBLEM
Wally was among several longtime city residents of an urban community who enjoyed a sense of security from having a police headquarters nearby. When a newspaper reported that the police administration wanted to close the old station house and build a new one somewhere else, Wally and his neighbors were sure their community would suffer.

ACTION
Wally got a copy of the new plan, and talked to some experts about the costs and benefits of renovating the old headquarters building as opposed to building a new one. He wrote to the mayor with his findings, describing the neighborhood concerns. To form a coalition of community support, Wally contacted political clubs and religious, business, and community leaders in the area. He made presentations to his block association, passing out copies of the letter he had written. After creating a "Committee to Save the Police Station," Wally built an advisory group and designed a letterhead with their names. He circulated petitions at neighborhood fairs, persuaded community organizations to sign resolutions, and made presentations to the city's budget committee. With each contact, he augmented a mailing list. Eventually a community group was so impressed that it offered to serve as a formal sponsor. When a new mayor took office, Wally fired off several letters with the neighborhood's concerns. After several years, his efforts paid off: plans for a new building were shelved, and preparations to renovate the old one began.

Defining the issue is the first step in organizing for action. Research the subject to find out the history of the issue, who has the authority to make the decision that you want, who else has expressed an interest, and how change can be effected. Merely complaining is not enough; you need to be specific about the results you seek.

Organizational Tips for Getting Started

Organizational meetings allow you to present your ideas to a wider community. Here are some tips for making such meetings productive:

✔ *Plan a presentation.* Keep it to the point and respect people's time.

✔ *Target a core group.* Try to identify a small group of committed, like-minded people.

✔ *Be pragmatic.* Set specific goals that deal with the primary objective.

✔ *Stick to an agenda.* If other issues arise, postpone them until the meeting's end.

✔ *Take notes.* Record ideas and resolutions, and distribute notes later.

✔ *Mediate.* Assign one group member to lead or monitor the discussions.

✔ *Get names and numbers.* Prepare a sign-in sheet to ensure you will be able to reach volunteers after the meeting.

✔ *Identify special skills.* Find people or parties who can help in specific ways, such as providing particular expertise.

✔ *Locate helpful contacts.* Ask for names of helpful public officials and private executives.

✔ *Set deadlines.* When someone agrees to take on a task, set a date for completion.

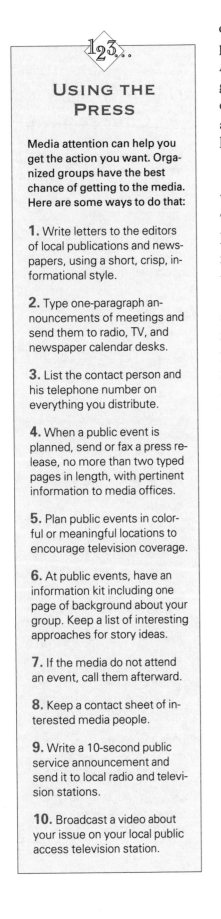

123

USING THE PRESS

Media attention can help you get the action you want. Organized groups have the best chance of getting to the media. Here are some ways to do that:

1. Write letters to the editors of local publications and newspapers, using a short, crisp, informational style.

2. Type one-paragraph announcements of meetings and send them to radio, TV, and newspaper calendar desks.

3. List the contact person and his telephone number on everything you distribute.

4. When a public event is planned, send or fax a press release, no more than two typed pages in length, with pertinent information to media offices.

5. Plan public events in colorful or meaningful locations to encourage television coverage.

6. At public events, have an information kit including one page of background about your group. Keep a list of interesting approaches for story ideas.

7. If the media do not attend an event, call them afterward.

8. Keep a contact sheet of interested media people.

9. Write a 10-second public service announcement and send it to local radio and television stations.

10. Broadcast a video about your issue on your local public access television station.

Set out the problem in writing—even if it is a single sheet of paper. Set a time and place for a meeting of interested people. Post notices in public places and community newspapers. After you give the people who come together some background, brainstorm for ideas toward resolution. Encourage everyone, without criticism, to contribute suggestions for action. Then sort through them, evaluating which are the most likely to be successful.

UTILIZING TEAMWORK

When building an organizational effort, you need teamwork. Through consensus, create a group plan of action that establishes reasonable priorities. Start with the least complex actions first. If problems arise between group members, try to keep the focus on the issue and away from personalities.

If your first steps do not get results, keep going down your action list. There are many group activities that can have a positive impact. Depending on the problem you have or action you want, you can set up community mediation, seek new legislation and lobby for it, plan a protest or march, get signatures on a petition, start a lawsuit, write a local ballot initiative, testify at public hearings, boycott a product, or take your case to the media.

Keeping lines of communication open in a group or among groups is challenging, but critical to the exchange of information and general cohesiveness. Set up a telephone tree in which each member takes responsibility to contact another. Consider using an answering service, creating a mailing list, or using an electronic message system. Committed leadership will be essential to your organizing efforts. The time involved may well be extensive, but the results can be impressive.

ACCESS TO INFORMATION

If information is power, the federal and provincial access to information acts are power tools. In the belief that governments should not operate in secrecy, the federal government and a number of provincial governments enacted freedom-of-information legislation in the 1980s. The legislation entitles individuals to examine and copy government information compiled and held by government departments and public institutions and agencies and, in some provinces, by private companies.

The information may be in the form of reports, photographs, films, microfilms, letters, memos, even computerized data. Classified defense department and cabinet meeting documents, personnel files, private business information, bank records, certain law enforcement records, and any information that might threaten an individual's safety or public security are exempt.

You can request to see government files by writing directly to the agency that holds the records. Put "Access to Information Act Request" at the top of the letter. Identify the records as specifically as possible, including all facts about the place, time, events, or subject of the records. Since you may be charged a search fee and copying cost, ask to be advised of the expenses in advance. A fee may be waived if your request serves the public interest. (Records of court proceedings are public in most cases and can be viewed without any formalities.) If your request is denied because the information falls under an exception, you can seek an agency review. See also RESOURCES, page 469.

Voting Power

Voting power is a dynamic and, in a democracy, an essential means of getting action. Voting, of course, expresses your approval of particular policies or candidates. If you maximize your voting power, voting can also become a way to get change. Contact candidates while they are running and find out their position on issues of concern to you.

Get involved in campaigns. Help your candidates get petitions signed, raise money, and appeal to other voters. Voting is not limited to government—the political process includes parent-teacher associations, boards of condominiums, and employee committees. Consider running for office yourself.

After an election, keep in touch with candidates. See that they are invited to community events. Volunteer to be a member of a board or committee that is forming. Go to public information meetings. When you need help with a problem, this groundwork will put you in a good position to approach the officeholder. You might have an idea for new legislation that will solve a problem. Put your ideas on paper and take them to your legislator. You or your legislator can get involved in lobbying, or trying to secure the support of other legislators who will be critical to the success of your project.

Winning at City Hall

You may not be able to "beat city hall," as the old phrase suggests, but by doing your homework, you can win a few battles there. Your local town government may be exactly where you need to go to get action on vital issues. Many essential decisions including those concerning schools, safety, garbage collection, environment,

Writing an Effective Call for Action

After marshaling local support for a cause or reform that you feel strongly about, you can broaden your influence by writing personal action letters to legislators, corporate leaders, and others in influential positions. Here are some suggestions for writing a letter that can get results:

✔ *Be polite but firm.* Take the time to find the proper salutation for the person you are addressing: "The Honorable Carol Brown" for example, if you are writing your Member of Parliament. (Most dictionaries and etiquette books list accepted salutations.) Throughout the letter, maintain a polite tone, but make it clear that you know what you are talking about.

✔ *Be specific.* Tell the leader exactly what action you are seeking. If you are urging acceptance of a piece of legislation, use the bill number. Be brief and to the point.

✔ *Get personal.* Lend credibility to your request by giving details about yourself that explain why the action you seek is important to you. You may be a working mother, for example, urging support of funding for a local after-school center.

✔ *Be persuasive.* Make a clear argument in support of the action.

✔ *Don't be shy.* Ask the person you are addressing to make a specific commitment or response.

But Is It "the Law"?

There are many layers of law, each building on another. Here are the various sources of law.

✔ *The Canadian Constitution.* Canada's Constitution like that of Great Britain is not contained in one document as is the case in the United States. The foundation of all Canadian law is the British North America Act (1867) and amendments, the Constitution Act (1982), and other documents such as the Statute of Westminster (1931).

✔ *Federal laws.* Statutes by the federal government—legislation on matters such as old age pensions and interprovincial trade, for example—apply to people in every province.

✔ *Provincial laws.* Provincial legislatures enact laws on matters within their jurisdiction, such as education.

✔ *Local ordinances.* Cities and towns pass laws on matters such as traffic and zoning in their communities.

✔ *Regulations.* Government agencies make regulations, such as building codes, that are enforced as law.

✔ *Court decisions.* Judges often base their decisions on case law—previous legal interpretations in similar cases.

✔ *Common law.* Certain well-established legal concepts—oral contracts, for example—are treated as law.

✔ *Private agreements.* People can enter into voluntary agreements, or contracts, to set rules for specific situations.

animals, welfare, property, and recreation, are made at the local level. Local public officials such as the mayor and city council members are the elected officials who make those decisions.

To understand your local bureaucracy, and to find the person to help you, you might literally call city hall. Look in your local telephone book for a listing of city departments and call the one that appears most likely to handle the problem in question. In addition, you might check with nongovernment organizations and your local library, to find references for local agencies and officials.

Try to secure the name of the appropriate local official and his direct telephone number. When you call, if you get no immediate assistance, ask your contact for the name of a person who can help you. If you need to send a request in writing, fax it or deliver it personally to avoid mailroom delay.

HELPING POLITICIANS HELP YOU

Meeting face to face with elected officials is one of the most effective ways to get your message across and to convince them to take action on matters that are important to you. If you can establish a working relationship with a key person on the elected official's staff, it will be very helpful.

If you succeed in scheduling a meeting with the elected official or staff person, get two to five people to go with you. Pick a lead person to introduce the topic with a short prepared presentation. This is a one-sided forum: you have the floor. You will not have it long, so you must be convincing. Have copies of backup materials that you can leave.

If an elected official agrees with you, make yourself available for support by offering to speak at community meetings or to be available to the media for comment.

OPEN-MEETING LAWS

Attending meetings of decision-makers is another way to create an impact. Often, government agencies are required to make their decisions in public meetings. The laws entitle you to know when and where meetings by government agencies, boards, and councils are being held, and to attend if you wish to.

The presence of citizens at a meeting—whether a zoning board or a budget meeting—can change its course. Often you can corner bureaucrats or media people and make connections that might otherwise be difficult to acquire. In some cases, you can ask to be placed on the agenda to speak. You also can pass around literature that will educate decision-makers and other citizens about your issue. By making the effort to educate people about your concerns, you can stand up for your rights and make a difference in your community.

RESOURCES

General Sources

The following resources may be useful to you in researching and exercising many aspects of your rights. Write, fax, or call the organizations for further information.

Adoption Council of Canada
P.O. Box 8442, Station T
Ottawa, Ont. K1G 3H8
(613) 235-1566
Fax: (613) 788-5075
This council provides information and referrals for adoptions in Canada.

Adult Children of Alcoholics (ACA)
20 Bloor Street E, P.O. Box 75061
Toronto, Ont. M4W 3T3
A national organization, ACA has a speakers service, and publishes a magazine, Serenity, *and a newsletter.*

Associated Credit Bureaus of Canada
814 Gadwell Court
Orleans, Ont. K1E 2L1
(613) 830-7866
Fax: (613) 230-4053
This organization provides credit reporting and collection services for members.

Association of Canadian Pension Management (ACPM)
1075 Bay Street, Suite 730
Toronto, Ont. M5S 2B1
(416) 964-1260
Fax: (416) 964-0567
The ACPM represents private corporate pension plan sponsors in dealings with governments. It publishes a newsletter and has a speakers service.

Bank of Canada
234 Wellington Street
Ottawa, Ont. K1A 0G9
(613) 782-8537
Fax: (613) 782-7713
Canada's national bank implements banking policy and provides bank notes.

Bank of Nova Scotia
Scotia Plaza
44 King Street W
Toronto, Ont. M5H 1H1
(416) 866-6161
Most chartered banks offer special deals to people 60 and older—to 59-year-olds in the case of the Bank of Nova Scotia. It, as well as the Bank of Montreal, Canadian Imperial Bank of Commerce, Royal Bank, and Toronto-Dominion Bank, also distributes free pamphlets on wise buying and money management. Check with your local branch.

Blue Cross
Travel and health insurance may be purchased from this company. Regional offices are listed below.

Blue Cross of Atlantic Canada
644 Main Street, P.O. Box 220
Moncton, N.B. E1C 1E2
(506) 853-1811

Blue Cross/MSA
2025 West Broadway, P.O. Box 9300
Vancouver, B.C. V6B 5M1
(604) 737-5700

Blue Cross of Ontario
185 The West Mall
Suite 600, P.O. Box 2000
Etobicoke, Ont. M9C 5P1
(416) 626-1688
1-800-865-2583
Fax: (416) 626-0997
Fax: 1-800-893-0997

Blue Cross Quebec
550 Sherbrooke Street W
Suite 160
Montreal, Que. H3A 1B9
(514) 286-8400

Canada Deposit Insurance Corporation (CDIC)
50 O'Connor Street, 17th Floor
Ottawa, Ont. K1P 5W5
(613) 996-2081
Fax: (613) 996-6095
This Crown corporation insures deposits such as savings and chequing accounts, term deposits such as

Guaranteed Income Certificates and debentures issued by loan companies, money orders, bank drafts, certified cheques and drafts, and traveler's cheques issued by member banks, trust companies, and loan companies.

Canada Mortgage and Housing Corporation (CMHC)
700 Montreal Road
Ottawa, Ont. K1A 0P7
(613) 748-2000
Fax: (613) 748-2098
This Crown corporation is involved in several programs to improve housing for aboriginal peoples, the elderly, and the disabled. It oversees the construction of residential housing for a variety of home buyers, administers National Housing Act loans and grants, and insures mortgages borrowed from private lenders.

Canada Post Corporation
2701 Riverside Drive, Suite E0322
Ottawa, Ont. K1A 0B1
(613) 734-7575
Fax: (613) 734-7726
A crown corporation, Canada Post annually processes and delivers more than 11 billion letters and parcels.

Canada Safety Council
1010 Thomas Spratt Place
Ottawa, Ont. K1G 5L5
(613) 739-1535
Fax: (613) 739-1566
A nonprofit organization, the council is dedicated to reducing death and injury by preventing accidents and health hazards in the home, workplace, recreational areas, and on the road.

Canadian Advertising Foundation (CAF)
350 Bloor Street E, Suite 402
Toronto, Ont. M4W 1H5
(416) 961-6311
Fax: (416) 961-7904
CAF, a regulatory board for advertisers and agencies, uses its regional Advertising Standards Council to

police its industry and investigate consumer complaints.

Canadian Association for Community Care

45 Rideau Street
Ottawa, Ont. K1N 5W8
(613) 241-7510
Fax: (613) 242-5923
This federally supported, national association (formerly known as HomeSupport Canada and the Canadian Long Term Care Association) promotes community care health services such as home-based care and meals programs. The organization supports community-care providers through research, education and training, advocacy and policy development, and liaison with govern-ment and other organizations.

Canadian Association of Home Inspectors

P.O. Box 22010
RPO Capri Centre
Kelowna, B.C. V1Y 9N9
This national association of insured, independently employed home build-ing inspectors has chapters in British Columbia, the Prairies (Calgary), Quebec, and central and eastern Ontario. It may be able to give you names of building inspectors in your area.

Canadian Association of Retired Persons (CARP)

27 Queen Street E, Suite 1304
Toronto, Ont. M5C 2M6
(416) 363-8748
Fax: (416) 363-8747
This organization seeks to foster and advance the interests of Canadians 50 years and older. Members can take advantage of group rates and discounts in purchasing services such as insur-ance, travel, and financial consulta-tion. The association has a speakers service and publishes a newspaper, CARP News.

Canadian Automobile Association (CAA)

1145 Hunt Club Road, Suite 200
Ottawa, Ont. K1V 0Y3

(613) 247-0117
Fax: (613) 247-0118
A non-profit federation of motor clubs, the CAA provides its members with emergency road service, technical automotive advice and services, and travel information.

Canadian Bankers Association

Commerce Court W
30th Floor, P.O. Box 348
Toronto, Ont. M5L 1G2
(416) 362-6092
Fax: (416) 362-7705
This bankers' association provides free information on the banking system and the chartered banks. The publications contain useful consumer information.

Canadian Cancer Society

10 Alcorn Avenue, Suite 200
Toronto, Ont. M4V 3B1
(416) 961-7223
Fax: (416) 961-4189
A national organization with divisions in all provinces and territories, the society supports education, research, and patient services programs.

Canadian Council of Better Business Bureaus

7330 Fisher Street SE, Suite 368
Calgary, Alta. P2H 2H5
(403) 531-8686
Fax: (403) 415-1752
This is the licensing and coordinating authority of Better Business Bureaus (BBBs). The nonprofit bureaus, funded by local businesses, promote self-regulation of the marketplace, offer consumer information, and help resolve disputes between business and consumers.

Canadian Council on Health Facilities Accreditation

1730 St. Laurent Boulevard
Suite 430
Ottawa, Ont. K1G 5L1
(613) 738-3800
Fax: (613) 738-3755
The council, previously called the Canadian Council on Hospital Accreditation, promotes efficient use of health resources and permits health

care organizations to voluntarily par-ticipate in an accreditation program based on national standards.

Canadian Direct Marketing Association (CDMA)

1 Concorde Gate, Suite 607
Toronto, Ont. M3C 3N6
(416) 391-2362
Fax: (416) 441-4062
This professional, self-regulatory association helps customers resolve problems with direct mail marketers. Consumers who do not want unsolicited direct mail advertising can have their names removed from one or all mailing lists by making a written request to the CDMA.

Canadian Federation of Labour (CFL)

107 Sparks Street, Suite 300
Ottawa, Ont. K1P 5B5
(613) 234-4141
Fax: (613) 234-5188
This organization is the national voice of Canadian workers whose interests it promotes through nonpartisan involvement, especially at the political level.

Canadian Human Rights Commission

Place de Ville, Tower A
320 Queen Street, 13th Floor
Ottawa, Ont. K1A 1E1
(613) 943-9505
The commission seeks to promote the knowledge of human rights, effec-tively resolve individual complaints, and reduce barriers to equality in employment.

Canadian Life and Health Insurance Association Inc.

1 Queen Street E, Suite 1700
Toronto, Ont. M5C 2X9
(416) 777-2221
1-800-268-8099
Fax: (416) 777-1895
This trade association (formerly known as the Canadian Life Insurance Association) provides a free answering service for consumer questions or complaints.

Canadian Medical Association (CMA)

1867 Alta Vista Drive
Ottawa, Ont. K1G 3Y6
(613) 731-9331
Fax: (613) 731-9013
Maintaining high standards of medical education and professional ethics is a priority of the CMA, the national association of Canada's physicians. The CMA also represents and coordinates the work of the provincial medical associations and societies. It offers members guidelines on various topics, produces several scientific publications, and has copublished several authoritative books on health care and Canadian medical practice for the general public.

Canadian Medical Protective Association (CMPA)

875 Carling Avenue
Ottawa, Ont. K1S 5P1
(613) 725-2000
Fax: (613) 725-1300
The CMPA provides professional liability for physicians.

Canadian Nurses Association (CNA)

50 Driveway
Ottawa, Ont. K2P 1E2
(613) 237-2133
Fax: (613) 237-3520
This national association represents nurses on nursing and health issues in dealings with governments and other organizations.

Canadian Order of Chartered Accountants

277 Wellington Street W
Toronto, Ont. M5V 3H2
(416) 977-3222
Fax: (416) 977-8585
This organization, also known as the Chartered Accountants of Canada, sets accounting and auditing standards for business and government, publishes professional literature, and develops continuing education programs for its members.

Canadian Organization of Small Business Inc. (COSBI)

P.O. Box 11246, Station Main
Edmonton, Alta. T5H 3J5
(403) 423-2672
Fax: (403) 423-2751
Membership in this national organization is open to small independent businesses and service providers to small business. COSBI supports and promotes the interests of small businesses and business professionals, lobbies governments on their behalf, provides a speakers service, maintains a library, and publishes the Voice of Business *magazine and a newsletter.*

Canadian Payments Association (CPA)

50 O'Connor Street, Suite 1212
Ottawa, Ont. K1P 6L2
(613) 238-4173
Fax: (613) 233-3385
CPA membership consists of banks, trust companies, and other financial institutions such as credit unions. The CPA operates a national clearing and settlement system for cheques, direct deposit, and other paper and electronic payments.

Canadian Pension Commission

Daniel J. MacDonald Building
P.O. Box 9900
Charlottetown, P.E.I. C1A 8V6
Fax: (902) 566-8879
This commission handles inquiries about veterans' disability pensions.

Canadian Pensioners Concerned Inc

830 McLean Street
Halifax, N.S. B3H 2T8
This organization, with regional divisions in Alberta, Nova Scotia, Ontario, and Quebec, is concerned with seniors' issues and legislation affecting seniors.

Canadian Radio-television and Telecommunications Commission (CRTC)

Les Terrasses de la Chaudière
1 Promenade du Portage, 5th Floor
Hull, Que. K1A 0N2
(819) 994-5366

As regulator of the broadcasting and telecommunications industries, the CRTC regulates telephone company rates and services, licenses broadcasters, is responsible for the character of advertising on the medium, must give all political parties fair access, and must ensure that radio and television programs do not encourage stereotyping of the sexes, races, or cultures.

Canadian Real Estate Association

344 Slater Street, Suite 1600
Ottawa, Ont. K1R 7Y3
(613) 237-7111
Fax: (613) 234-2567
The professional association of the real estate industry sets professional, competency, and profitability standards for members, and can provide statistics on housing sales.

Canadian Standards Association (CSA)

178 Rexdale Boulevard
Rexdale, Ont. M9W 1R3
(416) 747-4058
Fax: (416) 747-2475
An independent, nonprofit organization, the CSA is a leader in standard development. CSA certification indicates a product complies with specific standards for safety and performance. In addition to regional offices and laboratories across Canada, the CSA also maintains several offices overseas.

Canadian Textiles Institute

66 Slater Street, Suite 1720
Ottawa, Ont. K1P 5H1
(613) 232-7195
Fax: (613) 232-8722
This organization represents dyers and finishers as well as manufacturers of fibers, yarns, fabrics and other textile-related products.

Colleges of Physicians and Surgeons

These provincial organizations—they are known as medical boards in Nova Scotia and Newfoundland, and as a professional corporation in Quebec—license physicians and regulate the practice of medicine. All licensed physicians in a given province are members of the provincial body. The colleges set standards and investigate complaints by the public.

College of Physicians and Surgeons of Alberta

10180—101 Street, Suite 900
Edmonton, Alta. T5J 4P8
(403) 423-4764

College of Physicians and Surgeons of British Columbia

1807—10th Avenue W
Vancouver, B.C. V6J 2A9
(604) 733-7758

College of Physicians and Surgeons of Manitoba

494 St. James Street
Winnipeg, Man. R3G 3J4
(204) 774-4344

College of Physicians and Surgeons of New Brunswick

One Hampton Road, P.O. Box 628
Rothesay, N.B. E2E 5A7
(506) 658-0959

College of Physicians and Surgeons of Ontario

80 College Street
Toronto, Ont. M5G 2E2
(416) 961-1711

College of Physicians and Surgeons of Prince Edward Island

199 Grafton Street
Charlottetown, P.E.I. C1A 1L2
(902) 566-3861

College of Physicians and Surgeons of Saskatchewan

211—4th Avenue S
Saskatoon, Sask. S7K 1N1
(306) 244-7355

Corporation professionnelle des médecins du Québec

2170 boulevard René-Lévesque O
Montreal, Que. H3H 2T8
(514) 933-4441

Newfoundland Medical Board

15 Rowan Street
St. John's, Nfld. A1B 2X2
(709) 726-8546

Provincial Medical Board of Nova Scotia

5248 Morris Street
Halifax, N.S. B3J 1B4
(902) 422-5823

Commonwealth War Graves Commission

66 Slater Street, Suite 1707
Ottawa, Ont. K1A 0P4
(613) 992-3224
Fax: (613) 995-0431
Established in 1917, this commission marks and maintains the graves of fallen servicemen, builds memorials, and keeps records.

Consumers Association of Canada (CAC)

307 Gilmour Street
Ottawa, Ont. K2P 0P7
(613) 238-2533
This national nonprofit organization with regional offices in most provinces, provides advice and information on consumer goods and services, has a product testing program, and presents the consumer's point of view to government regulatory bodies.

Credit Union Central of Canada

300 The East Mall, 5th Floor
Toronto, Ont. M9B 6B7
(416) 232-1262
Fax: (416) 232-9196
Formerly known as the Canadian Cooperative Credit Society, Credit Union Central maintains a national liquidity facility for the country's credit unions and cooperative movement. As national trade association for credit unions, it provides administrative, legislative, and developmental support.

Equifax Canada Inc.

7171 rue Jean-Talon E
Montreal, Que. H1M 3N2
(514) 493-2470
Fax: (514) 493-2402
The country's largest credit bureau, Equifax has offices in every region and major city in the country.

Federal Business Development Bank (FBDB)

5 Place Ville Marie, 4th Floor
Montreal, Que. H3B 5E7
(514) 283-5904
Fax: (514) 496-8036
With branches in some 75 cities coast to coast, the FBDB offers a variety of services such as loans, venture financing, loan guarantees, export receivable financing, and management services, to small and medium-size businesses. The FBDB also operates a program, which gives counseling assistance to small enterprises with accounting, marketing, production, or other business-related difficulties.

Federal Court of Canada

Supreme Court Building
Kent and Wellington streets
Ottawa, Ont. K1A 0H9
(613) 996-6795
Fax: (613) 952-7226
This court has both trial and appeal divisions, and although both are in Ottawa, the court will conduct hearings or trials anywhere in the country. As a rule, the trial division shares jurisdiction with provincial courts over cases in which the federal court is the plaintiff, or cases dealing with shipping, patents and trademarks, aeronautics, and interprovincial matters. Its appeal division hears appeals of judgments from its trial division, and reviews certain decisions and orders of federal administrative boards and commissions. The Tax Court, which deals with Revenue Canada decisions, is another division of the Federal Court.

Infertility Awareness Association of Canada

396 Cooper Street, Suite 201
Ottawa, Ont. K2P 2H7
(613) 234-8585
Fax: (613) 234-7718
The purpose of this organization is to assist and support those with infertility problems. It does this through information seminars, support groups, and various information programs.

Insurance Bureau of Canada

181 University Avenue, 13th Floor
Toronto, Ont. M5H 3M7
(416) 362-2031
Fax: (416) 361-5952
Most of Canada's general insurers belong to this trade association, which exists to protect the industry and the public from insurance crime. The

bureau will take disciplinary action against members who practice unethical behavior.

International Air Transport Association (IATA)
2060-2000 Peel Street
Montreal, Que. H3A 2R4
(514) 844-6311
Fax: (514) 844-5286
This organization promotes safe, regular, and economical air transport. It provides a forum for developing industry standards and coordinating international fares and rates. reports is open to the public.

International Association for Medical Assistance to Travellers (IAMAT)
40 Regal Road
Guelph, Ont. N1K 1B5
(519) 836-0102
Fax: (519) 836-3412
Info Line: (416) 652-0137
IAMAT provides travelers with information on world immunization requirements, tropical diseases, and malaria risk. It can also provide the names of English-speaking physicians in some 500 cities worldwide.

International Centre for Human Rights & Democratic Development
63 rue de Bresoles
Montreal, Que. H2Y 1V7
(514) 283-6073
Fax: (514) 283-3792
This organization supports individuals and groups seeking civil, political, economic, and social rights.

International Civil Aviation Organization (ICAO)
400-1000 rue Sherbrooke W
Montreal, Que. H3A 2R2
(514) 285-8220
Fax: (514) 954-6077
This organization's extensive library of books, periodicals, and technical reports is open to the public.

Investment Dealers Association of Canada (IDA)
121 King Street W, Suite 1600
Toronto, Ont. M5H 3T9

(416) 364-6133
Fax: (416) 364-0753
This professional association of registered security dealers has regional offices in Calgary, Montreal, and Vancouver.

Last Post Fund Inc.
685 rue Cathcart, Suite 916
Montreal, Que. H3B 1M7
(514) 866-2727
1-800-465-7113
Fax: (514) 866-2147
This fund provides funds to ensure that eligible war veterans get a dignified funeral and burial.

Liberty Health
3500 Steeles Avenue E
Markham, Ont. L3R 0X4
(905) 946-4520
Fax: (905) 946-4927
This company offers comprehensive supplementary health insurance plans for Canadians and residents who are covered by Medicare.

Medical Information Bureau (MIB)
330 University Avenue
Toronto, Ont. M5G 1R8
A consortium of insurance companies, MIB prevents fraud in medical and life insurance business by checking the information that consumers submit when they apply for coverage. Call or write for more information and a free copy of your file.

Medical Research Council of Canada
Holland Cross Building
Tower B, 5th Floor
1600 Scott Street
Ottawa, Ont. K1A 0W9
(613) 954-1812
Fax: (613) 954-1800
This federal agency is responsible for funding health research in Canada.

The Mortgage Insurance Company of Canada
141 Adelaide Street W
Toronto, Ont. M5H 3L5
(416) 364-1650
Home buyers who borrow an RRSP mortgage from a self-directed RRSP

must have their mortgage insured either by this company or CMHC.

National Institute of Nutrition
265 Carling Avenue, Suite 302
Ottawa, Ont. K1S 2E1
(613) 235-3355
Fax: (613) 235-7032
The institute is dedicated to improving nutrition research and education. Toward this end it seeks to influence public policy on nutritional issues, and sponsors programs targeted to health professionals, media, educational institutions, government and industry.

Office of the Superintendent of Financial Institutions
255 Albert Street, 13th Floor
Ottawa, Ont. K1A 0H2
(613) 990-7788
Fax: (613) 952-8219
This government department safeguards policyholders, depositors, and pension plan members by regulating federal financial institutions and pension plans.

One Voice—The Canadian Seniors Network
350 Sparks Street, Suite 1005
Ottawa, Ont. K1R 7S8
(613) 238-7624
Fax: (613) 235-4497
This nonpartisan, nonprofit organization presents seniors' point of view to decision makers in government, industry, and business. It offers information on issues such as housing, health care, and pensions.

Ontario Association of Credit Counselling Services (OACCS)
P.O. Box 278
Grimsby, Ont. L3M 4G5
(905) 945-5644
1-800-263-0260
Fax: (905) 945-5644
This organization provides a forum for member agencies such as the Credit Counselling Services of Metro Toronto or Debt Counselling Services of London, Ont., to pursue their common goal of providing nonprofit credit counseling services to their communities.

**Royal Architectural Institute
of Canada**
55 Murray Street
Ottawa, Ont. K1N 5M3
(613) 241-3600
Fax: (613) 241-5750
*This professional group fosters public
awareness and appreciation of architecture and lobbies government on
architectural issues.*

Royal Canadian Legion
359 Kent Street
Ottawa, Ont. K2P 0R7
(613) 235-4391
Fax: (613) 563-1670
*This nonprofit organization, publisher
of the* Legion *magazine, assists
veterans and members of the armed
forces.*

**Royal Canadian Mounted Police
(RCMP)**
1200 Vanier Parkway
Ottawa, Ont. K1A 0R2
(613) 993-1204
Fax: (613) 990-6832
*RCMP officers, commonly known
as "Mounties," enforce federal law
across Canada, provincial and
municipal legislation in all provinces
and territories outside Ontario
and Quebec, and serve as Canadian
liaison officers in dozens of foreign
capitals.*

**Royal College of Physicians and
Surgeons of Canada (RCPSC)**
774 Echo Drive
Ottawa, Ont. K1S 5N8
(613) 730-8177
Fax: (613) 730-8830
*The college sets out requirements of
specialty training in medical, laboratory, and surgical specialties and
subspecialties, and accredits specialty
residency programs.*

**St. Elizabeth Visiting Nurses'
Association**
698 King Street W
Hamilton, Ont.,L8P 1C7
(905) 522-6887
Fax: (905) 522-5579
*This organization provides nursing
care and counseling in the home.*

*Specialty programs include palliative
care, foot care, early obstetrical
discharge, and psychiatric patient
monitoring.*

Standards Council of Canada
45 O'Connor Street, Suite 1200
Ottawa, Ont. K1P 6N7
(613) 238-3222
Fax: (613) 995-4564
*This corporation promotes voluntary
standardization in Canada with
a view to advancing the national
economy and maintaining the
health and safety of workers and
the public.*

Supreme Court of Canada
Supreme Court Building
Kent and Wellington streets
Ottawa, Ont. K1A 0J1
(613) 995-4330
Fax: (613) 996-3063
*This federal court rules on civil and
criminal cases and advises on constitu-
tional matters.*

Tax Court of Canada
Centennial Towers, 200 Kent Street
Ottawa, Ont. K1A 0M1
(613) 992-0901
Fax: (613) 957-9034
*This federal court rules on taxation
appeals.*

**Underwriters' Laboratories of
Canada (ULC)**
7 Crouse Road
Scarborough, Ont. M1R 3A9
(416) 757-3611
Fax: (416) 757-9540
*ULC develops classifications and
specifications for products posing a
risk of accident or fire or liable to
cause property damage. It tests and
certifies devices, materials, systems,
and services.*

Victorian Order of Nurses
5 Blackburn Avenue
Ottawa, Ont. K1N 8A2
(613) 233-5694
Fax: (613) 230-4376
*Visiting nurses help individuals
and families cope with health
problems.*

Visiting Homemakers Association
170 Merton Street
Toronto, Ont. M4S 1A1
(416) 489-2500
*The association provides trained
homemakers, working under social
worker supervision, to help the
elderly, handicapped, and others
in crisis.*

The War Amputations of Canada
2827 Riverside Drive
Ottawa, Ont. K1V 0C4
(613) 731-3821
1-800-467-2677
Fax: (613) 731-3234
*This organization provides programs
and services for all Canadian amputees.*

**The War Amputations of Canada
Key Tag Service**
140 Merton Street
Toronto, Ont. M4S 1A5
(416) 488-0600
1-800-268-8821
*The Key Tag Service of the War
Amputations of Canada provides
confidentially coded key tags and a
lost key return service for motorists.
The service relies on donations, which
provide a wide range of services for
all Canadian war amputees and child
amputees.*

Government Sources

Agriculture and Agri-Food Canada
Sir John Carling Building
930 Carling Avenue
Ottawa, Ont. K1A 0C5
(613) 759-1000

**Citizenship and Immigration
Canada**
200 St. Catherine Street
Ottawa, Ont. K2P 2K9
(613) 995-0362
Fax: (613) 995-7425

Department of Finance Canada
Esplanade Laurier, East Tower
140 O'Connor Street, 21st Floor
Ottawa, Ont. K1A 0G5
(613) 992-6923
Fax: (613) 947-8331

Department of Justice Canada
Justice Building, Room 116
239 Wellington Street
Ottawa, Ont. K1A 0H8
(613) 957-4222
Fax: (613) 954-0811

Environment Canada
Terrasses de la Chaudière
10 Wellington Street, 4th Floor
Hull, Que. K1A 0H3
(819) 997-2992
Fax: (819) 997-1781

**Federal Superintendent
of Insurance, Ottawa**
See Office of the Superintendent
of Financial Institutions,
page 473

Health Canada
Brooke Claxton Building
Address locator: 0909-D
Tunney's Pasture
Ottawa, Ont. K1A 0K9
(613) 957-3051
Fax: (613) 941-4541

**Human Resources Development
Canada**
Place du Portage, Phase IV
140 Promenade du Portage
4th Floor
Hull, Que. K1A 0J9
(819) 994-2548

Industry Canada
C.D. Howe Building
235 Queen Street
6th Floor, Room 643-D
Ottawa, Ont. K1A 0H5
(613) 954-2752
Fax: (613) 941-3085

National Defence
South Tower, 101 Colonel By Drive
Ottawa, Ont. K1A 0K2
(613) 992-4581

Natural Resources Canada
580 Booth Street
Ottawa, Ont. K1A 0E4
(613) 995-0947
*(This department was formerly
called Energy, Mines and
Resources.)*

Pension Appeals Board
P.O. Box 8567, Station T
Ottawa, Ont. K1G 3H9
(613) 995-0612
Fax: (613) 995-6834
*This tribunal hears appeals of deci-
sions by the ministries of Revenue,
Employment and Immigration, and
the Canada Pension Plan.*

Revenue Canada
14th Floor, Albion Executive Tower
25 Nicholas Street
Ottawa, Ont. K1A 0L5
(613) 957-8819
Fax: (613) 941-9395

Transport Canada
Place de Ville, Tower C
330 Sparks Street, 26th Floor
Ottawa, Ont. K1A 0N5
(613) 990-2309
Fax: (613) 995-0351

Veterans Affairs Canada
Dominion Building
97 Queen Street, Room 205
P.O. Box 7700
Charlottetown, P.E.I. C1A 8M9
(902) 566-8609
Fax: (902) 368-0460

Index

A

B

J

V

Vacation
 renting a car, 436-437
Vacation homes, 80
 see also Second homes
Veteran Independence
 Program, 205
Veterans Administration, 166
Veterans' Affairs
 income security plans, 333
Veterans benefits, 166
Veterans hospitals, 190
Veterans' Independence
 Program, 261
Veterinarians, 158-159
Victims of Crime Board
 rights, 446
Victorian Order of Nurses,
 215
Video cameras, 406
Videocassette recorders
 (VCRs), 406
Visa, 368
Visiting Homemakers
 Association, 204

W

Warehouse clubs, 422
Warranties, 383-384
 credit cards and, 384
 express, 383

full, 383
 implied, 384
 limited, 383
 red flags on, 383
 understanding, 383
 violations, 384
Water, 62
 see also Drinking water
Wills and estates, 134, 155,
 342-348
 being named executor, 346
 challenges to, 343
 changing your will, 344
 children, 342, 345
 debts, 344
 estate plans, 342
 executors, 347
 giving away power, 346
 making a new will, 342
 preparing a will, 343-345
 transferring property,
 345-346
 trusts, 347-348
 when you inherit, 348
Wise consumer, 378-379
Work for hire, 232
Work orders, 46
Work stoppage clause, 48
Workers compensation, 166,
 168
 contractors, 45
 coverage, 236-237
 disability payments, 236
 filing a claim, 237
 quitting your job, 237
Working for the government,
 260-261
Working at home, 267-268

World Health Organization
 abortion, 103
 travel, 438
Written agreements
 domestic partnerships, 134

X Y Z

X-rays
 and dentistry, 180

You and your doctor, 172-181
Young Offenders Act
 children's rights, 114
 criminal courts, 115
Your car, 349-375
Your health care, 169-224
Your home and community,
 9-96
Your marriage and family,
 97-168
Your rights in action, 439-468
Your rights as a patient,
 182-188
Your rights as a traveler,
 434-438
Youth
 car insurance, 367
 employment, 246

ZIFT (zygote intra-fallopian
 transfer), 104
Zoning laws, 14, 42-43, 51
 mobile homes, 86-87
 senior citizens, 85

NELSON BROTT
1945-1996

*O*n July 11, 1996, Nelson Brott lost his long and courageous battle with chronic *heart disease.* Know Your Rights *constitutes the final chapter of the Reader's Digest's collaboration with this extraordinary jurist and author.*

A graduate of Montreal's Sir George Williams (now Concordia) and McGill universities, Nelson loved the law and its traditions. Admitted to the Quebec Bar in 1972, he was always conscious of the law's remedial role in society and had little patience for those who would abuse its procedures.

A pioneer of the Quebec Legal Aid system, he deemed it imperative that the law be made accessible to all and valued his collaboration with Reader's Digest as a means of attaining that worthy objective. In 1987, he undertook to serve as legal consultant for a Reader's Digest publication featuring the 2,000 most commonly asked legal questions. In November of that year, he suffered a near-fatal heart attack and in March 1988 received a heart transplant at the Royal Victoria Hospital in Montreal. It was during his convalescence that he researched and wrote the Reader's Digest Legal Question and Answer Book, *which was ultimately published in 1989. Nelson never missed an opportunity to express his gratitude to the medical professionals who prolonged his life. Nor did he ever fail to credit his relationship with Reader's Digest for providing a vital lifeline to the world of normalcy during those periods of fear and discomfort that attended his convalescence.*

By 1994, Nelson had recovered sufficiently to resume his duties as a trial lawyer for a Legal Aid office in Montreal. Neither his heavy case load nor periodic medical setbacks prevented him from researching and writing the Reader's Digest Legal Problem Solver, *which was published that same year. He began working on* Know Your Rights *in 1995 and had completed a large portion of the book before he died.*

No one of good will was ever ill at ease in Nelson's company. Perhaps it was the full head of prematurely gray hair, which invariably gave him an avuncular demeanor. Or, better still, the hearty handshake and abundant good humor, which made everyone feel at home in his book-lined office or among the cheerful clutter of his living room.

ROSS ROBINS

A graduate of Sir George Williams (now Concordia) University, Montreal, and the Faculty of Law at the Université de Sherbrooke, Sherbrooke, Que., Ross Robins was admitted to the Bar of Quebec in 1987.

Since then, Mr. Robins has specialized in civil litigation and has pleaded before numerous civil and administrative tribunals. Since 1993, he has devoted a substantial part of his practice to labor and disciplinary law.

From 1990 to the present, Mr. Robins has taught at Concordia University, where he is a part-time instructor in civil law in the departments of Management and Accountancy.

PHOTO CREDITS: Jennifer Besse (p. 494), Mike Haimes (p. 495)
FILM WORK: Allard Photo-Litho Inc.
PRINTING: Interglobe Inc.
BINDING: Metropole Litho Inc.
PAPER: Les Papiers Graphiques Rolland